Learning Programming Using Visual Basic .NET

Williams E. Burrows

University of Washington

Joseph D. Langford

Xylo, Inc.

McGraw-Hill Irwin

Boston   Burr Ridge, IL   Dubuque, IA   Madison, WI   New York   San Francisco   St. Louis
Bangkok   Bogotá   Caracas   Kuala Lumpur   Lisbon   London   Madrid   Mexico City
Milan   Montreal   New Delhi   Santiago   Seoul   Singapore   Sydney   Taipei   Toronto

McGraw-Hill Higher Education

A Division of The **McGraw-Hill** *Companies*

LEARNING PROGRAMMING USING VISUAL BASIC .NET
Published by McGraw-Hill/Irwin, an imprint of the McGraw-Hill Companies, Inc. 1221 Avenue of the
Americas, New York, NY, 10020. Copyright © 2003, 2000, 1998, 1997 by the McGraw-Hill Companies, Inc.
All rights reserved. No part of this publication may be reproduced or distributed in any form or by any means,
or stored in a database or retrieval system, without the prior written consent of The McGraw-Hill Companies,
Inc., including, but not limited to, in any network or other electronic storage or transmission, or broadcast for
distance learning.

   Some ancillaries, including electronic and print components, may not be available to customers outside
the United States.

This book is printed on acid-free paper.

domestic   1 2 3 4 5 6 7 8 9 0 QPD/QPD 0 9 8 7 6 5 4 3 2
international 1 2 3 4 5 6 7 8 9 0 QPD/QPD 0 9 8 7 6 5 4 3 2

ISBN 0-07-245196-3

Publisher: *George Werthman*
Sponsoring editor: *Steve Schuetz*
Developmental editor: *Sarah Wood*
Editorial Assistant: *Jennie Yates*
Marketing manager: *Greta Kleinert*
Media producer: *Greg Bates*
Project manager: *Natalie J. Ruffatto*
Production supervisor: *Gina Hangos*
Senior supplement producer: *Rose M. Range*
Senior digital content specialist: *Brian Nacik*
Cover design: *Asylum Studios*
Interior Design: *Artemio Ortiz, Jr.*
Typeface: *11/13 Berkeley Book*
Compositor: *Cecelia G. Morales*
Printer: *Quebecor World Dubuque Inc.*

Library of Congress Cataloging-in-Publication Data

Burrows, William E.
   Learning programming using Visual Basic .NET / William E. Burrows, Joseph D. Langford.
      p. cm.
   Includes index.
   ISBN 0-07-245196-3 (alk. paper) -- ISBN 0-07-115146-X (international : alk. paper)
   1. Microsoft Visual BASIC. 2. BASIC (Computer program language) I. Langford,
Joseph D. II. Title.
QA76.73.B3 B87 2003
05.2'762--dc21

                                                                          2002069238

INTERNATIONAL EDITION ISBN 0-07-115146-X
Copyright © 2003. Exclusive rights by The McGraw-Hill Companies, Inc. for
manufacture and export. This book cannot be re-exported from the country to which it is sold by
McGraw-Hill.
   The International Edition is not available in North America.

www.mhhe.com

InformationTechnology

At McGraw-Hill Higher Education, we publish instructional materials targeted at the higher education market. In an effort to expand the tools of higher learning, we publish texts, lab manuals, study guides, testing materials, software, and multimedia products.

At McGraw-Hill/Irwin (a division of McGraw-Hill Higher Education), we realize that technology has created and will continue to create new mediums for professors and students to use in managing resources and communicating information to one another. We strive to provide the most flexible and complete teaching and learning tools available as well as offer solutions to the changing world of teaching and learning.

McGraw-Hill/Irwin is dedicated to providing the tools for today's instructors and students to successfully navigate the world of Information Technology.

■ **Seminar Series** McGraw-Hill/Irwin's Technology Connection seminar series offered across the country every year demonstrates the latest technology products and encourages collaboration among teaching professionals.

■ **McGraw-Hill/Osborne** This division of The McGraw-Hill Companies is known for its best-selling Internet titles, *Internet & Web Yellow* Pages and the *Internet Complete Reference*. For more information, visit Osborne at www.osborne.com.

■ **Digital Solutions** McGraw-Hill/Irwin is committed to publishing digital solutions. Taking your course online doesn't have to be a solitary adventure, nor does it have to be a difficult one. We offer several solutions that will allow you to enjoy all the benefits of having your course material online.

■ **Packaging Options** For more information about our discount options, contact your McGraw-Hill/Irwin Sales representative at 1-800-338-3987 or visit our website at **www.mhhe.com/it.**

Contents

CHAPTER FOUR   **Performing Calculations and Manipulating Data: Expressions   129**

CHAPTER FIVE   **Specifying Alternate Courses of Action: Selection Statements   181**

CHAPTER SIX

Reducing Program Complexity: General Sub Procedures and Developer-Defined Functions   229

CHAPTER SEVEN

Repeating Processing Tasks: Loop Structures   281

Preface

Goal

This is a text designed primarily to teach sound programming fundamentals. This is an important point: many Visual Basic texts focus on the "cool Visual Basic gizmos" and, in doing so, fail to teach the programming concepts that are common to all languages. That is why we titled our text *Learning Programming Using Visual Basic .NET,* not *Learning Microsoft Visual Basic .NET.* We think this distinction is important because languages come and go, but the fundamental concepts underlying the programming process stay fairly constant.

If teaching programming fundamentals is the primary goal, then why have we chosen Visual Basic .NET and not some other language? The rationale is simple: we feel that Visual Basic .NET is the language that facilitates our main goal by being relatively easy to learn without the overly complex syntax and semantic rules found in some other languages. We have been using various versions of Basic since the language was created at Dartmouth in the mid-1960s because we have always felt that programming fundamentals are the most important concepts to teach a beginning developer.

In fact, when Microsoft first introduced Visual Basic, we were initially hesitant to adopt it because it required us to attend to the graphical user interface and the components with which the GUI is constructed, and we felt that it would distract us from our primary goal. However, the excitement demonstrated by our students when they could build "real" applications using Visual Basic convinced us that we had to accept the challenge of focusing on programming fundamentals *and* include the additional instruction on the "gizmos" of the GUI.

If you look at the table of contents, you will see that we introduce Visual Basic .NET components in sections of the text where the underlying programming concepts are being discussed. For example, we talk about the RadioButton in the chapter on decision making and we talk about the ListBox in the chapter dealing with iteration. We have found that students can better understand a control by seeing it in a context where its function makes sense.

Pedagogical Design

Having over 40 years of combined teaching experience in the programming field, we have developed a number of pedagogical philosophies that have found their way into this text. The first is the observation that one learns to program by programming. We tell our students, "This is not a spectator sport." Therefore you will find a number of examples throughout the text. The code for these examples is available on the course website as well as the CD that accompanies the book and we encourage students to run the examples and to experiment. We would like to point out that when we create an example, it is generally designed to demonstrate a single concept. Therefore, the examples are not bulletproof because the bulletproofing code would just distract from the concept being demonstrated.

We have included 12 projects throughout the text and 5 comprehensive projects at the end of the text that, for the most part, are small applications. Within these projects we add the code that should make the application more robust and user-friendly. The projects within each chapter generally focus on material presented in that specific chapter. In the earlier chapters these projects provide a great deal of help on how to solve the problem and how to write the code. In later chapters the amount of detailed help is gradually reduced, challenging the student to do more independent thinking. The comprehensive problems differ in two ways. First, they generally require material from several chapters. Second, they include less "help" in terms of explaining what to do and how to do it. This makes them more challenging than the projects within each chapter.

We also include a number of exercises within each chapter. These are either short-answer questions or questions that require a small amount of code to be written by the student. We find that giving students a chance to test their understanding of concepts every few pages helps them move through the material with a greater understanding. We include answers to selected exercises in an appendix.

Each chapter ends with a set of questions designed to review the new concepts introduced within the chapter and a set of end-of-chapter programming problems that again focus on the new material from the chapter.

We also have chosen to link the topical material sequentially. That is, most chapters rely on an understanding of the preceding chapters. This allows us to go into greater depth and still retain our focus on fundamentals, because we need not wonder about the reader's background at any point in the text.

Visual Basic .NET

Now that we have established that this is book is about programming fundamentals, we need to say some words about Visual Basic .NET. Visual Basic .NET is a significant update to the previous version and it is "cool." It has been enhanced to make it as powerful as Microsoft's other two major development languages: Visual C++ .NET and C# .NET. In making this decision, Microsoft chose to introduce some significant changes to Visual Basic .NET and had to balance the historical focus of Basic with the object paradigm. These changes impact those who are already familiar with Visual Basic 6.0, but for someone new to Visual Basic they make little difference. Since we assume that you are learning to program, you have likely not seen earlier versions of Visual Basic. But you should be aware that much of what you will be learning is different, and most feel better, than what those who used earlier versions of Visual Basic learned.

Microsoft has chosen to configure Visual Basic .NET so that it is philosophically consistent with earlier versions. That is, they have set the default settings so that the beginner need not worry too much about data types. We have embraced this philosophy and have written all our code using the default settings. Instructors who wish to enforce stricter programming standards such as strong typing can do so by having their students change the default settings appropriately.

Visual Basic .NET also provides the ability to create Web Applications using Microsoft's ASP.NET technology. While we focus our attention on building Windows Applications (client solutions), we include a chapter that provides background and fundamentals of building Web Applications.

Visual Basic .NET also includes a number of tools for building sophisticated enterprisewide solutions. While these tools and features are very useful and powerful, they are beyond the scope and goals of this text.

Special Features

We have included material in this text that we think adds significantly to its value, particularly when using Visual Basic .NET to build solutions to business problems. This material includes a thorough presentation of relational databases and using Visual Basic .NET and ADO.NET to process relational databases. We also have included a chapter on XML (eXtensible Markup Language) and show how to process XML data as an alternative to data from a relational database.

As mentioned earlier, we also include a chapter on building Web Applications with Visual Basic .NET and ASP.NET. When considering the design for this text, we initially considered building the entire text around Web Applications instead of Windows Applications. However, after considering the logistics of requiring access to IIS to run the Web Applications and keeping our main goal of teaching programming fundamentals in mind, we elected to focus on Windows Applications and then include one chapter at the end of the text to introduce Web Applications. Ideally, students will have a firm understanding of the fundamentals at that point so that we can focus only on the differences between Windows and Web Applications.

Finally, while we briefly cover the concepts relating to traditional arrays, we chose to go into more detail on three classes in Visual Basic .NET that provide a set of "collection" objects. These include the ArrayList, SortedList, and Hashtable collection classes. As software evolves and becomes more object-oriented, fewer developers will be building solutions from scratch and will instead be assembling solutions from predefined class libraries. We believe that our approach is consistent with this philosophy.

Ancillary Material

The text comes with a student CD that includes Visual Basic .NET projects for all of the examples in the text as well as databases needed in problems and projects. There is also a full version of Visual Basic .NET that accompanies this text so that students may install and use Visual Basic .NET on their home computers while taking a course. Students will be required to register the product with Microsoft during the installation process.

The course website, found at www.mhhe.com/it/burrowsvbnet, contains a number of links to support materials. In addition to the code for all the examples, the course website includes an errata page in case any errors are found in the text; a link to the Microsoft Developer Network (MSDN), where documentation on Visual Basic .NET as well as documentation on other Microsoft Developer tools can be found; a link to PowerPoint slides that are available to instructors; and links to other sites of interest to Visual Basic .NET developers.

Material for instructors includes an Instructor's Manual that has a section summarizing the major differences between VB 6.0 and Visual Basic .NET and solutions to all the examples, exercises, end-of-chapter material, and all projects. Finally, a test bank is available for use by instructors. All this material is available either on a CD or at the course website.

Acknowledgments

There are so many people responsible for creating this text that it is hard to mention each one personally. However, there are a number of people who deserve special recognition. First we would like to thank Marc L. Berkenfeld and **Dan Rahmel** for their excellent technical editing of the text. In addition, Dan Rahmel provided extremely helpful suggestions on content and pedagogy as well as providing much of the end-of-chapter material.

Avner Aharoni deserves special recognition and thanks for not only providing extremely detailed technical and content editing, but also acting as a sounding board for ideas and approaches used throughout the book. Being a recent graduate of the University of Washington MBA program as well as a current Microsoft employee gave him a unique perspective from which to base his insightful suggestions. Avner was also responsible for several of the appendices dealing with Microsoft IIS, XSLT, and SQL. Amar Nalla assisted Avner with several of the appendices.

The editorial and production team at McGraw-Hill Higher Education also deserve recognition and thanks for all their help. This includes Publisher George Werthman, Associate Editor Steve Schuetz, and Developmental Editor Sarah Wood. Project Manager Natalie Ruffatto did an excellent job keeping the project on schedule and coordinating the many activities associated with editing, design, and production of the book. Copy editor Betsy Blumenthal did a remarkable job turning the rough wording of a couple of "hackers" into fine English.

Another special thanks goes to Cecelia G. Morales, who was the compositor of this text as well as its three previous editions. Her attention to detail and her skill at page layout add immense value to the text and significantly enhance the reader's experience.

Lastly we would like to thank the undergraduate Information Systems students at the University of Washington Business School for all their thoughtful suggestions and feedback over the years. The value of having direct student input into the process of creating a textbook is hard to overestimate.

Of course, even with all the help we received on the text, we accept full responsibility for any errors that might have found their way into the text.

PROBLEM SOLVING AND THE OBJECT-ORIENTED PARADIGM

Programming a computer to solve a problem provides a unique experience and challenge. Fredrick P. Brooks Jr., in his classic work titled *The Mythical Man-Month: Essays on Software Engineering,* provides us with the following viewpoint:

> The programmer, like the poet, works only slightly removed from pure thought-stuff. He builds his castles in the air, from air, creating by exertion of the imagination . . . Yet the program construct, unlike the poet's words, is real in the sense that it moves and works, producing visible outputs separate from the construct itself. It prints results, draws pictures, produces sounds, moves arms. The magic of myth and legend has come true in our time. One types the correct incantation on a keyboard, and a display screen comes to life, showing things that never were nor could be.

Creating a computer-based solution to a problem can be very challenging, at times frustrating, and also very rewarding. It provides the developer an opportunity to exercise creativity and make "real things" out of ideas. It can indeed be mystical.

This chapter describes the processes of solving problems with the intention of using a computer to actually carry out the solution steps. Solutions to some problems that we find easy to solve ourselves can be remarkably challenging when we need to specify a set of steps that will be carried out by the computer.

This chapter introduces you to a way of thinking about the world using the object paradigm. This is a way of developing programming solutions using classes and objects and is considered by many to be a superior approach to computer modeling of real-life things.

Finally, the chapter begins to introduce you to Visual Basic .NET and how Visual Basic .NET relates to problem solving and the object paradigm.

Objectives

After studying this chapter, you should be able to

- Understand some fundamental problem-solving concepts and be able to formulate algorithms using pseudocode.

- Realize that writing down the steps needed to solve a problem is not always an easy task.

- Understand what an event-driven environment is and how it impacts problem solutions.

- Describe how classes and objects work in the object paradigm.

- Use and understand the basic vocabulary of the object paradigm.

- Differentiate between visual and nonvisual software components.

- Begin understanding how Visual Basic .NET fits into the event-driven and object paradigms.

1.1 Problem Solving

We use the computer in many different ways. These include, but are not limited to, communicating using electronic mail and chat systems, writing papers and reports using a word processor, solving mathematical problems using a spreadsheet, finding useful data using database programs and the Internet, and entertaining using games and audio and video players. Note that all of these activities solve a specific type of problem (writing, Internet communication, etc.) and use *software,* or **programs to support the problem-solving activity.**

In this section we look at the general area of problem solving with a focus on solving a simple problem. We will investigate how one actually solves the problem, that is, the steps associated with solving the problem, and relate this activity to using a computer to solve the problem.

Sample Problem

We start with a very simple problem—one that we can all solve without really giving the problem much thought. In fact, the problem is so easy to solve that we might have a hard time communicating to someone else the steps that we go through to find the solution.

Problem Description

You are given five numbers as follows:

$$18 \quad 23 \quad 10 \quad 53 \quad 08$$

The problem is to find the largest number in the set of numbers. Give it a try. What's your answer? Hopefully you said 53! As we said earlier, the problem was not that hard. Notice that the problem was stated in terms of "what" you needed to do (find the largest number). It was not stated in terms of "how" you solve the problem—that was left for you to figure out. This distinction between "what" needs to be done and "how" you will arrive at the solution is important. As we will see later, the job of the developer is to figure out the "how" part of the overall problem-solving activity.

The question we next pose will likely be harder than the first question. The question we would like you to ponder is this, "How did you solve the problem?" That is, what steps did you follow to arrive at the correct answer?

Describing Your Solution

To get a feeling for problem solving via programming a computer, let us assume that in addition to your ability to describe how you would solve the problem, you must communicate your understanding to someone else who does not speak the same natural language you speak. For example, assume your native language is French and you must instruct someone who speaks German on how to solve the problem. We will assume that you have learned German and are fairly fluent in speaking the language but are naturally more comfortable using your native French language skills.

There are three steps that you need to complete in order to communicate your solution to your German-speaking friend. These are

1. Solving the problem yourself.

2. Formulating your solution approach in your natural languge (French in this example.)

3. Translating the solution from step 2 above into the other language (German in this case).

Step 1 is critical—if you cannot solve the problem yourself, there is no way you can instruct someone else on how to solve the problem. This may sound strange, but we sometimes see people trying to accomplish steps 2 and 3 when they do not know how to solve the problem. It is really just a waste of time in this case. Sometimes, like our sample problem, we can solve the problem without any thought. In other cases, we might have do some research or possess special training in order to be able to solve the problem. For example, if the problem statement asked us to determine the correct trajectory of a spacecraft so that it could land on Mars, most of us would need to do considerable research.

Step 2 can be the most challenging step of all and it is here that problem solving really takes place. We need to develop a method or set of steps that, if we follow them correctly, will produce the answer.

Let us look at our specific problem. Here are the numbers again:

18 23 10 53 08

It is likely that you looked at the five numbers and just said, "The number 53 is the largest!" What did you actually do? Perhaps you compared the first number with the second number and noted that since 23 is larger than 18, the answer is not 18. Note that you can say nothing about the 23 yet. Perhaps you then compared 23 with 10 and eliminated the 10. Continuing this process, you would compare 23 with 53 and observe that since 23 is less than 53, 23 is now eliminated from the solution. Finally you compared 53 with 8 and eliminated the 8. Since you are now out of numbers to compare to 53, you conclude that 53 is the largest.

To be honest, however, it is unlikely you consciously went through anything like this level of detail. Instead you just looked at the numbers and said 53. This brings up an issue that can be difficult. Would it be acceptable to formulate step 2 as "just look at the numbers and find the largest"? All you have done is restated the problem in terms of "what" to do; you have not come up with a statement of "how" to do it. After translating "just look at the numbers and find the largest" into German, what if your German-speaking associate responded by saying, "I don't know how to do that!" Again, think of the Mars landing problem. If I told you that my description of how to calculate the trajectory was "using the appropriate equations from physics and orbital dynamics, find the trajectory," you would likely come back and ask for more specific information. Remember that we are taking a problem statement (what to do) and trying to come up with a statement of "how" to solve the problem. The amount of detail we provide depends to a large extent on the abilities of the person (or machine) who receives the translation for the third step of our process.

Let us describe a precise set of steps that will find the largest number. We do so using English (our native language) and a brief outline style.

1. Write down the first number on a piece of paper. Identify the number as the "largest number so far." Observe that if your list contained only one number, this would be your answer.

2. Repeat the following steps until there are no more numbers.
   a. Take the next number from the list.
   b. Compare this new number to the number you have written down as the largest number so far. If this new number is bigger than the one written on the paper, erase the number on the paper and replace it with the new number.
   c. Return to step 2(*a*).

3. After completing step 2, the answer is the last number you have written down on your piece of paper.

This solution approach is sometimes called the "largest so far" solution approach because it requires you to remember the biggest number you have seen so far. When you run out of numbers, the largest so far is the largest overall because you have now seen all the numbers. The three-step process above is written using what is called *pseudocode* (**false code**). It contrasts with "real" code, the output of our third general problem-solving step, that is, translating the solution from one language to another. Webopedia.com defines pseudocode as follows:

> An outline of a program, written in a form that can easily be converted into real programming statements. Pseudocode cannot be compiled or executed, and there are no real formatting or syntax rules. It is simply one step—an important one—in producing the final code. The benefit of pseudocode is that it enables the developer to concentrate on the algorithms [defined below] without worrying about all the syntactic details of a particular programming language. In fact, you can write pseudocode without even knowing what programming language you will use for the final implementation.

Finally we need to take the pseudocode from problem-solving step 2 and translate the solution into the final target language (German in our example). Notice that this pseudocode works for number lists of any length. It works for five numbers or for five million numbers and, in both cases, we just have to remember one number (biggest so far) and compare it to one number in the list. It also works for finding the smallest number in a list by simply changing the comparison in step 2(*b*) to a "less than" comparison.

As mentioned in the definition of pseudocode above, the formal name for **the set of steps used to solve a problem** is *algorithm.* The real "art" of programming is the ability to use one's creativity and knowledge to come up with algorithms to solve a problem.

Algorithms[1]

There are several definitions of algorithm. TechEncyclopedia.com defines an algorithm as follows:

---

[1] According to Webopedia.com, the term *algorithm* was named after an Iranian mathematician, Al-Khawarizmi.

A set of ordered steps for solving a problem, such as a mathematical formula or the instructions in a program. The terms algorithm and logic are synonymous. Both refer to a sequence of steps to solve a problem.

A similar definition of algorithm comes from Webopedia.com.

A formula or set of steps for solving a particular problem. To be an algorithm, a set of rules must be unambiguous and have a clear stopping point. Algorithms can be expressed in any language, from natural languages like English or French to programming languages like Visual Basic.

We use algorithms every day. For example, a recipe for baking a cake is an algorithm. Most programs, with the exception of some artificial intelligence applications, consist of algorithms. Inventing elegant algorithms—algorithms that are simple and require the fewest steps possible—is one of the principal challenges in programming.

What we need to do is come up with the pseudocode for our algorithm and then translate this into the appropriate language of the problem solver. In a programming context, the problem solver is the computer and the language will be a programming language like Visual Basic .NET. This means that we are presented with two challenges: developing a correct solution in pseudocode and then translating that into the correct grammar (syntax) of Visual Basic .NET.

Exercise 1.1

Assume that you have three numeric values identified as A, B, and C. Write the pseudocode that results in placing the three values in order from smallest to largest. For example, if A = 10, B = 5, and C = 8, your algorithm should report that the correct order is B, C, A.

Exercise 1.2

You have two boxes labeled A and B that each can hold a single value. For example, you might have

A [35]   B [10]

Each box can hold only one value at a time. This means that if you put the value 20 into the box labeled A, the prior value 35 will be destroyed. Write an algorithm to swap or exchange the contents of the two boxes and communicate this algorithm using pseudocode. When your algorithm is done, your boxes should look like

A [10]   B [35]

You may assume that you have several "empty" boxes that each can hold one value and you may use these boxes if needed.

Exercise 1.3

You are given a list of five values identified as follows:

List Order	1st	2nd	3rd	4th	5th
Values	36	40	12	16	24

Create two different algorithms that reverse the values and write these algorithms as pseudocode. When the algorithms are finished, you should have

List Order	1st	2nd	3rd	4th	5th
Values	24	16	12	40	36

Be sure that the algorithms work for both an odd and an even number of values. You may create another list of numbers if needed, but the final result must be in the original list. You also may assume that you have several "empty" boxes that each can hold one value and you may use these boxes if needed.

Getting Data and Displaying Results

Most algorithms need data to work with. It is also important to be able to display the results of an algorithm in a meaningful and attractive format. These tasks are part of any programming application. While they are generally not considered part of the algorithm itself, they still are very important in the final solution to the problem.

The accuracy of input data is critical. An acronym that has been around computing for a long time is GIGO, which stands for "garbage in, garbage out." If you provide bad data to an algorithm, then the output of that algorithm will also be flawed. In many programs, a considerable amount of programming effort is devoted to testing and validating data supplied by the user of the application.

The results of an algorithm can range from a single numeric value to a complex graph or something even more complex like a video image. Often the results of an algorithm are usable only after they have been formatted in a way that the user can easily interpret. This often requires additional algorithms that take the results from the original problem solution and create a complex display. Again, a considerable amount of programming effort can be devoted to this activity.

You can now see the major tasks that comprise a computer-based solution to a problem. These can summarized as

- Write the appropriate computer code to accept and validate the data to be processed by the algorithm. This step also can include code to inform the user of any errors that are detected and provide an opportunity to correct those errors.

- Write the appropriate computer code to implement the algorithm, that is, process the data in a way that solves the problem at hand.

- Write the appropriate code to format the results generated by the algorithm in such a way as to enhance its usefulness to the user.

The initial version of these tasks must exist in the mind of the developer who often uses pseudocode to write down the logic necessary to complete them. The primary motivation behind this is to provide a means for arriving at the logical steps without having to worry about the specific rules and grammar associated with any formal programming language. When the algorithm is well understood in its pseudocode version, the developer then translates the solution into the formal programming language for testing and debugging (fixing the errors). It is important to follow this process regardless of the difficulty of the problem to be solved. Experienced developers always follow the process, although with experience comes the ability to do some simple problems in their heads. Beginners should not attempt to solve the problem in their heads—they should write down the pseudocode, verify that it is correct, and then translate it into programming code.

1.2   The Event-Driven Problem-Solving Environment

Most computer applications that you use today are *event driven.* This means that the **application performs actions based on events detected by the application** and otherwise just sits in what appears to be an idle state waiting for an event. A sample of user-generated events include clicking on a button named "OK", typing text into a field named "Zip Code", or clicking on a drop-down list of state abbreviations. A sample of events generated by something other than the user includes detecting the arrival of an email message or observing that a certain number of seconds have passed without any user interaction.

How does an event-driven environment impact problem solving? The answer is it helps the problem solver organize his solution into small segments of code associated with each event. For example, if the user is entering a value for a zip code field, there might be an event that is detected each time the user types a character. By including a small segment of code called an event handler or event procedure, the program can see what the user entered and if the value is invalid, reject the keystroke and inform the user of the problem. Another example might be an event handler that is executed when a new email message arrives at the user's computer. This event handler might notify the user of this event by generating a sound or causing something on the user's screen to flash.

Creating an event handler involves the same problem-solving concepts we discussed earlier. That is, first create an algorithm and pseudocode to solve the problem the event handler is intended to solve and then translate the pseudocode into actual program code.

Thus, in an event-driven environment, one organizes the solution to a problem around a series of events that reflect things to which the program should react. One important principle in software engineering states that the solution to a large problem should be broken down into small units, each of which focuses on one specific aspect of the problem and is independent of the other units. In an event-driven environment, this principle is easier to follow because there is a natural partitioning of code into units associated with each specific event. In Chapter 6 we will expand this concept and see how we can write small units of code that are not necessarily associated with an event.

Exercise 1.4

For a computer application that you are familiar with such as Microsoft Word or Excel, describe five different events that you think the application responds to.

1.3   Using the Object-Oriented Paradigm in Problem Solving

Over the years, the process of software engineering has evolved ways of looking at problems and organizing the code that is used to solve them. We just saw an example of this in the context of event-driven solutions and event procedures. Another major change has been the growing acceptance of what is called the object-oriented paradigm. In this section we will define what this paradigm is and why it is considered to be a superior way of constructing software solutions. We include a discussion of classes, objects, and class hierarchies.

Classes and Objects

Suppose you are solving a problem with your company's payroll system. In developing the solution to this problem, you obviously will be dealing with employees since it is they who are being paid. Also assume that your company has both employees who are paid by the hour (Hourly)[2] and those who are paid based on a fixed salary (Salaried). How are you going to think about these two types of employees? You know that each employee has an employee number and a name. For example, Table 1.1 shows three employees.

It is clear from this table that you have to somehow store data (employee number and name) about each employee and that all employees, regardless of their type, have these two pieces of data. There are additional data related to the employees but the additional data differ for each type of employee. For example, Hourly employees have an hourly rate and number of hours worked, while Salaried employees have an annual salary. These additional data are shown in Table 1.2.

We therefore can conclude that one thing we need to do for any employee is store some data describing that employee. What else is needed? What about the weekly gross pay due an employee? This is not a piece of data, but instead it is the result of a calculation. It could be a simple calculation (hours times rate) or it could involve more complex logic such as adjusting the hourly rate for hours in excess of 40 (overtime for example). In other words, there is an algorithm associated with paying the employee.

So we conclude that there are now two things we need for an employee: data describing the employee as well as algorithms associated with the employees and payroll. How are we to deal with these two distinct things? One alternative keeps these concepts separate. Data are stored in a database and algorithms (logic) are part of the software that processes payroll. In this paradigm, the software processes the data and generates the results (gross pay). This type of organization is called ***procedural programming*** and is **characterized by the separation of data and program logic.** Procedural programming was the dominant paradigm used throughout most of the history of programming and is still being used.

TABLE I.I Data on three employees

Employee Number	Name
1234	Joe
4321	Sue
3232	Chris

TABLE I.2 Employee data for both Hourly and Salaried employees

Employee Number	Name	Hourly Rate	Hours Worked	Annual Salary
1234	Joe	12.50	40	—
4321	Sue	—	—	52000
3232	Chris	15.00	45	—

---

2   It is a common convention to capitalize the first letter of a class name.

Another alternative is a single software component known as an ***object*** that **combines the data and program logic.** This is referred to as ***object-oriented programming*** (OOP). In OOP, since the **data and the program logic for each employee are in the same object** (sometimes referred to as a capsule), the program that uses the object does not need to know about the object's logic; it only needs to include the instructions to ask the object itself to determine its gross pay. In the object paradigm, we generally use the term ***behavior*** to **represent the algorithm or logic associated with an object.** Object orientation is actually very natural; it reflects things you see in nature all the time. For example, suppose you have a dog and have trained it to respond to the command "Speak." When you give the command Speak, your dog responds with a bark or two. Consider this to be the behavior associated with the command Speak. In the object paradigm, the command Speak would be referred to as a method or behavior of the Dog object. Thus, ***methods*** **describe the behavior associated with an object.** Your dog also would have a name, for example, Spot. So we say that the Dog object ***encapsulates*** **(holds in its capsule)** both data (Name: Spot) and behavior (Speak).

What is a class? A ***class*** is simply a **definition or template that defines how objects are created, that is, what will the data and methods of objects created from the class possess.** Have you had the experience of making cookies from scratch? You may have used a cookie cutter, like a tree or a snowman, to create the shapes of the cookies. You roll out the dough and press the cookie cutter into the dough. Each time a new "tree" cookie is created, each of these tree cookies is identical. In this analogy, the cookie cutter is the template (the class definition) and each cookie is an object created from the template. An ***instance of a class*** is **another name for an object.** We say that an object is ***instantiated*** from the class when a **new object is created.** The data are called ***instance variables*** because **they are included in each instance (each new object) created from the class template.** The methods are likewise called ***instance methods*** because **they exist for each instance created from class.**

Of course, our cookie cutter analogy is oversimplified. A class definition defines both the data and behavior of each object instantiated (created) from it. When using the object paradigm in solving problems, one of the main activities involves identifying and defining the classes that are needed to solve the problem.

Note that in many cases, a class also can define **special methods and data that are not related to objects instantiated from the class template.** They are called ***class methods*** and ***class constants.*** The class provides access to these methods and constants without the need to instantiate an object. For example, in Visual Basic .NET, the Math class provides a method to calculate the square root of a number and a constant for the number π (pi). A developer can access both this method and constant without ever instantiating an object from the Math class.

Finally, recognize that each object instantiated from a class has identical data elements and methods. However, the values of the data elements will likely differ from object to object. Figure 1.1 shows a graphical representation of our three employee objects. Note that they all contain the five data elements and all have a method named computeGrossPay(). However, the values of the five fields are not necessarily the same from object to object.

The class design that generated the three objects in Figure 1.1 is not a good design. One problem relates to the fact that both Hourly and Salaried employees are represented by the same object. This causes each object to include data from the other; this is not a good idea because it wastes valuable memory and disk storage. A second problem relates to how we use the same computeGrossPay() method for all three objects when we know that the logic for computing gross pay

FIGURE 1.1

Three Employee Objects

Employee Number: 1234 Name: Joe Hourly Rate: 12.50 Hours Worked: 40 Annual Salary: —	Employee Number: 4321 Name: Sue Hourly Rate: — Hours Worked: — Annual Salary: 52000	Employee Number: 3232 Name: Chris Hourly Rate: 15.00 Hours Worked: 45 Annual Salary: —
computeGrossPay()	computeGrossPay()	computeGrossPay()

is different for the two types of employees. Both of these problems will be resolved by using class hierarchies.

Exercise 1.5

Create a definition for a Product class. Make up several data elements and methods that you think might be found in such a class. After creating the class definition, create two sample objects using this class definition.

Class Hierarchies

You are likely already familiar with a method used by biologists and others to classify various things that they deal with. For example, consider the information in Figure 1.2.

This classification scheme demonstrates what we call an "is-a" type relationship. That is, when you move up the hierarchy, you can insert the phrase "is a." So you can say that a primate "is a" mammal and a shrew "is a(n)" insectivore. This "is-a" relationship is important because it reveals important information about the lower elements in the hierarchy. For example, mammals share the following characteristics: they breathe air, give live birth to their young, produce milk, have hair, and are warm blooded. This means that since a primate is a mammal, it shares (or inherits) these five characteristics. In addition, any element below mammal, regardless of its distance, exhibits the "is-a" relationship with mammal; for example, since a human is a primate and a primate is a mammal, then a human exhibits the five characteristics of all mammals.[3]

Also note that even though elements in the hierarchy at the same level (humans, lemurs, and marmosets) share the same five characteristics of all mammals, they are indeed different. That is, there are characters within each classification (such as walking erect or having an opposable thumb) that differentiate elements at the same level.

What, you may ask, does this have to do with the object paradigm and problem solving? Let us return to our employee example where we identified both Hourly and Salaried employees. Consider the diagram in Figure 1.3.

FIGURE 1.2

Sample Classification of Mammals

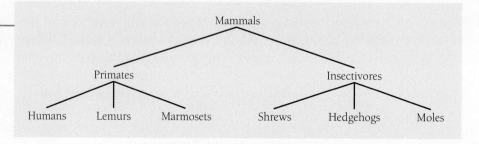

3   Since this is not a biology text, we will ignore the exceptions like the duck-billed platypus.

FIGURE 1.3

Classification of Employees

Using the "is-a" relationship, we can say that an Hourly "is a(n)" Employee and we also can say that a Salaried "is a(n)" Employee. This means that these two types of employees share everything defined for an Employee, but there are also things that are different between them. Looking back at Table 1.2, we see that all three employees have an employee number and name. However, only the Hourly employees have an hourly rate and hours worked, while only the Salaried employees have an annual salary. What we see is a very natural way to define the classes that represent our various employees. Figure 1.4 shows a class diagram using the notation of the UML (Unified Modeling Language).[4] This diagram uses a rectangle to represent a class with the class name at the top. Data elements are shown below the line.

Here we see the Employee class at the top, for which two data elements are defined: employee number and name. Since the Hourly class is a(n) Employee, it also includes these two fields. In addition, the Hourly class defines two data elements of its own: hourly rate and hours worked. Thus the Hourly class includes four data elements: employee number and name (from Employee) and hourly rate and hours worked (from Hourly). Similarly, the Salaried class includes the two data elements from the Employee class plus an annual salary data element from the Salaried class.

Notice that as far as data elements are concerned, the Hourly class and the Salaried class are different (although they both include an employee number and name element because they are both Employees). Here we have created a class design that eliminates the problems identified with the objects in Figure 1.1.

Before we go any further, we should introduce some additional terminology relating to classes and class hierarchies. Figure 1.5 shows an annotated version of Figure 1.4 with some definitional terms included.

FIGURE 1.4

A UML Class Diagram

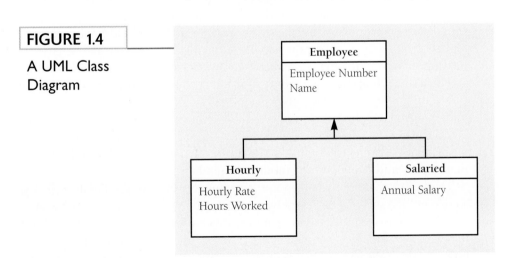

---

4   The Unified Modeling Language (UML) is a language for specifying, visualizing, constructing, and documenting the artifacts of software systems, as well as for business modeling and other nonsoftware systems. The UML represents a collection of best engineering practices that have proven successful in the modeling of large and complex systems. A full discussion of UML is beyond the scope of this text. For more information on UML, go to www.uml.org.

FIGURE 1.5

Some Terminology
Used in a Class
Diagram

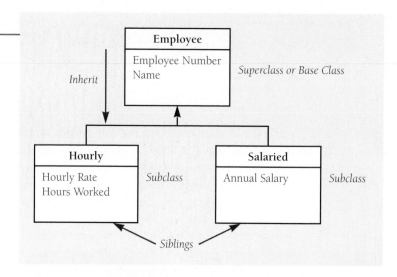

Using this terminology, we say that the Hourly class is a **subclass** (or **descends from**) the Employee class. We also can say that the Employee class is the **superclass** (or base class) of both the Hourly and Salaried classes because it **contains data and behavior common to the subclasses.** Both subclasses (Hourly and Salaried) inherit the data elements (as well as the methods, as we will see shortly) from their superclass (Employee). **Inheritance describes the process whereby a subclass takes on all the data elements and behaviors of the superclasses to which it is related.** This inheritance extends up through all the levels. This means that if you have three classes (class A at the top, class B as a subclass of A, and class C as a subclass of B), then class C inherits all the data and methods from class B (including all the data and methods class B inherited from class A).

The term **member** is often used to **describe the contents of a class.** You can say "data member" if you are referring to a data element defined in a class and you can say "behavior member" if you are talking about a method of the class. Using the unqualified term "members" implies you are talking about both the data and behavior of a class. As mentioned earlier, we also differentiate between instance and class data and behavior. We use the terms "instance members" and "class members" to describe these two concepts when differentiating between data and behavior is not important (but differentiating between instance and class is important).

The term **sibling** describes **any two or more classes that descend from the same superclass.** The siblings share members inherited from the common superclass but can, and almost always do, include either additional members or modified behavior. In this regard, we say that a subclass **extends** a superclass. This means that the **subclass includes everything the superclass had (via inheritance) plus additional and/or modified members.**

There is another important concept regarding class hierarchies. Recall in the last section we said that objects are software components that are created from the class template or class definition. For example, we could instantiate an Hourly object that would include the data members employee number, name, hourly rate, and hours worked. We also could instantiate a Salaried object. Now we ask the question: would we ever want to instantiate an Employee object? Going back to the biology example, would we ever want to instantiate a mammal? If we did, what would we have? What exactly is an employee or a mammal? In reality, we usually do not want to actually create an object from a class that has descendents. This is because the "real thing" is the descendent. For example, the real mammal is the human because its superclasses (primate and mammal) are incomplete—they lack sufficient data and behavior to be a "real" thing. In other words, we need to extend the superclasses sufficiently before we have the real thing. So why do we have the superclasses at all? Give this some thought. Isn't this just a convenient way of providing a place to define all the common data and behavior of the subclasses? That is, by putting the definitions that are common to all the subclasses in one superclass, then we do not need redundant definitions within the subclasses.

We use the term *abstract class* to describe **classes that cannot be used to instantiate objects but provide a base class to store the common data and behavior of all of its descendents.**

Exercise 1.6

Create a UML class diagram for Bank accounts. There should be two types of accounts: Saving and Checking. Both account types include a customer number, customer name, and account balance. Saving accounts include an interest rate and checking accounts have a check-writing fee. Your diagram should include only the data elements (you may ignore any methods).

Exercise 1.7

Create a UML class diagram for Customers. There are two types of customers: Credit and Cash. Each customer is identified with a customer identifier. You also need to store the name, address, and total sales to date for each customer. In addition, credit customers include a credit limit as well as an interest rate. Your diagram should include only the data elements (you may ignore any methods).

Benefits of Using Object Orientation in Problem Solving

Using the object paradigm in problem solving has many advantages. First of all, using classes to represent real things reflects the very natural way humans think. We can see classes (and their associated objects) in everyday life. If we ask a purchasing manager what the things she deals with on a day-to-day basis are, she might say employees, products, customers, and suppliers. All of these can be represented easily with a set of classes and subclasses.

Another advantage of using classes and objects is the ease with which an organization can use the same class definition in many different applications. For example, the same customer class used by the sales application might find its way into the accounts receivable application module of the accounting application. This supports the concept known as *code reuse*, **the ability to reuse the same objects in many different applications.**

Using class hierarchies also has several advantages. First, when we create a new subclass, we automatically inherit all the members from the superclass. This makes the job of creating a new subclass very easy. Figure 1.6 shows our original Employee class hierarchy with an additional type of employee added.

This new Commissioned employee automatically inherits all the members from the Employee class, so all we are left to define are the things that are special to the Commissioned class. In fact, subclassing is sometimes referred to as *specialization* because a **subclass is a specialized version of its superclass.**

An additional benefit of using class hierarchies and inheritance is that if we discover a problem in one of the superclasses, we can fix this problem and all of the descendents automatically will inherit this correction. This makes maintaining applications in the object paradigm easier and more efficient.

FIGURE 1.6

Adding a Commissioned Employee to the Class Hierarchy

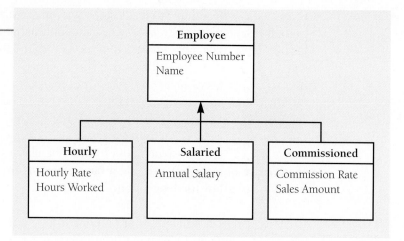

FIGURE 1.7

Class Diagram with the computeGross-Pay() Method Added

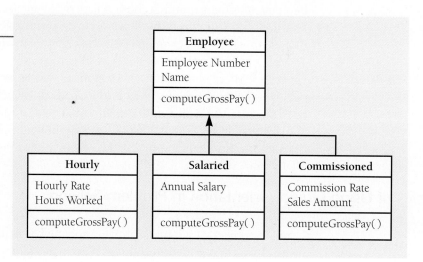

Finally, one of the greatest benefits of using the object paradigm is the ability to take advantage of a concept known as polymorphism. This is a difficult concept, but well worth looking at. Figure 1.7 shows our now-familiar Employee class hierarchy but it has added the computeGrossPay() behavior we talked about earlier. Note that in a UML class diagram, methods are shown in their own section below the definition of data elements.

All three of the subclasses include the computeGrossPay() method, but each actually does the computation differently. In the Hourly class, we will multiply hourly rate times hours worked, in the Salaried class, we will divide the annual salary by 52 (assuming we are calculating weekly salary), and in the Commissioned class, we will multiply the sales amount times the commission rate.

What will the computeGrossPay() method contain for the abstract class Employee? Remember, this class is just a place to put common data and behavior. The answer is simple—it will contain nothing! That's right, it will be empty because if you think about it, there is no way to know in advance whether you will be instantiating an Hourly, a Salaried, or a Commissioned object. We use the term *abstract method* to describe **any method in an abstract class whose definition is empty.** However, the superclass requires this empty definition in order for polymorphism to work. It is too early in this text to explain why we need to do this, so for now let us just accept this statement as true.

Suppose that we want to processes a collection of employees and compute their gross pay. Assume the employee objects (with their data and behavior) are stored in a database and include any combination of Hourly, Salaried, and Commissioned employees. We can write some pseudocode to process the collection of objects and print out their employee number, name, and gross pay. The pseudocode is

1. *Repeat this step for each Employee object that exists in the database.*
   a. *Get an Employee object from the database. Refer to it as emp.*
   b. *Print the requested information:*
      Print emp.Employee Number, emp.Name, emp.computeGrossPay()
2. *Perform any additional processing and then terminate.*

The pseudocode should be fairly easy to understand except for some notation. When we say "emp.Name," we are referring to the value of the Name data element in the object referred to as "emp." The same is true for "emp.Employee Number"— this is the value of the Employee Number data element for the object referenced by "emp." Finally, the notation "emp.computeGrossPay()" asks the specific object, whether it is an Hourly or a Salaried object, to compute its gross pay according to the rules that it knows. So if "emp" refers to an Hourly object, then hourly rate times hours worked is computed. If "emp" refers to a Salaried object, then annual salary divided by 52 is computed, and so on.

The statement "emp.computeGrossPay()" demonstrates **polymorphism.** The **same method (computeGrossPay()) has different behavior depending on the type of object (Hourly, Salaried or Commissioned) to which "emp" is referring.**

How would this same procedure look in a procedural program without objects? Table 1.3 shows what the data might look like for five different employees.

The pseudocode for processing this set of data from a database (one row at a time) would be

1. *Repeat while rows remain to be processed*
   a. *Read a row of data.*
   b. *If Employee Type = "Hourly" then*
      compute grossPay = Hourly Rate × Hours Worked
   c. *If Employee Type = "Salaried" then*
      compute grossPay = Annual Salary / 52
   d. *If Employee Type = "Comm" then*
      compute grossPay = Comm Rate × Sales
   e. *Print Employee Number, Name, grossPay*
2. *Perform any additional processing and then terminate.*

Notice how much actual "logic" is in this second procedural version of the pseudocode compared to the object-oriented version. More importantly, imagine that the company adds three more types of employees. What happens to the

TABLE 1.3 Employee data for Hourly, Salaried, and Commissioned employees

Employee Number	Employee Type	Name	Hourly Rate	Hours Worked	Annual Salary	Comm Rate	Sales
1234	Hourly	Joe	12.50	40	—	—	—
4321	Salaried	Sue	—	—	52000	—	—
3232	Hourly	Chris	15.00	45	—	—	—
5423	Comm	Ann	—	—	—	.12	32,400
6523	Salaried	Bob	—	—	26000	—	—

pseudocode for the object solution? The answer is nothing. Polymorphism takes care of the problem because each of the three new classes would include a method called computeGrossPay() that would compute the pay according to the correct set of rules.

What happens to the pseudocode in the second procedural version? The answer is a lot! You would have to add three more "If" questions with different formulas for computing gross pay. In a real-life situation, you likely would see many places where the procedural code differentiated between the types of employees and each one of these segments of code would have to be modified to reflect the three additional employee types.

So the final major benefit of the object paradigm is the ability to use polymorphic behavior to make program maintenance much easier and less error prone.

Exercise 1.8

Create the UML class diagram as described in Exercise 1.6. Add two methods, one named Deposit() and the other named Withdrawal(). Describe via pseudocode how these methods would operate for each class. Clearly state any assumptions that you make.

Exercise 1.9

Create the UML class diagram as described in Exercise 1.7. Add a method named MakeSale() that represents the sale of an item to a customer. Describe via pseudocode how this method would operate for each class. Clearly state any assumptions that you make.

Visual versus Nonvisual Components

Some objects (software components) can be seen on the **GUI** (**graphical user interface**). For example, Figure 1.8 shows a simple GUI where the user enters a name and then clicks on the button titled "Continue."

This sample GUI has an object called a TextBox and another object called a Button. These are objects created from the TextBox and Button classes. Each object has a number of data elements and methods associated with it. For example, the TextBox has a data element called the Text property that holds the information the user types into the box. The Button has a method named Hide() that causes the button to become invisible on the GUI.

Other objects, such as our Hourly, Salaried, and Commissioned employee objects, do not have a visual image. That is, the user does not see anything on the GUI associated with these objects. If the developer wants the user to see the contents of one of these nonvisual objects, then he must get the information from the object and then transfer it to the visible data element of one of the visual objects. For example, we might want to display the information for one of our Salaried objects. This might look like the screen in Figure 1.9.

FIGURE 1.8

A Sample GUI with a TextBox and Button Component

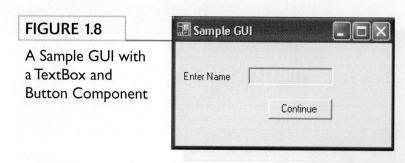

FIGURE 1.9

Displaying a Salaried
Object's Data
Elements

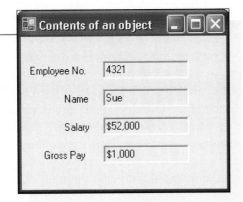

What you see on the GUI in Figure 1.9 are four TextBox objects (visual objects). As stated above, each of these objects has a data element called the Text property that holds the information seen on the screen. The developer has written some code to get the three data members from a Salaried object and transferred them to the TextBox's Text property. She also has executed the computeGrossPay() method and placed the result in the bottom TextBox's Text property. With this example you can see how the nonvisual Salaried object's contents can be displayed on the GUI—we have to use a visual component as the object to actually display the contents.

Most of the visual components you will use are provided by Microsoft and are part of Visual Basic .NET. Using Visual Basic .NET, you also can create your own visual component or create a new subclass of an existing visual component. In the latter case, you can add additional data or behavior methods to customize the component to your requirements. For example, you could create a subclass of the TextBox class that allowed only numeric values to be entered into its Text property.

Microsoft provides a number of nonvisual classes. These classes are generally considered utilities, that is, classes that provide the developer with behavior that is very useful in many different applications. As mentioned previously, there is a class called the Math class. This class includes a class data member that holds the constant for π. You can access this constant by saying Math.PI. The Math class also includes the class method (behavior) called Round(). This method rounds a value to a specified number of decimal places. For example, Math.Round(3.46, 1) produces the value 3.5 (3.46 rounded to one decimal place).

Other nonvisual classes generally are created by the developer and relate to the problem being solved. Our Employee, Salaried, Hourly, and Commissioned classes are examples of these.

Visual Basic .NET provides the developer with the ability to create or subclass either type of nonvisual component. There is also a market for what are called third-party component developers. These developers create both visual and nonvisual components and sell or license them to other developers. This brings up a very important point. By subclassing a component provided by Microsoft or a third-party developer (assuming the license permits such activities), you are able to leverage thousands of hours of development and testing at no cost. From a business perspective, this is a very important by-product of the object paradigm.

Exercise 1.10

Using an application you are familiar with such as Microsoft Word or Excel, identify five different types of visual objects (do not, for example, use five buttons) and indicate one event you think each might respond to.

1.4 Object Paradigm in Visual Basic .NET

We have now completed our general introduction to problem solving and the object paradigm. In the prior section we began looking at what Microsoft provides in terms of features and components within their Visual Basic .NET development environment. In this section we extend this discussion to introduce some of the terminology used by Microsoft relating to their implementation of the object paradigm.

The first thing about Visual Basic .NET that you should be aware of is that it supports both the procedural as well as the object-oriented programming paradigm and it does so in an event-driven environment.[5] This means that much of the code you write will be associated with various events. You will write events that respond to the user clicking on a button, or the user typing into a text box, or the user making a choice from a set of menu items. Within these event procedures, your code often will be procedural, so you can see a mixture of both paradigms.[6]

As mentioned in the previous section, Visual Basic .NET also supports the creation of both visual and nonvisual classes and fully supports the concepts of inheritance and polymorphism. Visual Basic .NET supports what is called **single inheritance.** This means that a **subclass can be related to one and only one superclass.** Some languages support *multiple inheritance* where a **subclass can be related to one or more superclasses.** Visual Basic .NET does not support multiple inheritance but provides an alternative using a technique called interfaces. However, this is beyond the scope of this text.

Your program needs to inform Visual Basic .NET when it wants access to a class to instantiate objects and use its methods and data elements. To do this, your program will "import" the class (we'll see the details later in the text). To make things easier and reduce the number of imports, Visual Basic .NET has defined a concept known as a *namespace.* A namespace **identifies a set of classes that are treated as a group.** If you import the namespace, then you have access to all the classes identified in that namespace. For example, if your code imports the System namespace, then you have access to the Math class and all of its methods and data elements (as well as over 75 other classes).

As we work our way through the remainder of the text, we will learn more about all these concepts and see the specific details that are needed to use them.

Chapter Summary

1. Problem solving with a computer requires that the developer first be able to solve the problem without using a computer. That is, she should have sufficient knowledge and expertise and be able to create an algorithm, or set of steps, that define how the problem will be solved. This algorithm should be written down as pseudocode that is unambiguous and sufficiently detailed so that it can be translated easily into the code of a particular programming language.

2. Creating algorithms is not easy. Often tasks that are easy for us to complete without a computer, such as finding the largest number in a list of numbers, can be challenging when you try to write down the steps so a computer can do the same thing.

---

[5] You might want to stop reading right here and try to describe for yourself exactly what this sentence means. There is a lot of content here.

[6] Most modern languages such as Java and C# .NET combine the procedural and object paradigms. The most popular object-only language used today is a language called SmallTalk.

3. In addition to the basic problem-solving algorithm, most computer applications also include code that is used to obtain input data for the algorithm as well as code to display the results. This additional code is generally not considered part of the basic algorithm but is still an important part of any computer-based solution.

4. An event-driven environment is one where the application responds to events generated by the user (such as clicking on a button) or by the system (such as the arrival of an email message). In an event-driven environment, the code used to solve the problem is organized into small units called event procedures that are designed to respond to each specific event.

5. Objects are software components created from a template called a class. Each class template defines data as well as behavior that each object created from the class possesses.

6. Classes can be arranged in hierarchies that define a set of "is-a" relationships. Superclasses (or base classes) are at the top of the hierarchy and subclasses descend from these superclasses. A subclass "is a" superclass. This means that all the data elements as well as behavior methods defined in the superclass are inherited (passed down) to the subclass.

7. The object paradigm and polymorphism (the same method generating different behavior depending on the specific class from which the object was created) provide a development environment that is very natural and one that helps produce solutions that are more flexible and easier to maintain compared to the more traditional procedural approach.

8. Classes can define objects that are either visual in nature (can be seen on the GUI) or nonvisual (cannot be seen directly on the GUI). Most classes created by developers to solve business problems are in the nonvisual category.

9. Visual Basic .NET creates event-driven solutions using a combination of the object and procedural paradigms that is typical of most modern programming languages. It includes support for creating both visual and nonvisual classes and also supports subclassing so that existing classes can be extended for specialized needs.

Key Terms

abstract class	inheritance	polymorphism
abstract method	instance method	procedural
algorithm	instance of a class	programming
behavior	instance variable	pseudocode
class	instantiate	sibling
class constant	member	single inheritance
class method	method	software
code reuse	multiple inheritance	specialization
encapsulates	namespace	subclass
event driven	object	superclass
extend	object-oriented	
GUI	programming	

End-of-Chapter Problems

1. What are the three steps you learned to follow in order to communicate how to solve a problem to a foreign-speaking friend (or computer)?

2. Explain the difference between pseudocode and actual program code.

3. Explain what is meant by the term *algorithm* and describe an example of one.

4. What is an event-driven program? Provide a few examples of events that may occur on a computer.

5. How does an "instance of a class" relate to an "object"?

6. Explain what is meant by polymorphism. Give an example where polymorphism could be used.

7. What is an abstract method? Would an abstract method be more likely to be used in a superclass or a subclass?

8. Does Visual Basic .NET directly support single inheritance or multiple inheritance?

9. Can Visual Basic .NET use the object-oriented programming paradigm or the procedural paradigm or both? Most Visual Basic .NET programs are written using which of these methods?

10. What is the difference between a visual and a nonvisual component? Give an example of each type.

CHAPTER TWO

CREATING SIMPLE VISUAL BASIC .NET WINDOWS APPLICATIONS

Modern software development usually involves the use of something called an *integrated development environment* or **IDE.** The IDE **includes tools to write code, build a graphical user interface (GUI), and test and debug applications.** In this chapter we focus on the Visual Basic .NET IDE.

We begin this chapter with a brief overview of the application construction process—that is, how the developer uses the Visual Basic .NET IDE to complete a project after identifying the user requirements and designing the new application. This overview provides a framework for the remainder of the chapter.

Next we turn our attention to design issues. We start with the basic structure that all VB projects possess. We then present an overview of **Visual Basic .NET controls[1]—the objects that appear on the user interface**—and examine three controls in detail: the Button, Label, and TextBox controls. We also take a brief look at the Windows Form control. These controls are sufficient to begin designing applications.

We then examine the MsgBox statement, which provides a way to alert the user to some condition using a separate window. We also examine the InputBox() function, which provides a way to get information from the user as the program executes.

We conclude with a project that brings together much of the material and provides an opportunity to put the concepts and techniques together in a working application.

Objectives

After studying this chapter, you should be able to

- Design and construct simple complete applications from scratch.

- Explain the structure of Visual Basic .NET projects.

- List the characteristics of several Visual Basic .NET controls—the objects that appear on the user interface—and the uses for which each is appropriate.

- Identify the purpose of each major tool of the Visual Basic .NET IDE.

- Explain basic programming practices that contribute to the readability of programs.

---

1   The terms *control* and *component* (as used in Chapter 1) are used interchangeably throughout this text.

2.1 | From New Solution to Finished Application

We begin this section by examining the construction process from a new Visual Basic .NET solution to a finished application in the user's hands. We then introduce Visual Basic .NET's modes of operation and discuss how the developer uses them to build, execute, and test the solution.

Overview of the Construction Process

Figure 2.1 illustrates the major steps in the application construction process. The developer begins by starting Visual Basic .NET, which initially presents a Start page for creating a new project or opening an existing one. The developer then proceeds to build the project (part of the overall solution). Visual Basic .NET has three modes of operation for building a project—design, run, and break—which we will discuss later in this section.

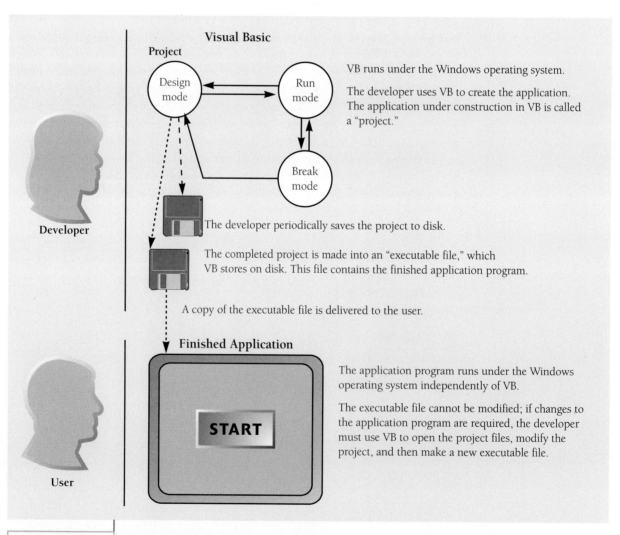

Visual Basic

Project

Design mode — Run mode

Break mode

Developer

VB runs under the Windows operating system.

The developer uses VB to create the application. The application under construction in VB is called a "project."

The developer periodically saves the project to disk.

The completed project is made into an "executable file," which VB stores on disk. This file contains the finished application program.

A copy of the executable file is delivered to the user.

Finished Application

START

User

The application program runs under the Windows operating system independently of VB.

The executable file cannot be modified; if changes to the application program are required, the developer must use VB to open the project files, modify the project, and then make a new executable file.

FIGURE 2.1

Visual Basic .NET Project and Finished Application

The time needed for the developer to build the complete application depends on its complexity. A simple application can be constructed in a few minutes, while a complex application may take a team of developers months to build. In any case, the developer periodically saves the solution on disk while building it.

When finished building the solution and its project(s), the developer saves it on disk one last time, then instructs Visual Basic .NET to add it to a deployment project that creates an executable distribution file. **An *executable file* is a file on disk that contains the finished application program, which the computer can execute independently of Visual Basic .NET.** A copy of the executable file is delivered to the user, who can then run the application on another computer.

Two observations regarding this process are critical. First, the user need not know anything about Visual Basic .NET to use the program. All the user knows is to expect a working program from the developer. Second, the contents of the executable file are unintelligible to humans and cannot be easily modified.[2] If changes to the application are required, the developer typically must use Visual Basic .NET to open the solution's project files, modify them as required, save the solution again, make a new executable file, and then give a copy of the new executable file to the user.

Because the executable file cannot be modified, the solution's project files are the chief repositories of the developer's work. Typically, when you buy a software package, you receive only an executable file. This enables you to run the application but prevents you from looking at its internal details to learn how it works or to modify it; only the developers who have the project files are able to do this.

Visual Basic .NET's Three Modes

The developer typically constructs a solution's projects a piece at a time, by building some of its user interface and adding some of the processing scripts for this part of the user interface, then testing this work before going on. Processing scripts contain the program logic used in the application. The term ***source code* is often used to describe the processing scripts**. Visual Basic .NET has three modes of operation to support this piece-at-a-time approach. As shown in Figure 2.1, the three modes are called design mode, run mode, and break mode. The developer can switch between them as shown by the solid arrows in the figure.

Design Mode
***Design mode* enables the developer to build and modify the project.** Some of the tasks it allows the developer to perform are

- Placing, arranging, and customizing the appearance of buttons, labels, and so forth, on a form.

- Writing processing scripts (code).

- Saving the solution.

- Making an executable file.

---

2   The computer instructions contained in the executable file are in ***machine language,*** which is **the language of 0s and 1s that the computer operates with internally.**

Run Mode

Run mode **enables the developer to run the project and interact with it just as a user would.** That is, in run mode Visual Basic .NET executes the solution just as Windows would execute an executable file.

The solution does not have to be complete for the developer to use run mode. Typically, the developer uses design mode to build a piece of the solution, then switches to run mode to evaluate whether the new piece operates correctly. The developer then switches back to design mode and either corrects problems discovered using run mode or starts building the next piece of the project.

The developer also may use run mode to show the user how the (unfinished) solution operates. This gives the user a chance to evaluate the solution and provide suggestions for improvement, which the developer may then be able to incorporate into the project.

Break Mode

Break mode **enables the developer to temporarily suspend execution of the running solution and examine the status of its processing scripts including values of variables being used by the scripts.** This capability helps the developer with *debugging,* which is **the task of determining the cause of the problem when the solution does not run as expected.** Debugging techniques are discussed in Appendix A.

After examining the status of the solution's processing scripts, the developer can switch back to run mode, which causes Visual Basic .NET to resume executing the solution where it left off (at the point when the developer switched to break mode), or to design mode to make changes in the processing scripts or build the next piece of the project.

Design Time and Run Time

When Visual Basic .NET is in design mode, the project is said to be at design time. When Visual Basic .NET is in run mode or break mode, the project is said to be at run time. These terms are useful because while building the project (at design time) the developer must be able to visualize how it will appear and behave when the computer executes it (at run time).

The difference between design time and run time is important in locating and correcting errors. Visual Basic .NET can detect some kinds of programming errors—for example, spelling errors—at design time, as the developer types the processing script. Visual Basic .NET immediately alerts the developer when it finds such an error, and the developer can correct the error on the spot. Other kinds of programming errors become apparent only at run time, when the computer executes the processing script. Here the developer has to determine what circumstances arose at run time to cause the processing script to fail. As an example, suppose the processing script performs a calculation using a number entered by the user at run time. The processing script might work fine when the number is positive but fail when the number is negative. The developer thus has to determine how to modify the processing script back at design time so that it won't fail at run time.

2.2 | **Overview of Controls**

One of the ways Visual Basic .NET helps developers create user-friendly applications is by providing a standard set of controls that they can incorporate into their programs. Standard controls make it easier for users to learn and run new programs. Just by its appearance, a user knows roughly what a standard control's purpose is, how it behaves, and the kinds of actions to which it might respond.

Categories of Controls

Visual Basic .NET controls fall into five general categories of fundamental functions, listed in Table 2.1. For each category, the table lists the controls that are typically used in the Primary Controls column and other controls that can be used (but are typically not used) in the Others column. Be aware that this is an incomplete list of Visual Basic .NET Windows Forms controls. The most common controls are show in the table.

In some situations the developer may want a single control to serve more than one purpose. For example, a text box can be used to get input data, display results, and trigger processing, and in a specific situation there could be practical reasons for using it for all three. However, when using a control for multiple purposes, the developer must be careful that the result will not confuse the user.

Table 2.1 Categories of Visual Basic .NET Windows Forms controls

Category	Primary Controls	Others
Trigger: Initiate processing	Button MainMenu Timer	TextBox PictureBox ListBox Form
Input: Get data from user	TextBox RadioButton CheckBox ListBox ComboBox	Various dialog boxes TrackBar
Output: Display results to user	Label DataGrid ListView PictureBox	TextBox ListBox Scroll bars Form
Organize: Group other controls	Form GroupBox Panel TabControl	PictureBox
Data Access: Interface with databases	Entire Data Group DataGrid	

The Correct Control for the Job

Part of designing a good **graphical user interface (GUI)** for an application is choosing controls to satisfy user requirements. In some situations selecting the correct control requires careful judgment, and experience is the best guide. New Visual Basic .NET developers who lack experience should abide by the conventional uses of controls and make exceptions only when there is good reason.

As an analogy, consider each type of control to be like a tool in a toolbox. Users and developers alike recognize tools by their appearance and understand that different tools are good for different tasks. A carpenter knows that it's possible to drive a nail using a wrench, but it's generally much more difficult and you are more likely to bend nails and injure your hands than if you use a hammer. Similarly, a developer can make a TextBox control work in situations for which a Label control is really appropriate, but doing so is unwise. For example, consider an order-entry application. The user enters a product number, and the application automatically looks up and displays the price of that product. The appropriate control for displaying the price is the Label; it displays text well, and, indeed, it can do nothing else. The text box, on the other hand, can display results, but its primary purpose is to accept user input. Thus, if the developer chooses to use a text box instead of a label, the user, knowing that text boxes allow user input, might mistakenly infer that the displayed price could be changed. Using the proper control will avoid the possibility of this type of confusion. Pay attention to popular programs such as Microsoft Word and Excel and use them as a guide for the generally acceptable use of the various controls. By closely examining these programs, the beginning developer can leverage some of the knowledge of more experienced user interface designers and learn from their choices.

In this chapter we introduce the Button, Label, and TextBox controls. You can see from Table 2.1 that with just these three controls, we will have a way of getting user input and we will be able to trigger processing steps and display results in a well-organized fashion. We also will cover two additional ways of getting user input and displaying results using the InputBox function and MsgBox statement. Most of the other controls in Table 2.1 will be introduced at appropriate times as we proceed through the text.

2.3 The Visual Basic .NET Development Environment

In this section we look at the Visual Basic .NET integrated development environment (IDE). It is important that you become familiar with the IDE so you can be efficient and effective in creating your solutions. The IDE for Visual Basic .NET is the same as all the other tools available within the Visual Studio .NET suite, so once you learn the IDE, you may apply that knowledge to the other tools.

Getting Started

When you first start Visual Basic .NET, you will likely[3] see the Start Page as shown in Figure 2.2.

---

[3] We say "likely" because the IDE is very customizable. If you are using a computer in a lab, the people who used the IDE before you may have changed it from the standard configuration.

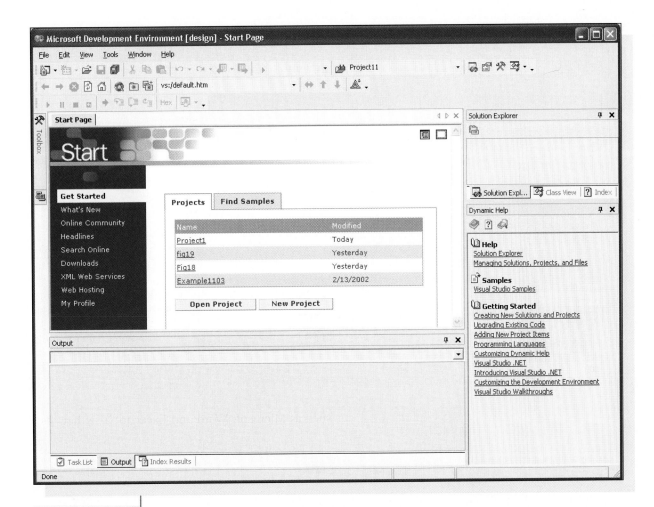

FIGURE 2.2

The Visual Basic
.NET Start Page

From the *Start Page* **you can open an existing project or create a new project** (we will talk about what a project is shortly). You can see that the most recent projects are shown on the Start Page. You also can perform a number of activities from the list on the left side of the screen. If you click on the *My Profile* **option, you can tell the IDE how you plan to use it and it will set things up in a way that is most useful for you.** Figure 2.3 shows the My Profile page. You can see that it has been set up for a Visual Basic Developer. You also can indicate what you want to have happen when you first start the IDE. After setting your profile, you can click on the Get Started item in the left pane to go back to the Start Page.

Visual Basic .NET Solution Structure

Every application you create using Visual Basic .NET will be organized as a "solution." Microsoft's Help system states that "To efficiently manage the items that are required by your development effort, such as references, data connections, folders, and files, Visual Studio .NET provides two containers: solutions and projects. An interface for viewing and managing these containers and their associated items, Solution Explorer, is provided as part of the integrated development environment (IDE). A *solution* **container can contain multiple projects** and a *project* **container typically contains multiple items.**" *Items* are **files that comprise your project, such as forms, source files, and classes.** As we talk more about building a solution, we will refer to these definitions to give concrete examples of the concepts they represent.

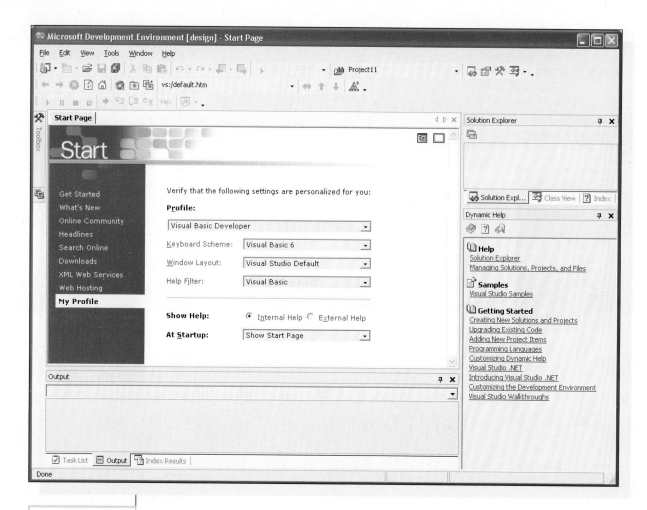

FIGURE 2.3

Setting the User Profile

Main Tools Used in Visual Basic .NET

The IDE has a number of tools used by the developer to support the creation and testing of solutions. Figure 2.4 identifies the main tools we will be using in this text. Later we show you how to open a project so that you can see the Visual Basic .NET IDE shown in Figure 2.4 Next we cover each tool in some detail.

Menu

The menu is just like any other menu in a Windows application. One thing to be aware of is the menu items can change as you select different windows on the IDE. This happens often when you select the Designer window. We'll discuss the various menu items as we use them.

Toolbar

The toolbar provides a way of accessing common menu items by clicking on a toolbar icon. Again, this is just like other Windows applications such as Microsoft Word or Excel. You can add/delete items in the toolbar by right-clicking on the toolbar and selecting the appropriate choice from the pop-up menu.

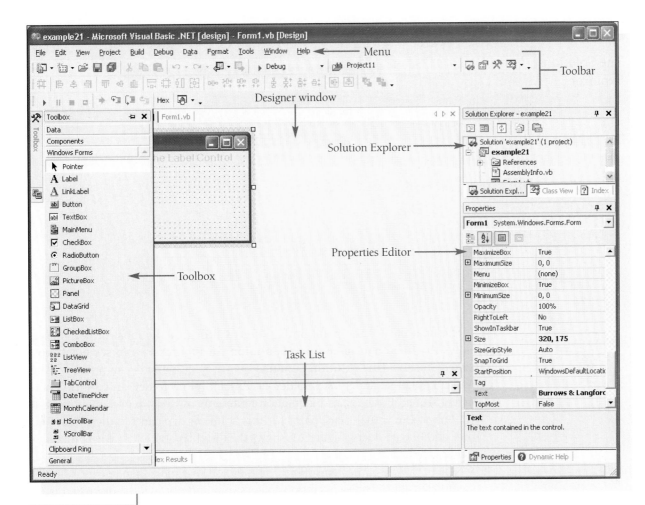

FIGURE 2.4

The Main Tools Used in the Visual Basic .NET IDE

Solution Explorer

The *Solution Explorer* **provides a view of the files associated with the solution.** Figure 2.5 shows a larger image of the Solution Explorer.

The two View buttons show either the code (the Visual Basic .NET statements that you write) or the Designer window (where you build your GUI, for example). The Refresh button just refreshes the Solution Explorer. The Show All Files button shows all the files associated with the solution. When you are not showing all the files (like in Figure 2.5), the IDE suppresses files that are generally not important to the developer. The Properties button causes the Properties Editor to show (if it is not already visible). The Auto Hide button (the pushpin icon) locks the window open (as we see here with the pushpin "pushed in" so the window stays open all the time). If you look back at Figure 2.4, you will see the pushpin for the Toolbox not pushed in. We'll explain that when we get to the Toolbox.

The Selection tabs at the bottom demonstrate that you have a choice of windows available in this same area. You can show the Solution Explorer (as we see in Figure 2.5) and also the Class View or the Help system's Contents or Index. Be warned that deciding what windows get grouped together can be changed by the user, so you may not always see the tab groups as shown here.

FIGURE 2.5

The Solution
Explorer

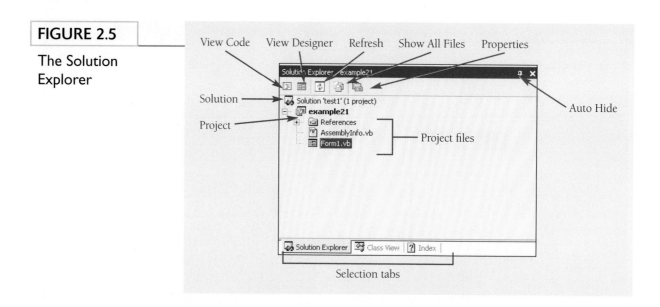

The final part of the Solution Explorer is probably the most important—it shows the files that make up the solution. In Figure 2.5, we see a solution named "test1". This solution contains one project named "example21". The project contains a References folder, an AssemblyInfo folder, and a form component named Form1. The indentation represents ownership or containment. If we look at the actual disk folder for this solution, we can see these files and some additional folders. Figure 2.6 shows the disk files and folder where the solution is saved.

Note that some of the items (Form1 and Project) use more than one file with different extensions. The two support folders (bin and obj) will be discussed later.

Properties Editor

The *Properties Editor,* shown in Figure 2.7, **provides a place for the developer to change the value of properties associated with the controls used in the design.** Recall from Chapter 1 the discussion of classes and methods associated with those classes. In designing a Visual Basic .NET GUI, the developer creates objects (also called controls or components) by dragging them out of the Toolbox

FIGURE 2.6

Contents of the
Folder Named test1

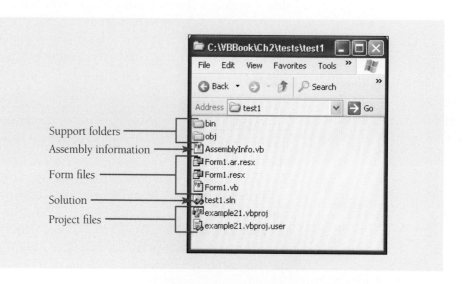

FIGURE 2.7

The Properties
Editor

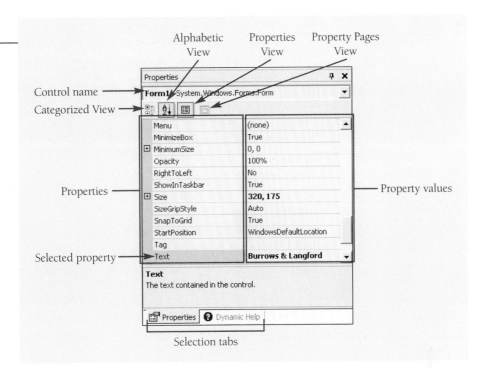

(more on that later) onto the Designer window. Once these objects are in the Designer window, their properties (referred to as instance variables) can be seen and changed in the Properties Editor. As you can see in Figure 2.7, the property names are shown on the left side and property values are shown on the right side. The name "Property Editor" is derived from the fact that the tool provides a place for the developer to edit or change the value (at design time) of the properties associated with each component on the Designer window.

To edit a property, you first click on its name in the list on the left and then change the value on the right. Some property values contain text (like the Text property that is selected in Figure 2.7) and in this case you just type whatever new text is appropriate. Other properties can have only a certain value selected from a defined list of choices. In this case you will see a drop-down list from which you select your choice. Finally, some properties are changed from a separate dialog box. If you click on a property value and a button with ellipses (...) appears, then clicking on the button displays the dialog box. Figure 2.8 shows the three types of control values.

Be aware that not all of a control's properties are shown (sometimes referred to as "exposed") in the Properties Editor at design time. Some properties are available only at run time. Also be aware that the IDE displays property values that have

FIGURE 2.8

Editing a Property's
Value

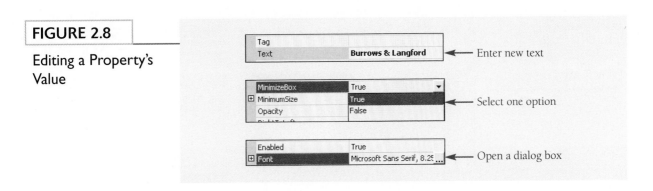

been changed from their initial default values using bold font. So as you scroll through the properties and look at their values, you can easily see which values you have changed.

We will address the Dynamic Help tab later.

Task List

The *Task List* **provides a place to record things that you need to do or be reminded of.** In Figure 2.9 you can see three tasks. The middle one—"I finished this task"—has been completed (checked off). The top task is linked to a specific line of code (line number 100 in Form1.vb). When you look at the Code window, you will see that this line has been marked so you know there is a task associated with it. The third task is one that is not linked to any line of code and has not yet been completed.

Like previous windows, this window has two additional tabs: the Output tab and a tab labeled Index Results. This last tab is used with the Help system. In this case, the developer looked for information on "solutions, overview" and the Help system found several entries. The list of entries shows up in the Index Results tab.

Toolbox

The *Toolbox,* shown in Figure 2.10, **contains all the "tools" or components that can be placed into the Designer window.**

We will be focusing on the design of a Windows application using Windows Forms, so you see the controls associated with Windows Forms in Figure 2.10. The various category tabs shown in the figure can change as the developer selects different components in the Designer window. Note that in Figure 2.10, the GUI Design Tab (see Figure 2.13) was the selected item in the Designer window, so you see the category tabs that are related to the GUI.

Note that the pushpin is on its side here. This is meant to indicate that the pin is not pushed in. With this setting, the Toolbox is not always open but instead expands and contracts (like a window shade) on the left margin of the screen. Figure 2.11 shows the Toolbox in its contracted and expanded views. To expand the Toolbox, just place the cursor over it.

In Figure 2.11 you also see the *Server Explorer* identified. This **provides access to servers connected to your computer** (both local and remote). Figure 2.12 shows the Server Explorer in its expanded view. We will not work with the Server Explorer until Chapter 8.

You switch between the Toolbox and Server Explorer by placing the mouse arrow over the appropriate icon (either the two computer screens or the crossed wrench and hammer).

FIGURE 2.9

The Task List
Window

FIGURE 2.10

The Toolbox

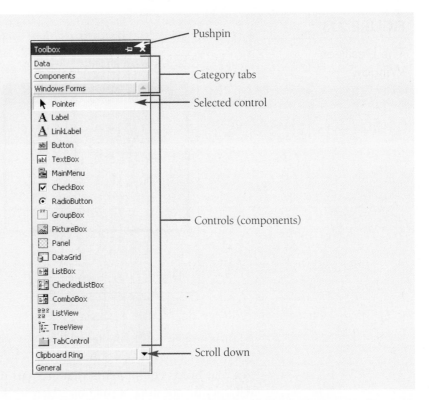

- Pushpin
- Category tabs
- Selected control
- Controls (components)
- Scroll down

FIGURE 2.11

The Toolbox in Its
Contracted and
Expanded Views

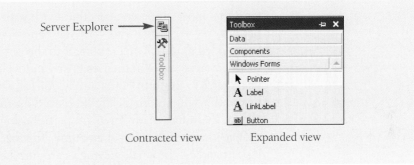

Server Explorer

Contracted view   Expanded view

FIGURE 2.12

The Server Explorer

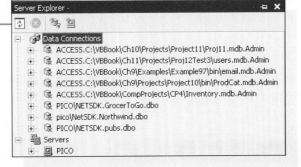

Designer Window

The *Designer window* **is where the developer builds the GUI, writes code, and accesses other components.** In Figure 2.13 you see the Designer window showing a Form component named Form1.vb. This form is where the GUI is built and now shows a single Button control (Button1). The "[Design]" after the form name indicates that the form is in design mode (you are able to add/delete/edit controls

FIGURE 2.13

The Designer
Window

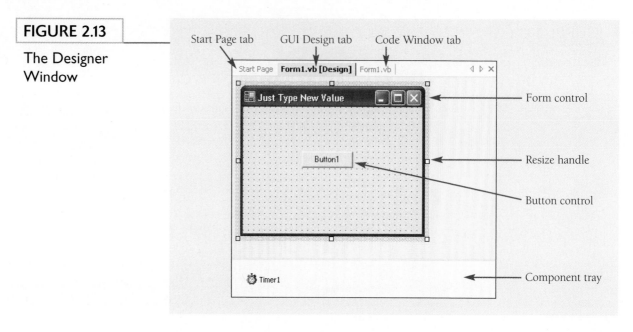

Start Page tab   GUI Design tab   Code Window tab

Form control

Resize handle

Button control

Component tray

and their properties). To the left of the active tab you see the Start Page tab. If you
click in this tab, you will see the Start Page. At the bottom you see the *component
tray.* This **holds components that are part of the project but not part of the
GUI** (they do not show at run time). Here we see a Timer control that can be used
to initiate an action based on the passing of a time interval. We will see in Chapter 8 that most of the controls that work with databases are placed in the component tray. Also be aware that the component tray is not shown unless you
have added a non-GUI component to the project.

To place a control in the Designer window, first click on it in the Toolbox and
then drag it to the form. Alternatively, you can double-click on a control in the Toolbox and it will automatically be placed on the form. Once it is there you can
change the values of any of its properties using the Property Editor. You also can
change its size or location at any time. To resize a control, you click on one of the
resize handles, the small rectangles around the border of the control (see Figure
2.13), and move it in the direction of the size change. To change the location,
just click on the component and move it around. As you can see in Figure 2.14,
you will see the cursor change to four arrows when you hover over the control.

Code Window

The *Code window* **is where you write your Visual Basic .NET program statements (code).** The Code window is shown in Figure 2.15. The IDE writes some

FIGURE 2.14

The "Move
Component"
Cursor Shape

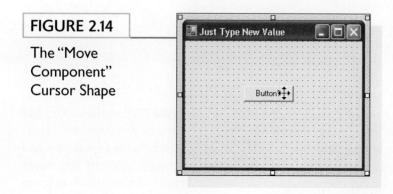

code for you. The area identified as "Windows Form Designer generated code" is where the IDE places this code. You can click on the expansion sign (+) next to this area and see the code; however, it is not a good idea to modify this code. It can result in a program that simply stops working. In fact, unless you are really confident of what you are doing, the best idea is to just keep this area in its default collapsed view. In addition to the IDE writing the code in this section, it also has written the first line of code:

> Public Class Form1
>   Inherits System.Windows.Forms.Form

Again referring to the class concepts discussed in Chapter 1, this statement means that a new class named "Form1" is being created. This new class is a descendent of the class named System.Windows.Forms.Form and inherits all the members from this class. You should not directly modify this statement either.

In Figure 2.15 you see a method named Button1_Click. The IDE wrote the first and last lines of this method (**Private Sub … End Sub**) and you should not modify them. As the developer, you are responsible for the code inside the method. This method is executed (run) when the user "clicks" on the button named Button1. We call this the Click event for the button because it is executed when a Click event is detected by the system when the cursor is on top of the button (it "handles" the event). The first line of code shows this in the Handles clause:

> Private Sub Button1_Click(…) Handles Button1.Click

For the time being, we will ignore the information between the opening and closing parentheses after the word "Click".

Note the asterisk after the file name in the tabs at the top of the window. The asterisk means that there are changes in the form (either the GUI or the code) that have not been saved to disk. As soon as you save the form, the asterisks go away.

The Class Name and Method Name drop-down lists are used to select predefined methods for any object you have in your design. Although we have not yet covered Button and TextBox controls, we can see how the Class and Method Name lists work. Consider the simple user interface in Figure 2.16. Here you see a Button control named Button1 and a TextBox control named TextBox1.

If we click on the View Code icon on the Solution Explorer (see Figure 2.5), we see the Code window shown in Figure 2.17. You can see "Form1" shown in

FIGURE 2.15

The Code Window

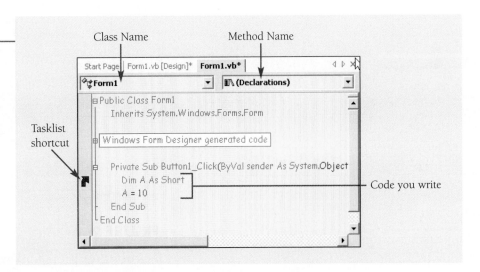

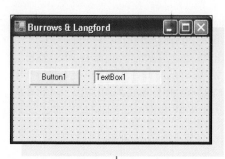

FIGURE 2.16

A Simple User Interface with a
Button and a Text Box

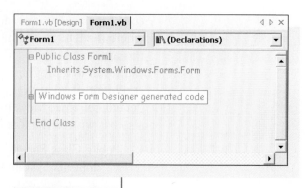

FIGURE 2.17

The Code Window

the Class Name box and "(Declarations)" in the Method Name box. Form1 is a form object and represents the actual window that contains the button and text box as we saw in Figure 2.16. (Declarations) is not a method name, but instead represents an area in the code where the developer can define a variety of items (don't worry now about this—it will be covered later).

If we pull down the Class Name list, we see all the objects currently defined for the project. Figure 2.18 shows this list. Note the presence of both Button1 and TextBox1 in this list.

If we select TextBox1 from the Class Name list and then pull down the Method Name list, we see all the methods that are defined for objects from the TextBox class. Figure 2.19 shows this list. Recall from Chapter 1 that methods represent behavior associated with an object. In this case the behavior represents event handlers—methods that respond to events associated with a particular control. For example, you can see the method "Enter" in Figure 2.19. This event is executed when the user clicks on TextBox1, that is, makes the text box active so he can type something in it. In the sections that follow, we will be explaining the various events for each component in more detail. For now, just recognize that the Class Name and Method Name drop-down lists are where you go, when you are working in the Code window, to find the objects you have added to your user interface and their methods.

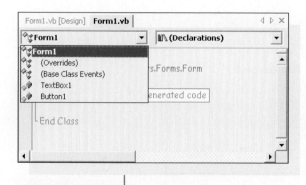

FIGURE 2.18

The Objects Shown in the Class Name
Drop-Down List

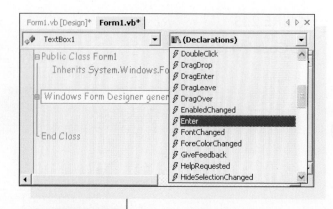

FIGURE 2.19

Methods Available for TextBox1

FIGURE 2.20

Ways to Access the
Help System

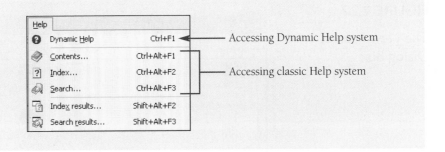

Accessing Dynamic Help system

Accessing classic Help system

Help System

There are two methods of getting help within the IDE. The first is the classic method where you pull down the Help menu and select either Contents…, Index…, or Search…. Figure 2.20 shows the Help menu. Recall from Figure 2.5 that you also can access these options from the tabs in the Solution Explorer.

The classic Help system lets you look at various broad categories (Contents), search for a specific keyword (Index), or perform a more complex search (Search). The *Dynamic Help* **system watches what you are doing and provides you with a continuously updated list of help topics.** Figure 2.21 shows Dynamic Help (available as a tab in the Properties Editor). In the image on the left, the cursor was on the keyword "Dim" in the Code window in Figure 2.15. In the image on the right, the cursor was on the "10" in the next line of code. You can clearly see that the first three help topics are different because the IDE has determined which topics would most likely be helpful based on what the developer was doing.

Saving a Solution

You need to save your solution and all that it contains on a regular basis. Until your work is saved to disk, you are vulnerable to losing it if something goes wrong (power failure, fatal error, etc.). When you first start Visual Basic .NET and indicate that you want to create a new project, you will be asked to specify the name of the folder that will store the solution and all of its files. Figure 2.22 shows the New Project dialog box. It is important that you get the information in this dialog box entered correctly or you may have problems later. *The first, and most important, rule is that each project should be in its own separate folder.* Do not try to store a project and all of its files in a folder that already stores a project.

In Figure 2.22 you can see that the Windows Application template has been selected. We will be using Windows Applications throughout this text (except in Chapter 11, where we will select the ASP.NET Web Application template). A

FIGURE 2.21

Dynamic Help
Constantly Updates
the Relevant Help
Topics

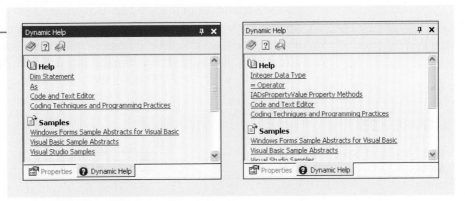

FIGURE 2.22

The New Project
Dialog Box

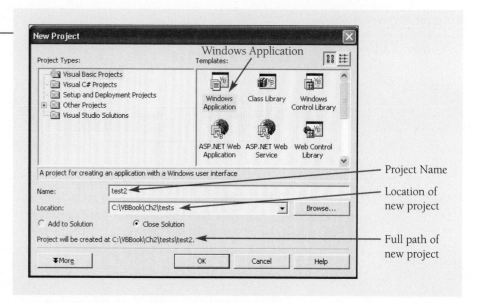

***Windows Application* is designed to run on the computer the user is using (called the client).** The name of the project (test2 in this example) becomes a new folder within the location you specify. You can see this in the full path of the new project. One mistake that is often made is to forget that the project name becomes a folder name within the location path. People who forget this often add the name to the location manually, that is, they enter

C:\VBBook\Ch2\tests\test2

in the Location box. If they did this, then the actual project would use the following path:

C:\VBBook\Ch2\tests\test2\test2

because if the developer adds the project name to the path and the IDE also does this, we end up with a duplicate. So watch the area identified as "Project will be created at" carefully and make sure you verify that it is correct before clicking on the OK button.

Once you have created a project folder, Visual Basic .NET will continue to use that folder to save additional files that might be created as you build your solution. ***Unless you really know what you are doing, do not change the locations where Visual Basic .NET wants to store them.*** In this spirit, we advise that you not use the Save As... save option in the File menu. There is no reason to use this unless you want to change the name or location of a file. As just stated, you should not be changing a file's location and you can change a file name within the IDE by right-clicking on the file in the Solution Explorer and selecting Rename from the pop-up menu. Doing this means that Visual Basic .NET can keep track of the change and no problems will ensue. To remove any temptation to use Save As..., we suggest you do all of your saving from the Save and Save All Toolbar icons and not use the File menu. Figure 2.23 shows the Save and Save All Toolbar icons.

FIGURE 2.23

The Save and Save
All Toolbar Icons

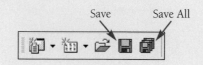

Summary

We have now seen many of the features of the Visual Basic .NET IDE. Of course, we have not seen everything. We will see more features as they become important in subsequent chapters. We also encourage you to experiment on your own to see what other features are available that might be helpful to you.

In the sections that follow, we will introduce some of the controls needed to write simple programs. We will conclude with a project where we write a small application using the controls that will be introduced. Just as with the IDE, we encourage experimentation. The best way to learn to program is to program. Reading about programming is an important first step, just like reading about driving a car is important, but both activities cannot be learned without hands-on experience.

2.4 Introducing the Windows Form Control

The **Windows Form control is basically the window that the user sees when the application is running.** Many applications include more than one form, with each form devoted to a particular display of information or engaging the user in a specific dialog. When you first create a Windows Application new project, the IDE will automatically create a Windows Form for you. Initially we will just be using this form to hold or "contain" the other controls as we introduce them.

At this point we will not concern ourselves with the form control in any detail. Later, in Section 3.4, we return to the form control and cover its details in full.

2.5 The Button Control

The **Button control** is one of the most common controls found on a user interface. Its **primary function is to react to the click of the user and perform a task associated with the name of the button that is displayed on its face.**

Appearance and Use

The Button control appears as a rectangular-shaped control on a form. Its face can contain text, an image, or both. Figure 2.24 shows several Button controls with a variety of text and images. The face of the button should clearly indicate what will happen if the button is pressed. In Figure 2.24 some of the buttons do not achieve this goal (what does Button1 do?).

FIGURE 2.24

Several Button Controls with Different Appearances

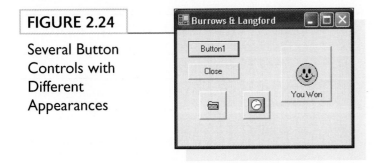

Properties

There are a number of properties for all controls that are rarely used, especially by those just learning to program. With that in mind, as we present the properties for various controls, we will limit our list to those controls that are most commonly used. We encourage the reader to investigate and experiment with other properties but limit the number in the tables to make it easier to find and use the most common properties. Table 2.2 shows a list of the most common properties of the Button control.

Most of the properties in Table 2.2 are available for every control, so we will take some time now and explain them in detail. However, in future tables showing properties, we will not show these properties again since that would be redundant. We limit the properties in future tables to ones that are unique or particularly important for the control being described.

We start with the Name property. Note that the properties are shown in alphabetic order with the exception of this one. We do this because we want to make sure the important information about the name is the first thing seen in the table. First, let's talk about what the name is for. When you view code, you see the name of the control in code that relates to that control. If you look back at Figure 2.15 that showed the Code window, you see the event named Button1_Click(…). This is because the button was named "Button1." In addition, if you refer to a control in the lines of code you write, your reference uses the name also.

Table 2.2 Common properties of the Button control

Property	Action
Name	(btn) Used to identify control in code. Gets or sets the name of the control.[4]
BackColor	Gets or sets the background color for the control.
BackgroundImage	Gets or sets the background image displayed in the control. Results in a wallpaper effect on the background.
Enabled	Gets or sets a value indicating whether the control can respond to user interaction.
Font	Gets or sets the font of the text displayed by the control.
ForeColor	Gets or sets the foreground color of the control. Foreground color is used to color the font.
Image	Gets or sets the image that is displayed on a Button control.
ImageAlign	Gets or sets the alignment of the image on the Button control.
TabIndex	Gets or sets the tab order of the control within its container.
TabStop	Gets or sets a value indicating whether the user can give the focus to this control using the TAB key.
Text	Gets or sets the text associated with this control. The text is what appears on the face of the button.
TextAlign	Gets or sets the alignment of the text on the Button control.
Visible	Gets or sets a value indicating whether the control is displayed.

---

4   "btn" is used as a prefix to the actual name of the control. It is part of the naming conventions to be explained later.

It is very important that controls have names that are meaningful. This makes the code much more readable and, therefore, much more maintainable. For example, if asked what the Click event named Button1_Click() did, it would be hard to provide an answer. However, if I asked what the event named ComputePayment_Click() did, one would likely say that it computes the payment.

In addition to giving controls names that are meaningful, we adopt the convention of prefixing each control with a generic three-letter prefix that identifies the class of the control. For the Button control, this prefix is btn (always lowercase). In our properties tables we will show the three-letter prefix in parentheses as you can see in Table 2.2. This helps us tell what type of control we are talking about. So if we name a button as btnComputePayment, we know it's a button (btn) that computes the payment. When we teach our programming course, we give students who follow this naming convention points for doing so because it really makes a difference in the code's readability.

The BackColor and BackgroundImage properties deal with what you see in the background. The two buttons in Figure 2.25 show how these impact a button's appearance. Note how hard it is to read the text on the right button.

The Enabled and Visible properties serve similar functions. The Visible property is pretty clear: if its value is True, then the control can be seen, and if it is False, the control cannot be seen. Clearly the user cannot click on a button that cannot be seen. The Enabled property does not cause a button to disappear, but it does stop the user from clicking on it. Figure 2.26 shows two buttons with one enabled and the other not enabled. As you can see, setting this property to False causes the visual image to change and provides a visual clue to the user that clicking on the button will not produce any action.

The next two properties are Font and ForeColor. Font determines the type and size of the font shown on the face of the button and ForeColor determines its color. Figure 2.27 shows a Button control that uses 12-point Comic Sans MS font that is white in color. The BackColor has been set to black.

Next we look at the Image and ImageAlign properties. The Image property value refers to a file storing an image. In Figure 2.28, you see a dialog box that is used to select the file.

The ImageAlign property is set by using a small template that gives you a very easy-to-understand set of choices. Figure 2.29 shows setting the alignment of the image to be centered in both the vertical and horizontal directions.

The TabIndex and TabStop properties deal with what happens when the user presses the [TAB] key on the keyboard. Many users like to press the [TAB] key to move to another control instead of using the mouse. The value of the TabIndex

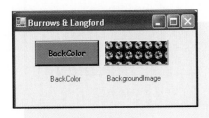

FIGURE 2.25

Changing the BackColor and BackgroundImage Properties

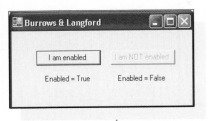

FIGURE 2.26

The Effect of the Enabled Property

FIGURE 2.27

Changing the Font and Fore-Color Properties

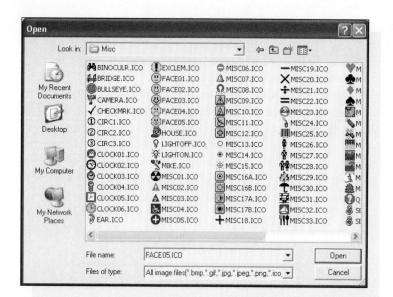

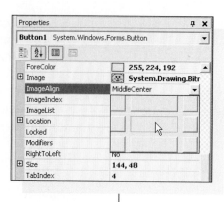

FIGURE 2.29

Setting the Alignment to Be Vertically and Horizontally Centered

FIGURE 2.28

Selecting a File to Be Used to Define the Image Property Value

property determines the order in which controls will be visited as the user presses the TAB key. The TabStop property (equal to either True or False) determines if a control will be in the tab sequence or not. Any control with its TabStop property set to false will be skipped as the user presses the TAB key.

The TabIndex property starts at zero and goes up by one with each additional control. The default values are allocated as you add new components. So the first component added will have a TabIndex of 0, the second one added will have a TabIndex of 1, and so on. The default value of the TabStop property is True. In Figure 2.30, we have shown four buttons and modified their TabIndex and TabStop properties. The blue arrows indicate how the buttons are visited as the user presses the TAB key.

Finally, we cover the Text and TextAlign properties. The Text property value determines what is displayed on the face of the button. This can include nothing (often done when you already have an image). The TextAlign property is just like the ImageAlign property that determines both the vertical and horizontal alignment. Figure 2.31 shows an example of these two property values.

This concludes the discussion of the common properties of the Button control. We remind you that most of these same properties are available on the other

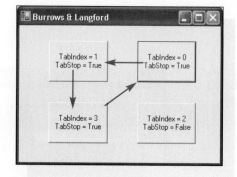

FIGURE 2.30

Effect of the TabIndex and TabStop Properties

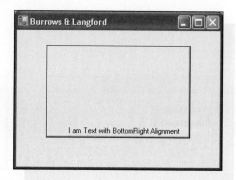

FIGURE 2.31

Demonstration of the Text and TextAlign Properties

controls we will be using and behave the same way. Thus, keep this section in mind as you read about the other controls because we will not be repeating this level of detail.

Exercise 2.1

Exercises are either short-answer questions or small programming problems designed to help you assess your understanding of material just presented. Answers to selected Exercises are found in Appendix E.

For this exercise, create a user interface with Button controls that look like

Exercise 2.2

Create a user interface with Button controls that look like

Events

As we discussed in Chapter 1, components in the event-driven environment are able to respond to events detected within the processing environment. One such event is the Click event that is generated when the user clicks the mouse button. Whatever component is under the mouse pointer at that time is then sent a Click event. As a developer, you can write an event handler for that component, that is, code that is executed when the event is detected. Most components can handle many events. However, just as was the case with properties, we usually write event handlers for only a small number of the total possible events. The Button control is always associated with the Click event. It may respond to other events on occasion, but this is rare and we will discuss only the Click event in this text.

Let's assume you have placed a Button control on your form and named it btnPressMe and changed the value of its Text property to "Press Me". This simple interface is shown in Figure 2.32.

We now want to write a Click event for this Button control. Be aware that if we have a button and no Click event defined for it, then if the user clicks on the button, nothing will happen. The easiest way to get started is to double-click on the button. This will open up the Code window and also create the first and last

FIGURE 2.32

Simple Interface with a Single Button Control

FIGURE 2.33

The Code Window
Showing the New
Click Event for Our
Button

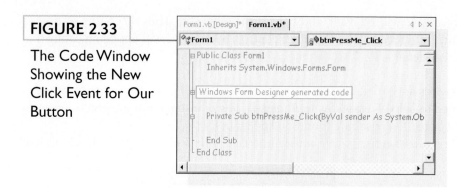

FIGURE 2.33

The Code Window
Showing the New
Click Event for Our
Button

statements of the Click event. Figure 2.33 shows the results of this action. Note that when we show code in future figures, we usually will limit it to just the event we are studying, not the entire Code window.

You can see in this figure how Visual Basic .NET has used the value of the Name property to name the Click event handler. You also can see code between the parentheses in the first line of the event handler. This code is defining what we call parameters. We wait until Chapter 6 to discuss parameters in detail, but, for now, just be sure you do not modify them or else the event handler will likely stop working correctly.

We now want to add some code in the Click event to make it do something. Since we are just starting to learn Visual Basic .NET, there is not much we can do that does not involve statements that we have not learned yet. In this case we'll simply change the value of the Text property for the Button control. This is not very realistic but kind of fun. When the user clicks on the Button control, we will change the value of the Text property to "Thanks!" To do this, we add the statement

    btnPressMe.Text = "Thanks!"

between the first and last statements of the Click event. The Code window now shows what we see in Figure 2.34.

We'd now like to test out the solution. To do this, we can either select Start from the Debug menu or click on the Start icon on the Toolbar. Figure 2.35 shows the Start tool on the Toolbar.

After the application starts, you'll see the form with the original value of the Text property. Clicking on the button changes the value. Additional clicking does not appear to do anything, but actually each click causes the event to be called. It's just that after the first click, the procedure is changing "Thanks!" to "Thanks!" so you see no difference. Figure 2.36 shows the before and after click images.

Let's go back and talk about the statement we wrote:

    btnPressMe.Text = "Thanks!"

FIGURE 2.34

The New Statement
in Our Click Event

```
Private Sub btnPressMe_Click(ByVal sender As System.Ob
    btnPressMe.Text = "Thanks!"
End Sub
```

FIGURE 2.35

The Start Icon on
the Toolbar

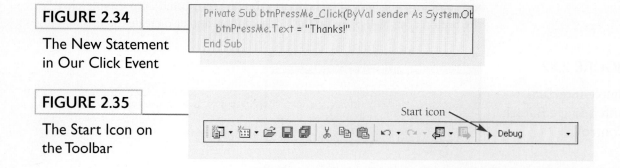

FIGURE 2.36

Running Application before and after Clicking on the Button Control

Before the click

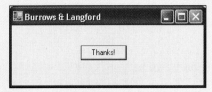

After the click

This is called an assignment statement because the information on the right of the equal sign (called a string constant in this case) is assigned to the entity on the left of the equal sign (in this case the Text property of the control named btnPressMe). Note that we refer to a property of a control by using the syntax[5]

controlName.propertyName

In our example, the control is named btnPressMe and we are referring to the Text property, so we say **btnPressMe.Text**. Assignment statements are used very often in programming and we will cover them in depth in Chapter 3.

To stop running the application, click on the close box (small **X** in the upper-right of the Form window) or select Stop Debugging from the Debug menu.

As you type in the Code window, you will see the impact of a technology Microsoft calls *IntelliSense.* This **helps the developer by checking spelling and providing suggestions on what to include in a statement**. One of the more useful features is the List Members feature. This shows you a list of all possible members (properties and methods) for a specific object. For example, as you type the assignment statement we have been talking about, you will notice the member list pop up after you type the period after the control name as shown in Figure 2.37.

The icons to the left of each member tell you if the member is a property or a method. In Figure 2.37, the icon next to BackColor denotes a property and the icon next to BringToFront denotes a method. To find the member you want, you can either scroll down to find it or type the first letter of the property; for example, type a "T" if you want the Text property. The list will automatically scroll down to the first "T." Once you see the member in the list, just double-click on it and it will be entered into the code for you.

FIGURE 2.37

The List Members Pop-Up Menu from IntelliSense

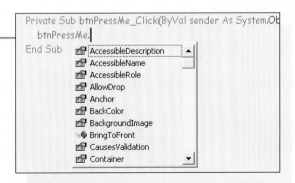

5   *Syntax* **refers to the rules associated with a grammatically valid construct.** All languages, both natural languages (like English or Spanish) and programming languages, have a set of syntax rules defined for them. In the case of natural languages, we use the term *grammatical rules* instead of the term *syntax.*

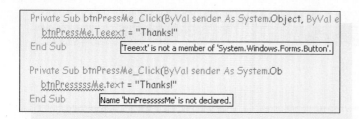

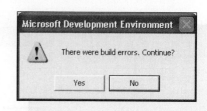

FIGURE 2.38

Two Different Typing Errors and Their Associated Pop-Up Explanations

FIGURE 2.39

Error Dialog Displayed If Your Program Includes Syntax Errors

FIGURE 2.40

The Task List Showing the Details of a Syntax Error

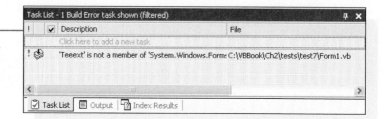

If you spell something wrong, you will see a squiggly line under the problem. If you place the cursor over the problem, a window will appear telling you what the problem is. Two spelling errors are shown in Figure 2.38.

These are examples of syntax errors, and the program will not run if it includes any syntax errors. If you try to run the program with the errors uncorrected, you will see the error dialog as shown in Figure 2.39. A build error is generated as Visual Basic .NET attempts to translate your program into internal machine language for execution. If it finds a syntax error, then this translation process cannot proceed. You should click on No in almost all cases when you see this error.

After clicking on No in the error dialog box, you can see an explanation in the Task List as shown in Figure 2.40. So either look for the squiggly lines in your code or just run it and then look in the Task List to find your syntax errors.

We have now seen how the Button control is defined and how an event handler is programmed to respond to the user clicking on the button. We also have seen how to enter code, interpret errors, and use the IntelliSense feature to help write our code. We now turn our attention to some additional controls.

Exercise 2.3

Explain in your own words why a Click event gets executed.

Exercise 2.4

Is a button with its Text property set to "btnDoIt" a good idea? Explain.

2.6 | The Label Control

The *Label control* is used to display information to the user. The user cannot interact with a Label control.[6] We use the Label control to either label other controls or show the answer to a calculation or something similar. For example,

---

6 Actually you could write event handlers that would react to user actions for the Label, but unless there is a very good reason to do so, you should not do this. Users do not expect any interaction and if they see it, they will likely be very confused.

FIGURE 2.41

The Visual Basic .NET
Find Dialog Box

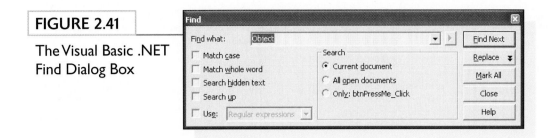

Visual Basic .NET has a dialog box used to find and replace text within the code. This is shown in Figure 2.41. Almost all the text you see on the dialog box is labels, such as the words "Find what:" at the upper left of the dialog box. These labels are identifying what check boxes and radio buttons (under "Search") mean.

Appearance and Use

The Label control is a rectangular area that can be filled with text. You have some control of the size and alignment of the text and have an option to include a border around the label.

Properties

Table 2.3 provides a list of commonly used properties for the Label control. Remember that many of the properties discussed for the Button control also apply to the Label control.

The Font, ForeColor, Image, ImageAlign, Text, and TextAlign properties are all the same as in Table 2.2. The Text property is the most-used property for the Label control. Setting its value at design time provides a label for a component and setting its value at run time provides an opportunity to display an answer as the program runs. The Label control does not have a TabStop property because it is meant to display information and not obtain it from the user.

Property	Action
Table 2.3 Common properties of the Label control	
Name	(lbl) Gets or sets the name of the control.
AutoSize	Gets or sets a value indicating whether the control is automatically resized to display its entire contents.
BorderStyle	Gets or sets the border style for the control.
DataBindings	Gets the data bindings for the control.
Font	Gets or sets the font of the text displayed by the control.
ForeColor	Gets or sets the foreground color of the control.
Image	Gets or sets the image that is displayed on a label.
ImageAlign	Gets or sets the alignment of an image that is displayed in the control.
Text	Gets or sets the text associated with this control.
TextAlign	Gets or sets the alignment of text in the label.

FIGURE 2.42

Available Border
Styles for a Label
Control

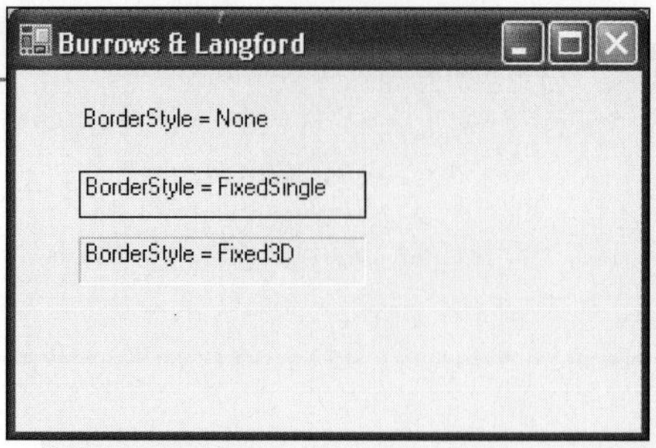

Note that we name Label controls using the lbl prefix. The AutoSize property will automatically size the label depending on the value of the Text property. If the AutoSize property value is True, automatic sizing will occur, and if the value is False, the size is fixed.

The BorderStyle property determines whether a border will be included. Figure 2.42 shows three Label controls with the three border options. Be careful about using the Fixed3D style because it looks very much like a TextBox control (discussed next) and the function of the two controls is very different.

The DataBindings property is used in association with databases. It is possible to display a value from a database directly in the Text property of a Label control using this Property. We will wait and discuss the DataBindings property in Chapter 8.

Events

As mentioned before, we almost never write event handlers for the Label control.

Example 2.1

USING THE LABEL CONTROL

Before we start this example, we would like to explain some things about examples in this text. Examples are small applications designed to demonstrate and explain one or two specific points relating to topics just covered. You will find the code for each example on the CD that accompanies the text or you can download the code from the text's website. We encourage you to experiment with these examples to help increase your understanding of the concepts. Note that the examples are not complete applications and therefore are easy to "break." That is, it is quite possible for the user to cause an example to generate an error that will stop the program (don't hesitate trying to cause such an error—no harm will be done to the computer). You might even try adding code to prevent the error from occurring. We provide this information so that you do not think that the examples have not been tested— they just are not intended to be what some call "bullet proofed."

Now we turn our attention to Example 2.1. This example has two buttons and three labels. You can see the example as it executes in Figure 2.43. You can see in the figure that one of two messages is displayed to the user depending on which button was clicked. The messages are being placed in the Text property of a Label control named lblAnswer.

If you look at Figure 2.43, you also will see two other labels. One is at the top of the window and contains the text "Example 2.1 Using . . ." The second Label control is above the two buttons and its Text property is set equal to "Are you confused?" Here we see the two primary uses of the Label control. The label named lblAnswer shows an example of using a label at run time to show a message to the

FIGURE 2.43

Example 2.1 at Run Time

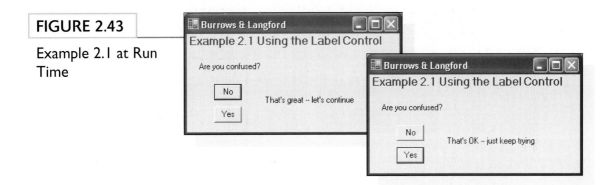

Table 2.4 Controls used in Example 2.1		
Type	**Property**	**Setting**
Button	Name	btnNo
Button	Name	btnYes
Label	Name	Label1
	Text	Example 2.1 Using the Label Control
Label	Name	Label2
	Text	Are you confused?
Label	Name	lblAnswer
	Text	" "
Form	Name	Form1
	Text	Burrows & Langford

user. The other two labels are just "labeling" information for the user and their Text property values never change.

Table 2.4 shows the controls on the form and the values of properties that have been changed at design time.

There are two things we would like to point out in Table 2.4. First, the two Label controls that are not changing while the program runs have names assigned by the IDE (Label1 and Label2), while the Label control whose Text value changes while the program runs is given a more meaningful name (lblAnswer). The difference is based on the reason why we name controls—to make the code easier to read and maintain. Since the first two labels will never be referenced in the code, giving them meaningful names does not enhance the code readability. On the other hand, the third label will appear twice in the code—once for each button's Click event. We name it to make the code easier to read. The second point is to note that the value of the Text property for the third button has been set equal to "". This is called the "empty string."[7] You enter the empty string in the Property Editor by highlighting the existing text and pressing the Delete key. We set this Label's Text property equal to the empty string at design time so that when the application starts running, nothing is shown in lblAnswer.

The code for this example is shown in Figure 2.44. We need two event handlers: one for responding to the user clicking on the No button (btnNo) and the other for responding to the user clicking on the Yes button (btnYes).

---

7   A string is a type of data that just stores characters. We discuss the concept of a data type and specifics of various data types in Chapter 3.

FIGURE 2.44

Code for the Two
Button Controls in
Example 2.1

```
Private Sub btnNo_Click(ByVal sender As System.Object, ByVal e As Sy
    lblAnswer.Text = "That's great -- let's continue"
End Sub

Private Sub btnYes_Click(ByVal sender As System.Object, ByVal e As S
    lblAnswer.Text = "That's OK -- just keep trying"
End Sub
```

Hopefully you can see how easy it is to read this code given our naming conventions. The Click events are for Buttons (btn prefix)—one for clicking on No and the other for clicking on Yes. Within each event we are placing information into a Label (lbl).

We have now seen a control that responds to the user clicking on it (a Button) and another control (a Label) whose content (Text property) is displayed on the user interface and whose content can either be static (not changing) or dynamic (changes as the program runs). We are missing a control that allows the user to provide information to the program as the program runs. There are a number of ways to achieve this goal, but we start with the TextBox control.

Exercise 2.5

Would it ever make sense to set a Label control's Text property to the empty string? Explain.

Exercise 2.6

Using the Internet, go to a site that supports icon images (.ico) such as http://www.coolarchive.com/icons.cfm and download two "smiley face" icons. Place them into the folder for Example 2.1. Modify Example 2.1 so that it shows the smiley faces instead of text in the label. Consider having two label controls and using their Visible properties in association with the Click events for the two Button controls.

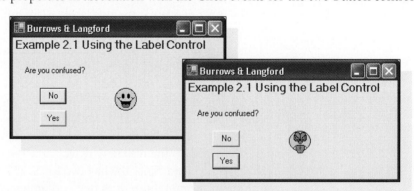

2.7   The TextBox Control

The *TextBox control* **provides an area for the user to type while the program executes.** This information can then be used by the application's code as it executes.

Appearance and Use

The TextBox is a rectangular area that provides the user a place to type. It is possible to limit what the user types, to limit the user to a single line or multiple lines (with or without scroll bars), and to surround the TextBox with a border.

Properties

The common properties of the TextBox control are shown in Table 2.5.

As you can see in Table 2.5, there are quite a few properties that prove to be commonly useful. We will briefly review all of these now but reserve a more in-depth discussion for some of them until later in the text. Also, some of the properties, such as the TextLength property, are only available at run time (you will not see them in the Property Editor).

The value of the Text property is used most often as it represents what the user typed in the TextBox control. There are a number of properties that affect the appearance of the text in the TextBox and are all related to the Multiline property. If the Multiline property value is set to True, then you can control the following aspects of the TextBox. You can control how the ENTER and TAB keys are

Table 2.5 Common properties of the TextBox control

Property	Action
Name	(txt) Gets or sets the name of the control.
AcceptsReturn	Gets or sets a value indicating whether pressing ENTER in a multiline TextBox control creates a new line of text in the control or activates the default button for the form.
AcceptsTab	Gets or sets a value indicating whether pressing the TAB key in a multiline TextBox control types a tab character in the control instead of moving the focus to the next control in the tab order.
AutoSize	Gets or sets a value indicating whether the height of the control automatically adjusts when the font assigned to the control is changed.
BorderStyle	Gets or sets the border type of the TextBox control.
CharacterCasing	Gets or sets whether the TextBox control modifies the case of characters as they are typed.
Font	Gets or sets the font of the text displayed by the control.
Lines	Gets or sets the lines of text in a TextBox control.
MaxLength	Gets or sets the maximum number of characters the user can type into the TextBox control.
Modified	Gets or sets a value that indicates that the TextBox control has been modified by the user since the control was created or its contents were last set.
Multiline	Gets or sets a value indicating whether this is a multiline TextBox control.
PasswordChar	Gets or sets the character used to mask characters of a password in a single-line TextBox control.
ReadOnly	Gets or sets a value indicating whether text in the text box is read-only.
ScrollBars	Gets or sets which scroll bars should appear in a multiline TextBox control.
SelectedText	Gets or sets a value indicating the currently selected text in the control.
SelectionLength	Gets or sets the number of characters selected in the text box.
SelectionStart	Gets or sets the starting point of text selected in the text box.
Text	Gets or sets the current text in the text box.
TextAlign	Gets or sets how text is aligned in a TextBox control.
TextLength	Gets the length of text in the control.
WordWrap	Indicates whether a multiline TextBox control automatically wraps words to the beginning of the next line when necessary.

handled (AcceptsReturn and AcceptsTab), whether scroll bars (none, vertical, horizontal, or both) are permitted (ScrollBars), and, in a related area, whether the TextBox supports word wrapping (WordWrap). You also can use the Lines property to easily enter multiple lines of text at design time.

Control of what the user types is shared between properties and events. The CharacterCasing property will automatically change whatever the user types to either uppercase or lowercase; MaxLength controls the maximum number of characters the user can type; and ReadOnly property, when set to True, prevents the user from typing into the TextBox. We will discuss these events shortly.

The PasswordChar property lets you set a character (like an asterisk) that will be displayed as the user enters a character. The actual characters the user typed will be in the Text property, but the user interface will show the PasswordChar.

The TextLength property is used during run time to see how many characters exist in the TextBox. The Selection... properties (SelectedText, SelectionStart, and SelectionLength) all provide information at run time regarding what the user has selected or highlighted in the TextBox control.

We will try out some of these properties in examples that follow.

Events

The TextBox control typically responds to the events described in Table 2.6.

The term *focus* means that the user is currently working with the specific control. Focus can be set by the user clicking on a control or using the TAB key to get to the control. There is always only one control that has focus and as a new control receives focus, two events occur. One is the Leave event for the control that is losing focus and the other is the Enter event for the control that is getting the focus. For example, if the focus is currently on txtBefore and the user clicks on txtAfter, a Leave event would be generated for txtBefore and then an Enter event would be generated for txtAfter. The Enter and Leave events can be useful for determining if the user has entered valid information into a TextBox.

The KeyPress event is fired each time the user types a character in the TextBox control. This can be very useful for determining and possibly controlling what the user types as he or she types, unlike the Leave event, where the user's typing can only be checked after he or she has finished typing and moved to another control.

These three events are fairly complex and we delay their discussion until Chapter 6.

Methods

The TextBox control has a number of methods available for it that help the developer manipulate the text in the TextBox. Table 2.7 shows the most common of these methods.

Table 2.6 Common events for the TextBox control

Event	Trigger
Enter	Occurs when the input focus for the control is received.
KeyPress	Occurs when a key is pressed while the control has focus.
Leave	Occurs when the input focus leaves the control.

Table 2.7 Common methods of the TextBox control

Method	Behavior
AppendText	Appends text to the current text of the text box.
Clear	Clears all text from the TextBox control.
Copy	Copies the current selection in the text box to the Clipboard.
Cut	Moves the current selection in the text box to the Clipboard.
Paste	Replaces the current selection in the text box with the contents of the Clipboard.
Select	Selects text within the control.
SelectAll	Selects all text in the text box.
Undo	Undoes the last edit operation in the text box.

You can see some methods that are usually associated with text in a word processing context. These include the Cut, Copy, and Paste methods. These methods are associated with the Selection... property values discussed earlier.

The AppendText method adds text to the end of the text that is already associated with a TextBox. For example, if the Text property of a TextBox named txtStory contained "Once upon a time, there was ", the statement

> **txtStory.AppendText("a big bad wolf.")**

would cause the Text property value to be "Once upon a time, there was a big bad wolf." Notice that the syntax for referring to a method is

> *controlName.method(...)*

This is the same syntax as when we refer to a control's property. That's why the pop-up list from the IntelliSense system shows both properties as well as methods.

Example **2.2**   **MODIFYING USER INPUT**

In this example we use the CharacterCasing and PasswordChar properties of the TextBox to modify the user input in two different ways. The hypothetical application accepts a license code (such as a software license code) and a corresponding security code to validate the license. The license consists of letters and digits and all the letters are uppercase letters. However, the user may be careless and enter lowercase letters not realizing that there may be a problem with that. To prevent this problem, the application accepts both lower and uppercase letters but automatically shifts them to uppercase.

The security code should be displayed on the form in a way an unauthorized person looking at the screen could not recognize. However, within the running application, the security code must be the original characters typed by the user. Figure 2.45 shows the application at run time. Note that the user typed lowercase letters in the License field although we see them displayed as uppercase. The characters typed by the user in the Security Code TextBox were replaced with asterisks, but as you can see in the labels under the "View Entries" button, the original characters were retained.

In addition to the labels used for identification purposes, the application contains two TextBox controls, two Label controls, and a Button control. The properties whose values were changed and their values are shown in Table 2.8.

FIGURE 2.45

Example 2.2 at
Run Time

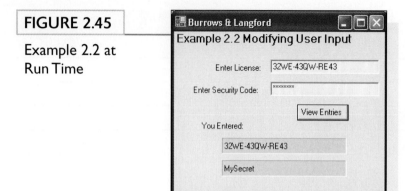

Table 2.8 Control properties and values for Example 2.2

Control	Property	Setting
TextBox	Name	txtLicense
	CharacterCasing	Upper
	Text	""
TextBox	Name	txtSecCode
	PasswordChar	"*"
	Text	""
Label	Name	lblLic
	BackColor	Gainsboro (from the Web tab)
	BorderStyle	Fixed3D
	Text	""
Label	Name	lblCode
	BackColor	Gainsboro (from the Web tab)
	BorderStyle	Fixed3D
	Text	""
	TextAlign	MiddleLeft
Button	Name	btnViewEntries
	Text	View Entries
	TextAlign	MiddleLeft

FIGURE 2.46

Code for the
Button Control in
Example 2.2

```
Private Sub btnViewEntries_Click(ByVal sender As System.Object, ByV
    lblLic.Text = txtLicense.Text
    lblCode.Text = txtSecCode.Text
End Sub
```

The code for the Button control is shown in Figure 2.46. As you can see, the Text property of **txtLicense** stores the uppercase version of the information typed by the user. This is confirmed when the Text property is displayed in the Label control **lblLic**. It also should be clear that the Text property of **txtSecCode** stores that information entered by the user although the text box shows asterisks. These two behaviors were controlled using the CharacterCasing property in **txtLicense** and the PasswordChar in **txtSecCode**.

Example **2.3**   USING A MULTILINE TEXTBOX AND SELECTION... PROPERTIES

This example uses a TextBox named should **txtWords** with its Multiline property set to True and its ScrollBars property set to Vertical. You can see this in Figure 2.47. There are also three Button controls. Each of these controls displays one of the three Selection... properties associated with the TextBox control. They use a Label control named lblInfo to show the information.

The code for the three Button controls is shown in Figure 2.48. Notice how the three Button controls reference SelectedText, SelectionStart, and SelectionLength properties of the multiline text box.

If you click on the Show Selected Start and Show Selected Length buttons with the word "is" selected as in Figure 2.47, you will see values 5 and 2 shown. We will cover character processing in detail in Chapter 4, but be aware that a string of characters is numbered from left to right starting at zero. That is why the word "is" starts in position 5:

```
This is
0123456
```

One more point about Example 2.3. The image you see in Figure 2.47 is exactly what you should expect to see. If you select the word "is" and then click on Show Selected Text, you will see the correct selection in the Label but the word "is" in the text box will not be highlighted as you see in the figure. This is because when you click on the Button control, focus moves to that control and focus leaves the TextBox control. A TextBox control that does not have focus cannot show a selection. The way we got the image in Figure 2.47 was to first select "is", then click on the Show Selected Text button, and then select the word "is" again. We thought the explanation would be clearer if you saw the word selected in the TextBox and shown in the Label. You might agree and wonder how to make this happen without this bit of "trickery." The answer is to use a pop-up menu (we have not covered that yet).

FIGURE 2.47

Example 2.3 at Run Time

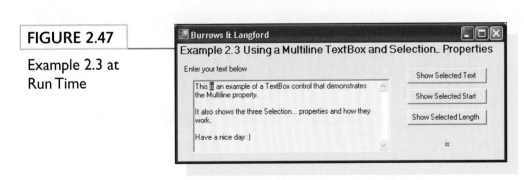

FIGURE 2.48

Code for Example 2.3

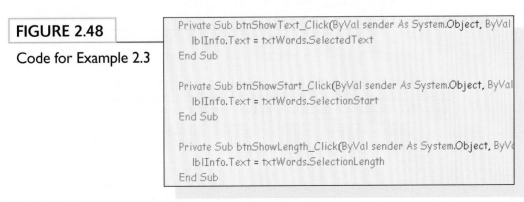

```
Private Sub btnShowText_Click(ByVal sender As System.Object, ByVal
    lblInfo.Text = txtWords.SelectedText
End Sub

Private Sub btnShowStart_Click(ByVal sender As System.Object, ByVal
    lblInfo.Text = txtWords.SelectionStart
End Sub

Private Sub btnShowLength_Click(ByVal sender As System.Object, ByV
    lblInfo.Text = txtWords.SelectionLength
End Sub
```

Example 2.4   COPYING SELECTION FROM ONE TEXTBOX TO ANOTHER

In this example we look at the Copy() and Paste() methods associated with the TextBox control. As you can see from the sequence of steps in Figure 2.49, the user is able to select some text in the TextBox labeled "Top" and then copy it to the TextBox labeled "Bottom." You also can do the same thing going from the bottom to the top TextBox. Note that when the selected text is placed in the destination text box, it is placed where the cursor is located, not at the end of the existing text.

Recall that methods define behavior. The Copy() method copies the selected text for the associated TextBox and places it on the ClipBoard. What is the **ClipBoard?** It is just **an object created and managed by Visual Basic .NET for the purpose of temporarily storing text.** It can be accessed only by certain methods defined by the TextBox and other classes. The Paste() method does just the opposite—it places the contents of the ClipBoard into a TextBox at the current insertion point. The current insertion point is where the user clicked and is shown with a vertical bar (just like in a word processing application). Figure 2.50 shows the application with the insertion point visible. Note that this is the same as the SelectionStarts parameter we saw in Example 2.3.

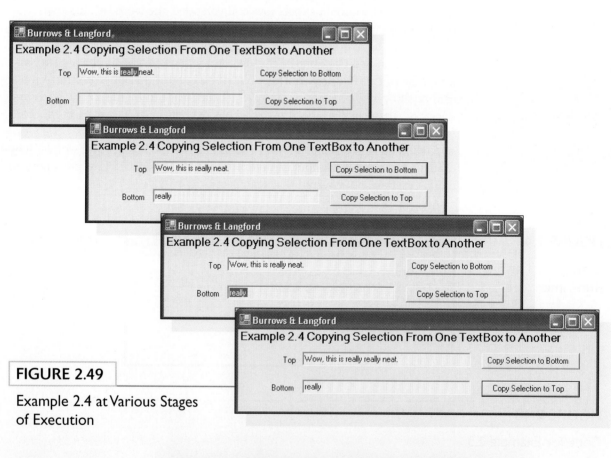

FIGURE 2.49

Example 2.4 at Various Stages
of Execution

FIGURE 2.50

Showing the
Insertion Point

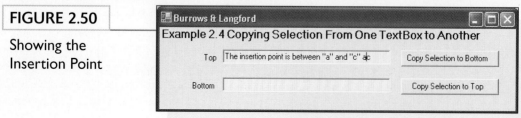

FIGURE 2.51

Code for Example 2.4

```
Private Sub btnTopToBot_Click(ByVal sender As System.Object, ByVal
    txtTop.Copy()
    txtBottom.Paste()
End Sub

Private Sub btnBotToTop_Click(ByVal sender As System.Object, ByVal
    txtBottom.Copy()
    txtTop.Paste()
End Sub
```

The code that performs these copy/paste operations is shown in Figure 2.51. Note that we first copy the selected text from one of the TextBox controls to the ClipBoard and then follow that by pasting the contents of the ClipBoard to the other TextBox control.

You may not have thought about this, but it should be clear from the code we have seen so far that the statements of code are executed in a specific sequence. We use the term "flow of control" to describe the order the statements are executed. The flow of control shown so far is called sequential because we start with the first statement and execute the statements one at a time from top to bottom. Note that the order of these statements is very important in this example (we must copy before we paste). Later in the text we will examine two addition types of control flow called selection and iteration.

Exercise 2.7

Modify Example 2.3 so that it when the user clicks on the Show Selected Text button (btnShowText), the newly selected text is added to the prior selected text. For example, if the user originally selects the word "is" and then clicks on btnShow-Text, the Label lblInfo would show "is". If the user then selects the word "how" and then clicks on btnShowText, the Label lblInfo would show "ishow".

Exercise 2.8

Modify Example 2.4 so that the selection is moved, not copied from one TextBox to the other one. For example, if the original text was "Wow, this is really neat." and the user selected the word "really", then, after clicking on the appropriate button, the text would read "Wow, this is neat." In addition, the word "really" would be placed at the end of the text in the other Label control. Change the Text property of the Button controls to reflect this new behavior.

2.8 The MsgBox Statement and InputBox Function

We have now seen the TextBox and Label components that are used to get information from the user and to display information to the user. We now turn our attention to two alternate ways of performing the same tasks. However, these new methods are based on a different philosophy. In the case of the Label control, the user was free to read or ignore information displayed on the form. There are cases where this is not desirable. For example, if an error has occurred, then the developer might want the user to know this and not let her continue until she has acknowledged that she is aware of the problem. We can use the MsgBox statement to do this.

In a similar way, the InputBox() function shows the user a new form on which to enter some information. The user must enter the information before he can continue with the application.

MsgBox Statement

MsgBox stands for "message box." The **MsgBox statement causes a new window to open that contains a message. The window stays open until the user has acknowledged it by clicking on one of its buttons.** MsgBox is a statement, like the assignment statement that we saw earlier. This means that it is a separate line of code within our application. The syntax of the MsgBox statement is

MsgBox("A prompt", Buttons, "A title")

The "things" between the parentheses are called arguments. Commas separate arguments, so we see three arguments. The first argument is a message displayed to the user in a new window that opens up—it is the "message" in the box. The second argument indicates display information such as what icons and buttons to display within the message box. The third argument represents the title used in the title bar at the top of the message box.

Figure 2.52 shows the message box displayed with the following statement:

MsgBox("Hello World", MsgBoxStyle.Exclamation, "My Creative Title")

As you can see, the prompt is "Hello World". We call this a string constant because it is enclosed in quotes. The Button constant, **MsgBoxStyle.Exclamation**, causes the exclamation point in the yellow triangle to be displayed. This is a "predefined symbolic constant" defined within the MsgBoxStyle class. We cover predefined symbolic constants in Chapter 3. Finally, the title is the string constant "My Creative Title".

The execution of the program that displayed the message box in Figure 2.52 paused until the user clicked on the OK button. As stated earlier, this is supposed to get the user's attention. In fact, some programming languages use the term *alert box* instead of message box.

FIGURE 2.52

An Example of a
Message Box

Private Sub btnShowMessage_Click(ByVal sender As System.Object, ByVal e As System.EventArgs) Handles btnShowMessage.Click
    MsgBox(

MsgBox (**Prompt As Object**, [Buttons As Microsoft.VisualBasic.MsgBoxStyle = MsgBoxStyle.OKOnly], [Title As Object = Nothing]) As Microsoft.VisualBasic.MsgBoxResult
Prompt:
String expression displayed as the message in the dialog box. The maximum length of Prompt is approximately 1024 characters, depending on the width of the characters used. If Prompt consists of more than one line, you can separate the lines using a carriage return character (Chr(13)), a linefeed character (Chr(10)), or a carriage return-linefeed character combination between each line.

FIGURE 2.53

IntelliSense Help Provided When Entering a MsgBox Statement

It would be helpful to see how the IntelliSense system helps you remember what to enter when you type a statement like this. Figure 2.53 shows the Code window as we start to type the MsgBox statement. The arguments are shown in the Help window with the argument you are currently entering shown in bold with an explanation below it. Note also that some of the arguments are surrounded with square brackets [ ]. This indicates that the argument is optional. You can leave out any or all of the optional arguments and Visual Basic .NET will use a predefined default value. If you leave out an optional argument but want to include the next, you must still include the comma for the argument you left out. For example, if you leave out the Buttons argument shown in Figure 2.53 but want a title, you would say **MsgBox("Hi", ,"My Title")**.

After entering the first argument and typing a comma, IntelliSense provides additional help for the next argument. Figure 2.54 shows the IntelliSense help for the Buttons argument. The help text states that you provide a "Numeric expression that is the sum of values . . ." This means that if you want to select more than one choice from the pop-up list, you need to add them together. This "sum" will be used by the system to decide what to display.

Assume you want the Critical icon and also want three buttons: an Abort, a Retry, and an Ignore button. The Critical constant is the third from the top and the three-button choice is the top constant. We need to add them together to get the behavior we want. Figure 2.55 shows the code for this as well as the resulting message box.

Figure 2.55 also shows how to continue a statement across more than one line in the Code window. The underscore character (_), preceded by a space,

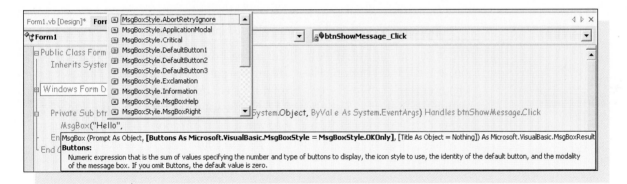

FIGURE 2.54

IntelliSense Help for the Buttons Argument

FIGURE 2.55

Adding the Button Arguments to Get Several Choices

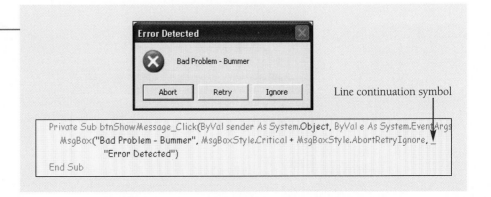

Line continuation symbol

represents line continuation. This means that the information on the next line is part of the statement on the previous line. We always indent the continued line so that it is easier to see.

Note that code in Figure 2.55 has no way of determining which one of the three buttons the user pressed and this is probably not good. We will see how to handle this situation when we get to Chapter 5 and learn about decision making within the code.

InputBox() Function

A "function" is something that "takes on a value." For example, there is a square root function available in Visual Basic .NET. This function takes on the value of the square root of a number it is given. For example, if you give the square root function the number 5, it returns the value 2.2361. The number we give the function, the 5 in this case, is called the argument, like we just saw in the MsgBox statement. The value we get back is called the return value. We look at a number of different functions in Chapter 4.

Here we look at our first function, the InputBox() function. The **InputBox() function** displays a new window that includes a prompt and a text box for the user to type a response to the prompt. The syntax of this function is shown via IntelliSense in Figure 2.56.

From the syntax definition in Figure 2.56 you can see that you are required to supply a prompt as an argument. The Title and DefaultResponse arguments are optional as are the XPos and YPos arguments. Figure 2.57 shows an InputBox. This InputBox was created with the following code:

InputBox("What's your name?", "Get Name", "none")

Notice that an InputBox includes a text box for user data entry, an OK button, and a Cancel button. These are always part of the InputBox. The user types whatever is relevant in the text box and then clicks on OK (or Cancel). The information the user types into the text box is the value "returned by" this function. A question that comes up is "what to do with this information?" The answer is it must be stored somewhere, or printed, or used in some way. The code in Figure 2.58

InputBox (**Prompt As String**, [Title As String = ""], [DefaultResponse As String = ""], [XPos As Integer = -1], [YPos As Integer = -1]) As String
Prompt:
  String expression displayed as the message in the dialog box. The maximum length of Prompt is approximately 1024 characters, depending on the width of the characters used. If Prompt consists of more than one line, you can separate the lines using a carriage return character (Chr(13)), a linefeed character (Chr(10)), or a carriage return–linefeed character combination between each line.

FIGURE 2.56

Syntax of the InputBox Function

FIGURE 2.57

An Example
InputBox

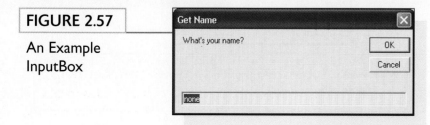

FIGURE 2.58

Code to Store Value
Returned from
InputBox() Function

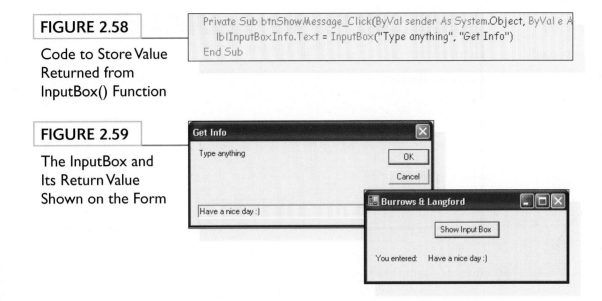

```
Private Sub btnShowMessage_Click(ByVal sender As System.Object, ByVal e A
    lblInputBoxInfo.Text = InputBox("Type anything", "Get Info")
End Sub
```

FIGURE 2.59

The InputBox and
Its Return Value
Shown on the Form

takes the information supplied by the user and uses it to change the Text property of a Label control.

When the application runs, the InputBox and the form are shown in Figure 2.59.

Although useful, be careful about using the InputBox() function. Users like to be able to supply information in an order they define. That is, if you have five TextBox controls on a form, the user should be able to fill them out in any order and then click on a button indicating she is done entering the information. If you use the InputBox() function, the order of data entry is determined by the order the developer chooses to display the input boxes. This is generally undesirable and should be avoided. The other problem with the InputBox() function is it only provides a single TextBox control for user data entry. In Chapters 3 and 6 we look at ways to design your own dialog boxes, which provide a much more flexible way of obtaining user information.

Exercise 2.9

Explain how you can continue a statement in the Code window.

Exercise 2.10

Create a small project that displays the following message box when the user clicks on a Button control.

2.9 Project 1: Creating a Simple Windows Application

Each chapter contains at least one project. Projects are more involved than examples and include most of the concepts presented in the chapter. This project is a tutorial-type project where you follow a set of steps to complete the solution. Most projects are not tutorial in nature. Instead they first describe the problem,

FIGURE 2.60

The Completed
Solution to Project 1

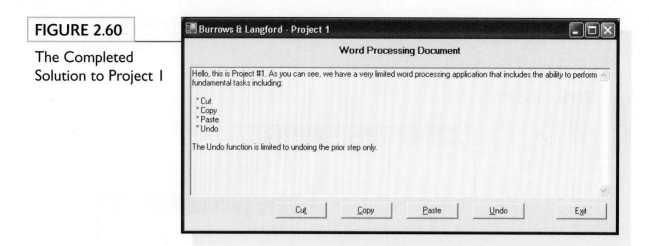

then talk about the design of the solution, and finally give information on construction of the solution. In the early chapters, the projects provide much more detail than in the later chapters. The rationale for this is the expectation that as you learn more about programming, you will be able to do more on your own.

You should read each project even if you do not plan to create a solution using Visual Basic .NET. Projects often expand on ideas and at times introduce new concepts. For example, this project introduces the End statement and the use of Access keys for Button controls.

In Project 1 you will build a very limited word processing application. The completed solution is shown in Figure 2.60.

As stated earlier, this project is presented in a step-by-step tutorial fashion.

1. Start Visual Basic .NET and create a new Windows Application from the Start Page. Figure 2.61 shows what you should see.[8] In the figure the name of the project is MyProject1. The Location is something for you to determine. It could be a floppy disk (a: drive), the computer's desktop, a folder you created prior to starting the project, or the default location provided by Visual

FIGURE 2.61

Creating the New
Project

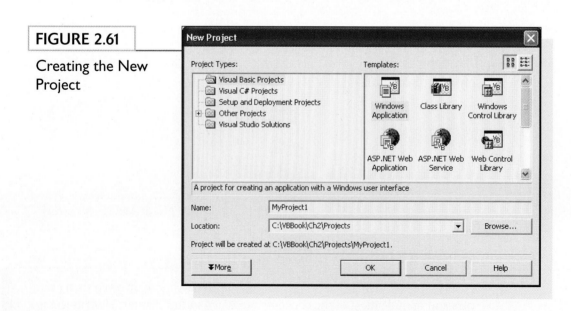

---

[8] You may see some additional choices in the Project Types: box depending on what was initially installed as part of Visual Studio .NET.

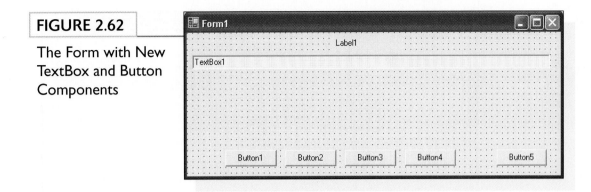

Basic .NET. Be sure to note where the project is being saved (see the "Project will be created at" information near the bottom of the dialog box).

After supplying information on the new project, click on the OK button.

2. You should now see a new project with a single form. Use the resize handles to make the form a little wider and shorter than the initial size. The actual size is not too important because you can always change it later.

3. With the form selected, go to the Toolbox and double-click on a TextBox component. Resize and relocate the TextBox as shown in Figure 2.62. Following this, add a Label control and five Button controls. Relocate these controls as shown in the figure.

4. We will now set the properties of the various controls. Table 2.9 shows each control and the properties and values you need to set.

5. After completing step 4, rearrange and resize the controls as shown in Figure 2.63. Note the Access keys defined for the Button controls. The & used in the Text property of a control makes the character following it the *Access key.* **This**

Table 2.9 Property values for the controls in Project 1

Control	Property	Setting	Control	Property	Setting
Label1	Text	Word Processing Document	Button2	Name	btnCopy
	Font—Size[9]	9.75		Text	&Copy
	Font—Bold	True	Button3	Name	btnPaste
TextBox1	Name	txtDocument		Text	&Paste
	Multiline	True	Button4	Name	btnUndo
	Scrollbars	Vertical		Text	&Undo
	Text	""	Button5	Name	btnExit
Button1	Name	btnCut		Text	E&xit
	Text	Cu&t[10]	Form1[11]	Text	Put your name here

[9]   To set the font, click on the expander icon (+) by Font. You should then see the Size and Bold properties and their values. You can also click on the ellipses in the Font property value box to open the Font dialog box. Here select size 10 but note that it gets changed to 9.75 in the actual Size property value box.

[10]   The ampersand (&) denotes an Access key. See discussion in the text.

[11]   To select the Form control, click on any part of the Form not occupied by another component.

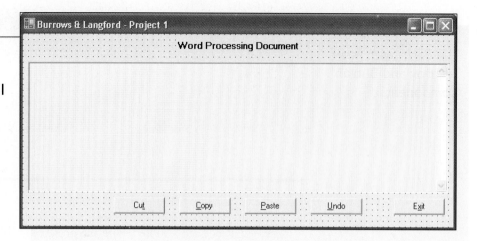

FIGURE 2.63

The Final Version of the Graphical User Interface for Project 1

means that the user can access the control by pressing the ALT key followed by the specific Access key. Since the Text property of btnCut is "Cu&t", this makes the "t" the Access key. When the program is running, if you press ALT+t, the cut operation will take place.

As a way of making the interface look nice, experiment with the Format menu items or their Toolbar equivalents.

6. Now would be a good time to click on the Save All icon on the Toolbar. It is always a good idea to save your work frequently in order to reduce the risk of losing everything.

7. We now need to add the code for the Button controls. There are two ways to create a Click event for a Button control. One way is to double-click on a button in the Form Designer and the Code window will open with the opening and closing statements for the button's Click event. The other way is to use the Class Name list in the Code window to select the specific Button control. Then use the Method Name list to select the Click event. This also will show the opening and closing statements for the button's Click event in the Code window. For this project we suggest you try both approaches since you have five buttons that have Click events. Figure 2.64 shows the code for the four text-processing buttons.

8. We now need to write the code for btnExit. The way we do this is execute the **End statement. This statement causes the application to stop executing.**

FIGURE 2.64

Code for the Four Text-Processing Buttons in Project 1

```
Private Sub btnCut_Click(ByVal sender As System.Objec
    txtDocument.Cut()
End Sub

Private Sub btnCopy_Click(ByVal sender As System.Obje
    txtDocument.Copy()
End Sub

Private Sub btnPaste_Click(ByVal sender As System.Obj
    txtDocument.Paste()
End Sub

Private Sub btnUndo_Click(ByVal sender As System.Obj
    txtDocument.Undo()
End Sub
```

```
Private Sub btnExit_Click(ByVal sender As System.Obje
    End
End Sub
```

FIGURE 2.65

Code to Terminate the Execution
of the Application

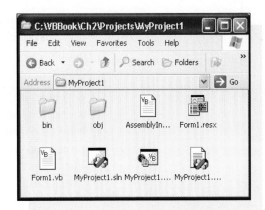

FIGURE 2.66

The MyProject1 Project Folder
and Its Contents

It consists of just the single word "End". Figure 2.65 shows the Click event.

9. Time to save the application again by clicking on the Save All icon.

10. Now that all the code is completed, scan it carefully for any errors. Look for the squiggly lines under any code that indicate problems. If you see any, fix them using the description of the problem provided by the IntelliSense system.

11. Now run and test the application. Start the application running by either selecting Start from the Debug menu, clicking on the Start icon on the Toolbar, or pressing F5. Try out all the functions to make sure they work. Also press the ALT key to see the Access keys. Make sure they work also.

12. When you are done, you should have a folder with your solution stored inside. The contents of the folder for our solution is shown in Figure 2.66. Your solution folder should be similar (the names of the files might be different).

For if you want to move your project to another computer, move the entire project (MyProject1) folder using Windows tools such as Copy/Paste or the Send To file option.

Exercise 2.11   What can you do as a developer to give the user the opportunity to stop a running application besides having him or her click on a Form control's close (**X**) icon?

Exercise 2.12   Read Section 6.8 and then modify Project 1 so that it includes a File menu with an Exit option and an Edit menu with Cut, Copy, Paste, and Undo options. Replace the behavior in the five Button controls with these five menu options.

Chapter Summary

1. An application under construction in Visual Basic .NET is called a project. When the project is complete, the programmer creates an executable file that contains the finished application. A copy of the executable file is given to the user, who can run the application without knowing anything about Visual Basic .NET.

The executable file cannot easily be modified. When changes are required, the programmer must make the changes in Visual Basic .NET using the project files, then create a new executable file for the user.

2. Visual Basic .NET has three modes of operation. Design mode allows the developer to build or modify the project. Run mode allows the developer to execute the project in order to see whether it works correctly. Break mode allows the developer to pause Run mode execution to examine the status of the project's event procedures, which helps in the process of debugging. When Visual Basic .NET is in design mode, the project is at design time; and when Visual Basic .NET is in run or break mode, the project is at run time.

3. The Visual Basic .NET IDE consists of a number of tools to help the developer. These include the Solution Explorer, the Properties Editor, the Task List, the Toolbox, and the Designer window used to design the GUI and also the code (the Visual Basic .NET statements).

4. During the design phase of the application creation process, you should choose descriptive names for every important control defined and any control whose name appears in an event procedure.

A good descriptive name for a control always begins with the standard three-letter prefix for the type of control. This naming practice makes event procedures easier to read because the name of the control indicates what type of control it is.

5. The Windows Form control is used to contain the other GUI controls. A control is an object that sits on top of the form. A property is an attribute that defines some characteristic of the control. Each type of control can respond to a number of different kinds of events. An event is a signal, generated at run time, that indicates something has happened to which the program must respond. An event procedure is a script containing instructions the computer will follow when an event occurs for the control.

6. The Button control allows the user to trigger a processing step via a Click event. The Label control displays text used to either identify another component on the GUI or provide some information while the program runs. The TextBox control provides a way for the user to enter information at run time that can then be processed by the program.

7. The MsgBox statement provides an alternate way of displaying information to the user. It is best to use this statement when it is important that the user read the information. The program execution pauses while the message box is displayed and only resumes after the user has clicked on a button on the message box.

The InputBox() function provides an alternate way of getting information from the user. This function returns the value entered by the user to the executing program. The InputBox() function should be used with caution since it tends to interrupt the user and requires him to do things in a predefined sequence.

Key Terms

Access key	ClipBoard	controls
break mode	Code window	debugging
Button control	component tray	design mode

Designer window	items	Solution Explorer
Dynamic Help	Label control	source code
End statement	machine language	Start Page
executable file	MsgBox statement	syntax
GUI	My Profile	Task List
IDE	project	TextBox control
InputBox() function	Properties Editor	Toolbox
integrated development	run mode	Windows Application
environment	Server Explorer	Windows Form
IntelliSense	solution	

End-of-Chapter Problems

1. Explain the reason for creating an executable file from a project. Can changes be made to the executable to modify the application?

2. What is the break mode used for?

3. What is the difference between design time and run time? Describe a possible error that could occur in run time that would not be caught by the development system at design time.

4. Name three Visual Basic .NET controls and describe the basic functionality of each.

5. In the development IDE, what does a project contain? What does a solution contain? Does a solution contain multiple projects or does a project contain multiple solutions?

6. It is recommended that you avoid changing the names of the files used by your project. To prevent accidental file name changes, what save options is it suggested that you use?

7. In the Name property of a control, a three-letter prefix should be used to identify the control type. What are the three-letter prefixes for the Button, Label, and TextBox controls? Why use these prefixes?

8. What is the Properties Editor used for? Is every property available to a control displayed in the Properties Editor?

9. Name the events that execute when a control receives focus and when a control loses focus.

10. Name and describe the statement that is used to quit a program without the user clicking on the Window's close box.

Programming Problems

1. Create a Visual Basic .NET project that has a form with a TextBox control, a Button control, and a Label control. The TextBox control should accept user entry. Write code that allows the user to click a button to copy the text in the text box and place it in the Text property of a Label control. Don't forget to name all of the controls with their proper prefixes.

2. Create a form that provides a button that activates an InputBox and allows the user to enter text. Store the text received from the InputBox in a label on the form. Create a second button that uses the MsgBox statement to display the typed information.

3. Create a form with two TextBox controls and a Label control. Place code in the Enter events of each TextBox that sets the Text property of the label to state which control now has the focus.

4. Create a new application with a form that has two text boxes and two buttons. Call the first text box txtCut and the second txtPaste. Likewise, name the first button btnCut2Characters and the second btnPaste. Add the logic needed to make the Cut button select the first two characters from the txtCut TextBox and cut them to the ClipBoard. Make the Paste button paste the characters in the ClipBoard to the Paste TextBox control. While in design mode, set the default Text property of txtCut to "1,2,3,4,5,6,7,8,9," so there will be initial text to cut to the ClipBoard.

5. Create a Visual Basic .NET project that has a form with a TextBox control and a Button control. In design mode, use the Lines property of the TextBox to enter three lines of default text. Be sure to first turn on the Multiline, Accepts-Returns, and AcceptsTab properties.

   Within a TextBox control, setting the SelectionLength property to a value greater than the length of the current text will automatically adjust the property value to the existing text length. Therefore, if you set the value to 65536, you can be assured that all of the text within the text box will be selected. Add code to the Click event of the button that will select all of the text in the text box and copy it to the ClipBoard.

THREE

REPRESENTING DATA

Constants and Variables

The project we introduced in Chapter 2 had limited processing capabilities. Its purpose was to introduce the Visual Basic .NET environment and the structure of Visual Basic .NET programs and to demonstrate how Visual Basic .NET's controls operate. Beginning with this chapter, we turn our focus to the job of composing event procedures that perform more sophisticated processing tasks. In this chapter we focus specifically on *data items*—**facts or quantities that describe things and that are processed by our programs.** Examples would be an employee name, a tax rate, or a product price.

We must specify the characteristics of each data item in our programs for Visual Basic .NET to correctly input, process, and output the item. For example, we want to handle a product price differently than a customer name, because the price is a number and is likely to be needed in arithmetic calculations, whereas the customer name is not. We begin this chapter by examining how data items are defined in Visual Basic .NET programs and how to specify the characteristics of data items.

In addition to studying data items, we continue our work with Visual Basic .NET project structure. The projects we create in this chapter have more than one form, and they build on the simple structure of the project presented in Chapter 2.

In Chapter 2 we stated that a Visual Basic .NET project can have many forms, and each form can have many controls and associated event procedures. Can a data item defined in one event procedure be accessed by statements in a second event procedure? The answer to this question is determined by the data item's *scope*—**the domain of procedures that are allowed to access the data item.**

Objectives

After studying this chapter, you should be able to

- Differentiate between numeric and string data.

- Determine whether a data item should be a constant or variable.

- Code constants and variables in event procedures.

- Describe the characteristics and uses of standard data types.

- Create projects that consist of several forms.

- Explain scope and describe the domain of variables in procedures and forms.

3.1 Data Categorization

The data manipulated by a Visual Basic .NET program fall into two broad categories: numeric and string. They differ in both form and use.

1. *Numeric data* **must contain only numbers,** whereas *string*[1] *data* **can contain any symbol.**

2. Numeric values can be used in arithmetic calculations, but string values cannot.

When you analyze a problem to be solved by a computer program, one of the first things you must do is decide which facts and quantities will be represented as data items. Then you must determine whether each data item should be numeric or string. The computer will not manipulate data items correctly if you do not identify them correctly. Therefore, we begin our discussion of data by explaining how you can determine which data items should be numeric and which should be string.

If the value of a real-world quantity contains letters, it must be represented as string data. For such cases the numeric-versus-string decision is easy.

Real-World Quantity	Example Value
A person's name	Jane Arbor
A person's address	321 Alder Ave.

However, many real-world quantities look like numbers, and you could represent them as either numeric or string.

Real-World Quantity	Example Value
The weight of a shipping container to be loaded on a truck, in tons	9.35
The population of a city or town in a state	85783
The dollar amount of an item in an invoice	109.95
A ZIP code (U.S. 5-digit postal code)	98765
A Social Security number	123456789
A phone number	12065551212

If you use a data item in arithmetic calculations, you should make it numeric. If the data item is never used in arithmetic, you should make it string.[2] Thus, you must evaluate how each data item will be used in the program.

The operators of a trucking company will want to know the total weight carried by a truck. To do this, a program would have to add the weights of the shipping containers loaded on the truck. A program used by a marketing department to track demographics would want to accumulate the population totals for various cities.

[1] Visual Basic .NET uses the term *string* to represent a string of characters.
[2] Actually, there are other reasons for selecting numeric rather than string. A developer might make a data item numeric instead of string, even if it will never be used in arithmetic, if doing so saves a significant amount of storage space. We leave such considerations for experienced developers to debate.

A company using a computer billing program would expect dollar amounts for items sold to be added on an invoice. All of these quantities should be numeric data.

How about a ZIP code? This real-world quantity looks like a number—it contains only digits—but we seldom think of adding up ZIP codes.

Suppose you are writing a program for your mail-order company, and you decide to represent your customers' ZIP codes as numeric data. This will work as long as all your customers reside in the United States. But postal codes in some other countries contain letters and therefore cannot be represented as numeric data. Your program may work perfectly until the day when you get your first international customer, at which time the program fails. Unless you are on your toes, you may not immediately see the cause of the failure.

String data are more flexible than numeric data in the values they can represent, as long as arithmetic is not required. For example, Social Security numbers and phone numbers, like ZIP codes, are never used in arithmetic. An added benefit of choosing to make these strings is that we can insert hyphens, parentheses, spaces, and other characters to format them so that they are easier for humans to read. *Formatting* is the **process of adding characters (such as dollar signs or commas) to a data item to make it easier for humans to read.**

Real World Quantity	Example Formatted Value
A Social Security number	123-45-6789
A phone number	1 (206) 555-1212

Although string data cannot be manipulated mathematically, they can still be processed. For example, a list of names and addresses could be sorted by ZIP code in a program being used by an advertising company.

After deciding whether a data item should be numeric or string, the Visual Basic .NET developer must identify the data item as a constant or a variable. Figure 3.1 depicts this decision-making process. We discuss constants in Section 3.2 and variables in Section 3.3.

3.2   Constants

In a program, a *constant* is a **data item whose value is specified at design time and cannot change at run time.** A program can manipulate both numeric constants and string constants. Figure 3.2 shows that a constant is either literal or symbolic.

FIGURE 3.1

Decisions Required to Specify a Data Item in Visual Basic .NET

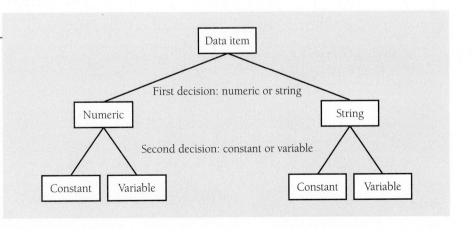

FIGURE 3.2

Classification of Constants in Visual Basic .NET

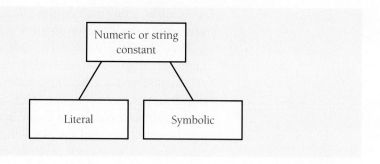

A *literal constant* is **simply a value.** A *symbolic constant* is a **descriptive name that the developer substitutes for a literal constant.** Using symbolic constants improves program readability because the developer reading the program code attaches the real-world meaning to his or her interpretation of the code.

As you can see from Figures 3.1 and 3.2, there are actually four different kinds of constants:

- Numeric literal constants.

- String literal constants.

- Numeric symbolic constants.

- String symbolic constants.

We discuss each of these next.

Literal Constants

An example of a numeric literal constant is 123, and an example of a string literal constant is "John Doe". A numeric literal constant can be used in arithmetic calculations but can contain only certain symbols (digits, decimal point, and an optional sign). A string literal constant cannot be used in arithmetic but can contain any symbol.

Writing Numeric Literal Constants

You must follow a few rules to specify valid numeric literal constants in your programs.[3] For the most part, Visual Basic .NET's rules conform to ordinary usage in writing numbers. The following are valid numeric literal constants in Visual Basic .NET:

$$1.23 \quad +123 \quad .1 \quad -6 \quad 8.9E{-}6 \quad 0.0000089 \quad 8.9E{+}3$$

The first four of these are straightforward. A numeric constant that begins with a digit, a plus sign, or a decimal point is a positive number. A numeric constant that begins with a minus sign (this is the same as the hyphen key on your keyboard) is a negative number. Visual Basic .NET treats the constant .1 the same as 0.1 (it ignores the leading 0).

The constant 8.9E–6 illustrates scientific notation in Visual Basic .NET: the E– is read as "times 10 to the minus." This is the same as 8.9×10^{-6}. The notation

---

[3] Windows allows you to specify the country format, which affects, among other things, the way numbers appear. In this text we have chosen to use the U.S. format, for which the "decimal point" is the period. If you choose the German format, for example, the "decimal point" will be a comma.

$\times\ 10^{-6}$ means "move the decimal point six places to the left." Thus, the constants 8.9E–6 and 0.0000089 are treated identically by Visual Basic .NET. The last example, 8.9E+3, is equivalent to 8.9×10^3, which is the same as 8900.

Scientific notation is convenient shorthand for representing very large and very small numbers. By using it, the developer eliminates the likelihood of miscounting the number of leading or trailing zeros. The difference between .0000089 and .000089 is not as readily apparent to a human as the difference between 8.9E–6 and 8.9E–5. Note that computers seldom err when counting 0s but humans frequently do, and an error of a factor of 10 can have disastrous effects in many applications.

The familiar practice of using commas in large numbers is disallowed in Visual Basic .NET; 2,123,234 is not a valid numeric constant in Visual Basic .NET. Nor are other characters, such as spaces or dollar signs, allowed in numeric constants.

Writing String Literal Constants

A string literal constant begins with a quote mark and ends with a quote mark.[4] Whenever you see quote marks in a program statement, you have found a string literal constant. Quote marks always occur in pairs. The symbols between the quote marks specify the value of the string constant. Visual Basic .NET accepts any symbol you can type (digit, letter, space, punctuation mark, etc.) to put between the quotes.

The quote marks merely serve to mark the beginning and end of the string constant and are not themselves part of the value. Thus, a person's name might be represented in a program as the string literal constant "Jane Arbor" and a person's address as "321 Alder Ave." If you want to place a quote mark within a string constant, you cannot just type it in the middle of a string constant because Visual Basic .NET would interpret it as the matching (terminating) quote mark for the opening quote.

To solve this problem, Visual Basic .NET provides an alternative. If you place two quote marks next to each other within a string constant, then it will not cause any confusion for Visual Basic .NET and the two adjacent quotes will be inserted into the string as a single quote. For example, if you create a string constant as "He said, ""Stop thief!"" in a very loud voice", this will create the string constant: He said, "Stop thief!" in a very loud voice. Note that the two sets of adjacent quote marks each become a single quote mark in the actual string constant.

Symbolic Constants

A symbolic constant is a descriptive name that the developer associates with a literal constant, allowing the developer to use the descriptive name instead of the literal constant. To demonstrate the purpose of symbolic constants, suppose the program requires a data item equal to 0.087 to be used in arithmetic calculations. The developer could simply use the numeric literal constant 0.087 everywhere it is needed in the program, but this is a poor idea. For one thing, it is not clear what real-world quantity 0.087 represents. The computer doesn't mind this, but it makes the program difficult for developers to understand and this can make the program more difficult to maintain.

Suppose the number 0.087 represents a sales tax rate. The developer could make the program more readable by associating the descriptive name

---

4 In this text we use the term *quote marks* to describe what some call double quotes ("). We use the term *single quote* as the same as apostrophe (').

SALESTAXRATE with the value 0.087, and subsequently using this descriptive name instead of the cryptic value 0.087.

Creating/Choosing Symbolic Constant Names

As a developer, you choose the symbolic constant name, but the name you choose must conform to certain rules. The first rule is that symbolic constant names can be no longer than 255 characters. These can include letters, digits, or the underscore (_) character, but the first character must be a letter. Spaces, commas, and other punctuation marks are not allowed in constant names. In addition, **certain combinations of characters, called *reserved words*, are not allowed as constant names because they form parts of the Visual Basic .NET language itself.** Reserved words, also called *keywords*, include Sub, If, End, and Print. Visual Basic .NET ordinarily displays keywords in a different color than non-keywords.[5]

As a general rule, you should avoid digits and use all capital letters in symbolic constant names. Capitalizing all letters makes it easier to recognize symbolic constants in your code.

You now know enough about string and numeric constants to see how they differ and why you would choose one or the other for a particular data item. We now turn our attention to the constant definition statement, which is the vehicle for specifying the symbolic constants you use in a program and identifying whether they are numeric or string.

The Constant Definition Statement

To create a symbolic constant in a procedure, at the top of the procedure you write a *constant definition statement* (**also called a *Const statement*) that begins with the keyword Const, followed by the symbolic name, then an optional type declaration, then an equal sign, and finally the literal value.** Each of the four constant definition statements that follow defines a symbolic constant.

```
Const SALESTAXRATE = 0.087
Const DRIVEEMPTY = "Please insert disk in drive A."
Const ZIPCODE As String = "98195"
Const MINIMUMAGE As Integer = 21
```

Following these statements in a procedure, you can use any one of the four symbolic constants to refer to the actual literal value.

Notice the first two examples above do not use the optional type declaration while the last two do. If the optional type declaration is omitted, the type (numeric or string) of a symbolic constant is determined by the type of the literal constant on the right-hand side of the equal sign. In this case, if the literal constant is numeric, then the symbolic constant is also numeric. If the literal constant is string, then the symbolic constant is also string. If the optional type declaration, for example, As String or As Integer, is included, the type of the constant will match the explicit type specified. We discuss the standard data types in the next section on variables.

---

5   You can specify the color Visual Basic .NET uses for keywords by selecting Options… under the Tools menu. Within the Environment folder you will see "Fonts and Colors." Clicking on this option will allow you to change fonts and colors for a number of categories.

Run Time: How the Computer Uses Symbolic Constants

Whenever Visual Basic .NET first begins executing a procedure, it creates an empty table of symbolic constants. Then, when Visual Basic .NET executes a constant definition statement, it adds a row to the table showing the name and the value of the new symbolic constant. For example, suppose Visual Basic .NET is executing a procedure that contains two of the constant definition statements presented earlier. After it has executed both of these, its table of symbolic constants will appear as follows.

Constant Name	Value
SALESTAXRATE	0.087
DRIVEEMPTY	"Please insert disk in drive A."

What happens when the computer subsequently executes a statement that contains a symbolic constant name? It first goes to its table of symbolic constants to look up the value that corresponds to the symbolic constant name. It substitutes this value for the name, and then executes the statement just as if the statement had originally contained the literal value.

Advantages of Using Symbolic Constants

Symbolic constants have two advantages over literal constants:

1. They can make the program easier for humans to understand.

2. They reduce the chance of inconsistencies in the program.

To see these advantages in action, consider the Click event in Figure 3.3. This figure shows the code that is executed when the user clicks on the button named btnDoSomething. Can you figure out what is happening with this code?

The code in this figure is harder to read because the choices of names for the two label components are vague, though you still might be able to figure out its function. However, if you thought that you were looking at a calculation of sales tax and a calculation of the total amount to be collected, you would be wrong.

Look now at the code in Figure 3.4. In this code, the literal constants have been replaced with symbolic constants. Can you now figure out what is being computed?

Using symbolic constants as shown in Figure 3.4 not only increases the code's readability (the first mystery label is holding the tax amount and the second is holding a new sales amount based on a projected growth rate factor), but also enhances the code's maintainability. For example, since both constants just happen to be equal to each other in this example, it would be very easy to change the

```
Private Sub btnDoSomething_Click(ByVal sender As System.O
    lblMystery1.Text = txtSalesAmt.Text * 0.087
    lblMystery2.Text = txtSalesAmt.Text * (1 + 0.087)
End Sub
```

FIGURE 3.3

A Mystery Click Event with
Literal Constants

```
Private Sub btnDoSomething_Click(ByVal sender As System.Object, ByVal e A
    Const SALESTAXRATE = 0.087
    Const PROJECTEDGROWTHRATE = 0.087
    lblMystery1.Text = txtSalesAmt.Text * SALESTAXRATE
    lblMystery2.Text = txtSalesAmt.Text * (1 + PROJECTEDGROWTHRATE)
End Sub
```

FIGURE 3.4

Replacing Literal Constants with Symbolic Constants

wrong literal constant in Figure 3.3 if only one of them needed to be changed. However, it is much less likely that a similar error would be made with the code in Figure 3.4.

Note that as a standard convention, you place constant definition statements right after the event procedure's Private Sub statement so that they are easy to find.

Literal versus Symbolic Constants

When should you use literal constants, and when should you use symbolic constants? As a general rule, code should contain no literal constants except the zero-length string ("") and numbers that are an integral part of a formula. For example, using the literal constant 7 as the number of days in the week or 12 as the number of months in a year would be fine since they would never change (as compared to a tax rate that might change often).

Typical Uses of Symbolic Constants

Symbolic constants are good for representing facts and quantities that do not change during program execution but may change over time. Typical examples are

- The prime interest rate.

- The overtime rate such as time and a half or double time.

- The number of lines per page a particular printer produces.

Predefined Symbolic Constants

Visual Basic .NET provides a large set of predefined symbolic constants. Many of these constants are made available via constants within the classes. For example, the Math class supports the constants E, which specifies the natural logarithmic base, and PI, which specifies the ratio of the circumference of a circle to its diameter. These constants are referred to with the syntax Math.E and Math.PI (class name dot constant name). Another example is the Color class, which supports constants such as AliceBlue, Fuchsia, HotPink, and so on, referred to as Color.AliceBlue, Color.Fuchsia, and Color.HotPink. Notice that these constants do not follow the standard naming convention of using all uppercase letters. You will need to refer to the Visual Basic .NET Help system for more on the predefined symbolic constants.

Exercise 3.1

Write a statement that defines a symbolic constant representing the number of days in the month of January.

Exercise 3.2

Which of the following are not valid constant definition statements? Explain how they could be modified to make them valid.

```
Const OURNAMES = "Joe, Bill"
Const T1RATE = 1,544,000
Const ANNSOFFICEPHONE = 555 - 1234
Const MAX SPEED = 55
Const COMPOSER = Ludwig Van Beethoven
Const STARTINGCHECKNUMBER = 100
```

3.3 | Variables

***Variables* are used in a program to store data items and to retrieve the data during processing.** That is, variables allow us to represent data items whose values change at run time.

Variables can be either numeric or string. For example, in an insurance application, you could create a numeric variable called **Age** that would hold the age of the person applying for insurance coverage. Similarly, you could create a string variable called **ApplicantName** that would hold the applicant's first and last name. Although you would know at design time what type of data each variable would store, you would not be able to predict the value those variables would hold at run time. Therefore, you could not use constants for these data items.

In this section we discuss how to work with variables. The steps are to give the variable a symbolic name, to inform Visual Basic .NET of the characteristics of the data the variable will store, and to give the variable an initial value. The variable declaration statement—the counterpart to the constant definition statement—is the vehicle for doing this. We also will discuss how to use variables in procedures.

Variable Names

As with symbolic constant names, you choose the names for the variables you create. Visual Basic .NET places the same restrictions on variable names that it does on constant names: they can be no longer than 255 characters; and although they may contain letters, digits, or the underscore character, the first character must be a letter. Again, keywords are not allowed, nor are spaces, commas, and other punctuation marks.

You should choose descriptive names for your variables, that is, names that convey the real-world meanings of the values to be stored in the variables. Using descriptive names makes your program much easier for other developers to understand. (Visual Basic .NET does not attempt to interpret the meaning of variable names.)

Choosing descriptive variable names is simple. A variable to store the user's first name, for example, might be called **FirstName**. The programming convention we will use in this text is that we will use only letters, start each variable with an uppercase letter, and capitalize the first letter of each word within the variable name. This convention is called Pascal-casing and is the standard Microsoft recommends for Visual Basic .NET.

All of the following are valid variable names:

FleetSize	NumberOfSeminarParticipants	EmployeeNumber
WageRate	EmployeeName	ExtendedPrice
AverageAge	NumBidUnits	Depreciation
MaximumCapacity	YtdEarnings	X

The variable name **X**, of course, usually cannot be considered descriptive and should not be used unless the value being stored has no real-world meaning. Mathematical programs sometimes require variables like this (which mathematicians often call dummy variables), while they are rare in business programs. Also, instructors sometimes use variable names like **X** when they teach to reduce the amount they (and their students) have to write.

Observe that the convention for symbolic constant names is to use all capital letters, but the convention for variable names is to capitalize the first letter of the variable name and each embedded word within the variable name. Following these conventions in the code you write makes it easier to distinguish symbolic constants from variables.

Exercise 3.3

The following are not valid variable names:

Net-Pay   Item Price   Sub   3rdAlternate

How does each of these violate the variable-naming rules?

Standard Data Types

When deciding what variables are needed for a program, you also must decide whether they should contain numeric or string data. Remember, a value stored in a numeric variable can be used in arithmetic calculations, whereas a value stored in a string variable cannot.[6]

As you may be aware, internally the computer uses a binary language of ones and zeros (1s and 0s). Thus, by necessity, computer scientists have devised many different schemes for representing data as sequences of 1s and 0s. Each such scheme is called a data type. When you create a variable in a program, you have to specify a data type for it. Visual Basic .NET provides 12 different **predefined types, which are often called** *standard data types*.[7]

A variable's data type determines its characteristics, which include the kind of value it can store. Table 3.1 summarizes the characteristics of each type. There is only one string type, six numeric types, and a type that represents a true/false value. The developer must specify one of these types for each variable.

Number of Bytes

The "Number of Bytes" column of Table 3.1 shows the number of bytes of main memory that a variable of each type occupies. Each numeric type has a fixed size, but the size of a string variable depends on the value stored in it. For example, a variable of type Decimal occupies 16 bytes, regardless of the value stored in it, but a variable of type String occupies 10 bytes if the value stored in it is "board" and 30 bytes if the value is "QWERTY keyboard" (two bytes per character, counting every character, including spaces, commas, and other symbols).[8]

Range

Range **refers to the largest and smallest values that can be stored in a numeric variable of the given type.** For string variables, the range is the maximum length (number of characters) that can be stored.

---

[6] This statement is literally true. However, as we will see later, Visual Basic .NET sometimes will convert string values into their numeric equivalents automatically. This, however, is considered by some to be a bad idea (and is not supported in most other languages).

[7] Although there 12 standard data types, we will only discuss 8 of the most commonly used types here. See Visual Basic .NET's documentation for information on the other 4 types.

[8] Visual Basic .NET actually uses several more bytes in a String type to store the length of the string. We are ignoring these few extra overhead bytes in this discussion.

Table 3.1 Characteristics of the most common standard data types

Data Type	Number of Bytes	Range	Precision
Boolean	2 bytes	True or False	Not applicable
Decimal	16 bytes	+/–79,228,162,514,264,337,593,543,950,335 with no decimal point; +/–7.9228162514264337593543950335 with 28 places to the right of the decimal; smallest non-zero number is +/–0.0000000000000000000000000001	29 digits
Double	8 bytes	4.94065645841247E–324 to 1.79769313486231E+308 for positive values; –1.79769313486231E+308 to –4.94065645841247E–324 for negative values; and 0	15 significant digits
Integer	4 bytes	–2,147,483,648 to 2,147,483,647	10 digits; whole numbers only
Long	8 bytes	–9,223,372,036,854,775,808 to 9,223,372,036,854,775,807	19 digits; whole numbers only
Short	2 bytes	–32,768 to 32,767	5 digits; whole numbers only
Single	4 bytes	1.401298E–45 to 3.402823E+38 for positive values; –3.402823E+38 to –1.401298E–45 for negative values; and 0	7 significant digits
String	2 bytes per character	0 to approximately 2 billion Unicode characters	Not applicable

Precision

Precision **indicates how close together two numeric values can be before Visual Basic .NET cannot tell them apart.** Different numeric data types have different degrees of precision. For example, suppose we have two variables named **TestInt** and **TestLong**, of types Integer and Long, respectively. Further, suppose we try to store the number 1.2 in **TestInt** and the number 1.3 in **TestLong**. Variables of type Integer and Long (as well as Short) can store only integer values (whole numbers), so both variables **TestInt** and **TestLong** will actually store the number 1. We say that types Short, Integer, and Long are exact for integer values but that they round off fractional values; equivalently, we say that the precision is limited to whole numbers for variables of type Short, Integer and Long.

Decimal, Single, and Double all store fractional values, but with varying degrees of precision. Suppose we try to store the value 654321.123456 in three variables named **TestDec**, **TestSing**, and **TestDoub**, of types Decimal, Single, and Double, respectively. The values that actually get stored in these variables are

Variable	Type	Actual Value Stored	Explanation
TestDec	Decimal	654,321.123456	Full precision because the number uses less than 29 digits
TestSing	Single	654,321.1	Maximum of seven significant digits is reached.
TestDoub	Double	654,321.123456	Full precision, because 12 significant digits are fewer than the maximum of 15.

Single and Double are called *floating-point* **types because they store numbers using a scheme based on scientific notation.** They are able to store very large and very small numbers. The Decimal type is not a floating-point type. It uses a modified version of whole number representation with a scaling factor to record where the decimal point is located. The effect of these two internal representations impacts accuracy. We humans deal with numbers using the base 10 number system and the computer internally deals with numbers in the binary (base 2) number system. Thus, there is a conversion from base 10 to base 2 when a number is input into the computer and the opposite conversion from base 2 to base 10 when a number is output. The conversion process is guaranteed to be exact with whole numbers and so we expect no internal representation errors with the types based on whole numbers (Integer, Long, Short, and Decimal). The conversion process is not necessarily exact for numbers represented internally as floating-point numbers such as Double and Single (the value to the left of the decimal point will always be exact but the fraction part to the right of the decimal point may not be exact).

Speed of Arithmetic Calculation

Finally, note that the speed of arithmetic calculation differs for the different numeric types. As you would expect, the larger and more precise the number that can be stored, the more memory is required and the slower the arithmetic operations are.[9]

Choosing the Best Data Type for a Variable

Suppose that you know the characteristics of a real-world value you need to store in a variable and you have chosen a descriptive name for it. Which one of the eight data types should you choose? Table 3.2 contains a set of decision rules to help you select the best type for the variable. To use this table, scan the left-hand column until you find the first description that matches the characteristics of the real-world value to be stored.

As an example, suppose we need a variable to store a city's population. We reject type String because we may want to use a city population in arithmetic. It is not a dollar amount, so we reject type Decimal. A city population is a whole number, and it is possible for a city's population to exceed 32,767 but it is less than 2 billion, so we choose type Integer.

Exercise 3.4

What value is actually stored in a variable of type Single if we try to store the value 0.0000123456789 in it?

Exercise 3.5

Suppose you need a variable to store the user's height, in centimeters. Which type would you choose for this variable? Explain your answer.

Exercise 3.6

Suppose you need a variable to store a five-digit ZIP code. Will type Short work? Suppose you need a variable to store a nine-digit ZIP code. Will type Integer work? Explain. What if the nine-digit ZIP code also included a dash between

---

9 It takes the computer very little time to perform any simple arithmetic calculation. You will notice the speed difference for the different types only if your program performs thousands, or perhaps millions, of arithmetic operations.

Table 3.2 Decision rules for choosing a variable's data type

Nature of Value to Be Stored	Best Type	Reasons
Something that is either true or false	Boolean	Most efficient storage for a true/false entity.
Sequence of characters; not involved in arithmetic; may include letters and special characters	String	Only choice if value contains letters; more flexible if not involved in arithmetic.
Dollar amount	Decimal	Can store $ and ¢; no round-off error with arithmetic; arithmetic reasonably fast.
Whole number: Always < 32,767 (see footnote 10)	Short	Less memory required; faster arithmetic than other numeric types.
Always < 2,147,483,647	Integer	Less memory and faster than Long.
May be ≥ 2,147,483,647	Long	
Number with fractional part: Seven digits sufficient; < 10^{38}	Single	Slower arithmetic and possible representation errors, but guaranteed number of significant digits regardless of size of value.
More than seven digits of significance; ≥ 10^{38}	Double	

the fifth and sixth characters (using a total of 10 characters)? Would this have an impact on the data type you would choose?

Declaring Variables: The Dim Statement

To create a variable, you write a *variable declaration statement* (also called a *Dim statement*), **which begins with the keyword Dim, followed by the name of the variable to be declared, then the keyword As, the data type for the variable, and finally an optional equal sign and initial value.** The following are valid variable declaration statements:

```
Dim ContainerWeight As Integer
Dim CityPopulation As Integer
Dim InvoiceAmount As Decimal = 10
Dim EmployeeName As String = "none"
Dim ZipCode As String
```

The placement of a Dim statement determines where the variable that is declared may be used. We will cover this issue later in Section 3.6.

If you leave off the optional equal sign and initial value as in the first two examples above, the variable will be initialized with a default value. For numeric variable types the default value is zero. For the String type, the default value is the zero-length or empty string. This is a string with no characters and is created with two adjacent quote marks (""). If you include the explicit initialization as in the third and fourth examples above, the variable will be initialized to whatever you specify after the equal sign.

---

10   For all numeric values, consider the value shown to be an absolute value, that is, < 32,767 means that the value is between −32,767 and +32,767.

Declaring Multiple Variables in One Dim Statement

It is possible to declare multiple variables in a single Dim statement. For example, these three Dim statements could replace the five Dim statements in the preceding example:

```
Dim ContainerWeight, CityPopulation As Integer
Dim InvoiceAmount As Decimal = 10, EmployeeName As String = "none"
Dim ZipCode As String
```

In the first Dim statement above, both variables will be declared as Integer types with default initial values of 0. The second Dim statement creates both a Decimal and a String variable with initial values as shown.

Exercise 3.7

The following are not valid variable names:

Net-Pay   Item Price   Sub   3rdAlternate

In Visual Basic .NET, edit any event procedure and add a Dim statement declaring a variable named **Net-Pay** of type Integer. Then place the cursor over the variable name; what is the exact error message that Visual Basic .NET displays when you try this?

Try to declare variables having the other three names shown here. What error message does Visual Basic .NET display for each?

Exercise 3.8

In Visual Basic .NET, edit any event procedure and add the following Dim statement, which contains the misspelled word "Decmal".

Dim MySalary As Decmal

Then run the program and execute the event procedure. What error message does Visual Basic .NET display?

Exercise 3.9

What problem do you think some U.S. businesses had with their programs when they changed from five-digit to nine-digit ZIP codes?

Using Variables: The Assignment Statement

To change the value stored in a variable you use an assignment statement. It is called an assignment statement because storing a value in a variable is sometimes described as assigning a value to a variable. Our program examples have included assignment statements. Now we will see what constitutes a valid assignment statement and how it causes the computer to act at run time.

Syntax of the Assignment Statement

The term *syntax* **means the correct grammatical form of an element of a programming language.** The syntax of the assignment statement is

$$variablename = expression$$

The italicized words represent positions at which the developer provides specific details to customize the statement. Thus, a valid ***assignment statement* consists of a variable name, followed by an equal sign, followed by an expression.** You must create the variable using a variable declaration statement before you can use the variable in an assignment statement. The equal sign is called the assignment operator. The *expression* **may be a constant or a variable, or it may combine constants and variables using such operations as addition and subtraction.** As you will see in Chapter 4, you can compose quite complicated expressions. In this chapter we work with simple expressions.

The following is an example of a valid assignment statement:

ContainerWeightA = 1000

Run Time: The Effect of the Assignment Statement

To execute an assignment statement, the computer performs two steps.

1. It evaluates the expression on the right-hand side of the equal sign to determine its value. That is, it determines the value of the expression.

2. It stores the value of the expression in the variable named on the left-hand side of the equal sign. That is, it changes this variable's value.

To demonstrate how this process works, let us examine the actions of the computer as it executes the following two statements:

Dim ContainerWeightA As Short
ContainerWeightA = 1000

When it executes the Dim statement, the computer creates the variable **ContainerWeightA** and initializes its value to the default value of zero. Next, the computer executes the assignment statement. To do this, it performs the following sequence of steps.

1. Computer determines value of expression to be 1000.

2. Computer stores 1000 in variable on left-hand side (changes its value).

The net effect of executing this assignment statement is to change the value stored in the variable **ContainerWeightA** to 1000.

The action of the assignment statement may seem trivial, but you should study it carefully. It is easy to confuse assignment statements with algebraic expressions, and the action of the assignment statement is completely different. You will have difficulty understanding even the simplest programs if you do not interpret assignment statements correctly.

Run Time: How the Computer Evaluates Expressions

When the expression in an assignment statement is just a literal constant, as in our example, the value of the expression is just the value of the constant. But what is the value of the expression when the expression is a variable? What is it when the expression combines constants and variables using addition and subtraction? In such cases, evaluating the expression is a two-step process.

In the first step, the computer carefully determines the identity of each component of the expression: it identifies the literal constants, the symbolic constants, and the variables, as well as any addition and subtraction symbols. In performing this step, it replaces each symbolic constant and variable with its value.

In the second step, the computer performs any specified operations (e.g., addition and subtraction) to arrive at the expression's value. The following example demonstrates how the computer evaluates expressions.

Example 3.1   SIMPLE ASSIGNMENT STATEMENTS

The purpose of this example is to observe the action of a variety of simple assignment statements. The form used in this example is shown in Figure 3.5. The form has just two important controls: a button (btnAssignmentTest) and a label (lblTotal). The Click event procedure for btnAssignmentTest is shown in Figure 3.6. At run time, when the user clicks on btnAssignmentTest, the computer begins executing btnAssignmentTest_Click; it executes one statement at a time, from top to bottom.

When the computer executes the constant definition statement, it adds a row to its symbolic constant table, setting the value of the symbolic constant METRICTON to the literal constant value 1000.

Then it executes the three Dim statements. These statements declare and initialize the variables **ContainerWeightA**, **ContainerWeightB**, and **TotalWeight** to the value zero.

Next, the computer executes the first assignment statement. To do this, it performs this sequence of steps:

1. Computer replaces constant name by its value.

2. Computer determines value of expression to be 1000.

3. Computer stores 1000 in variable on left-hand side (changes its value from 0 to 1000).

The computer next executes the second assignment statement. To do this, it performs this sequence of steps:

1. Computer replaces variable name by its value (now equal to 1000).

2. Computer determines value of expression to be 1000.

3. Computer stores 1000 in variable on left-hand side (changes its value from 0 to 1000).

The computer executes the third assignment statement. To do this, it performs these steps:

1. Computer replaces the variable names by their values.

2. Computer adds 1000 and 1000, determines value of expression to be 2000.

3. Computer stores 2000 in variable on left-hand side (changes its value from 0 to 2000).

The final assignment statement is a little different from the others: it has a control property, instead of a variable, on the left-hand side. You may recall seeing statements like this in examples earlier. The net effect of this statement is to display the value

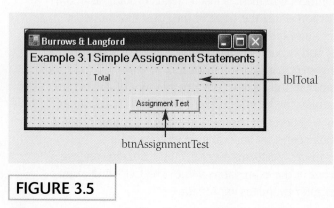

FIGURE 3.5

Form and Controls for Example 3.1

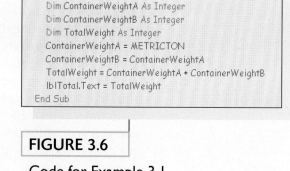

```
Private Sub btnAssignmentTest_Click(ByVal sender As Syste
    Const METRICTON = 1000
    Dim ContainerWeightA As Integer
    Dim ContainerWeightB As Integer
    Dim TotalWeight As Integer
    ContainerWeightA = METRICTON
    ContainerWeightB = ContainerWeightA
    TotalWeight = ContainerWeightA + ContainerWeightB
    lblTotal.Text = TotalWeight
End Sub
```

FIGURE 3.6

Code for Example 3.1

of variable **TotalWeight** on the user interface in the Text property of the label named lblTotal. When the computer executes this statement, it performs these steps:

1. Computer replaces variable name by its value.

2. Computer determines value of expression to be 2000.

3. Computer converts the value 2000 to the string "2000" and stores it in the Text property of the Label control, which displays it on the user interface.

Changing Variable Values during Execution

As you have seen, you can instruct the computer to do two things with a variable:

1. *Store a value in the variable*—the previous value in the variable will be overwritten (irretrievably lost) by this operation. To store a value in a variable, place the variable on the left-hand side of an assignment statement.

2. *Retrieve the value from the variable*—this operation will not change the value in the variable. It is done either to use this value in a calculation or processing step or to display it to the user. To retrieve the value from a variable, place the variable in an expression on the right-hand side of an assignment statement.

These are the only two things that you can do with a variable. You must understand these two ideas in order to be able to write correct assignment statements. For example, consider the following statement:

$$X = X + 1$$

Statements like this, where the same variable name appears both in the expression and on the left-hand side, are used very frequently in programs.

What does this statement do? Suppose that the variable X had the value 5 stored in it before the statement above was executed. To execute the assignment statement, the computer performs this sequence of steps:

1. Computer replaces variable name by its value (5 in this case).

2. Computer performs addition, determines value of expression to be 6 (5 + 1).

3. Computer stores 6 in the variable on left-hand side (changes X's value to 6).

Regardless of the value in X when the statement is executed, the statement's net effect is to increase the value stored in X by 1.

To test your understanding of the assignment statement's action, let's work through a complete event procedure. This event procedure, which is associated with a button named btnAssignmentQuiz on a hypothetical form, is shown below.

```
Private Sub btnAssignmentQuiz_Click(...)
    Dim A As Short
    Dim B As Short
    Dim C As Short
    A = 5
    A = A + A
    B = A - 6
    C = A + B
    B = B + C
    B = B - A
    B = B + 1
    lblQuiz.Text = B
End Sub
```

Before reading further, see if you can figure out what value will be displayed in the Label control (lblQuiz) when the event procedure is finished executing. That is, what value does the variable **B** hold at the end of the procedure?

How did you do? Let's go through the procedure one statement at a time and see what happens. After executing the three Dim statements, the three variables **A**, **B**, and **C** are declared with initial values of 0. Executing the statement **A** = 5 changes the variable **A** to be equal to 5. Next, the computer executes the statement **A** = **A** + **A**. To do this, it performs these steps:

1. Computer replaces variable name on the right-hand side by its value (5 in this case).

2. Computer performs addition and determines value of expression to be 10.

3. Computer stores 10 in variable on left-hand side (the variable **A**).

The net effect of executing this statement is to change the variable **A** to be equal to the value 10. After executing the statement **B** = **A** − **6**, the variable **B** now stores the value 4 (10 − 6). At this point the variable values are **A** = 10, **B** = 4, and **C** still equals zero.

After executing the statement **C** = **A** + **B**, the variable **C** is set equal to 14 (10 + 4). And after executing the statement **B** = **B** + **C**, the variable **B** is set equal to 18 (4 + 14).

The three variables values are **A** = 10, **B** = 18, and **C** = 14. Executing the statement **B** = **B** − **A** sets the variable **B** equal to 8. Finally, after executing the statement **B** = **B** + 1, the variable **B** is equal to 9. The final statement in the event procedure, **lblQuiz.Text** = **B**, stores the value of the variable **B** in the Text property of lblQuiz. Thus, the value 9 is displayed on the user interface.

You can see how tedious operations like this are for humans to perform. It is very easy to make a mistake. However, the computer never tires of performing these operations and gets them right every time.

Assignment Statements with Strings

You can use the assignment statement to store the result of string manipulations in string variables just as you store the result of arithmetic calculations in numeric variables. The main difference is that string expressions tend to be simpler than numeric expressions. To illustrate, the Click event procedure for a hypothetical button named btnStringAssignment is shown next.

```
Private Sub btnStringAssignment_Click(...)
    Dim FirstName As String
    Dim LastName As String
    Dim FullName As String
    FirstName = "Benjamin"
    LastName = "Franklin"
    FullName = FirstName & LastName
    lblName.Text = FullName
End Sub
```

This event procedure manipulates strings using statements similar to those we have seen that manipulate numbers. The & (ampersand) symbol in the expression of the third assignment statement is called the ***concatenation operator***: **it joins two string values together, end-to-end, to form a single string value.**

After executing the three Dim statements, the three variables **FirstName**, **Last-Name**, and **FullName** are declared and set equal to the default initial value for strings (the empty string). Executing the statement **FirstName** = "Benjamin" changes the variable **FirstName** to be equal to the string "Benjamin".

After executing the statement **LastName** = "Franklin", the variable **LastName** is equal to the string "Franklin". To execute the statement **FullName** = **FirstName** & **LastName**, the computer performs the following steps:

1. Computer replaces variable names on the right-hand side by their values.

2. Computer performs string concatenation and determines value of expression to be "BenjaminFranklin".

3. Computer stores "BenjaminFranklin" in variable on left-hand side (**FullName** now stores the string "BenjaminFranklin").

The final assignment statement in the event procedure, **lblName.Text** = **FullName**, displays the value "BenjaminFranklin" on the user interface.

The Type Mismatch Error

Numeric variables can store numeric values but cannot store string values. So what happens when the computer tries to execute the following event procedure?

```
Private Sub btnTypeMismatchA_Click(...)
    Dim X As Integer
    X = "12a"        ' This will cause a type mismatch
    lblX.Text = X
End Sub
```

When the computer tries to execute the statement **X** = "12a", it fails. Because "12a" does not have the correct form for a number, it cannot be stored in a numeric variable. This mistake—**trying to store string data in a numeric variable**—is known as a *type mismatch error.* The computer stops executing the project and displays the error message shown in Figure 3.7.

Note that the error message is referring to an invalid "cast" exception. The term *exception* **is used to describe an error that occurs while the program is running.** The term *cast* **is used to describe the process of converting one type to another.** In this case, for the assignment statement to work, the string ("12a") must be cast into an Integer type for the assignment to take place. The system is unhappy because this cast fails. Also be aware that it is not wrong to store a String type as a numeric variable as long as the string looks like a valid number (like "12").

The type mismatch error is an example of a *run time error*—**a condition arising during execution of a statement that prevents the computer from successfully executing the statement.** Note that while Visual Basic .NET can

FIGURE 3.7

Error Message Due to a Type Mismatch Error

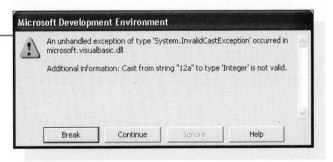

detect some errors at design time (e.g., when you try to type a variable name containing a space), it cannot detect the type mismatch error at design time.

Visual Basic .NET will try to make an assignment statement work even if the types on the left- and right-hand sides are different.[11] That is, it will try to cast the expression on the right side of the assignment operator so that it is compatible with the data type of the variable on the left side.

In order to fix the problem, the developer must modify the code, either by changing the Dim statement so that **X** is declared to be type String, by changing the assignment statement so that the expression is numeric instead of string (e.g., 12 instead of "12a"), or by adding a Try/Catch block.

The Try/Catch Block

A *Try/Catch* **block is used to detect and handle exceptions that are detected while the program is running.** The term *throw an exception* **means to indicate when a problem has been detected at run time.** All exceptions must be caught (we say *catch an exception*); that is, **someone (either the developer or the system) must supply code to do something when an exception is thrown.** In the example above, the developer did not supply any code, so the exception was caught by the system, and the error message in Figure 3.7 is what the system did to respond to that exception.

The developer uses the Try/Catch block to catch exceptions and handle them instead of letting the system handle them. This results in more meaningful error messages (more meaningful to the user of the application). The basic logic underlying this can be summarized in pseudocode as:

1. *Try*
   Include a block of code here that might throw an exception.
2. *Catch*
   Include code here to handle the exception. Skip if no exception is thrown.
3. *Continue with any remaining code.*

The syntax of the Try/Catch block can get rather involved. We introduce the simplest form here and will expand this later as needed. The example above can be modified to use a Try/Catch block as follows:

```
Private Sub btnTypeMismatchA_Click(...)
    Dim X As Integer
    Try
        X = "12a"        ' This will cause a type mismatch
        lblX.Text = X
    Catch
        lblX.Text = "You entered an illegal value for an integer"
    End Try
End Sub
```

---

11 Visual Basic .NET can be set to force the developer to always perform the type conversions herself, that is, to specify an explicit type casting for an assignment operation. Changing the value of the Option Strict setting to "ON" does this. By default, it is set to "OFF". You can access this setting by right-clicking on the project name in the Solution Explorer and selecting Properties from the pop-up menu. You will find the setting in the Build tab of the Common Properties section.

The Try block includes the two assignment statements that attempt to assign something first to the variable **X** and then to the Text property of the label lblX. An exception might be thrown from the first assignment statement. The Catch block "catches an exception" if thrown in the Try block. Here the program is informing the user via the label's Text property that an illegal value was being converted from String to Integer.

The example above is not very realistic. A more realistic example would be the user (at run time) trying to store a value into a numeric variable. The Text properties of all components are String type, so storing the Text property of a text box into a numeric variable requires a cast (implicit or explicit). Consider the following code:

```
Private Sub btnFindSqrt_Click(...)
    Dim N As Integer
    Try
        N = txtN.Text
        lblSqrtN.Text = Math.Sqrt(N)
    Catch
        lblSqrtN.Text = "Input value not legal"
    End Try
End Sub
```

Here the user enters a value into the text box txtN. If this is a valid number, that is, if an exception is not thrown while it is being cast into an Integer, then the square root will be calculated using the Sqrt() method from the Math class. Otherwise an exception will be thrown and caught and the message "Input value not legal" will be displayed in the label lblSqrtN.

One final comment regarding the Try/Catch block and the program's flow of control is in order. **Flow of control is a term used to describe the sequence in which statements are executed.** So far we have seen that statements are executed one after the other, starting with the first statement. This is called *sequential flow of control,* that is, **starting with the first statement, the statements are then executed in the physical sequence provided by the developer.** The Try/Catch block can modify this sequential flow of control. Here is how it works. The first statement in the Try block is executed and following statements are executed in sequence. If no exception is thrown, then the statements in the Catch block are skipped and flow of control continues with the first statement after the End Try statement. However, if an exception is thrown while executing a statement in the Try block, flow of control is immediately transferred to the first statement in the Catch block and any remaining statements in the Try block (after the one that threw the exception) are skipped. When all the statements in the Catch block are done executing, flow of control continues with the first statement after the End Try statement.

Control Properties in Assignment Statements

Most control properties can be used just like variables in assignment statements. Thus, if a control property appears on the left-hand side of an assignment statement, then the computer stores the result of the expression in the specified property of the specified control. For example, the assignment statement

```
lblCPUPrice.Text = 1450
```

causes the value 1450 to be stored in the Text property of the control named lblCPUPrice. Note that the number 1450 must be cast to a String for this assignment to work. Also be aware that there cannot be a cast exception in this case because all numbers can be successfully cast into Strings.

If a control property appears in the expression of an assignment statement, then the computer will retrieve the value from the specified property of the specified control to use in evaluating the expression.

There are only two differences between a control property and a variable:

1. To create a variable you must write a variable declaration statement; in contrast, you don't declare a control's properties. Visual Basic .NET automatically gives you a whole set of control properties when you place the control on the form.

2. Visual Basic .NET automatically links a control.property to some aspect of the control's behavior; for example, the value stored in a label's Text property is automatically displayed on the user interface. Variables are just symbolic names for storage locations in memory and have no direct connection to the user interface.

Note in particular that, like variables, every property has a type. For example, the Text property of labels is type String and therefore can store values containing any character.

Finally, the first of the two differences noted earlier between variables and control properties deserves emphasis. As a beginning developer you may be tempted to declare a property of a control, using a Dim statement. Suppose you place a Label control on the form and set its Name property to lblPrice. If you write the variable declaration statement

Dim lblPrice.Text As Decimal

it will be rejected by Visual Basic .NET.

You also should never use a variable name beginning with one of the conventional three-letter prefixes for control names (e.g., btn, lbl, txt, and so forth). This is not illegal unless you also have a control with the same name, but it is very misleading and makes the program hard to read.

Why Use Variables?

Since control properties can be used like variables in a program, why do you need variables? When you try to write a useful, user-friendly program, you find that variables are essential. Sometimes a program needs to perform intermediate calculations that should not be displayed to the user. Since control properties are automatically linked to the user interface, you do not want to use them to store the results of intermediate calculations. Variables are ideal for storing such results because they have no direct connection to the user interface.

Similarly, in a well-designed application, values displayed on the user interface will be nicely formatted. But quite often, formatting a value for display requires introducing symbols (such as dollar signs) that Visual Basic .NET does not allow in arithmetic calculations. Thus, it is typical to use variables to hold unformatted values for calculation, and then, when it is time to display a result, retrieve the value from its variable, format it, and store it in a control property. We discuss formatting values for display in Chapter 4. Finally, since you cannot declare the type of any control property, the use of variables permits better matches between the type of a variable and how you plan to use it.

Example **3.2**

USING VARIABLES TO STORE INTERMEDIATE RESULTS

In this example we show a simple form for calculating the price of a computer. The computer consists of a CPU, a monitor, and a keyboard. Each of these units is priced separately. An example of the user interface is shown in Figure 3.8.

You can see that there are four values supplied by the user in text boxes. Three of these values are used in the calculations shown at the bottom of the form. It should be clear from the user interface that the button contains the code for performing the calculations. You also should wonder how the taxes are being calculated because there is no input component for the user to enter a tax rate.

The code for the button is shown in Figure 3.9. Let's examine this code. First note that all the variables are Decimal type because they are all storing dollars and cents and we want to be sure there are no representation errors. Also note that the tax rate is defined as a symbolic constant. This constant is also a Decimal type, not because it represents dollars and cents, but because we want to be sure that it too does not have any representation errors.

The main logic is all within the Try block. This is where cast exceptions due to type mismatch errors might occur. If the user enters any nonnumeric values, an exception will be thrown and caught in the Catch block. Here a message box is displayed to inform the user of his error, as shown in Figure 3.10.

FIGURE 3.8

User Interface for Example 3.2

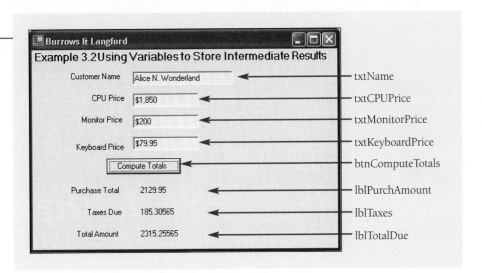

FIGURE 3.9

Event Procedure for btnComputeTotals_Click

```
Private Sub btnComputeTotals_Click(ByVal sender As System.Ob
    Const SALESTAXRATE As Decimal = 0.087
    Dim CpuPrice, MonitorPrice, KeyboardPrice As Decimal
    Dim TotalPurchAmt, TaxDue, GrandTotal As Decimal
    Try
        CpuPrice = txtCPUPrice.Text
        MonitorPrice = txtMonitorPrice.Text
        KeyboardPrice = txtKeyboardPrice.Text
        TotalPurchAmt = CpuPrice + MonitorPrice + KeyboardPrice
        TaxDue = TotalPurchAmt * SALESTAXRATE
        GrandTotal = TotalPurchAmt + TaxDue
        lblPurchAmt.Text = TotalPurchAmt
        lblTaxes.Text = TaxDue
        lblTotalDue.Text = GrandTotal
    Catch
        MsgBox("Please enter only valid numeric values")
    End Try
End Sub
```

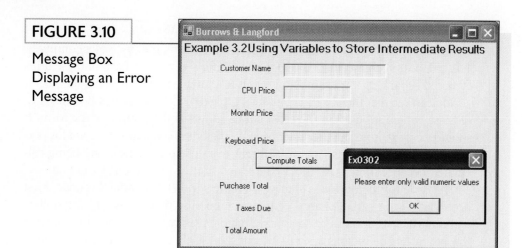

FIGURE 3.10

Message Box
Displaying an Error
Message

Look back at Figure 3.8 and notice that the user entered dollar amounts in the form "$1,850". You also can see that this did not throw an exception. We can therefore conclude that Visual Basic .NET is able to cast the string "$1,850" into the Decimal value 1850 without throwing an exception. Finally notice how all arithmetic was performed using numeric variables. While you could have used the actual Text properties of the text boxes in the expressions, you would not have control over the numeric type to which Visual Basic .NET cast the values before performing the arithmetic. It is better to use variables and retain the control of types yourself.

Exercise 3.10

Describe, using everyday words, the net effect of the assignment statement X = X + 1.

Exercise 3.11

Show the value of the variable X after it has executed the following two statements.

```
Dim X As Short = 10
X = X
```

What is the net effect of the statement X = X?

Exercise 3.12

The event procedure below contains the same statements as the event procedure btnAssignmentQuiz_Click discussed in the text, but the statements have been rearranged. What value is displayed in lblQuiz when btnRearrangedAssignments_Click is executed?

```
Private Sub btnRearrangedAssignments_Click(...)
    Dim A As Short
    Dim B As Short
    Dim C As Short
    C = A + B
    B = B + 1
    A = 5
    B = A - 6
    A = A + A
    B = B + C
    B = B - A
    lblQuiz.Text = B
End Sub
```

Exercise 3.13   An event procedure contains the following three variable declaration statements:

```
Dim FirstName As String
Dim LastName As String
Dim FullName As String
```

The same event procedure also contains the following assignment statements:

```
FirstName = "William"
LastName = "Gates"
FullName = FirstName & LastName
```

What value is stored in the variable **FullName** after these three assignment statements are executed?

Exercise 3.14   Immediately after the following three assignment statements are executed, the variable **FullName** holds the value "BenjaminFranklin".

```
FirstName = "Benjamin"
LastName = "Franklin"
FullName = FirstName & LastName
```

How can you modify the third assignment statement above so that a space appears between the first and last names in the value stored in **FullName**?

Exercise 3.15   What value will be displayed in lblLetters when the following event procedure is executed?

```
Private Sub btnRearrangedAssignments_Click(...)
    Dim A As String
    Dim B As String
    Dim C As String
    A = "X"
    B = "O"
    A = A & B
    B = A & B
    A = B & A
    C = "OOOOO"
    lblLetters.Text = C & A
End Sub
```

Exercise 3.16   What value is stored in the variable TestDifference after the following statements are executed?

```
Dim TestNumberA As Single
Dim TestNumberB As Single
Dim TestDifference As Single
TestNumberA = 2.3456789
TestNumberB = 1.2345678
TestDifference = TestNumberA - TestNumberB
```

What value would be stored in **TestDifference** if the three variables were all type Decimal instead of Single? Type Long? Type Double?

Exercise 3.17   In the code that follows you will see the statement:

```
'statement block
```

Any statement that starts with an apostrophe is a comment. Visual Basic .NET ignores comments—they are for developers to read. Comments are generally used to help the human reader better understand the Visual Basic .NET code. Complete the following event procedure by writing a sequence of statements that, when used in place of the commented statement block, will cause the last two statements to display 2 in lblX and 1 in lblY. The statements you write should contain no constants. Do not modify or move any other statements in the event procedure.

Hint: Consider the value of the three variables immediately after it executes the statement Y = 2. Then consider values before the final two assignment statements can be executed. Be sure to check that your solution works correctly!

```
Private Sub btnExchange_Click(...)
    Dim X As Integer
    Dim Y As Integer
    Dim Z As Integer
    X = 1
    Y = 2
    'statement block
    lblX.Text = X
    lblY.Text = Y
End
```

Option Explicit

Visual Basic .NET has an option that removes the requirement that you declare all variables. However, this option is not set by default. We highly recommend (read *insist*) that you do not change this option. If you do change this[12] to a value of "OFF" (normally it is set at "ON"), then Visual Basic .NET cannot find typographical errors in your variable names.

If you make a typographical error and Option Explicit is ON, then the misspelled variable name will show a squiggly line under it. If you place your cursor over this, a message will appear giving you further explanation of the problem. Figure 3.11 shows how typographical errors appear in the Code window.

The following practices can both reduce your effort when typing statements and help you avoid typographical errors.

*   First, be sure to create and name the important controls before working on event procedures.

FIGURE 3.11

Event Procedure with a Typo in a Variable Name

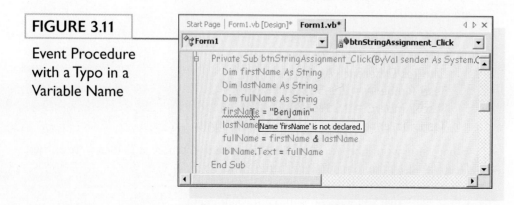

- Second, type constant definition and variable declaration statements before any other statements, being sure to follow the conventions for capitalization of symbolic constant and variable names.

Assuming that Option Explicit is ON, these practices give Visual Basic .NET something to work with as far as determining if you are spelling things correctly. In addition, be aware that changing the name of a control after you have written code that uses its original name can at times cause the program to fail.

3.4 | The Windows Form Control

Up to this point we have seen the form only as the background of our user interface. While the form always plays this role, it can do much more. In fact, the **Form control is what organizes a project in terms of the appearance and functionality of its user interface, its constants and variables, and its storage on disk.** We are creating Windows Applications here and the type of form we are using is called a Windows Form. We also can create Web Applications with Visual Basic .NET and there the form is called a Web Form. We introduce Web Applications and Web Forms in Chapter 11.

Appearance and Use

What happens if a project is large? In particular, suppose there are more controls than can comfortably fit on a single form. Making the controls smaller and packing them more closely together is a bad idea because it makes the program hard to use. The solution is to use multiple forms in the design and construction of the project. Each form should have an objective, or theme, that the user easily comprehends. Each form should contain all the controls necessary for that objective, and the form should have a clear and attractive layout. Because of their ability to contain other controls, forms are often referred to as "container controls." Later we will see other container controls that can be placed on a form; you can have containers within containers.

During program execution, each form is a user interface window. These are ordinary windows that are familiar to Microsoft Windows users. By establishing the number, content, and appearance of forms in a project, and also the timing with which forms are presented to the user at run time, the developer controls the overall organization and behavior of the project as experienced by the user.

All forms have the same basic components, which are labeled in Figure 3.12. The Reduce and Enlarge buttons allow the user to change the size of the form. At

FIGURE 3.12

Anatomy of a Form

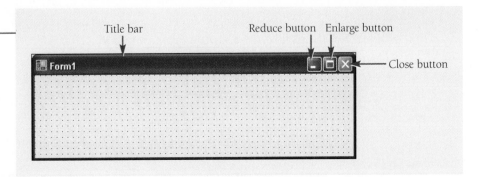

run time, if the user clicks on a form's Reduce button, the form "collapses" into an icon on the Taskbar. In order to see the form again, the user can click on this icon. If the user clicks on a form's Enlarge button, the form will expand to fill the entire screen. The user can change the form back to its original size and location by clicking the Enlarge button a second time. If the user clicks on the Close button, the form is removed from the screen (and execution of the application ends if this was the only form on the screen).

Properties

The properties of the Form control that the developer typically sets are listed in Table 3.3. There are additional properties that allow the developer to refine the form; check the Visual Basic .NET documentation if you are interested in these.

Events

While the form's primary purpose is to help organize a project, it also is capable of responding to certain events. The most common of these are the Activate and Load events for a form. At run time only one form is active at any given time. The

Table 3.3 Properties of the Form control

Property	Specifies
(Name)	*(frm) A unique name for the Form control.* As developer, you use this property to distinguish forms from one another in a multiple-form project. The form's Name property is distinct from the name of the form file that saves the form on disk. As with the Name property for other controls, the user is completely unaware of the form's Name property.
AcceptButton	*The accept button is the button that is clicked whenever the user presses the* (ENTER) *key.* Choose the button that you want to take on this role from the drop-down list. You can use this property to allow the user to quickly navigate a simple form by allowing the user to simply press the (ENTER) key when finished instead of manually clicking a button with the mouse.
BackColor	*The background color of the form.* To change the BackColor setting, select BackColor in the Properties window and then click on the down-arrow button at the right end of its settings box. This will bring up a dialog with three tabs: Custom, Web, and System. Choose a tab and simply click on the color you wish to use.
CancelButton	*The cancel button is the button that is clicked whenever the user presses the* (ESC) *key.* Choose the button that you want to take on this role from the drop-down list.
ControlBox	*A Boolean property that dictates whether the control box button is displayed (true) or hidden (false).* The default is true. When set to false, only the window's Text appears on the Title bar.
Font	*The font inherited by all controls added to the form.* Can be overridden for any control by setting that control's Font property.
MaximizeBox	*A Boolean property that dictates whether the maximize button is displayed (true) or hidden or disabled (false).* The default is true.
MinimizeBox	*A Boolean property that dictates whether the minimize button is displayed (true) or hidden or disabled (false).* The default is true.
Text	*The descriptive text that is displayed at the left end of the form's Title bar.* Use this to describe the objective or theme of the form.

active form is the form with which the user can interact. The user can click on a control on the active form and the control's event procedure will be executed. The active form always has its Title bar highlighted to indicate its active status.

When a user switches from using one form to another, an *Activate event* occurs for the form that becomes active. Thus, you can write an Activate event procedure that performs a particular processing task every time the form becomes active. As an example of this, some forms are always cleared each time they are presented to the user; to accomplish this, the developer places the code that clears the form in the form's Activate event procedure.

The Load event enables the developer to control how much of the computer's memory the project occupies at run time. Doing this may affect the program's speed of execution. Let us now briefly examine these issues.

Forms and Main Memory

In a large project with many forms, it is possible to use up much of the computer's main memory (RAM) at run time. To mitigate this problem, Visual Basic .NET allows you to design a project such that at run time only one or just a few forms are in main memory at any given time. The remaining forms are stored on the computer's disk.

To make such a project work, the developer writes code that loads a form when it is needed. To load a form means to transfer it from disk storage to main memory. The developer also writes code that unloads (disposes of) the form when the user is finished working with it. Unloading a form makes the main memory that it occupied available for other forms.

You will learn about the statements that perform the load and dispose actions later. In a project with only one form, Visual Basic .NET automatically loads the form when program execution first begins.

Each time a form is loaded, a *Load event* occurs for the form. Thus, you can write a Load event procedure that performs a particular processing task every time the form is loaded. The term *initialization* refers to tasks that are performed when an activity first starts. Thus, we say that the Load event procedure is commonly used to initialize various aspects of the form.

Run Time Speed

The process of transferring data or code between disk storage and main memory is very slow compared with the speed of processes occurring in main memory. Thus, developers generally try to minimize the amount of loading and unloading of forms. This also is why users and developers alike prefer to have computers with large main memories.

Forms and Disk Storage

Forms are also Visual Basic .NET's primary way of organizing the storage of a project on disk. When you save the project, Visual Basic .NET creates one file for each form. For each of these form files, Visual Basic .NET asks you to specify a file name, to which Visual Basic .NET appends the extension ".vb". Note that the name of the form file is different from the form's Name property. This difference is illustrated in Figure 3.13.

A form file contains information about the form, including the form's properties, all the controls (and their properties) that reside on the form, and all the event procedures associated with all the controls on the form.

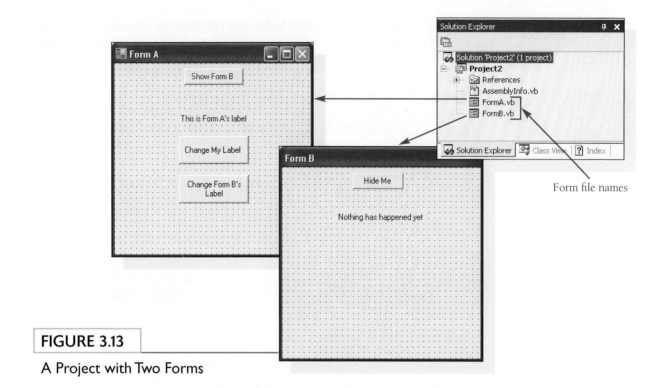

FIGURE 3.13

A Project with Two Forms

Forms and Code Windows

Each form in a project has its own Code window. The Code window's Class Name box shows the Name property of the form to which it belongs. It will show only the event procedures for the controls that reside on that form. Figure 3.14 shows the Code windows for the forms frmTestA and frmTestB depicted in Figure 3.13.

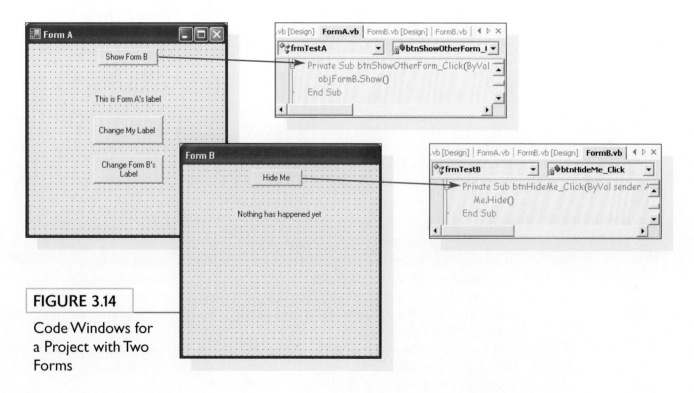

FIGURE 3.14

Code Windows for a Project with Two Forms

Form as a Class

When you are working with a form in the form Designer window, you are actually creating a class template. The components you add such as buttons and text boxes are added to the class definition. The events you program, such as Click events for buttons or form events such as the form Activate method, are methods added to the form class. In addition, the form you create inherits many properties and methods from its superclasses. You can see this by looking at any form's Code window and noting that a class is being created. Figure 3.15 shows a Code window for a form that includes only the code created by Visual Basic .NET.

The fact that you are creating a form class means that you will need to create actual form objects when you want to use multiple forms within a project. For example, assume you have two forms named frmMain and frmOther. frmMain is the main form and it has a button on it named btnShowOther. The code for the button's Click event would be

```
Private Sub btnShowOther_Click(...)
    Dim ObjFormOther As New frmOther()
    ObjFormOther.Show()
End Sub
```

Let's see what is happening in these two lines of code. In the Dim statement you are asking for a new object to be instantiated from your class definition. The object will be called **ObjFormOther** and the class template that will be used to create this object is frmOther. The keyword "New" in the Dim statement instructs Visual Basic .NET to create (instantiate) a new object from the class. This is our first real look at the process of creating objects within our code. It might be a good idea to go back to Chapter 1 and review the object paradigm concepts and see how they are related to what we are doing here.

The line of code after the Dim statement is asking the new object (**ObjForm Other**) to execute its Show() method. The behavior of the Show() method results in the object being loaded into memory and displayed on the GUI.

A common mistake is to not differentiate the class (frmOther) from the object (**ObjFormOther**). The class does not have a Show() method but the object does. That is, there is no class method named Show() but there is an instance method named Show(). So it would be wrong to say

```
frmOther.Show()
```

Keep this in mind—you need to first instantiate an object from the class template before you can use object methods.

FIGURE 3.15

Code Window for a Form Class Definition

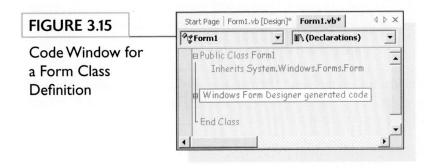

3.5 Project 2: Using Multiple Forms

In this project we examine how forms establish the structure of a project. We also demonstrate the mechanics of building and managing a project with more than one form.

This project is not a useful application; rather, it is a tutorial that lays the foundation for multiform applications and introduces the concepts needed to work with forms. Project 3 builds on this foundation to construct a simplified payroll application.

This project consists of the two forms shown earlier in Figures 3.13 and 3.14. The user can switch between the two forms and also modify a control property on one form by clicking a button on the other. When you complete this project, you should understand how to use multiple forms and how forms can communicate with each other.

Begin as follows.

1. Create a file folder in which to save this project before beginning work on it. This is particularly important for projects with multiple forms, because the number of files belonging to the project can be large.

2. Launch Visual Basic .NET and create a new Windows Application project. Store it in the folder you created in Step 1. As usual, Visual Basic .NET automatically gives you one Windows Form to start with to which it gives the default name Form1.

3. Be sure the form is selected by clicking on it and then, using the Properties window, change the form's Name to frmTestA and change its Text to "Form A". Observe how these changes appear in the Solution Explorer window and on the form.

4. Create a second form by selecting Add Windows Form... from the Project menu. In the Add New Item dialog box, click on the Windows Form icon in the Template pane and click on Open. Observe that Visual Basic .NET makes an entry for the new form in the Solution Explorer window. Using the Properties window, set the Name property to frmTestB and change its Text to "Form B".

Notice that you can see only one form at a time, but you can click on the tabs at the top of the Designer window to switch between forms. If you have a large enough screen, you can direct the system to display both forms next to each other. To do this, click on the Form2.vb tab to select it, then choose New Vertical Tab Group from the Window menu. The two forms should be displayed next to each other as shown in Figure 3.16.

5. On frmTestA, place a button with Name btnShowOtherForm and Text "Show Form B". On frmTestB, place a button with Name btnHideMe and Text "Hide Me". After doing this, your forms should appear as shown in Figure 3.17.

Note that in a single project, you cannot have two forms with the same Name. On a single form, you cannot have two controls with the same Name. But you can have two controls with the same Name if they are on different forms. The ability to reuse control names is useful in large projects created by teams of developers. For example, if you create one form and I create another, we don't have to bother to make sure we choose different names for controls that may perform similar functions. In fact, it may even help us understand each other's work if we do use the same names for controls that perform similar tasks.

FIGURE 3.16

Displaying Two
Vertical Tab Groups

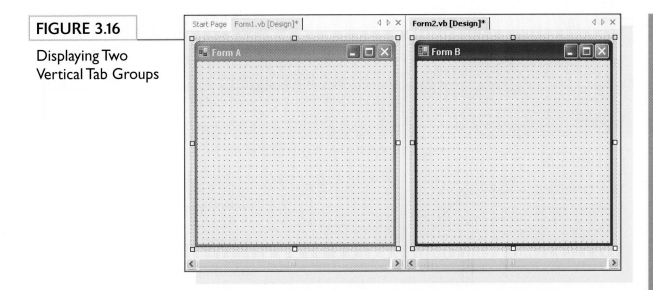

FIGURE 3.17

Project 2 Forms
with Buttons

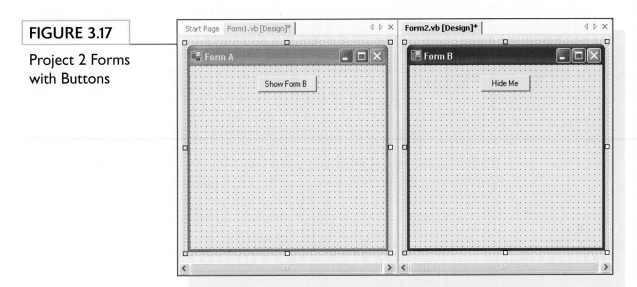

6. Select frmTestA and look at the list of objects in the drop-down Object box at the top of the Properties window. Then select frmTestB and look at the list of objects in the Object box of the Properties window. Note that the Properties window displays only objects belonging to the selected form.

7. Run the project. A dialog box will be displayed telling you that there are build errors and asking if you want to continue—say No. You'll see an error message displayed in the Task List window shown in Figure 3.18.

Double-click on this error message and the dialog box shown in Figure 3.19 will be displayed.

Every project requires one and only one form to be specified as the one to show when the application starts running. Since there are two forms, there is ambiguity that Visual Basic .NET wants you to resolve. In this case, select frmTestA and click on OK. Run the project again and this time frmTestA should show on the GUI. You can click on the button but nothing will happen because no code has been written for the button's Click event.

8. End execution.

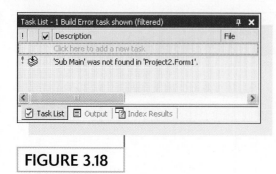

FIGURE 3.18

Task List Window Showing
the Build Error

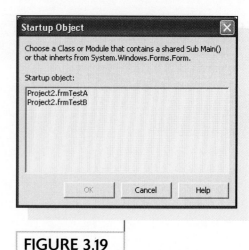

FIGURE 3.19

Specifying the Startup Object

9. Right-click on the project name in the Solution Explorer (see Figure 3.20) and select Properties from the pop-up menu.

10. On the Property Pages dialog box, select the General tab and observe that there is a Startup object drop-down list. Figure 3.21 shows this dialog box. This dialog box is an alternate way to set the startup object. For this project, leave frmFormA as the startup object.

11. Next, create Click event procedures for the buttons as shown in Figure 3.22. There are three lines of code that you need to add. The first is the Dim statement added right after the "Windows Form Designer generated code" box on frmTestA. We will explain why this line is placed here in the next section. The second line, also in frmTestA, is the only line in the btnShowOtherForm_Click() event. This statement uses the Form class's Show() method to cause the form to be loaded into memory and shown on the GUI. The third and final line of code is in the Click event btnHideMe_Click() on frmTestB. The statement Me.Hide() needs an explanation. The special identifier Me

FIGURE 3.20

Pop-up Menu that
Results from Right-
Clicking on the
Project Name

FIGURE 3.21

Property Pages
Dialog Box Used to
Set the Startup
Object

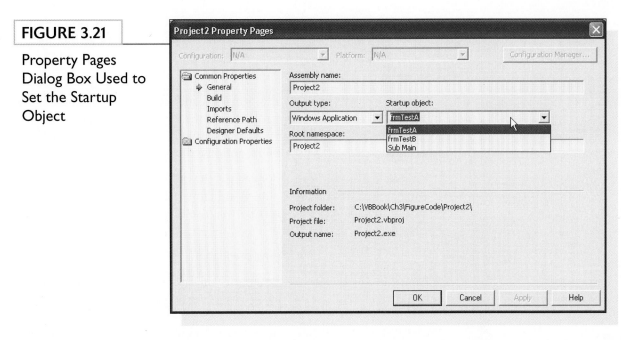

FIGURE 3.22

Click Event
Procedures that
Show and Hide
frmFormB

refers to the form object where the code is held, that is, the current object where the reference Me is found. Since the statement Me.Hide() is in the form object **ObjFormB**, then it is **ObjFormB** that becomes hidden.

12. After creating the event procedures, make sure that frmTestA is the startup form and then run the program. Click the buttons to see their effect.

13. End execution.

Notice that when we refer to an object and its properties or methods, we use the same syntax. That is, we say "object.property" and "object.method". For example, a text box has a Text property and a method called AppendText() that appends text to the end of the current contents of the Text property. We might see code like the following where the first line refers to a property and the second line refers to a method:

```
txtInformation.Text = "Be careful in the rain"
txtInformation.AppendText(" and in the snow.")
```

14. Now save the project by selecting Save All under the File menu.

At this point, you should know (*a*) how to specify the startup form, (*b*) that there can be only one active form at a time, and (*c*) that an event procedure can cause another form to become active. We now turn our attention to making an event procedure on one form manipulate a control on another form.

1. Add one label and two buttons to frmTestA and set their properties as shown in Figure 3.23. Set their Text properties to the text you see in the figure. You may have to resize the buttons. As also shown in Figure 3.23, add a label to frmTestB and also set the Form's ControlBox property to false.

2. Add a Click event procedure for each of the buttons on frmTestA. The code for these two Click events is shown in Figure 3.24.

   Note the syntax differences between setting the text property for the local label:

   lblTest.Text = "I am changing my own label"

   versus setting the Text property for a label that is located on another form:

   ObjFormB.lblTest.Text = "Changed from Form A"

   We have seen the first case many times now, but in order to reference a component on another form (technically a member of a different object), we

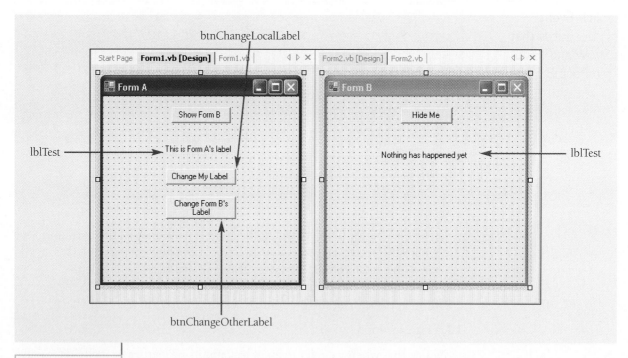

btnChangeLocalLabel

lblTest

lblTest

btnChangeOtherLabel

FIGURE 3.23

Controls for frmTestA and frmTestB

FIGURE 3.24

Code for the Click Events for the Two Buttons on frmTestA

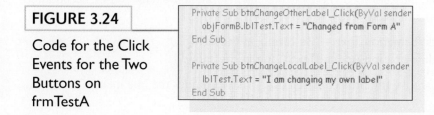

```
Private Sub btnChangeOtherLabel_Click(ByVal sender
    objFormB.lblTest.Text = "Changed from Form A"
End Sub

Private Sub btnChangeLocalLabel_Click(ByVal sender
    lblTest.Text = "I am changing my own label"
End Sub
```

need to start with a reference to the object, then a reference to one of its components, and finally a reference to the property or method of the specific component. These three references are separated by a period.

3. Run the program and verify that it works as you expect.

4. End execution, then save the project. Use the Save All option.

5. Finally, create a third form and observe the new entry that appears in the Solution Explorer window. Now suppose you change your mind and you no longer want this form. How can you eliminate it from the project? Highlight the entry for this form in the Solution Explorer window and then select Delete under the Edit menu. Observe the change in the Solution Explorer window.

Exercise 3.18

Using the forms from Project 2, change frmTestB's ControlBox property back to true. Run the project, show Form B, and then hide it using the Hide Me button. Repeat these steps except this time, close Form B by clicking on the **X** (the Close button) on the far right of the title bar. Then click on the Show Form B button. What happens? Can you think of an explanation?

The Hide() method of the form simply makes the form invisible but it is still stored in memory. This means that it can be shown a second and subsequent times. However, the Close button does not just hide the form, it also unloads it from memory (it is disposed of or thrown into an imaginary garbage heap). Since it is no longer in memory, the Show() method will not work because there is no longer an object being referenced by **ObjFormB**. An error message similar to "Cannot access a disposed object…" will be generated. Whenever you see such a message, it means that your object reference like **ObjFormB** is no longer referring (pointing) to a valid object.

3.6   Variable Scope

Can a variable that is declared inside one procedure be accessed by statements inside a different procedure? What if one of these procedures belongs to one form and the other belongs to a different form? These are important questions, especially when we contemplate trying to construct and maintain large projects. The answers are determined by Visual Basic .NET's rules for a ***variable's scope,* the domain within which a variable can be accessed.** The scope of a variable is the set of all code that can refer to it. A variable's scope is determined by where and how the variable is declared. There are four levels of variable scope. In increasing size of domain these are called block-level scope, procedure-level (local) scope, module-level scope, and global scope.

Block- and Procedure-Level Scope

Any variable that is declared inside a procedure has *procedure-level scope.* It is described as being "local to" the procedure in which it is declared, and it can be accessed only by statements within that procedure. In addition, the scope can be narrowed even further and restricted to a single block of code within a procedure. A code block is any set of statements that end with the keyword End, Catch, Loop, or Next. The only block statement we have seen so far is the Try/Catch block. Example 3.3 demonstrates block-level scope.

Example **3.3**

BLOCK SCOPE

Consider the code shown in Figure 3.25. The variable **N** is being declared within the Try part of a Try/Catch block. It's scope is restricted to the Try block only—the Catch statement marks the end of the block. Note the squiggly line under the variable **N** in the Catch block. This indicates a syntax error. If you place the cursor over the error, you see the message "The name 'N' is not declared." This means that the variable **N** is not known outside the block in which it was declared. How can you expand the scope? You need to declare the variable in a block with larger scope. In this case, you need to expand the scope to be local to the entire procedure.

The revised code would look like that in Figure 3.26. With the declaration moved out of the Try block, its scope is now extended to the entire procedure. Figure 3.27 identifies the three blocks in this example. Note that two of the blocks (Try and Catch) are nested inside the other block. The way variable scope works is simple: a variable declared in a block is visible within that block, including any nested blocks. But it is not visible outside the block where it was declared.

FIGURE 3.25

A Variable N Declared with Block Scope

```
Private Sub btnShowN_Click(ByVal send
    Try
        Dim N As Integer = 1
        N = N + 1
    Catch
        MsgBox(N)
    End Try
End Sub
```

FIGURE 3.26

Variable N's Scope Expanded to Procedure-Level

```
Private Sub btnShowN_Click(ByVal send
    Dim N As Integer = 1
    Try
        N = N + 1
    Catch
        MsgBox(N)
    End Try
End Sub
```

FIGURE 3.27

Visual Indication of Block Structure

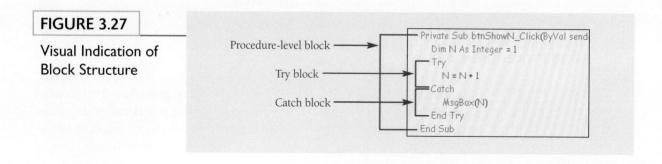

Procedure-level block ⟶

Try block ⟶

Catch block ⟶

```
Private Sub btnShowN_Click(ByVal send
    Dim N As Integer = 1
    Try
        N = N + 1
    Catch
        MsgBox(N)
    End Try
End Sub
```

FIGURE 3.28

Form and Controls
for Example 3.4

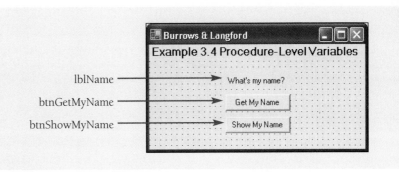

FIGURE 3.29

Code for Example 3.4

```
Private Sub btnGetMyName_Click(ByVal sender As
    Dim MyName As String
    MyName = "John Doe"
End Sub

Private Sub btnShowMyName_Click(ByVal sender A:
    Dim MyName As String
    lblName.Text = MyName
End Sub
```

Example **3.4**   **PROCEDURE-LEVEL VARIABLES**

In this example we explore the scope of two variables, each defined in a different event procedure and therefore local to that procedure (procedure-level scope).

Consider the Visual Basic .NET project consisting of one form with a label (lblName) and two buttons (btnGetMyName and btnShowMyName) as shown in Figure 3.28.

The Click event procedures for the two buttons are shown in Figure 3.29. Both have a variable named **MyName**. If you run the application, click on btnGet-MyName (which causes "John Doe" to be stored in **MyName**), and then click on btnShowMyName, will "John Doe" appear in the label text? The answer is no. The variable **MyName** in event procedure btnGetMyName_Click has no relationship to the variable **MyName** in event procedure btnShowMyName_Click. Although they have the same name, they are actually two different variables, representing two different locations in main memory.

Module-Level Variables

Just as two employees in an office sometimes agree to share files, we sometimes want two procedures on a form to share a variable. In this case we create a variable of *module-level* **scope by using an ordinary Dim statement placed in the form's declarations section instead of inside a procedure.** The scope of a module-level variable is the set of all procedures associated with the form. That is, any statement in any procedure belonging to the form can access a module-level variable.

If you look at the code in Figure 3.30 taken from Project 2, you see a perfect example for the need to share a variable between two procedures. The variable **ObjFormB** is used in the procedure btnShowOtherForm_Click() as well as the procedure btnChangeOtherLabel_Click(). In order to be able to do this, the variable had to be declared outside either procedure but within the form's declaration section.

```
Public Class frmTestA
    Inherits System.Windows.Forms.Form

    Windows Form Designer generated code

    Dim objFormB As New frmTestB()

    Private Sub btnShowOtherForm_Click(ByVal sender
        objFormB.Show()
    End Sub

    Private Sub btnChangeOtherLabel_Click(ByVal send
        objFormB.lblTest.Text = "Changed from Form A"
    End Sub
```

FIGURE 3.30

Code from Project 2 with the
Variable ObjFormB Having Module-
Level Scope

```
Public Class Form1
    Inherits System.Windows.Forms.Form

    Windows Form Designer generated code

    Dim MyName As String

    Private Sub btnGetMyName_Click(ByVal sender As
        MyName = "John Doe"
    End Sub

    Private Sub btnShowMyName_Click(ByVal sender A
        lblName.Text = MyName
    End Sub
```

FIGURE 3.31

Code for Example 3.5

Example 3.5   **MODULE-LEVEL VARIABLES**

Let us modify the previous example by deleting the two procedure-level variable declarations and making **MyName** a module-level variable. The objective is to see how the program behavior differs with module-level scope compared with procedure-level scope. The modified code is shown in Figure 3.31.

If you run this program, click on btnGetMyName, and then click on btnShowMyName, "John Doe" will appear in the label Text because both event procedures share the variable. The first event procedure stores a value in the string variable **MyName**, and the second event procedure retrieves that value from **MyName**.

Note that if you run Example 3.5 again, but click on btnShowMyName first and then click on btnGetMyName, the result will be different! Since string variables are initially set to the zero-length string when they are declared, clicking first on btnShowMyName results in the zero-length string being displayed.

Example 3.6   **HIDDEN MODULE-LEVEL VARIABLES**

Often a given procedure accesses both procedure-level variables and module-level variables. This example demonstrates what happens if the developer uses the same variable name (same spelling) for both a procedure-level variable and a module-level variable. In Example 3.6 the form has two labels (lblMyName and lblYourName) and two buttons. This form and its controls are shown in Figure 3.32. The code is shown in Figure 3.33.

Note carefully that btnGetNames_Click has no procedure-level variables, but btnShowNames_Click has a procedure-level variable with the same name as one of the module-level variables. If you run this program, click on btnGetNames, and then click on btnShowNames, will "John Doe" appear in lblMyName and "Jane Smith" in lblYourName? The answer is no. The reason has to do with how Visual Basic .NET handles the situation where the same variable name occurs as both a procedure-level variable and a module-level variable. We focus on this issue next.

FIGURE 3.32

Form and Controls
for Example 3.6

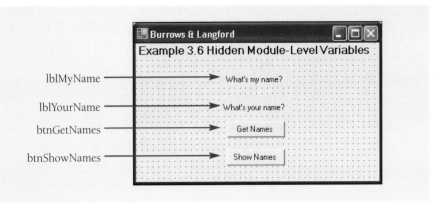

FIGURE 3.33

Code for Example 3.6

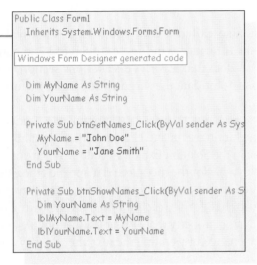

```
Public Class Form1
    Inherits System.Windows.Forms.Form

Windows Form Designer generated code

    Dim MyName As String
    Dim YourName As String

    Private Sub btnGetNames_Click(ByVal sender As Sys
        MyName = "John Doe"
        YourName = "Jane Smith"
    End Sub

    Private Sub btnShowNames_Click(ByVal sender As S
        Dim YourName As String
        lblMyName.Text = MyName
        lblYourName.Text = YourName
    End Sub
```

In Example 3.6, the procedure-level variable **YourName** in btnShowNames_Click is a different variable than the module-level variable **YourName**. They have no relationship to each other even though they have the same name. The question, then, is which variable will the assignment statement **lblYourName.Text = Your-Name** use: the procedure-level variable or the module-level variable? Visual Basic .NET's rule for this is that a procedure will always use the procedure-level variable if it exists. This is sometimes stated as "A procedure-level variable hides a module-level variable with the same name." Thus, event procedure btnShowNames_Click is "unaware" that the module-level variable **YourName** even exists.

Be aware that this "hiding" does not apply to procedure-level variables with block- and procedure-level scope. Within a procedure, it is not legal to declare a block-level variable using the same name as a variable with procedure-level scope.

Global Variables

Suppose we have two procedures that belong to different forms. Can they share a procedure-level variable? It should be clear that they cannot. Since they are on different forms, they cannot share module-level variables either. Each form has its own declarations section, and variables declared in a form's declarations section belong only to that form.

Of course there is a way for procedures on different forms to share a variable. **Variables that can be shared across all forms have *global scope.*** To create a variable with global scope, declare it using a Public statement in the declarations section of a module.

The Public Statement

The Public statement is identical to the Dim statement except it uses the keyword Public instead of Dim. The ***Public statement* is used to create a global variable.**

You typically create a module to hold the declaration statements for global variables (in Chapter 6 we will see an alternative approach).

Modules

A ***module,* also called a code module, is identical to a form except that it has no user interface window,** and therefore, no controls and no event procedures. What does that leave? A declarations section.[13] You can think of a module as a repository for data that need to be shared by forms; that is, a repository for global variables.

To create a Module, select Add Component… under the Project menu and then click on the Module icon and click on Open. Visual Basic .NET makes an entry for the module in the Solution Explorer window. When you save the project, Visual Basic .NET creates a file for the module and it appends the extension .vb. You can remove an unwanted module from the project the same way you remove a form from the project. And, like forms, each module has its own Code window. Each module also has a Name property that appears in the module at the top of its Code window and can be changed by editing the text after the keyword Module.

Example 3.7   GLOBAL VARIABLES

In this example that uses two forms, we create a global variable and see how this variable can be accessed in two event procedures. Figure 3.34 shows the two forms and the Solution Explorer window. The code is shown in Figure 3.35.

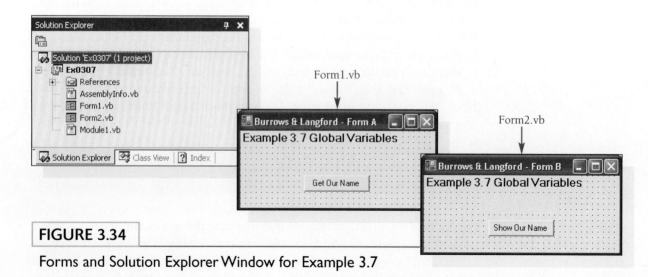

FIGURE 3.34

Forms and Solution Explorer Window for Example 3.7

13   In Chapter 6 we will see that modules and forms can (and usually do) also have general procedures.

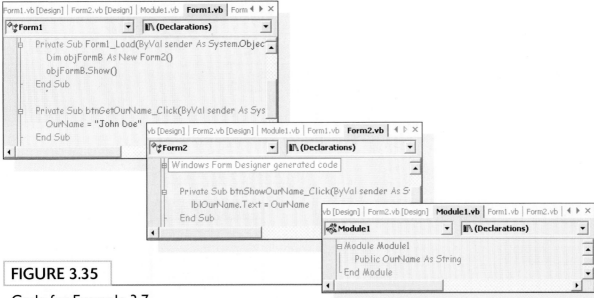

FIGURE 3.35

Code for Example 3.7

There is one global variable, named **OurName**. Because **OurName** is global, it can be used by any event procedure in the project, regardless of which form the event procedure is on.

If you run this program, click on btnGetOurName on Form A, and then click on btnShowOurName on Form B, "John Doe" will appear in the label Text on Form B because the event procedures share the global variable. The first event procedure stores a value in **OurName**, and the second event procedure retrieves that value from **OurName**.

Hiding Global Variables

As with module-level variables, a procedure-level variable in a procedure "hides" a global variable with the same name; that is, the procedure will always use the procedure-level variable if it exists. Similarly, a module-level variable declared in a form's declarations section will "hide" (from all the procedures on the form) a global variable with the same name. This behavior can be described thus: "A procedure always uses the closest variable with the specified name." Procedure-level is closer than module-level, which in turn is closer than global.

Procedure-Level, Module-Level, and Global Scope

It may take you a while to digest these scope rules. Rest assured, they do make development of large applications much easier. It may help you to experiment with Project 2, adding a few procedure-level, module-level, and global variables as in the preceding examples.

Figure 3.36 consolidates the relationships between event procedures, forms, modules, and variable scope. In this figure, the blue border indicates the project boundary; the green borders indicate form and module boundaries; and the orange borders indicate event procedure boundaries. A project consists of one or more forms and modules. Each form and module is stored on disk in its own file. A form comprises a user interface window, a declarations section, and a number of procedures. A module comprises a declarations section.

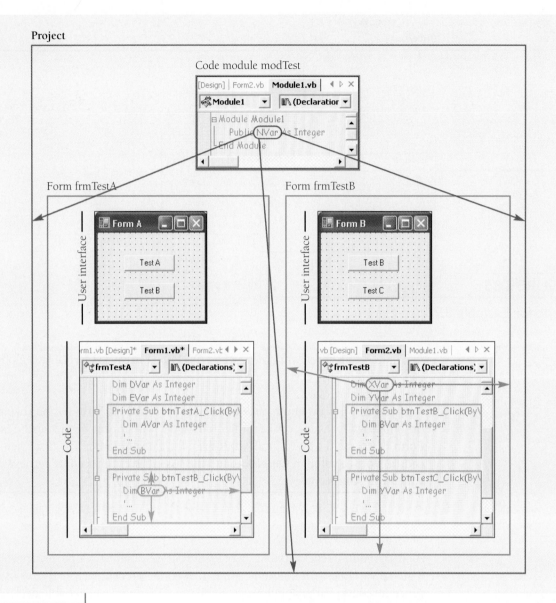

FIGURE 3.36

Three Levels of Variable Scope

Global variables are declared in the declarations section of a module using the Public statement. A global variable can be accessed by the code in any event procedure anywhere in the project. In Figure 3.36 this is depicted by the blue arrows emanating from variable **NVar**, which extend to the project boundary in all directions.

A module-level variable is declared in the declarations section of a form using a Dim statement. It can be accessed by any procedure on the same form as the declarations section containing the Dim statement. The scope of a module-level variable is depicted by the green arrows emanating from variable **XVar**, which extend only to the boundary of frmTestB.

A procedure-level variable is declared in a procedure using a Dim statement. It can be accessed only in the procedure in which it is declared. The scope of a procedure-level variable is depicted by the orange arrows emanating from variable **BVar** in btnTestB_Click, which extend only to the boundary of btnTestB_Click.

There is no conflict between control btnTestB on frmTestA and btnTestB on frmTestB. Similarly, there is no conflict between the two variables **BVar** in the two corresponding event procedures. The module-level variable **YVar** in frmTestB will not be accessible in event procedure btnTestC because of the procedure-level variable with the same name.

Project Structure

Now that you've been introduced to projects with multiple forms and modules, this is a good time to look at Visual Basic .NET project structure. Figure 3.37 includes the components we've discussed in this chapter. Observe that each form has one declarations section and one or more controls. Each module has only a declarations section. A module is necessary if the project requires global variables, which can only be the case if the project has more than one form.

Exercise 3.19

A hypothetical form has two buttons named btnA and btnB and three labels named lblC, lblD, and lblE. The code for the declarations section and all event procedures on the form is as follows.

```
Dim W As Integer
Dim X As Integer
Private Sub btnA_Click(...)
    Dim Y As Integer
    Dim Z As Integer
    W = 3
    X = 6
    Y = W + X
    Z = 4
    lblC.Text = X
    lblD.Text = Y
    lblE.Text = Z
End Sub
Private Sub btnB_Click(...)
    Dim X As Integer
    Dim Y As Integer
    Y = W + X
    lblC.Text = W
    lblD.Text = X
    lblE.Text = Y
End Sub
```

FIGURE 3.37

Structure of Visual Basic .NET Projects

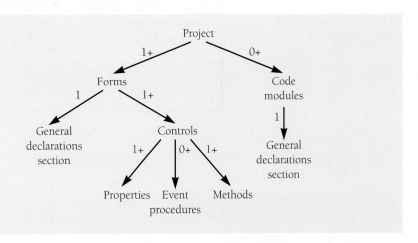

When the program runs, the user first clicks on btnA and then clicks on btnB. What values do lblC, lblD, and lblE display immediately after the user clicks on btnA? What values do they display immediately after the user clicks on btnB?

Exercise 3.20   Modify Project 2 as follows. Place a button named btnGetMyName on frmTestA and a button named btnShowMyName on frmTestB. Then declare a variable named **MyName**, write a Click event procedure for btnGetMyName that stores your name in **MyName**, and write a Click event procedure for btnShowMyName that retrieves the value from **MyName** and displays it on frmTestB in lblTest's Text.

3.7   Variable Lifetime

When an application stops executing, the values of all variables are lost. But what happens to a procedure's procedure-level variables when the procedure is finished? Remember that after the procedure finishes (that is, after the End Sub statement is executed), the application may still be executing. To answer this question, we must investigate *variable lifetime,* **which is the period of time a variable exists.**

Example 3.8   **LIFETIME OF PROCEDURE-LEVEL VARIABLES**

This example demonstrates what happens to the value of a procedure-level variable when an event procedure finishes. Consider the form with a label and a button in Figure 3.38.

The Click event procedure for the button is shown in Figure 3.39. At run time, what does the label display after you click on btnLocalLifetimeTest once? What does the label display after you click on btnLocalLifetimeTest a second time?

Let us consider the first time this event procedure is executed. The Dim statement creates the variable named **X** and initializes it to 0. The next statement retrieves the value stored in **X**, which is 0, and stores it in the Text property of the Label control. Hence the label will display the value 0. The next statement stores the value 15 in the variable **X** and then the event procedure ends (but the project remains running, waiting for the user to act again).

FIGURE 3.38

Form and Controls for Example 3.8

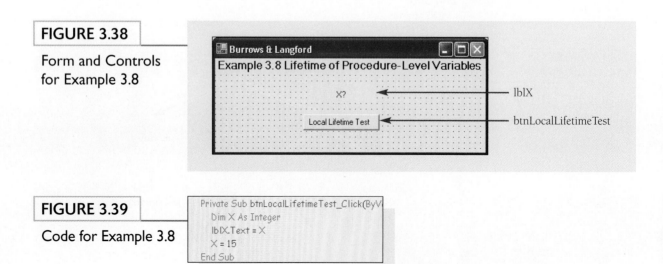

FIGURE 3.39

Code for Example 3.8

```
Private Sub btnLocalLifetimeTest_Click(ByV
    Dim X As Integer
    lblX.Text = X
    X = 15
End Sub
```

What happens when this event procedure is executed the second time? You might expect that the assignment statement **lblX.Text = X** causes the value 15 to be displayed in the label, because the value 15 was stored in **X** at the end of the first execution of the event procedure. But what actually happens is that the label displays the value 0 again. Why?

Every time a procedure is executed, Dim statements are executed and variables are declared and initialized. Subsequent statements in the procedure may change the values stored in the variables. Then, when the end of the procedure is reached, Visual Basic .NET destroys the procedure's variables.

This behavior is sometimes described thus: "Procedure-level variables live only while their procedure is executing." In effect, a procedure-level variable cannot "remember" anything prior to the start of its procedure's execution. Each time an event occurs, the event procedure's procedure-level variables are created from scratch and initialized, with no memory of prior values.

In contrast to procedure-level variables, module-level and global variables "live" longer. A module-level variable lives as long as the module is in memory. Hiding a module does not remove it from memory. The only way to remove a module from memory is to execute the module's Dispose() method. Global variables live as long as the application is running.

Example 3.9

LIFETIME OF MODULE-LEVEL VARIABLES

In this example, we modify the code from Example 3.8 to demonstrate how the lifetime of module-level variables differs from that of procedure-level variables. The code for this example is shown in Figure 3.40. In this code the scope of **X** is module-level instead of procedure-level.

When program execution begins, Visual Basic .NET creates the variable **X** and initializes it to 0.

The first time the user clicks on btnModuleLevelLifetimeTest, the value 0 is retrieved from the module-level variable **X**, and 0 is displayed in the label. Next, the value 15 is stored in the module-level variable **X**. The next time the user clicks on btnModuleLevelLifetimeTest, the value 15 is retrieved from the module-level variable **X** and 15 is displayed in the label. Next, the value 15 is stored in the module-level variable **X** (again). And the same thing happens each subsequent time the user clicks btnModuleLevelLifetimeTest. The module-level variable is destroyed when program execution ends.

Static Variables

Sometimes as a developer you want a variable to have the scope of a procedure-level variable so that it can be accessed only by its own procedure, yet to have the lifetime of a module-level variable, so that it can retain its value from one execution of

FIGURE 3.40

Code for Example 3.9

```
Dim X As Integer
Private Sub btnModuleLevelLifetimeTest_Cli
    lblX.Text = X
    X = 15
End Sub
```

FIGURE 3.41

Code for Example 3.10

```
Private Sub btnStaticLifetimeTest_Click(ByVal se
    Static X As Integer
    lblX.Text = X
    X = X + 1
End Sub
```

the procedure to the next. To achieve this behavior you declare a *static variable,* **inside the procedure, using the keyword Static instead of the keyword Dim.**

Visual Basic .NET gives special treatment to static variables. It stores them separately from the procedure-level variables so that they are not destroyed when the end of the procedure is reached. In addition, Visual Basic .NET allows only the procedure in which the static variable is declared to access it.

Be aware that variables with block-level scope within a procedure have a lifetime just like a procedure-level variable. If you use Dim to declare the variable, its lifetime will be as long as the block is executing. If you use Static to declare the block-level scope variable, its lifetime will be extended to the lifetime of the application.

Example 3.10

STATIC VARIABLES

In this example we see how to make the lifetime of a procedure-level variable extend beyond the termination of the procedure in which the variable is declared. The code for this example is shown in Figure 3.41. The variable **X** is declared as static. Describing the behavior of this event procedure is left as an exercise.

Exercise 3.21

In Example 3.10, what will be displayed in the Text of lblX the first time btnStaticLifetimeTest is clicked? The second time? The third? Explain.

3.8 Constant Scope

Symbolic constants have the same levels of scope as variables; that is, they can have block-level, procedure-level, module-level, or global scope. The only difference is you must add the access qualifier Public to the constant definition for a global constant. For example, **to create a global constant, add the** *Public Const statement*

Public Const MINUTESPERDAY = 1440

to a module.

Exercise 3.22

Generally, it is a good idea to minimize the scope of variables in a project. Why? On the other hand, it is a good idea to maximize the scope of symbolic constants in a project. Why?

3.9 Project 3: A Simple Payroll Application

In creating this project, you'll combine what you've learned about constants, variables, data types, project structure, and scope.

The project is a simple payroll application with a main form, one form for each of two employees, and a single summary form for both employees. This is not a good design for an actual payroll application, because if the company had

100 employees, the project would need 100 form files. We will refine the design features developed here in more sophisticated applications in later chapters.

Description of the Application

This application uses the hours worked and the hourly pay rate for two employees to compute each employee's gross pay, employment tax, and net pay. In addition, the application computes summary information that aggregates the three calculated values for both employees.

The application starts by showing the user a main form that provides three options. Figure 3.42 shows this form. When the user clicks on either of the Show Employee buttons, the appropriate employee form is displayed.

The form for employee 1 is shown in Figure 3.43. When the user clicks the Compute button, the program takes the values the user enters for hours worked and hourly rate, then computes and displays the following values in the lower three boxes:

- Gross Pay is the product of hours worked and hourly rate.

- Tax Due is the product of gross pay and the tax rate.

- Net Pay is gross pay minus tax due.

The Close button causes the form to be hidden. Notice that this form does not have a close box (set the form's ControlBox property to false), so the user must click on the Close button to make it disappear. A similar form exists for employee 2.

When the user clicks on the Show Summary button located on the main form, a summary form is displayed. Figure 3.44 shows this form.

When the user clicks the Update Totals button, the program totals the gross pay for the two employees using the gross pay values previously computed on the employee forms and displays this result in the top box. It similarly computes and displays the total tax due and total net pay for the two employees.

The tax rate, which is 17 percent, is the only data we assume are known at design time.

FIGURE 3.42

The Main Form for Project 3

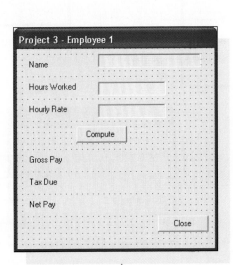

FIGURE 3.43

Employee Form User Interface

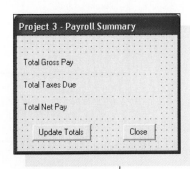

FIGURE 3.44

Summary Form User Interface

Design of the Application

To successfully construct any project, you have to make some decisions regarding controls, properties, constants, variables, and scope. You should make these decisions before beginning to construct the project.

We have already made some design decisions by sketching out the forms and controls in Figures 3.42 through 3.44. We now need to give these controls names and note property values that are not obvious. Figure 3.45 shows property settings for the controls on the employee and summary forms.

The tax rate is the only constant in the project. What should its scope be? The tax rate is the same for all employees, so it should be a global constant.

What variables are needed in the project, and what should their scope be? In the Compute event procedure on the Employee forms, we need to store the hours worked and hourly rate, so we need one variable for each. We also need to compute gross pay, tax due, and net pay and these too require variables. These variables can all have procedure-level scope. However, gross pay, tax due, and net pay also are needed on the summary form (that displays totals), so we need to be able to access them from the summary form. Since variables that have procedure-level scope cannot be accessed by another procedure, we need to create three variables that have global scope for each employee. These three variables store the same information as the procedure-level variables.

Since the project requires a global constant and several global variables, you will have to create a module. A good name for the module is GlobalDefs, and a good

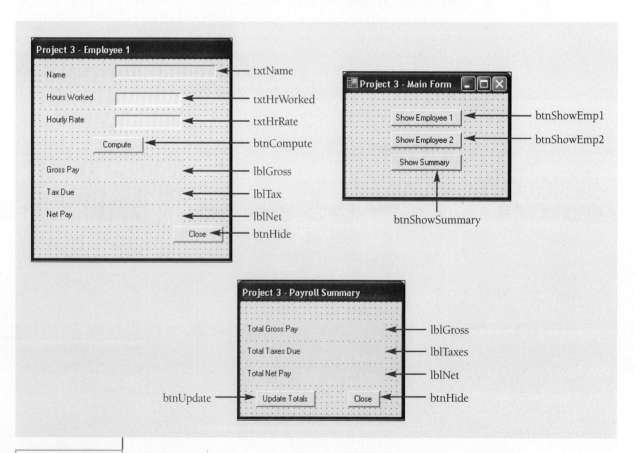

FIGURE 3.45

Main, Employee, and Summary Form Controls

FIGURE 3.46

Constants and
Variables in
Project 3

```
Module GlobalDefs
    Public Const TAXRATE = 0.17
    Public emp1Gross, emp1Tax, emp1Net As Decimal
    Public emp2Gross, emp2Tax, emp2Net As Decimal
End Module
```

name for its file is Globals.vb. Figure 3.46 depicts the constants and variables in the project.

Construction of the Application

When you're ready, open a new project. Begin by creating a module and declaring the global constant and global variables. It makes sense to do this before working on forms since all of the forms have code that use these constants and variables.

When you initially opened the new project, Visual Basic .NET automatically created a form, to which it gave the default name Form1. Change the form's Name property to "frmEmp1" and its Text to "Project 3 - Employee 1" (do not include the quotes). On this form you will now create and place the controls as they appear in Figure 3.45.

First create the six labels you see on the far left-hand side of the form. Then add the three textboxes. Give these textboxes names as shown in Figure 3.45. You also need to clear the Text property by selecting the existing text and pressing the DELETE key.

You next need to add and name the three labels on the lower right of the form. These also need their Text properties cleared. Finally add the two buttons as shown in Figure 3.45.

Next create the btnCompute_Click event procedure that computes and displays the employee's gross pay, tax due, and net pay, and stores them into the global variables. Figure 3.47 shows the code for this procedure. *After completing this step save the project.*

You also need to write the Click event for the Close button. Figure 3.48 shows this code.

```
Private Sub btnCompute_Click(ByVal sender As System.Object, ByVal e As Sys
    Dim hrWorked, hrlyRate As Decimal
    Dim gross, tax, net As Decimal
    Try
        hrWorked = txtHrWorked.Text
        hrlyRate = txtHrRate.Text
        gross = hrWorked * hrlyRate
        tax = gross * TAXRATE
        net = gross - tax
        emp1Gross = gross
        emp1Tax = tax
        emp1Net = net
        lblGross.Text = gross
        lblTax.Text = tax
        lblNet.Text = net
    Catch
        MsgBox("Please enter valid numbers for hourly rate and hours worked")
    End Try
End Sub
```

```
Private Sub btnHide_Click(ByVal sender
    Me.Hide()
End Sub
```

FIGURE 3.48

Code for btnHide_Click

FIGURE 3.47

Code for btnCompute_Click for First Employee

You next need to create a form for the other employee. We'll do some copy/paste to make this process easier. First, be sure that you have frmEmp1 active in the design window. You should notice that the actual form file is highlighted in the Solution Explorer window. Right-click on the highlighted file in the Solution Explorer and select Copy from the pop-up menu. Then right-click on the project folder in the Solution Explorer and select Paste from the pop-up menu. Figure 3.49 shows these two actions.

Figure 3.50 shows the Solution Explorer after doing the paste operation. Observe that the icon for the copy of the form is visually different from the original. This is due to the fact that you copied everything including the class name (resulting in duplicate class names). You need to fix this so that you will have a second form useable for a second employee.

Open the Code window for the copy of the form and look at the code at the top. It should say

```
Public Class frmEmp1
    Inherits System.Windows.Forms.Form
```

You need to edit this by replacing **frmEmp1** with **frmEmp2** as follows

```
Public Class frmEmp2
    Inherits System.Windows.Forms.Form
```

FIGURE 3.49

Copying an Existing
Form and Pasting
Copy into Project

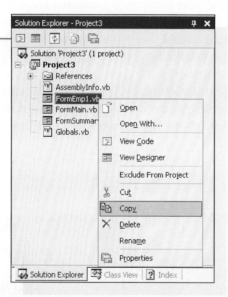

FIGURE 3.50

Solution Explorer
with a Copy of
FormEmp1

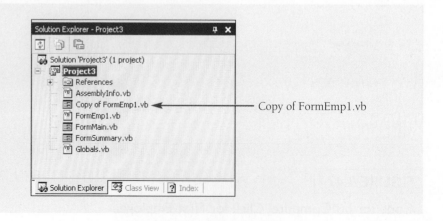

Copy of FormEmp1.vb

At this point you should have an exact copy of the form for the first employee. You need to make a couple of small edits to the code for the btnCompute_Click event. Edit the references to the three global variables by changing the 1s to 2s. Also change the Text property of the Form to read "Project 3 - Employee 2". When you are done, the code for the second employee's btnCompute_Click event should look like that in Figure 3.51.

Now create the summary form. Change the form's name to frmSummary and its Text to "Project 3 - Payroll Summary". Create and name the controls for this form as shown in Figure 3.45. Then create the Click event procedures for the command buttons. The code for these procedures is in Figure 3.52. Save the program again.

Finally you need to create the main form. After adding the form, name it "frmMain" and set its Text to "Project 3 - Main Form". Add and name the three buttons shown on Figure 3.45. Finally, add the code for both the objects in the declaration section as well as the three Click events. Figure 3.53 shows this code.

FIGURE 3.51

Code for
Employee 2's
btnCompute_Click
Event

```
Private Sub btnCompute_Click(ByVal sender As System.Object, ByVal e As Sys
    Dim hrWorked, hrlyRate As Decimal
    Dim gross, tax, net As Decimal
    Try
        hrWorked = txtHrWorked.Text
        hrlyRate = txtHrRate.Text
        gross = hrWorked * hrlyRate
        tax = gross * TAXRATE
        net = gross - tax
        emp2Gross = gross
        emp2Tax = tax
        emp2Net = net
        lblGross.Text = gross
        lblTax.Text = tax
        lblNet.Text = net
    Catch
        MsgBox("Please enter valid numbers for hourly rate and hours worked")
    End Try
End Sub
```

```
Private Sub btnHide_Click(ByVal sender As Syste
    Me.Hide()
End Sub

Private Sub btnUpdate_Click(ByVal sender As Sys
    Dim totGross, totTax, totNet As Decimal
    totGross = emp1Gross + emp2Gross
    totTax = emp1Tax + emp2Tax
    totNet = emp1Net + emp2Net
    lblGross.Text = totGross
    lblTaxes.Text = totTax
    lblNet.Text = totNet
End Sub
```

FIGURE 3.52

Event Procedures for the Summary Form

```
Dim objEmp1 As New frmEmp1()
Dim objEmp2 As New frmEmp2()
Dim objSummary As New frmSummary()

Private Sub btnShowEmp1_Click(ByVal sender As
    objEmp1.Show()
End Sub

Private Sub btnShowEmp2_Click(ByVal sender As
    objEmp2.Show()
End Sub

Private Sub btnShowSummary_Click(ByVal sender
    objSummary.Show()
End Sub
```

FIGURE 3.53

Code for the Main Form (frmMain)

It is almost time to run the application. Save it before you start these last steps.[14] Before you run the application, be aware that the system does not know which form to use at startup. You can either set the startup form (frmMain) now (Project → Properties) or just run the application. If you just run the application, it will tell you it needs a startup form; just double-click on the error message in the Build Error task list and set frmMain from the ensuing dialog box.

Once started, play with the application. Verify that it is working correctly. Be sure to test the Try/Catch blocks by entering invalid numeric data into the textboxes. Finally, after you are done and things are working, do a final save and smile—you've just completed a nontrivial application.

This project demonstrates how an application can use multiple forms and illustrates the use of global variables and constants to share data between forms. The construction steps also demonstrate shortcuts (copy/paste) that are useful when two or more forms are very similar.

Exercise 3.23

In Project 3, how can you verify that the results displayed by your summary form are correct?

Exercise 3.24

Suppose you are part of a team of programmers who will cooperate to construct a large project. Is it important for the team to decide in advance on the module-level and global variables and constants that will be part of the project? Explain.

Chapter Summary

1. There are two basic kinds of data items: numeric data items that can be used in arithmetic and string data items that cannot be used in arithmetic. Data items are represented in a program as either constants or variables.

2. Constants are data items that cannot change while the program is executing. Constants can be represented literally (the constant value itself) or symbolically (a descriptive name that represents the value). Symbolic constants must be defined using the Const statement. Using symbolic constants makes a program easier to read and maintain and reduces the likelihood of inconsistent values for the same constant in a program.

3. Variables are symbolic names for memory locations. Unlike constants, the values of variables can and often do change during program execution. Variables can be string or numeric. Numeric variables are further classified into specific types, which include Short, Integer, Long, Decimal, Single, and Double. Variables must be declared with a variable declaration statement, which specifies the name of the variable and its type. The Dim statement is one kind of variable declaration statement.

4. Expressions are combinations of variables, constants, and operators that produce a value. The + operator adds two numeric values and the * operator multiplies two numeric values. The & operator concatenates (joins end-to-end) two string values.

---

14 We recommend saving projects fairly often in case something goes wrong. It's hard enough work doing these things once, but having to do them more than once is even worse.

5. An assignment statement is used to store the value of an expression into a variable or a control property. The syntax of the assignment statement is

$$variablename = expression$$

or

$$control.property = expression$$

The expression on the right-hand side of the equal sign is evaluated and reduced to a single value. This value is then stored in the variable or control property on the left-hand side of the equal sign.

6. A project can have more than one form, but Visual Basic .NET allows only one form to be active at a time. The active form is the form with which the user can interact and is visually identified by the color of the Title bar. Forms also can be loaded into main memory (from disk) and unloaded from main memory. The process of loading and unloading forms can be used to conserve main memory at run time. One form can access a control on another form. This is done by qualifying the reference to a control by adding the name of the form object to the name of the control. The syntax is

$$formObjectName.controlName.property$$

7. The Show method causes a form object to become the active form. Its syntax is

$$formObjectName.Show$$

8. A variable's scope is the domain within which the variable can be accessed. There are three levels of scope: procedure-level, module-level, and global. A variable with procedure-level scope is known and accessible only within a single procedure. Procedure-level variables are declared using a Dim statement placed in the procedure. These variables can have their scope further narrowed by declaring the variable within a block. This creates block-level scope that limits visibility of the variable to the block.

A variable with module-level scope is known and accessible to any procedure of a given form or module. The Dim statement used to declare the variable is placed in the declarations section of the form or module.

A variable with global scope is known and accessible to any procedure of the project. To declare a global variable, a Public statement must be placed in the declarations section of a module. The Public statement is just like the Dim statement except the word Dim is replaced with the word Public.

If a procedure has a procedure-level variable whose name is the same as a module-level variable, the procedure uses the procedure-level variable and ignores the module-level variable. The general rule is that a procedure always uses the closest variable with the specified name (where procedure-level is closer than module-level, which in turn is closer than global).

9. Variable lifetime refers to how long a variable exists. Module-level variables exist until the module is removed from memory (disposed). Global variables exist during the entire execution of the program. In contrast, procedure-level variables exist only during the execution of the procedure in which they are declared. When the procedure starts to execute, its procedure-level variables are created and initialized. When the procedure terminates, the procedure-level variables are destroyed (their values are lost). To make procedure-level variables retain their values from one execution of the procedure to the next, declare the variable within the procedure using the Static statement instead of the Dim statement.

Key Terms

Activate event	Form control	sequential flow of
active form	global scope	control
assignment statement	initialization	standard data types
cast	keywords	static variable
catch an exception	literal constant	string data
concatenation operator	Load event	symbolic constant
constant	module	syntax
constant definition	module-level scope	throw an exception
statement	numeric data	Try/Catch
Const statement	precision	type mismatch error
data item	procedure-level scope	variable
Dim statement	Public Const statement	variable declaration
exception	Public statement	statement
expression	range	variable lifetime
floating-point types	reserved words	variable scope
flow of control	run time error	
formatting	scope	

End-of-Chapter Problems

1. For each of the following real-world quantities, write a Dim statement that declares an appropriate variable. State any assumptions you make.
   a. A part number that consists of four digits followed by two letters (e.g., 4745XY).
   b. The number of units sold for an item on an invoice.
   c. The comments entered into an employee's job evaluation form.
   d. The asking price of a home listed for sale.
   e. The number of acres purchased for a commercial building site, which is the result of a geometrical calculation using the site's corner points.

2. Write the Visual Basic .NET statement that increases by 5 the value stored in the integer variable **n**.

3. Assume that you want a variable that is declared in a Click event procedure to retain its value each time the procedure is executed. What is the correct way to accomplish this?

4. Explain the difference between module-level scope and global scope for a variable.

5. The following Visual Basic .NET statement calculates the final balance of a $100 investment at the end of three years, assuming an 8 percent interest rate and annual compounding.

   finalBalance = 100 * (1 + 0.08) ^ 3

   In the statement, * means multiply and ^ means "raised to the power of." Suppose we want to modify this statement to use in a real program. Of the values on the right side of the equal sign, which should be represented as variables, which as symbolic constants, and which as literal constants? Explain.

6. Suppose that the event procedures associated with two controls on the same form need to access the same variable. Explain how you would make this possible.

7. Suppose that you are in the process of choosing the type for a variable, and you have narrowed the choices to Decimal and Double. Identify the important factors that you should consider when deciding whether the variable should be typed as Decimal or as Double.

8. What value will be stored in the variable **N** at the end of the third time the following Click event procedure is executed?

   ```
   Private Sub btnExample_Click(...)
       Dim N As Integer
       N = N + 1
   End Sub
   ```

9. Do variables declared with global scope need to be declared as static variables if you want their values to be retained as the program executes? Explain.

10. Which of the following declares three Decimal and two String variables?
    a. Dim X, Y, Z As Decimal, A, B As String
    b. Dim X, Y, Z As Decimal
        Dim A, B As String
    c. Dim X As Decimal
        Dim Y As Decimal
        Dim Z As Decimal
        Dim A As String
        Dim B As String
    d. both b and c
    e. a, b, and c

Programming Problems

1. Create a form with one button and four Label controls. Program the button's Click event procedure to store the numeric value 875426.4796752 in four variables, one each of type Integer, Decimal, Single, and Double. Then have the Click event procedure display the values of the four variables in the four labels. Run the program and observe the result. Now, change the declaration of the variable of type Integer to type Short and run the program again. What happens? Explain.

2. Create a form that has three buttons and one Label control. The first button should set a Short variable named **firstVar** to the value 105. The second button should set a Short variable named **secondVar** to the value 200. The third button should compute the sum of the two variables and display the result in the Label control.

3. Create a project with two forms. Then declare a global variable; this global variable should be the only variable in the project. On the first form, create four buttons. The first button should store the value 11 in the global variable. The second button should change the value of the global variable to 22. The third button should display the value of the global variable in a Label control. The fourth button should show the other form.

   The second form should be identical to the first form, except that its first two buttons should set the global variable to 33 and 44, instead of 11 and 22. Run the program and experiment by clicking its buttons in various orders.

4. For this problem you are to create a multiform application that manipulates and displays the values of several variables. The form shown below (Form A)

has buttons that manipulate variables named **N**, **K**, **X**, and **A**, and labels that display the values of these variables. Clicking on "Add 10 to N" should increase the value of the variable **N** by 10 and then display the value of **N** in its label. Thus, if you click this button repeatedly, the label should display 10, 20, 30, and so on. Similarly, clicking on "Add 20 to K" should increase the value of the variable **K** by 20 (20, 40, 60, etc.). Clicking on "Add 100 to X" should add the constant 100 to the variable **X** and then display the value of **X** in its label; however, instead of showing 100, 200, 300, and so forth, this label should show 100, 100, 100, and so on. Finally, clicking on "Add 5 to A" and "Add 15 to A" should add 5 and 15, respectively, to the variable **A**. This action should be cumulative: for example, clicking on "Add 5 to A" first should change **A** to 5; then clicking on "Add 15 to A" should change **A** to 20, and so forth.

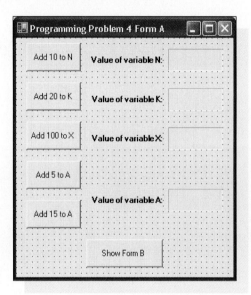

The Show Form B button should display the following form (Form B). Clicking the Show Variable K button should cause the value of the variable **K** (as seen on Form A) to be displayed (the two values should be the same).

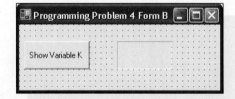

Your solution should use minimal scope for each variable. That is, if procedure-level scope works, it should be used instead of module-level or global scope. If procedure-level scope will not work but module-level scope will, then you should use module-level scope, not global. Use global scope only if it is the only scope that works.

Do not allow any controls on Form A to refer to controls on Form B or vice versa—use only variables to store and access values.

5. In this chapter you learned how to concatenate two or more strings with the ampersand (&) operator. If you concatenate two strings with a carriage return/linefeed character between them (for example "a" & CRLF & "b"),

the new string will be displayed with the first string on one line and the second string on another. Microsoft includes the carriage return/linefeed character as a constant much like a mathematical constant. To simplify the long name, you can declare a local constant with the following line:

Const CRLF = Microsoft.VisualBasic.ControlChars.CrLf

Create a form with TextBox controls and matching labels to accept input for "Full Name", "Address", "City", "State", and "Zip". On the form, put a label at the bottom that has room for three lines of text. Create a button with "Update Label" as the Text property setting. Write the proper code to concatenate all of the text from the text boxes into the bottom label. The name should appear on the first line of the label, the address on the second, and the city/state/ZIP on the third.

6. The last chapter showed you how to use the InputBox() function to accept user input. For this problem you will create a multiform application where the first form displays a simple button to activate an InputBox and use the results to personalize the second form. Create the first form with a single button on it. Create a second form (named frmPersonal) with a label in the center and set the Name property of the label to lblPersonal. On the first form, at the module level, create an object reference to the second form. For the button, write the code necessary to concatenate the text string "Hello, " with the results of the InputBox() function. The code should place the completed string in the label on the second form and then display that form.

CHAPTER

FOUR

Expressions

In Chapter 3 we discussed the different ways data items can be represented in programs. We also discussed the assignment statement that stores the value of an expression in a variable. We stated that expressions specify calculations or manipulations with data, and we gave a number of simple examples of expressions. However, many applications must frequently perform complex operations on data, so in this chapter we extend what we know about expressions.

Expressions are made up of constants, variables, operators, and functions. The *operators* and *functions* specify how the data are to be manipulated, and the *constants, variables* and *control properties* provide the data. Operators and functions are part of the programming language. Thus, in order to write powerful expressions, you must become familiar with the operators and functions provided by the Visual Basic .NET language.

The three kinds of expressions that are typically used include

- *Arithmetic expressions* **used to perform arithmetic calculations**.

- *String expressions* **used to manipulate string data**.

- *Logical expressions* **used to select an appropriate action from a set of possible actions**.

An arithmetic expression is made up of numeric constants and variables and arithmetic operators and functions. Arithmetic operators include addition, subtraction, multiplication, and division as well as others. An example of an arithmetic function is the square root function; if you give the number 4 to the square root function, the function returns the value 2. As we saw in Chapter 3, the Math class provides a number of arithmetic functions.

A string expression is made up of string constants and variables and string operators and functions. We briefly discussed the string concatenation operator, "&", in Chapter 3. The format function that is used to format values for display is an example of a string function.

A logical expression is made up of numeric, string, and Boolean constants and variables, comparison operators, logical operators, and logical functions. A logical expression "evaluates to" (a phrase discussed later in this chapter) either True or False. As an example, you can use a logical expression in a program to determine whether an invoice total exceeds $100.

We begin this chapter by introducing operators and functions, showing how they can be used to construct expressions, and giving examples of how they are used. Next, we discuss arithmetic and string expressions and introduce the commonly used operators and functions for each. We then discuss logical expressions. The chapter concludes with a project that combines many of the topics in this and previous chapters to create a multipurpose financial calculator.

Objectives

After studying this chapter, you should be able to

- Describe the operators and functions used to create arithmetic, string, and logical expressions.

- Explain why errors such as overflow and roundoff occur and how to avoid them.

- Write logical expressions using comparison operators and logical operators to enable your programs to make simple choices while executing.

4.1 Using Expressions, Operators, and Functions in Visual Basic .NET Statements

Each line of a procedure is one statement,[1] and an expression is often part of a statement. An **expression instructs the computer to manipulate specific data in a specific way**, and the result of this manipulation is a single value. The **statement then tells the computer what to do with the value that results from the expression**—for example, store it in a particular variable or display it on the user interface.

We construct expressions from values, operators, and functions. A **value** is a constant, a variable, or a control property. An **operator is a symbol that specifies a common operation, such as addition or multiplication.** A **function is a descriptive name that specifies a less familiar or more complex operation than those performed by operators, such as computation of the square root of a number.** Figure 4.1 shows the relationship between statements, expressions, values, operators, and functions.

We now describe statements, expressions, and the components of expressions to help you learn to use them in event procedures that manipulate data.

Statements

Statements differ in the kinds of actions they specify and in their syntax. For example, we can easily distinguish a Dim statement, which is used to declare a variable, from an assignment statement, which is used to store a value in a variable or a control property.

Some statements, such as Try, have no expressions. Others, like the assignment statement, require exactly one expression. Still other statements allow multiple expressions.

At run time, to execute a statement containing one or more expressions, the computer performs the following two steps, in order:

1. It evaluates the expressions, one at a time, arriving at a single value for each expression.

---

1   This is not entirely true. It is possible to split a long statement across several lines. However, in that case you would see a line-continuation character (the underscore symbol, _) and know that you were looking at one statement.

FIGURE 4.1

Statements,
Expressions, and
the Components
of Expressions

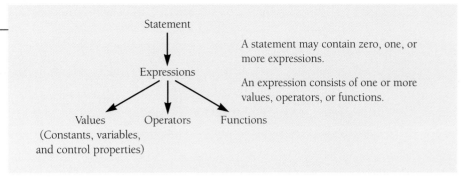

FIGURE 4.2

Steps in Execution
of the Assignment
Statement

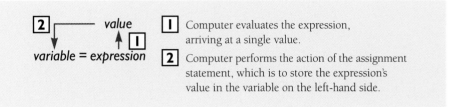

2. It performs the action specified by the statement, which entails doing something with the value(s) obtained in step 1.

Figure 4.2 illustrates these steps for the assignment statement.

Expressions

An expression is either a single value or a combination of values, operators, and/or functions that reduce to a single value. For example, 2 is an expression, and 2 + 3 is also an expression. When the computer encounters the expression 2 in a statement, it understands it to be the number 2. When the computer encounters the expression 2 + 3 in a statement, it performs the addition to arrive at the number 5. **Performing the calculation or manipulation specified by an expression is called** *evaluating the expression.* For example, we say that 2 + 3 evaluates to the value 5.

Evaluating expressions is step 1 in the execution of a statement. To evaluate an expression, the computer

1. Obtains the data to be manipulated by identifying the value of each constant in the expression and retrieving the value from each variable and control property in the expression.

2. Performs the specified manipulations, one at a time, using the values obtained in step 1.

The resulting value is always either numeric, string, or Boolean.
As mentioned before, there are three kinds of expressions:

- Arithmetic expressions that specify ordinary arithmetic calculations. The result of an arithmetic expression is always a numeric value. An example is 2 + 3, which evaluates to 5.

- String expressions that manipulate or combine string values. The result of a string expression is always a string value. An example is "A" & "B", which evaluates to "AB".

- Logical expressions that represent True/False questions. The result of a logical expression is always a Boolean value True or False. An example is 2 < 3, which evaluates to True.

We form complex expressions by combining variables and constants with operators and functions. We describe operators and functions next.

Operators

An operator is a symbol that specifies a common operation such as addition or multiplication. The plus sign (+) is the addition operator and the asterisk (*) is the multiplication operator.

Most operators are *binary operators*, **so called because they combine the two values on either side of them into a single value.**[2] The addition operator is a binary operator. In the expression 2 + 3, the addition operator adds the value on its left to the value on its right, arriving at the single value of 5. **A few operators affect only the value on their right; they are called *unary operators*.**[3] In the expression –2, the minus sign is called the negation operator; since there is no value on its left side, it simply makes the 2 negative. The negation operator is unary.

Many operators are easy to understand because their use in Visual Basic .NET is equivalent to their everyday use. For example, everyone is familiar with the binary subtraction operator, as in 3 – 2.

Functions

A function is a descriptive name that specifies a more complex operation than that performed by an operator. In Visual Basic .NET, function names are always followed by parentheses. Examples of functions are Math.Sqrt(), which computes the square root of a number, and Math.Abs(), which computes the absolute value of a number.

To make the Math.Sqrt() function compute the square root of a number, place the number between its parentheses. For example, if a procedure contains the statements

```
Dim X As Single
X = Math.Sqrt(4)
```

then after the assignment statement is executed, the variable **X** will store the value 2.

The **value between the parentheses is called the *argument* of the function.** A function manipulates or performs a calculation with its argument, then returns the result.[4] The phrase "returns the result" means that the function becomes the result; that is, the computer replaces the function with the result just as the computer replaces a variable name with its value. **We also call the resulting value of**

---

2   The *bi* in binary means "two."

3   The prefix *uni* means "one."

4   At this point, think of a function as a black box, meaning a device that accepts an input and produces an output. We need to understand the input and the output, but we don't need to know how the black box transforms the input into the output. The square root function accepts a number as the input and produces the square root of the number as its output. We don't need to know how the output value was actually computed.

the function the *return value.* In the preceding example, the Math.Sqrt() function computes square roots, and its argument is 4; thus, Math.Sqrt(4) becomes the value 2. We use the phrases "Math.Sqrt(4) returns the value 2," "Math.Sqrt(4) becomes the value 2," and "Math.Sqrt(4) takes on the value 2" interchangeably.

The argument of a function is itself an expression. The computer first evaluates the argument—the expression between the parentheses—to arrive at a single value and then performs the action of the function upon this value. Suppose a procedure contains the following statements:

```
Dim X As Single
Dim Y As Single
Y = 7
X = Math.Sqrt(2 + Y)
```

What value will **X** hold after the second assignment statement executes? When the computer executes this second assignment statement, it performs the following steps:

1. Computer replaces variable name by its value (7).

2. Computer performs the specified manipulations: it adds 2 + 7 to get 9; then the function computes the square root ($\sqrt{9} = 3$).

3. Computer stores 3 in the variable **X**.

More Complicated Expressions

Operators and functions can be combined to compose complicated expressions, as illustrated by the following statements:

```
Dim X As Single
Dim Y As Single
Y = 7
X = Y - Math.Sqrt(Y + 9) + 5 + Math.Sqrt(2 + Y)
```

What value does **X** hold after the second assignment statement executes? When the computer executes this statement, it

1. Retrieves the value of the variable **Y** (7) and makes this the interim answer.

2. It computes **Y** + 9 (16) and passes this value to the Sqrt() function, which returns 4.

3. Subtracts 4 from the interim solution (7) and saves a new interim solution of 3.

4. It adds 5 to the interim solution (3), making the interim solution 8.

5. It adds 2 to **Y** (7), getting 9, and passes this value to the Sqrt() function, which returns 3.

6. It adds 3 to the interim solution (8), arriving at the expression's final value of 11.

7. It stores 11 in the variable **Y**.

Notice that we are evaluating this expression from left to right. Soon we will see some rules that might change this left-to-right order.

Because the argument of a function is itself an expression, a function's argument also can be complex. It may include another function, for example, as illustrated by the following statements:

```
Dim X As Single
Dim Y As Single
Y = 7
X = Math.Sqrt(10 + Math.Sqrt(Y + 29))
```

What value does **X** store after the second assignment statement executes? To execute this statement, the computer performs these steps:

1. Retrieves the constant 10 and makes this the interim solution.

2. Adds **Y** + 29 (7 + 29), getting 36. It passes 36 to the Sqrt() function, which returns the value 6.

3. It adds 6 (from step 2) to 10 (the current interim solution), making the interim solution 16. It passes the number 16 to the Sqrt() function, which returns the value 4 (making this the final value of the expression).

4. It stores the expression value (4) in the variable **X**.

Let's look at a complete event procedure that illustrates the use of operators and functions to perform a moderately complex calculation. This event procedure is executed when the user clicks on a button named btnCalculateHypotenuseLength. The procedure calculates the length of a right triangle's hypotenuse given the lengths of the other two sides. The calculation uses the Pythagorean theorem from geometry, which states that if the sides of the right triangle have lengths A and B, then the length of the hypotenuse, C, is equal to the square root of $A^2 + B^2$.

The program has five variables. Variables **A** and **B** store the lengths of the two sides. Variables **ASquared** and **BSquared** store the results of computing the squares of the sides. Variable **C** stores the length of the hypotenuse, which is computed using the Pythagorean formula. The results are presented to the user using the Text properties of three labels on the form. The code for the procedure is as follows:

```
Private Sub btnCalculateHypotenuseLength_Click()
    Dim A As Single
    Dim ASquared As Single
    Dim B As Single
    Dim BSquared As Single
    Dim C As Single
    A = 3
    B = 4
    ASquared = A * A
    BSquared = B * B
    C = Math.Sqrt(ASquared + BSquared)
    lblA.Text = A
    lblB.Text = B
    lblC.Text = C
End Sub
```

Expressions as a Part of Statements

An expression can never appear on a line by itself in a procedure. That is, an expression by itself is never valid; an expression is always part of a larger statement.

You will never see the following sequence of statements in a working Visual Basic .NET program.

```
Dim X As Single
Dim Y As Single
7              ' Not a valid statement
Math.Sqrt(Y)    ' Not a meaningful statement
```

Intuitively, we know that 7 by itself is a simple enough expression for the computer to evaluate, but a valid statement, in addition, always will tell the computer what to do with the result. For example, an assignment statement can have an arbitrarily complicated expression on the right-hand side of the equal sign, and after the computer evaluates the expression, it knows what to do with the result: store it in the variable specified on the left-hand side of the equal sign. The line with **Math.Sqrt(Y)** is a valid statement (it will be accepted as correct syntax) but it is not meaningful because it does not say what to do with the result of the function.

Exercise 4.1

What values are stored in the variables X, Y, and Z after the following statements execute?

```
Dim X As Single
Dim Y As Single
Dim Z As Single
X = Math.Sqrt(5 + 20)
Y = 5 + Math.Sqrt(X + 11)
Z = Math.Sqrt(X + 2 + Y) + Math.Sqrt(4)
```

4.2 Arithmetic Expressions

For the most part, arithmetic operators and functions are similar to their counterparts in ordinary arithmetic, but to write arithmetic expressions skillfully you must learn precisely how they are used in Visual Basic .NET. In this section we describe arithmetic operators and functions and demonstrate their use.

Arithmetic Operators and Operator Precedence

Of the arithmetic operators listed in Table 4.1, only one requires explanation. **The exponentiation operator raises the first number to the power of the second number.** Thus, $3 \wedge 2$ means 3^2, and $2 \wedge 5$ means 2^5, and so on. The numbers can

Table 4.1 The arithmetic operators

| Operator | | Example | |
Symbol	Name	Expression	Result
+	Addition	3 + 1	4
–	Subtraction	3 – 1	2
*	Multiplication	3 * 2	6
/	Division	3 / 2	1.5
^	Exponentiation	3 ^ 2	9

have fractional parts, so, for example, 2.25 ^ 0.5 ($2.25^{1/2}$ or $\sqrt{2.25}$) will compute the square root of 2.25.

Although arithmetic operators are used in Visual Basic .NET expressions pretty much the same as in ordinary algebra, you must compose complicated expressions with care, since the order in which the operations are performed will affect the result. For example, for the expression

$$-1 + 2 * 4 - 4 / 2 * 3 \wedge 2 + 3$$

is the result 3, 6.9835, –8, or something else?

As in ordinary algebra, you can use parentheses to force the order in which operations are performed: the operations in the innermost parentheses are evaluated first, then the operations in the next innermost parentheses, and so on. In the absence of parentheses, Visual Basic .NET follows an *operator precedence rule* **that specifies arithmetic operations to be performed in the following order:**

1. Exponentiations

2. Unary negations

3. Multiplications and divisions

4. Integer divisions

5. Modulus operations

6. Additions and subtractions

We will delay the discussion of integer division and modulus operations for a moment and just focus on the other operators.

If two or more operators at the same precedence level occur in an expression, they are evaluated from left to right. For example, if an expression contains both a multiplication and a division operator, the left-most one is performed first.

We will now apply the operator precedence rules to evaluate our expression

$$-1 + 2 * 4 - 4 / 2 * 3 \wedge 2 + 3$$

1. Evaluate all exponentiations. 3 ^ 2 yields the intermediate result of 9 so we now have

$$-1 + 2 * 4 - 4 / 2 * 9 + 3$$

2. Evaluate unary minus. The –1 is identified as negative 1, so we now have

$$-1 + 2 * 4 - 4 / 2 * 9 + 3$$

3. Evaluate multiplications and divisions from left to right. First 2 * 4 yields the intermediate result of 8, so we now have

$$-1 + 8 - 4 / 2 * 9 + 3$$

Then 4 / 2 yields the intermediate result of 2 and we have

$$-1 + 8 - 2 * 9 + 3$$

Finally 2 * 9 yields the intermediate result of 18 and our expression becomes

$$-1 + 8 - 18 + 3$$

4. Finally we apply additions and subtractions from left to right. –1 + 8 yields the intermediate result of 7 and we have

$$7 - 18 + 3$$

Next 7 – 18 yields the intermediate result of –11 and our expression is

$$-11 + 3$$

Finally –11 + 3 yields the final result of –8.

Of course, when you create an application, your goal is to make the computer perform a calculation that you need to have performed. One way to proceed is to study the operator precedence rule and arrange your arithmetic expression accordingly so that all operations are performed in the correct order. However, a better way to proceed is to write your expression in the clearest, most natural order you can, based on your experience with ordinary arithmetic, and use parentheses for added clarity and to override the operator precedence rules when necessary. This makes the expression easier to read, which in turn adds to the readability and maintainability of the program.

For example, a human can understand the expression we have been using as an example much more readily if it is written in the following form:

$$(3 - 1) + (2 * 4) - ((4 / 2) * (3 \wedge 2))$$

Exercise 4.2

What value results when the computer evaluates this numeric expression?

$$3 + 5 * 10$$

Exercise 4.3

Write a modified version of the expression in Exercise 4.2 to yield the value of 80.

Exercise 4.4

What values are displayed by the following event procedure?

```
Private Sub btnSimpleArithmetic_Click()
    Dim X As Single
    Dim Y As Single
    Dim Z As Single
    X = 2 + 3
    MsgBox(X)
    Y = 7 * X
    MsgBox(Y)
    Z = X + Y / 10 + 2 ^ 3
    MsgBox(Z)
    X = X + 1
    MsgBox(X)
    MsgBox(X + 1)
    MsgBox(X)
End Sub
```

Integer Division

Visual Basic .NET provides two operators for performing division with integers. The *integer division operator* **calculates how many times one integer goes into another, ignoring the remainder. The modulus operator** *Mod* **calculates the remainder produced when one integer is divided by another.** These operators are shown in Table 4.2.

If we divide 33 by 12, the answer is 2 with a remainder of 9. The Visual Basic .NET expression 33 \ 12 evaluates to 2, the number of times 12 goes into 33

Table 4.2 Integer arithmetic operators

Operator		Example	
Symbol	Name	Expression	Result
\	Integer division	33 \ 12	2
Mod	Mod (remainder or modulo)	33 Mod 12	9

(ignoring the remainder). The Visual Basic .NET expression 33 Mod 12 evaluates to 9, the remainder after dividing 33 by 12.

Be sure to note the difference between the integer divide symbol, \, which is sometimes called a backslash, and the ordinary division symbol, /, which is sometimes called a slash. The result of integer division is always an integer, while the result of ordinary division may have a fractional part.

Also, remember that in the operator precedence rule, the \ operator comes after multiply and divide and the Mod operator comes after \.

Exercise 4.5

What values will the following event procedure display?

```
Private Sub btnIntegerDiv_Click()
    MsgBox(18 / 4)
    MsgBox(18 \ 4)
    MsgBox(18 Mod 4)
End Sub
```

Example **4.1**

USING CYCLIC SEQUENCES

Many programs simulate cyclical events such as changes in the seasons of the year, the schedule of a sales representative visiting clients, or the dividing of a group of students into teams. To solve such problems with the computer, programs use the Mod operator to generate a sequence of numbers matching the real-world event. As an example of this kind of calculation, the event procedure in Figure 4.3 generates the sequence 1, 2, 3, 0, 1, 2, 3, 0, 1, 2, 3, . . . As the user clicks btnCycleTest successively, the program counts and computes the remainder. This program is said to "count modulo 4."

Notice that the variable **C** is declared as static in the procedure. This is necessary to insure that it does not get reset to zero each time the button is clicked.

Exercise 4.6

Modify btnCycleTest_Click in Example 4.1, without changing the assignment statement lblCycle.Text = **C**, so that it produces the sequence 1, 2, 3, 4, 1, 2, 3, 4, . . ., instead of the sequence 1, 2, 3, 0, 1, 2, 3, 0, . . .

FIGURE 4.3

Code for Example 4.1

```
Private Sub btnCycleTest_Click(ByVal sender As System.Objec
    Static C As Integer
    C = (C + 1) Mod 4 ' produces sequence 1,2,3,0,1,2,3,,0, ...
    lblCycle.Text = C
End Sub
```

Arithmetic Functions

Visual Basic .NET's Math class contains a number of arithmetic functions that make it easy to perform common mathematical calculations such as square roots or logarithms. In addition, Visual Basic .NET has several additional arithmetic functions built in that are not part of the Math class. To perform a calculation using a function, include the function in an expression. Be sure to preface the function name with the class name Math if the function comes from that class. Some common arithmetic functions are listed in Table 4.3. In this section we describe these functions, starting with Abs(). We've already seen how Math.Sqrt() works in Section 4.1.

Math.Abs() and Math.Sign()

The Abs() function returns the absolute value of its argument (i.e., it removes the sign and makes the value positive). The Sign() function is useful when you can ignore the value of a number but need to know its sign. Sign() takes on the value −1 if its argument is negative, 0 if its argument is 0, and 1 if its argument is positive. This function might be used, for example, to determine whether a customer's credit balance has gone negative.

Fix()

The Fix() function truncates a number with a fractional part; that is, it throws away the fractional part and returns just the integer part. Several functions are variations on Fix(), including Int() and CInt(). None of these three functions are members of the Math class, so you do not preface them with the class name Math. Int() returns the largest integer less than or equal to its argument. The values returned by Fix() and Int() are the same except when the argument is negative: Fix(−4.3) returns the value −4 and Int(−4.3) returns the value −5. CInt() rounds its argument up or down to the nearest integer. If the fractional part of its argument is exactly .5, then CInt() rounds it to the nearest even integer; for example, CInt(3.5) returns 4 and CInt(2.5) returns 2.

Table 4.3 Common arithmetic functions

| Function | | Example | |
Name	Description	Expression	Result
Math.Sqrt()	Square root	Math.Sqrt(4)	2
Math.Abs()	Absolute value	Math.Abs(−4)	4
Math.Sign()	Sign	Math.Sign(−3.5)	−1
Fix()	Integer part	Fix(4.28745)	4
Math.Exp()	Exponential (natural)	Math.Exp(1)	2.718282
Math.Log()	Natural logarithm	Math.Log(2.71828)	0.9999993
Rnd()	Random number (0 to < 1)	Rnd()	0.3845683

Math.Exp() and Math.Log()

Exp() and Log() compute natural exponents and logarithms. That is, they perform the operations with *e*, sometimes called *Euler's number*, as the base. Exp() computes *e* raised to the power of its argument: Exp(*X*) returns the value e^X. The Log() function is the inverse of Exp(): Log(*Y*) returns the value *X* for which e^X is equal to *Y*.

The quantity *e* may be accessed from the Math class as Math.E (approximately equal to 2.718282). It occurs very frequently in mathematics and science, and less frequently in business applications. Nonetheless, business applications do sometimes need to be able to compute exponentials and logarithms. For example, they can be used to project growth trends for sales or stock prices.

Rnd()

The Rnd() function generates random numbers, which are often necessary for business simulations. For example, we might want to simulate the arrival of customers to a bank, and we can use random numbers to produce random arrival times for the customers. Every time Rnd() is evaluated, it returns a different random fraction (greater than or equal to 0 and less than 1).

Example 4.2

GENERATING RANDOM NUMBERS

In this example, we look at a procedure that generates random numbers ranging from 0 to 10. The event procedure is shown in Figure 4.4. Each time you click on btnRandomTest, a new random number is computed and displayed. If you end execution and run the program again, you will see that it produces the same sequence each time the program is executed.

The repeated sequence is useful in some simulations because repeatability allows you to check, and recheck, the result. But the repeated sequence is inappropriate in other situations. To make the computer produce a different sequence of random numbers each time the program runs, use the following statement:

Randomize()

This statement needs to be executed only once, before the first time Rnd() is executed. A good place for it is in the Load event procedure for the form.

You might need to generate random integers that range between specific lower and upper limits. For example, you might need to generate random integers between 1 and 52 in a card game program. You can use the following expression for this:

*Int((UpperBound − LowerBound + 1) * Rnd() + LowerBound)*

As an example, the following statement stores a random integer in the range 1 to 52 (inclusive) in the variable **RndCard**.

RndCard = Int(52 * Rnd() + 1)

FIGURE 4.4

Code for Example 4.2

```
Private Sub btnRandomTest_Click(ByVal sender As System
    MsgBox(10 * Rnd())
End Sub
```

Type Conversion Functions

Visual Basic .NET has a number of functions that convert values from one type to another. For example, the CInt() function takes the argument and returns an integer value equal to the argument (rounding if necessary) of the Integer type. Type conversion is different than we saw earlier with functions such as Int() and Fix(). The return value of these two functions is the same type as the type of the argument. For example, consider the following lines of code:

```
Dim A As Double = 1.33
Dim B As Integer
B = Int(A) + CInt(A)
```

The answer stored in the variable **B** will be 2. During the evaluation of the expression, the first reference to the variable **A** (**Int(A)**) will be treated as a 64-bit Double equal to 1, but the second reference to the variable **A** (**CInt(A)**) will be treated as a 32-bit Integer equal to 1. This does not make a difference here, but there are cases where you actually want to convert one type to another. Table 4.4 shows some of the valid type conversion functions.

Avoiding Arithmetic Errors

Because of the inherent limitations of computer data types, your programs can produce mathematical errors if you do not write arithmetic expressions carefully. In this section we describe those limitations and note pitfalls you may encounter if you do not predict the results of your arithmetic expressions when designing your programs. We also describe programming practices that help you avoid these errors.

Overflow Errors

Recall that every numeric type has a largest possible value; for example, the largest value that can be stored in a variable of type Short is 32767. *Overflow* **occurs when the computer attempts to store a number that is larger than the variable can hold.** Most commonly, it occurs because the result of an expression at run time is larger than the developer anticipated when the type of the variable

Table 4.4 Type conversion functions

Function	Return Type
CBool()	Boolean
CDbl()	Double
CDec()	Decimal
CInt()	Integer
CLng()	Long
CShort()	Short
CSng()	Single
CStr()	String

was chosen at design time. Every developer encounters the overflow error from time to time, and it's best to get your initial experience with it in a small, simple program. It can occur with any type of numeric variable.

Example 4.3

OVERFLOW

The objective of this example is to show an overflow exception and how the computer reacts to it. In the event procedure shown in Figure 4.5, the user is asked to enter an integer, and the entered value is stored in the variable **X**. The variable **X** is then multiplied by 1000, and the result is stored in the variable **Y**.

What happens if the user enters the number 40 in the text box? The computer will store 40 in **X** and then evaluate the expression **1000 * X**, which results in 40000. Because 40000 is greater than 32767 (the largest value that can be stored in a variable of type Short), an overflow exception occurs when this result is stored in the variable **Y**. The error message Visual Basic .NET displays for overflow is shown in Figure 4.6.

If you click the Break button, Visual Basic .NET will switch to break mode, and you will see the Code window with the offending statement highlighted. If you click on Help, Visual Basic .NET simply explains what the three buttons do (this is not very helpful). Since an exception is being thrown, you can modify the code in Figure 4.5 by adding a Try/Catch block and dealing with the error yourself.

Roundoff Errors

Roundoff **occurs when floating-point values or variables (types Single and Double) are used in a program, because, as we discussed in Chapter 3, the computer cannot represent certain base-10 fractions exactly in base-2 using a finite number of bits.** Roundoff also occurs in manual computations. If you try to write the fraction ⅓ in base-10, the repeating fraction .3333333. . . results. At some point you decide to stop writing 3s, and so the number you write is not exactly equal to ⅓.

Because the computer rounds off fractional amounts, sometimes a program produces results that are inaccurate.

FIGURE 4.5

Code for Example 4.3

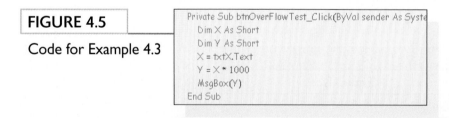

```
Private Sub btnOverFlowTest_Click(ByVal sender As Syste
    Dim X As Short
    Dim Y As Short
    X = txtX.Text
    Y = X * 1000
    MsgBox(Y)
End Sub
```

FIGURE 4.6

Overflow Error Message

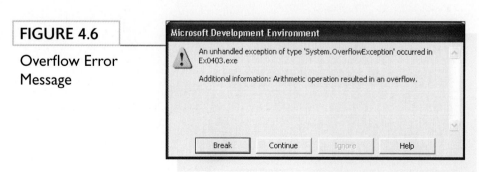

Microsoft Development Environment

An unhandled exception of type 'System.OverflowException' occurred in Ex0403.exe

Additional information: Arithmetic operation resulted in an overflow.

| Break | Continue | Ignore | Help |

FIGURE 4.7

Code for Example 4.4

```
Private Sub btnRoundoffTest_Click(ByVal sender As Syste
    Static X As Single
    X = X + 0.01
    lblResult.Text = X
End Sub
```

Example 4.4

ROUNDOFF

This example demonstrates how Visual Basic .NET can produce an incorrect answer due to roundoff. Consider the event procedure in Figure 4.7. This Click event increases the value stored in the variable **X** by 0.01 and then displays the result in a Label control. This is analogous to counting pennies: as you click on the button repeatedly, the label should display the numbers 0.01, 0.02, 0.03, and so forth. However, by the tenth execution of the procedure, the label actually displays 0.09999999, and if you keep clicking, you will see even more errors. This type of error might not be a problem in an application that estimates future sales, for example. However, most business programs that manipulate dollar amounts cannot tolerate errors like this. To correct the problem, Visual Basic .NET provides the Decimal data type. If you change the variable in this example to type Decimal, the roundoff error will not occur.

Problems Caused by Limited Significant Digits

In Chapter 3, Table 3.1 identified the precision of numeric data types and listed the number of significant digits for each type. The table also listed the range of each type. When performing arithmetic, the computer can process very large and very small numbers (range) but may not be able to keep all the digits due to limitations on the number of significant digits. For example, on September 6, 2001, the national debt was $5,774,086,630,858.16.[5] This number can be stored exactly in a variable of type Decimal. However, in a variable of type Single, it will be stored as 5.774087×10^{12}, which is equal to 5,774,087,000,000. This represents an error of $369,141.84!

We now look at an example that illustrates the loss of digits at run time.

Example 4.5

SIGNIFICANT DIGITS

This example adds two numbers and displays the result to 10 digits. Figure 4.8 shows the code. The Format() function that is discussed later in this chapter ensures that the exact value of **Z**, up to 10 digits, will be displayed. The first message box produces the answer, 10,000,000 – not the correct answer 10,000,002. This is due to the fact that any variable of type Single represents at most seven significant digits. The second message box produces the answer 100,000,000—not the correct answer of 100,000,002. The value 100,000,002 has nine significant digits, which is too much for the variable **Z**. The digits that cannot be represented are replaced with zeros. No overflow error occurs because the range of type Single allows values up to 3.4×10^{38}, and our answer is well below that limit.

---

5   Check the national debt any time at http://www.publicdebt.treas.gov/opd/opdpenny.htm.

FIGURE 4.8

Code for Example 4.5

```
Private Sub btnSignificantDigits_Click(ByVal sender As System.Object, ByVal
  Dim X, Y, Z As Single
  X = 5000001
  Y = 5000001
  Z = X + Y
  MsgBox(Format(Z, "#,###,###,###"))
  X = 50000001
  Y = 50000001
  Z = X + Y
  MsgBox(Format(Z, "#,###,###,###"))
End Sub
```

If you are writing an accounting application that has to keep track of dollar amounts exactly (to the penny), and the amounts may be greater than 99999.99, then type Single will not work. Type Decimal will work.

What is clearly a shortcoming of floating-point types in most business applications is actually a strength in many scientific applications and business simulations; the floating-point types automatically make a trade-off between the size and the precision of the numbers they store. Type Single can store numbers much larger and much smaller than type Decimal can. This is important when calculating physical quantities like the mass of the earth, 5.98×10^{24} kg. If a huge number like this is rounded off by a small amount, the result isn't going to cause geologists much of a problem. However, when you need extreme precision, you should be aware of the significant digits problem.

4.3 String Expressions

If you've worked with a word processing program to write letters or reports, you've experienced the manipulation of string data firsthand. For example, you've probably rearranged text by cutting and pasting and used commands to format the characters in your documents. In this section we describe how to manipulate strings using Visual Basic .NET's string operators and functions. These operators and functions allow you to program a variety of tasks, such as displaying messages to users in an attractive manner or searching text for a given sequence of characters.

String Operators

The only string operator in Visual Basic .NET is the & symbol, called the string concatenation operator. **To *concatenate* two values means to join them end-to-end, creating a single string.**

| Operator | | Example | |
Symbol	Name	Expression	Result
&	String concatenation	"ABC" & "123"	"ABC123"

The values to be concatenated can be any type (numeric or string), but the result of the concatenation operation will be a string. Note that if a value is numeric, Visual Basic .NET will automatically cast it to a String for you. For example, if variable **Num** is type Short and holds the number 123, then the result of the expression **Num & " Elm St"** will be the string value "123 Elm St".

FIGURE 4.9

Code for Example 4.6

```
Private Sub btnStringConcatenation_Click(ByVal sender As Sys
    Dim FirstName, LastName, FullName As String
    FirstName = txtFirstName.Text
    LastName = txtLastName.Text
    FullName = LastName & ", " & FirstName
    MsgBox("Your name is " & FullName)
    MsgBox("Hello, " & FirstName & LastName)
End Sub
```

Example 4.6

USING STRING CONCATENATION

This example demonstrates string concatenation. The user enters his or her first name and last name via a text box. When the Click event executes, they are stored in string variables and then concatenated, creating a new string in the form **LastName, FirstName**, which is then displayed to the user in a message box. The code for this example is shown in Figure 4.9.

The example shows two MsgBox statements that both use string concatenation. This illustrates a common practice: developers frequently want to display more than one data item in the message box, but the MsgBox statement allows only one expression for the message. Concatenating the data items produces a single value that can be displayed as the message.

Exercise 4.7

The message displayed by the second message box in Example 4.6 is unsatisfactory. Why is it unsatisfactory, and how can you fix it?

Functions Used with Strings

The most frequently used functions that deal with strings are listed in Table 4.5. In addition to these functions, the type conversion functions listed in Table 4.4 can convert a String into a specific numeric type and the CStr() function can convert any numeric type into a String.

Some functions take more than one argument. The arguments must be placed in the correct order, separated by commas. For example, Left("Theodolite", 4) works properly, but Left(4, "Theodolite") does not, because the Left() function requires its first argument to be string and its second argument to be numeric. Also, note that while many of our examples use constants as arguments, any expression of the correct type can be used as an argument.

Format()

In many programs, the developer wants to control the appearance of values that are displayed on the user interface. For example, dollar amounts should appear as $1,234.50 (the usual format in the United States) instead of 1234.5. The Format() function makes this easy. In its typical use, Format() converts a numeric value to string and formats it. It takes two arguments: the first is the numeric value and the second is the format specification that is type String. **The *format specification* specifies exactly how the result should appear.**

Visual Basic .NET provides a number of predefined formats for common situations, including General Number, Currency, and Percent. Many business applications use the Currency format specification to format dollar amounts.

Table 4.5 Common string functions

Function Name	Description	Example Expression	Result*
Format()	Convert to string with formatting	Format(3.5, "$#.00")	"$3.50"
Microsoft.VisualBasic.Left()[6]	Substring from left end	Microsoft.VisualBasic.Left("Theodolite", 4)	"Theo"
Microsoft.VisualBasic.Right()	Substring from right end	Microsoft.VisualBasic.Right("Theodolite", 4)	"lite"
Mid()	Substring from interior	Mid("Theodolite", 3, 4) Mid("Theodolite", 4)	"eodo" "odolite"
StrConv()	Converts a string according to the specified rule	StrConv("hello world", VbStrConv.UpperCase)	"HELLO WORLD"
Replace()	Replaces one substring with another	Replace("abracadabra", "a", "z")	"zbrzczdzbrz"
LTrim()	Trim spaces off left	LTrim(" Hello ")	"Hello "
RTrim()	Trim spaces off right	RTrim(" Hello ")	" Hello"
Trim()	Trim spaces off both	Trim(" Hello ")	"Hello"
Len()	Length of string	Len("Theodolite")	10
Space()	Generates a sequence of spaces	Space(4)	" "
InStr()	Substring search	InStr("arrows", "row")	3
Asc()	Convert character to ANSI code	Asc("A")	65
Chr()	Convert ANSI code to character	Chr(65)	"A"

*Note: All string results are shown enclosed in quotes. However, the quotes are not part of the result value.

Visual Basic .NET also provides format characters that you can use to construct your own custom specifications when none of the predefined formats is appropriate. These characters include the decimal placeholder (.), the thousands separator (,), and the digit place holders (# and 0). The # and 0 differ in how they treat leading and trailing zeros. The 0 placeholder displays a digit or a zero while the # placeholder displays a digit or nothing.

Now let's look at the use of format specifications in an example.

Example 4.7   USING THE FORMAT() FUNCTION

This example takes a user-supplied numeric value and then displays a series of message boxes with this number formatted in different ways. If you execute the event procedure in Figure 4.10 several times, enter a different number (positive, negative, with and without fractional parts, large and small) each time and note the results.

---

6   The Right() and Left() functions are also defined for the Form class. In order to resolve the ambiguity of the function names, you must qualify these function names with the namespace Microsoft.VisualBasic.

FIGURE 4.10

Code for Example 4.7

```
Private Sub btnFormatTest_Click(ByVal sender As System.Object, ByVal e As
    Dim TestNumber As Single
    TestNumber = txtTestNumber.Text
    MsgBox(TestNumber)
    MsgBox(Format(TestNumber, "Currency"))
    MsgBox(Format(TestNumber, "$#,##0.0000;($#,##0.0000)"))
    MsgBox(Format(TestNumber, "0.00%"))
    MsgBox(Format(TestNumber, "0000.###"))
End Sub
```

Format() also can be used to format strings, dates, and times. See the Visual Basic .NET documentation for further information.

Left(), Right(), and Mid()

In addition to joining strings, we often want to select portions of a string. In word processing, when you highlight a portion of a sentence or word for cutting or copying, you are selecting a substring. **A *substring* is a contiguous set of characters taken from another string.** To manipulate substrings in Visual Basic .NET, you use the Left(), Right(), and Mid() functions. Be sure to add the namespace qualifier, Microsoft.VisualBasic, in front of the Left() and Right() function names so that Visual Basic uses the correct String functions.

If the desired substring is located at an end of the given string, use Left() or Right(). Each of these functions requires two arguments: the first argument is the given string and the second argument is the number of characters in the desired substring. So **Left("Theodolite", 4)** returns the left-most four characters from the string "Theodolite", that is, "Theo", and **Right("Theodolite", 4)** returns the right-most four characters, "lite".

If the desired substring is somewhere in the middle of the string, use Mid(). In its typical use, this function takes three arguments: the first is the given string, the second is the character position of the start of the desired substring, and the third is the number of characters in the desired substring. Thus, **Mid("Theodolite", 3, 4)** says to start at character position 3 (the first "e") and extract four characters, "eodo".

When you want to extract a substring from the right end of the given string and you know the starting character position of the desired substring (instead of the number of characters in the desired substring) you can use Mid() with just two arguments. Thus, **Mid("Theodolite", 4)** returns the substring that starts at character position 4 (the "o") and extends to the right end: "odolite".

StrConv()[7]

The StrConv() function converts a string into a new string using a number of predefined conversion rules. The general syntax is StrConv(str-exp, conv-const). The argument "str-exp" is the string to be converted and the argument "conv-const" is one of the predefined constants on the following page.

---

[7] In addition to the StrConv() function, Visual Basic .NET has a function named UCase() that converts a string to uppercase and another function named LCase() that converts a string to lowercase. These two functions may be used as alternatives to the StrConv() function.

Conversion Constant	Meaning
VbStrConv.UpperCase	Converts the string to uppercase characters.
VbStrConv.LowerCase	Converts the string to lowercase characters.
VbStrConv.ProperCase	Converts the first letter of every word in string to uppercase.

So **StrConv("seattle mariners baseball team", VbStrConv.ProperCase)** produces the string "Seattle Mariners Baseball Team".

LTrim0, RTrim0, and Trim0

LTrim() removes spaces from the left end only, RTrim() from the right end only, and Trim() from both ends. Each of these functions takes only one argument, which must be type String, and removes only leading/trailing spaces, not embedded spaces.

Example 4.8

TRIMMING SPACES

The event procedure in Figure 4.11 demonstrates the effect of LTrim(), RTrim(), and Trim(). If you run this example, the composer name in each message box will clearly illustrate what each function does (you should see the spaces before and after the composer's name get trimmed).

Len0

The Len() function takes as an argument a string and returns the number of characters in the string. Be sure to note that this count includes every character, including letters, digits, spaces, punctuation, and special characters. For example, **Len("Quick, jump!")** is 12.

Space0

The Space() function takes one numeric argument that indicates the number of space characters to generate. For example, **Space(80)** returns a string consisting of 80 spaces.

InStr0

The InStr() function performs a string search operation. It takes two arguments: a base string and a substring that we want to try to find within the base string. InStr() searches through the base string, proceeding from left to right, and stops

FIGURE 4.11

Code for Example 4.8

```
Private Sub btnTrimTest_Click(ByVal sender As System.Object, ByVal e As Sy
    Dim Composer, Country As String
    Composer = "    Bela Bartok    "
    Country = "Hungary"
    MsgBox("Composer " & Composer & " was a native of " & Country)
    MsgBox("Composer " & LTrim(Composer) & " was a native of " & Country)
    MsgBox("Composer " & RTrim(Composer) & " was a native of " & Country)
    MsgBox("Composer " & Trim(Composer) & " was a native of " & Country)
End Sub
```

when it encounters a match or reaches the end of the base string. If the search is successful, InStr() returns the character position at which the match was found; if unsuccessful, it returns the number 0.

For example, InStr("Eventful adventure","advent") returns the number 10, since the string "advent" occurs starting at position 10 in the first string (the base string); but InStr("Eventful adventure","venturi") returns the number 0.

Sometimes the second string occurs more than once in the base string. Using InStr() as described above, you can find only the first occurrence. There is, however, a second form of InStr() that enables you to find all occurrences. This form takes three arguments: the first is the character position at which to start the search, the second is the base string, and the third is the substring to locate within the base. The search again proceeds through the base string from left to right, and stops when InStr() encounters a match or encounters the end of the base string.

For example, InStr(1,"Eventful adventure","vent") returns the number 2, which is the first occurrence of "vent" that the search encounters when it begins the search at position 1. But InStr(3,"Eventful adventure","vent") returns the value 12, which is the first occurrence of "vent" that the search encounters when it begins the search at position 3 (which is past the start of the first "vent" in "Eventful"). Finally, InStr(13,"Eventful adventure","vent") returns 0. Code similar to the following could be used to perform this multiple search:

```
FirstPos = InStr(1,"Eventful adventure","vent")
SecondPos = InStr(FirstPos + 1,"Eventful adventure","vent")
ThirdPos = InStr(SecondPos + 1,"Eventful adventure","vent")
```

When this code is executed, **FirstPos** equals 2, **SecondPos** equals 12, and **ThirdPos** equals 0. Although this code works, it is not general; that is, it only works when trying to find the substring "vent" in the string "Eventful adventure" three times. A better solution uses string variables instead of string constants as the arguments. An even better solution also would search for the substring as many times as it might occur and not be limited to just three searches.

By default, the searches are *case sensitive,* meaning that **they consider lowercase and uppercase letters to be different.** Thus, InStr("BAH!","ah") returns 0 because "ah" is different from "AH". When using the three-argument form of InStr() you can make the search case insensitive by including the numeric constant CompareMethod.Text as a fourth argument. For example, InStr(1,"BAH!","ah", CompareMethod.Text) returns 2. You also can change the Option Compare parameter to "Text" to make the search case insensitive.

Example 4.9

MANIPULATING NAMES

The event procedure in Figure 4.12 uses the string functions Left(), Mid(), Trim(), and InStr(). Its manipulation of first and last names is similar to, but more sophisticated than, what we saw in Example 4.6. Assume that we have the situation

---

FIGURE 4.12

Code for Example 4.9

```
Private Sub btnNameReversal_Click(ByVal sender As System.Object, ByVal e
    Dim WholeName, FirstName, LastName As String
    Dim CommaPos As Short
    WholeName = txtName.Text
    CommaPos = InStr(1, WholeName, ",")
    FirstName = Trim(Mid(WholeName, CommaPos + 1))
    LastName = Trim(Microsoft.VisualBasic.Left(WholeName, CommaPos - 1))
    MsgBox("Welcome, " & FirstName & " " & LastName)
End Sub
```

where the user enters the name "Beethoven, Ludwig Van" in the text box. The InStr() function will find the comma at position 10.

It then uses the position of the comma (**CommaPos**) to split the name into first name and last name.

Asc() and Chr()

Internally, the computer represents string data as a sequence of numeric codes, with one code for each character in the string. The coding scheme used by Visual Basic .NET is called Unicode. Unicode uses 2 bytes (16 bits) to store each character. Using 2 bytes for each character allows a total of 65,536 different characters. **Another coding scheme, called *ANSI*, uses one byte (8 bits) to store each character.** ANSI defines 256 different characters. The 256 characters of the ANSI coding scheme are identical to the first 256 characters in the Unicode coding scheme. Table 4.6 shows these 256 characters and their numeric values.

The characters in positions 0 through 31 of the ANSI table are *nonprintable characters* that, as their name implies, cannot be printed or displayed (for example, in a label) but that control certain computer operations. Table 4.6 shows short descriptive names (orange) for each of the nonprintable characters.

The Asc() function takes as its argument a single-character string and returns the character's numeric code using the ANSI table. For example, **Asc("a")** returns the number 97. Why is this function named Asc()? Because the predecessor to the ANSI code was ASCII (American Standard Code for Information Interchange). The ASCII code uses only seven bits and therefore can represent only 128 characters. In fact, the first half of the ANSI code is identical to the ASCII code.

The Chr() function does the opposite of Asc(): it takes a number as its argument and returns the character that resides at that position in the ANSI table. For example, **Chr(65)** returns the string "A".

Now let's look at three examples that demonstrate how the Chr() and Asc() functions help us manipulate strings in our programs.

| Example 4.10 | **USING CARRIAGE RETURN AND LINE FEED** |

In the early days of computing, people used Teletype machines to interact with the computer. These devices were much like typewriters in that they had a printing mechanism—called the carriage—that moved across the paper from left to right. When the user pressed the key labeled [RETURN], the carriage would return to the left edge of the paper and the paper would be advanced one line. The terms used to describe these actions were carriage return and line feed. Although your computer screen does not have a carriage, these terms are still used. *Carriage return* **means move the screen cursor to the left of the text field, and *line feed* means move down one row in the text field.**

Carriage return and line feed are supported by two nonprintable ANSI characters. The carriage return, abbreviated cr, has numeric code 13, and the line feed, lf, has numeric code 10. Together, these characters make it possible to display multiple lines in a message box or label Text, as illustrated by the event procedure in Figure 4.13.

Because the carriage return and line feed characters are nonprintable, one of the ways of specifying them in expressions is to use the Chr() function. The message box displayed by this example is shown in Figure 4.14.

Table 4.6 Ansi code

0	null	32	space	64	@	96	`	128		160		192	À	224	à
1	soh	33	!	65	A	97	a	129		161	¡	193	Á	225	á
2	stx	34	"	66	B	98	b	130	,	162	¢	194	Â	226	â
3	etx	35	#	67	C	99	c	131	ƒ	163	£	195	Ã	227	ã
4	eot	36	$	68	D	100	d	132	„	164		196	Ä	228	ä
5	enq	37	%	69	E	101	e	133	…	165	¥	197	Å	229	å
6	ack	38	&	70	F	102	f	134	†	166	|	198	Æ	230	æ
7	bell	39	'	71	G	103	g	135	‡	167	§	199	Ç	231	ç
8	backspace	40	(	72	H	104	h	136	^	168	¨	200	È	232	è
9	tab	41	)	73	I	105	i	137	‰	169	©	201	É	233	é
10	lf	42	*	74	J	106	j	138	S	170	ª	202	Ê	234	ê
11	vt	43	+	75	K	107	k	139	‹	171	«	203	Ë	235	ë
12	ff	44	,	76	L	108	l	140	Œ	172	¬	204	Ì	236	ì
13	cr	45	-	77	M	109	m	141		173	-	205	Í	237	í
14	so	46	.	78	N	110	n	142		174	®	206	Î	238	î
15	sl	47	/	79	O	111	o	143		175	¯	207	Ï	239	ï
16	dle	48	0	80	P	112	p	144		176	°	208	Δ	240	∂
17	dc1	49	1	81	Q	113	q	145	'	177	±	209	Ñ	241	ñ
18	dc2	50	2	82	R	114	r	146	'	178	²	210	Ò	242	ò
19	dc3	51	3	83	S	115	s	147	"	179	³	211	Ó	243	ó
20	dc4	52	4	84	T	116	t	148	"	180	´	212	Ô	244	ô
21	nak	53	5	85	U	117	u	149		181	µ	213	Õ	245	õ
22	syn	54	6	86	V	118	v	150	–	182	¶	214	Ö	246	ö
23	etb	55	7	87	W	119	w	151	—	183	·	215	×	247	÷
24	can	56	8	88	X	120	x	152	~	184	¸	216	Ø	248	ø
25	em	57	9	89	Y	121	y	153	™	185	¹	217	Ù	249	ù
26	sub	58	:	90	Z	122	z	154	s	186	º	218	Ú	250	ú
27	escape	59	;	91	[	123	{	155	›	187	»	219	Û	251	û
28	fs	60	<	92	\	124	|	156	œ	188	¼	220	Ü	252	ü
29	gs	61	=	93	]	125	}	157		189	½	221	Ý	253	ý
30	rs	62	>	94	^	126	~	158		190	¾	222	Φ	254	φ
31	us	63	?	95	_	127	delete	159	Ÿ	191	¿	223	β	255	ÿ

FIGURE 4.13

Code for
Example 4.10

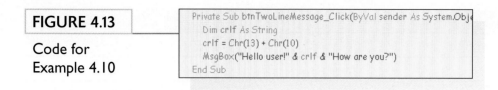

```
Private Sub btnTwoLineMessage_Click(ByVal sender As System.Obj
    Dim crlf As String
    crlf = Chr(13) + Chr(10)
    MsgBox("Hello user!" & crlf & "How are you?")
End Sub
```

FIGURE 4.14

Message Box with
Two Lines Created
Using Carriage
Return and Line
Feed

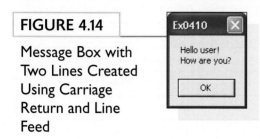

Ex0410

Hello user!
How are you?

OK

Example 4.11

USING MULTIPLE-LINE MESSAGES AND vbCrLf

Because developers frequently need to use the carriage return/line feed combination, Visual Basic .NET provides a predefined constant named vbCrLf whose value is equal to Chr(13) & Chr(10). This example demonstrates the use of this constant (see Figure 4.15). It embellishes the two-line message in Example 4.10 with strings consisting of 10 asterisks. The message box displayed by this example when the user enters "Nixon, Richard" in the text box is shown in Figure 4.16.

Example 4.12

USING SIMPLE ENCRYPTION

As an example of the power of the Asc() and Chr() functions, consider the problem of encrypting messages. **An *encrypted message* is a message that has been encoded into a different set of characters.** One reason for encryption is to protect the privacy of a message during transmission. The encrypted message will be unintelligible to anyone who gains access to it but does not know the coding scheme. Businesses use encryption when sending sensitive data such as financial transactions over a network.

FIGURE 4.15

Code for
Example 4.11

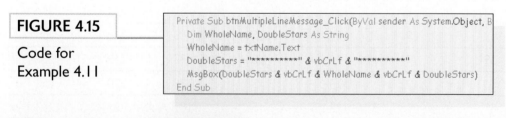

```
Private Sub btnMultipleLineMessage_Click(ByVal sender As System.Object, B
    Dim WholeName, DoubleStars As String
    WholeName = txtName.Text
    DoubleStars = "**********" & vbCrLf & "**********"
    MsgBox(DoubleStars & vbCrLf & WholeName & vbCrLf & DoubleStars)
End Sub
```

FIGURE 4.16

Example 4.11
Message Box

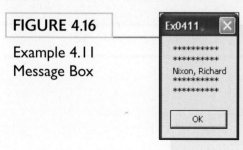

Ex0411

****
****
Nixon, Richard
****
****

OK

FIGURE 4.17

Code for
Example 4.12

```
Private Sub btnCaesarCipher_Click(ByVal sender As System.Object, ByVal e
    Dim Letter As String
    Letter = txtLetter.Text
    lblPlainText.Text = lblPlainText.Text & Letter
    lblCipherText.Text = lblCipherText.Text + Chr(Asc(Letter) + 3)
    txtLetter.Text = ""
End Sub
```

The encryption procedure transforms the original message, called plaintext, into an unintelligible form, called ciphertext. The sender and receiver agree in advance on the transformation method, and the recipient, of course, must be able to transform the ciphertext back into plaintext. The transformation method must be clever enough that a third party, who isn't told the details of the method, can't easily decipher the cipher (i.e., transform the ciphertext back into plaintext).

One of the first encryption methods ever devised is called the Caesar cipher. In this method each letter in the plaintext is shifted by three positions in the alphabet; that is, "A" is changed to "D", "B" to "E", and so on. This is easily accomplished using the Asc() and Chr() functions along with a simple addition operation as illustrated in Figure 4.17.

Before each time the procedure btnCaesarCipher_Click is executed, the user is expected to enter a letter into the text box. This letter is concatenated to the Text property of the label lblPlaintext. Then the letter is converted to its ANSI code, which is then increased by 3 and converted back into an ANSI character, and this converted character is concatenated to the Text property of the label lblCiphertext.

There is nothing special about the number 3; as long as both the sender and receiver agree in advance on the number, any shift amount will work. Knowing the shift amount, the receiver can easily transform the ciphertext back into plaintext.

Replace()

The Replace() function searches a string for the occurrence of a substring and replaces the substring with a second substring. It works just like the search and replace function found in most word processing programs. The first argument is a string expression that will be searched; the second argument is the substring being searched for, and the third argument is the replacement substring that will replace the substring used as the second argument. For example, the function **Replace("VB is cool. VB is also awesome", "VB", "VB .NET")** produces the string "VB .NET is cool. VB .NET is also awesome".

There are three additional optional arguments. A fourth (optional) argument indicates where in the original string to start the search. If you leave this off, the search starts at character position 1 of the original string. The fifth (optional) argument is a numeric value indicating how many substring replacements to perform. If omitted, the function will make all the replacements it can find. The sixth (optional) argument is used to indicate if the search is case sensitive. By default, the search is case sensitive.

Exercise 4.8

Write a Click event procedure for a button that shortens the value displayed by a Label control named lblTest by removing one character from its right end. For example, suppose lblTest.Text initially holds the value "visual". The first time the user clicks the button, the value in lblTest.Text should be changed to "visua"; the second time the user clicks the button, lblTest.Text should be changed to "visu"; the third time "vis"; and so on.

Your event procedure should work regardless of the value initially displayed by lblTest. You can assume the user will not click the button if the value in lblTest.Text is the zero-length string, that is, it is empty.

Exercise 4.9

Repeat Exercise 4.8, but make your event procedure remove the character from the left end instead of the right end. For example, if lblTest.Text holds the value "visual" before the user clicks the button, then it should hold the value "isual" after the user clicks the button.

Exercise 4.10

What is the length of the zero-length string, **Len("")**?

Exercise 4.11

In btnCaesarCipher_Click in Example 4.12, what happens if the user enters more than one letter in the text box? Run the example to find out.

Exercise 4.12

Write a procedure that performs the inverse operation of btnCaesar Cipher_Click in Example 4.12. That is, the user should enter the letters in ciphertext, and your event procedure should display the corresponding plaintext letters.

Exercise 4.13

In btnCaesarCipher_Click (Example 4.12), what characters are the letters X, Y, and Z transformed into?

Exercise 4.14

Modify btnCaesarCipher_Click (Example 4.12) so it performs a cyclic shift. That is, it should transform X into A, Y into B, and Z into C, and all other letters should still be shifted up by three characters.

Exercise 4.15

Modify your solution to Exercise 4.14 so that it still performs a cyclic shift, but the amount of the shift is given by a symbolic constant named SHIFTAMOUNT. For example, if SHIFTAMOUNT is equal to 4, then W, X, Y, and Z should be transformed into A, B, C, and D, respectively, and all other letters should be shifted up by four characters. Your event procedure should work properly for any value of SHIFTAMOUNT between 1 and 25.

Exercise 4.16

Suppose we wanted to modify the btnCaesarCipher_Click event procedure (Example 4.12) to allow the user to enter the whole plaintext string in the text box instead of entering a single letter at a time. We have not seen all the Visual Basic .NET statements to make this possible. Write down instructions you would give to an assistant to perform this task manually using the ANSI table and pencil and paper. Be specific—assume the assistant can follow directions precisely but doesn't have the ability to fill in any missing information in your instructions.

4.4 The Try/Catch Block Revisited

We first saw the use of the Try/Catch block in Chapter 3, where it was used to detect and react to an exception that was thrown at run time. In Chapter 3 we presented a simplified version and in this section we will expand the definition of the Try/Catch block and see how this expanded definition is helpful.

Assume you have the code shown in Figure 4.18. There is a possibility of two different errors that could be generated by this code. The first would be the result of the user entering a value that is not a valid number. This would cause an

FIGURE 4.18

A Simple Procedure to Compute a Square Root

```
Private Sub btnComputeSqrt_Click(ByVal sender As System.Object, ByVal e
    Dim N As Short
    Dim S As Double
    N = txtUserValue.Text
    S = Math.Sqrt(N)
    lblSqrt.Text = S
End Sub
```

FIGURE 4.19

Adding a Try/Catch Block to Detect and Catch the Possible Exceptions

```
Private Sub btnComputeSqrt_Click(ByVal sender As System.Ob
    Dim N As Short
    Dim S As Double
    Try
        N = txtUserValue.Text
        S = Math.Sqrt(N)
        lblSqrt.Text = S
    Catch
        MsgBox("What do we tell the user here?")
    End Try
End Sub
```

InvalidCastException to be thrown. The other error is possible if the user enters a value that is a valid number, but is larger than 32767. This could cause an OverflowExecption to be thrown.

If we add a Try/Catch block as we saw in Chapter 3, we would see code like that in Figure 4.19. The problem with this is we end up in the Catch block regardless of which exception was thrown, so we are left with a problem of what to tell the user. If we say something like "There's either an overflow or invalid number", then it's up to the user to decide which error occurred (if the user even knows what we mean).

Since multiple errors are common, the Try/Catch block has a way of handling the situation. Here is pseudocode of full syntax of the Try/Catch block.

```
Try
        ' Starts a structured exception handler.
        ' Place executable statements that may generate
        ' an exception in this block.
Catch [optional filters]
        'This code runs if the statements listed in
        ' the Try block fail and the filter on the Catch statement is True.
[Additional Catch blocks]
Finally
        'This code always runs immediately before
        ' the Try statement exits.
End Try
        ' Ends a structured exception handler.
```

The difference we see here is the ability to provide more than one Catch block with each having a different "filter." We also see the Finally block that defines a segment of code that is executed no matter what happens in the Try or Catch blocks. We'll start with a discussion of the multiple filtered Catch blocks.

One form of a filter is based on the exception that is thrown. For example, you could say:

```
Catch OE As OverflowException
        MsgBox("The number you entered is too large (max 32767)")
```

This would catch an OverflowException. Note how the error message can be much more direct. The identifier **OE** is an object reference to the actual error object that was thrown.[8] The actual identifier (**OE** in the case) is an arbitrary value determined by the developer just like any other variable name. The Exception class includes a number of properties such as Message and Source. It also includes methods such as GetBaseException() and ToString(). The Message property holds the actual error message that the system would display if the exception were not caught. The Source property details the name of the application or the object that causes the exception. The GetBaseException() method gets the original exception that was thrown and the ToString() method returns a string describing the exception.

Since we have two possible exceptions that we need to catch, we simply add two filtered Catch blocks, one for the OverflowException and another for the InvalidCastException. Figure 4.20 shows this code.

The order of the catch blocks can be important (although it is not important in Figure 4.20). The flow of control has the Catch blocks executed from top to bottom. The first catch block that is valid for the particular exception is the one and only one that is executed. If you have an unfiltered Catch block, that is, one that has no filter (like the one in Figure 4.19), the unfiltered catch block will catch any exception. So if you have multiple Catch blocks, never put the unfiltered one first because it will catch all exceptions and the remaining Catch block(s) will never get executed.

Also note the Finally block in Figure 4.20. This block of code is executed regardless of what happens in the Try and/or the Catch blocks. In this code, the message box displaying "Hello Mom :)" will always be displayed. In the example in Figure 4.20 the Finally block serves no useful function except for demonstrating the concept. It is typically used when the code in the Try block has made a connection to some nonsharable resource such as a database or an Internet IP address. In situations such as this, it is important to release the resource for others to use regardless of whether an exception was thrown or not.

It is also possible to create and "throw" your own exceptions. This might be necessary if you detect a problem that does not normally cause an exception. For example, assume you want to make sure that the values in a TextBox are valid numbers **and** are not empty. An exception will be thrown if the user enters a

---

FIGURE 4.20

Using Multiple Catch Blocks

```
Private Sub btnComputeSqrt_Click(ByVal sender As System.Object, ByVal e
    Dim N As Short
    Dim S As Double
    Try
        N = txtUserValue.Text
        S = Math.Sqrt(N)
        lblSqrt.Text = S
    Catch oe As OverflowException
        MsgBox("The number you entered is too large (max 32767)")
    Catch ice As InvalidCastException
        MsgBox("You must enter a valid numeric value")
    Finally
        MsgBox("hello Mom :)")
    End Try
End Sub
```

---

8   This is why it's called "throwing an exception." When an exception is detected, a new object is instantiated from a subclass of the Exception class. This object is then "thrown" to be caught by an exception handler.

value in the TextBox that is not numeric if you try to store the contents of the TextBox into a numeric variable. However, storing an empty TextBox into a numeric variable does not cause an exception to be thrown.

To handle this situation you can create your own exception object. This is done with a Dim statement as follows:

Dim *identifier* **As New Exception**(*MessageString*)

where *identifier* is the name of the Exception object and *MessageString* is a message associated with the exception object. You may then "throw" this exception with a Throw statement. Its syntax is

Throw *ExceptionObject*

The following code segment checks to see if a TextBox is empty and if it is, creates and throws an exception. It also catches this exception as well as any other exceptions. (*Note:* We cover the if statement in Chapter 5.)

```
Dim Income As Double
Try
    If txtIncome.Text = "" Then
        Dim MyException As New Exception("Empty field not valid")
        Throw MyException
    End If
    Income = txtIncome.Text
    lblIncome.Text = Income
Catch Ex As Exception
    MsgBox(Ex.Message)
End Try
```

An empty TextBox causes the exception to be created and thrown. The "Catch" statement catches this exception and the MsgBox() statement will display the message "Empty field not valid".

4.5 Project 4: A Present Value Calculator

This project uses arithmetic expressions, string expressions, and text boxes to create a present value calculator. It also addresses the issue of testing, that is, verifying that the project works correctly before giving the finished application to the user.

Present value is a measure of the value of a future cash flow in today's dollars. To see why this measure is useful, consider the choice you'd make if someone offered you $1,000 today or $1,000 a year from now. If you accept the $1,000 today, you can deposit it in an interest-bearing account or invest it— and a year from now you'll have more than $1,000. The difference in the value of money over time is measured by present value. Financial analysts often use present value to compare investments offering different payments over time to determine which is the most profitable.

The present value calculator we develop in this section answers the question, "What amount would you have to invest today in order to accumulate a given amount in the future?" The user has to input the time period of the investment, the interest rate, and the **amount of money to be accumulated, called the** *future value*.

FIGURE 4.21

User Interface for
Project 4

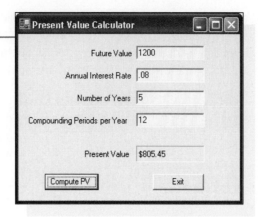

Description of the Application

The form for this application appears in Figure 4.21. The user first enters values
into the text boxes for Future Value, Annual Interest Rate, Number of Years, and
Compounding Periods/Year and then clicks the Compute PV button. The computer uses the input values to calculate the present value (PV) using the following formula:

$$PV = FV/(1 + r/m)^{(n \times m)}$$

where: FV is the future value.
r is the annual interest rate.
n is the number of years.
m is the number of compounding periods/year.

For the number-of-compounding-periods-per-year parameter, if the user enters
12, this means that interest is compounded monthly; if he or she enters 4, then
the interest is compounded quarterly; and so forth.

Design of the Application

As always, before beginning construction of the project, you have to make some
decisions regarding controls, properties, constants, variables, and scope. Figure
4.22 shows property settings for the controls on the form.

FIGURE 4.22

Present Value
Calculator Controls

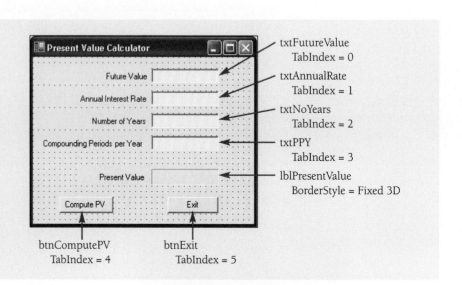

Table 4.7 Variables in the present value calculator	
Variable Name	Type
PresentValue	Decimal
FutureValue	Decimal
InterestRate	Decimal
NumberOfPeriods	Short
NumberOfPeriodsPerYr	Short

Since all calculations are performed in a single event procedure (Compute PV), all constants and variables in the project can be local to that event procedure. Are any symbolic constants needed? In this case, the answer is no since the only constant used is the value 1 and it is a part of the formula that never changes. Note that defining a symbolic constant named **ONE** that is equal to 1 does not make the code more readable or maintainable.

What variables are needed? Use a variable for each quantity involved in the calculation (i.e., for each quantity in the present value formula). Table 4.7 shows good names and types for these variables.

Construction of the Application

As always, start the project by creating a new folder in which to save it. As you proceed, be sure to save periodically.

Open a new project and place the controls on the form. Arrange the controls and set their properties as in Figure 4.22. Next, create the Click event procedure for the Exit button. This event procedure should contain the single statement End, which simply causes execution to terminate.

Run the program and verify that the (TAB) key moves the focus from control to control and that clicking the Exit button causes the program to terminate. You can change the TabIndex property of a control if you want to change its position in the tab cycle.

Next, create the Click event procedure for the Compute PV button (see Figure 4.23). This procedure stores the values from the text boxes in the appropriate variables and then calculates the present value using the present value formula. It then displays the present value formatted as a dollar amount. After you've completed this event procedure, run the program and verify that it works properly.

FIGURE 4.23

Click Event Procedure for the Compute PV Button

```
Private Sub btnComputePV_Click(ByVal sender As System.Object, ByVal e As System.EventArgs) Hand
    Dim PresentValue, FutureValue As Decimal
    Dim InterestRate As Single, NoOfYrs As Short
    Dim PeriodsPerYr As Short
    Try
        FutureValue = txtFutureValue.Text
        InterestRate = txtAnnualRate.Text
        NoOfYrs = txtNoYears.Text
        PeriodsPerYr = txtPPY.Text
        PresentValue = FutureValue / (1 + InterestRate / PeriodsPerYr) ^ (NoOfYrs * PeriodsPerYr)
        lblPresentValue.Text = Format(PresentValue, "Currency")
    Catch
        MsgBox("Please enter valid numeric values for each parameter")
    End Try
End Sub
```

Table 4.8 Tests for verifying present value calculations

Input Values				Result
Future Value	Annual Interest Rate	Number of Years	Compounding Periods per Year	Present Value
1	0%	1	1	1
1	1%	0	1	1
1	12%	.08333	1	Approximately 0.5
1	1%	100	1	Almost 0

Testing the Application

It is always important to test a program thoroughly before users start to rely on it. How can you be sure the present value displayed by your program is correct? The calculations are complicated enough that you shouldn't take this for granted.

One way to test this program is to compare the results it produces with results produced by another program that is known to be correct. You might, for example, have a spreadsheet or calculator that performs the same calculation. For simple problems like this, you also can compute some answers by hand.[9]

If you don't have another program to use as a check, you should at least perform some commonsense checks. You usually can develop checks like this by examining the formulas used in the calculations. Table 4.8 shows some simple checks that were derived from the present value formula. For example, the last check simply means that if the interest rate is high and the number of compounding periods is high, then the present value will be low.

A final comment regarding testing and user-friendliness is in order. Users commonly expect to see interest rates in two different forms: as decimal numbers (0.12) or as percentages (12 percent). The user interface shown in Figure 4.21 does not tell the user which form to use. If the expressions in your event procedure assume one form and the user employs the other form, the computed result will be incorrect.

A well-designed user interface accepts all reasonable input, or else informs the user of the required format of values. It also displays error messages when the user fails to provide data in a format that the program can accept. Thus, while testing you should test for the program's response if the user enters bad data. We will see how to program these checks in later chapters.

4.6 Logical Expressions

Almost all computer programs have to perform tasks that involve selecting an action from several alternative actions. For example, depending on the value of an account balance, a billing program might have to select an action that would cause an overdue-payment notice to be sent. And depending on the number of hours worked, a payroll program might have to pay a higher rate for some of the hours (overtime hours). Logical expressions, as mentioned earlier, are used in

---

9   Visual Basic .NET has a built-in function named PV(). It too computes the present value. You might want to use this function to test the correctness of your program.

programs to evaluate the conditions (account balance overdue or hours greater than 40) that dictate the correct action to select. In this section we examine logical expressions, and we will see their full utility in Chapter 5.

A logical expression, sometimes called a Boolean expression, always evaluates to either the value True or False. The simplest logical expressions use **comparison operators to compare one value to another.** Using *logical operators* **to combine results from comparisons** can form more powerful logical expressions.

Comparison Operators

The comparison operators, which compare two expressions, are shown in Table 4.9. The result of a comparison is always either True or False.

Most often developers use comparison operators to compare two variables or a variable and a constant. It's unlikely that you would see the comparison 2 < 3 in an actual program, because the developer knows in advance that this expression is True, so there's no reason to make the computer evaluate it.

As an example of a useful comparison, consider the following: **Price < 10.** As with any expression containing variables, to evaluate this expression the computer will first retrieve the value stored in the variable **Price.** If this value is less than 10, the result of the expression is True; otherwise it is False.

If you compare one numeric value to another numeric value, the result is the same as in algebra; for example, the expression 2 < 3 is True. You can compare a string value to a numeric value if the string value has the form of a number; in this case, Visual Basic .NET casts the string value to numeric before performing the comparison. Thus, the expression "2" < 3 is True. However, if you attempt to compare a string value to a numeric value and the string value does not have the form of a number, Visual Basic .NET throws an InvalidCastException. For example, the expression "2a" < 3 would throw this exception.

Comparing two string values is a little more complicated than comparing two numeric values.

Table 4.9 Comparison operators

Operator		Example*	
Symbol	Name	Expression	Result
<	Less than	a < b	True
		b < b	False
<=	Less than or equal to	b <= b	True
		b <= –4	False
>	Greater than	–2 > b	False
		c > a	True
>=	Greater than or equal to	a >= a	True
		a >= 5	False
=	Equal to	b = b	True
		b = c	False
<>	Not equal to	b <> b	False
		b <> c	True

*Assume numeric variables a, b, and c have been declared and contain the values 2, 3, and 4, respectively.

Comparison of Strings

Strings are ranked alphabetically, much as words are arranged in a dictionary. There are, however, some differences between Visual Basic .NET's dictionary order and what you might think of as dictionary order. These differences are a result of the way Visual Basic .NET interprets uppercase and lowercase letters and nonletter symbols. These are treated according to the ANSI table. In technical language, we say that the ANSI code defines Visual Basic .NET's *collating sequence*—**the idea of an alphabetical order extended to include all 256 symbols of the ANSI table.**

To compare two string values, Visual Basic .NET first compares the first character of one to the first character of the other. If they are not equal, then the smaller string value is the one whose first character has the lower ANSI value. If they are equal, then Visual Basic .NET compares the second character from one string to the second character of the other string. If these characters are not equal, then the smaller string value is the one whose second character has the lower ANSI value. If they are equal, then Visual Basic .NET compares the third character from one string to the third character of the other string, and so on.

This process can end in three ways. In the first case, Visual Basic .NET finds the first instance (from the left) where corresponding characters in the two strings are different, and identifies the smaller of the two strings accordingly. This case would arise in the comparison of **"VISIBLE"** to **"VISUAL"**; the first three characters are identical, but the fourth characters differ, and since "I" comes before "U" in the ANSI table, **"VISIBLE"** is less than **"VISUAL"**.

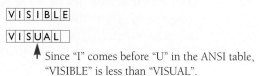

Since "I" comes before "U" in the ANSI table,
"VISIBLE" is less than "VISUAL".

In the second case, Visual Basic .NET reaches the end of one string (no more characters) before identifying any different characters and before reaching the end of the other string. This would arise in the comparison of **"VISUAL"** to **"VISUALLY"**; the first string is six characters long, the first six characters of the two strings are identical, and the second string is longer than six characters. In this case, the shorter string is the lesser of the two.

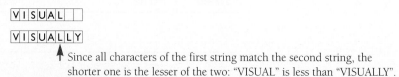

Since all characters of the first string match the second string, the
shorter one is the lesser of the two: "VISUAL" is less than "VISUALLY".

In the third case, Visual Basic .NET reaches the end of both strings at the same time without identifying any different characters. An example of this case is the comparison of **"HELLO, USER"** to **"HELLO, USER"**. In this case the strings are equal.

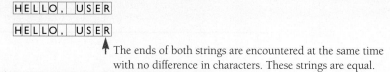

The ends of both strings are encountered at the same time
with no difference in characters. These strings are equal.

Finally, note that every character, including spaces, digits, punctuation marks, and other special symbols, is used in string comparisons, and the case of the letters (lowercase versus uppercase) counts. For example, the string **"lex icon"** is less than the string **"lexi con"** because the space character (position 32 in the ANSI table) comes before the "i" (position 105) in the ANSI table. Note also that

FIGURE 4.24

Code for
Example 4.13

```
Private Sub btnComparisonTest_Click(ByVal sender As System.O
    Dim Price As Decimal, GoodPrice As Boolean
    Price = 5 + Rnd() * 10
    GoodPrice = Price < 10
    MsgBox("Is " & Price & " a good price? " & GoodPrice)
End Sub
```

all uppercase letters appear before all lowercase letters in the ANSI table. Thus, for example, "SMALL" is less than "small".

Example 4.13

TRUE AND FALSE

You can make a logical expression easier to interpret by storing its result in a descriptively named variable of type Boolean. Figure 4.24 shows a procedure that illustrates this point. The variable **Price** is set equal to a random number ranging from 5 to 14.9999. Remember that the Rnd() function returns a value less than 1 and greater than or equal to 0. The logical expression **Price < 10** will be True if the value stored in **Price** is less than 10. Otherwise the logical expression will be False. The result is stored in the variable **GoodPrice**, so **GoodPrice** will be True if price is less than 10. That is, **Price < 10** means that you got a good price.

Example 4.14

ASSIGNMENT VERSUS EQUALITY COMPARISON

Assignment statements with comparison operators can sometimes look a little confusing, because in Visual Basic .NET the equal sign plays two roles: assignment operator and equality comparison operator. Consider the event procedure in Figure 4.25, which is entirely valid.

Any statement that begins with a variable (or control property) followed by an equal sign is an assignment statement, and the first (i.e., left-most) equal sign in an assignment statement is always the assignment operator. Everything to the right of the assignment operator is the expression, and any equal sign in an expression is a comparison operator. So the assignment statement in Figure 4.25 is perfectly valid. However, you can write it more clearly by using parentheses:

ExactlyTwenty = (Age = 20)

Exercise 4.17

What does the message box display?

```
Private Sub btnZeroLengthStringTest_Click()
    Dim X As String
    Dim Y As Boolean
    Y = (X = "")
    MsgBox(Y)
End Sub
```

FIGURE 4.25

Code for
Example 4.14

```
Private Sub btnEquityTest_Click(ByVal sender As System.O
    Dim Age As Short
    Dim ExactlyTwenty As Boolean
    Age = txtAge.Text
    ExactlyTwenty = Age = 20
    MsgBox("Exactly twenty? " & ExactlyTwenty)
End Sub
```

Exercise 4.18

Consider the following event procedure.

```
Private Sub btnAgeThreshold_Click()
    Dim Age As String
    Dim UnderTwenty As Boolean
    Age = txtAge.Text
    UnderTwenty = (Age < "20")
    MsgBox("Under twenty? " & UnderTwenty)
End Sub
```

There is no cast exception, since the variable **Age** is type String and is compared to the string value "20". However, does this event procedure perform as it should? What happens if the user is less than 10 years old? What happens if the user is older than 99 years old? Explain.

Exercise 4.19

What will the message box display?

```
Private Sub btnComparisons_Click()
    Dim A As String
    Dim X As Boolean
    Dim Y As Boolean
    Dim Z As Integer
    A = "study"
    Z = 10
    X = (5 < Z)
    Y = (A >= "stupefy")
    MsgBox(X & Y & Z)
End Sub
```

Exercise 4.20

What will the message box display?

```
Private Sub btnComparisons_Click()
    Dim A As String
    Dim B As String
    Dim C As Single
    Dim D As Integer
    Dim X As Boolean
    A = "cran"
    B = "crankshaft"
    C = -0.5
    D = 2
    X = ((A & "berry") < B) * (-3 ^ 3) + (((D / 2) = 1) + 3)
    MsgBox(X)
End Sub
```

Logical Operators

Logical operators, as mentioned earlier, combine simple logical expressions to create more complex logical expressions. Suppose a multinational firm wants to identify job candidates who have more than five years of business experience. To do this, a program might have the statement

```
Qualified = (YearsExperience > 5)
```

Table 4.10 Common logical operators

Symbol	Operator Name	Example* Expression	Result
Not	Not (negation)	Not (a < b)	False
		Not (a >= b)	True
And	And (conjunction)	(a < b) And (b < c)	True
		(−2 < b) And (4 = b)	False
		(a > b) And (b <= b)	False
		(−2 >= b) And (c < b)	False
Or	Or (disjunction)	(a < b) Or (b < c)	True
		(−2 < b) Or (c = b)	True
		(a > b) or (b <= b)	True
		(−2 >= b) Or (c < b)	False

* Assume numeric variables a, b, and c have been declared and contain the values 2, 3, and 4, respectively.

What if this firm wants to identify job applicants who speak at least three languages? To do this, a program might have the statement

> Qualified = (NumberOfLanguages >= 3)

But what if the firm wants a candidate who has both qualifications? This is where a logical operator helps. In a program that evaluates candidates who satisfy both requirements we might see the statement

> Qualified = (YearsExperience > 5) And (NumberOfLanguages >= 3)

This expression uses the binary And operator to join the simple comparisons **YearsExperience > 5** and **NumberOfLanguages >= 3**. The entire expression evaluates to True if both comparisons evaluate to True, and it evaluates to False if either one or both of the comparisons are False.

The most common logical operators are shown in Table 4.10. There are other logical operators (Xor, Eqv, and Imp) that are less commonly employed.

The unary Not operator takes the value of the expression to its right and negates it; Not True evaluates to False, and Not False evaluates to True.

Result of Not A

A	Not A
TRUE	FALSE
FALSE	TRUE

The And and Or operators are both binary. The result of And'ing two expressions is True if both of the expressions are True, and False if either one or both of them are False.

Result of A And B

	B	
	TRUE	FALSE
A TRUE	TRUE	FALSE
FALSE	FALSE	FALSE

The result of Or'ing two expressions is True if either one or both of them are True, and False if they are both False.

Result of A Or B

		B	
		TRUE	FALSE
A	TRUE	TRUE	TRUE
	FALSE	TRUE	FALSE

EXAMPLE 4.15

USING LOGICAL OPERATORS

The event procedure in Figure 4.26 evaluates whether the user is between 10 and 20 years old, inclusive. To evaluate the expression **(10 <= Age) And (Age <= 20)**, the computer first evaluates the left-most comparison, **10 <= Age**, to arrive at True or False, then evaluates the right-most comparison, **Age <= 20**, to arrive at True or False, then And's these two Boolean values. If they are both True then the final result is True; otherwise the final result is False.

Observe that there is more than one way to write the logical expression in Example 4.15 and still get the same result: **(20 >= Age) And (10 <= Age)**, for example. However, one expression that will not yield the same result is **10 <= Age <= 20**. To evaluate this expression, Visual Basic .NET will first compare **10 <= Age**, arriving at True or False, and then compare the result of this comparison to 20. In either case the result is True. In other words, this expression is worthless because it always gives the result True.

This is an easy trap for beginning Visual Basic .NET developers to fall into, because from algebra we are used to writing expressions like

$$10 \leq x \leq 20$$

In fact, the computer will not notify you of this error because it is syntactically correct. As a developer you have to be careful to remember to write out one comparison at a time, then use the logical operators And or Or to join the comparisons appropriately.

Large and complex logical expressions can be constructed and may be time-consuming to understand. Also, the values on either side of the comparison operators can be large arithmetic expressions. In such expressions Visual Basic .NET will perform all the arithmetic operations first, then the comparison operations, and then the logical operations (first Nots, then Ands, and finally Ors). As with arithmetic expressions, it makes sense to use parentheses to keep the expression easy to read.

FIGURE 4.26

Code for Example 4.15

```
Private Sub btnRangeCheck_Click(ByVal sender As System.Obje
    Dim Age As Short
    Dim BetweenTenAndTwenty As Boolean
    Age = txtAge.Text
    BetweenTenAndTwenty = (10 <= Age) And (Age <= 20)
    MsgBox("Between 10 and 20? " & BetweenTenAndTwenty)
End Sub
```

Exercise 4.21   Is the following expression True or False?

$$(\text{Not } (3 < 2) \text{ And } (5 < 7 - \text{Math.Sqrt}(16))) \text{ Or } (\text{Not } (2 * 5 + 1 > 3))$$

Exercise 4.22   In Example 4.15, what happens if the developer mistakenly types Or instead of And in btnRangeCheck_Click? Explain.

Exercise 4.23   Change the statement

$$\text{Qualified} = (\text{YearsExperience} > 5) \text{ And } (\text{NumberOfLanguages} >= 3)$$

so that a candidate is still considered to be qualified if he or she meets the specified requirements, but now any candidate who speaks six or more languages (regardless of years of experience) is also considered to be qualified.

Exercise 4.24   What will the message box display?

```
Private Sub btnLogicalOperators_Click()
    Dim A As Integer
    Dim B As Integer
    Dim C As Integer
    Dim D As Integer
    Dim X As Boolean
    Dim Y As Boolean
    Dim Z As Boolean
    A = 2
    B = 3
    C = 4
    D = 5
    X = Not (A < B)
    Y = (A < B) And (C > D)
    Z = (A < B) Or (C > D)
    MsgBox(X & Y & Z)
End Sub
```

Logical Functions

The two most frequently used logical functions are listed in Table 4.11.

Table 4.11 Common logical functions

| Function | | Example* | |
Name	Description	Expression	Result
IsNumeric()	Check for valid number	IsNumeric("12a")	False
IIf()	Immediate If	IIf(b < a, a + b, a * b)	6

*Assume numeric variables a and b have been declared and contain the values 2 and 3, respectively.

IsNumeric()

The IsNumeric() function takes one argument and returns True or False according to whether the argument has the form of a valid number. This function uses the same rules that Visual Basic .NET uses when it casts a string from the Text property of a text box into a numeric value when storing into a numeric variable. Thus, **IsNumeric("12a")** returns False, while **IsNumeric("12")** returns True. The argument can be any type, although in practice it usually will be type String (because we already know that a numeric type stores only numeric values).

IsNumeric() can be useful for avoiding casting exceptions. Suppose that an application requires the user to enter a number. Directly storing the user's input into a numeric variable will result in an invalid cast exception if the user makes a mistake. As an alternative, the program can first store the user's input in a string variable (so there will be no chance of a cast exception), and then use IsNumeric() to evaluate whether the value is a valid number. If it is, the value can be safely stored in the numeric variable, and, if not, the user can be notified of the mistake. We will see examples of this kind of user input validation in Chapter 5.

IIf()

The Immediate If function, IIf(), provides a way for your program to make simple decisions. Given two expressions, the function chooses which one to evaluate. As we will see in Chapter 5, most programs have to make decisions, and Visual Basic .NET provides sophisticated statements for handling more complex decisions.

The IIf() function takes three arguments: the first is a logical expression, and the second and third can be string or numeric expressions. The action of IIf() is as follows. It first evaluates the logical expression (its first argument) to arrive at True or False. If the outcome is True, it then evaluates and returns the result of the second argument; otherwise it evaluates and returns the result of the third argument. An illustration of this action follows:

$$IIF(LogicalExpression, Expression1, Expression2)$$

First evaluate LogicalExpression:
If True, IIF() takes on the value of ⎯⎦
If False, IIF() takes on the value of ⎯⎦

In the example **IIf(b < a, a + b, a * b)** in Table 4.11, the logical expression **b < a** is False, so the third argument, **a * b**, is evaluated, and its result, 6, is returned.

Example **4.16**

USING THE IIF() FUNCTION

The event procedure in Figure 4.27 illustrates the use of the IIf() function. In this example, the user enters two string values into the text boxes. The IIf() function compares the first string (**A**) to the second string (**B**). If **A** is less than **B**, then string **A** is displayed. If **A** is not less than **B**, then string **B** is displayed.

FIGURE 4.27

Code for
Example 4.16

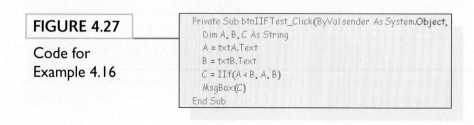

```
Private Sub btnIIFTest_Click(ByVal sender As System.Object,
    Dim A, B, C As String
    A = txtA.Text
    B = txtB.Text
    C = IIf(A < B, A, B)
    MsgBox(C)
End Sub
```

Simply put, this procedure displays via a message box the lesser of two strings that are input via text boxes.

Exercise 4.25

In Example 4.15, modify btnRangeCheck_Click so its message box displays

Between ten and twenty? Yes

if the user's age is between ten and twenty, and

Between ten and twenty? No

if the user's age is not between ten and twenty.

4.7   Project 5:   Financial Calculators

This project provides a platform for a number of different financial calculators. The application includes a calculator to compute the depreciation of an asset, another calculator to compute the monthly payments of a loan, and a third calculator to compute the future value of an annuity.

When a company purchases an asset, it is allowed to depreciate the asset over its useful life. Assets have an initial value and a salvage value. The difference between these two amounts is the amount that can be depreciated. The annual depreciation amount is generally used to reduce the taxes paid by the firm. One of the several depreciation methods used is called the sum-of-the-years'-digits depreciation method. In this method, the annual depreciation value of the asset is calculated with larger amounts in the early life of the asset and lesser amounts in the later years of the life of the asset.

We are all aware of the details of a loan. Someone gives you some money (loan amount) and you agree to repay that person over time. Of course, the person making the loan generally expects to get back more money than the amount loaned; this extra amount is the interest on the loan. Our loan calculator accepts the loan amount, the interest rate paid by the borrower, and the number of years agreed upon to repay the loan. It then calculates the monthly payment amount.

Finally we have a calculator that computes the future value of an annuity. We assume that you are investing the same amount of money annually at a given interest rate. This calculator will tell you the amount of money you will have at the end of a specified number of years. For example, if you invest $1,000 a year at an 8 percent rate, what will your investment be worth at the end of 10 years?

Description of the Application

Figure 4.28 shows the user interface for this application. As you can see, there are a main form and three additional forms—one for each of our calculators. Any one or all of the calculators may be open at once and the user can move freely between them. Also note the similarity in the layout of the three calculators. Having a consistent look and feel is an important factor in user interface design.

If you look at the interest rate fields in the Loan Payment and Future Value calculators, you will see that the user can enter an interest rate as a decimal number (.08) or as a percent (whole number) 10 for 10%. The code detects which form the users chose to use and adjusts it accordingly using a simple rule we will talk about later.

FIGURE 4.28

User Interface for
Project 5

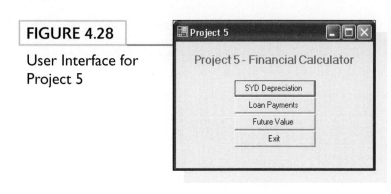

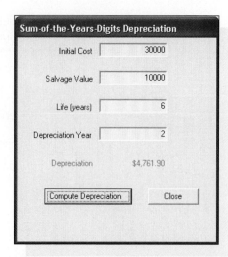

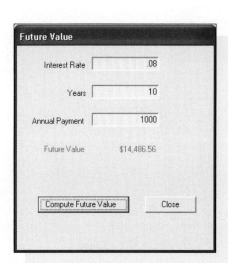

Design of the Application

This project has four forms. The controls and their names are shown in Figure 4.29 while the property settings are shown in Table 4.12.

Visual Basic .NET includes a number of very useful financial functions including functions that perform the calculations we need for this application. That means that the main job of the developer is to get the data from the user interface and then execute the correct function taking care of any exceptions that might be thrown by the application and then finally formatting and displaying the results.

Since none of the forms interact with each other, and since each calculation takes place in a single Click event, there is no need for variables that have a scope wider than procedure-level.

Construction of the Application

You may construct the application in a number of different ways. We will first build the main form and then add/test one calculator form at a time. Begin by creating a new Visual Basic .NET Windows Application project. Use the form created with this project as the main form (frmMain). Add and name all the components and then add the Click event procedures as shown in Figure 4.30. Notice in this project that the form objects are being instantiated with procedure-level scope and procedure-level lifetime. This means that each time one of the buttons

FIGURE 4.29

Forms and Their
Controls and Names
for Project 5

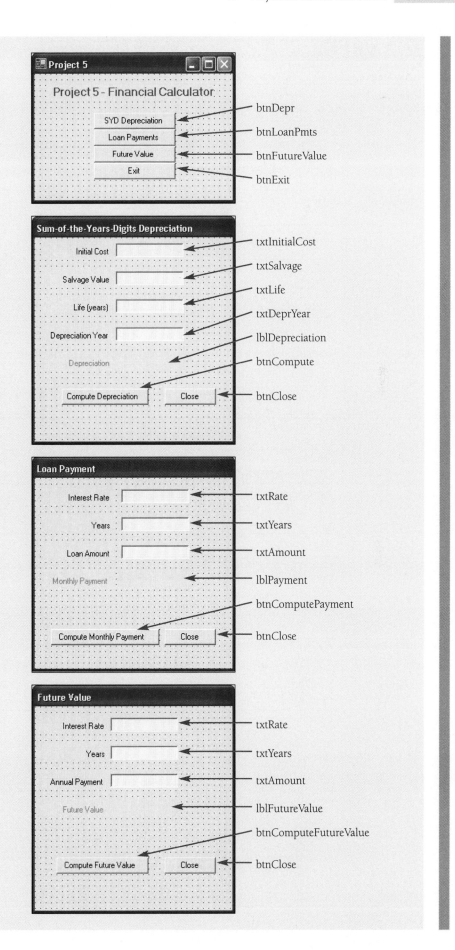

Table 4.12 Properties of various controls in Project 5

Form	Control	Property = Value
frmMain	frmMain	StartPosition = CenterScreen Text = Project 5
	btnDepr btnLoanPmts btnFutureValue btnExit	Text = SYD Depreciation Text = Loan Payments Text = Future Value Text = Exit
frmFV	frmFV	ControlBox = False Text = Future Value
	btnClose btnCompute	Text = Close Text = Compute Future Value
	lblFV	ForeColor = Red Text = "" TextAlign = MiddleRight
	txtPayment	Text = "" TextAlign = Right
	txtRate	Text = "" TextAlign = Right
	txtYears	Text = "" TextAlign = Right
frmPayment	frmPayment	ControlBox = False Text = Loan Payment
	btnClose btnComputePayment	Text = Close Text = Compute Monthly Payment
	lblPayment	ForeColor = Red Text = "" TextAlign = MiddleRight
	txtAmount	Text = "" TextAlign = Right
	txtRate	Text = "" TextAlign = Right
	txtYears	Text = "" TextAlign = Right
frmSYD	frmSYD	ControlBox = False Text = Sum-of-the-Years-Digits Depreciation
	btnClose	Text = Close
	btnCompute	Text = Compute Depreciation
	lblDepreciation	ForeColor = Red Text = "" TextAlign = MiddleRight
	txtDeprYear	Text = "" TextAlign = Right
	txtInitialCost	Text = "" TextAlign = Right
	txtLife	Text = "" TextAlign = Right
	txtSalvage	Text = "" TextAlign = Right

FIGURE 4.30

Code for frmMain

```
Private Sub btnExit_Click(ByVal sender As System
    End
End Sub

Private Sub btnDepr_Click(ByVal sender As System
    Dim objfrmSYD As New frmSYD()
    objfrmSYD.Show()
End Sub

Private Sub btnLoanPmts_Click(ByVal sender As Sy
    Dim objfrmPayment As New frmPayment()
    objfrmPayment.Show()
End Sub

Private Sub btnFutureValue_Click(ByVal sender As
    Dim objfrmFV As New frmFV()
    objfrmFV.Show()
End Sub
```

is clicked, a new form object will be instantiated. When we get to the code of the forms themselves, you'll see how we ensure that the memory used by the forms is released as soon as the user closes the form.

After finishing the main form, we turn our attention to the payment calculator. Start by adding a new Windows Form to your project. Name the form and then add and name the components as shown in Figure 4.29 and Table 4.12. Then add the code shown in Figure 4.31. Note several things about this code. First, we use the Dispose() method in btnClose_Click instead of the Hide() method we used earlier. The Hide() method basically makes the form invisible but it remains in memory. The Dispose() method causes all resources (including memory) to be released for reuse. In this application we choose to release memory when the user closes the calculator. Second, notice the use of the IIF() function to adjust the interest rate. We use a simple rule that states, "If the interest rate value entered by the user is greater than 1, we divide the value by 100 to move the decimal point accordingly." Thus, a value entered as 8 will be transformed to .08 while a number entered as .08 will not be modified.

We have two exceptions that need to be caught: an ArgumentException that means the Pmt() function is unhappy with what we pass it and an InvalidCastException that we have seen before. We include an unfiltered catch at the end in case

FIGURE 4.31

Code for
frmPayment

```
Private Sub btnComputePayment_Click(ByVal sender As System.
    Dim rate, amount, payment As Decimal
    Dim years As Short
    Try
        rate = txtRate.Text
        years = txtYears.Text
        amount = txtAmount.Text
        rate = IIf(rate > 1, rate / 100, rate)
        payment = Pmt(rate / 12, years * 12, -amount)
        lblPayment.Text = Format(payment, "C")
    Catch ex1 As ArgumentException
        MsgBox("Invalid values for this calculation")
    Catch ex2 As InvalidCastException
        MsgBox("Please provide numeric values only")
    Catch
        MsgBox("Unexpected error" & Err.Description)
    End Try
End Sub
```

FIGURE 4.32

Code for frmSYD

```
Private Sub btnCompute_Click(ByVal sender As System.Object,
    Dim cost, salvage, life, period, depreciation As Decimal
    Try
        cost = txtInitialCost.Text
        salvage = txtSalvage.Text
        life = txtLife.Text
        period = txtDeprYear.Text
        depreciation = SYD(cost, salvage, life, period)
        lblDepreciation.Text = Format(depreciation, "C")
    Catch ex1 As InvalidCastException
        MsgBox("Please provide numeric values only")
    Catch ex2 As ArgumentException
        MsgBox("Invalid values for this calculation")
    Catch
        MsgBox("Unexpected error" & Err.Description)
    End Try
End Sub
```

an exception is thrown that we do not anticipate. The reference "Err.Description" stores the description of the error. Including this in the message box helps you understand what went wrong so the problem can be handled better in the future.

Finally, note that we need to divide the interest rate by 12 and multiply the years by 12. This is necessary because we are dealing with annual rates and years but our payment is monthly. The adjustments you see are taking that into account (annual rate / 12 = monthly rate and years * 12 = number of months). Also note that the Format() function is using a predefined format specification of "C" instead of "Currency". This is a valid alternative (as well as "c") and it saves some typing.

You should now run the application to see if there are any errors. Be prepared for Visual Basic .NET telling you that it needs help deciding which form to use as the startup form. Make the main form the startup form. Once all errors are corrected, try some values and see if the calculator is giving you reasonable results.

Code for the depreciation calculator is shown next in Figure 4.32. This code is very similar in structure and style to the previous form. Note that the value entered in the text box txtDeprYear and stored in the variable **Period** represents the year (from 1 to life) for which the user wants to see the depreciation.

The final Windows Form is used to compute the future value. Its code is very similar to that of the payment calculator with two exceptions. First, since we are dealing with annual investments and annual rates, there is no need to adjust for monthly calculations by dividing or multiplying by 12. Second, we need to use a different function. The function we need is the future value function, FV(). The syntax of this function is

FV(Rate, NoOfPeriods, Payment)

We leave the coding of this form's two event procedures for you to complete.

Chapter Summary

1. Expressions are used as part of a statement—they are not statements themselves. For example, the assignment statement uses an expression on the right-hand side of the equal sign.

Expressions can be either numeric, string, or logical. When evaluated, a numeric expression produces a single number as its value, a string expression produces a single string value, and a logical expression produces either True or False.

2. Expressions consist of constants, variables, operators, and functions. An operator is a symbol that specifies a simple operation, such as addition. A function is a descriptive name that specifies a more complex operation, such as the square root calculation.

    Function names always end in parentheses; for example, the name of the square root function is Math.Sqrt(). Functions take arguments and return values. Arguments are expressions that specify the values to be used by the function, and are placed between the parentheses. For example, in Math.Sqrt(4), the argument is 4 and the returned value is 2.

3. Arithmetic expressions are composed of numeric constants, variables, arithmetic operators, and functions. Arithmetic expressions are evaluated using an operator precedence rule, which specifies a particular order in which operations are to be performed. You can override the operator precedence rule by using parentheses, since parenthesized parts of the expression are always evaluated first.

    When the computer evaluates arithmetic expressions, it is possible for arithmetic errors to occur. An overflow error occurs when the computer attempts to store the result of an expression in a variable that does not have the capacity to hold the result. Roundoff errors occur with variables of type Single and Double. The impact of roundoff errors must be evaluated in the context of the problem being solved by the program.

4. String expressions are composed of string constants and variables and string operators and functions. Visual Basic .NET's string concatenation operator & (the ampersand) joins (concatenates) two values end to end. String functions are very frequently used in creating applications with Visual Basic .NET.

    Two functions used with strings provide access to the ANSI table. Chr() takes a numeric argument and returns its equivalent ANSI character. This function may be used to specify nonprintable characters in a string. Asc() takes a single character (string) as the argument and returns its equivalent ANSI number.

5. Logical expressions consist of variables, constants, comparison operators, logical operators, and logical functions. A logical expression has the form of a True/False question. That is, a logical expression evaluates to either True or False. The logical operators Not, And, and Or can be used to combine logical expressions to form a more complex logical expression.

6. Comparison of numeric values is straightforward, but comparison of string values is more complex. String values are compared character by character beginning at the left-most character, using the ANSI table to determine which character is smaller. Two strings are equal if they are the same length and contain identical characters.

7. The logical function IIf() is used to select one of two expressions depending on the value of a logical expression. The function's first argument is the logical expression. If this logical expression evaluates to True, then the function takes on the value of the expression defined by the second argument. If the logical expression evaluates to False, then the function takes on the value of the expression defined by the third argument.

Key Terms

ANSI
argument
arithmetic expression
binary operator
carriage return
case sensitivity
collating sequence
comparison operator
concatenation
encrypted message
evaluating the expression
exponentiation operator

expression
format specification
function
future value
integer division operator
line feed
logical expression
logical operator
Mod operator
nonprintable character
operator

operator precedence
    rule
overflow
present value
return value
roundoff
statement
string expression
substring
unary operator
value

End-of-Chapter Problems

1. Convert the following algebraic expressions into valid Visual Basic .NET expressions.

   a. $\dfrac{A + B}{C}$

   b. $\sqrt{A^2 + B^2}$

   c. $\dfrac{A + B \times C}{X - Y}$

   d. $\dfrac{[A + B]^2}{\sqrt{X \times Y - Z}}$

   e. $A + [B \times C - D] \times E$

2. Evaluate each of the following Visual Basic .NET expressions. That is, determine the result of the computation that will be performed by the computer. Assume that all the variables are declared as type Single and that A = 10, B = 2, C = 5, D = 25, and E = 3.

   a. A + B * C + D

   b. A ^ B + (D / C) ^ E

   c. A / B * C / D / E

   d. A ^ 2 + B ^ 2 / C

   e. D / (A + C + E – B) ^ B

3. Evaluate each of the following string expressions. That is, determine the result of the manipulation that will be performed by the computer. Be aware that there may be syntax or run time errors in one or more of the expressions. Assume that all the variables are declared as type String and that A = "Apple", B = "Banana", C = "Apply", and D = "banana".

   a. A & Chr(115)

   b. Microsoft.VisualBasic.Left(B, 2) & Microsoft.VisualBasic.Right(C, 4)

   c. Mid(C, 2, 3)

   d. InStr(D, "ana", 3)

4. Evaluate each of the following logical expressions. That is, determine whether they evaluate to True or False. Assume that all the variables are declared as type Integer and that A = 10, B = 50, C = 0, and D = 100.

   a. (A < B) And (C = 0)

   b. B >= D Or B <= A

   c.   10 <= B <= D

   d.   B > A And (A = 0 Or B <= 50)

   e.   Not C And (D >= B) Or A = 100

5. Evaluate each of the following logical expressions. That is, determine whether they evaluate to True or False. Assume that all the variables are declared as type String and that A = "Apple", B = "Banana", C = "Apply", and D = "banana".

   a.   A > B

   b.   B = D

   c.   A < C And B > D

   d.   A > "annual" Or B <> "Fruit"

   e.   "Apricot" <= B <= "Kumquat"

6. What code would be needed to display a message of "Greater than zero" or "Less than or equal to zero" in a MsgBox depending on the value held in a variable named "Result"?

7. For the following numbers, which data type (Single, Double, or Decimal) would be most appropriate?

   a. $23,819,305,917,631.75 in an accounting application.

   b. $9,308,983,238,544 for estimated U.S. gross domestic product for 1999.

   c. 5.9736×10^{24} for the mass of the Earth.

   d. $458,439,211,069 in an economic simulation.

   e. 4.5×10^{51} for the kilometers to a distant star.

8. Take each of the following numbers and apply the functions Abs, Sign, Fix, CInt, and Sqrt. What are the results?

   a.   12

   b.   –8

   c.   10.12

   d.   10.17

   e.   –10.12

   f.   –10.17

9. If a random statement read **(Rnd()*67) + 8**, what are the upper and lower bounds that the random number may fit into? What would the Randomize() statement do to the numbers returned?

10. Describe what you think would happen and then test each of the following Replace() statements when used on the string "The time has come." in variable **myString**:

   a.   myString = Replace(myString, "i", "o")

   b.   myString = Replace(myString, "e", "plete", 14)

   c.   myString = Replace(myString, "t", "L", 5, 1)

   d.   myString = Replace(myString, "E", "ee", 1, , CompareMethod.Binary)

Programming Problems

1. Create a Visual Basic .NET form that has two text boxes, each identified by a label. The captions of the labels should read "ANSI Character" and "ANSI Code." Then create two buttons with captions "Convert Code to Character" and "Convert Character to Code."

Program the Click event procedures of these two buttons to perform the appropriate conversions. When the user clicks the Convert Code to Character button, the code value in the ANSI Code text box should be used to determine the corresponding ANSI character, and this character should be placed in the ANSI Character text box. The reverse operation should be performed when the user clicks the Convert Character to Code button.

2. Create a Visual Basic .NET project that computes the economic order quantity (EOQ) using the fixed order quantity lot size decision rule. This rule helps retailers, manufacturing managers, and so forth, determine the number of units to order each time a particular item must be ordered because of low stock. The EOQ is the most economical quantity possible under a certain set of conditions. The equation for computing the economic order quantity is

$$EOQ = \sqrt{\frac{2RS}{kC}}$$

where S is the cost to prepare an order.
R is the annual demand.
C is the cost per unit.
k is the cost rate of carrying $1 of inventory per year.

Your project should let the user enter values for S, R, C, and k, and it should have a button that the user clicks to compute and display the EOQ.

3. Create a Visual Basic .NET project that compares two string values entered by the user. The form should have two text boxes with corresponding labels captioned "String 1" and "String 2", and a button captioned "Compare Strings". At run time, the user should first enter values into the text boxes, and then click the button. The button's event procedure should then compare the two values in the text boxes and accordingly display either the message "String 1 is less" or the message "String 2 is less".

4. Create a Visual Basic .NET project that implements Find and Find Next operations similar to those found in word processors. The form should have a Text box control and two buttons. The figure below shows the user interface after the user has typed a memo in the text box and then initiated a search for the word "look".

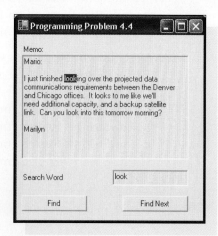

When program execution begins, the Find button should be visible but the Find Next button should not be visible. The user first enters text into the text box at the top of the form and then enters text in the second text box to search for in the top text box. After the text has been entered, clicking on the Find button causes the following actions to occur:

a. The text in the second text box is stored in a variable named **Target**.

b. A search is performed to find the location of the first occurrence of **Target** in the top text box, and the result of the search is stored in a variable named **FoundPos**.

c. If the search is successful (**FoundPos > 0**), then the occurrence of **Target** in the top text box is highlighted.

d. The Find Next button is made visible if the search is successful and invisible if the search is unsuccessful.

The preceding figure shows an example of how the form might appear after the user types text in the top text box, clicks Find, and enters the word "look" as the target. Subsequently clicking the Find Next button should cause the same actions as clicking the Find button, except the search should try to find the next occurrence of **Target** (instead of the first occurrence). For example, if the user clicks the Find Next button on the form shown above, the appearance of the text box should change as shown below.

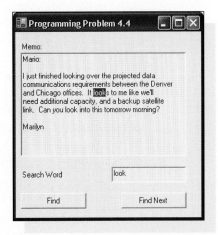

Hint 1: The following sequence of statements accomplishes the action of step c given earlier, assuming the TextBox control is named txtMemo.

```
txtMemo.SelStart = IIf(FoundPos > 0, FoundPos - 1, 0)
txtMemo.SelLength = IIf(FoundPos > 0, Len(Target), 0)
txtMemo.SetFocus()
```

Hint 2: What scope should variables **Target** and **FoundPos** have?
Hint 3: See the discussion in the text on using InStr() for multiple searches.

5. Create a Visual Basic .NET project that computes the future value of a given dollar amount. An example user interface is shown below.

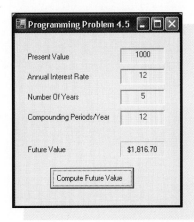

The formula for computing the future value is:

$$FV = PV \times (1 + AnnualRate/PerPerYr)^{(Years \times PerPerYr)}$$

where **AnnualRate** is the annual interest rate and **PerPerYr** is the number of compounding periods per year.

The annual rate must be a fraction in the formula given above. For example, for a 10 percent rate the number .10 should be used in the formula. If the user enters a number greater than 1 (as shown above), the program should divide the value by 100 to locate the decimal point at the correct place (the value 12 in the example was divided by 100 and the resulting value .12 was used in the calculation).

6. Create a Visual Basic .NET project that uses the Rnd() function to simulate a slot machine. The slot machine should use three large Label controls (with red text about 36 points tall) for the wheels in this game of chance. A button can act as the pull lever to start the game. Each wheel should have three different possible values since more values means you'll almost never win! Instead of placing the random number generated by a pull in each slot, use the Chr() function to add the number to an ANSI value to display a more interesting character or letter.

Use a module level variable that increments with each pull and a label to display the number of player tries. Finally, you'll need to create a label at the bottom of the form to tell the player whether it was a winning pull. *Hint:* Use the IIf() statement with Boolean operators to determine if all wheels matched for a winning pull.

SPECIFYING ALTERNATE
COURSES OF ACTION

Selection Statements

Most applications need to be able to select an appropriate action from several alternatives, depending on certain conditions that occur in the data. For example, an accounts receivable program must be able to handle overpayments and when they occur, it reacts by producing refund checks.

With the exception of programs that included the IIF() function, in the programs we wrote in previous chapters the procedures always performed the same actions, regardless of the data they processed. This is because, up to this point in our use of Visual Basic .NET, statements within a procedure have been executed one at a time, from top to bottom, and no statements have ever been skipped.

But suppose we wanted to include sales tax, varying from city to city and from state to state, in an order entry application? We would need the program to examine the customer's address and select the appropriate tax rate for that address. For this, we need new Visual Basic .NET statements that allow us to ask a question (where does the customer live?) and, based on the answer, choose the appropriate course of action. Under these circumstances, statements are still executed one at a time and in top-to-bottom order, but some statements are skipped (at least sometimes). This makes sense because the answer to the question can be different each time the procedure is executed.

In this chapter we show how a program can select alternate courses of action depending on the data to be processed. Two statements make this possible: the If...Then...Else statement and the Select Case statement. In addition, we introduce Visual Basic .NET controls that make it easy to design GUIs that allow the user to indicate choices such as whether an employee wants optional life insurance. Typically, the program responds to this kind of input by selecting an action that corresponds to the user's choice.

Objectives

After studying this chapter, you should be able to

- Construct programs that select alternative actions using the If...Then...Else and Select Case statements.

- Compare the Select Case statement with the If...Then...Else statement and describe situations for which each is appropriate.

- Create GUIs using the MsgBox() function and three new controls—RadioButton, GroupBox, and CheckBox—that present a set of options to the user and allow the user to input choices.

5.1 The Decision-Making Process

We make so many decisions each day that it is easy to overlook the process we go through to choose one option instead of another. But when writing a program that must select one action from several alternatives, we must be very precise in how we construct the decision criterion and write the alternative actions. Therefore, we begin our investigation of programs that make choices by looking carefully at the structure of decisions.

If you look closely at the decision-making process, you will see that the action you take depends upon the *conditions* of the situation. As represented by Figure 5.1, each condition has two or more possible *outcomes,* and for each possible outcome there is an appropriate *action*.

To demonstrate how these steps work, consider a program that checks to see whether a student is eligible to register for a course. For example, assume that a student must take Intro to Business Computing before taking Intro to Programming. The condition is, has the student passed Intro to Business Computing? If the outcome is yes, then the appropriate action is to allow the student to enroll in Intro to Programming. If the outcome is no, then the appropriate action is to deny the student permission to enroll.

In a program,

- A *condition* is represented as an expression.

- An *outcome* corresponds to a value produced when the computer evaluates the expression.

- An *appropriate action* is specified as a group of statements.

At design time the developer has to specify the condition, its possible outcomes, and the appropriate action for each outcome. At run time, the computer evaluates the condition (an expression), identifies the outcome, and then executes the group of statements for that outcome.

5.2 The If...Then...Else Statement

The *If...Then...Else statement* allows a program to handle situations having two outcomes. Accordingly, the statement has three parts:

1. The condition.

2. The statements to perform for the first outcome.

3. The statements to perform for the second outcome.

FIGURE 5.1

Elements of a Decision in a Program

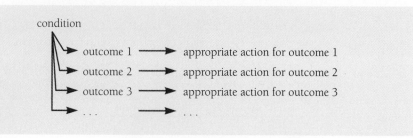

We begin this section by examining the syntax and action of the If…Then…Else statement and looking at an illustrative example. We then discuss the task of reading and writing If…Then…Else statements, and briefly discuss logical expressions in the context of If…Then…Else statements. Finally, we look at a variation of the If…Then…Else statement.

Syntax and Action of If…Then…Else

The If…Then…Else statement has the following syntax:

If *condition* **Then**
    statementblock1
Else
    statementblock2
End If

The italics indicate positions at which you, as developer, provide specific details to customize the statement. The reserved word If marks the top of the If…Then…Else statement, and the reserved words End If marks its bottom. The reserved word Then separates the *condition* from *statementblock1*, and the reserved word Else separates *statementblock1* from *statementblock2*. Be aware that Visual Basic .NET will automatically insert the End If statement after you have entered the If statement. This feature can be disabled (see Options… under the Tools menu) if you do not like it.

The condition is a logical expression that you provide. Recall that a logical expression always evaluates to either True or False. Hence, the If statement's condition allows only two outcomes.

A *statement block* is any sequence of zero or more statements. If…Then…Else requires you to provide two statement blocks. *Statementblock1* is used for outcome True, and *statementblock2* is used for outcome False.

Run Time: The Effect of the If…Then…Else Statement

The action of the If…Then…Else statement is as follows. When the computer executes the If statement, it first evaluates the condition and determines whether its outcome is True or False. If the outcome is

- True: the computer executes the statements in *statementblock1*, one at a time, in top-to-bottom order, then skips to the statement following End If.

- False: the computer skips immediately to Else, executes the statements in *statementblock2*, one at a time, in top-to-bottom order, then resumes at the statement following End If.

Returning to the concept "flow of control" we introduced earlier, this type of flow of control is called "selection." So now we have seen both sequential and selection flow of control. Note that the description above is describing sequential flow of control within a statementblock. We are not limited to sequential flow within a statementblock but we will delay a discussion of this issue until we get to Section 5.3.

FIGURE 5.2

Code for Example 5.1

```
Private Sub btnGuessMe_Click(ByVal sender As Syste
    Dim Target, Guess As Short
    Target = 1 + Int(6 * Rnd())
    Guess = txtGuess.Text
    If Guess = Target Then
        Beep()
        MsgBox("Correct - congratulations")
    Else
        MsgBox("Incorrect - bummer")
    End If
End Sub
```

Example 5.1

USING THE IF...THEN...ELSE STATEMENT

The event procedure in Figure 5.2 uses an If...Then...Else statement to implement a simple guessing game. The variable **Target** is set to a random integer ranging from 1 to 6. Then the value the user has entered in the TextBox (an integer between 1 and 6) is stored in the variable **Guess**.

The If...Then...Else statement evaluates the condition, which determines whether the user's guess and the random target are equal. If they are equal, the computer beeps and displays a message box offering congratulations. If not, it displays a message box indicating that the guess did not match the random target.

Figure 5.3 shows the components of the If...Then...Else statement in btnGuessMe_Click. Figure 5.4 shows the action of the statement when the condition evaluates to True and when it evaluates to False; in each case the statements that are executed are shaded. Note that the reserved words Then, Else, and End If don't cause the computer to perform any action; they merely serve to delimit—mark the beginning and end of—the two statement blocks.

Figure 5.4 shows a color bar after the End If statement. This indicates that when the If...Then...Else statement finishes executing either *statementblock1* or

FIGURE 5.3

Components of If...Then...Else Statement in Example 5.1

Condition

```
If Guess = Target Then
    Beep
    MsgBox "Correct -- congratulations!"      } Statementblock1
Else
    MsgBox "Incorrect -- bummer!"    } Statementblock2
End If
```

FIGURE 5.4

Action of If...Then...Else Statement in Example 5.1

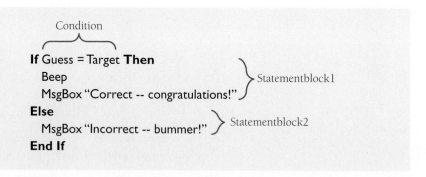

Condition True
```
If Guess = Target Then
    Beep
    MsgBox "Correct!"
Else
    MsgBox "Incorrect!"
End If
```

Condition False
```
If Guess = Target Then
    Beep
    MsgBox "Correct!"
Else
    MsgBox "Incorrect!"
End If
```

statementblock2, the program continues executing at the first statement after the End If statement.

Note that in Example 5.1 it is impossible to say whether the condition will be True or False until the user enters a guess and clicks on the button. It will be True only if the number entered by the user just happens to be equal to the number stored in the variable **Target**.

As developers, we want our code to be easy to understand, so we should emphasize the presence of If...Then...Else statements. Developers do this by indenting the statement blocks in the interior of If...Then...Else. In fact, this indentation is so important that Visual Basic .NET will do this indentation automatically (unless you tell it not to—not a good idea).

| **Exercise** 5.1 |

Suppose the user of the program in Example 5.1 wants to make a correct guess in as few tries as possible. The user clicks on btnGuessMe and enters a guess between 1 and 6, and repeats this until the guess is correct. Consider the following two guessing strategies:

> **Strategy A: Guess the same number every time.**
>
> **Strategy B: Guess a different number each time.**

Which strategy is better? That is, which strategy will help the user make a correct guess in fewer tries? Explain.

| **Exercise** 5.2 |

Suppose we modify Example 5.1 by making the variable **Target** module-level instead of local to btnGuessMe_Click and moving the statement **Target = 1 + Int(6 * Rnd())** from btnGuessMe_Click to Form_Load. Now answer Exercise 5.1's question again, assuming the code has been modified as suggested.

Meta Statements

The If...Then...Else statement is our first example of a compound statement, meaning that a single If...Then...Else statement may contain many individual statements. That is, there are two statement blocks, and each statement block can contain one or more statements.

Compound statements can be harder to understand than simple statements. For example, the simple statement

```
GrossPay = HoursWorked * HourlyRate
```

is easy to understand—it has a single action. The compound If...Then...Else statement

```
If Guess = Target Then
    Beep()
    MsgBox("Correct -- congratulations!")
Else
    MsgBox("Incorrect -- bummer!")
End If
```

is harder to understand because it specifies multiple alternative actions. However, you might describe this If...Then...Else statement with a phrase like "Process user's guess and display result." This phrase captures the essence of the compound statement. **When we describe a compound statement with a single phrase, we say that the phrase is a *meta statement*.** "Meta" means to "go

beyond or transcend." A meta statement goes beyond the individual statements and describes the concept represented by those statements.

In the design phase, while developing the logic of our code, using the meta statement lets us understand what the code accomplishes without having to constantly keep in mind the details of how the code accomplishes it. In the current example, what the code does is "process the user's guess and display the result." We need to examine how the code accomplishes this only when we write the code and when we modify what it does.

Problem Solving and Pseudocode

A major part of designing any project is writing the code that performs the tasks needed to satisfy the user requirements. Developers often use the term **problem solving for the process of writing code that performs a required task.** Problem solving can be quite challenging.

Meta statements can facilitate the problem-solving process. To illustrate this, consider the following narrative description of the user requirements for a computerized guessing game.

> When the user clicks on a button, the computer generates a random integer between 1 and 6, inclusive, and then accepts the user's guess. If the guess is correct, the computer beeps, then displays the message "Correct -- congratulations!" If the guess is incorrect, the computer displays the message "Incorrect -- bummer!"

Pretend for a moment that you have not already seen the code for Example 5.1 and that you need to write the code that implements this guessing game. How do you proceed?

By reading the above narrative, you can get a firm understanding of *what* the application should do without concern for exactly *how* the program code will accomplish the tasks. As we said in Chapter 1, it is critical that you reach this level of understanding before trying to write the code. You may find this hard to believe, but developers often cannot resist the temptation to start writing code before they have this understanding.

It is not always easy to translate user requirements directly into Visual Basic .NET code. As an intermediate step, developers sometimes use pseudocode—or "false" code. It's not real code because it does not follow any strict rules of syntax. Recall that **pseudocode is an English-like outline that is easy to write and easy to translate into real code.**

Let's look at some pseudocode for the guessing-game problem.

> *generate random integer between 1 and 6*
> *obtain user's guess via a text box*
> *determine whether guess is correct and respond accordingly*

The first two lines of this pseudocode are easy to translate into actual Visual Basic .NET statements because we've used similar statements many times, and because they are simple (not compound) statements. The third line represents a meta statement. That is, it describes what will eventually become a compound statement (If...Then...Else).

Often we expand a meta statement in pseudocode after we have written our first draft. The idea is to start with a very broad overview of what needs to be done, and then refine this with more and more detail until finally we write the actual

Visual Basic .NET code. The advantage of this approach is that it enables us to think about the problem-solving steps without worrying about rules of syntax.

Let's revise our pseudocode to expand the meta statement into more detail.

> *generate random integer between 1 and 6*
> *obtain user's guess via a text box*
> *If user's guess = random integer Then*
> > *beep*
> > *display congratulations*
> *Else*
> > *display condolences*
> *End If*

Now we can easily translate this pseudocode into a working event procedure like the code in Figure 5.2.

This example is typical of the process that developers follow to translate the user requirements for an application into working code. In the first pass, the pseudocode may be a simple list of fairly vague actions. In each subsequent pass the pseudocode is refined a little, and it begins to look more and more like actual program statements. The translation from pseudocode to Visual Basic .NET statements is smoother if you include Visual Basic .NET reserved words (such as If, Then, Else, and End If) in your pseudocode. You might also consider adding some of the pseudocode as comments to the actual Visual Basic .NET code to help make the code easier to understand.

Most problems have more than one solution, and different developers may think about the same problem in different ways. For example, one developer might create the following pseudocode when translating the guessing-game description into working code.

> *obtain user's guess via a text box*
> *generate random integer between 1 and 6*
> *If user's guess <> random integer Then*
> > *display condolences*
> *Else*
> > *beep*
> > *display congratulations*
> *End If*

The user will not be able to tell the difference between the two solutions. However, the fact that different developers think about the same problem in different ways contributes to the difficulty of understanding someone else's code. This, in turn, increases the cost of maintaining applications in the real world.

To make it easy for someone else to read your programs, use common sense in designing and coding problem solutions. For example, humans usually compare two quantities for equality rather than comparing them for inequality, so unless there are other reasons for using an inequality, the equality comparison will seem simpler.

Exercise 5.3

Modify btnGuessMe_Click in Example 5.1 so that each time the user enters a guess and the button is clicked, the computer displays the total number of guesses the user has taken and the number of guesses that were correct.

Exercise 5.4

Modify btnGuessMe_Click in Example 5.1 so that the user still enters a guess and clicks the button each time, but now when the user guesses correctly, it displays its congratulations, displays the number of guesses taken, and ends execution of the program (using the End statement). When the user's guess is incorrect, the event procedure should merely display condolences.

Exercise 5.5

An automobile insurance company allows customers to pay the amount of the insurance, called the premium, in one of two ways: twice a year or monthly. Each month the insurance company sends the customer a bill showing the balance (equal to the premium minus the total amount paid to date) and the minimum amount due. The minimum amount due is equal to the lesser of the following two quantities: (1) the balance and (2) the premium divided by 6.

The company is creating a Visual Basic .NET form to process customer payments. Assume the form has module-level variables named **Premium** and **Balance**, and that these have been initialized to the correct amount for a given customer. Also assume that the form has Label controls named lblBalance and lblAmount-Due, and their Text properties also have been initialized appropriately. The initializations might be performed in the Form_Load event procedure as shown below. (In a real application the premium and balance would be obtained from a database.)

```
Private Sub Form1_Load(ByVal sender ...)
    Premium = 435
    Balance = Premium
    lblBalance.Text = Format(Balance, "currency")
    lblAmountDue.Text = Format(Premium / 6, "currency")
End Sub
```

Write a Click event procedure for a button named btnProcessPayment that does the following:

1. Gets the amount paid from a TextBox, then updates the balance by subtracting the amount paid from it.

2. If the balance is now greater than or equal to 0, makes lblBalance display the balance, and lblAmountDue display the minimum of the following two quantities: (a) the balance and (b) the premium divided by 6.

3. If the balance is now negative, makes lblBalance display the absolute value of the balance followed by "CR" (to indicate credit) and makes lblAmountDue display $0.00.

Be sure to format all dollar amounts.

Using Logical Expressions in If...Then...Else Statements

Since the condition of the If...Then...Else statement is a logical expression, you can apply what you learned about logical expressions in Chapter 4. Recall the example used in that chapter of a multinational firm that wants to identify job candidates who have more than five years of business experience and who also speak at least three languages. To evaluate whether or not a candidate satisfies these requirements, we wrote the following logical expression:

(YearsExperience > 5) And (NumberOfLanguages >= 3)

We can use this expression as the condition of an If...Then...Else statement.

If (YearsExperience > 5) And (NumberOfLanguages >= 3) Then
 'statementblock to set up interview with candidate
Else
 'statementblock to display message that candidate does not meet requirements
End If

Alternatively, we can store the result of the logical expression in a Boolean variable, and then use the variable in the condition of the If…Then…Else statement.

Qualified = ((YearsExperience > 5) And (NumberOfLanguages >= 3))
If Qualified = True Then
 'statementblock to set up interview with candidate
Else
 'statementblock to display message that candidate does not meet requirements
End If

Using a descriptive name for the variable makes the program easier to read. And if the result of the logical expression is needed in more than one place in the program, then evaluating it once and storing it in a variable can eliminate potential inconsistencies as well as shorten the program.

Exercise 5.6

It is possible to write event procedure btnGuessMe_Click in Example 5.1 without any variables. Rewrite the If…Then…Else statement to accomplish this. Is the resulting code easier or harder to understand than when variables are used?

If…Then

Some decisions have two outcomes, only one of which requires processing. Consider, for example, a payroll program that computes overtime. If the condition determines whether a worker has put in extra hours, then a True outcome requires the calculation of the worker's extra pay, and a False outcome does not. In such situations we use Visual Basic .NET's If…Then statement.

The syntax of the If…Then statement is

> **If** *condition* **Then**
> *statementblock*
> **End If**

Its action is as follows. When the computer executes the If statement, it first evaluates the condition and determines whether its outcome is True or False. If the outcome is

- True: the computer executes the statements in the *statementblock*, one at a time, from top-to-bottom, then resumes at the statement following End If.

- False: the computer skips immediately to the statement following End If.

The If…Then statement is a simplified version of the If…Then…Else statement. If…Then…Else is useful when the two outcomes dictate either action A or action B. If…Then is useful when the two outcomes dictate either action A or no action. Because they are otherwise identical, in the remainder of the text we will refer to If…Then…Else and If…Then collectively as If statements.

Exercise 5.7

Complete the following event procedure by providing the statement block that will ensure that the message displayed in the message box is always correct. For example, if the user enters 3 and 5 in the TextBoxes txtX and txtY, respectively, then the message should read "3 <= 5", and if the user enters 7 and 4, then the message should read "4 <= 7".

Recall that a statement block is any sequence of zero or more statements. It may include If statements.

Do not modify, move, or add any statements before or after *statementblock*.

```
Private Sub btnSort_Click()
    Dim X As Integer
    Dim Y As Integer
    Dim Z As Integer
    X = txtX.Text
    Y = txtY.Text
    'statementblock
    MsgBox(X & " <= " & Y)
End Sub
```

Exercise 5.8

Complete the following event procedure by providing the statement block that will ensure that the message displayed in the message box is always correct. For example, if the user enters the numbers 3, 5, and 6 in the three TextBoxes txtX, txtY, and txtZ respectively, the message should read "Sequence 3, 5, 6 is in ascending order", but if the user enters 7, 4, 2 the message should read "Sequence 7, 4, 2 is not in ascending order".

Recall that a statement block is any sequence of zero or more statements. It may include If statements.

Do not modify, move, or add any statements before or after *statementblock*.

```
Private Sub btnVerifyAscending_Click()
    Dim X As Integer
    Dim Y As Integer
    Dim Z As Integer
    Dim Sequence As String
    Dim BlankOrNot As String
    X = txtX.Text
    Y = txtY.Text
    Z = txtZ.Text
    'statementblock
    Sequence = "Sequence " & X & "," & Y & "," & Z
    MsgBox(Sequence & " is " & BlankOrNot & " in ascending order")
End Sub
```

Exercise 5.9

Suppose that a user of the Caesar cipher encryption scheme (discussed in Example 4.12) needs to encrypt an entire sentence. A user employing the event procedure below would be wise to omit the spaces between words. Explain why.

```
Private Sub btnCaesarCipher_Click()
    Dim Letter As String
    Letter = txtNextLetter.Text
    txtNextLetter.Text = ""
    lblPlaintext.Text = lblPlaintext.Text & Letter
    lblCiphertext.Text = lblCiphertext.Text & Chr(Asc(Letter) + 3)
End Sub
```

Now modify btnCaesarCipher_Click so that the user can include spaces without "giving the code away." That is, modify it so that it shifts only the alphabetic characters "A" through "Z" and "a" through "z". All nonalphabetic characters in the plaintext should appear unchanged in the ciphertext.

5.3 Nested If Statements

Frequently a statement block in the interior of an If statement contains another If statement. In fact, the "inner" If statement may have yet another If in its interior, and on and on. **If statements that are arranged in this way, with one containing another, are called** *nested* **or** *embedded.*

As an example, consider the problem of determining whether a sequence of three numbers is in ascending or descending order. The event procedure in Figure 5.5 provides a partial solution to this problem. Looking at the event procedure you can see that the comment must be replaced by a statement block whose action is to store an appropriate value ("ascending" or "descending") in the string variable **AscOrDesc**.

The statement block has to make a choice, because we do not know in advance what sequence of numbers the user will enter. The problem description identifies only two possible outcomes: the sequence is in either ascending or descending order. If you think about it, you will see that there is another possibility: the user might enter 5, 8, and 1 that is neither in ascending nor descending order. In this third case we would probably like the program to display the message "Sequence 5, 8, 1, is in neither ascending nor descending order."

How do we handle this decision that has three outcomes? A common way of proceeding when faced with a new problem is to focus on only a part of the problem first, write out its solution in pseudocode, then assess whether it is possible to build on the partial solution. Consider the following pseudocode:

```
If (X < Y) And (Y < Z) Then
      AscOrDesc = "ascending"
Else
      what now? we know it's not ascending
End If
```

This pseudocode is actual Visual Basic .NET code except for the second interior statement block "what now? we know it's not ascending." Can we translate this statement block into working Visual Basic .NET statements?

Given that the sequence is not ascending, it must be either descending or neither. That is, at the position of "what now? we know it's not ascending," we still have a decision, but now there are only two possible outcomes: either the sequence

FIGURE 5.5

Partial Solution to Ascending/ Descending Problem

```
Private Sub btnDetermineAscDesc_Click(ByVal sender As System.Object
    Dim X, Y, Z As Integer
    Dim Sequence, AscOrDesc As String
    X = txtX.Text
    Y = txtY.Text
    Z = txtZ.Text
    ' Statement block
    Sequence = "Sequence " & X & ", " & Y & ", " & Z
    MsgBox(Sequence & " is in " & AscOrDesc & " order.")
End Sub
```

is descending, or it is neither ascending nor descending. We know how to handle a two-outcome decision with an If…Then…Else statement, so we can write our If statement as

```
If (X < Y) And (Y < Z) Then
    AscOrDesc = "ascending"
Else
    If (X > Y) And (Y > Z) Then
        AscOrDesc = "descending"
    Else
        AscOrDesc = "neither ascending nor descending"
    End If
End If
```

This is a solution to the problem.

As you can see, indentation is even more important when using embedded If statements. Each If statement has its own Else and its own End If. To keep clear which Elses and End Ifs belong to which Ifs, the "I" in If should line up vertically with both the "E" in its Else (if it has one) and the "E" in its End If, and the statement blocks in the interior should be indented. Again, unless you disable this feature, Visual Basic .NET will automatically produce this indentation.

Embedded If statements are frequently used this way to handle decisions with more than two outcomes. They are used so frequently that Visual Basic .NET provides a shortcut syntax that you should use when the statement block following Else begins with an If. The code in our example can be written more clearly using this shortcut as follows.

```
If (X < Y) And (Y < Z) Then
    AscOrDesc = "ascending"
ElseIf (X > Y) And (Y > Z) Then
    AscOrDesc = "descending"
Else
    AscOrDesc = "neither ascending nor descending"
End If
```

Note carefully that there is now only one If, one Else, and one End If. The ElseIf belongs to the If above it in the same way that the Else belongs to the If above it. When it can be used, this syntax is preferable to a nested If because it is easier to see the conditions and outcomes.

The shortcut syntax can be extended to handle any number of outcomes. There are only two restrictions: (1) there can be only one Else and (2) no ElseIfs can follow the Else; that is, the Else must represent the last (bottom) outcome.

The syntax for a decision with five outcomes follows:

```
If condition1 Then
    statementblock1
ElseIf condition2 Then
    statementblock2
ElseIf condition3 Then
    statementblock3
ElseIf condition4 Then
    statementblock4
Else
    statementblock5
End If
```

As before, exactly one of the statement blocks in this structure will be executed. Visual Basic .NET evaluates the conditions in order (starting at the top and proceeding through subsequent ElseIfs) and stops at the first one that evaluates to True. Visual Basic .NET then executes the corresponding statement block and resumes at the statement following End If. If none of the conditions evaluate to True, then Visual Basic .NET executes the statement block following Else.

Example 5.2

USING SHORTCUT SYNTAX FOR EMBEDDED IF STATEMENTS

A labor union bases its wage rate for a particular job class on number of months of service.

Wage Rate Categories Based on Months of Service	Wage Rate
< 3	$ 9.75
≥ 3 and < 6	10.25
≥ 6 and < 12	11.00
≥ 12 and < 24	12.50
≥ 24	14.75

We need a Click event procedure that has the user enter the number of months of service, then determines the corresponding wage rate from the table, stores it in a module-level variable named **WageRate**, and displays it in a message box (we assume in a real application that the variable **WageRate** would be used in other procedures and that is why we made it module-level scope). The solution is shown in Figure 5.6.

After the value for **MonthsOfService** is retrieved from the TextBox, it is tested to see which wage rate category it belongs to. For example, if the user enters 10, the first condition (**MonthsOfService < 3**) is False, so the first ElseIf condition is evaluated. Its condition (**MonthsOfService < 6**) is also False, so the next ElseIf condition is evaluated. Its condition (**MonthsOfService < 12**) is True, so **WageRate** is set equal to 11. This completes execution of the If statement, so the MsgBox statement is executed next.

Figure 5.7 shows a very poor solution to the same problem. It produces the same result as the solution in Figure 5.6, but is much longer than necessary.

FIGURE 5.6

Code for Example 5.2

```
Dim WageRate As Decimal
Private Sub btnLookupWageRate_Click(ByVal sender As System.Object,
    Dim MonthsOfService As Short
    MonthsOfService = txtMonthsOfService.Text
    If MonthsOfService < 3 Then
        WageRate = 9.75
    ElseIf MonthsOfService < 6 Then
        WageRate = 10.25
    ElseIf MonthsOfService < 12 Then
        WageRate = 11.0
    ElseIf MonthsOfService < 24 Then
        WageRate = 12.5
    Else
        WageRate = 14.75
    End If
    MsgBox("Wage rate is " & Format(WageRate, "Currency"))
End Sub
```

FIGURE 5.7

Poor Solution to
Wage Rate Problem

```
Dim WageRate As Decimal
Private Sub btnLookupWageRate_Click(ByVal sender As System.Object
    Dim MonthsOfService As Short
    MonthsOfService = txtMonthsOfService.Text
    If MonthsOfService < 3 Then
        WageRate = 9.75
        MsgBox("Wage rate is " & Format(WageRate, "Currency"))
    ElseIf MonthsOfService >= 3 And MonthsOfService < 6 Then
        WageRate = 10.25
        MsgBox("Wage rate is " & Format(WageRate, "Currency"))
    ElseIf MonthsOfService >= 6 And MonthsOfService < 12 Then
        WageRate = 11.0
        MsgBox("Wage rate is " & Format(WageRate, "Currency"))
    ElseIf MonthsOfService >= 12 And MonthsOfService < 24 Then
        WageRate = 12.5
        MsgBox("Wage rate is " & Format(WageRate, "Currency"))
    Else
        WageRate = 14.75
        MsgBox("Wage rate is " & Format(WageRate, "Currency"))
    End If
    MsgBox("Wage rate is " & Format(WageRate, "Currency"))
End Sub
```

Also, it is redundant in two ways. As always, these redundancies create potential for the program to behave inconsistently, which may annoy the user or cause the program to produce incorrect results. Try to spot the redundancies.

One redundancy is the repetition in the conditions. The constant 3, for example, occurs in *condition1,*

MonthsOfService < 3

and in *condition2,*

(MonthsOfService >= 3) And (MonthsOfService < 6)

In *condition2,* it is not necessary to check whether the months of service is greater than or equal to 3. Why? The computer evaluates *condition1* first, and if *condition1* is True, it executes *statementblock1,* and then jumps to the statement following End If. The computer will evaluate *condition2* only if *condition1* is False; but this means that **MonthsOfService** must be greater than or equal to 3, and so there is no need to check this as part of *condition2.*

The other redundancy is the message box statement that occurs in the statement block of every outcome. Any time you see the same statement occur in every statement block of an If structure, try to remove it from the statement blocks and place it either before or after the If structure. After all, if the statement will be executed regardless of the outcome, it is probably not necessary to handle it as part of the decision.

Example 5.3   **USING NESTED IF STATEMENTS**

This example illustrates that sometimes it is better not to use the shortcut syntax for embedded If statements. You must use common sense to determine the most readable and maintainable form of the If statements.

An automobile insurance company uses a customer's risk factors to compute the premium for the customer's policy. As an intermediate step, it computes a "risk rate" based on the customer's age and sex.

Age	Risk Rate	
	Male	Female
≤ 18	.34	.26
>18 and <21	.28	.22
≥ 21	.22	.18

We need a procedure that has the user enter a customer's sex and age, and then determines the risk rate for the customer, stores the risk rate in a module-level variable named **RiskRate**, and displays it. The event procedure in Figure 5.8 is one solution to this problem.

An alternative solution uses ElseIfs as follows. This solution contains more redundancy than the solution in Figure 5.8.

```
If (Sex = "Male") And (Age <= 18) Then
    RiskRate = 0.34
ElseIf (Sex = "Male") And (Age < 21) Then
    RiskRate = 0.28
ElseIf (Sex = "Male") Then
    RiskRate = 0.22
ElseIf (Sex = "Female") And (Age <= 18) Then
    RiskRate = 0.26
ElseIf (Sex = "Female") And (Age < 21) Then
    RiskRate = 0.22
Else
    RiskRate = 0.18
End If
```

FIGURE 5.8

Code for Example 5.3

```
Dim RiskRate As Decimal
Private Sub btnLookupRiskRate_Click(ByVal sender As System
    Dim Sex As String
    Dim Age As Integer
    Sex = txtGender.Text
    Age = txtAge.Text
    If Sex = "Male" Then
        If Age <= 18 Then
            RiskRate = 0.34
        ElseIf Age < 21 Then
            RiskRate = 0.28
        Else
            RiskRate = 0.22
        End If
    Else
        If Age <= 18 Then
            RiskRate = 0.26
        ElseIf Age < 21 Then
            RiskRate = 0.22
        Else
            RiskRate = 0.18
        End If
    End If
    MsgBox("Risk rate is " & RiskRate)
End Sub
```

Exercise 5.10

In Example 5.3, what happens if the user enters "male" instead of "Male"? Explain. Suggest a way to modify the code so this doesn't happen. *Hint:* Use the StrConv() or UCase() function.

Exercise 5.11

What happens in Example 5.3 if the user makes any typographical errors when attempting to enter "Male" or "Female"? Explain. With what we have covered so far, suggest a way to modify the code so this doesn't happen.

Exercise 5.12

A credit card company sends monthly bills to its customers. The bill shows the customer's balance (amount owed) and minimum amount due. The minimum amount due is computed from the balance as follows. If the balance is less than $0 (meaning the customer has overpaid), then the minimum amount due is $0. If the balance is between $0 and $20, inclusive, the minimum amount due is equal to the balance. If the balance is greater than $20, the minimum amount due is equal to the larger of the following two quantities: $20 or 2 percent of the balance.

Write a Click event procedure for a button that has the user enter a customer's balance, then computes and displays the corresponding minimum amount due.

5.4 The *MsgBox()* Function

Applications frequently display dialog boxes containing combinations of buttons like OK and Cancel, or Yes and No, to allow the user to make simple choices. **The *MsgBox() function* displays a message box on the screen and waits for the user to click one of the buttons; then it returns a value that indicates which button the user clicked.** This value can then be used by decision-making code to select an action that corresponds to the user's choice.

The syntax of the MsgBox() function is

MsgBox*(message, mbStyle, title)* **As MsgBoxResult**

This looks a lot like the syntax of the MsgBox statement. The difference in their actions is that the MsgBox statement does not provide any indication of which button the user clicked.

Now let's look at the *mbStyle* argument in more detail. In addition to specifying an icon style for the message box, the (numeric) value of *mbStyle* specifies the combination of buttons to be displayed in the message box. The six different button combinations are listed in Table 5.1 along with the value of *mbStyle* that produces them.

Table 5.1 MsgBox() button combinations

Symbolic Constant (Value)	Button Combination
MsgBoxStyle.AbortRetryIgnore (2)	The message box contains Abort, Retry, and Ignore buttons.
MsgBoxStyle.OKOnly (0)	The message box contains an OK button.
MsgBoxStyle.OKCancel (1)	The message box contains OK and Cancel buttons.
MsgBoxStyle.RetryCancel (5)	The message box contains Retry and Cancel buttons.
MsgBoxStyle.YesNo (4)	The message box contains Yes and No buttons.
MsgBoxStyle.YesNoCancel (3)	The message box contains Yes, No, and Cancel buttons.

Table 5.2 MsgBox() return values	
Symbolic Constant (Value)	Description
vbOK (1)	OK button was pressed.
vbCancel (2)	Cancel button was pressed.
vbAbort (3)	Abort button was pressed.
vbRetry (4)	Retry button was pressed.
vbIgnore (5)	Ignore button was pressed.
vbYes (6)	Yes button was pressed.
vbNo (7)	No button was pressed.

The value returned by the MsgBox() function indicates which button the user clicked. The type of this return value is indicated in the "As" clause that follows the parenthetical list of parameters. In this case, the return type is an enumeration[1] called MsgBoxResult. Table 5.2 lists the return values in the MsgBoxResult enumeration.

As an example, the statement

Response = MsgBox("You've taken 10 guesses. Quit now?", MsgBoxStyle.YesNo)

causes the computer to display the message box shown in Figure 5.9, then wait for the user to click one of the buttons. If the user clicks Yes, the MsgBox() function returns vbYes, and if the user clicks No, it returns the value vbNo.

To specify an icon for the message box, we use one of the values MsgBoxStyle.vbCritical, MsgBoxStyle.vbQuestion, MsgBoxStyle.vbExclamation, or MsgBoxStyle.vbInformation for the *mbStyle* argument. To specify both an icon and a particular combination of buttons, use *mbStyle* equal to the sum of the constant for the icon and the constant for the button combination. For example, to make the message box show both a question icon (vbQuestion) and the Yes and No button combination (MsgBoxStyle.YesNo), use *mbStyle* equal to (vbQuestion + MsgBoxStyle.YesNo). Thus, the statement

Response = MsgBox("You've taken 10 guesses. Quit now?", _
vbQuestion + MsgBoxStyle.YesNo)

displays the message box in Figure 5.10.

FIGURE 5.9

Message Box
Showing Yes and No
Buttons

---

[1] Enumerations provide a convenient way to work with sets of related constants and to associate constant values with names. For example, you can declare an enumeration for a set of integer constants associated with the days of the week and then use the names of the days rather than their integer values in your code.

FIGURE 5.10

Message Box with
Yes and No Buttons
and a Question
Mark Icon

FIGURE 5.11

Code for Example 5.4

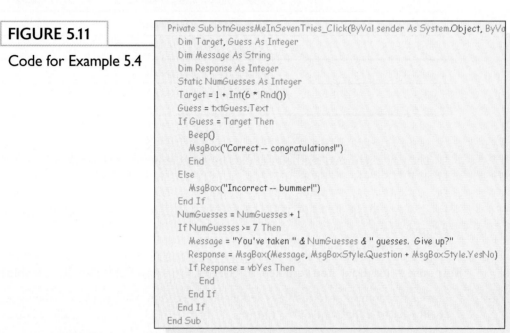

```
Private Sub btnGuessMeInSevenTries_Click(ByVal sender As System.Object, ByVa
    Dim Target, Guess As Integer
    Dim Message As String
    Dim Response As Integer
    Static NumGuesses As Integer
    Target = 1 + Int(6 * Rnd())
    Guess = txtGuess.Text
    If Guess = Target Then
        Beep()
        MsgBox("Correct -- congratulations!")
        End
    Else
        MsgBox("Incorrect -- bummer!")
    End If
    NumGuesses = NumGuesses + 1
    If NumGuesses >= 7 Then
        Message = "You've taken " & NumGuesses & " guesses.  Give up?"
        Response = MsgBox(Message, MsgBoxStyle.Question + MsgBoxStyle.YesNo)
        If Response = vbYes Then
            End
        End If
    End If
End Sub
```

Example 5.4   **USING THE MSGBOX() FUNCTION**

The event procedure in Figure 5.11 modifies the guessing game from Example
5.1. When the user guesses correctly, it displays congratulations and then terminates
execution. It also counts the number of guesses the user has made, using the static variable **NumGuesses**; if this count reaches 7, it displays a message and gives the
user the option of quitting. If the user chooses to quit, program execution terminates.

5.5   The RadioButton Control

Many programs have options from which the user must select exactly one. For
example, in a medical records system the user needs to specify the sex (male or
female) of the patient. Visual Basic .NET's *RadioButton control,* **which ensures
that the user will select only one option**, is simple and very effective in such
situations.

Appearance and Use

Figure 5.12 identifies the RadioButton tool and shows a RadioButton control on
the form at design time. Visually, a RadioButton appears as descriptive text next
to a circle. At run time, the user selects a RadioButton by moving the cursor

FIGURE 5.12

RadioButton Tool
and Control

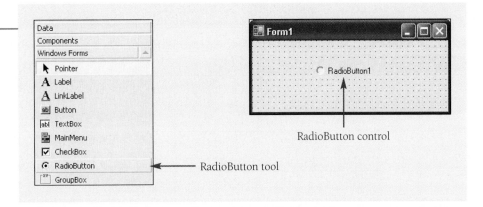

RadioButton tool

RadioButton control

atop either the text or the circle, then clicking the mouse. Visual Basic .NET acknowledges the user's selection by placing a dot in the circle.

If the user subsequently selects a different RadioButton, Visual Basic .NET automatically erases the dot from the previously selected RadioButton and moves it to the newly chosen RadioButton. Thus, the user is able to select only one option from a group of RadioButtons. The developer often provides a Button control to let the user initiate processing after making a choice.

Like the TextBox control and Button control, the RadioButton control is capable of receiving the focus. The user can move the focus among RadioButton controls using the mouse or any of the arrow keys.

To demonstrate the use of RadioButtons, let us work with a computerized replica of the U.S. Individual Income Tax Return (Form 1040). The Filing Status section of this form presents the taxpayer with five options. The taxpayer is required to specify exactly one of them. If RadioButtons are used, this section might appear as in Figure 5.13.

When you design an application with RadioButtons, be sure to keep the number of options the user has to choose from small, no more than seven or so. This is an important rule of thumb for designing GUIs. Researchers in the field of psychology have long known that most people cannot keep more than about seven items in their short-term memory and, as a result, it is difficult for them to make a selection if the list of options is longer than that.

Properties

Table 5.3 lists some properties of the RadioButton control. In terms of its role in a program's operation, the Checked property is the RadioButton's most used property. This property is Boolean: it has two allowable settings, True and False. As a result, the RadioButton control is a natural partner of the If statement. The

FIGURE 5.13

User Interface for
Filing Status Section
of Income Tax Form

Figure 5.13

- Single
- Married filing joint return
- Married filing separate return
- Head of Household
- Qualified widow(er) with dependent child

Table 5.3 Properties of the RadioButton control

Property	Value
Name	(rad) *Gets or sets the name of the control.*
Appearance	*Gets or sets the value that determines the appearance of the RadioButton control.* Choices are Normal (default) and Button. The Button choice makes the RadioButton look like a regular Button control.
CheckAlign	*Gets or sets the location of the check box portion of the RadioButton control.* Includes all combinations of the three vertical and three horizontal choices. Default is MiddleLeft.
Checked	*Gets or sets a Boolean value indicating whether the control is checked.*
Enabled	*Gets or sets a Boolean value indicating whether the control is enabled.*
FlatStyle	*Gets or sets the flat style appearance of the RadioButton control.* The four choices are Flat, Popup, Standard (default), and System.
Image	*Gets or sets the image that is displayed on a RadioButton control.* Specifies the path to an image that is placed in the text portion of the control. Typically used instead of text to identify an option (such as a picture of a man instead of the text "Male" and a picture of a woman instead of the text "Female".)
ImageAlign	*Gets or sets the alignment of the image on the RadioButton control.* Includes all combinations of the three vertical and three horizontal choices. Default is MiddleCenter.
Text	*Gets or sets the text associated with this control.*
TextAlign	*Gets or sets the alignment of the text within the text portion on the RadioButton control.* Includes all combinations of the three vertical and three horizontal choices. Default is MiddleLeft.
Visible	*Gets or sets a Boolean value indicating whether the control is visible.*

event procedure that processes the user's selections can use a RadioButton's Checked property as the condition of an If statement.

Events

The RadioButton control is capable of responding to the CheckedChanged event. This event occurs when the value of the Checked property changes. Often, however, the RadioButton's CheckedChanged event procedure is not used to perform major processing tasks. Instead, the RadioButton control is used just as a means of getting input from the user, and the user initiates processing by clicking on a Button control.

Example 5.5 USING RADIOBUTTONS

An automobile insurance company uses a computer program to compute a driver's premium. The premium is based on the risk rate that in turn depends on the driver's age and sex. The user must specify either male or female, and RadioButtons are a good way to accomplish this. Figure 5.14 shows the user interface.

The user first selects the appropriate RadioButton, and then clicks the Button. The Click event procedure for btnComputeRiskFactor is shown in Figure 5.15. The condition **radMale.Checked = True** will be True if the user selected the Male option; otherwise it will be False.

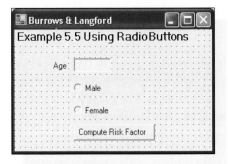

FIGURE 5.14

User Interface for Insurance Risk
Rate Program

```
Dim RiskRate As Decimal
Private Sub btnComputeRiskFactor_Click(ByVal sender As Sy
    Dim Age As Integer = txtAge.Text
    If radMale.Checked = True Then
        If Age <= 18 Then
            RiskRate = 0.34
        ElseIf Age < 21 Then
            RiskRate = 0.28
        Else
            RiskRate = 0.22
        End If
    ElseIf radFemale.Checked = True Then
        If Age <= 18 Then
            RiskRate = 0.26
        ElseIf Age < 21 Then
            RiskRate = 0.22
        Else
            RiskRate = 0.18
        End If
    Else
        MsgBox("Did not make Male/Female selection.")
        End
    End If
    MsgBox("Risk rate is " & RiskRate)
End Sub
```

FIGURE 5.15

Code for Example 5.5

An equivalent way of writing the logical expression in

If radMale.Checked = True Then

is as

If radMale.Checked Then

You may think that this syntax is not valid because it is not comparing rad-Male.Checked to another value. However, these two alternatives are identical as far as Visual Basic .NET is concerned. In the first alternative, radMale's Checked property is retrieved and then compared to the logical constant True. If they are equal, Visual Basic .NET evaluates the logical expression to the value True and then executes the "True action" of the If statement. The second one looks at the current contents of radMale's Checked property and if it is True, executes the "True action" of the If statement. In the first case we are comparing True = True and getting True as a result. In the second case we are also getting a result of True but this time directly from the Checked property.

Note that we include a condition for the case in which neither RadioButton is selected. Why do we do this? Suppose we did not provide it; then what would happen if neither RadioButton were selected when the user clicked the button? Since the Checked property of both RadioButtons would be False, none of the actions in the If statement would be executed. Thus, the module-level variable **RiskRate** would not be modified, and its value would be whatever value was left over from the previous execution of the procedure. This would be a very serious error in the code because the program would produce an incorrect risk rate and the user would be unaware of the error. To be safe, you should always include an outcome in decision-making code for the user's failure to make a selection.

Exercise 5.13

Suppose you have a project consisting of a single form with several RadioButtons, and the Checked properties of all of the RadioButtons have been initialized to False. When program execution begins, how many of the RadioButtons will be selected (i.e., how many will have a dot)? Which one(s)? Create a simple Visual Basic .NET project to find out.

Exercise 5.14

Suppose that you have just finished an application and given it to a user to try out. Your application requires the user to answer a Yes/No question, and you have provided RadioButtons for this purpose. The user complains that a text box is preferable because typing is quicker than positioning the mouse. How do you respond to this criticism?

5.6 The GroupBox Control

Some programs require the user to answer more than one question. For example, on the U.S. Income Tax form, taxpayers are asked two Yes/No questions:

- Do you want $3 to go to this fund?

- If a joint return, does your spouse want $3 to go to this fund?

The answers to these questions are easily processed using four RadioButtons. The interface for this part of the tax form might appear as in Figure 5.16. However, Visual Basic .NET allows only one RadioButton to be selected at any given time. If we put these four RadioButtons on the same form as the Filing Status RadioButtons, then there will be a total of nine RadioButtons on the form, only one of which can be selected. But there are really three separate questions. What we need is a way to inform Visual Basic .NET of this fact, so that Visual Basic .NET will allow one RadioButton to be selected for each question. **The *GroupBox control* allows you to group RadioButtons to correspond to categories of items, so that the user can select exactly one item in each category.**[2]

Appearance and Use

Visually, the GroupBox control appears as a rectangle surrounding the controls it groups together. Descriptive text can be used with the rectangle to help identify the "group" to which the contents relate. Figure 5.17 identifies the GroupBox tool and shows a GroupBox control on the form at design time.

To group RadioButtons, you may either drag them into a GroupBox or draw them in the GroupBox in the first place. You can always drag a RadioButton in or out of the GroupBox. To verify that a RadioButton is in the GroupBox, you can drag the whole GroupBox around the form (at design time) and all RadioButtons within the GroupBox container will move with it.

FIGURE 5.16

User Interface for Campaign Fund Section of Income Tax Form

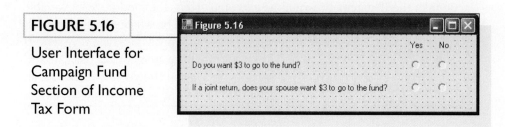

---

2   The GroupBox control can contain other types of controls besides RadioButtons and is often referred to as a "container control."

FIGURE 5.17

GroupBox Tool and
Control

GroupBox tool   GroupBox control

Properties

Table 5.4 lists some important properties of the GroupBox control.

Events

The GroupBox control is capable of responding to Click events. However, the
GroupBox's Click event procedure is seldom used to perform major processing
tasks. The GroupBox control's fundamental purpose is to organize the controls on
a form.

With the GroupBox control we can add the questions about Presidential Election Campaign contributions to the U.S. Individual Income Tax Return form.
The form shown in Figure 5.18 contains three GroupBox controls. The rectangle
surrounding the text "Presidential Election Campaign" is a Label. The filing status GroupBox has its Text property set to "Filing Status", and the other two
GroupBox controls have empty Text properties.

The names of the GroupBox and RadioButtons on this form are shown in
Table 5.5. If you look carefully at the RadioButton names, you can discern a
common naming convention. All of them begin with rad. But the next few letters

Table 5.4 Properties of the GroupBox control

Property	Value
Name	(grp) *Gets or sets the name of the control.*
Enabled	*Gets or sets a Boolean value indicating whether the control is enabled. If the GroupBox is not enabled (value set to False), then all the controls it contains also are not enabled.*
FlatStyle	*Gets or sets the flat style appearance of the group box control. The four choices are Flat, Popup, Standard (default), and System.*
Text	*Gets or sets the text associated with this control.*
Visible	*Gets or sets a Boolean value indicating whether the control is visible. If the GroupBox is not visible (value set to False), then all the controls it contains also are not visible.*

GroupBox	RadioButtons
Table 5.5 Main controls for user interface of Figure 5.18	
GroupBox	RadioButtons
grpPECYou	radPECYouYes
	radPECYouNo
grpPECSpouse	radPECSpouseYes
	radPECSpouseNo
grpFilingStatus	radFSSingle
	radFSMarriedJoint
	radFSMarriedSeparate
	radFSHeadOfHousehold
	radFSWidower

FIGURE 5.18

Expanded User
Interface for
Income Tax Return
Application

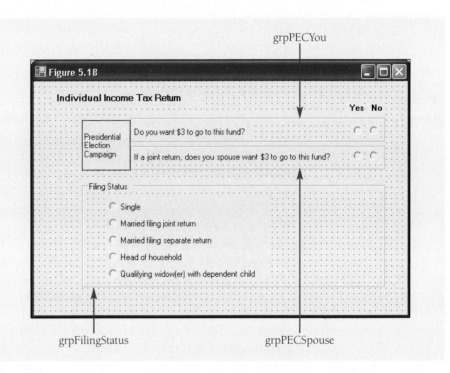

of these names are an abbreviation that suggests the name of the GroupBox in which the RadioButton resides. This is a simple trick to help the developer keep track of which RadioButtons reside in which GroupBox.

We know that when the user selects a RadioButton at run time, Visual Basic .NET sets its Checked property to True, places a dot in the button, and generates a CheckedChanged event. But the RadioButton also can be selected in code by executing an assignment statement such as the following:

radPECYouYes.Checked = True

When this statement executes, Visual Basic .NET places a dot in the RadioButton and generates a CheckedChanged event.

Setting a RadioButton's Checked property in code often can be used to good effect, as our next example illustrates.

Example 5.6

USING THE RADIOBUTTON'S CHECKEDCHANGED EVENT

The three separate questions on the income tax form in Figure 5.18 are not entirely independent of one another. The event procedures in Figure 5.19 make the user aware of this. Event procedure radFSSingle_CheckedChanged disables the Election Campaign question that a single taxpayer cannot answer, and event procedure radFSMarriedJoint_CheckedChanged enables it again for a married taxpayer.

Event procedure radFSSingle_CheckedChanged is executed when the user selects filing status Single. It performs the following actions:

* It deselects the two RadioButtons radPECSpouseYes and radPECSpouseNo by setting their Checked properties to False.

* It disables the GroupBox control (by setting its Enabled property to False). This has the effect of disabling the controls in the GroupBox (radPECSpouseYes and radPECSpouseNo) so that the user cannot select either of them. This also changes their appearance to light gray, which provides a visual cue to the user that this question does not apply.

Figure 5.20 shows the effect, at run time, when the user selects filing status Single.

Event procedure radFSMarriedJoint_CheckedChanged is executed when the user selects filing status Married filing joint return. This event procedure undoes the effect of radFSSingle_CheckedChanged, which is necessary because the question "If a joint return, does your spouse want $3 to go to this fund?" is again applicable. The user can switch back and forth between the two filing statuses, each time observing the applicability or nonapplicability of the choice regarding his or her spouse's $3.

FIGURE 5.19

Code for Example 5.6

```
Private Sub radFSSingle_CheckedChanged(ByVal sender
    grpPECSpouse.Enabled = False
    radPECSpouseYes.Checked = False
    radPECSpouseNo.Checked = False
End Sub

Private Sub radFSMarriedJoint_CheckedChanged(ByVal s
    grpPECSpouse.Enabled = True
End Sub
```

FIGURE 5.20

User Interface When User Selects Filing Status Single

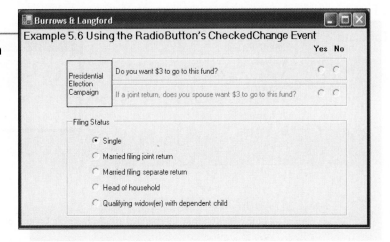

5.7 | The CheckBox Control

Users sometimes have to make decisions that require selecting a combination of options from a set of alternatives. For example, in a real estate application, the user may be asked to specify whether the houses to be viewed should have a garden, a garage, and/or a view. Any combination of these options is valid. For such situations, **where a combination of options may be selected, Visual Basic .NET provides the *CheckBox control.***

Appearance and Use

Figure 5.21 identifies the CheckBox tool and shows a CheckBox control on the form at design time. A CheckBox appears as descriptive text next to a square. At run time, the user selects a CheckBox by moving the cursor atop either the text or the square, then clicking the mouse. Visual Basic .NET acknowledges the user's selection by placing a check mark in the square. The user can remove the check mark by clicking on it again; this action is called deselection.[3]

Functionally, the essential difference between RadioButtons and CheckBoxes is that RadioButtons impose the restriction that the user selects only one option, whereas CheckBoxes do not. This is an important difference. Users rely on the visually different appearance of RadioButtons and CheckBoxes to quickly infer whether they are allowed to select only one option or several. Thus, a developer who uses CheckBoxes when RadioButtons are appropriate will construct programs that users find confusing.

Properties and Events

The commonly used properties of the CheckBox control are similar to those of the RadioButton control. Table 5.6 shows some of the commonly used properties.

The three properties Checked, CheckState, and ThreeState need a little explanation. The difference between being checked and unchecked should be clear. However, the CheckState value of Indeterminate is generally not clear. In this state, the check box is checked (so the value of the Checked property is True); however,

FIGURE 5.21

CheckBox Tool and Control

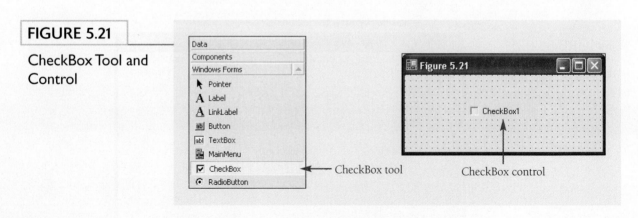

CheckBox tool   CheckBox control

---

3   Any type of action that alternately turns something on and off is called a toggle.

Table 5.6 Properties of the CheckBox control

Property	Value
Name	*(chk) Gets or sets the name of the control.*
CheckAlign	*Gets or sets the horizontal and vertical alignment of a check box on a CheckBox control.* Includes all combinations of the three vertical and three horizontal choices. Default is MiddleLeft.
Checked	*Gets or sets a Boolean value indicating whether the CheckBox is in the checked state.*
CheckState	*Gets or sets the state of the CheckBox.* Possible values are Checked, UnChecked, or Indeterminate.
Enabled	*Gets or sets a Boolean value indicating whether the control is enabled.*
Text	*Gets or sets the text associated with this control.*
TextAlign	*Gets or sets the alignment of the text on the CheckBox control.* Includes all combinations of the three vertical and three horizontal choices. Default is MiddleLeft.
ThreeState	*Gets or sets a Boolean value indicating whether the check box will allow three check states rather than two.* Determines if the user can select the Indeterminate state. Default value is False.
Visible	Gets or sets a Boolean value indicating whether the control is visible.

the check mark itself will not be the normal color, but instead gray. This is generally used in an application to indicate that the user may have selected a subset of options. For example, in a Help system, there may be five different categories of help. A CheckBox indicating the user's selection of these five options might be UnChecked, meaning no help categories were selected; Checked, meaning that all help categories were selected; and Indeterminate, meaning that a subset of the five options (but not all of them) were selected. The ThreeState property indicates whether the user can click on the CheckBox to set its state to Indeterminate. When this property is set to False, the user is not able to cause the Indeterminate state by clicking (but you, as the developer, can write code to change the state to Indeterminate regardless of the value of the ThreeState property).

Like the RadioButton, the CheckBox can respond to a CheckedChanged event.

Example 5.7

USING CHECKBOXES

The U.S. Individual Income Tax Return (Form 1040) contains an Exemptions section. In our computerized application, this section might appear as shown in Figure 5.22. The taxpayer may check neither, one, or both of the boxes for Yourself and Spouse.

A subsequent step in the income tax form requires counting the number of exemptions claimed by the filer. The event procedure in Figure 5.23 performs this task; it stores the result in a procedure-level variable named **NumberOfExemptions** and displays it. Observe that the code works correctly for every possible combination of check marks in the two boxes.

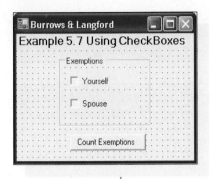

FIGURE 5.22

User Interface for Example 5.7

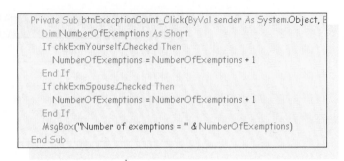

FIGURE 5.23

Code for Example 5.7

Exercise 5.15

Is it ever necessary to group CheckBoxes using a GroupBox control? If so, why? If not, would it hurt to group them anyway, or might it help? Explain.

Exercise 5.16

A form contains two CheckBoxes (chkA and chkB), two RadioButtons (radX and radY), and a Button (btnShowTotals). The code for this form is shown below. Note that two of the controls, chkB and radY, do not have event procedures (which means that no code is executed when the user clicks on them). When program execution begins, both of the CheckBoxes are clear (they don't have check marks in them). The user then clicks on the controls in the following order:

> chkA, chkB, chkA, radX, radY, radX, btnShowTotals

Show the values that are displayed by the message boxes in btnShowTotals_Click.

```
Dim TotalA As Integer
Dim TotalX As Integer
Private Sub chkA_CheckedChanged(ByVal sender ...)
    If chkA.Checked = True Then
        TotalA = TotalA + 10
    Else
        TotalA = TotalA - 5
    End If
End Sub
Private Sub radX_CheckedChanged(ByVal sender ...)
    If radX.Checked = True Then
        TotalX = TotalX + 10
    Else
        TotalX = TotalX - 5
    End If
End Sub
Private Sub btnShowTotals_Click(ByVal sender ...)
    MsgBox("Total A = " & TotalA)
    MsgBox("Total X = " & TotalX)
End Sub
```

5.8 | **The Select Case Statement**

As we have seen, a single If statement can only handle a condition having two outcomes. We can handle conditions having more than two outcomes with embedded If statements. Visual Basic .NET's *Select Case statement* **can handle conditions with multiple outcomes** and in many situations is easier to read than embedded If statements.

Like the If…Then…Else statement, the Select Case statement is a compound statement, meaning it can contain many individual statements. Also, as with If…Then…Else, you can conceptualize the Select Case statement as a single meta statement to help you think about the logic used to solve a problem.

Syntax and Action of Select Case

The Select Case statement spans more than one line in a procedure. The statement itself has several parts and multiple statement blocks. Its syntax is as follows:

```
Select Case testexpression
Case expressionlist I
    statementblock I
Case expressionlist2
    statementblock2
...
Case expressionlistN
    statementblockN
Case Else
    statementblock
End Select
```

An example Select Case statement is

```
Select Case MonthAbbr
    Case "JAN", "MAR", "MAY", "JUL", "AUG", "OCT", "DEC"
        DaysInMonth = 31
    Case "APR", "JUN", "SEP", "NOV"
        DaysInMonth = 30
    Case "FEB"
        DaysInMonth = 28
    Case Else
        MsgBox(MonthAbbr & " is not a valid month abbreviation.")
End Select
```

The test expression (the string variable **MonthAbbr** in the example) may be any numeric or string expression. An *expression list* ("APR", "JUN", "SEP", "NOV" in the example) is simply a list of expressions separated by commas. If the test expression is numeric, then the expressions in each list are generally numeric; and if the test expression is string, then the expressions in each list are generally strings.

Note that the test expression in Select Case is different from the condition in If…Then…Else. The test expression in Select Case can be any numeric or string expression, whereas the condition in If…Then…Else must be a logical expression. Also be aware that Case Else is optional.

Run Time: The Effect of the Select Case Statement

When the computer executes the Select Case statement, it first evaluates the test expression and then attempts to match the resulting value with one of the values from the expression lists. That is, it starts searching at the top expression list and proceeds through subsequent expression lists, stopping at the first value that matches. Visual Basic .NET then executes the corresponding statement block and resumes at the statement following End Select. If none of the expression lists matches the test expression result, Visual Basic .NET executes the Case Else statement block, then resumes at the statement following End Select. If Case Else is omitted and none of the expression lists matches the test expression result, then nothing happens, that is, none of the statement blocks is executed.

As with the If statement, you improve the readability of your code by using appropriate indenting. Unless you disable this feature, Visual Basic .NET will automatically indent the parts of the Select Case statement appropriately.

Example 5.8

USING THE SELECT CASE STATEMENT

This example shows how the Select Case statement presented earlier works. The complete event procedure containing this statement is shown in Figure 5.24. Although it is very simple, it demonstrates how Select Case is useful for decisions that can be described as "classifications" or "groupings." In this example, the user enters a month abbreviation that is stored in variable **MonthAbbr**. This variable is then used as the test expression in the Select Case statement. The variable **DaysInMonth** is set according to which expression list contains the value stored in **MonthAbbr**.

Exercise 5.17

In Example 5.8, what happens when the user enters "Mar" or "mar" instead of "MAR"? How can you modify the code so that it treats these three inputs identically?

Exercise 5.18

In Example 5.8, if the user enters "ARG", the message "ARG is not a valid month abbreviation" is displayed, and then the message "ARG has 0 days" is displayed. Modify btnMonthDays_Click so that it does not display the latter (meaningless) message when the user enters an invalid month abbreviation.

FIGURE 5.24

Code for Example 5.8

```
Private Sub btnMonthDays_Click(ByVal sender As System.Object, ByVa
    Dim MonthAbbr As String
    Dim DaysInMonth As Integer
    MonthAbbr = txtMonth.Text
    Select Case MonthAbbr
        Case "JAN", "MAR", "MAY", "JUL", "AUG", "OCT", "DEC"
            DaysInMonth = 31
        Case "APR", "JUN", "SEP", "NOV"
            DaysInMonth = 30
        Case "FEB"
            DaysInMonth = 28
        Case Else
            MsgBox(MonthAbbr & " is not a valid month abbreviation.")
    End Select
    MsgBox(MonthAbbr & " has " & DaysInMonth & " days.")
End Sub
```

Ranges

In the previous example, the expression lists were simply lists of distinct values. But Select Case also allows you to specify ranges of values in your expression lists. There are two variations:

1. Two expressions separated by the keyword To. For example, the range

8 To 10

will match the test expression value if it is between 8 and 10, inclusive.

2. The keyword Is, followed by a comparison operator, followed by an expression. For example, the range

Is <= 10

will match the test expression value if it is less than or equal to 10.

Be aware that logical operators such as And and Or are syntactically legal in the Select Case statement but generally do not produce the results you would expect. The comma separating two or more expressions in the expression list is conceptually the same as a logical "or". For example, **10 To 20, 33, Is > 100** will capture values between 10 and 20 (inclusive), *or* 33, *or* greater than 100. The keyword "To" is logically equivalent to "and". But the actual logical operators And and Or should be avoided.

Ranges are illustrated by the event procedure in Figure 5.25, which is a version of our simple guessing game that uses a "loaded die." In our previous version each integer from 1 through 6 had an equal chance of coming up, because the random integer was generated by the statement **Target = 1 + Int(6 * Rnd())**. A Select Case statement has replaced this statement. Recall that the Rnd() function returns a random fraction between 0 and 1. In this example there is a 20 percent chance of **Target** equaling 1, a 10 percent chance of **Target** equaling 2, and so on. This is why we called the die "loaded."

FIGURE 5.25

Event Procedure for "Loaded Die" Guessing Game

```
Private Sub btnGuessMeLoaded_Click(ByVal sender As System.O
    Dim Target, Guess As Short
    Select Case Rnd()
        Case Is < 0.2
            Target = 1
        Case 0.2 To 0.3
            Target = 2
        Case 0.3 To 0.6
            Target = 3
        Case 0.6 To 0.75
            Target = 4
        Case 0.75 To 0.9
            Target = 5
        Case Else
            Target = 6
    End Select
    Guess = txtGuess.Text
    If Guess = Target Then
        Beep()
        MsgBox("Correct - congratulations")
    Else
        MsgBox("Incorrect - bummer!")
    End If
End Sub
```

Visual Basic .NET will not complain if the ranges in two or more expression lists overlap; it will simply execute the statement block for the first case it matches. This can be important. For example, the number 0.6 appears in two consecutive ranges in Figure 5.25. If we had used

Case 0.61 To 0.75

instead of

Case 0.6 To 0.75

so that there was no overlap, then there would have been a "gap" between 0.6 (the upper bound of the one range) and 0.61 (the lower bound of the next range). Consequently, if the random number happened to be 0.605, it would fall into this gap. Since it would not be covered by either Case, it would be handled by the Case Else, which is probably not what we would have intended.

Working with numeric expressions as in the previous code is straightforward. It is clear what values lie in the "To" range. But what about string expressions? Consider the following Select Case statement:

```
Select Case Letter
    Case "A" To "H"
        MsgBox("First Group")
    Case "I" To "P"
        MsgBox("Second Group")
    Case Else
        MsgBox("Third Group")
End Select
```

What does the range "A" to "H" include? It includes any string that begins with the letter "A" through "G" plus the single letter "H"; examples are "Apple", "BANANA", "Dawg House", and "Grocery". Visual Basic .NET uses the ANSI table to define the values included in the range with string expressions.

Another interesting version of our guessing game is shown in Figure 5.26. It uses the "Is" variation for specifying ranges. This version generates a random target when the form is loaded. The user tries to guess the number. If the guess is wrong, the message says whether it was too high or too low. This additional information should help the user with the next guess because it eliminates some possible numbers.

FIGURE 5.26

Event Procedure for Modified Guessing Game

```
Dim Target As Short
Private Sub Form1_Load(ByVal sender As System.Object, ByVal
    Randomize()
    Target = 1 + Int(6 * Rnd())
End Sub

Private Sub btnGuessMeGuided_Click(ByVal sender As System.O
    Dim Guess As Integer = txtGuess.Text
    Select Case Guess
        Case Is < Target
            MsgBox("Guess too low.")
        Case Is > Target
            MsgBox("Guess too high.")
        Case Else
            Beep()
            MsgBox("Correct - congratulations")
    End Select
End Sub
```

FIGURE 5.27

Letter Categories

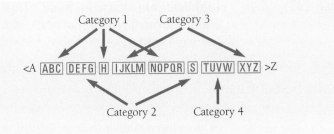

A single expression list can contain both ranges and individual expressions, separated by commas. Expression lists of this type are useful in situations where a single outcome corresponds to a collection of "scattered" items. As an example of this, suppose the letters of the alphabet (capital letters only) are divided into four categories as shown in Figure 5.27. Observe that each letter belongs to exactly one of the categories. The event procedure in Figure 5.28 takes a letter and displays the category to which the letter belongs.

As we pointed out earlier, the Select Case syntax does not require the Case Else; it is optional. However, even when the expression lists prior to Case Else cover all possible outcomes, as in Figure 5.28, it is still a good idea to have a Case Else. This practice helps to identify problems that may arise due to unanticipated outcomes that even experienced developers encounter in complicated programs.

Even if a developer successfully handles all possible outcomes when originally creating the program, at some point in the future the program may need to be modified and new outcomes added. If the developer overlooks one of the cases at that time, he or she will be thankful for including the Case Else at the outset.

Exercise 5.19

In the code in Figure 5.25, which is the most likely value of Target? The most unlikely?

Exercise 5.20

The ranges in the Select Case statement in Figure 5.25 contain redundant data. Rewrite the ranges in this Select Case statement using Is instead of To in order to eliminate this redundancy. Which form is more readable? Explain.

Hint: The second expression list, **0.2 To 0.3**, can be written as **Is <= 0.3**. Remember that Visual Basic .NET does not mind if ranges overlap.

FIGURE 5.28

Event Procedure that Determines a Letter's Category

```
Private Sub btnLetterCategories_Click(ByVal sender As
    Select Case txtLetter.Text
        Case Is < "A", Is > "Z"
            MsgBox("Not a capital letter")
        Case Is <= "C", "H", "N" To "R"
            MsgBox("Category 1")
        Case "D" To "G", "S"
            MsgBox("Category 2")
        Case "I" To "M", Is >= "X"
            MsgBox("Category 3")
        Case "T" To "W"
            MsgBox("Category 4")
        Case Else
            MsgBox("Unanticipated value")
    End Select
End Sub
```

Exercise 5.21

In the guessing-game example in Figure 5.26, what is the largest number of guesses an intelligent user of btnGuessMeGuided_Click might reasonably take to guess correctly? Explain.

If versus Select Case

Select Case is similar to embedded If statements, except that the outcome of the decision is determined by a single expression at the top. In contrast, an embedded If has one condition at the top and one for each ElseIf, and each of these conditions is a separate expression. Thus, embedded If structures allow for much greater complexity than Select Case.

As a developer, when should you use embedded Ifs and when should you use Select Case? The following decision rules may help you choose:

- If a decision has only two outcomes and the condition can be expressed as a single logical expression, then the If statement is easier to read than a Select Case. The developer has only to understand the condition, and the two statement blocks are readily apparent because of indentation.

- If a decision has multiple outcomes that depend only on a single expression, Select Case is usually easier to read than nested If statements.

- If the outcomes depend on a number of conditions that may be independent of one another, then the flexibility of embedded If statements makes them the better choice.

Exercise 5.22

Solve Exercise 5.12 using Select Case instead of embedded If statements. Which approach is better? Explain.

5.9 | The Exit Sub Statement

Suppose you are designing an application in which the user is supposed to enter some data and then click a button to invoke a procedure to process the data in some way. What should the event procedure do if it discovers that one or more of the input values are not valid and therefore the processing cannot be carried out? Most likely the procedure should notify the user via a message box and then stop and wait for the user to correct the data. How would you write the code to implement this behavior?

Visual Basic .NET provides the **Exit Sub statement for decisions where one of the appropriate actions is to perform no further processing.** When executed, this statement causes execution to skip all subsequent statements and jump directly to End Sub.

The Exit Sub statement is not limited to If…Then…Else and Select Case statements, but it is most often used within these statements. It also might be found in the Catch block of a Try/Catch statement.

As an example, consider again procedure btnMonthDays_Click, repeated in Figure 5.29. This event procedure responds poorly if the user enters an invalid month abbreviation. For example, if the user enters the month abbreviation "GEB", it will display the message "GEB has 0 days" in the final message box.

```
Private Sub btnMonthDays_Click(ByVal sender As System.Object, ByVa
  Dim MonthAbbr As String
  Dim DaysInMonth As Integer
  MonthAbbr = txtMonth.Text
  Select Case MonthAbbr
    Case "JAN", "MAR", "MAY", "JUL", "AUG", "OCT", "DEC"
      DaysInMonth = 31
    Case "APR", "JUN", "SEP", "NOV"
      DaysInMonth = 30
    Case "FEB"
      DaysInMonth = 28
    Case Else
      MsgBox(MonthAbbr & " is not a valid month abbreviation.")
  End Select
  MsgBox(MonthAbbr & " has " & DaysInMonth & " days.")
End Sub
```

FIGURE 5.29

Poorly Handled Case Else

```
Private Sub btnMonthDays_Click(ByVal sender As System.Object, ByVa
  Dim MonthAbbr As String
  Dim DaysInMonth As Integer
  MonthAbbr = txtMonth.Text
  Select Case MonthAbbr
    Case "JAN", "MAR", "MAY", "JUL", "AUG", "OCT", "DEC"
      DaysInMonth = 31
    Case "APR", "JUN", "SEP", "NOV"
      DaysInMonth = 30
    Case "FEB"
      DaysInMonth = 28
    Case Else
      MsgBox(MonthAbbr & " is not a valid month abbreviation.")
      Exit Sub
  End Select
  MsgBox(MonthAbbr & " has " & DaysInMonth & " days.")
End Sub
```

FIGURE 5.30

Exit Sub Statement

The problem is that the message box statement at the end of the procedure is always executed, but it makes no sense to display its message if the entered value is invalid. We would like to modify the event procedure so that this statement is executed only if the entered value is valid. How?

The following looks like a possibility. We can put the MsgBox statement inside an If statement whose condition determines whether the entered value was valid. Here's some code that uses this approach.

```
Select Case MonthAbbr
    Case "JAN", "MAR", "MAY", "JUL", "AUG", "OCT", "DEC"
        DaysInMonth = 31
    Case "APR", "JUN", "SEP", "NOV"
        DaysInMonth = 30
    Case "FEB"
        DaysInMonth = 28
    Case Else
        MsgBox(MonthAbbr & " is not a valid month abbreviation.")
End Select
If DaysInMonth > 0 Then
        MsgBox(MonthAbbr & " has " & DaysInMonth & " days.")
End If
```

Right after the End Select statement, the variable **DaysInMonth** will hold zero if the entered value is invalid—because the Dim statement initializes **DaysInMonth** to zero (by default)—and we can test for this value in the If statement.

This strategy yields a poor solution to the problem. Its obvious weakness is that the condition of the If statement fails to say what it means. However, even if you can infer that **DaysInMonth > 0** *really* means that the entered value is valid, you have to read the entire Select Case statement and all of its statement blocks to make sure this will work. That is, you have to be sure that all of the valid cases set **DaysInMonth** to some value greater than 0, and that the Case Else does not.

Figure 5.30 shows an alternative solution that uses Exit Sub. This solution is much easier to understand. The Case Else handles the invalid entry by displaying an appropriate message and then skipping the rest of the procedure by using Exit Sub.

5.10 Project 6: An Inventory Replenishment Simulation

Companies that produce and distribute goods monitor their inventory closely. For each item they have to decide

- When to order more units (that is, how low should the item's inventory be allowed to fall before an order is placed to replenish it).

- What quantity to order.

We can describe the flow of inventory in a retail store as follows: The store manager orders an initial quantity of some good and puts it on the shelves. As customers buy small quantities of it over time, the manager monitors the number of units remaining in stock (its inventory of the good). Several factors affect the manager's decision of when and how much to order.

The manager places an order to the store's suppliers before the inventory hits zero because it typically takes some time (called *lead time*) for the ordered goods to be delivered. If the inventory actually falls to zero, the store may lose sales and create customer dissatisfaction.

The store wants to avoid large inventories because it has to pay its supplier at the time of delivery but does not earn any revenue until its own customers buy the goods off the shelf. This time lag between paying and getting paid represents an actual cost (called *holding cost*) to the store. On the other hand, the store tries not to order too frequently, because deliveries are not free (there is an ordering cost).

Businesses facing the trade-off between inventory costs and lost sales due to shortages typically employ the following kind of policy: Let the inventory fall until it drops below some quantity, *L*; then order however many units are needed to bring the inventory back up to another quantity, *H*. The numbers *L* and *H* are carefully chosen and depend on the customer demand, holding and ordering costs, and lead time. Of course, they are always chosen so that *L* is less than *H*.

Description of the Application

We want a program that simulates the interaction between a store, its customers, and its supplier. We should be able to use the program to learn how this interaction works, and also to find good values of *L* and *H* by experimenting. Let us make the following simplifying assumptions:

- The store sells only one good.

- Customers pay $6 for each unit of the good they buy.

- Each period of time, customers demand between 0 and 5 (random) units of the good.

- The store cannot sell more units than it has in stock; thus, the number of units actually sold in any period of time is equal to the lesser of the demand and the inventory.

- Each period of time, the store incurs a holding cost of $0.50 for each unit of the good in stock.

- The ordering cost is $20 and the unit cost is $2; that is, the cost for the store to order *N* units from its supplier is $(20 + 2 * N).

- The lead time for an order is a minimum of two periods and may be as long as six periods. It is randomly distributed in this range.

The simulation should (1) generate customer sales, (2) employ the (L, H) inventory policy just described to replenish inventory, (3) generate the delivery lead times, and (4) keep track of and display the store's cash and inventory. To highlight the ordering process, the simulation should beep every time an order is placed. At the start of the simulation, the store should have $100 cash and zero inventory, and the simulation should end after 50 time periods elapse.

Design of the Application

To simulate time periods, we introduce the Timer control available within Visual Basic .NET. This control will "fire" at fixed intervals (that we can specify). Each time it "fires," it calls an event procedure. We can use this event procedure to initiate processing of the "real-world" event we are trying to simulate.

The Timer control has two properties of interest in addition to its Name property (tmr prefix). These include the Boolean Enabled property and the Interval property. If the Enabled property is set to True, then the timer "fires" once every interval. The exact interval is determined by the value of the Interval property. It uses units of milliseconds (1/1,000 of a second), so if you want the Timer to fire once a second, you would set the Interval property equal to 1,000 (1,000/1,000 = 1 second).

When the Timer "fires," it calls an event called the Tick() event. We write the code that is supposed to execute at the specified time interval in this Tick() event.

The application requires only one form. The user interface should display the quantities: cash, inventory, and current period number. It also should have two text boxes for the user to enter the values for L and H, and a button for the user to start the simulation. Figure 5.31 shows a sample form with its controls.

The three timers control the events of the simulation. Let's look at each one and decide what should happen when its Tick() event occurs.

Event procedure tmrPeriod_Tick() is executed once every second and represents one period in the simulation. This procedure is responsible for keeping track of the current period number, stopping the simulation after 50 periods,

FIGURE 5.31

User Interface for Project 6

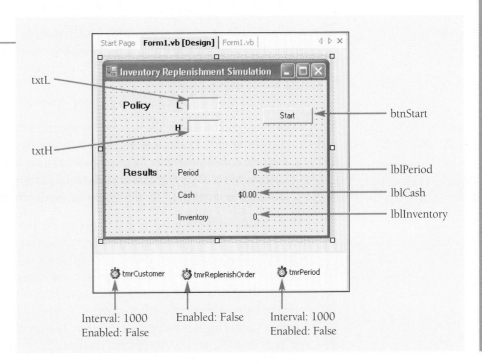

applying holding costs, and checking the level of inventory to see if a new order needs to be placed. Let's write some pseudocode to better understand the logic involved.

> *If period number = 50 then end the simulation*
> *Add one to the current period number*
> *Decrease cash by subtracting unit holding cost times current inventory*
> *Update the labels displaying the period number and the cash*
> *Place a new order if necessary*

This pseudocode is complete except for the last step, which is a meta statement. "Place a new order if necessary" can be expanded as follows:

> *If current inventory < lower limit (L) and a new order has not already been placed Then*
> > *Set order quantity = upper limit (H) − current inventory*
> > *Set lead time = minimum lead time plus a random interval*
> > *Set the Interval property of tmrReplenishOrder to the lead time*
> > *Enable tmrReplenishOrder*
> > *Beep*
> *End If*

Event procedure tmrCustomer_Tick() is executed once every second (once every period) and represents the customer demand for the good. This event procedure is responsible for generating a random demand, processing the amount sold based on this demand, adjusting cash and inventory levels to reflect the sale, and updating the cash and inventory displays on the form. Again, pseudocode may be helpful.

> *Set demand = random integer between 0 and max demand defined for the simulation*
> *Set sale amount = minimum of demand and current inventory*
> *Increase cash by adding sale amount times price*
> *Decrease current inventory by sale amount*
> *Update labels displaying cash and current inventory*

The final Tick event procedure, tmrReplenishOrder_Tick(), simulates the arrival of a replenishment order. This timer's Interval property was set by tmrPeriod when that event procedure detected that the inventory level had dropped below the minimum amount (*L*).

Pseudocode for the tmrReplenishOrder procedure is as follows:

> *Reduce cash by subtracting the fixed order cost and the unit cost times the number of units in the order (defined by tmrPeriod)*
> *Increase current inventory by the number of units in the order*
> *Update labels displaying cash and current inventory*
> *Disable this timer (wait for the tmrPeriod procedure to enable it again)*

The last step may need some explanation. We place an order in the tmrPeriod procedure by setting the Interval and Enabled properties of tmrReplenishOrder. When the Tick event for tmrReplenishOrder occurs (the order arrives), we disable tmrReplenishOrder because we don't want another order to be placed until the tmrPeriod procedure detects the circumstances that justify a new order.

There are two other event procedures that need to be coded. One is for the button that starts the simulation (btnStart). This procedure reads the values of *L* and *H* from the two text boxes txtL and txtH and stores them in variables. It then disables the two text boxes and enables both the period and customer timers (tmrPeriod and tmrCustomer) to start the simulation.

Finally, there are two initialization steps that need to take place when the simulation first starts. The cash balance and current inventory level must be set to 100 and 0, respectively, and the labels that display these values also must be initialized. We'll use the Form_Load event procedure to perform these steps.

We conclude the design section with a discussion of the data and variables used in the simulation. There will be five variables with module-level scope. These are

Variable	Type
Cash	Decimal
Inventory	Short
OrderQuantity	Short
Low	Short
High	Short

These variables have module-level scope because they are used in several procedures. For example, **Cash** and **Inventory** are used by the tmrCustomer, tmrPeriod, tmrReplenishOrder, and Form_Load procedures. The variable **OrderQuantity** is set by tmrPeriod and used later by tmrReplenishOrder. **Low** and **High** are set by btnStart and used later by tmrPeriod.

Symbolic constants implement the assumed numeric values. These symbolic constants are

Symbolic Constant	Numeric Value
MAXDEMAND	5
PRICETOCUSTOMER	6
ORDERFIXEDCOST	20
ORDERMARGINALCOST	2
HOLDINGCOSTPERUNIT	0.5
MINLEADTIME	2
MAXLEADTIME	6
INITIALCASH	100
INITIALINVENTORY	0
SIMULATIONLENGTH	50

Construction of the Application

Begin by creating a folder for the project. Start Visual Basic .NET, place the controls on the form, and set the properties of the controls as indicated in Figure 5.31.

Begin coding by declaring the module-level variables and constants. Figure 5.32 shows the declarations section of the form. Figure 5.33 shows the code for the btnStart_Click and Form_Load procedures, which are straightforward.

```
Dim Cash As Decimal
Dim Inventory As Integer
Dim OrderQuantity As Integer
Dim Low As Integer
Dim High As Integer
Const MAXDEMAND = 5
Const PRICETOCUSTOMER = 6
Const ORDERFIXEDCOST = 20
Const ORDERMARGINALCOST = 2
Const HOLDINGCOSTPERUNIT = 0.5
Const MINLEADTIME = 2
Const MAXLEADTIME = 6
Const INITIALCASH = 100
Const INITIALINVENTORY = 0
Const SIMULATIONLENGTH = 5
```

```
Private Sub btnStart_Click(ByVal sender As System.Object, ByVal e As
    Low = txtL.Text
    High = txtH.Text
    txtL.Enabled = False
    txtH.Enabled = False
    tmrPeriod.Enabled = True
    tmrCustomer.Enabled = True
End Sub

Private Sub Form1_Load(ByVal sender As System.Object, ByVal e As Sy
    Cash = INITIALCASH
    Inventory = INITIALINVENTORY
    lblCash.Text = Format(Cash, "currency")
    lblInventory.Text = Inventory
End Sub
```

FIGURE 5.32

Declarations Section of Form

FIGURE 5.33

btnStart_Click and Form1_Load Event Procedures

Next we code the Tick() events. Procedure tmrPeriod_Tick() is in Figure 5.34. If you compare this code to the pseudocode given earlier, you'll see a great deal of similarity. Let's compare some of the pseudocode and actual code. The pseudocode for placing a new order was

> *If current inventory < lower limit (L) and a new order has not already been placed Then*
> > *Set order quantity = upper limit (H) – current inventory*
> > *Set lead time = minimum lead time plus a random interval*
> > *Set the Interval property of tmrReplenishOrder to the lead time*
> > *Enable tmrReplenishOrder*
> > *Beep*
> *End If*

FIGURE 5.34

Code for
tmrPeriod_Tick()
Event Procedure

```
Private Sub tmrPeriod_Tick(ByVal sender As System.Object, ByVal e As System.EventA
    Static PeriodNumber As Integer
    Dim LeadTime As Integer
    If PeriodNumber = SIMULATIONLENGTH Then
        tmrPeriod.Enabled = False
        tmrCustomer.Enabled = False
        tmrReplenishOrder.Enabled = False
        MsgBox("End of simulation.  Cash = " & Format(Cash, "currency"))
        End
    End If
    PeriodNumber = PeriodNumber + 1
    Cash = Cash - Inventory * HOLDINGCOSTPERUNIT
    lblPeriod.Text = PeriodNumber
    lblCash.Text = Format(Cash, "currency")
    If (Inventory < Low) And (tmrReplenishOrder.Enabled = False) Then
        OrderQuantity = High - Inventory
        LeadTime = MINLEADTIME + Int((MAXLEADTIME - MINLEADTIME + 1) * Rnd())
        tmrReplenishOrder.Interval = 1000 * LeadTime
        tmrReplenishOrder.Enabled = True
        Beep()
    End If
End Sub
```

The actual code for the If statement is

```
If (Inventory < Low) And (tmrReplenishOrder.Enabled = False) Then
    OrderQuantity = High - Inventory
    LeadTime = MINLEADTIME + Int((MAXLEADTIME - MINLEADTIME + 1) _
                          * Rnd())
    tmrReplenishOrder.Interval = 1000 * LeadTime
    tmrReplenishOrder.Enabled = True
    Beep()
End If
```

The logical expression **tmrReplenishOrder.Enabled = False** tests to see if no order is pending. If this timer's Enabled property is True, then an order has already been placed and the simulation is waiting for the order to arrive. The expression **MINLEADTIME + Int((MAXLEADTIME - MINLEADTIME + 1) * Rnd())** generates a random integer ranging between **MINLEADTIME** and **MAXLEADTIME**.

The next two statements enable tmrReplenishOrder and set its interval equal to the lead time (recall that the Interval property must be in milliseconds). The effect of this is to place an order that will arrive at some random time in the future.

Now code the tmrCustomer_Tick() event procedure (Figure 5.35). Compare this code to the pseudocode.

> *Set demand = random integer between 0 and max demand defined for the simulation*
> *Set sale amount = minimum of demand and current inventory*
> *Increase cash by adding sale amount times price*
> *Decrease current inventory by sale amount*
> *Update labels displaying cash and current inventory*

There is a very close correlation between the two.

The final timer event is tmrReplenishOrder_Timer (see Figure 5.35). Notice that the last statement of this procedure disables the timer. This prevents the timer from activating again (since otherwise the event occurs repeatedly) unless it is re-enabled by the tmrPeriod procedure.

After coding the procedures, run the simulation to be sure that it works. After verifying that it works, experiment with different values of *L* and *H* to see if you can maximize the cash position at the end of the simulation. Watch the inventory level as time goes by and you'll get a better feel for how to adjust the values of *L* and *H*.

FIGURE 5.35

Code for
tmrCustomer_Tick() and
tmrReplenishOrder_Tick()
Event Procedures

```
Private Sub tmrReplenishOrder_Tick(ByVal sender As System.Object, ByVal e As
    Cash = Cash - ORDERFIXEDCOST - ORDERMARGINALCOST * OrderQuantity
    Inventory = Inventory + OrderQuantity
    lblCash.Text = Format(Cash, "currency")
    lblInventory.Text = Inventory
    tmrReplenishOrder.Enabled = False
End Sub
```

```
Private Sub tmrCustomer_Tick(ByVal sender As System.Object, ByVal e As Syste
    Dim Demand As Integer
    Dim SaleAmount As Integer
    Demand = Int((MAXDEMAND + 1) * Rnd())
    SaleAmount = IIf(Demand < Inventory, Demand, Inventory)
    Cash = Cash + SaleAmount * PRICETOCUSTOMER
    Inventory = Inventory - SaleAmount
    lblCash.Text = Format(Cash, "currency")
    lblInventory.Text = Inventory
End Sub
```

Chapter Summary

1. To make a decision, we first evaluate a condition and determine its outcome. The correct action to perform depends upon that outcome. This basic decision-making process needs to be mimicked in programs that select alternative courses of actions.

2. The logic used in procedures that specify alternative courses of action can be complex. It is difficult to get the logic correct and worry about statement syntax at the same time. To simplify their thinking, developers use pseudocode. Pseudocode is an English-like outline that describes the logical steps in a problem solution. It helps the developer to focus on the logic of the solution without concern for syntax rules.

3. A complex compound statement may be more easily understood as a single statement, called a meta statement, that goes beyond the individual statements to describe the concept represented by those statements.

4. The If…Then…Else statement gives a program the ability to choose one of two actions based on a condition. The condition can be any logical expression (recall that logical expressions evaluate to either True or False). The developer specifies one or more statements, called a statement block, to be executed if the outcome is True, and another statement block to be executed if the outcome is False.

   The If…Then…Else statement has a variation that uses the ElseIf clause to extend the number of conditions that a single If…Then…Else statement can support.

   Either statement block of the If…Then…Else statement can include another If…Then…Else statement, creating nested If statements.

5. Three Visual Basic .NET controls are associated with the GUI and the user's ability to make choices. The RadioButton control presents the user with a set of options from which to select exactly one. The RadioButton that is chosen has its Checked property set to True.

   The GroupBox control allows the developer to group RadioButtons to correspond to different categories of items. This allows the user to select exactly one option from each category.

   The CheckBox control allows the user to select multiple options from a set of options—any combination of zero, one, or more CheckBoxes at the same time.

6. The Select Case statement is designed to handle the situation where a single condition can have more than two outcomes. It can be used to identify a set of categories and specify the processing associated with each category.

7. Finally, the Exit Sub statement makes it possible to stop executing a procedure before it is completed. This might be necessary because some condition has been detected for which the appropriate action is to skip the rest of the procedure.

Key Terms

appropriate action	embedded If statement	If…Then…Else state-
CheckBox control	Exit Sub statement	ment
condition	GroupBox control	meta statement

MsgBox() function
nested If statement
outcome

problem solving
pseudocode
RadioButton control

Select Case statement
statement block

End-of-Chapter Problems

1. What function do the keywords Then, Else, and End If perform in the context of the If…Then…Else statement?

2. What is a meta statement? What is its value to a developer/problem solver? How are meta statements and pseudocode similar? How are they different?

3. A university uses the following tuition table to determine a student's quarterly tuition:

	Residence Status	
	In-State	Out-of-State
Undergraduate	$ 450	$ 780
Graduate	1,250	3,275
Professional	2,300	5,200

Assume that you have a variable called **ResStatus** that holds the value 1 for in-state students and the value 2 for out-of-state students. Also assume that you have a variable **ClassStanding** that holds 1 for undergraduates, 2 for graduates, and 3 for professional students. Given this information, write an If…Then…Else statement that sets the variable **Tuition** equal to the appropriate value based on the current values of **ResStatus** and **ClassStanding**. Now do the same thing using a Select Case statement. Comment on the two alternative approaches.

4. Explain when you would use RadioButtons for user input and when you would use CheckBoxes.

5. What important function does the GroupBox control serve? How does the GroupBox control relate to both RadioButtons and CheckBoxes?

6. Using the Select Case statement and ranges, construct the correct Visual Basic .NET statement to implement this table.

Age	Risk Factor
≤ 2	.03
> 2 and < 10	.07
≥ 10 and ≤ 30	.15
> 30	.12

The statement should set the variable **RiskFactor** to its proper value depending on the current value of the variable **Age**. Assume that the value stored in variable **Age** is a whole number.

7. In question 6, does it make any difference if you assume that the variable **Age** is declared as type Short versus one of the floating-point types (either Single or Double)? Explain.

8. Assume you have the segment of Visual Basic .NET code shown here.

```
Dim Letter As String

Select Case Letter
    Case "A" To "H"
        MsgBox("In the first third")
    Case "I" To "P"
        MsgBox("In the middle third")
    Case "Q" To "Z"
        MsgBox("In the final third")
    Case Else
        MsgBox("Not in any group")
End Select
```

Given this code, assume that the **Letter** variable holds the value "B". What message would be displayed? Explain why Visual Basic .NET makes this decision. (*Hint:* Think about ANSI codes.) Now assume that the **Letter** variable holds the value "b". What message would be displayed? Explain.

9. Describe how a Select Case statement will handle the overlap of two ranges. For example, how would the Select Case react to a number that fell in the overlap of the **Case 1 To 5** and **Case 5 To 10** statements? If there is a gap in the selection range, how should a Select Case statement be constructed to catch missed values?

10. The MsgBox function can be used for more than simply an OK dialog box. Write a Select Case statement that displays a message for each selection that might be returned in the **Response** variable of this statement:

```
Response = MsgBox("Setup file not found.", MsgBoxStyle.AbortRetryIgnore + _
            MsgBoxStyle.Critical, "File Missing")
```

Programming Problems

1. Assume that you own a small deli that sells bagels. You want a simple program that computes the price of a purchase based on what the customer orders. A sample user interface is shown below.

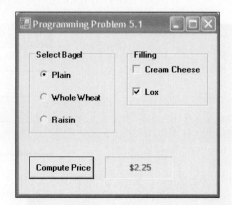

You charge $1.75 for a plain bagel, $1.95 for a whole-wheat bagel, and $2.15 for a raisin bagel. In addition, you add $.50 if customers want lox on the bagel and $.75 for cream cheese (they might want both). Write the code so that after the customer's preferences are input, clicking on the Compute Price button will cause the price to be computed and displayed as shown above.

2. Construct a menu calculator as shown below. Bagels cost $2.25. Selecting lox adds $1.20 to the price, and cream cheese adds $1.00. A spinach salad costs $2.75 and a chef salad costs $3.25. Sodas are $1.25 regardless of type. A sample user interface is shown below.

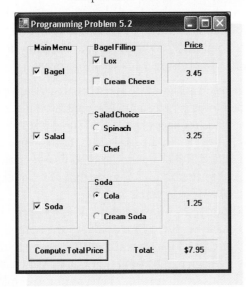 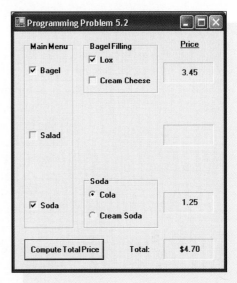

The form should not show the options if the main selection has not been made. In the right-hand figure, salad has not been selected, so the Spinach and Chef options are not displayed.

The price should be cleared whenever a main selection is "deselected." In the two figures shown, the deselection of Salad caused the "3.25" to be cleared from the price column. However, the total price does not have to be updated automatically—you can assume that the user will click on the Compute Total button to recalculate the total.

When a main selection has been deselected and then selected again, the project should clear the options. In the figure below, the Bagel selection was deselected and then reselected. As you can see, the Lox option has been cleared and the price is correct for just a Bagel.

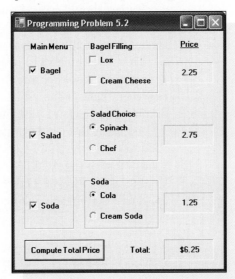

Finally, be aware that the Bagel options behave differently from the Salad options. The Bagel options are cumulative; that is, you can select both, and the price should reflect this. In contrast, the Salad options are mutually exclusive; you will only have one or the other (and there will be no price until the user selects one). See Exercise 5.15 for a hint as to one way to implement the Bagel options.

3. Complete the requirements of problem 2, but have the total price update automatically. That is, remove the Compute Total button and have the project update the total price as the individual selection prices change.

    Hint: Think about using a TextChanged event.

4. A company needs a program to help calculate the yearly bonus for each employee. The bonus is determined by considering several different factors. The first factor is the number of years a person has been employed by the firm. Being employed for 1 to 5 years adds $100 to the bonus, being employed for 6 to 10 years adds $200 to the bonus, and being employed for 11 or more years adds $350 to the bonus. Assume that years of experience are always rounded up to the nearest whole number.

    In addition to years of experience, an employee's job grade is considered. For job grade Level I, $75 is added to the bonus; for Level II, $100 is added to the bonus; and for Level III, $125 is added to the bonus. Also, if an employee has participated in community service, then an additional $100 is added to the bonus. And, finally, 5 percent of the employee's current salary is computed and added to the bonus. The sum of all these values represents the yearly bonus.

    Create a Visual Basic .NET project to solve this problem. Use Check-Boxes, RadioButtons, GroupBox controls, and TextBoxes as appropriate. Try to use controls that make it difficult for the user to make typographical errors when inputting data.

5. Validating data input is an important part of many applications. In this problem you will implement some simple data validation operations. Use TextBoxes to get the name, the salary, the years of experience, the department code, and the job title of a hypothetical employee. Add a Button that when clicked, should display either the word "Valid" or the words "Not valid" next to each TextBox.

    Names should be less than 18 characters long. A valid salary must be between $10,000 and $150,000, inclusive. Valid years of experience must be greater than or equal to zero and less than or equal to 75.

    There are three valid department codes: PROD, ACCTG, and MKTG. Your project should ensure that only these three codes are marked as valid. However, the user should be able to enter the codes using either uppercase or lowercase (review string functions to get an idea of how to do this).

    Assuming that the department code is valid, the title needs to be validated. Valid titles for the PROD department are MGR, SUPERVISOR, and STAFF. Valid titles for the ACCTG department are MGR, AUDITOR, and STAFF. Valid titles for the MKTG department are ACCT REP and SALES REP (note that there is a single blank between SALES and REP). Again, allow the user to enter titles using either uppercase or lowercase.

6. Many applications now include instant conversion of numeric values between systems of measure. For example, in most Page Setup dialog boxes, even if a margin setting reads "1.5 in" for 1.5 inches, the value "5 cm" can be entered

directly in the text box for a new setting in centimeters. Using the Right() function, write an application that checks text the user entered and converts it from either inches to centimeters or centimeters to inches.

Create a new form and place a TextBox, a Button, and a Label control on it. When the user clicks the Convert button, obtain the text from the TextBox and use an If...Then...ElseIf...Else structure to determine if the last two characters of the string are "CM" or "IN" or to display a MsgBox instructing the user on the proper entry format.

Once the type is determined, place the string minus the final two characters in a variable of Double type. Use the following conversion factors to display the converted number (with the proper suffix) in the label: 1 centimeter = 0.3937 inch and 1 inch = 2.54 centimeters. Don't forget to enclose the conversions within a Try/Catch structure to capture any unexpected errors.

REDUCING PROGRAM COMPLEXITY

General Sub Procedures and Developer-Defined Functions

A project can contain many event procedures, and the processing tasks performed by each of them can be complicated. Three important considerations help us design, construct, and maintain complex programs:

1. We can understand complex tasks more readily by breaking them into smaller "subtasks."

2. We can make the meaning of each subtask clear by giving it a descriptive name.

3. We can avoid duplication of effort, as well as potential inconsistencies, by finding processing tasks that have subtasks in common. For example, the subtask "print a check" may be involved in both payroll processing and accounts payable processing.

The following event procedure illustrates points 1 and 2:

```
Private Sub btnPayEmployee_Click(…)
    GetEmployeeData()
    ComputeGross()
    ComputeDeductions()
    ComputeNet()
    PrintCheck()
End Sub
```

The processing task performed by btnPayEmployee_Click consists of five subtasks. Each of the five statements in the event procedure refers to a different general sub procedure. **A general sub procedure contains the statements necessary to perform a single subtask** (such as printing a check) **and is given a descriptive name** (PrintCheck). Since the descriptive name stands for several actual statements, it is like a *meta statement* in pseudocode. That is, the descriptive name goes beyond the individual statements of the general sub procedure to describe the concept represented by those statements.

If more than one event procedure needs to perform the same subtask, they can share the general sub procedure. The following event procedure and btnPayEmployee_Click together illustrate point 3. Both event procedures refer to the same general sub procedure named PrintCheck.

```
Private Sub btnPayInvoice_Click(…)
    GetInvoiceData()
    PrintCheck()
End Sub
```

General sub procedures allow us to create **reusable code—that is, code that can be used by more than one procedure.** One developer figures out the statements necessary to accomplish a given subtask and records them as a descriptively named general sub procedure. Subsequently, other developers can use that general sub procedure whenever they create a procedure that requires the subtask. This way we avoid constantly "reinventing the wheel."

In this chapter we examine general sub procedures in detail: how they work and how to create them. We also examine *developer-defined functions*: you can write your own functions, which you can then use just as you use Visual Basic .NET's predefined functions, such as the square root function Math.Sqr(). Our study of general sub procedures and functions includes an important mechanism for sharing data known as *parameter passing*.

We then discuss how code modules help in organizing projects by acting as containers for general sub procedures and developer-defined functions.

We also use our understanding of general sub procedures and parameter passing to extend our mastery of the user interface. We examine the KeyPress event, whose event procedure uses parameter passing to determine which key the user pressed. We then discuss the Enter and Leave events that are natural partners of the KeyPress event because applications commonly allow the user to press certain keys (e.g., ENTER) to move the focus from one control to another.

We examine the topic of *form modality,* in which the user can be forced to respond to a request on one form before being allowed to move to another form (as we have seen with message boxes). From a flow of control perspective, the statement that achieves this (a variation of the Show method) works much as general sub procedures work.

Finally we look at how a developer creates and programs main menu items.

Objectives

After studying this chapter, you should be able to

- Share code by creating general sub procedures and functions.

- Use parameters to share data between procedures and functions.

- Use code modules to organize code for reusability.

- Use three new events—KeyPress, Enter, and Leave—that are useful for data editing and for causing the user interface to respond when the user activates or deactivates a control.

- Use the concept of form modality to decide the best way to display forms to the user.

- Create and program main menus within an application.

6.1 General Sub Procedures

As mentioned in the introduction, a general sub procedure contains the statements necessary to perform a single subtask. Each event procedure that requires the subtask "calls" or "invokes" the general sub procedure by its name. To illustrate how general sub procedures can improve the organization of a program and to demonstrate how procedures are used in projects, we begin this section by rewriting the U.S. Individual Income Tax Return application from Chapter 5. We then examine precisely how general sub procedures work and how to create them.

Using General Sub Procedures in a Project

We can improve the design of the computerized income tax application by placing statements that are common to multiple processing steps in a general sub procedure. Figure 6.1 shows the user interface we developed for this application in Chapter 5. Recall that the three separate questions appearing on this form are not independent of one another: in particular, the question "If a joint return, does your spouse want $3 to go to this fund?" applies to users who select "Married filing joint return" but not to those who select "Single".

The program we created in Chapter 5 has two Click event procedures, shown in Figure 6.2, that implement a visual cue to show the user when the second question is not applicable. They work by appropriately setting the Checked property of the Yes/No RadioButtons and the Enabled property of the GroupBox that holds them. When the user selects filing status "Single", the second Presidential Election Campaign question changes to gray (not enabled). If the user selects filing status "Married filing joint return", the appearance of the user interface reverts to Figure 6.1.

When we turn to the user requirements for linking the Presidential Election Campaign question to the three remaining filing status categories, we find that they are like the "Single" filing status category: the question "If a joint return, does your spouse want $3 to go to this fund?" does not apply. Thus, we should create

FIGURE 6.1

User Interface for Income Tax Return Application

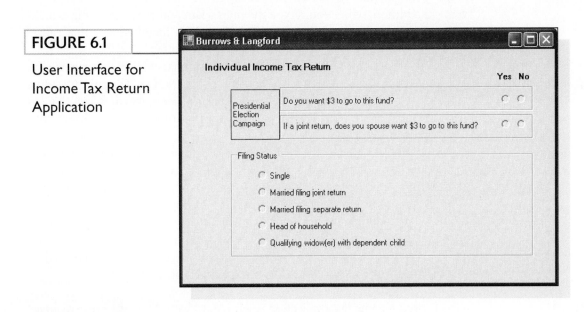

FIGURE 6.2

Event Procedures for Income Tax Return Application

```
Private Sub radFSSingle_CheckedChanged(ByVal send
    grpPECSpouse.Enabled = False
    radPECSpouseYes.Checked = False
    radPECSpouseNo.Checked = False
End Sub

Private Sub radFSMarriedJoint_CheckedChanged(ByV
    grpPECSpouse.Enabled = True
End Sub
```

FIGURE 6.3

Income Tax Program
with General Sub
Procedure

```
Private Sub radFSMarriedJoint_CheckedChanged(ByVal sender
    grpPECSpouse.Enabled = True
End Sub

Private Sub WithdrawPECSpouseQuestion()
    grpPECSpouse.Enabled = False
    radPECSpouseYes.Checked = False
    radPECSpouseNo.Checked = False
End Sub

Private Sub radFSSingle_CheckedChanged(ByVal sender As Sy
    WithdrawPECSpouseQuestion()
End Sub

Private Sub radFSMarriedSeparate_CheckedChanged(ByVal se
    WithdrawPECSpouseQuestion()
End Sub

Private Sub radFSHeadOfHousehold_CheckedChanged(ByVal s
    WithdrawPECSpouseQuestion()
End Sub

Private Sub radFSWidower_CheckedChanged(ByVal sender As
    WithdrawPECSpouseQuestion()
End Sub
```

CheckedChanged event procedures for radFSMarriedSeparate, radFSHeadOf-Household, and radFSWidower, which are identical to radFSSingle_Click.

Adding these new CheckedChanged event procedures makes the code substantially longer, adding three more statements for each new CheckedChanged event. In addition, when you retype the lines again and again, you might make a typographical error or omit a line, introducing an inconsistency that causes one event procedure to execute differently from the others.

We can shorten the program and eliminate the chance of inconsistencies by placing the common statements in a general sub procedure. The sub procedure will have a descriptive name that will appear in each event procedure that requires its subtask. In Figure 6.3 the general sub procedure is named WithdrawPEC-SpouseQuestion.

The descriptive name WithdrawPECSpouseQuestion is easy to interpret. Now when we want to know what happens when the user clicks the "Head of household" option RadioButton, the answer is immediately apparent; the event procedure contains only one statement, and it is descriptive.

This example illustrates how a program can be simplified with a general sub procedure. In order to write your own general sub procedures, you must understand how execution flows from an event procedure to the general sub procedure and back to the event procedure. We turn to this topic next.

Exercise 6.1

In the revised income tax application (Figure 6.3), would it make sense to create a general sub procedure containing the statements that are currently in event procedure radFSMarriedJoint_Click? If so, explain why and suggest a name for it.

Execution of General Sub Procedures

Even if you agree that the code in Figure 6.3 looks good, it may not be obvious to you exactly how it executes at run time. By looking at the code alone, how can you tell which are event procedures and which are general sub procedures? Does it matter? Which statement is executed when?

You can determine whether a procedure is an event procedure or a general sub procedure from its name. The names of event procedures always end with an underscore followed by the type of event (such as radFSMarriedJoint_Checked-Changed); whereas the names of general sub procedures do not. Because of our convention for naming controls, the names of event procedures begin with a three-letter prefix for the type of control to which the event procedure belongs. Since general sub procedures are not associated with controls, their names do not begin with a prefix for a control type.

From now on we will often use only the term *procedure,* trusting that you can tell from the procedure's name whether it is an event procedure or a general sub procedure. Note that a printout of the code in a Visual Basic .NET project does not explicitly distinguish between event procedures and general sub procedures. Programmers have to be able to recognize which are event procedures and which are general sub procedures in order to understand how the processing steps are performed.

We know that to execute an event procedure, the computer executes its statements one at a time, from top to bottom. How does the computer execute a statement that is just the name of a general sub procedure? It performs the following steps:

1. Transfers execution from the event procedure to the named general sub procedure.

2. Executes the statements in the general sub procedure from top to bottom.

3. Returns execution to the event procedure and resumes with the event procedure's next statement.

Figure 6.4 illustrates this process. When the user clicks the RadioButton named radFSSingle, the computer begins executing the statements in event procedure radFSSingle_CheckedChanged. The numbers in Figure 6.4 indicate the order in which statements are executed. The arrows show the flow of execution between the procedures.

The statement numbered 2 in Figure 6.4 is sometimes referred to as a **procedure call** because it calls, or invokes, the specified procedure—in this case, WithdrawPECSpouseQuestion. In the example shown, radFSSingleModified_CheckedChanged is the calling procedure and WithdrawPECSpouseQuestion is the called procedure.

FIGURE 6.4

Flow of Execution in Programs with General Sub Procedures

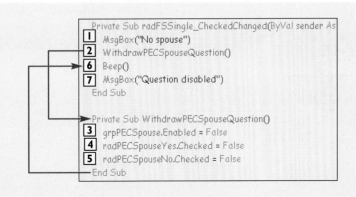

```
Private Sub radFSSingle_CheckedChanged(ByVal sender As
 1  MsgBox("No spouse")
 2  WithdrawPECSpouseQuestion()
 6  Beep()
 7  MsgBox("Question disabled")
   End Sub

Private Sub WithdrawPECSpouseQuestion()
 3  grpPECSpouse.Enabled = False
 4  radPECSpouseYes.Checked = False
 5  radPECSpouseNo.Checked = False
   End Sub
```

Exercise 6.2
Analyze the following code (i.e., explain what it does) and sketch the flow of execution as in Figure 6.4.

```
Private Sub btnCallsQuiz_Click(...)
    lblConcat.Text = ""
    DisplaySomething()
    lblConcat.Text = lblConcat.Text & "E"
    DisplayAnotherThing()
    lblConcat.Text = lblConcat.Text & "HING"
End Sub
Private Sub DisplayAnotherThing()
    lblConcat.Text = lblConcat.Text & "T"
End Sub
Private Sub DisplaySomething()
    lblConcat.Text = lblConcat.Text & "S"
    lblConcat.Text = lblConcat.Text & "OM"
End Sub
```

Local Variables in General Sub Procedures

General sub procedures can access module-level and global variables just like event procedures. They also have their own procedure-level variables, and, for general sub procedures and event procedures alike, procedure-level variables in one procedure have no relationship whatsoever to procedure-level variables in any other procedures, regardless of their names. We now illustrate this rule with examples, because the flow of execution between the calling and the called procedure can make procedure-level variables seem confusing at first.

Recall that a procedure's procedure-level variables are created when the procedure begins executing and are destroyed when its End Sub statement is encountered. A procedure-level variable exists until the procedure's End Sub statement is encountered, even if the flow of execution moves to another procedure because of a procedure call. That is, transferring execution to another procedure has no effect on the calling procedure's procedure-level variables. An example of this behavior is illustrated by the code in Figure 6.5. Before reading further, try to number the statements in Figure 6.5 in the order in which they execute (as in Figure 6.4) when the user clicks the button named btnTestCall.

When the user clicks on btnTestCall, the computer starts executing btnTestCall_Click. It first creates the procedure-level variable **X**, then stores the value 100 in **X**, and then calls the general sub procedure named TestProcedure. This call transfers execution to TestProcedure. The computer beeps, displays a message box,

FIGURE 6.5

Code Demonstrating Local Variable's Lifetime

```
Private Sub btnTestCall_Click(ByVal sender As System.Objec
    Dim X As Integer
    X = 100
    TestProcedure()
    MsgBox("X = " & X)
End Sub

Private Sub TestProcedure()
    Beep()
    MsgBox("This is a test procedure")
End Sub
```

FIGURE 6.6

Code Showing Multiple Procedure-Level Variables with the Same Name

```
Private Sub btnTestMultipleCalls_Click(ByVal sender As Syst
    Dim x As Short = 100
    TestProcedureA()
    TestProcedureB()
    MsgBox("TestMultipleCalls_Click: X = " & x)
End Sub

Private Sub TestProcedureA()
    Dim X As Short = 200
    TestProcedureB()
    MsgBox("TestProcedureA: X = " & X)
End Sub

Private Sub TestProcedureB()
    Dim X As Short = 300
    MsgBox("TestProcedureB: X = " & X)
End Sub
```

and then encounters the End Sub in TestProcedure that returns execution to btnTestCall_Click. It then executes the statement

MsgBox("X = " & X)

Will **X** still hold the value 100?

The answer is yes. TestProcedure has no effect on the variable **X** because **X** is local to btnTestCall_Click. Therefore, **X** continues to exist until the End Sub statement in its procedure, btnTestCall_Click, is encountered.

A procedure can call another procedure that in turn can call a third procedure that in turn can call a fourth procedure, and so on. Each procedure can have its own procedure-level local variables, as illustrated by the code in Figure 6.6. Before reading further, try to predict what values will be displayed and in what order when the user clicks on btnTestMultipleCalls. Note that TestProcedureB is called twice, once by TestProcedureA and once by btnTestMultipleCalls_Click.

When btnTestMultipleCalls_Click starts to execute, it creates a procedure-level variable **X** and sets it equal to 100. It then transfers execution to procedure TestProcedureA. This procedure creates its own procedure-level variable **X** and sets its value to 200. At this point in the execution of the program there are two procedure-level variables, as depicted below.

btnTestMultipleCalls_Click		TestProcedureA	
Variable	**Value**	**Variable**	**Value**
X	100	X	200

TestProcedureA now transfers execution to TestProcedureB. TestProcedureB creates a procedure-level variable named **X** and sets it equal to 300. Now there are three local variables:

btnTestMultipleCalls_Click		TestProcedureA		TestProcedureB	
Variable	**Value**	**Variable**	**Value**	**Variable**	**Value**
X	100	X	200	X	300

The MsgBox statement in TestProcedureB is executed, displaying the value 300. The End Sub statement destroys TestProcedureB's procedure-level variables and returns execution to TestProcedureA (the procedure that called TestProcedureB).

FIGURE 6.7

Flow of Execution
for Code in
Figure 6.6

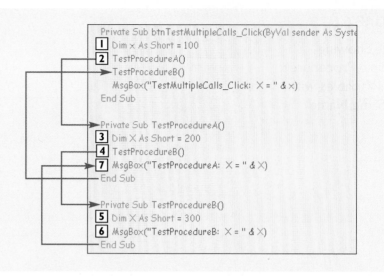

```
Private Sub btnTestMultipleCalls_Click(ByVal sender As Syste
 1  Dim x As Short = 100
 2  TestProcedureA()
    TestProcedureB()
    MsgBox("TestMultipleCalls_Click: X = " & x)
 End Sub


 Private Sub TestProcedureA()
 3  Dim X As Short = 200
 4  TestProcedureB()
 7  MsgBox("TestProcedureA: X = " & X)
 End Sub


 Private Sub TestProcedureB()
 5  Dim X As Short = 300
 6  MsgBox("TestProcedureB: X = " & X)
 End Sub
```

Now the MsgBox statement in TestProcedureA is executed, displaying the value 200. This procedure's End Sub statement is then encountered, which destroys Test-ProcedureA's procedure-level variables and returns execution to procedure btn-TestMultipleCalls_Click (the procedure that called TestProcedureA). Now only procedure-level variables exist for the event procedure btnTestMultipleCalls_Click.

btnTestMultipleCalls_Click

Variable	Value
X	100

Figure 6.7 shows the flow of execution that brought us to this point in the execution of the program.

Next, btnTestMultipleCalls_Click calls TestProcedureB, and TestProcedureB again creates a procedure-level variable **X** and sets it equal to 300. The variables that now exist are as follows:

btnTestMultipleCalls_Click		**TestProcedureB**	
Variable	Value	Variable	Value
X	100	X	300

The MsgBox statement in TestProcedureB is executed, displaying the value 300. The End Sub statement destroys TestProcedureB's procedure-level variables and returns execution to btnTestMultipleCalls_Click. Finally, the MsgBox statement in btnTestMultipleCalls_Click is executed, displaying the value 100. Then its End Sub statement is encountered that destroys its procedure-level variables.

The variable **X** in TestProcedureA is a different variable from **X** in TestProcedureB, even though both variables have the same name. We could rewrite this code, using **Y** instead of **X** in TestProcedureA, and **Z** instead of **X** in TestProcedureB, but the program would operate identically.

Exercise 6.3

Predict what values the following code displays, and in what order, when the user clicks on btnScopeQuiz. Note the module-level variable named **X**.

```
        Dim X As Integer
        Private Sub btnScopeQuiz_Click(...)
            Dim Y As Integer
            Dim Z As Integer
            Y = 2
            Z = 5
            X = Y + Z
            MsgBox(X & Y & Z)
            SQuizProcedureA()
            SQuizProcedureB()
            MsgBox(X & Y & Z)
        End Sub
        Private Sub SQuizProcedureA()
            Dim X As Integer
            Dim Y As Integer
            Y = Y + 4
            X = X + Y
            MsgBox(X & Y)
        End Sub
        Private Sub SQuizProcedureB()
            Dim Y As Integer
            Dim Z As Integer
            Y = Y - 1
            Z = 3
            X = X + Y + Z
            MsgBox(X & Y & Z)
        End Sub
```

General Sub Procedures and Project Structure

In this section we discuss how general sub procedures are handled by the Visual Basic .NET programming environment and examine their position in the hierarchical structure of projects. We start by showing how to locate a general sub procedure in the Code window, and then discuss the scope of a procedure (i.e., which procedures are able to call it). Finally, we discuss code modules that act as containers for general sub procedures and can be used in more than one project.

Locating a General Sub Procedure in the Code Window

In the Visual Basic .NET programming environment, the Code window is where we enter and view event procedures—but it is also where we enter and view general sub procedures. A general sub procedure is called *general* because, unlike an event procedure, it is not associated with any control. In fact, a general sub procedure is actually a method of the Form class where it is defined.

We can find any desired procedure simply by scrolling up and down until we see its heading. However, when the Code window contains many procedures, it can be difficult to find the desired one using this method. In that case, we use the Code window's Class Name and Method Name boxes.

Suppose we are working with our computerized income tax application. The project has one form, and the form has several controls. Five of its RadioButtons have CheckedChanged event procedures, and there is one general sub procedure named WithdrawPECSpouseQuestion.

Recall that to view an event procedure—say, radFSMarriedJoint_Checked-Changed—we

1. Select the name of the control, radFSMarriedJoint, in the Code window's Class Name box.

2. Select the event, CheckedChanged, in the Method Names box.

This is depicted in Figure 6.8.

However, the name of a general sub procedure will never appear in the Code window's Class Name box, because the Class Name box lists only classes (and a general sub procedure is actually a method). To view a general sub procedure—say, WithdrawPECSpouseQuestion—we

1. Select Form1 in the Code window's Class Name box.

2. Use the Method Name box to select the name of the general sub procedure, WithdrawPECSpouseQuestion.

This is depicted in Figure 6.9.

FIGURE 6.8

Selecting an Event Procedure in the Code Window

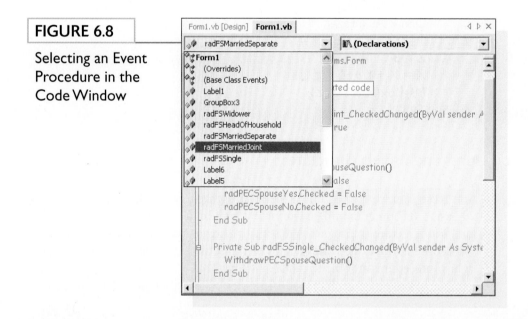

FIGURE 6.9

Selecting a General Sub Procedure in the Code Window

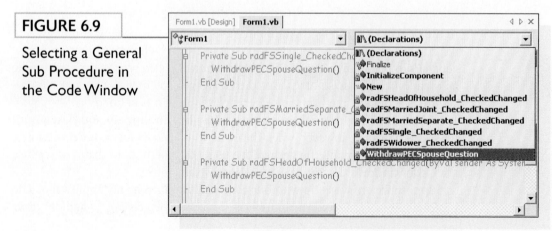

Procedure Scope

Like variables and constants, procedures—both event procedures and general sub procedures—have scope. A procedure's *scope* determines which procedures are able to invoke it. A procedure is *private* if it begins with the keyword Private. **A *Private procedure* is module-level, which means that it can be invoked by all procedures in the same form (class) but cannot be invoked by any procedure in a different form (class).** A procedure is *public* if it begins with the keyword Public. **A *Public procedure* is global, which means that it can be invoked by all procedures in all forms (classes) of the project.** There are several other options in terms of scope, but they are beyond the scope of this text.

As with variables, it is a good idea to limit the scope of procedures that you create. That is, every procedure should be private unless it is intended to be invoked by procedures in other forms.

Procedure scope applies to event procedures as well as general sub procedures. (Note that all the event procedures we have seen so far have begun with the keywords Private Sub.) In fact, as long as scope allows it, any procedure can invoke any other procedure regardless of whether they are event procedures or general sub procedures.

You may wonder why we even need general sub procedures if event procedures can call other event procedures. Why not just use event procedures? Remember that an event procedure is associated with a specific event for a specific control, for example, a Button's Click event. General sub procedures are not directly related to any single control and often perform processing that is independent of the concept of controls, such as placing a set of names into alphabetical order.

Example 6.1 — USING A PUBLIC GENERAL SUB PROCEDURE

This example illustrates a public general sub procedure. It has two forms, shown in Figure 6.10. The code is shown in Figure 6.11. Form A has two procedures: a private event procedure named btnBeepTime_Click and a public general sub procedure named displayTime. Form B has a private event procedure named btnQuietTime_Click. Both event procedures invoke the public general sub procedure that resides in form A.

Observe that btnBeepTime_Click (on form A) does not have to qualify the procedure name to invoke displayTime because it too resides on form A. However, btnQuietTime_Click (on form B) does have to qualify the procedure name to invoke displayTime because displayTime resides on a different form.

Procedure displayTime uses Visual Basic .NET's built-in Now() function to determine the current time and the Format() function with the predefined format specification "Medium Time" to format the current time.

FIGURE 6.10

Forms and Controls for Example 6.1

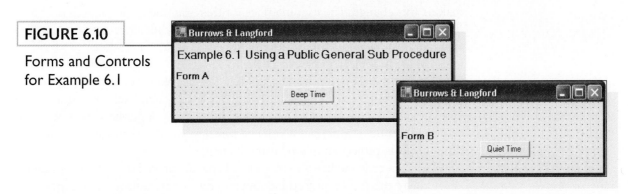

FIGURE 6.11

Code for Example 6.1

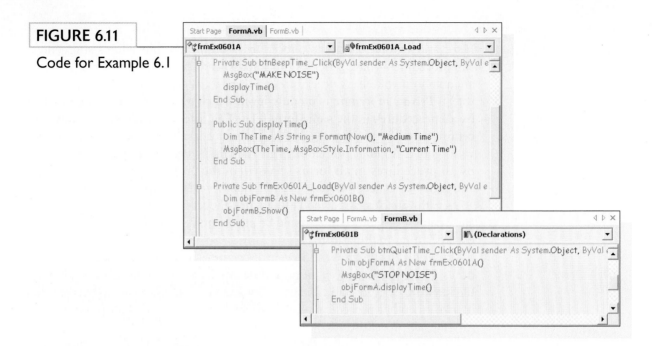

Code Modules

In Chapter 3 we saw how to use a code module as a place to declare global variables and symbolic constants. The code module has another purpose: it can contain general sub procedures. Even though forms can contain general sub procedures, we often use code modules to improve the project's organization.

Forms and code modules both serve to help organize a project, and they behave similarly in most respects. However, a code module cannot contain event procedures because it has no user interface window to hold the associated controls.

Many processing tasks are generic in the sense that they are not associated with any particular control and can be used by more than one form. Specifically, event procedures on many different forms—possibly forms in many different projects—may require the same processing task. To allow these event procedures to share code, a developer creates a general sub procedure that performs the processing task and places it in a descriptively named code module. This code module can then be included in many different projects.

Example 6.1 contains a general sub procedure named displayTime that displays the current time, nicely formatted, in a message box. In Example 6.1, procedure displayTime resides in one of the forms. However, the task performed by displayTime could be useful in many different applications.

By moving displayTime into a code module, we make it easy to include this functionality in other projects. Figure 6.12 shows the code for Example 6.1 after making this change. The user interface for this example is the same as in Example 6.1 (see Figure 6.10). The user cannot tell any difference between the two examples. The only difference is in the organization of the code.

The code module's Name property appears in its Code window's Title bar. In Figure 6.12, the code module is named modTime. Note carefully that the event procedures in the forms do not have to qualify the general sub procedure name with the name of the code module in which it resides. A public general sub procedure in a code module can be invoked by any procedure in any form or code module of the project simply by using its name.

Note that a code module also may include private procedures. These procedures are used by the public procedures but for various reasons are not exposed to the users of the code modules.

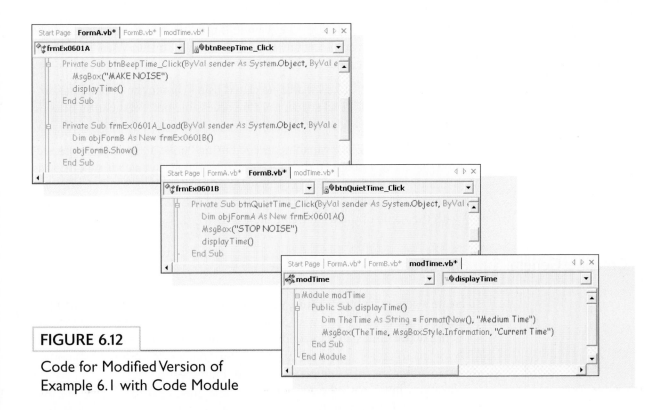

FIGURE 6.12

Code for Modified Version of
Example 6.1 with Code Module

Project Structure

Now is a good time to incorporate our understanding of general sub procedures into our view of project structure. Figure 6.13 is an expanded version of Figure 3.37 that includes the scope of variables, procedures, and properties.

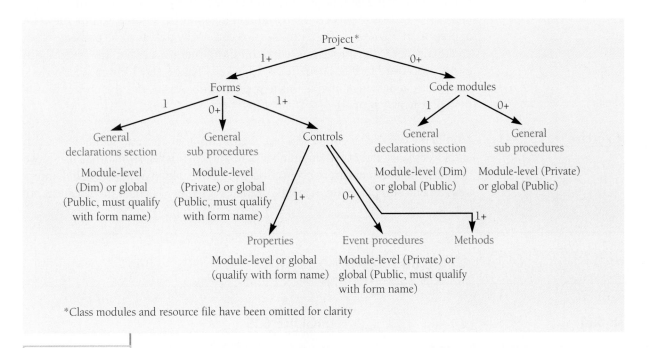

FIGURE 6.13

Structure of Visual Basic .NET Projects

The key terms Public, Private, and Dim in this figure are intended to highlight the close analogy between procedure scope and variable scope in Visual Basic .NET. The analogy can be summarized as follows:

- Private procedures, like variables declared using Dim in the declarations section, have module-level scope: they are accessible only in the form or code module that contains them.

- Public procedures, like variables declared using Public in the declarations section, have global scope. If the procedure or variable is in a code module, it is accessible anywhere in the project without qualifying its name. If the procedure or variable is in a form, it can be accessed by qualifying its name with the name of the form that contains it.

Creating General Sub Procedures

To create a general sub procedure, first bring up the Code window for the form or code module in which you wish to place the procedure. Being sure that the cursor is not within an existing procedure, enter the header for the sub procedure. If you want to create a general sub procedure named WithdrawPECSpouse-Question, enter the information as shown in Figure 6.14.

When you finish with the closing parenthesis, just press the (ENTER) key and Visual Basic .NET will complete the procedure ending for you. Figure 6.15 shows this.

To complete the general sub procedure you need only enter its statements, just as you would for an event procedure.

Always choose descriptive procedure names. Good procedure names often include a verb indicating the action performed by the procedure and a direct object indicating the entity on which the action is performed.

Exercise 6.4

Modify the project for Example 5.6 that contains the income tax application before introducing general sub procedures, as follows: First, modify the code by creating general sub procedure WithdrawPECSpouseQuestion, so that the code appears as in Figure 6.3. Then run the project to verify that it works properly. Next, create a general sub procedure containing the statements that are currently in event procedure radFSMarriedJoint_CheckedChange and have radFSMarried-Joint_CheckedChange invoke this new procedure. Again, run the project to verify that it works properly.

Exercise 6.5

Modify the code for Example 5.2 (see Figure 5.6) that computes and displays an employee's wage rate based on number of months of service, as follows: First, move the entire If statement from event procedure btnLookUpWageRate_Click into a new general sub procedure named ComputeWageRate. Then, at the If statement's

```
  Private Sub WithdrawPECSpouseQuestion()
End Class
```

FIGURE 6.14

Adding a New Sub Procedure Named
WithdrawPECSpouseQuestion

```
  Private Sub WithdrawPECSpouseQuestion()

    End Sub
End Class
```

FIGURE 6.15

New General Sub Procedure in
the Code Window

original location, place the name of the new general sub procedure. Finally, make the variable **MonthsOfService** module-level instead of local, so that both procedures btnLookUpWageRate_Click and ComputeWageRate can access it. Run the project to verify that it works properly.

Exercise 6.6

Modify the code for Example 5.8 (see Figure 5.24) that computes and displays the number of days in any desired month, as follows: First, make the variables **MonthAbbr** and **DaysInMonth** module-level instead of local. Then create a general sub procedure named FindNumDaysInMonth that performs the task of looking in variable **MonthAbbr** to find a month abbreviation, then determining the number of days in that month and storing this result in variable **DaysInMonth**. Finally, modify event procedure btnMonthDays_Click to invoke the new general sub procedure instead of using the Select Case statement directly. Run the project to verify that it works properly.

6.2   Procedures with Parameters

Suppose that you wanted to write a general sub procedure that prints a check. Suppose the calling procedure possesses the data for the dollar amount and the name of the payee to appear on the check. How can the calling procedure communicate these data to the general sub procedure? We have already worked with one approach: module-level or global variables. However, there is a better approach, called *parameter passing*, **in which we can pass local data between the calling procedure and the called procedure.**

Parameter passing offers more flexibility than using module-level or global variables. To set the stage for our work with parameters, we discuss the drawbacks of sharing data using module-level and global variables, and then observe how using parameters corrects these problems.

Drawbacks of Module-Level and Global Variables

Although module-level and global variables allow procedures to share data, this process has two serious drawbacks. To illustrate, suppose that two or more procedures in a project need to share data, and we create a global variable for this purpose. The first drawback is that every procedure in the project has access to this variable, even if only two or three should have access to it. Thus, the possibility exists that a procedure that really should not have access to the data item will modify it, causing trouble for those procedures that legitimately rely on that data item. The inadvertent change of a variable is very common and very troublesome in large projects with many procedures. When a data item gets corrupted, it is difficult to discover the procedure that is corrupting it.

The second drawback is that the procedures wanting to share data using the global variable have to "know" its name. That is, the exact name of this variable must appear in the code of these procedures. As a result, the procedures will be able to share data only through this particular variable. This approach is inflexible, particularly when the developer has identified a processing subtask that is generic. Lack of flexibility is an obstacle to the goal of reusable code. Of course, the same arguments can be applied to module-level scope; while the scope is narrower, it is still too wide unless every procedure in the form needs to share it.

Consider the following code:

```
Dim MyInitials As String

Private Sub ReverseTwoCharString()
    MyInitials = Microsoft.VisualBasic.Right(MyInitials, 1) & _
                    Microsoft.VisualBasic.Left(MyInitials, 1)
End Sub

Private Sub btnReverseMyInitials_Click(...)
    MyInitials = txtInitials.Text
    ReverseTwoCharString()
    MsgBox("Your reversed initials are: " & MyInitials)
End Sub
```

This code uses the module-level variable **MyInitials** to facilitate the sharing of data between the event procedure btnReverseMyInitials_Click and the general sub procedure ReverseTwoCharString. The event procedure gets the user's initials and stores them in **MyInitials**. It then calls procedure ReverseTwoCharString. Procedure ReverseTwoCharString retrieves the value from **MyInitials**, performs the reversal (putting the original left character on the right of the new string and the original right character on the left of the new string), and stores the result back in **MyInitials**. Execution then returns to the event procedure, where the reversed initials are displayed using the MsgBox statement.

The code is clear and concise, but the variable name **MyInitials** makes no sense inside procedure ReverseTwoCharString. Imagine we wanted a new event procedure to obtain and then reverse the two digits of a person's age. Since the procedure ReverseTwoCharString uses the module-level variable **MyInitials**, this new event procedure would be

```
Private Sub btnReverseMyAge_Click(...)
    MyInitials = txtAge.Text
    ReverseTwoCharString()
    MsgBox("Your reversed age is: " & MyInitials)
End Sub
```

While this works, it is confusing. Storing the user's age in a variable named **MyInitials** makes no sense.

| Exercise 6.7 | What happens if the user enters three or more letters, instead of two, in txtInitials in btnReverseMyInitials_Click? What can you say about this use of procedure ReverseTwoCharString? What can you say about the name of procedure ReverseTwoCharString? Explain. |

Parameter Passing

If we can somehow "send" the two characters to be reversed directly to the general sub procedure, then we can make the general sub procedure truly generic. By generic, we mean that the procedure will work and will be easy to understand when it is used to reverse any string consisting of two characters. Parameter passing allows us to do this. The calling procedure hands the called procedure a

FIGURE 6.16

Code for Reversing
Two Characters
Using a Parameter

```
Private Sub btnReverseMyAge_Click(ByVal sender As System.Object, By
    Dim MyAge As String = txtAge.Text
    ReverseTwoCharString(MyAge)
    MsgBox("Your reversed age is: " & MyAge)
End Sub

Private Sub btnReverseMyInitials_Click(ByVal sender As System.Object,
    Dim MyInitials As String = txtInitials.Text
    ReverseTwoCharString(MyInitials)
    MsgBox("Your reversed initials are: " & MyInitials)
End Sub

Private Sub ReverseTwoCharString(ByRef TwoChars As String)
    TwoChars = Microsoft.VisualBasic.Right(TwoChars, 1) & _
              Microsoft.VisualBasic.Left(TwoChars, 1)
End Sub
```

variable ByRef,[1] and the called procedure then uses the variable as if it were one of its own local variables. When the called procedure is finished executing, it hands the variable back to the calling procedure. This sharing lasts only while the called procedure is executing.

Figure 6.16 shows the program that reverses two initials (or two digits of an age), modified to use parameter passing. In the next few sections we describe how parameter passing works.

Parameter Lists

Procedure headings contain important information, and they are about to become even more important to us because they identify the parameters being passed. In every procedure heading, the parentheses following the procedure's name surround a *parameter list*, **a list of data items that the procedure expects any calling procedure to send it.** If these parentheses were empty, this means that no parameters were used. But note that procedure ReverseTwoCharString in Figure 6.16 does specify a parameter.

Private Sub ReverseTwoCharString(ByRef TwoChars As String)

Parameter list

This parameter list specifies the following:

1. Any procedure calling ReverseTwoCharString must provide a variable of type String. This variable is called an *argument,* and we say that the argument is passed from the calling procedure to the called procedure.

2. Inside procedure ReverseTwoCharString, this variable is referred to as **TwoChars** (the *parameter*), regardless of what its name is in the calling procedure.

3. The keyword ByRef means that the argument and the parameter are actually two names for the same variable. Anything that procedure ReverseTwoChar-String does with the parameter it refers to as **TwoChars** actually happens with the argument passed to it by the calling procedure. That is, **TwoChars** is not a separate variable; it is just another name for the variable passed to procedure ReverseTwoCharString. We will cover this topic in more depth later.

The variable in the procedure call is referred to as an *argument,* and the corresponding variable in the procedure heading is called a *parameter.* In Figure 6.16, the variable **MyInitials in the statement **ReverseTwoCharString(MyInitials)** is an**

[1] The keyword ByRef will be discussed shortly.

argument. The variable **TwoChars** in the heading **Private Sub ReverseTwoCharString (ByRef TwoChars As String)** is a parameter. Using the terms *argument* and *parameter* helps to clarify discussions of parameter passing.

Procedure Calls with Parameters

Developers sometimes draw arrows on source code printouts to highlight parameter passing. This is illustrated in Figure 6.16. In procedure btnReverseMyInitials_Click, the statement

> **ReverseTwoCharString(MyInitials)**

invokes procedure ReverseTwoCharString and provides it with the string variable **MyInitials** (**MyInitials** is the argument). Procedure ReverseTwoCharString then begins executing, and it uses the variable **MyInitials**, but refers to it as **TwoChars** instead of **MyInitials**.

Similarly, in procedure btnReverseMyAge_Click in Figure 6.16, the call

> **ReverseTwoCharString(MyAge)**

invokes procedure ReverseTwoCharString and provides it with the string variable **MyAge**. Procedure ReverseTwoCharString then begins executing, and it uses the variable **MyAge**, but refers to it as **TwoChars** instead of **MyAge**.

Analyzing Procedures That Use Parameters

In order to fully understand parameter passing, it is often helpful to "hand-check," that is, simulate execution of the code by hand. When you hand-check code, you should heed the following practices to help you keep track of the details:

- Execute statements one at a time, in the same order the computer does.

- Place a number next to each statement as you execute it so that later you can review the order in which statements were executed.

- Write down variables to keep track of the value stored in each variable. Be sure to create a different variable for each procedure's procedure-level local variables, for each form or code module's module-level variables, and for the global variables.

- Create the new variable and initialize it when a variable declaration statement is executed.

- Draw a line through a variable's old value and write the new value below it when a variable's value changes. This way, the current value in the variable is always obvious. This also enables you to review your work when you're finished and contemplate the effect of individual statements.

- Finally, draw a line through any procedure-level variables when their lifetime has expired (usually when the procedure finishes).

Exercise 6.8

Hand-check procedure btnParameterQuiz1_Click and show its output.

```
Private Sub btnParameterQuiz1_Click(...)
    Dim BuildUp As String
    BuildUp = "From "
    QuizProcedureA(BuildUp)
    QuizProcedureB(BuildUp)
```

```
        BuildUp = BuildUp & "sentence."
        MsgBox(BuildUp)
    End Sub

    Private Sub QuizProcedureA(ByRef Message As String)
        Message = Message & "short "
    End Sub

    Private Sub QuizProcedureB(ByRef Phrase As String)
        Phrase = Phrase & "words emerges a "
        QuizProcedureA(Phrase)
    End Sub
```

Exercise 6.9   Hand-check procedure btnParameterQuiz2_Click and show its output.

```
    Private Sub btnParameterQuiz2_Click(...)
        Dim X As Integer
        X = 1
        QuizProcedureC(X)
        X = X + 1
        QuizProcedureD(X)
        X = X + 1
        MsgBox(X)
    End Sub

    Private Sub QuizProcedureC(ByRef Y As Integer)
        QuizProcedureD(Y)
        Y = Y + 10
    End Sub

    Private Sub QuizProcedureD(ByRef Z As Integer)
        Z = Z + 100
    End Sub
```

Multiple Parameters

You can write procedures that receive and process more than one parameter. The parameter list is the key to this. Every parameter list must contain five important pieces of information:

1. The *number* of arguments that the calling procedure must provide.

2. The *types* of the arguments that the calling procedure must provide.

3. The *sequence* of the arguments that the calling procedure must provide.

4. The *names* the arguments are referred to as *inside* the called procedure.

5. Whether the parameter and argument represent the same variable or whether the parameter is storing a local copy of the argument's value.

To examine these in more depth, consider the following sub procedure heading statement

Private Sub Demo(ByRef A As Integer, ByRef B As String, ByRef C As Double)

This sub procedure shows three parameter names (**A**, **B**, and **C**). It also shows their types (Integer, String, and Double). Finally, each parameter is preceded by ByRef, which means that the parameters will be making references to the actual arguments in the calling procedure.

This information defines exactly how any procedure calling this sub procedure must arrange the arguments it passes. To call Demo, the calling procedure must pass three arguments; their types must be Integer, String, and Double in that order; and any changes made to the corresponding parameter within the Demo sub procedure will change the value in the corresponding argument.

Consider the following segment of code:

Dim X As Integer, Y As String, Z As Double
Demo(X, Y, Z)

Private Sub Demo(ByRef A As Integer, ByRef B As String, ByRef C As Double)

As this shows, the calling code passes three variables (**X**, **Y**, and **Z**) as arguments to Demo. The names of these variables can be whatever makes sense within the calling procedure; however, their types must correspond with the types specified in Demo. That is, they must be Integer, String, and Double in that order.

The practice of drawing arrows between the arguments and corresponding parameters helps show that the sequence of the arguments and parameters is important and it also shows the relationships between each argument and parameter name. In this example, argument **X** and parameter **A** refer to the same variable (**X** in this case), argument **Y** and parameter **B** refer to the same variable (**Y** in this case), and argument **Z** and parameter **C** refer to the same variable (**Z** in this case). Any changes to either **A**, **B**, or **C** within Demo will actually be changing the arguments **X**, **Y**, and **Z**.

Note that this can sometimes get confusing. For example, the following is legal:

Dim C As Integer, A As String, B As Double
Demo(C, A, B)

Private Sub Demo(ByRef A As Integer, ByRef B As String, ByRef C As Double)

Here the argument/parameter association is argument **C** is associated with parameter **A**, argument **A** is associated with parameter **B**, and argument **B** is associated with parameter **C**. This means that any reference to parameter **B** within Demo actually refers to the argument **A** in the calling procedure.

When you enter a procedure call into your Visual Basic .NET code, you will note that the code helper displays the parameter values for you. Figure 6.17 shows an example of this.

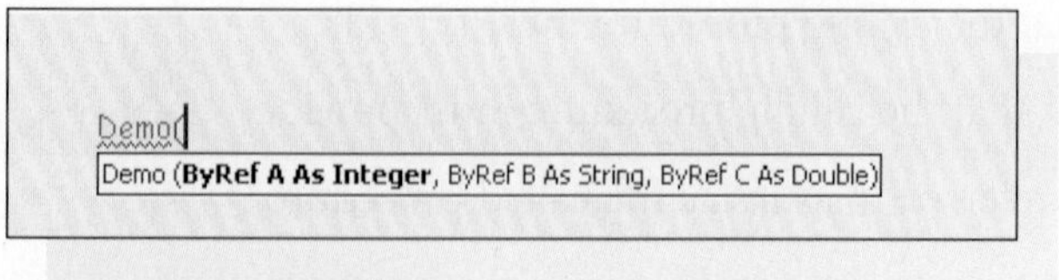

Demo(
Demo (**ByRef A As Integer**, ByRef B As String, ByRef C As Double)

FIGURE 6.17

Code Helper Showing the
Procedure's Parameters

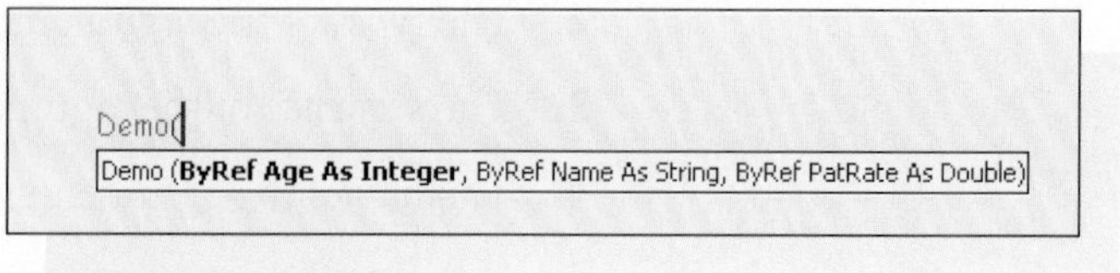

Demo(
Demo (**ByRef Age As Integer**, ByRef Name As String, ByRef PatRate As Double)

FIGURE 6.18

Code Helper Showing Better
Parameter Names

This shows that the types of the arguments must be Integer, String, and Double. The parameter names (A, B, C) mean very little in this procedure. However, if you use better names as parameters, that is, names that help the user know what is expected, then both the parameter types as well as their meanings can be derived from the code helper. Figure 6.18 shows an example of this.

Exercise 6.10

Hand-check procedure btnMultipleParametersTest_Click and show its output.

```
Private Sub btnMultipleParametersTest_Click(...)
    Dim A As Integer
    Dim B As Integer
    Dim C As Single
    A = 2
    B = 4
    SimpleCalculations(A, B, C)
    MsgBox("A = " & A)
    MsgBox("B = " & B)
    MsgBox("C = " & C)
End Sub

Private Sub SimpleCalculations(ByRef X As Integer, ByRef Y As Integer, _
                               ByRef Z As Single)
    Dim W As Single
    W = X + Y
    X = X + 1
    Y = Y * 2
    Z = (X + Y) / W
End Sub
```

Exercise 6.11

Suppose we modify Exercise 6.10 by changing the statement

SimpleCalculations(A, B, C)

in procedure btnMultipleParametersTest_Click to

SimpleCalculations(B, A, C)

What values will the message boxes display? Can you figure this out without having to work through the code by hand?

Exercise 6.12

Write a procedure named Swap that performs the task of exchanging the values stored in two variables of type Single. If your procedure is correctly written, the message boxes in the event procedure below should display the same two numbers that the user enters in the TextBoxes, but in reverse order.

```
Private Sub btnSwapTest_Click(...)
    Dim A As Single
    Dim B As Single
    A = txtA.Text
    B = txtB.Text
    Swap(A, B)
    MsgBox(A)
    MsgBox(B)
End Sub
```

Exercise 6.13

Given the following code, predict what values will be displayed, and in what order, when the user clicks on btnParmQuiz.

```
Private Sub btnParmQuiz_Click(...)
    Dim A As String
    Dim B As String
    Dim C As String
    Dim D As String
    A = "maga"
    B = "zine"
    C = "busi"
    D = "ness"
    Rearrange(C, D)
    MsgBox(A)
    MsgBox(B)
    MsgBox(C)
    MsgBox(D)
End Sub

Private Sub Rearrange(ByVal A As String, ByVal B As String)
    Dim C As String
    Dim D As String
    C = Mid(A, 2, 2)
    D = Mid(B, 2, 2)
    A = Microsoft.VisualBasic.Left(A, 1) & Microsoft.VisualBasic.Right(A, 1) & _
        Microsoft.VisualBasic.Left(B, 1) & Microsoft.VisualBasic.Right(B, 1)
    B = C & D
End Sub
```

Exercise 6.14

Suppose we modify Exercise 6.13 by changing the statement

```
Rearrange(C, D)
```

in procedure btnParmQuiz_Click to

```
Rearrange(A, B)
```

What values will the message boxes display? Can you figure this out without having to work through the code by hand?

Passing by Reference and Passing by Value

We have seen that using the *ByRef keyword*, **short for "By Reference," in front of a parameter means that the parameter and its corresponding argument refer to the same variable,** that is, they both refer to the argument in the calling procedure. Short of extending the scope of a variable, using ByRef is the only way a sub procedure can change the value it is passed by the calling procedure.

However, there are times when the sub procedure does not need to change the value of the argument, that is, it just needs to use the value while doing something such as a calculation. For this **Visual Basic .NET provides the *ByVal* keyword to specify explicitly in the parameter list that the called procedure cannot change the value stored in a variable passed to it.** To do this, simply place the keyword ByVal before the parameter name.

FIGURE 6.19

A Procedure That Adds Two Numbers

```
Private Sub Add(ByVal A As Short, ByVal B As Short, ByRef C As Integer)
    C = A + B
End Sub
```

In the called procedure, the ByVal parameter is a local copy of the argument that was passed by the calling procedure. That is, the ByVal parameter in the parameter list is

1. Created when the called procedure begins executing, and is considered to be a local variable within the procedure.

2. Initialized to the value of the corresponding argument in the call.

Subsequently, this variable is just like any other local variable in the called procedure. It has *no connection* with any other variables in the project, and it goes away like other local variables when the procedure's End Sub is encountered. It is essentially a disconnected copy of the argument.

Consider the procedure in Figure 6.19. Here the procedure is passed two Short values (**A** and **B**). It adds them together and stores the result in the Integer **C**. Notice that while the procedure needs the values of **A** and **B** to compute the sum, it does not intend to change their values. In fact, if the procedure Add did change these two values, the user of the procedure would likely not be happy. This would be equivalent to using a MsgBox() procedure such as **MsgBox("The sum is " & Sum)** to display the value of **Sum** but in addition to displaying the value of **Sum**, the value also was changed inside the MsgBox() procedure. By using ByVal to qualify the parameters **A** and **B**, there is no way that their values can accidentally be changed because the procedure Add is just working with a copy of the arguments, not the actual arguments themselves.

On the other hand, the parameter **C** *must be* a ByRef parameter. If it were not, there would be no way for the sum to be returned to the calling procedure.

Using ByVal is considered "safer" than using ByRef because there is no way to accidentally change the argument value inside the procedure if the corresponding parameter is qualified with ByVal. In fact, Visual Basic .NET considers ByVal to be the default parameter modifier. If you enter a new sub procedure and fail to qualify a parameter with ByRef or ByVal, the system will automatically add the ByVal (safer) qualifier. This means that you must explicitly specify ByRef in order to get this type of argument/parameter association.

Exercise 6.15

Given code below, indicate what is printed for each of the MsgBox statements in btnStart_Click.

```
Dim A As Integer
Dim B As Integer

Private Sub btnStart_Click(...)
    Dim X As Integer
    Dim Y As Integer
    X = 10
    Y = 20
    DoSomething(X, Y)
    MsgBox(X & " - " & Y)
    DoSomethingElse(X, Y)
    MsgBox(X & " - " & Y)
    MsgBox(A & " - " & B)
End Sub
```

continues

```
Public Sub DoSomething(ByVal A As Integer, ByRef B As Integer)
    Static K As Integer
    K = K + 1
    A = K
    B = B * K
    A = 50
End Sub

Public Sub DoSomethingElse(ByRef K As Integer, ByRef J As Integer)
    Dim B As Integer
    B = 100
    K = A
    J = 13
    DoSomething(J, K)
    A = A + 1
End Sub
```

Exercise 6.16

Given code below, indicate what is printed for each of the MsgBox statements in btnExam1_Click.

```
Dim A As Integer
Dim B As Integer

Private Sub btnExam1_Click(...)
    Dim A As Integer
    Dim C As Integer
    A = 10
    B = 25
    C = 4
    procA(A, B, C)
    MsgBox(A & "-" & B & "-" & C)
    procB(A, B, C)
    MsgBox(A & "-" & B & "-" & C)
    procC(C)
    MsgBox(A & "-" & B & "-" & C)
End Sub

Public Sub procA(ByRef X As Integer, ByVal Y As Integer, ByRef Z As Integer)
    Dim A As Integer
    A = 100
    X = A
    Y = A
    Z = 200
End Sub

Public Sub procB(ByVal A As Integer, ByRef B As Integer, ByRef C As Integer)
    Dim T As Integer
    T = A
    A = B
    B = T
    C = 33
End Sub
```

```
Public Sub procC(ByRef Z As Integer)
    Dim C As Integer
    C = B
    A = 199
    Z = 833
    procA(Z, A, C)
End Sub
```

Passing Expressions

The calling procedure can pass an expression instead of a variable to the called procedure. That is, the argument can be an expression. We can call the Add() procedure shown in Figure 6.19 using the following statement

> Add(3, 4, Answer)

Whenever expressions are used as arguments, the corresponding parameters are treated as ByVal regardless of what is specified. Using ByRef in these cases makes no sense. Can you explain why?

Correcting Common Mistakes in Parameter Passing

Beginning developers often make mistakes when using parameter passing. In this section, we describe the most common errors and how to correct them. We organize the discussion by the error messages Visual Basic .NET will display if you make these errors.

Argument Not Specified

When the number of arguments provided by a procedure call does not match the number of parameters in the called procedure's parameter list, an *Argument Not Specified* error occurs. This is a syntax error and will show up in the Code window. The code in Figure 6.20 illustrates this error. The procedure call has no arguments, but Demo's parameter list specifies two parameters. The program will not run with this error.

When you see this error message, count the number of parameters in the called procedure's parameter list, then count the number of arguments in the call and determine which must be corrected.

FIGURE 6.20

Argument Not Specified Error

```
Private Sub btnTester_Click(ByVal sender As System.Object, ByVal e As System.EventA
    Dim X As Short = 10, Y As String = "Hello"
    Demo()
End Sub   Argument not specified for parameter 'B' of 'Private Sub Demo(ByRef A As Short, B As String)'.

Private Sub Demo(ByRef A As Short, ByVal B As String)
    'simple procedure to show argument/parameter errors
End Sub
```

Invalid Cast Exception

When the types of the arguments in the procedure are not compatible with the types in the parameter list, an *invalid cast exception* can occur. The code in Figure 6.21 illustrates this error. The String argument **Y** is associated with the Short parameter **A** and the Short argument **X** is associated with the String parameter **B**. This is not necessarily an error with the default Visual Basic .NET settings. That is because, as we have seen earlier, Visual Basic .NET tries to cast one type to another. In this case, when the code is executed, Visual Basic .NET tries to cast the value of argument **Y** ("Hello") to a Short. This will fail with an invalid cast exception (see Figure 6.22). Note, however, that if the value of the argument **Y** was "34", then the cast would have succeeded and no exception would be thrown. In addition, the argument **X** that stores the number 10 would be successfully cast into the String parameter **B** without any problems.

When you see this error message, compare—one by one and from left to right—the types specified in the parameter list with the types of the arguments provided by the call. If the arguments are variables, you must find their Dim statements to determine their types. To help you identify the problem, you can sketch lines on a printout of the source code that go from the parameter list, through the call, to the Dim statements.

When you receive an invalid cast exception, you must eliminate the mismatch. Change the type of either the argument in the call or the parameter in the parameter list, whichever is appropriate. Also check to see that the arguments are not out of order.

Arguments Out of Order

The arguments in a call are associated with the parameters in the parameter list by position, not by name. The developer who wrote the code in Figure 6.23 made a mistake in writing the procedure call. Visual Basic .NET displays the same invalid cast exception we just saw because the value of the argument **Name** ("Bill") cannot be cast into a Short.

To fix the type mismatch problem, you might first try to change the Dim statements in the calling procedure, making **Age** type String and **Name** type Short. This

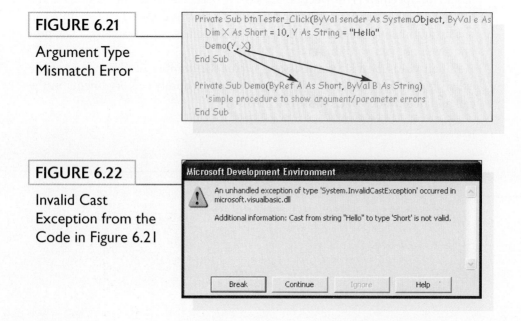

FIGURE 6.21

Argument Type Mismatch Error

```
Private Sub btnTester_Click(ByVal sender As System.Object, ByVal e As
    Dim X As Short = 10, Y As String = "Hello"
    Demo(Y, X)
End Sub


Private Sub Demo(ByRef A As Short, ByVal B As String)
    'simple procedure to show argument/parameter errors
End Sub
```

FIGURE 6.22

Invalid Cast Exception from the Code in Figure 6.21

Microsoft Development Environment

An unhandled exception of type 'System.InvalidCastException' occurred in microsoft.visualbasic.dll

Additional information: Cast from string "Hello" to type 'Short' is not valid.

| Break | Continue | Ignore | Help |

FIGURE 6.23

Code with Error
Due to Parameters
and Arguments Not
Being in the Correct
Corresponding
Positions

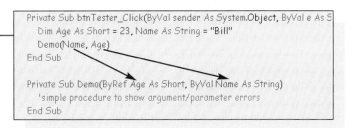

```
Private Sub btnTester_Click(ByVal sender As System.Object, ByVal e As S
    Dim Age As Short = 23, Name As String = "Bill"
    Demo(Name, Age)
End Sub

Private Sub Demo(ByRef Age As Short, ByVal Name As String)
    'simple procedure to show argument/parameter errors
End Sub
```

would eliminate the type mismatch, but would cause worse problems because the variables would have the incorrect data types. The real problem lies in the fact that the arguments in the procedure call are in the wrong order.

Another problem can result if a developer orders the arguments in a call incorrectly and the arguments are the same data type. In this case, the program executes incorrectly but there is no error message to warn of the problem. This is the worst possible situation.

To keep errors like this from going undetected, it is important to thoroughly test the code by entering values with known answers and verifying that the code produces the correct answers. The fact that a program produces no error messages does not necessarily mean it works correctly.

Conflict between Parameter Name and Local Variable Name

Visual Basic .NET does not allow you to declare a local variable in the called procedure that has the same name as a parameter in the procedure's parameter list. Figure 6.24 shows variable **Age** as both a parameter and a local variable in the sub procedure Demo. You can see that this error is detected by Visual Basic .NET at design time and the application will not run until you have corrected the problem.

General Sub Procedures versus Event Procedures

Although general sub procedures and event procedures have many similarities, there are two important differences. First, an event procedure is always associated with a control. We have discussed this fact already, but now is a good time to review its implications.

- The naming conventions differ. Event procedure names begin with the name of the associated control, followed by an underscore character, and ending with the type of event. General sub procedure names do not have this form.

- Event procedures cannot be located in code modules.

FIGURE 6.24

Local Variable
Conflicting with
Parameter

```
Private Sub btnTester_Click(ByVal sender As System.Object, ByVal e As S
    Dim Age As Short = 23, Name As String = "Bill"
    Demo(Name, Age)
End Sub

Private Sub Demo(ByRef Age As Short, ByVal Name As String)
    Dim Age As Short
    'simple pr 'Age' is already declared as a parameter of this method.
End Sub
```

Second, for a general sub procedure the developer creates the procedure heading, including the parameter list, whereas for an event procedure, Visual Basic .NET creates the procedure heading. The developer is allowed to modify the parameter list for a general sub procedure. However, Visual Basic .NET does not allow the developer to modify the parameter list for an event procedure.

Most event procedures use parameters. For these event procedures Visual Basic .NET creates the procedure heading, complete with the parameter list. As a developer, you may be tempted to modify the parameter list in order to add or delete a parameter, but Visual Basic .NET does not allow this.

Exercise 6.17

Modify your solution to Exercise 6.5 as follows: First, make both variables **WageRate** and **MonthsOfService** local to event procedure btnLookUpWageRate_Click instead of module-level. Then modify the heading for general sub procedure ComputeWageRate by adding parameters for the wage rate and months of service (be sure to specify ByVal or ByRef as appropriate). Finally, modify the procedure call by adding **WageRate** and **MonthsOfService** as arguments. Run the project to verify that it works properly.

Exercise 6.18

Modify your solution to Exercise 6.6 as follows: First, make both variables **MonthAbbr** and **DaysInMonth** local to event procedure btnMonthDays_Click instead of module-level. Then modify the heading for general sub procedure FindNumDaysInMonth by adding parameters for the month abbreviation and the number of days in the month (be sure to specify ByVal or ByRef as appropriate). Finally, modify the procedure call by adding **MonthAbbr** and **DaysInMonth** as arguments. Run the project to verify that it works properly.

General Sub Procedures versus Event Procedures and the Object Paradigm

Historically, Visual Basic has differentiated general sub procedures, developer-defined functions (see Section 6.3), and event procedures as we have done so far in this and previous chapters. However, it is valuable to relate these concepts to the object paradigm discussed in Chapter 1 of the text. Let us look at the complete code listing for a very simple form. Figure 6.25 shows this code.

Using the code in Figure 6.25, we can see that what Visual Basic .NET has built for us is a class named frmSimple. This class is a subclass of the System.Windows.Forms.Form class. Within this class, we see two methods that have been defined. These include the btnDemo_Click() method and the Demo() method. Note that the btnDemo_Click() method "Handles btnDemo.Click". This means that this

FIGURE 6.25

Complete Code Listing for a Simple Form

```
Public Class frmSimple
    Inherits System.Windows.Forms.Form

    Windows Form Designer generated code

    Private Sub btnDemo_Click(ByVal sender As System.Object, _
            ByVal e As System.EventArgs) Handles btnDemo.Click

    End Sub
    Private Sub Demo(ByVal A As Integer)
        MsgBox("Hello - I am Sub Demo with A = " & A)
    End Sub
End Class
```

method will be called when the system detects a Click event on the component named btnDemo. In contrast to the btnDemo_Click() method, the Demo() method does not "handle" anything. Thus, it is not associated with any events generated and detected by the system. This means that the only way for the Demo() method to be called is from another method (such as the btnDemo_Click() method).

In the vocabulary of the Object paradigm, what we have created is a form class and two new methods (note that within the section marked "Windows Form Designer generated code" there are several more methods defined for this class). The difference between the two methods we have created is one handles a specific event (an event procedure in Visual Basic .NET vocabulary) and the other is not associated with an event (a general sub procedure in Visual Basic. NET vocabulary).

With this clarification in mind, we now turn our attention to developer-defined functions that, as one might suspect, are also methods of the form class that behave somewhat differently than sub procedures.

6.3 | Developer-Defined Functions

In Chapter 4 we discussed Visual Basic .NET's built-in functions. These functions, such as Math.Sqr() and Chr(), perform some manipulation on an argument and return a result. Recall that these built-in functions were always used in expressions. For example, we saw the statement

lblHypotenuse.Text = Math.Sqr(ASquared + BSquared)

In Visual Basic .NET, the developer can create custom functions—called ***developer-defined functions*—to perform calculations or string manipulations.** In this section we show how to write and use developer-defined functions.

Almost everything we know about general sub procedures also applies to functions. Specifically,

- Functions are not associated with any control (they handle no events).

- Functions have parameter lists just like general sub procedures.

- Variables declared inside the function are local to the function.

The main difference between a general sub procedure and a developer-defined function is that, like Visual Basic .NET's built-in functions, the developer-defined function returns a value.

Let's look at an example of a developer-defined function. The code in Figure 6.26 shows a function named Add() that performs the same processing task as the

FIGURE 6.26

A Developer-
Defined Function
Named Add()

```
Private Sub btnTester_Click(ByVal sender As System.Object, ByVal e As Sy
    Dim X As Short = 10, Y As Short = 12, Z As Short
    Z = Add(X, Y)
    MsgBox("Sum = " & Z)
End Sub


Private Function Add(ByVal A As Short, ByVal B As Short) As Integer
    Return A + B
End Function
```

general sub procedure named Add() used in previous examples (see Figure 6.19). Notice how event procedure btnTester_Click invokes the function: the name of the function appears on the right-hand side of an assignment statement (i.e., in the expression), just like one of Visual Basic .NET's built-in functions:

Z = Add(X,Y)

When the computer executes this assignment statement, it first goes to the right-hand side (as always) to evaluate the expression. It encounters the name of the function, Add(). When the computer encounters the name of a function in an expression, it transfers execution from the current procedure to the named function (passing it any specified arguments). We describe this operation as invoking or calling the function.

When the function is finished executing, it returns its result, and the flow of execution returns to the calling procedure where it left off. In this example, when function Add() is finished executing, execution resumes with the MsgBox() statement in btnTester_Click.

Notice how the function returns its result to the calling procedure. A function includes a Return statement followed by an expression. In this case we have

Return A + B

This causes two things to happen. First, the function stops executing and flow of control returns to the calling procedure. Second, the function itself is set equal to the value of the expression in the Return statement. You may see now why we use the terminology "a function returns a value." Note that a function can only return the value of a single expression.

Developer-defined functions differ from general sub procedures in several ways. An obvious difference is that developer-defined functions begin with the keyword Function and end with the keywords End Function.

Another difference is in the function heading: a type specification follows the parameter list.

Private Function Add(ByVal A As Short, ByVal B As Short) As Integer

This specifies the type of the value returned by the function. Since the job of procedure Add() is to take two values of type Short and add them together, its return value is Integer. If the return value were Short, then an overflow could occur because a Short type uses 16 bits (an Integer type stores 32 bits). You may specify any of the types we have discussed as the return type of a function.

Observe that the two parameters are qualified with the ByVal qualifier. This means that copies of the arguments are being used within the function. If we were to change the value of either **A** or **B** within the function, the value of the corresponding arguments would not be changed. Since a function's primary job is to return a value, it would be unusual to have any ByRef parameters. In fact, the version of the Add() procedure in Figure 6.19, where there was an additional ByRef parameter needed to get the answer back from the procedure, is actually a bad example of a procedure. Anytime the objective of your code is to return a value, that code should be in the form of a function, not a procedure.

If you put the function name in an expression inside the same function, when the computer tries to evaluate the expression it will invoke the function again instead of retrieving a value. That is, the function will invoke itself. This is legal and is called a recursive call. Recursion can be useful but is beyond the scope of this text.

FIGURE 6.27

Code for Example 6.2

```
Private Sub btnHandling_Click(ByVal sender As System.Object, ByVal e As Sys
    Dim TotalPurchase As Decimal = txtAmount.Text
    MsgBox("Handling charge: " & HandlingCharge(TotalPurchase))
End Sub

Private Function HandlingCharge(ByVal OrderAmount As Decimal) As Decimal
    Select Case OrderAmount
        Case Is < 10
            Return 2.95
        Case Is < 25
            Return 3.95
        Case Is < 100
            Return 4.95
        Case Else
            Return 5.95
    End Select
End Function
```

Example 6.2

USING A DEVELOPER-DEFINED FUNCTION

The code in Figure 6.27 contains a simple arithmetic function. The function computes the handling charge for orders processed by a mail-order company. The amount of the charge depends on the amount of the order; thus, the function contains a Select Case statement. The function examines the order amount, determines the appropriate charge, and stores this value in the function name that becomes the value returned by the function.

Observe in Figure 6.27 that the Return statement occurs in multiple statements within the function. Note also that the type of the function's return value is Decimal. Because the function does not modify the value stored in the argument passed to it, **OrderAmount** is specified as a ByVal parameter.

Creating Functions

To create a function, follow the same steps that you followed to create a general sub procedure. Just be sure to use the keyword Function instead of Sub; Visual Basic .NET will take care of adding the correct End Function statement.

6.4 Code Modules

So far we have seen code modules used to declare module-level and global variables and to store general sub procedures. They also can store developer-defined functions. We now examine two additional uses of code modules.

Sub Main

Recall that Visual Basic .NET allows you to specify a startup form that is the form that Visual Basic .NET automatically displays when program execution begins. As an alternative, you can use *Sub Main* **to specify that Visual Basic .NET begin execution of the program by executing a general sub procedure.** To use Sub Main, first select the project in the Solution Explorer, then choose Properties

FIGURE 6.28

Specifying Sub Main in Visual Basic .NET's Project Properties Window

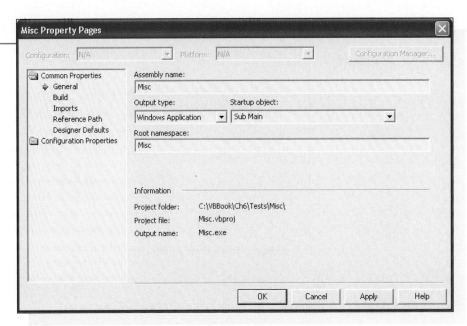

under the Project menu, and in the Misc Property Pages dialog box that Visual Basic .NET displays, select General under Common Properties. Then, in the Startup Object box, select Sub Main, as shown in Figure 6.28.

After specifying Sub Main as the startup object, you must create a public general sub procedure named Main in a code module. It can be in any code module, but you must not have more than one procedure named Main, even if they are in different code modules. Then, when program execution begins, Visual Basic .NET will not load any form but instead will find the procedure named Main and begin executing it.

What might you use procedure Main for? You could use it to initialize global variables or properties of controls on different forms before showing one of the forms using the Show method. If the project has multiple forms, you might want the program to decide which form to display first. That is, you can have decision-making statements in procedure Main that determine the order in which to present the various forms to the user. This provides more flexibility than specifying a startup form at design time.

Libraries

General sub procedures and developer-defined functions make it possible to create reusable code. One developer writes a procedure or function to perform a given task, and subsequently other developers can use this procedure or function whenever they require the task it performs. In practice, developers have found that such reusable code is essential for successfully building maintainable, large systems.

Programmers try to organize reusable code for easy access. To do this, they identify categories of processing tasks, create one code module for each category, and arrange the reusable procedures and functions in the code modules appropriately. Processing tasks might be broken into categories such as financial calculations, database processing, graphic image processing, user interface operations, statistical calculations, and so forth. **A collection of code modules organized this way, according to categories, is called a *library*.**

The code module for financial calculations, for example, contains all the previously written general sub procedures and functions having to do with financial calculations. If a developer has to create a new application that involves financial operations, then she should become familiar with the content of this code module to take advantage of code that has already been written.

6.5 The KeyPress Event

We now turn our attention to Visual Basic .NET controls and some additional events. Unlike previous event procedures we have seen where we did not pay any attention to the event's parameters, we will now use our knowledge regarding parameters to focus on events where using the parameters is valuable.

In this section we examine the ***KeyPress event,*** **which enables your programs to respond to keystrokes made by the user.** This capability might be useful, for example, in determining whether the user is entering valid characters.

Any control that can have the focus is capable of responding to the KeyPress event that occurs when the control has the focus and the user presses an ANSI key. (Non-ANSI keys such as SHIFT, CTRL, ALT, and the arrow keys will not cause the KeyPress event.) Typically, you will write decision-making statements in the KeyPress event procedure to determine which key the user pressed and to perform appropriate processing steps.

The empty template for a KeyPress event procedure for a TextBox control named txtSSN follows. Recall that Visual Basic .NET creates the entire procedure heading for event procedures, including the parameter list.

```
Private Sub txtSSN_KeyPress(ByVal sender As Object, _
    ByVal e As System.Windows.Forms.KeyPressEventArgs) _
    Handles txtSSN.KeyPress

End Sub
```

Every KeyPress event procedure specifies an object reference parameter named **e** from the System.Windows.Forms.KeyPressEventArgs class. This class includes a number of properties that are useful for determining what is happening as the key is pressed. At run time, when the KeyPress event occurs, Visual Basic .NET first stores information about the key the user pressed in the object reference **e**, and then begins executing the statements inside the KeyPress event procedure.

The KeyPress Event for TextBox Controls

Programmers frequently write KeyPress event procedures for TextBox controls. As mentioned previously, one use of KeyPress is to validate user input. For example, if the user is supposed to enter a numeric value in the TextBox, we can use the KeyPress event to prevent the user from entering letters.

Ordinarily, when a TextBox control has the focus and the user presses a key, the character is immediately appended to the TextBox's Text property. However, when the TextBox has a KeyPress event procedure, the sequence of events includes execution of the event procedure, as follows:

1. The user presses a key.

2. Visual Basic .NET stores the ANSI character of the key in the KeyChar property of the object reference parameter **e**. This can be retrieved by using **e.KeyChar**.

3. Visual Basic .NET begins executing the KeyPress event procedure.

4. While the KeyPress event is executing, the code can set the (Boolean) Handled property of the object reference parameter **e** to either True or False, that is, **e.Handled = True**. If this property is set to True, then the system does not process the event. The effect of this is the character never gets placed into the TextBox. If the Handled property is set to False or not set at all within the event procedure (it is False by default), the system processes the event when the KeyPress event is done.

Essentially the KeyPress event sits between the pressing of the key on the keyboard and the system displaying the character in the TextBox. By handling the event (**e.Handled = True**), the system never sees it and thus the character does not get placed in the TextBox. We can use this behavior to reject characters that we do not want in a TextBox.

The code in Figure 6.29 shows a KeyPress event procedure for a TextBox that allows the user to enter a Social Security number (SSN). An SSN consists of nine digits (ignoring the dashes). Since a Social Security number consists of digits only, the user should not be allowed to enter other characters, such as letters, punctuation, and so forth. Setting the Handled property to True in those cases nullifies the user's keystroke. The Beep alerts the user that he pressed an invalid key.

While the action of the KeyPress event is straightforward, it may not be possible to define some of the characters that we want to identify in a Case clause as string constants. For example, the code in Figure 6.29 restricts the user to entering only digits. It considers BACKSPACE an illegal character. This is probably not a good idea! However, we cannot put a BACKSPACE between quotes as we did with the 0 and 9. Instead, we must look up the numeric ANSI value of BACKSPACE and then convert it to a character using the Chr() function. Thus, our Case clause in Figure 6.29 that allows a BACKSPACE as well as any digit would be

```
Case "0" To "9", Chr(8) ' character is OK
```

You should refer back to Table 4.6 for the numeric values of the nonprintable ANSI characters. Note that your code would be more readable if you defined a symbolic constant for the backspace character:

```
Const BACKSPACE = Chr(8)
...
Case "0" To "9", BACKSPACE ' character is OK
```

FIGURE 6.29

Using KeyPress to Restrict SSN Input to Digits Only

```
Private Sub txtSSN_KeyPress(ByVal sender As Object, ByVal e As System.Win
    Select Case e.KeyChar
        Case "0" To "9" 'character is legal - do nothing
            Exit Sub
        Case Else 'reject character by handling event here
            Beep()
            e.Handled = True
    End Select
End Sub
```

FIGURE 6.30

Code That Manages SSN in the Form DDD-DD-DDDD

```
Private Sub txtSSN_KeyPress(ByVal sender As Object, ByVal e As System
    Const BACKSPACE = Chr(8)
    Dim N As Short = Len(txtSSN.Text)
    Select Case e.KeyChar
        Case BACKSPACE ' OK any time
        Case "0" To "9" ' digits OK but not in positions 4 or 7
            If N = 3 Or N = 6 Then ' digit in the wrong place
                Beep()
                e.Handled = True
            Else
                Exit Sub
            End If
        Case "-" ' be sure it is the correct location
            If N = 3 Or N = 6 Then
                Exit Sub ' because it is in right position
            Else
                Beep()
                e.Handled = True ' reject dash if not in right position
            End If
        Case Else
            Beep()
            e.Handled = True
    End Select
End Sub
```

Example 6.3

ALLOWING DIGITS, BACKSPACES, AND DASHES

The procedure in Figure 6.29 allows only digits. In this example, we expand the KeyPress event to also allow BACKSPACE as well as dashes (but only in the correct positions). In other words, we want the following format to be enforced (where D means a digit):

DDD-DD-DDDD

Note that the dashes are located in character positions 4 and 7.

The code in Figure 6.30 shows such a KeyPress event. To enforce the maximum of 11 characters in the TextBox, we have set the TextBox's MaxLength property to 11 at design time.

The only "tricky" thing to remember regarding this code is that it is called *before* the character is placed in the TextBox. When the length of the Text property is equal to 3, we know that we are looking at a character that will be the fourth character if we allow the event to be handled by the system. Therefore, if **N** = 3 and we are looking at a dash coming in, we allow it to enter and become the fourth character. Likewise, if **N** = 3 and we see a digit coming in, we reject it (we handle the event here) because the digit would become the fourth character.

The SendKeys Class

Many applications allow the user to move the focus from one TextBox to another using either the ENTER key or the TAB key. Visual Basic .NET provides the TabStop and TabIndex properties so that you can easily enable the user to switch between controls using the TAB key, but you have to do a little coding to enable the user to switch between controls using the ENTER key.

The problem with using the ENTER key as an equivalent to the TAB key is that Visual Basic .NET has already defined the behavior of ENTER for the TextBox control if the system handles the key press. This predefined behavior adds a new line of text to the TextBox (this assumes that the Multiline property is True).

FIGURE 6.31

KeyPress Event Procedures That Make Pressing ENTER Move the Focus to the Next Component

```
Private Sub txtDemo_KeyPress(ByVal sender As Object, ByVal e As Systen
  Const ENTER = Chr(13)
  Select Case e.KeyChar
    Case ENTER ' Enter key detected
      SendKeys.Send("{Tab}") ' send a tab instead
      e.Handled = True ' reject the Enter character
  End Select
End Sub
```

What we need to do is intercept the ENTER key and replace it with another key. To do this we need to take advantage of the SendKeys class.

You can write code that sends any keystroke to the application using the *SendKeys class.* The code in Figure 6.31 illustrates how the Send method of the SendKeys class can be used in a KeyPress event to allow the user to press ENTER to move the focus to the next control in the tab sequence. The ANSI code for the ENTER key is 13. When this character is detected, a TAB character is sent instead and then the event is marked as being handled. All other keystrokes are ignored by this code and are thus handled by the system.

The common nonprintable keystrokes that one might want to send are displayed in Table 6.1.

Table 6.1 Codes for nonprintable keystrokes for the Send() method

Key	Code
BACKSPACE	{BACKSPACE}, {BS}, or {BKSP}
BREAK	{BREAK}
CAPSLOCK	{CAPSLOCK}
DEL or DELETE	{DELETE} or {DEL}
↓	{DOWN}
END	{END}
ENTER	{ENTER}or ~
ESC	{ESC}
HELP	{HELP}
HOME	{HOME}
INS or INSERT	{INSERT} or {INS}
←	{LEFT}
NUMLOCK	{NUMLOCK}
PAGE DOWN	{PGDN}
PAGE UP	{PGUP}
PRINT SCREEN	{PRTSC} (reserved for future use)
→	{RIGHT}
SCROLL LOCK	{SCROLLLOCK}
TAB	{TAB}
↑	{UP}

6.6 The Enter and Leave Events

Any control that can have the focus is capable of responding to the Enter and Leave events. **The *Enter event* occurs for a control when the control receives the focus. The *Leave event* occurs for a control when the control loses the focus** (because the focus is moved to another control). Both events can be caused by user actions (clicking the mouse on a control, pressing (TAB), or pressing an access key) or by execution of a statement containing the Focus method.

The developer can use the Enter and Leave events to make an application behave more intuitively for the user. For example, the user might enter a customer number in a TextBox and then click or tab to another TextBox. This action causes the Leave event to occur for the Customer Number TextBox. As a result, the developer can write a Leave event procedure that uses the customer number to look up the customer's name and address from a database and then fills this information into TextBoxes on the form. From the user's perspective, the user enters a customer number and then moves to another TextBox, and the application automatically fills in the customer's name and address.

The code in Figure 6.32 illustrates a technique for conveying information about program execution to the user. The form contains two TextBoxes (one for a Name and another for an SSN), a Label, and a Button. When the user clicks on the Name TextBox (txtName), event procedure txtName_Enter is executed. This causes the phrase "Please enter your full name (Last, First, Middle Initial)" to be displayed in the label (lblExplanation). If the user clicks on the SSN TextBox (txtSSN), then the explanation changes to "Please enter your SSN (xxx-xx-xxxx)". This technique informs the user what type of entry is expected in the currently active TextBox.

Each time a TextBox loses the focus, the explanation label is cleared. This ensures that a message will not linger after the user moves on to another control (perhaps the Button).

Exercise 6.19

Suppose you have provided a TextBox control to allow the user to enter a Social Security Number without the dashes. Write the code that will ensure that the entry has no fewer than nine digits (since an SSN always consists of exactly nine digits) before allowing the focus to leave the TextBox. *Hint:* Check out the Focus method.

FIGURE 6.32

Code That Tells User
What to Enter

```
Private Sub btnProcess_Click(ByVal sender As System.Object, ByVal e As System.E
    MsgBox("Now processing data.")
End Sub

Private Sub txtName_Enter(ByVal sender As Object, ByVal e As System.EventArgs)
    lblExplanation.Text = "Please enter your full name (Last, First, Middle Initial)"
End Sub

Private Sub txtName_Leave(ByVal sender As Object, ByVal e As System.EventArgs)
    lblExplanation.Text = ""
End Sub

Private Sub txtSSN_Enter(ByVal sender As Object, ByVal e As System.EventArgs)
    lblExplanation.Text = "Please enter your SSN (xxx-xx-xxxx)"
End Sub

Private Sub txtSSN_Leave(ByVal sender As Object, ByVal e As System.EventArgs)
    lblExplanation.Text = ""
End Sub
```

6.7 | Modal versus Modeless Forms

As we know, most real-world applications have multiple forms, with each form having a particular objective or theme. In most such applications, the developer must carefully design and control the order in which forms are presented to the user. Otherwise, if the user is allowed to navigate through the forms at random, the application looks confusing, is unnecessarily complicated, and is difficult to use. One approach for controlling how a form is displayed is *form modality*.

When a *modal form* is shown, controls on other forms do not react to user actions; the user must first respond to the modal form. A modal form must be hidden before the controls on other forms can be used. **When a *modeless form* is displayed, both its controls and the controls on other forms can react.** When you work through Examples 6.4 and 6.5, you will observe the differences.

Example 6.4   USING MODELESS FORMS

This example has three forms. The startup form contains a Label control named lblStep and a Button named btnShowForms. The other two forms each contain a Button named btnDone. Given the code in Figure 6.33, can you predict what will happen when the user clicks on btnShowForms? (Recall that the Show method is used to display a form on the screen and the Hide method is used to remove a form from the screen.)

After clicking on btnShowForms, the user will see both frmTestA and frmTestB (as well as the original form), and lblStep on the startup form will display "C". The user can click between any of the three forms to make them active.

This behavior may seem a bit surprising. It occurs because the computer executes the statements in btnShowForms_Click one after another without pausing. That is, when a form is shown as a modeless form, the flow of control in the procedure showing the form continues as the new form is shown. The most recently "shown" form is on top.

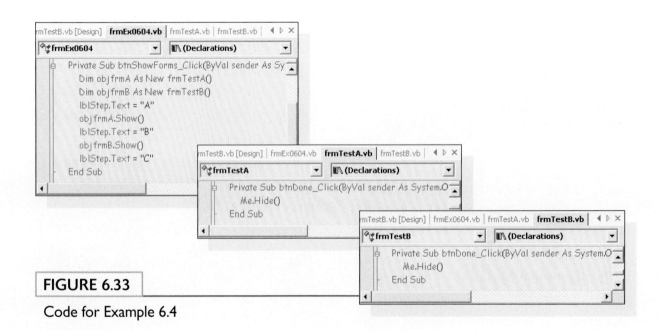

FIGURE 6.33

Code for Example 6.4

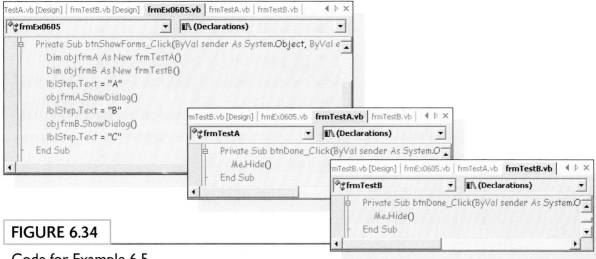

FIGURE 6.34

Code for Example 6.5

Example 6.5 USING MODAL FORMS

Example 6.5 also has three forms. The only difference between it and Example 6.4 is in btnShowForms_Click where the Show() method is replaced with the Show-Dialog() method. Figure 6.34 shows this code. Now after clicking on btnShow-Forms, the user will see frmTestA, and lblStep on the startup form will display "A".

To execute the statement

objfrmA.ShowDialog()

the computer shows objfrmA, then suspends further execution of the event procedure btnShowForms_Click until objfrmA is hidden (using the Hide method). Clicking btnDone on objfrmA executes the Hide method for the form, and execution of btnShowForms_Click resumes.

While objfrmA is shown, the computer can execute procedures on objfrmA, but no user input is allowed on any form other than objfrmA until after objfrmA is hidden (at which time control returns to btnShowForms_Click).

The forms objfrmA and objfrmB are said to be modeless in Example 6.4 and modal in Example 6.5. Note that objfrmA and objfrmB are identical in the two examples; what differs is the type of Show method in the startup form.

Modal Forms

A message box is the simplest example of a modal form. It displays a message and an OK button, and control does not return to the procedure containing the Msg-Box statement until the user clicks the OK button (that hides the message box).

The File dialog window is also modal. When the user selects Open from the File menu of any Windows application, the application displays the File Open window. The user is expected to select a file and then click either the Open or the Cancel button. If the user tries to move to a different form without first clicking either Open or Cancel, the application just beeps. This is an important feature, because the user could not be certain whether the file opened if he or she could switch to a different form before completing the file operation.

Presenting a Sequence of Forms

Suppose you want the program to present a sequence of forms to the user. This is common, and it often happens that the appropriate sequence depends on one or more choices the user makes. To do this using modeless forms, the first form has to have the code to show the second form, the second form has to have the code to show the third form, which in turn has to have the code to show the fourth form, and so on. Using modal forms, all the code that controls the sequence of presentation of forms can be conveniently located in a single procedure.

6.8 The MainMenu Control

It is relatively easy to add a main menu to any Visual Basic .NET application. You need to add a MainMenu component and then program Click events for the various menu items. Figure 6.35 shows the MainMenu tool and a MainMenu component at design time.

If you right-click on the MainMenu control in the component tray and select Edit Menu from the pop-up menu, the form will show a box in the upper-left where you will be able to enter both main menu items and subitems. Figure 6.36 shows this before any items have been entered.

We will construct a very simple menu here. Figure 6.37 shows the three menu items and their submenus at design time. Notice in the Special menu how a text area is open to the right of the Dinner sub item. This is how you get submenus into the overall menu design.

When you click on a menu item at design time, you can see its properties. We have named the five menu items that we will program as follows: mnuFileExit, mnuSpecialFoodBreakfast, mnuSpecialFoodLunch, mnuSpecialFoodDinner, and mnuHelpAbout. With this naming convention it should be fairly obvious what menu item we are talking about. Also use the & character in the Text property of each menu item to define the access key. For example, the Text in the Exit menu is entered as E&xit so that the "x" is underlined and can be accessed by pressing the ALT key.

FIGURE 6.35

MainMenu Tool and Control

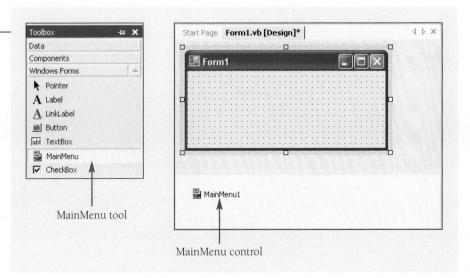

MainMenu tool

MainMenu control

FIGURE 6.36

Area to Create New
Menu Items

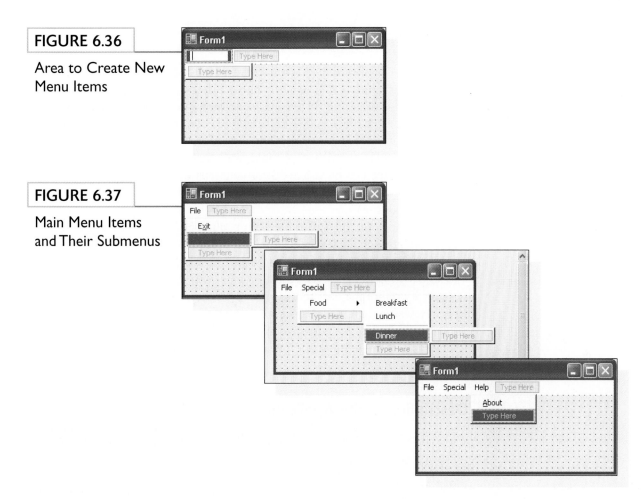

FIGURE 6.37

Main Menu Items
and Their Submenus

FIGURE 6.38

Click Events for the
Menu Items

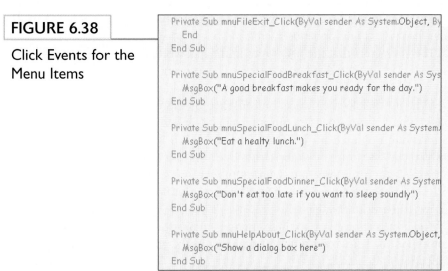

```
Private Sub mnuFileExit_Click(ByVal sender As System.Object, By
    End
End Sub

Private Sub mnuSpecialFoodBreakfast_Click(ByVal sender As Sys
    MsgBox("A good breakfast makes you ready for the day.")
End Sub

Private Sub mnuSpecialFoodLunch_Click(ByVal sender As System.
    MsgBox("Eat a healty lunch.")
End Sub

Private Sub mnuSpecialFoodDinner_Click(ByVal sender As System
    MsgBox("Don't eat too late if you want to sleep soundly")
End Sub

Private Sub mnuHelpAbout_Click(ByVal sender As System.Object,
    MsgBox("Show a dialog box here")
End Sub
```

Observe that there is a separator bar in the Special menu. This can be done by
right-clicking on a "Type Here" box and selecting Insert Separator from the pop-
up menu.

You can program only menu items that have no submenus. In our case, for
example, this means that we cannot program the Special menu item but we can
program the Breakfast item. The primary event you can program for a menu
item is a Click event. Figure 6.38 shows the code for our five Click events.

6.9 Project 7: User Authorization

Many business applications allow access to authorized users only. To do this, the application requires the user to identify himself or herself and also provide proof of identification. An obvious example is the program executed by a bank's automatic teller machine. Another example is a computerized registration application that enables students to enroll in classes for the upcoming term. Such an application would be worthless if I could easily fool it into thinking that I am you, because I could then enroll you in classes you don't want to take or drop you from classes you do want to take (in order to make room for me, if the class is full when I want to enroll in it).

A simple and common way to prevent unauthorized users from accessing a system is to assign each legitimate user a username and a password. The computer maintains a database that stores the username/password combination for each user.

To access the system, the user must provide both username and password. The username identifies the user to the system and is usually treated as public information. However, each user's password is secret; thus, the password serves as proof that the user is in fact the person identified by the corresponding username.

Such systems are familiar and present the user with a login window similar to that in Figure 6.39.

Description of the Application

We want to create reusable code to check user authorization. We can then include this code in any application we wish to restrict to selected users. When an application with this code begins executing, it should behave as follows.

First, the Login form should be displayed. The Login form's Text should read "Log in to the " followed by the name of the application that is using the user authorization code. In Figure 6.39, the application name is Student Registration System. The user then types in his or her username and password and clicks either OK or Cancel.

The characters that the user types in the Password TextBox are not displayed. Instead, the TextBox displays asterisks. This prevents other people from seeing a password by simply looking over the user's shoulder.

If the user clicks the Cancel button, then program execution ends. If the user clicks the OK button, the computer checks whether the username/password combination entered in the TextBoxes is valid. If it is valid, then the program displays the first form of the application (i.e., the user is allowed access to the application). If the username/password combination is not valid, the program displays a brief error message, then clears the TextBoxes on the login form and allows the user to try again.

The user is allowed up to three attempts to provide a valid username/password combination. If the combination entered on the third try is invalid, program execution ends.

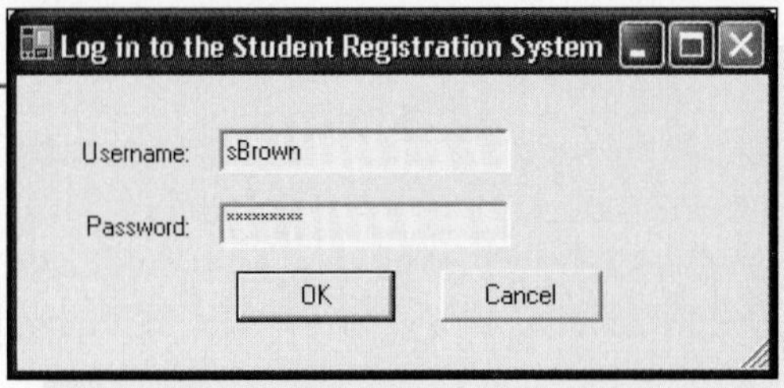

FIGURE 6.39

Sample Login Form

Finally, if the user succeeds in providing a valid username/password combination, then the application will want to know the username. In the case of a student registration system, for example, the application needs the username so it can record who is registering for the classes.

Design of the Application

We want the user authorization code to be easy to integrate into any application that needs it, and we want to structure it so that it can be "plugged into" any application without modification. Which form should be the startup form? Since the Login form is the first thing the user sees, we might consider making it the startup form for the application that uses it. However, if we do this, we'll have to write a statement somewhere in the Login form (or associated code) that loads the first form of the application when the user logs in successfully. Since this "first form" will have a different name for each application, this approach would require modifying our user authorization code for each application.

An alternative approach is to create a Sub Main in the application that needs to use our user authorization code, and have Sub Main invoke this code. This way our user authorization code will not require any modification to work with any application.

Our reusable code will be easiest to use if Sub Main needs to invoke only a single procedure or function in order to use it. Assuming this is possible, which should it be, a procedure or a function?

The net effect of our user authorization code will be either to end execution (if the user fails to provide a valid username/password combination) or to return control to the application, along with the valid username. If the user fails, execution can be ended by either a procedure or a function. If the user succeeds, there is only one value (the username) to be returned to the application, so a function appears to be appropriate. What is a good name for the user authorization function? How about AuthorizeUser()?

The proposed structure of the project as we have described it so far is illustrated in Figure 6.40. Because we want the user authorization code to work with any application, we must design it to operate independently of the details of the application. The vertical bar signifies this independence.

We can develop our ideas further by building on this figure. Sub Main must be in a code module, and its scope is Public. Since Sub Main invokes function AuthorizeUser(), the scope of AuthorizeUser() must be Public.

What is the type of the value returned by AuthorizeUser()? The value to be returned is a username, which commonly contains letters, digits, and other symbols, so let us use type String. Does function AuthorizeUser() have any parameters? AuthorizeUser() should receive the name of the application that invokes it, so it can set the Login form's caption. The user will enter the username and password into the TextBoxes on the Login form, so these should not be passed as parameters. Figure 6.41 is a refinement of Figure 6.40 that incorporates these ideas. The rectangles represent code modules and forms.

FIGURE 6.40

Application Code and User Authorization Code

Application Code		Reusable Code
Sub Main()		Function AuthorizeUser()
Application forms		Login form

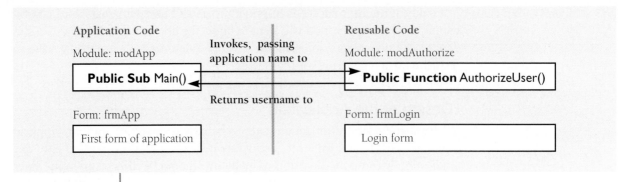

FIGURE 6.41

Refined Application Code and User Authorization Code

We need to examine the sequence of tasks to be performed by the user authorization code. Here is a list of the major tasks.

- Display a Login form similar in appearance to Figure 6.39. The user can click the Cancel button or enter username and password in the TextBoxes, then click OK.

- If the user clicks the Cancel button, then execution should end.

- If the user clicks the OK button, the username/password combination entered by the user should be checked to see whether it is valid. If it is valid, return the username. If it is not, display a message saying it is invalid, and display the login form again with cleared TextBoxes. (Remember to give the user at most three chances.)

Figure 6.42 shows another refinement of our figure, depicting these tasks and indicating the sequence in which they must be performed. Note that there are two tasks labeled 4, since the user may click either OK or Cancel, and there are two tasks labeled 5, since the username/password combination may or may not be valid. Let us use the information in this figure to write pseudocode for function AuthorizeUser().

```
Public Function AuthorizeUser (ByVal ApplicationName As String) As String
    set Login form's Text property to show application name
    show Login form ' step 2
    ' if this comment is reached user must have clicked OK at step 3
    If username/password is valid Then ' step 4
        Return username ' step 5
        Exit Function
    End If
    ' if this comment is reached username/password must have been invalid
    display message indicating invalid username/password
    show Login form, with clear TextBoxes ' step 5, user gets to try again
    If username/password is valid Then
        Return username
        Exit Function
    End If
    display message indicating invalid username/password
    show Login form, with clear TextBoxes
```

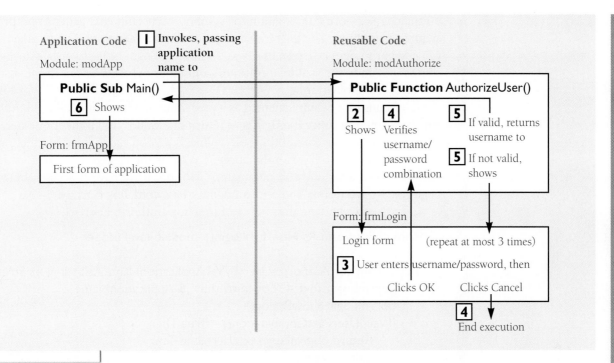

FIGURE 6.42

Sequence of Tasks in User Authorization

> *If username/password is valid Then*
> *Return username*
> *Exit Function*
> *End If*
> *display message indicating invalid username/password*
> *End ' user failed in all three attempts*
> *End Function*

Let's refine this pseudocode. Try to answer the following questions before reading further:

- Should the Login form be modeless or modal?

- In function AuthorizeUser(), how can we obtain the username/password entered by the user on the Login form?

- Given the username/password combination, how can we determine whether it is valid?

A good name for the Login form is frmLogin. It should be a modal form, because when the form is shown we need the values entered by the user before the next statement in function AuthorizeUser() can be executed. (Do you see now what the Click event procedure for frmLogin's OK button should do?)

The username/password entered by the user can be accessed (globally) by qualifying the names of the username and password TextBox controls by the name of the form object they reside on: objfrmLogin.txtUsername.Text and objfrmLogin.txtPassword.Text.

The description of the application says that the computer maintains a table of valid username/password combinations. In a real application, such a table would be maintained in a database. For the sake of this project, let us keep the valid username/ password combinations as symbolic constants in a general sub procedure or function. The task for this procedure or function will be to take the values objfrmLogin.txtUsername.Text and objfrmLogin.txtPassword.Text, then compare them to the symbolic constants and report whether or not they constitute a valid combination.

Should this task be implemented as a procedure or a function? It should probably be a function, since it only has to return one value: True if the user entered a valid combination, False otherwise. What is a good name for this function? How about ValidUserPassCombination()? What is the type of its return value? Boolean. Does it require any parameters? No, not if we have it access objfrmLogin.txtUsername.Text and objfrmLogin.txtPassword.Text directly.

Now we can complete the coding of function AuthorizeUser().

```
Dim objfrmLogin As New frmLogin() 'module-level scope

Public Function AuthorizeUser(ByVal ApplicationName As String) As String
    objfrmLogin.Text = "Log in to the " & ApplicationName
    objfrmLogin.ShowDialog()
    If ValidUserPassCombination() = True Then
        Return objfrmLogin.txtUsername.Text
        Exit Function
    End If
    MsgBox("Invalid username/password combination", vbExclamation)
    objfrmLogin.txtUsername.Text = ""
    objfrmLogin.txtPassword.Text = ""
    objfrmLogin.ShowDialog()
    If ValidUserPassCombination() = True Then
        Return objfrmLogin.txtUsername.Text
        Exit Function
    End If
    MsgBox("Invalid username/password combination", vbExclamation)
    objfrmLogin.txtUsername.Text = ""
    objfrmLogin.txtPassword.Text = ""
    objfrmLogin.ShowDialog()
    If ValidUserPassCombination() = True Then
        Return objfrmLogin.txtUsername.Text
        Exit Function
    End If
    MsgBox("Invalid username/password combination", vbExclamation)
    End
End Function
```

We leave the coding of function ValidUserPassCombination() to you as an exercise. For this project, assume that there are two authorized users, with usernames and passwords given in the symbolic constant definitions below.

```
Const USERNAME1 = "JSmith"
Const PASSWORD1 = "seCret"
Const USERNAME2 = "EAPoe"
Const PASSWORD2 = "Sc@red"
```

Note that if "JSmith" and "Sc@red" are the username and password, function ValidUserPassCombination() should return False. The only valid password corresponding to username "JSmith" is "seCret".

Remember that the function ValidUserPassCombination() requires no parameters, so its parameter list is empty. Also, since the function returns True or False, the type of its return value should be Boolean.

Construction of the Application

Create frmLogin, with an appearance similar to that shown in Figure 6.39, and write the Click event procedures for the two Buttons. Make the Password TextBox display asterisks instead of the characters that the user types by setting its PasswordChar property to an asterisk (*).

Make the OK button frmLogin's default accept button by setting frmLogin's AcceptButton property to btnOK. This allows the user to press (ENTER) as an alternative to clicking on the OK button. Note that a form can have only one default accept button.

Make the Cancel button frmLogin's default cancel button by setting frmLogin's CancelButton property to btnCancel. This allows the user to press the (ESC) key as an alternative to using the mouse to click on the Cancel button. Note that a form can have only one default cancel button.

Next, create functions AuthorizeUser() and ValidUserPassCombination() in a code module. Save this code module.

Create a mock-up of a student registration application. This should consist of a form and a code module. A good name for this form is frmRegistration, and it should appear as shown in Figure 6.43. It has a Label control to display the username if the user logs in successfully and a main menu that supports Exit under File. Save this form.

The code module should contain procedure Main. When program execution begins, Sub Main should invoke AuthorizeUser(), passing to it the string "Student Registration System". If the user logs on successfully, execution returns to Main, which should then store the username returned by AuthorizeUser() in objfrmRegistration.lblUser.Text and then show objfrmRegistration.

Save this code module. Then make Sub Main the startup object and run the application. If all goes well, the first thing you should see is the Login form. Click Cancel and verify that execution ends. Run the program again and enter "JSmith" and "seCret" in the Login form, then click OK. The application should respond by displaying the form in Figure 6.43, with lblUser showing "JSmith".

Run the program again, entering invalid username/password combinations and clicking OK, and verify that the application ends execution after three attempts.

Exercise 6.20

If the user enters an invalid username/password combination, which control will have the focus when the Login form is redisplayed? To be user-friendly, which control should have the focus? Modify the code to automatically give the focus to your chosen control the second and third times the Login form is displayed.

FIGURE 6.43

Form for Student Registration System Mockup

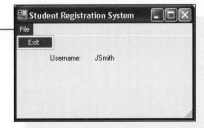

Chapter Summary

1. General sub procedures and developer-defined functions provide a way to break a programming solution into small parts that facilitate sharing of code (code reuse) and also facilitate the problem-solving process itself.

2. A general sub procedure performs a specific processing task. If the task is applicable in more than one program, then the same general sub procedure can be used in each program that needs it. In this way, developers in building projects can use a library of procedures performing common tasks.

3. Unlike event procedures, general sub procedures are not linked to any control on a form. They can be called (or invoked) from other general sub procedures or from event procedures by using the name of the procedure to be invoked as a statement. When they are called, the flow of control passes from the calling procedure to the sub procedure. When the end of the called procedure is reached, the flow of control returns to the calling procedure at the statement immediately following the call.

4. A developer-defined function returns a single value when it executes. As with built-in functions, this value may be any valid type. Also, as with built-in functions, developer-defined functions can be invoked only in expressions. This is consistent with the fact that they take on a value when they execute.

5. Both procedures and functions can use parameters to facilitate sharing of data between the calling and the called procedure or function. An argument is a variable in the calling procedure that is made available to the called procedure or function. Inside the called procedure or function this variable is referred to as a parameter. Corresponding arguments and parameters must be the same type. For example, if the first parameter in a sub procedure is type Integer, then the variable used as the first argument in the call also must be type Integer.

6. An argument can be passed to a procedure or function either by reference or by value. Passing by reference means that the parameter in the called procedure or function refers to the same variable as the argument—the parameter and the argument are the same variable. In contrast, passing by value causes the called procedure or function to make a local copy of the argument passed to it. Since the parameter is a copy of the argument—not the same variable—changing the value of the parameter does not affect the value of the argument. Passing by value is specified by placing the ByVal keyword before the parameter in the function or sub heading and passing by reference is specified by placing the ByRef keyword before the parameter.

7. The KeyPress event procedure has a parameter (**e**) in which Visual Basic .NET passes the ANSI character of the key that the user pressed. The developer can write code to test the value of this parameter and, depending on its value, perform appropriate actions.

The SendKeys Send() method can be used to change the character the user enters into a TextBox. If the KeyPress event handles the event by setting **e.Handled** to True, then the character the user entered does not get processed by the system and does not get placed into the TextBox. Otherwise, the character the user entered is handled by the system.

8. The Enter event occurs when the user gives the focus to a control by clicking on it, tabbing to it, or using an access key for the control. One use of the Enter event is to display an informative message when the user clicks on a control. The Leave event is just the opposite—it occurs when the focus leaves a control.

9. Form modality (modal or modeless) refers to the way forms behave when two or more are displayed at one time. When a modal form is shown, controls on other forms do not react to user actions; the user must respond to the modal form. A modal form must be hidden before the controls on other forms can be used. When a modeless form is displayed, both its controls and the controls on other forms can react.

Form modality is specified by the type of Show method used. If the Show method is used, the form will be modeless. If the ShowDialog method is used, then the form will be modal.

10. Applications can incorporate a main menu bar by using the MainMenu control. This control allows main menu items, submenus, and so forth. Menu items that have no submenu can be programmed with a Click event to respond to the user action.

Key Terms

argument	general sub procedure	parameter list
argument not specified error	invalid cast exception	parameter passing
	KeyPress event	Private procedure
ByRef keyword	Leave event	procedure call
ByVal keyword	library	Public procedure
developer-defined function	modal form	reusable code
	modeless form	SendKeys class
Enter event	parameter	Sub Main

End-of-Chapter Problems

1. Explain why using parameters to communicate data between a procedure or function and the associated calling procedure is superior to using global or module-level variables.

2. Write a function that computes and returns the present value of a given future amount of money. The function should be passed the future value (Decimal), the number of years (Integer), the number of times the interest is compounded each year (Integer), and the annual interest rate (Single).

The formula for present value (PV) is

$$PV = \frac{FV}{\left(1 + \dfrac{r}{m}\right)^{(n \times m)}}$$

where FV is the future value.

  n is the number of years.

  m is the number of times interest is compounded per year.

  r is the annual interest rate.

Be sure to specify that the function cannot modify the arguments passed to it.

3. Explain the difference between a parameter that is passed by value and one that is passed by reference.

4. Does it make sense to "pass by reference" a constant as an argument to a procedure?

5. Is it possible to define a function that has no parameters? Would you even want to do so? Explain.

6. Write a KeyPress event procedure for a TextBox named txtName that beeps and rejects all keystrokes that are not capital letters (A–Z) or dashes.

7. Explain the difference between modal and modeless forms. Give an example of when it would make sense to use each type.

8. You have a TextBox named txtPartNumber. You want to make sure that when the user finishes typing in the box (as indicated by clicking on another control), the TextBox has at least three characters in it. Write the appropriate event procedure to accomplish this.

9. What is a code module? How is the "code library" concept related to the concept of a code module?

10. What is the difference between a procedure and a function? Explain when it is appropriate to use each one.

Programming Problems

1. Modify Programming Problem 5 in Chapter 4 by including a code module that includes a function that computes the future value of a given present amount. The formula for future value (FV) is

$$FV = PV \times [1 + (i / m)]^{m \times y}$$

where PV is the present amount.
i is the annual interest rate.
m is the number of compounding periods per year.
y is the number of years.

Create a form that allows the user to input the four parameter values. After typing in the values, the user should click a Button to cause the future value to be computed and displayed on the form. The calculation should be performed using your function. Use Labels and TextBoxes as appropriate.

2. Create a Visual Basic .NET project that allows the user to provide the price of an item and the quantity sold. At the direction of the user, the project should then compute and display the gross sales amount (price times quantity), the discount, and the net sales amount. The discount should be computed using the table shown here.

Quantity	Discount
0–10	0%
11–25	5
26–100	8
101 +	10

Use a developer-defined function to determine the percentage discount figure.

3. You have a simple form with a TextBox for input as shown here.

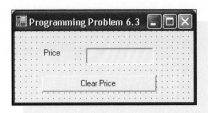

Write code that checks the user input in the Price TextBox and enforces all of the following rules:

a. Any digit is legal.

b. A maximum of one decimal point is legal.

c. A maximum of one dollar sign is legal as long as it is the first character.

d. Commas are legal (don't worry about where they are located).

If any illegal character is detected, have the system beep and reject it.

When the user clicks the Clear Price button, the Price TextBox should be cleared so that another test can be performed. Be sure that the mechanism you use to detect errors is also reset so that, for example, the new input can begin with another dollar sign.

4. Create a form as shown here.

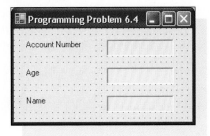

When the user enters data into the Account Number and Age TextBoxes, the system should automatically test for valid input, as prescribed by the table provided here.

Quantity	Valid Range
Account Number	1000 to 99999, inclusive
Age	0 to 99, inclusive

The test should be made as soon as the user clicks on the next TextBox. If an invalid value is detected, the system should display a message indicating the nature of the error, clear the TextBox, and then place the focus back on that TextBox (the user will not be able to leave a TextBox unless a valid value is entered). (*Hint:* See the Leave method.)

5. Create a Visual Basic .NET project that reorders three string values input by the user into sequence from the largest to the smallest. The form shown below uses TextBoxes for user input.

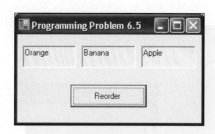 

Use a general sub procedure to perform the reordering. Remember that you can compare two string variables, and Visual Basic .NET will determine which one is larger based on the ANSI collating sequence. Be aware, though, that this reordering scheme is not a good, general-purpose solution for sorting. You will see a general solution later.

6. A university charges tuition based on the table shown here.

	Resident	Nonresident
Undergraduate	$35/credit	$65/credit
Graduate	$70/credit	$135/credit

Create a Visual Basic .NET project that allows the user to indicate resident or nonresident status, class standing, and number of credits. Then provide a way for the user to request that tuition be computed and displayed.

Provide appropriate controls for user input (TextBoxes, RadioButtons, CheckBoxes, etc.). Use a developer-defined function that determines the cost per credit given the student's residency status and class standing.

SEVEN

REPEATING PROCESSING TASKS

Loop Structures

Most applications have processing steps that must be performed repeatedly. An example is an order entry application that accepts and processes a list of items a customer wants to order. The program must process many items, and the steps required to process one item are identical to the steps required to process any other item. Indeed, the real power of the computer is not unleashed until it is put to work on repetitive tasks.

In a program, **the structure or flow of control used to execute a group of statements repeatedly is called a *loop*.** The loop structure controls how many times the statements are executed. In the order entry example, the developer determines the statements necessary to process one item and places those statements inside a loop. The developer composes the loop so that the statements are executed once for each item on the order form.

As we know, statements in a procedure always execute one at a time. To this point in our study of Visual Basic .NET, all statements have been executed in order, from top to bottom, with technically three exceptions: the If, the Select…Case, and the Try/Catch statements can cause certain statements to be skipped, depending on the value of a specified condition. Of course, we can view If and Select…Case as meta statements, and from this perspective they are not exceptions to the "top-to-bottom" rule at all. Like the If and Select…Case statements, a loop

- Has a top and a bottom that are clearly indicated by reserved words.

- Has a statement block in its interior.

- Technically, introduces an exception to the rule that statements are executed from top to bottom.

- When viewed as a meta statement, is not seen as an exception to the "top-to-bottom" rule.

In Visual Basic .NET there are two kinds of loops. The ***Do…Loop* structure executes the statement block in its interior repeatedly until a specified condition occurs. The *For…Next* structure executes the statement block in its interior a specified number of times.** It is important to use the appropriate loop for each given situation.

As we shall see, many programs must process lists of data items. Visual Basic .NET provides several such controls. We will look at the ListBox, ComboBox, and ListView controls that are used for maintaining and displaying lists of text data. Loops and these controls are natural partners.

Objectives

After studying this chapter, you should be able to

- Use the Do…Loop and For…Next structures and know when each structure is appropriate.

- Understand how nested loops operate.

- Construct user interfaces with the ListBox control, the ComboBox control, and the ListView control.

7.1 The Do...Loop Structure

Developers use the Do...Loop structure when they do not know how many times the statements inside the loop will be executed. For example, suppose you are writing a program that examines a list of credit card transactions in order to make sure there are no duplicate transactions. That is, your program looks for pairs of identical transactions (having the same date, time, and total charge amount for a customer). When the loop begins executing, you do not know when—or even if—a duplicate transaction will be found.

The Do...Loop structure has a number of variations in how it determines when to stop repeating the statements inside the loop. We will look at each of these variations in turn, then examine initialization and termination conditions.

Syntax and Action of the Do...Loop

Loops, like decision-making statements, consist of multiple statements. The Do...Loop consists of a minimum of three statements. The simplest has the following syntax:

> **Do**
>> *statementblock*
> **Loop**

The reserved word Do marks the top of the loop, and the reserved word Loop marks its bottom. Recall that a statement block is any sequence of zero or more statements.

To make loops more readable and understandable, developers indent the statement block (in the interior of the loop). Visual Basic .NET will do this automatically for you.

Run Time: The Effect of the Do...Loop Structure

The reserved word Do does not cause the computer to take any action; it simply marks the top of the loop. The statements in the loop's interior are executed one at a time, in order, from top to bottom. The reserved word Loop causes execution to go back up to the top of the loop—that is, back to the Do statement. Figure 7.1 illustrates this action. The net effect is that the statements inside the loop are executed repeatedly.

FIGURE 7.1

Action of the
Do...Loop

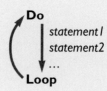

FIGURE 7.2

An Infinite Loop

```
Private Sub btnDoLoopTest_Click(ByVal sender As System
    Dim N As Short
    MsgBox("Pre-Do")
    Do
        MsgBox(N)
        N = N + 1
    Loop
    MsgBox("Post-Loop")
End Sub
```

Example **7.1**

USING A DO...LOOP

The event procedure in Figure 7.2 illustrates the use of Do...Loop. This event procedure executes, but it has the disadvantage of executing forever. **A loop that executes forever is called an *infinite loop*.** Nearly all developers have inadvertently created an infinite loop or two. How do you make it stop? You should click on the development environment to make it the active application (instead of your application that is in the infinite loop), then click on the Stop button.

Do While...Loop

Infinite loops are rarely desirable. Therefore, Visual Basic .NET provides variations of the Do...Loop that allow you to specify a condition—called the ***termination condition***—that terminates execution of the loop. The first variation is the *Do While...Loop,* which places the termination condition at the top of the loop. It has the following syntax:

> **Do While** *condition*
>   *statementblock*
> **Loop**

The reserved words Do While mark the top of the loop, and the reserved word Loop marks its bottom. The condition is a logical expression that the developer provides.

Run Time: The Effect of the Do While...Loop Structure

Each time the computer encounters Do While, it evaluates the condition.

- If the condition is False, **execution skips to the statement following the reserved word Loop, which we call *exiting the loop,*** or, equivalently, terminating it.

- If the condition is True, the computer executes the statements in the loop's interior one at a time and in order, from top to bottom. The reserved word Loop then causes execution to go back up to the top of the loop—that is, back to the Do While statement.

Each time the Loop statement sends execution back up to Do While, the computer executes the Do While statement again, by evaluating the condition, and then either exiting the loop or executing the statement block. The loop continues to execute "while the condition is true." Figure 7.3 depicts the action of the Do While...Loop.

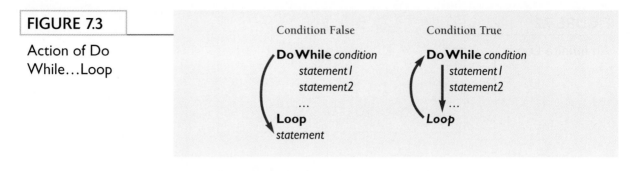

FIGURE 7.3

Action of Do While...Loop

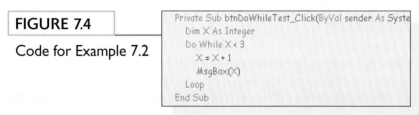

FIGURE 7.4

Code for Example 7.2

```
Private Sub btnDoWhileTest_Click(ByVal sender As Syste
    Dim X As Integer
    Do While X < 3
        X = X + 1
        MsgBox(X)
    Loop
End Sub
```

Example **7.2**   **USING A DO WHILE...LOOP**

The code in Figure 7.4 illustrates the Do While...Loop. Let us describe the execution of this code to make sure you understand its action. When the user clicks the Button named btnDoWhileTest, the statements inside event procedure btnDoWhileTest_Click begin to execute. The action of the Dim statement creates a local variable named **X** of type Integer and initializes it to 0. Then the Do While statement is executed. Its condition is **X < 3**. Since **X** holds the value 0, the condition (**0 < 3**) is True, so we proceed to execute the statements inside the loop.

The action of the assignment statement **X = X + 1** changes the value stored in **X** to 1. The message box then displays the value 1.

Next, we execute the Loop statement. **When the Loop statement sends execution back up to the Do While statement, we say that we have completed one** *iteration* **of the loop.** We execute the Do While statement by evaluating its condition. Since **X** holds the value 1, the condition (**X < 3**) is True, so we execute the statements inside the loop.

The assignment statement **X = X + 1** changes the value stored in **X** to 2. Then the message box displays the value 2. We then execute the Loop statement that sends execution back up to the Do While statement. We execute the Do While statement by evaluating its condition. Since **X** holds the value 2, the condition (**X < 3**) is True, so we execute the statements inside the loop. The assignment statement **X = X + 1** changes the value stored in **X** to 3 and the message box displays the value 3.

Next, we execute the Loop statement that sends execution back up to the Do While statement. We execute the Do While statement by evaluating its condition. Since **X** holds the value 3, the condition (**X < 3**) is False, so we exit the loop. The next statement to be executed is the statement following Loop, which is the End Sub. The net effect of the event procedure was to display three message boxes, containing the values 1, 2, and 3.

Coding the Loop Body

When coding **the statements in the interior of the loop**—sometimes called the *loop body*—keep the following factors in mind.

First, one or more statements in the loop body must eventually cause the condition to become False. Otherwise, the loop will execute forever. In Example 7.2, the statement X = X + 1, executed repeatedly, eventually caused the value of X to be 3, so that the loop's condition (X < 3) became False.

Second, the order of statements inside the loop affects the result of the loop. After a developer has decided on the loop's condition and the statements inside the loop, he or she must make sure that the statements in the interior of the loop are arranged in the correct order, and that the loop condition will cause the computer to exit the loop at the right time. To do this, the developer typically hand-checks the loop for a few iterations.

Third, it is possible for the loop to terminate immediately. That is, the condition can be False the first time the Do While statement is executed, so that the statements inside the loop are executed zero times. This behavior is sometimes appropriate.

Finally, a loop can be viewed as a meta statement. This is true because the computer begins executing the loop at its top (the Do While statement), and when it exits the loop, the next statement to be executed is the one right below the bottom of the loop (the Loop statement). As an example, the meta statement for the loop in Example 7.2 might be worded as "display the numbers 1, 2, and 3 in message boxes." The following examples strengthen some of these observations.

Example 7.3

ORDER OF STATEMENTS WITHIN A LOOP

The loop in Figure 7.5 differs from Example 7.2 only in that the order of the two statements inside the loop has been reversed. In this example, the message box statement executes before the variable X is incremented by 1. Therefore, during the first iteration of the loop, the value of X is still zero when the message box displays its value (recall that Example 7.2 incremented X before it was displayed).

Since this loop displays X before it is incremented, the values displayed by the message boxes will be 0, 1, and 2—not 1, 2, and 3 as was the case in Example 7.2.

Example 7.4

USING IMMEDIATE TERMINATION

The code in Figure 7.6 simulates a coin-tossing game. Each time a coin is tossed, it is equally likely to come up heads or tails. The event procedure keeps tossing the coin until it comes up tails, and then displays the number of heads that appeared before the first occurrence of tails.

```
Private Sub btnDoWhileTest_Click(ByVal sender As Syste
    Dim X As Integer
    Do While X < 3
        MsgBox(X)
        X = X + 1
    Loop
End Sub
```

FIGURE 7.5

Code for Example 7.3

```
Private Sub btnNumberOfHeads_Click(ByVal sender As S
    Dim Heads As Boolean
    Dim RunLength As Integer
    Heads = Rnd() <= 0.5
    Do While Heads
        RunLength = RunLength + 1
        Heads = Rnd() <= 0.5
    Loop
    MsgBox(RunLength & " heads in a row.")
End Sub
```

FIGURE 7.6

Code for Example 7.4

The assignment statement

Heads = Rnd() <= 0.5

stores True in the Boolean variable **Heads** if the random fraction returned by Rnd() is less than or equal to 0.5, and False otherwise. When this statement is executed the first time, **Heads** may be False; if so, when Do While is executed, its condition will be False, and the loop will be exited immediately.

The meta statement for this loop might be worded as "generate random numbers until you encounter one greater than 0.5, and count how many you generated."

Exercise 7.1

Modify Example 7.2 to display the numbers 1 through 10. Also modify Example 7.2 to display the even numbers from 2 to 20 (i.e., 2, 4, 6, 8, . . , 20).

Do...Loop While

The *Do...Loop While structure* works like the Do While...Loop structure except that the termination condition is at the bottom of the loop instead of at the top. This guarantees that the statements inside the loop are executed at least once, unlike the Do While...Loop, which may terminate immediately. The Do...Loop While has the following syntax:

> **Do**
> > *statementblock*
> **Loop While** *condition*

The reserved word Do marks the top of the loop, and the reserved words Loop While mark its bottom. The condition is a logical expression that the developer provides.

The reserved word Do does not cause the computer to take any action; it simply marks the top of the loop. The statements inside the loop are executed one at a time and in order, from top to bottom. Each time the computer encounters the Loop While statement, it evaluates the condition.

- If the condition is False, execution resumes at the statement following Loop While. That is, the computer exits the loop.

- If the condition is True, execution jumps back up to the top of the loop—that is, back to the Do statement.

As illustrated in Figure 7.7, each time the Loop While statement sends execution back up to Do, the computer executes the statements inside the loop again. It then encounters the Loop While statement again, which it executes by evaluating the

---

FIGURE 7.7

Action of Do...Loop While Structure

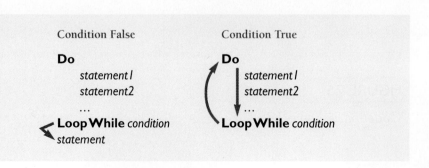

FIGURE 7.8

Code for Example 7.5

```
Private Sub btnGuessMe_Click(ByVal sender As System.Object, ByVal e As Syst
   Dim Target, Guess As Short
   Do
      Target = 1 + Int(6 * Rnd())
      Guess = InputBox("Enter a guess between 1 and 6, inclusive.")
      If Guess <> Target Then
         MsgBox("Incorrect - bummer!")
      End If
   Loop While Guess <> Target
   MsgBox("Correct - congratulations")
End Sub
```

condition and either exiting the loop or jumping back up to Do. The loop repeats "while the condition is true."

Example 7.5

USING DO…LOOP WHILE

The code in Figure 7.8 is a simple guessing game in which the computer generates a random integer between 1 and 6 and the user is asked to guess what the integer is. Do…Loop While is appropriate in this instance because in a guessing game the user should certainly be allowed to make at least one guess.

In contrast, the code in Example 7.4 simulates the number of times in a row a tossed coin comes up heads. We use the Do While…Loop there because if the first coin toss turns out to be tails, then we don't want the statements inside the loop to be executed (that would cause **RunLength** to be incremented to 1).

Exercise 7.2

Rewrite the event procedure in Example 7.5 using the Do While…Loop instead of the Do…Loop While. Your new event procedure should behave identically to that in Example 7.5. In particular, it should allow the user to make at least one guess. Which event procedure is easier to understand? Explain.

Exercise 7.3

Suppose we modify Example 7.5 by moving the statement

Target = 1 + Int(6 * Rnd())

from just after Do to just before Do. How will the game change? Explain.

Do Until…Loop and Do…Loop Until

The two final variations of the Do…Loop are **the *Do Until…Loop* structure, which has the termination condition at the top of the loop,** and the ***Do…Loop Until* structure, which has the termination condition at the bottom of the loop.**

The syntax and action of the Do Until…Loop are the same as the syntax and action of the Do While…Loop, with two exceptions:

1. There is an obvious difference in the keywords: Do Until instead of Do While.

2. The loop statements inside the Do Until…Loop are executed when the condition is False, and the loop is exited when the condition is True, which is just the opposite of the Do While…Loop.

The action of the Do Until…Loop is illustrated in Figure 7.9. This structure can be interpreted as "execute the statements inside the loop until the condition

FIGURE 7.9

Action of Do
Until...Loop
Structure

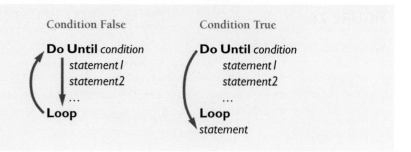

becomes True." In contrast, the Do While...Loop statement means "execute the statements inside the loop while the condition is True," or, equivalently, "execute the statements inside the loop until the condition becomes False."

Any loop you create using the Do While...Loop can also be written using the Do Until...Loop, and vice versa. It is necessary only to negate the condition. For example, if the original condition was **X = 3**, the negated condition will be **X <> 3**. Or if the original condition was **X > 3**, then the negated condition will be **X <= 3**. As an example of this, consider the event procedure in Example 7.2 that used the Do While...Loop. Figure 7.10 shows this event procedure written using the Do While...Loop and the Do Until...Loop. The two procedures behave identically.

Does it matter which you use? Since the two versions behave identically, the only issue is which one is easier to read. Quite often, as in the code in Figure 7.10, the difference is not significant.

Suppose, however, that you are writing pseudocode for a procedure to print employee paychecks. Which of the following do you prefer?

> *Do While there are more employees*
> > *get current pay data for an employee*
> > *print the employee's paycheck*
> *Loop*

or

> *Do Until there are no more employees*
> > *get current pay data for an employee*
> > *print the employee's paycheck*
> *Loop*

Both seem reasonable so far. But as you refine the pseudocode, you eventually will have to figure out how to express the condition as a logical expression. If you obtain the employee data from a database, you might use the database property EOF (end of file). Assume that an EOF property is set to True when the end of the database has been reached (no more employees to be processed) and to False when the end of the database has not been reached (still more employees to be processed).

FIGURE 7.10

Equivalent Do While
and Do Until Loops

```
Private Sub btnDoWhileTest_Click()      Private Sub btnDoUntilTest_Click()
    Dim X As Integer                        Dim X As Integer
    Do While X < 3                          Do Until X >= 3
        X = X + 1                               X = X + 1
        MsgBox (X)                              MsgBox (X)
    Loop                                    Loop
End Sub                                  End Sub
```

FIGURE 7.11

Action of Do...Loop Until Structure

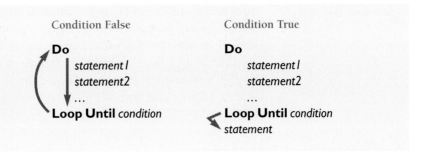

So the two versions of pseudocode become

> *Do While database.EOF = False*
> > *get current pay data for an employee*
> > *print the employee's paycheck*
> *Loop*

or

> *Do Until database.EOF = True*
> > *get current pay data for an employee*
> > *print the employee's paycheck*
> *Loop*

While the difference is not earth-shattering, in this case the Do Until...Loop is a little more straightforward because this loop's condition becomes True when database.EOF becomes True.

The same similarities and differences apply to the Do...Loop Until and the Do...Loop While structures. The action of the Do...Loop Until is illustrated in Figure 7.11.

Exercise 7.4

Complete the event procedure below by providing the statement block that performs the following tasks: First, ask the user to input a guess between 1 and 127. If the user's guess is less than the value stored in **Target**, display the message "Too low" and ask the user to input another guess between 1 and 127. If the user's guess is greater than the value stored in **Target**, display the message "Too high" and ask the user to input another guess between 1 and 127. Repeat this until the user's guess is equal to the value stored in **Target**. Store the number of guesses entered by the user in the variable named **Count**. These actions occur after the user clicks a single time on btnGuidedGuessMe.

Do not modify, move, or add any statements before or after the *statement-block*. Recall that a statement block consists of any sequence of zero or more statements. It may include decision-making statements and loops.

```
Private Sub btnGuidedGuessMe_Click()
    Dim Target As Integer
    Dim Guess As Integer
    Dim Count As Integer
    Target = 1 + Int(127 * Rnd())
    'statementblock
    MsgBox("It took you " & Count & " guesses.")
End Sub
```

Exercise 7.5

Write a complete Click event procedure for a Button named btnRunningSum that performs the following tasks: Ask the user to input numbers; compute the sum of the numbers as they are entered, until the sum becomes either less than −10 or greater than +10. Then display how many numbers the user entered and their final sum. Display only the final count and sum. Do not display the results of intermediate calculations. For example, if the user entered the numbers 3, 5, 1, and 7, your event procedure should display only the messages "You entered 4 numbers" and "The sum is 16".

Initialization and Termination

A common error is for the loop to perform one iteration more or one iteration less than desired. The error often stems from the initial value of a variable involved in the loop condition or from the loop condition itself. In Examples 7.2 and 7.3, the initial value of the variable **X** was 0 (as defined by the Dim statement). The following examples demonstrate the problem and show how to correct it.

Example 7.6   **INITIALIZATION AND TERMINATION**

The developer who wrote the event procedure in Figure 7.12 intended first to ask the user to input a number and then to display that many letters of the alphabet (starting at A). The code uses the Chr() function to convert an integer into a letter. The first letter of the alphabet, A, appears at position 65 in the ANSI table, and Visual Basic .NET can find this with the Asc("A") function call.

If the user enters the number 3 in response to the input box, the program should display the letters A, B, and C in separate message boxes. Unfortunately, it displays B, C, D, and E instead. This error is common when composing a loop. Actually there are two errors:

- The first value displayed is incorrect (B instead of A).

- The number of values displayed is incorrect (4 instead of 3).

What are the causes of these errors?
The statement

> **PositionInANSItable = Asc("A")**

just before the loop is said to *initialize* the variable **PositionInANSItable**, **meaning it defines the value that the variable initially holds when the loop begins executing.** Initialization statements are common before loops, because statements inside the loop often manipulate one or more variables and the correct operation of the loop often requires that a variable hold a particular value when the loop is first entered.

FIGURE 7.12

Code for Example 7.6

```
Private Sub btnPartOfAlphabet_Click(ByVal sender As System.Object, 
    Dim NumLetters As Short
    Dim PositionInANSItable As Short
    NumLetters = InputBox("How many letters would you like to see?")
    PositionInANSItable = Asc("A")
    Do Until PositionInANSItable > Asc("A") + NumLetters
        PositionInANSItable = PositionInANSItable + 1
        MsgBox(Chr(PositionInANSItable))
    Loop
End Sub
```

In this procedure we want to initialize the variable **PositionInANSItable** to 65. This way, the first letter displayed by the MsgBox statement will be A. However, since the statement

PositionInANSItable = PositionInANSItable + 1

occurs before the MsgBox statement, the letter B is the first letter displayed. This causes the loop to "start in the wrong place." One way to fix this problem is to change the initialization statement to

PositionInANSItable = Asc("A") - 1

After this change, the event procedure will display A, B, C, and D when the user enters 3 in response to the input box.

The remaining problem is that the loop displays one too many letters. It is quite common for a newly composed loop to iterate one too many or one too few times. In the code above, we can correct this problem by changing the loop condition to

PositionInANSItable >= Asc("A") - 1 + NumLetters

Example 7.7 ── CORRECTING EXAMPLE 7.6

The code in Figure 7.13 incorporates the suggested changes to the event procedure in Example 7.6 and operates correctly.

There is, however, a "cleaner" solution to the problems of Example 7.6, as Figure 7.14 illustrates. Here the initialization statement is the same as that of Example 7.6, and the loop condition is only slightly modified (> was changed to >=). The substantial change was to swap the order of the statements inside the loop.

FIGURE 7.13

Loop Now Executes Correct Number of Times with Correct Values

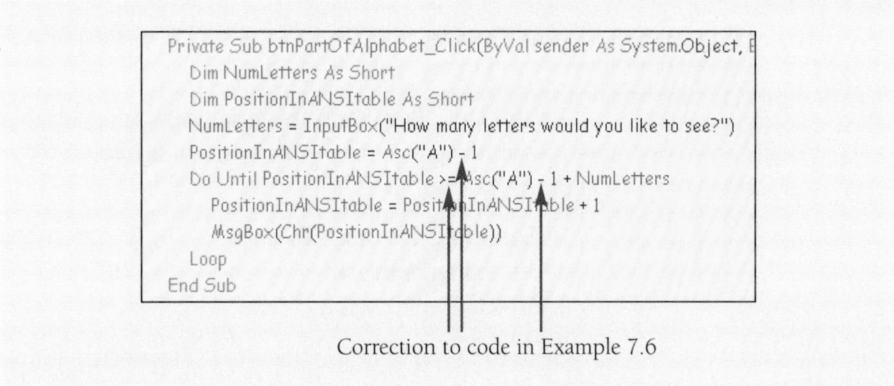

```
Private Sub btnPartOfAlphabet_Click(ByVal sender As System.Object, E
    Dim NumLetters As Short
    Dim PositionInANSItable As Short
    NumLetters = InputBox("How many letters would you like to see?")
    PositionInANSItable = Asc("A") - 1
    Do Until PositionInANSItable >= Asc("A") - 1 + NumLetters
        PositionInANSItable = PositionInANSItable + 1
        MsgBox(Chr(PositionInANSItable))
    Loop
End Sub
```

Correction to code in Example 7.6

FIGURE 7.14

Code for Example 7.7

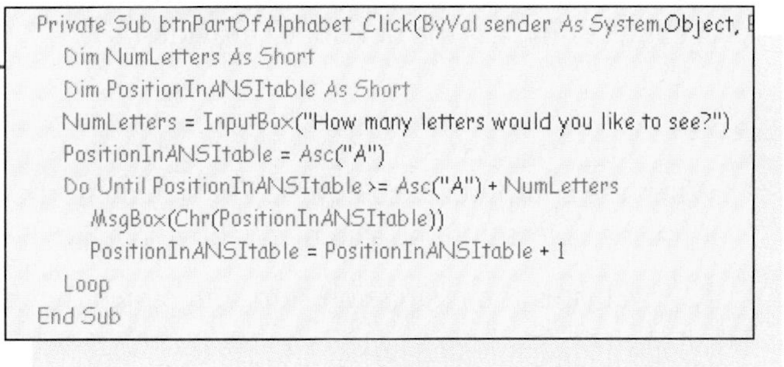

```
Private Sub btnPartOfAlphabet_Click(ByVal sender As System.Object, E
    Dim NumLetters As Short
    Dim PositionInANSItable As Short
    NumLetters = InputBox("How many letters would you like to see?")
    PositionInANSItable = Asc("A")
    Do Until PositionInANSItable >= Asc("A") + NumLetters
        MsgBox(Chr(PositionInANSItable))
        PositionInANSItable = PositionInANSItable + 1
    Loop
End Sub
```

From time to time you may create a loop that starts in the wrong place and has a termination condition that is off by one iteration. Some likely sources of the problem are

- An initialization statement that is off by one.

- A loop condition in which > may need to be changed to >=, or vice versa (or < may need to be changed to <=, or vice versa).

- The order of the statements inside the loop that may need to be reordered.

Don't try to change all three at once when fixing loop errors. Instead, hand-check a few iterations of the loop first and try to identify the source of the error. Then make one modification and test it. If this doesn't improve (or completely correct) the situation, undo the modification and try another.

Exercise 7.6

In Example 7.7, describe the output if the user enters −1 in response to the input box.

Exercise 7.7

Modify Example 7.2 to display the numbers 50 through 60, inclusive.

7.2 The For...Next Loop Structure

In contrast to Do...Loops, in which the number of repetitions of the loop body is unknown prior to processing, the For...Next loop is used when the developer can write an expression that specifies how many iterations the loop will perform. For example, suppose that we want a loop that computes the average grade for a class of 33 students. Each iteration of the loop processes a different student. Since there are 33 students in the class, we know that the loop will need to be executed 33 times.

Syntax and Action of For...Next

Like the Do...Loop and its variations, the For...Next loop consists of multiple statements that can be viewed as a single meta statement. The syntax of the For...Next loop is

> **For** *counter* = *start* **To** *end*
>   *statementblock*
> **Next**

The reserved word For marks the top of the loop, and the reserved word Next marks its bottom. **The *counter* is a numeric variable that the developer provides and that the loop uses to count iterations.** Both start and end are numeric expressions that the developer provides.

Run Time: The Effect of the For...Next Structure

When the computer executes the For statement the first time (that is, right after it finishes executing the statement above For), it

1. Evaluates the expression *start* and stores the result in the variable *counter.*

2. Evaluates the expression *end* to arrive at the ending value.

FIGURE 7.15

Action of the
For...Next
Structure

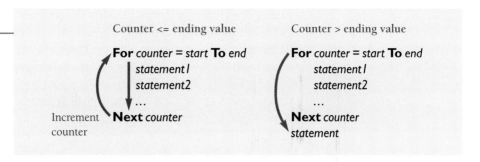

3. Compares the value stored in *counter* to the ending value, and
   a.   If the value stored in *counter* is greater than the ending value, then the computer exits the loop, and execution resumes at the statement following Next.
   b.   If the value stored in *counter* is less than or equal to the ending value, it executes the statements inside the loop one at a time, top to bottom.

When the computer executes the Next statement, it:

4. Increases the value stored in *counter* by 1.

5. Causes execution to go back up to the For statement.

After "jumping up" from Next to For, the computer executes the For statement by performing only step 3.

To fully understand the action of the For...Next loop, you must keep in mind that operations 1 and 2 are performed only once, when the computer enters the loop from above. These operations are the *initialization* operations of the For...Next loop.

The action of the For...Next loop, after the initialization operations have been completed, is depicted in Figure 7.15. This action may seem complicated, but if you work through the following examples, you will see that it is not difficult.

Example **7.8**

USING A FOR...NEXT LOOP

The code in Figure 7.16 illustrates the For...Next loop. Let us hand-check this example. The statements inside event procedure btnForNextTest_Click begin to execute after the user clicks on btnForNextTest. To mimic the action of the Dim statement, we create a local variable named **X** of type Integer and initialize it to 0. Then we execute the For statement. Since we've just entered the loop, we have to perform its initialization operations. Operation 1 stores the start value 1 in the counter variable **X**, and operation 2 determines the ending value to be 3.

To finish execution of the For statement, we compare the value stored in the counter **X** to the ending value. Since 1 is less than or equal to 3, we execute the loop body. The only statement inside the loop is the message box statement that displays the value 1.

Next, we execute the Next statement, which does two things: it increases the value stored in the counter **X** by 1 and it sends execution back up to the For

FIGURE 7.16

Code for Example 7.8

```
Private Sub btnForNextTest_Click(ByVal sender As System.Object, By
    Dim X As Short
    For X = 1 To 3
        MsgBox(X)
    Next
End Sub
```

statement. This time, we do not initialize the counter and end values when we execute the For statement; we simply perform operation 3, which compares the value stored in the counter **X** to the ending value. Since 2 is less than or equal to 3, we proceed to execute the statement inside the loop. The message box now displays the value 2.

We then execute the Next statement, which increases the value stored in **X** by 1, then sends execution back up to the For statement. To execute the For statement we compare the value stored in **X** to the ending value. Since 3 is less than or equal to 3, we execute the statement inside the loop. The message box displays the value 3.

We execute the Next statement, which increases the value stored in **X** by 1, then sends execution back up to the For statement. To execute the For statement we compare the value stored in **X** to the ending value. Since 4 is greater than 3 (is not less than or equal to 3), we exit the loop. The next statement to be executed is the statement following Next. Since this is the End Sub statement, we are finished executing the event procedure. We see that the net effect of the event procedure is to display the values 1, 2, and 3 in message boxes.

For…Next versus Do…Loop Variations

It is interesting to compare Example 7.8 with Example 7.2, which produced the same net effect but was written with a Do While…Loop structure instead of a For…Next structure. After working with a few examples using For…Next, you will discover that loops using For…Next are actually simpler than loops using Do…Loop.

When you see

For X = 1 To 3

at the top of a loop, you know immediately that

- The statements inside the loop will be executed three times.[1]

- The first time the statements inside the loop are executed, counter **X** will hold the value 1.

- The second time the statements inside the loop are executed, counter **X** will hold the value 2.

- The third time the statements inside the loop are executed, counter **X** will hold the value 3.

In contrast, when you see

Do While X < 3

at the top of a loop, you can only conclude that the statements inside the loop will be executed as long as **X** is less than 3. You'll have to look at statements above the loop to see what value **X** holds going into the loop (perhaps the loop statements will be executed 0 times), and you'll have to study the statements in the loop's interior to figure out how the value in **X** changes each time they are executed.

In some situations Do…Loop is appropriate and in others For…Next is appropriate. Choosing the correct one for each given situation will make your programs easier to understand and modify. Use For…Next when the number of iterations the loop will perform can be determined at the time the loop is entered, that is, when

---

1   Actually, it is possible for the loop to terminate early as a result of executing an Exit Sub statement or an Exit For statement (see Section 7.3) inside the loop.

counting the number of iterations is sufficient to determine when the loop should terminate. Use a variation of the Do...Loop only when the number of iterations the loop will perform depends on the results of executing the statements inside the loop that do not involve counting.

As a more practical example of the use of For...Next, consider the following function, which we designed in Project 7. The function gives the user up to three chances to successfully log into an application. Accordingly, you will find a statement block (colored) that occurs three times.

```
Public Function AuthorizeUser(ByVal ApplicationName As String) As String
    objfrmLogin.Text = "Log in to the " & ApplicationName
    objfrmLogin.ShowDialog()
    If ValidUserPassCombination() = True Then
        Return objfrmLogin.txtUsername.Text
        Exit Function
    End If
    MsgBox("Invalid username/password combination", vbExclamation)
    objfrmLogin.txtUsername.Text = ""
    objfrmLogin.txtPassword.Text = ""
    objfrmLogin.ShowDialog()
    If ValidUserPassCombination() = True Then
        Return objfrmLogin.txtUsername.Text
        Exit Function
    End If
    MsgBox("Invalid username/password combination", vbExclamation)
    objfrmLogin.txtUsername.Text = ""
    objfrmLogin.txtPassword.Text = ""
    objfrmLogin.ShowDialog()
    If ValidUserPassCombination() = True Then
        Return objfrmLogin.txtUsername.Text
        Exit Function
    End If
    MsgBox("Invalid username/password combination", vbExclamation)
    End
End Function
```

The function can be improved by using a loop, as follows:

```
Public Function AuthorizeUser(ByVal ApplicationName As String) As String
    Const MAXNUMBEROFATTEMPTS = 3
    Dim attempt As Integer
    objfrmLogin.Text = "Log in to the " & ApplicationName
    For attempt = 1 To MAXNUMBEROFATTEMPTS
        objfrmLogin.txtUsername.Text = ""
        objfrmLogin.txtPassword.Text = ""
        objfrmLogin.ShowDialog()
        If ValidUserPassCombination() = True Then
            Return objfrmLogin.txtUsername.Text
            Exit Function
        End If
        MsgBox("Invalid username/password combination", vbExclamation)
    Next
    End
End Function
```

The code is shorter and reduces the possibility of inconsistency. It is also easier to understand, because it clearly shows that the identical statement block is being performed three times; to be certain that this is true in the version without the loop you have to compare statements carefully. Also note how easy it is to change the maximum number of attempts if such a change is necessary.

If you look closely, you'll notice that in this modified version the TextBoxes on frmLogin are cleared before frmLogin is shown the first time. While not necessary, this doesn't hurt anything, either.

Example **7.9**

ENCRYPTION

As another example of using loops, consider the problem of encrypting an entire string of characters. The form for this example has one TextBox (txtPlaintext), one Button (btnEncryptMessage), and one Label control (lblCiphertext). The user enters a message in the TextBox and then clicks the Button that encrypts the message and displays the result in the Label.

Previously we created a function named Rotate() that "rotates" a capital letter by a specified number of positions in the alphabet. Function CaesarCipher() in Figure 7.17 takes a message as an argument, encrypts the entire message, and returns the ciphertext. It works by invoking function Rotate() repeatedly, one time for each letter in the message.

The For statement

> For C = 1 To Len(Plaintext)

sets up the counter variable **C** to start at 1 and stop at the last character in the variable **Plaintext**. For example, if **Plaintext** stored "VISUAL BASIC", then the counter **C** would start at 1 and end at 12. Inside the For…Next loop, the Mid() function is used to identify a single character. Thus, **Mid(Plaintext, C, 1)** returns the single character at location **C** in the variable **Plaintext**.

Exercise **7.8**

Modify Example 7.8 to display the numbers 1 through 10.

FIGURE 7.17

Code for Example 7.9

```
Private Sub btnEncryptMessage_Click(ByVal sender As System.Object, ByVal e As System.Ev
    lblCiphertext.Text = CaesarCipher(txtPlainText.Text)
End Sub

Private Function CaesarCipher(ByVal Plaintext As String) As String
    Const SHIFTSIZE = 3
    Dim Ciphertext, Letter As String
    Dim C As Short
    For C = 1 To Len(Plaintext)
        Letter = Mid(Plaintext, C, 1)
        Ciphertext = Ciphertext & Rotate(Letter, SHIFTSIZE)
    Next
    Return Ciphertext
End Function

Private Function Rotate(ByVal Letter As String, ByVal ShiftAmount As Integer) As String
    Dim PositionInAlphabet, RotatedPosition As Short
    PositionInAlphabet = Asc(Letter) - 65
    RotatedPosition = (PositionInAlphabet + ShiftAmount) Mod 26
    Return Chr(65 + RotatedPosition)
End Function
```

Exercise 7.9

Should the solution to Exercise 7.5 use For...Next or one of the variations of Do... Loop? Explain.

Exercise 7.10

Write a complete event procedure that simulates a coin-tossing experiment by performing the following tasks: First, ask the user to input the number of tosses. Then "toss a coin" that many times, counting the number that turn up heads. Finally, display a message box showing the fraction of tosses that turned up heads.

The Step Amount

The For...Next statement has a variation that allows you to specify **the amount by which the Next statement increases the counter variable—the** *step amount.* Its syntax is

For *counter* = *start* **To** *end* **Step** *increment*
    statementblock
Next

The action of this variation is the same as the For...Next loop described earlier, with the following exceptions:

- When the loop is first entered, the numeric expression *increment* is evaluated to arrive at the *step amount.*

- Each time the Next statement is executed, the computer increases the value stored in *counter* by the *step amount,* instead of by 1.

Thus, by specifying a step amount, you can make the loop "count by 2s," or by 3s, by 1.5s, or by any other number.

Example 7.10

USING A STEP AMOUNT

Figure 7.18 shows an event procedure that displays the numbers 50, 60, and 70 in message boxes. The step amount is 10.

Negative Step Amounts

You can make the For...Next loop count backward by specifying a negative step amount. When the step amount is negative, For...Next changes its rule for deciding when to exit the loop. As before, when the For statement is executed, the computer compares the value stored in *counter* to the *ending value.* But when the step amount is negative,

- If *counter is greater than or equal to the ending value,* the computer executes the statements inside the loop.

- If *counter is less than the ending value,* the computer exits the loop.

FIGURE 7.18

Code for
Example 7.10

```
Private Sub btnStepTest_Click(ByVal sender As System.O
    Dim X As Short
    For X = 50 To 70 Step 10
        MsgBox(X)
    Next
End Sub
```

FIGURE 7.19

Code for
Example 7.11

```
Private Sub btnNegativeStepTest_Click(ByVal sender As
    Dim X As Short
    For X = 30 To 0 Step -5
       MsgBox(X)
    Next
End Sub
```

That is, when the step amount is negative, the computer counts down from the starting value to the ending value. If the starting value is less than the ending value when the loop is first entered, the statements inside the loop will be executed 0 times.

Example 7.11 **USING NEGATIVE STEP AMOUNTS**

As an example of negative step amounts, Figure 7.19 shows an event procedure that counts backward from 30 to 0 by 5s.

Exercise 7.11

Modify Example 7.8 to display the even numbers from 2 to 20 (i.e., 2, 4, 6, 8, . . ., 20). Then modify Example 7.8 to display the even numbers from 20 down to 2 (i.e., 20, 18, 16, . . ., 2).

Exercise 7.12

What values are displayed by the following event procedure? Explain.

```
Private Sub btnAnnoyingLoop_Click()
    Dim N As Integer
    Dim StartVal As Integer
    Dim EndVal As Integer
    Dim StepAmount As Integer
    StartVal = 1
    EndVal = 10
    For N = StartVal To EndVal Step StepAmount
        MsgBox(N)
    Next
End Sub
```

Avoiding For...Next Errors

A developer must understand exactly how the For...Next loop executes to code a loop that will execute properly. It is possible to add statements to the loop body that will alter the loop's execution and produce unintended results. We discuss these pitfalls here.

Developers who forget that the start, end, and increment expressions are evaluated only when the loop is first entered might try to modify one or more of these values in the loop body. For example, the developer might try to change the end value in order to stop the loop. However, this will not work.

Example 7.12 **FOR...NEXT INITIALIZATIONS**

This example, shown in Figure 7.20, demonstrates the action of the For...Next loop and its initialization operation. It looks as if the assignment statements inside the loop will make the loop counter, **N**, run through the values from 100 to 200 by 10s. However, this is not what happens when the loop executes. The

FIGURE 7.20

Code for
Example 7.12

```
Private Sub btnInitializationOperations_Click(ByVal send
    Dim N, StartVal, EndVal, StepAmount As Short
    StartVal = 1
    EndVal = 3
    StepAmount = 1
    For N = StartVal To EndVal Step StepAmount
        MsgBox(N)
        StartVal = 100
        EndVal = 200
        StepAmount = 10
    Next
End Sub
```

loop will display the values 1, 2, and 3 because its initialization operation is performed only once, when the loop is first entered. At the time this loop is first entered, the start expression evaluates to 1, the end expression evaluates to 3, and the increment expression evaluates to 1.

It is true that the assignment statements inside the loop will change the values stored in the variables **StartVal**, **EndVal**, and **StepAmount**, but by the time these statements are executed the loop's initialization operation has already been performed; the *starting value, ending value*, and *step amount* used by the loop no longer have any connection to these variables.

To avoid confusion, do not place statements inside the loop that change the values stored in variables appearing in the *start, end,* and *increment* expressions.

Another potential problem arises from the fact that it is possible to include statements inside the loop that change the value stored in the *counter variable*. Unlike Example 7.12, where the *starting value, ending value,* and *step amount* cannot be changed within the loop, the value of the counter variable can be changed (but you should not do it).

Example 7.13

CHANGING THE COUNTER VARIABLE

The code in Figure 7.21 illustrates the confusion that can result when a statement that changes the value stored in the *counter* variable is included inside the loop. Can you predict what values this code will display?

Upon seeing the statement

    For N = 1 To 10

the developer wants to believe that the loop will be executed 10 times, with the loop variable starting at 1 and increasing by 1 each time the loop is executed. But the statement

    N = N + 3

inside the loop increases **N** by 3 each time the loop is executed. The loop itself increases **N** by 1 each iteration, so the net effect is to increase **N** by 4 each iteration.

FIGURE 7.21

Code for
Example 7.13

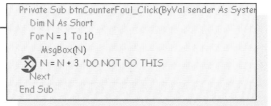

```
Private Sub btnCounterFoul_Click(ByVal sender As System
    Dim N As Short
    For N = 1 To 10
        MsgBox(N)
        N = N + 3  'DO NOT DO THIS
    Next
End Sub
```

The loop displays the values 1, 5, and 9. This is very deceptive and probably not what the developer intended.

As a result of the confusion that arises from a situation like that in Example 7.13, you should never include a statement in the interior of a For…Next loop that changes the value stored in the loop's *counter* variable. If you want to do something tricky like this, you should use one of the variations of Do…Loop instead of For…Next. Since the Do…Loop structure does not automatically initialize or increment any variables, you don't have to worry about "deceiving" yourself or other developers who read your Do…Loop code.

7.3 Exit Do and Exit For

Occasionally the statements in the interior of a loop make a decision for which the appropriate action is to exit the loop immediately. For such situations Visual Basic .NET provides the Exit Do and Exit For statements.

The *Exit Do statement* **is used inside a Do…Loop structure to cause execution to jump to the statement following the Loop statement.** Similarly, **the** *Exit For statement* **is used inside a For…Next loop to cause execution to jump to the statement following the Next statement.** The Exit For statement is illustrated in Example 7.14.

Example 7.14

USING EXIT FOR

Let us modify the guessing game so that it generates a random integer between 1 and 127, then gives the user up to seven tries to guess it. After each guess the procedure should inform the user whether the guess was correct, too high, or too low. With this modification, the user should be able to arrive at the right value fairly quickly. Figure 7.22 shows one solution to this problem using a For…Next loop and Exit For.

FIGURE 7.22

Code for
Example 7.14

```
Private Sub Form1_Load(ByVal sender As Object, ByVal e As System.Eve
    Randomize()
End Sub


Private Sub btnGuessMeQuickly_Click(ByVal sender As System.Object,
    Dim Target, Guess, Attempt As Short
    Target = 1 + Int(127 * Rnd())
    MsgBox("Guess the random integer between 1 and 127, inclusive.")
    For Attempt = 1 To 7
        Guess = InputBox("Enter a guess")
        Select Case Guess
            Case Target
                MsgBox("Correct -- congratulations!")
                Exit For
            Case Is > Target
                MsgBox("Too high")
            Case Else
                MsgBox("Too low")
        End Select
    Next
    If Guess <> Target Then
        MsgBox("You took too many guesses!")
    End If
End Sub
```

If the guess matches the target, a congratulatory message is displayed. Then the Exit For statement is executed, causing the loop to terminate, and the If statement following the loop is executed. Note that this If statement is executed regardless of whether the loop terminated normally (after seven iterations) or early via the Exit For. That is why the If statement checks whether **Guess <> Target**. If this condition is True, then the loop must have terminated normally after seven iterations, which means that the user did not guess correctly in seven tries.

7.4 Nested Loops

Often the statements in the interior of one loop include another loop. **Loops embedded inside other loops are called** *nested loops.* We might use nested loops in payroll processing. The outer loop would process employees (one iteration per employee), and the inner loop would accumulate the hours worked on each project for a given employee (one iteration per project).

Nested Do While...Loops have the following structure (the nested loop is in color):

```
Do While condition1
    statementblock1a
    Do While condition2
        statementblock2
    Loop
    statementblock1b
Loop
```

Note that the Do statements and the Loop statements occur in matched pairs. The inner Loop statement belongs to the inner Do statement, and the outer Loop belongs to the outer Do. Therefore,

• When the inner Loop statement is executed, it causes execution to jump up to the inner Do statement (its partner). When the outer Loop statement is executed, it causes execution to jump up to the outer Do statement (its partner).

• When the inner Do While's condition causes the computer to exit the inner loop, execution jumps to the statement following the inner Loop statement. Similar behavior holds for the outer Do While.

As with embedded Ifs, indentation is very important to the readability of your code. The "L" in Loop should line up vertically with the "D" in the Do it belongs to, and the statements in the interior of the loop should be indented. As with earlier indentation guidelines, Visual Basic .NET automatically enforces this indentation by default.

A procedure may have two loops, one of which entirely precedes the other. In this case, the loops are not nested. This is shown below.

```
Do While condition1
    statementblock1
Loop
    ...
Do While condition2
    statementblock2
Loop
```

In nested For...Next loops, as in nested Do...Loop statements, the For statements and Next statements occur in matched pairs. You cannot use the same counter variable for both the outer and inner loops. Nested For...Next loops have the following structure (the nested loop is in color):

> **For** *counter1* = *start1* **To** *end1*
>   *statementblock1a*
>   **For** *counter2* = *start2* **To** *end2*
>   *statementblock2*
>   **Next**
>   *statementblock1b*
> **Next**

Note that whenever loops are nested, one of the loops is inside the other. It is not possible for the loops to "cross" each other. That is, the following is not valid:

> **For** *counter1* = *start1* **To** *end1*
>   *statementblock1a*
>   **Do While** *condition1*
>   *statementblock2*
>   **Next**
>   *statementblock1b*
> **Loop**

Example 7.15   USING NESTED LOOPS

The procedure in Figure 7.23 shows an example of a nested For...Next loop. Remember that each loop behaves just like the previous examples. Try to predict what the event procedure will display.

The outer loop starts to execute with **X** equal to 1. While this loop is executing, the inner loop starts to execute. Since **X** equals 1, the inner For loop is actually

> For Y = 1 To 1   'because X = 1 at this point

The inner loop performs one iteration.

When the inner loop terminates, the outer **Next** statement is executed. This changes **X** to 2 and the outer loop repeats. The inner loop now starts over. Since **X** equals 2, the inner For statement is now actually

> For Y = 1 To 2   'because X = 2 at this point

This time the inner loop performs two iterations, with values of 1 and 2.

This process continues for **X** equal to 3 and **X** equal to 4. It is important to note that the inner loop always starts over for each iteration of the outer loop.

FIGURE 7.23

Code for
Example 7.15

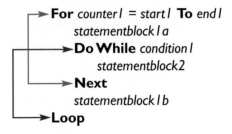

```
Private Sub btnNestedLoops_Click(ByVal sender As Syst
    Dim X, Y As Short
    For X = 1 To 4
        For Y = 1 To X
            MsgBox("X = " & X & " and Y = " & Y)
        Next
    Next
End Sub
```

7.5   The ListBox and ComboBox Controls

We now turn our attention to the GUI and two Visual Basic .NET controls that are often associated with loops. We first present a basic description of each control and then describe how they can be combined with loops for processing.

So far, all the controls we have encountered have displayed at most one value at a time. For example, the TextBox has a single property (the Text property) for storing and displaying information. Even if the TextBox has multiple lines, all these lines are associated with the single Text property. Labels are similar. The List-Box and ComboBox controls are different in that they can reference multiple text values.

You see this type of list when you open a file in any Windows application: the File Open dialog box presents you with a list of files and a list of directories that you can scroll through and use to select a file and directory.

The ListBox

To design a user-friendly GUI, you might want to **display a list of items from which the user makes a selection, and the *ListBox control* makes this easy.** The user can be limited to selecting a single item or allowed to select many items. For example, you might present the user with a list of state abbreviations. After the user selects a state or several states, the program then uses this in further processing. In this section we assume the user will be limited to selecting a single item; we will discuss multiple selection in Section 7.6.

Appearance and Use

A ListBox appears as a rectangle that displays rows of text. Each row is an item that the user may select. If the number of rows is too large to fit within the rectangle, Visual Basic .NET automatically provides a vertical scroll bar on the right side of the ListBox. Figure 7.24 identifies the ListBox tool and shows a ListBox control on the form at design time. At run time, the user selects an item by clicking on

FIGURE 7.24

ListBox Tool and Control

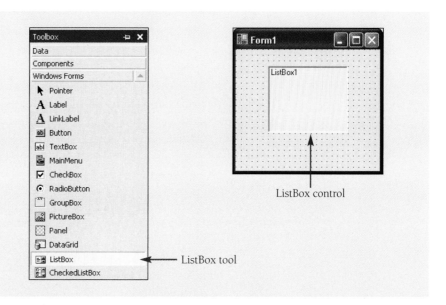

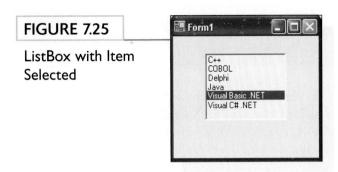

FIGURE 7.25

ListBox with Item
Selected

it with the mouse or by pressing an arrow key when the ListBox has the focus. Visual Basic .NET automatically highlights the currently selected item. An example of a ListBox at run time is shown in Figure 7.25.

ListBoxes can be used both as a means of obtaining input from the user and as a means of providing output to the user. For example, the ListBox in Figure 7.25 may be presenting the user with the names of programming languages being researched.

Properties

Some of the most common properties of the ListBox control are shown in Table 7.1. As you scan this table, you may find that some of the descriptions are difficult to understand. Some of the ListBox's properties are moderately complex, and we will illustrate them with examples.

Events

A user typically interacts with a ListBox as follows: The user first gives the List-Box the focus by tabbing to it or clicking the mouse on an item in it. Then the user presses arrow keys or uses the mouse to move the highlight to—that is, to select—a desired item. Finally, the user initiates some processing step involving the selected item.

Typically, the DoubleClick event that occurs when the user double-clicks on an item in the ListBox initiates processing of the selected item. The Click event cannot be used effectively for this purpose because it occurs every time the selected item changes; that is, pressing an arrow key as well as clicking the mouse causes the Click event to occur.

While the most common event used for a ListBox is the DoubleClick event, the ListBox control is also capable of responding to other events, such as KeyPress, Enter, and Leave. One event that is often useful is the SelectedIndexChanged. This event fires whenever the value of the SelectedIndex property is changed either by user action or statements being executed in the code.

Methods

There are two commonly used methods for the ListBox control and five commonly used methods associated with the ListBox control's Items property. This is the first control we have seen that has a property that itself is an object. The Items property, being an object, is associated with its own set of properties and methods. We will investigate five of its methods here. But first, we look at the two methods associated directly with the ListBox control.

Table 7.1 Properties of the ListBox control

Property	Value
Name	(lst) *Gets or sets the name of the control.*
HorizontalScrollbar	*Gets or sets a Boolean value indicating whether a horizontal scroll bar is displayed in the control.* Set to True to display a horizontal scroll bar in the control; otherwise, False. The default is False.
Items	*Gets the items of the ListBox.* This property is itself an object that has its own set of properties and methods. Use the methods of this object to manage the items shown in the ListBox.
MultiColumn	*Gets or sets a Boolean value indicating whether the ListBox supports multiple columns.* Multiple columns in a ListBox is not what one normally expects. If this property is True new items are added to the ListBox until it is full. When it is full, then additional items are added in a new column to the right. Essentially this means that instead of having vertical scrolling, new items are added in columns that expand to the right (requiring horizontal scrolling to see them). This type of behavior is commonly found in File Open dialog boxes.
SelectedIndex	*Gets or sets the zero-based index of the currently selected item in a ListBox.* Used when the SelectionMode is set to "One". Returns a value of −1 if no item is selected.
SelectedIndices	*Gets a collection that contains the zero-based indices of all currently selected items in the ListBox.* Used when the SelectionMode is set to "MultiSimple" or "MultiExtended".
SelectedItem	*Gets or sets the currently selected item in the ListBox.* Used when the SelectionMode is set to "One". Note that the "Item" is the actual item the user selected while the index is a zero-based integer index of the selected item.
SelectedItems	*Gets a collection containing the currently selected items in the ListBox.* Used when the SelectionMode is set to "MultiSimple" or "MultiExtended".
SelectionMode	*Gets or sets the method in which items are selected in the ListBox.* Possible values are None, One, MultiSimple, and MultiExtended. Essentially controls whether the user is limited to selecting zero, one, or many items. If many items are chosen, determines how these many items are selected.
Sorted	*Gets or sets a Boolean value indicating whether the items in the ListBox are sorted alphabetically.* Indicates that the items in the ListBox should be sorted regardless of the order they are entered.
Text	*Gets or searches for the text of the currently selected item in the ListBox.* Valid if SelectionMode is set to One.
UseTabStops	*Gets or sets a Boolean value indicating whether the ListBox can recognize and expand* (TAB) *characters when drawing its strings.* Setting to True allows the (TAB) character to behave as a tab within the ListBox.

The ListBox control includes two very useful methods: the FindString and FindStringExact methods. The FindString method is used to search the ListBox to find the first item that starts with a given string argument. Its syntax is

*lstBoxName.***FindString***(stringToSearchFor)*

This method searches beginning at the first item (index 0) until it finds a match. If it finds a match, it returns the index value of the item that starts with the *stringToSearchFor*. If the *stringToSearchFor* does not exist in the ListBox, then the method returns a value equal to the constant ListBox.NoMatches.

The FindStringExact method differs from the FindString method in that the *stringToSearchFor* must match the entire text within an item of the ListBox. It too returns either the index value of the item where the match was found or a constant equal to ListBox.NoMatches.

Table 7.2 Selected methods of the ListBox's Items property

Method	Behavior
Add(text)	Adds the *text* to the end of the list of items.
Insert(index, text)	Inserts the *text* at the index location indicated by *index*. The original item at that location and all items below it will be moved down to make room for the inserted item. Legal values of *index* range from 0 to the value of the Count property minus 1.
Remove(text)	Searches the items for an exact match of the *text*. If found, that item is removed from the list and all items below it shift up one spot. If the *text* is not found, nothing happens.
RemoveAt(index)	Remove the item at the specific *index* value and all items below it shift up one spot. Legal values of *index* range from 0 to the value of the Count property minus 1.
Clear()	Clears (removes) all the items from the ListBox. The value of the Count property is set to zero.

Both of these two methods include an alternate syntax that allows the search to begin at an item whose index is not zero. The syntax for this alternative for the FindString method is

lstBoxName.**FindString**(*stringToSearchFor, startIndex*)

The Items property of the ListBox control provides five methods that can be used to manage its items. These include the Add, Insert, Remove, RemoveAt, and Clear methods. A useful property of the Items property is the Count property, which is equal to the number of items in the Items collection. This property is read-only and is managed (updated) by the system as items are added and removed from the ListBox. Table 7.2 shows these methods and explains what they do.

Since the Items property is a property of the ListBox control, the syntax for accessing the methods of the Items property requires that you specify the name of the ListBox control, followed by a period, then the Items property, another period, and then any one of the Items property's methods. For example, to access the Clear() method, you would say

lstBoxName.**Items.Clear**()

Example 7.16   USING METHODS WITH THE LISTBOX CONTROL

This example illustrates the use of the ListBox's methods. Figure 7.26 shows the form at run time, just after the user has clicked the Add Items to List button. The code for this example also is shown in Figure 7.26.

Here are some things to try when you execute this example.

1. Click on Add Items to List. Then put the focus in the ListBox .

2. Change the item that is selected by pressing the ⬆ and ⬇ keys; then try pressing the Ⓐ, Ⓑ, Ⓒ, and Ⓓ keys (the first letters of items in the ListBox). The latter is a shortcut method of selecting items in the list based on the first letter of each item. What happens if you press Ⓑ several times?

3. Click on Add Items to List several times and observe the vertical scroll bar that appears. Visual Basic .NET automatically places the vertical scroll bar on the ListBox when it is needed. Click on Clear List.

4. Click on Add Items to List, select an item, then click on Remove Selected Item. Try clicking on Remove Selected Item when nothing is highlighted; were it

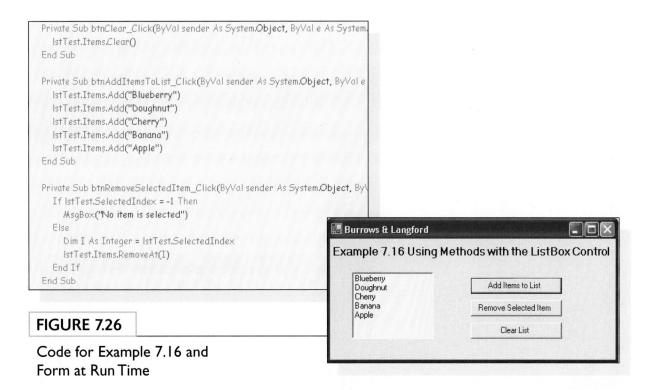

```
Private Sub btnClear_Click(ByVal sender As System.Object, ByVal e As System.
   lstTest.Items.Clear()
End Sub

Private Sub btnAddItemsToList_Click(ByVal sender As System.Object, ByVal e
   lstTest.Items.Add("Blueberry")
   lstTest.Items.Add("Doughnut")
   lstTest.Items.Add("Cherry")
   lstTest.Items.Add("Banana")
   lstTest.Items.Add("Apple")
End Sub

Private Sub btnRemoveSelectedItem_Click(ByVal sender As System.Object, By\
   If lstTest.SelectedIndex = -1 Then
      MsgBox("No item is selected")
   Else
      Dim I As Integer = lstTest.SelectedIndex
      lstTest.Items.RemoveAt(I)
   End If
End Sub
```

FIGURE 7.26

Code for Example 7.16 and
Form at Run Time

not for the If statement in btnRemoveSelectedItem_Click, this would cause a
run-time error. As shown in Table 7.1, when no item is selected, the Selected-
Index property is set to −1.

5. End execution, and at design time change the ListBox's Sorted property to
True. Then run the example again. Click Add Items to List two or three
times to see the effect. The order of the items in the list is determined by
the ANSI collating sequence.

Example 7.17

USING THE DOUBLECLICK EVENT

This example illustrates how the DoubleClick event can be used to initiate processing of the selected item.

The example employs two ListBoxes. Figure 7.27 shows the application at run
time. In this figure, the user has double-clicked on Doughnut in List A and it has
been copied to List B. The code for this example also is shown in the figure.

Here are some things to try when you execute this example.

1. Click on Add Items to List A. Then double-click on an item in List A and
observe the effect.

2. Press either the ↑ or ↓ key to change which item is selected in List A. Then
press the TAB key to move the focus to List B.

3. Press either the ↑ or ↓ key to change which item is selected in List B. Then
press TAB to move the focus back to List A.

Observe that both ListBoxes can have a selected item at the same time, but only
one ListBox can have the focus at any given time.

As we indicated earlier, the discussion so far has focused on ListBoxes where
the SelectionMode property has been set to One (or single selection). In Section
7.6 we investigate processing ListBoxes where multiple items are selected.

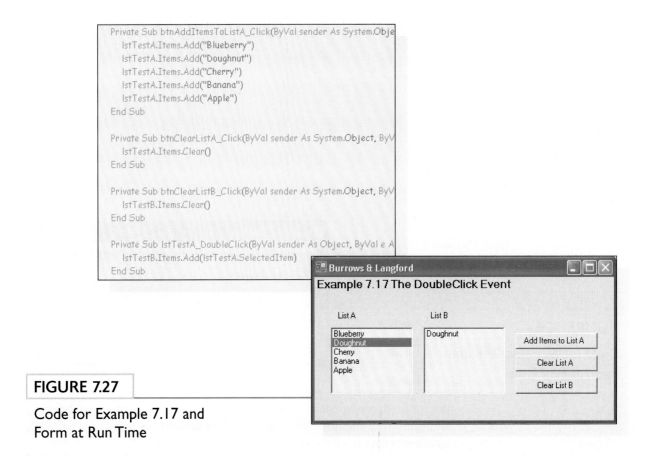

```
Private Sub btnAddItemsToListA_Click(ByVal sender As System.Obje
    lstTestA.Items.Add("Blueberry")
    lstTestA.Items.Add("Doughnut")
    lstTestA.Items.Add("Cherry")
    lstTestA.Items.Add("Banana")
    lstTestA.Items.Add("Apple")
End Sub

Private Sub btnClearListA_Click(ByVal sender As System.Object, ByV
    lstTestA.Items.Clear()
End Sub

Private Sub btnClearListB_Click(ByVal sender As System.Object, ByV
    lstTestB.Items.Clear()
End Sub

Private Sub lstTestA_DoubleClick(ByVal sender As Object, ByVal e A
    lstTestB.Items.Add(lstTestA.SelectedItem)
End Sub
```

FIGURE 7.27

Code for Example 7.17 and
Form at Run Time

The ComboBox

Many situations require the user to input a value that usually, but not always, comes from a predefined list of values. If the value does come from the predefined list of values, then we can save the user time and effort by providing a ListBox from which to select the value. If not, then we can provide a TextBox in which to type the value. **The *ComboBox* is a combination TextBox/ListBox that provides both a TextBox for entering the value and a ListBox of predefined values.**

Visually, a ComboBox appears as a thin TextBox next to a down-arrow button. Figure 7.28 identifies the ComboBox tool and shows a ComboBox on the form at design time. At run time, the user can click on the down arrow at the right of the control that causes a ListBox to drop down (i.e., appear below the TextBox). The user can then select an item in this list. When the user makes a selection, by clicking the mouse or pressing ENTER, the ListBox disappears and the value of the selected item is displayed in the TextBox. The user can edit the value in the TextBox if so desired. Alternatively, the user can simply type a value directly in the TextBox.

Properties

The ComboBox control has many of the properties of the ListBox control, but it does not have a SelectionMode property. It also has some of the properties of the TextBox control. The ComboBox's Text property holds the value displayed in its TextBox.

The ComboBox control's *DropDownStyle property* is described in Table 7.3. The three styles are shown in Figure 7.29.

FIGURE 7.28

ComboBox Tool and Control

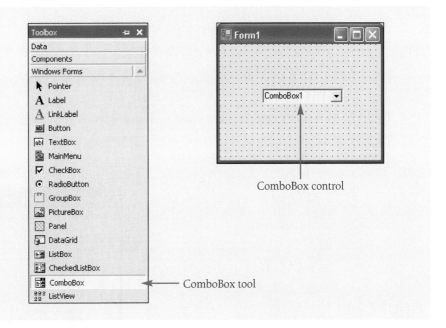

ComboBox control

ComboBox tool

Table 7.3 The ComboBox's DropDownStyle property

Property	Specifies
Name	(cbo) *Gets or sets the name of the control.*
DropDownStyle	*Gets or sets the style of the ComboBox.* Possible values are: **Dropdown.** This style has a TextBox next to a down arrow. Clicking on the down arrow at run time causes a ListBox to drop down. **Simple.** The ListBox is always displayed below the TextBox at run time. **DropDownList.** This style is like the Dropdown combo style except that the user cannot type in the TextBox; that is, the user can select only from the ListBox.

Dropdown style

Simple style

DropDownList style*

*Note: The DropDownList style has almost the same appearance as the Dropdown style. However, the user cannot type in the text box portion of the DropDownList.

FIGURE 7.29

Examples of the DropDownStyle Properties

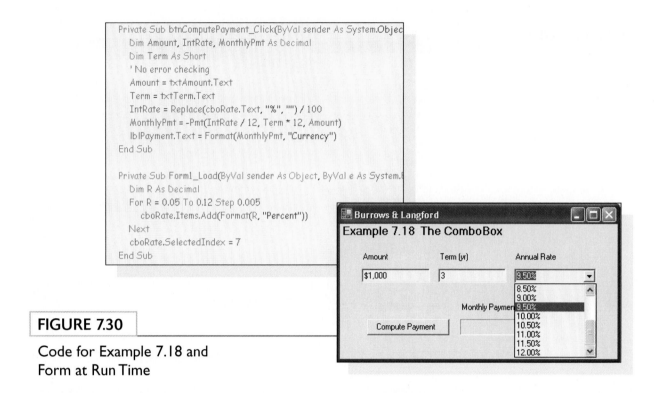

```
Private Sub btnComputePayment_Click(ByVal sender As System.Objec
    Dim Amount, IntRate, MonthlyPmt As Decimal
    Dim Term As Short
    ' No error checking
    Amount = txtAmount.Text
    Term = txtTerm.Text
    IntRate = Replace(cboRate.Text, "%", "") / 100
    MonthlyPmt = -Pmt(IntRate / 12, Term * 12, Amount)
    lblPayment.Text = Format(MonthlyPmt, "Currency")
End Sub

Private Sub Form1_Load(ByVal sender As Object, ByVal e As System.
    Dim R As Decimal
    For R = 0.05 To 0.12 Step 0.005
        cboRate.Items.Add(Format(R, "Percent"))
    Next
    cboRate.SelectedIndex = 7
End Sub
```

FIGURE 7.30

Code for Example 7.18 and
Form at Run Time

Events

The ComboBox control generally responds to the same events as the ListBox.

EXAMPLE **7.18**

USING THE COMBOBOX

This example shows how you might use a ComboBox to supply the interest rate to a simple loan payment calculator. Figure 7.30 shows the application while it is executing. Notice that the ComboBox that shows the interest rate is dropped down for the user to make a selection. The code for this application also is shown in the figure. The Form_Load procedure uses a For…Next loop and the Add method of the Items property to generate the interest rates and fill the ComboBox. Again, this is an ideal place to use For…Next loops.

The btnComputePayment_Click procedure uses Visual Basic .NET's built-in Pmt() function to compute the monthly payment.

The statement

IntRate = Replace(cboRate.Text, "%", "") / 100

takes the value from the TextBox portion of the ComboBox, replaces the "%" character with the empty string, and divides the value by 100 to convert it to a decimal interest rate.

7.6 Collections and the For Each…Next Structure

Referring back to Table 7.1 you will note that if the user was allowed to select multiple items, both the SelectedIndices and SelectedItems properties returned a "collection" of selected index values and selected items from the ListBox.

Although not mentioned in Table 7.1, the Items property of the ListBox control is also a collection. A ***Collection object* is an ordered set of items that can be referred to as a unit.** The Collection object provides a convenient way to refer to a related group of items as a single object. The items, or members, in a collection need only be related by the fact that they exist in the collection. We will discuss working with collections in greater detail in Chapter 10, but since the ListBox control provides collections, we introduce the concept here.

It should be clear to you that dealing with a ListBox that restricts the user to a single selection is very different from dealing with a ListBox that allows either type of multiple selection. If the SelectionMode property of the ListBox is set to MultiSimple, then the user can select an item by clicking on it and deselect a selected item by again clicking on it. That is, when the user clicks on an item in the ListBox, he toggles the selection on or off with each click. Each item in the ListBox is independent so any number or combination of items may be selected. If the SelectionMode property is set to MultiExtended, then the user can define a contiguous range of selected items either by clicking on the first item and dragging to the last item or by clicking on the first item and then SHIFT + clicking on the last item. In this mode, the user also can select/deselect any item by CTRL + clicking on an item.

Regardless of how the user selects multiple items, the question of how to process them needs to be answered. Visual Basic .NET provides the ***For Each...Next*** control structure to facilitate this. It **repeats a group of statements for each element in a collection.** The For Each...Next loop is entered if there is at least one element in the collection. Once the loop has been entered, the statements are executed for the first element in the collection; if there are more elements in the collection, the statements in the loop continue to execute for each element. When there are no more elements, the loop is terminated and execution continues with the statement following the Next statement.

The syntax of the For Each...Loop structure is

```
For Each object In collection
    statementblock
Next
```

Object is a variable that stores one item from the *collection*. Each time the loop repeats, the variable *object* refers to the next item in the *collection*. For example, if you had a collection named Students, you could access one student at a time from the collection with code like

```
Dim Student As Object
For Each Student In Students
    ' here Student refers to a specific student from the collection
Next
```

Example 7.19 demonstrates the use of collections as they are related to the List-Box control.

Example **7.19**   **WORKING WITH LISTBOX COLLECTIONS**

This example provides the user with the ability to copy either all of the items from lstDemoA to lstDemoB or just to copy the selected items from lstDemoA to lst-DemoB. Figure 7.31 shows the code for the example and the form at run time.

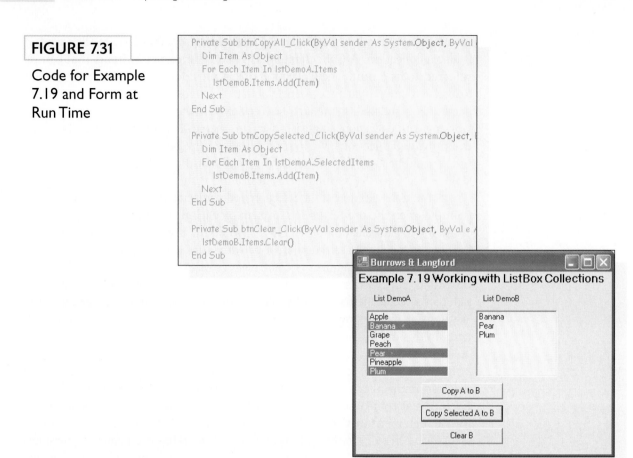

FIGURE 7.31

Code for Example 7.19 and Form at Run Time

The "Object" type referred to in the statement that declares the variable **Item**

> **Dim Item As Object**

is a type that has the ability to store any type of object. This can be string text as well as any other object. Since a variable of type "Object" can store any object, we generally use this type when referring to a specific element within a collection.

The only difference between the event procedures btnCopyAll_Click and btnCopySelected_Click is the collection being referenced in the For Each statement. In btnCopyAll_Click, the Items collection that contains all the items in the ListBox is processed. Each item of lstDemoA is extracted and added to the Items property of lstDemoB.

> **For Each Item In lstDemoA.Items**
>   **lstDemoB.Items.Add(Item)**
> **Next**

In btnCopySelected_Click, the SelectedItems collection is processed in the For Each loop. This collection contains zero or more values, depending upon how many items the user selected in lstDemA. Like the previous loop, each item in this collection is added to the Items property of lstDemoB.

> **For Each Item In lstDemoA.SelectedItems**
>   **lstDemoB.Items.Add(Item)**
> **Next**

As stated earlier, we will look at collections in greater detail in Chapter 10.

7.7 | The ListView Control

The *ListView control* **is a very flexible and somewhat complex control used to display lists of items that can include icons and/or text.** It also supports the ability to associate subitems with each item. Perhaps the most familiar use of this control is the right window of the Windows Explorer. Figure 7.32 shows two different views: one is the Large Icon view and the other is the Details view. This figure clearly shows the use of icons as well as text. In the *Details view,* it **also shows how the items can be displayed in a tabular form with rows and columns (including column headers).**

We will limit our discussion here to using the control for only one type of view, referred to as the Details view, and we will not use any icons. While this will be an incomplete exposure to the ListView control, it will provide a way to display information in a tabular form and also will provide a level of exposure to a moderately complex control.

Appearance and Use

Visually the ListView control appears as a rectangular area that can contain icons, text, or combinations of icons and text. Figure 7.33 identifies the ListView tool and shows a ListView control at design time.

Our use of this control is to display textual information in a row and column arrangement. The rows of the control are represented by an Items collection object just as in the case with the ListBox and ComboBox controls. The column

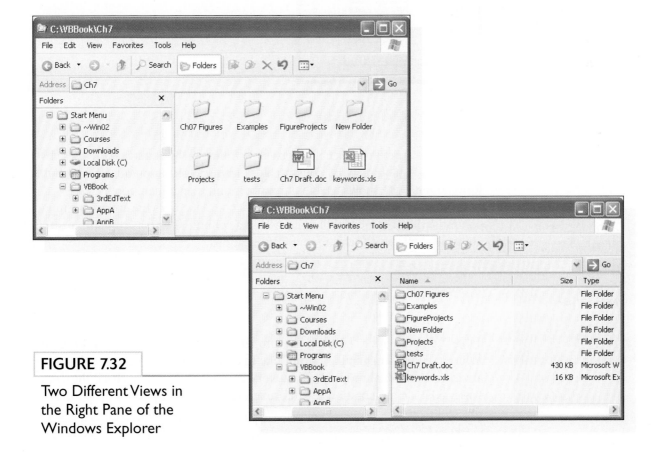

FIGURE 7.32

Two Different Views in the Right Pane of the Windows Explorer

FIGURE 7.33

ListView Tool and
Control

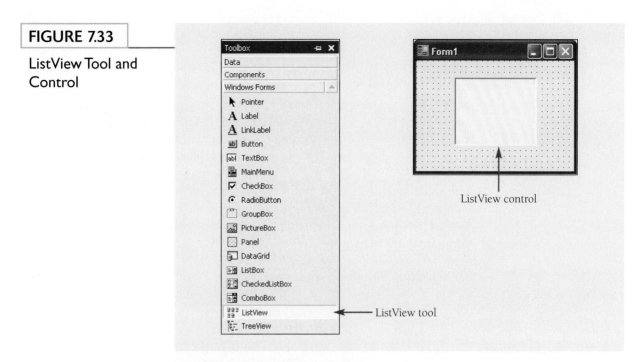

FIGURE 7.34

Table of Square
Roots Displayed in a
ListView Control

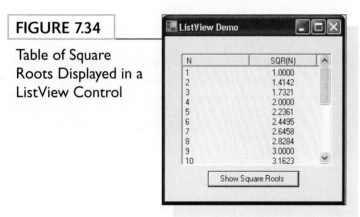

headers also are stored in a collection called Columns. By adding text to these two collections, a table may be constructed and displayed in an attractive tabular form. Figure 7.34 shows a table of numbers and their square roots.

Unlike the ListBox control, the ListView control includes the ability to support columns with control of alignment within a column as well as content. It is this ability that makes it useful in many applications.

Properties

Table 7.4 summarizes some of the properties of the ListView control that are focused on building tabular output like that in Figure 7.34. Be aware that there are many additional properties that work with icons. You may check the Visual Basic .NET documentation for information on these additional properties. In this table the term "item" is equivalent to a "row" in the table.

Table 7.4 Common ListView properties

Property	Action
Name	(lvw) *Gets or sets the name of the control.*
CheckBoxes	*Boolean property that gets or sets whether every item will display a checkbox next to it.*
CheckedIndices	*Gets a collection of the indices of the currently checked list items.*
CheckedItems	*Gets a collection of the currently checked list items.*
FullRowSelect	*Boolean property that gets or sets whether clicking an item will select only the item or the entire row the item is in.*
GridLines	*Boolean property that gets or sets whether grid lines are drawn between items and subitems.*
Items	*Gets a collection of the list items.*
MultiSelect	*Boolean property that gets or sets a value indicating whether multiple items in a ListView control can be selected at one time. A value of True produces a multiselection mode equivalent to the ListBox's MultiSelected mode*
Scrollable	*Boolean property that gets or sets whether scroll bars are visible or not.*
SelectedIndices	*Gets the indices of the currently selected list of items.*
SelectedItems	*Gets the currently selected list of items.*
Sorting	*Gets or sets the sort order of the items. Valid values are None (default), Ascending, and Descending.*
View	*Gets or sets the current view. Valid values are LargeIcon, SmallIcon, List, and Details. We will only cover the Details view.*

Events

Like the ListBox, the ListView component responds to both the DoubleClick and SelectedIndexChanged events. These events can be used along with the SelectedIndices and SelectedItems collections to determine what the user selected.

Example 7.20   **USING THE LISTVIEW CONTROL FOR TABULAR DISPLAY**

This example illustrates the application of the ListView component to display a table showing the future value (FV) factor for a number of years and different interest rates. The formula for the FV factor is

$$FVFactor = (1 + r)^n$$

where r is the annual interest rate and n is the number of years. Our code computes and displays the FV factors for interest rates and years specified by the user. Figure 7.35 shows the application as it is running.

The code for Example 7.20 is broken down into two parts and is shown in Figures 7.36 and 7.37. The code in Figure 7.36 is straightforward and does not need much explanation.

The code in Figure 7.37 is more complex and introduces several new concepts. In order to better understand this code, we will go through it line by line. Before we start analyzing the code, let us understand the basic philosophy underlying this code. Complex classes rely on other classes to help them do their

FIGURE 7.35

Example 7.20 during
Execution

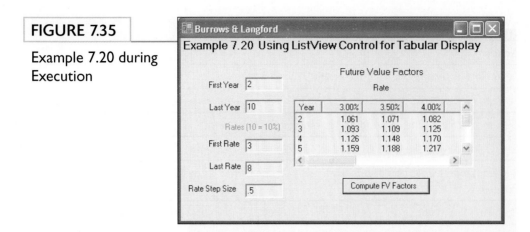

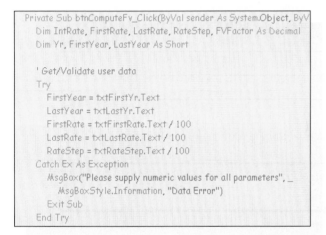

FIGURE 7.36

Code for Example 7.20 That Gets User Input

FIGURE 7.37

Code for Example 7.20 That Fills
the ListView Component

work. In the case of the ListView component, the management of its column headers and the management of its actual data items are each managed by objects instantiated from other classes. The object paradigm encourages this segregation of responsibilities and is considered good design. Now let us begin with the analysis of the code.

The first two lines of code from Figure 7.37 are fairly easy—we simply set the View property to "Details". Editing the View property at design time could also have done this.

```
' Set the view
lvwFVFactors.View = View.Details
```

Continuing with the code, we then deal with statements that create the column header information.

```
' Get a col header collection and fill it with col headers
Dim Col As New ListView.ColumnHeaderCollection(lvwFVFactors)
Col.Clear()
Col.Add("Year", 40, HorizontalAlignment.Right)
For IntRate = FirstRate To LastRate Step RateStep
    Col.Add(Format(IntRate, "Percent"), 60, HorizontalAlignment.Right)
Next
```

We first need to instantiate a ColumnHeaderCollection object (**Col**) to manage the column headings. When this object is created, the ListView component (lvwFVFactors) is passed as an argument. This results in the ColumnHeader-Collection object (**Col**) being associated with the ListView component (lvwFV-Factors) so that the particular column heading is for the particular ListView.

After the ColumnHeaderCollection object is created, its Clear() method is executed to clear any prior contents. This is needed in case the user clicks on the Button several times. Following this, the first column heading is added (the "Year" heading). The syntax of the Add() method for a ColumnHeaderCollection object is

Add(*headingString, width, alignment*)

The *headingString* is the actual string that goes into the heading. The *width* is the width of the column. It is often necessary to experiment with this number to find the correct width. The final argument, *alignment,* is a constant used to define the alignment of the column (Left, Center, or Right).

After adding the text for the first column, a For loop is used to fill in the interest rate values based on user input. The Add() method simply adds column headers in sequence from left to right. The Format() function is used to format the interest rates as percentage value.

After filling in the headings using the ColumnHeaderCollection object, it is time to fill in the body of the table.

```
' Get and fill the ListView with FV factors
Dim Row As ListViewItem
For Yr = FirstYear To LastYear
    ' Put year into first column of listview
    Row = lvwFVFactors.Items.Add(Yr)
    ' Now fill the remaining columns of the current row with FV Factors
    For IntRate = FirstRate To LastRate Step RateStep
        FVFactor = (1 + IntRate) ^ Yr
        Row.SubItems.Add(Format(FVFactor, "#.000"))
    Next
Next
```

This process uses a ListViewItem object reference referred to as **Row** in this code. The Dim statement creates the object reference but does not actually cause an object to be instantiated (because it does not include the keyword New). The nested loop structure generates the appropriate year/interest rate combinations. When the outer (year) loop starts, the ListViewItem object reference **Row** is set equal to an Item object within the ListView. This is equivalent to a row (this is why we chose the object reference name of "**Row**") in the table. The statement

```
Row = lvwFVFactors.Items.Add(Yr)
```

does two things. First, it adds a new Item (actually a row in the ListView) to the lvwFVFactors component and sets its value equal to the value of the variable

Yr. Second, it sets the object reference **Row** to refer to that Item. The Item reference is needed so that additional values (columns) can be added to the row.

In the inner loop, the future value factors are computed and then stored in the ListView component. Each Item of a ListView can be associated with a set of subitems. In this application, these subitems are treated as additional column information being added to a specific row. The statement

Row.SubItems.Add(Format(FVFactor, "#.000"))

performs this task. **FVFactor** is formatted and added to the Item object's (**Row**) SubItems collection.

7.8   Project 8:   Monthly Payment Schedule Application

When a customer borrows money from a lender, part of the contract includes a loan repayment schedule. The schedule shows the following: the monthly payment amount; the contribution of each payment to the principal (which reduces the loan balance) and to the interest; and the remaining loan balance at the end of the month. Many commercial financial software packages perform this type of calculation. However, the calculations are straightforward, so we can easily create our own. The user interface for our application is shown in Figure 7.38.

Description of the Application

From Figure 7.38 you can see that the application requires the user to first enter three values: the loan amount, the annual interest rate, and the number of years of the loan. When the user clicks the Update Schedule button, these values are used to compute and display the table on the left side of the form. Selecting Exit from the File menu causes program execution to terminate.

Design of the Application

The developer must decide early on what type of controls to use for user interaction with the application. The values for loan amount and number of years must provide the user with the option to enter practically any values. This eliminates controls such as a ListBox or ComboBox where predefined values must exist. The other likely choices are either the TextBox or InputBox. However, in an

FIGURE 7.38

User Interface for
Monthly Payment
Schedule Application

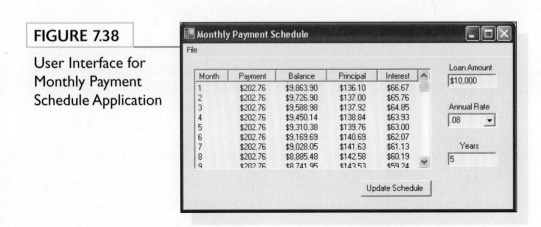

application like this, we want the user to see these values at all times and be able to easily change one or two of them and generate a new schedule at any time. With this in mind, TextBoxes are superior to the InputBox() function.

The annual interest rate presents a special problem. Users traditionally find it difficult to determine whether they should enter interest rates as percentages or as rates. For example, do they enter 8, 8%, or .08? Developers also seem to have a hard time wording the request so that it is clear to the user. These factors make the ComboBox a good alternative. The user can plainly see the format of the values. Our application, shown in Figure 7.38, expects the user to enter rates (e.g., .08). Another benefit of the ComboBox is that it provides a list of common rates, so the user may not need to type a number at all.

The payment schedule requires one line for each month. Thus we need a control that readily shows more than one line. The ListView fulfills this requirement perfectly.

The main piece of coding required by the application is the event procedure for the Update Schedule button. Good names for some of the variables needed by the procedure are **Years**, **LoanAmount**, **Rate**, **Payment**, **Balance**, **Month**, **MonthlyInterest**, and **MonthlyPrincipal**. Pseudocode for the procedure follows.

1. *Obtain values for* Years, LoanAmount, *and* Rate *from the appropriate controls on the form*
2. *Clear the ListView and set up the column headings*
3. *Compute* Payment *using Visual Basic .NET's Pmt() function (discussed below)*
4. *Set* Balance = LoanAmount
5. *For* Month = *1 To* Years * 12
    5.1 *Compute* MonthlyInterest = Balance * Rate / 12
    5.2 *Compute* MonthlyPrincipal = Payment – MonthlyInterest
    5.3 *Compute* Balance = Balance – MonthlyPrincipal
    5.4 *Add the month number (*Month*), the* Payment, *and the three computed amounts to the ListView*

Visual Basic .NET has many built-in financial functions in addition to the payment function, Pmt(). Some of these include IRR() (internal rate of return), PV() (present value), and NPV() (net present value). You should take some time to become familiar with these and others. The Pmt() function has the following syntax:

Pmt*(Rate, Nper, Pv)*

Rate is the periodic rate. Since our user specifies the rate as an annual rate, you need to divide this input value by 12 to get the monthly rate. *Nper* is the number of periods. Our user specifies the number of years, so you need to multiply this input value by 12 to get the number of months. *Pv* is the present value, which in our case is the loan amount. You should enter this into the function as a negative number so that your payments will have a positive sign. Payments and Pv always have opposite signs because they represent cash flowing in opposite directions.

Construction of the Application

The application is straightforward. Start by placing all the controls on the form and giving them appropriate names. Next, create the event procedure for the Exit menu item. Then compose the Form_Load event procedure to add the interest rate items to the ComboBox . Use a loop to generate the values (.05 to .15 in steps of .01). When the loop is done, set the SelectedIndex property to the interest rate you want displayed as the default.

Run the program and verify that the Annual Rate ComboBox contains the interest rate values, that your chosen default rate is selected, and that the ComboBox functions correctly. Next, create the event procedure for the Update Schedule button using the pseudocode presented earlier as a guide. Since this procedure does not share any data with other procedures, all variables should be local to the procedure. Your application should now be ready to run and test.

Chapter Summary

1. Loop structures are used to execute a group of statements repeatedly. Without loops, many types of problems could not be solved effectively.

2. There are two fundamental types of loops. In the first type, the number of iterations performed by the loop is unknown at the time the loop starts to execute. For this type of loop Visual Basic .NET provides the Do...Loop structure and its variations. In the second type of loop, the number of iterations performed by the loop is known at the time the loop starts to execute. For this type of loop Visual Basic .NET provides the For...Next structure.

3. Two variations of the Do...Loop structure are Do While...Loop and Do...Loop While. These structures continue to iterate "while a condition is true." The condition is any logical expression.

   The Do While...Loop and the Do...Loop While structures differ in where the condition is evaluated. In the Do While...Loop, the condition is evaluated at the beginning of the loop. If the condition is False initially, then the loop is terminated immediately—thus, it is possible for the loop to iterate zero times. In the Do...Loop While structure, the condition is evaluated at the end of the loop. Thus, the statements inside the loop will be executed at least one time.

4. Two other variations of the Do...Loop structure are Do Until...Loop and Do...Loop Until. These are identical to the While variations except that the condition used to control the loop is negated. For example, Do While X > 0 is equivalent to Do Until X <= 0. Whereas the Do While loop repeats "while a condition is true," the Do Until loop repeats "until a condition is true."

5. An important consideration of the Do...Loop variations is that the statements inside the loop must somehow change the values of the variables involved in the condition. For example, if the condition of a Do While loop is initially True, the loop starts to execute, and there must be a statement somewhere in the loop that can cause the condition to become False. Otherwise the loop will never stop iterating—it will be an infinite loop.

6. The For...Next loop structure uses a counter variable to control the number of iterations. When the For...Next loop begins to execute, it first sets its counter variable to a specified initial value. Before beginning each iteration, the loop compares the counter variable to an ending value. If the counter variable is greater than the ending value, the loop terminates. Otherwise, the body of the loop is executed. The loop then increments the counter variable by a specified step value, and the loop repeats as long as the value of the counter variable is less than or equal to the ending value.

7. Variations of the Do…Loop can be terminated early using the Exit Do statement. When this statement is executed, the loop is immediately terminated and execution continues with the first statement following the loop. Similarly, a For…Next loop can be terminated early using an Exit For statement.

8. The body of a loop can include another loop. In this case, the inner loop is called a nested loop. The nested loop operates independently of the outer loop and executes completely for each iteration of the outer loop.

9. The ListBox control provides a means of presenting the user with a list of items that can be selected. The selected item then can be used by the program in further processing. The developer can use the SelectionMode property to specify whether the user can select only one item or several items from the ListBox. If multiple selections are to be allowed, the developer can use the SelectedIndices and SelectedItems collections to determine which items were selected and the values of those selected items. To do this, the For Each… loop structure is used.

10. The ComboBox control is a combination of a ListBox and a TextBox. Thus, it combines the capabilities of a ListBox —providing a list of items for the user to select—with a TextBox in which the user can type a value if the list of items does not include what the user wants.

11. Both the ListBox and ListView components provide properties to access the items (and the indices of those items) selected by the user. These properties provide this information in a Collection. A collection is an object that stores zero or more items. To process a collection, one uses the For Each … structure. This structure loops through a collection once for each item within the collection.

12. The ListView component provides a way to display a list of icons (large and small) as well as text in a tabular form. Using the component to display tables of text involves adding text to the Items collection as well as adding text to each Items collection's SubItem collection. In addition, the table's heading is created by adding items to the component's ColumnHeaderCollection property.

Key Terms

Add method	Do Until…Loop	initialization
Clear method	structure	Insert method
Collection object	Do While…Loop	iteration
ComboBox	structure	ListBox control
counter	DropDownStyle property	ListView control
Details view	Exit Do statement	loop
Do…Loop structure	Exit For statement	loop body
Do…Loop Until	exiting the loop	nested loops
structure	For Each…Next	Remove method
Do…Loop While	structure	RemoveAt method
structure	For…Next structure	step amount
	infinite loop	termination condition

End-of-Chapter Problems

1. Study the following code segment (assume the variables have been declared appropriately).

```
Sum = 0
Count = 0
Do While X < 100
    Sum = Sum + X
    Count = Count + 1
Loop
Average = Sum / Count
```

What is wrong with this code? What needs to be done to fix it?

2. Explain the major difference between Do While...Loop and Do...Loop While. Can they be used interchangeably?

3. How are For...Next and Do While...Loop similar? How are they different?

4. Classify each of the following code segments as either "legal," "legal but not recommended," or "not legal." In all cases assume the variables have been declared appropriately.

   a.
   ```
   For i = 1 To 10
       i = i + 1
   Next
   ```
   b.
   ```
   For J = 1 To N
       X = InputBox("Enter a value")
       S = S + X
   Next
   ```
   c.
   ```
   For K = 1 To N
       For J = 1 To N
           MsgBox(K & J)
       Next
   Next
   ```
   d.
   ```
   For J = 1 To 10
       Do Until J > 5
           MsgBox(J)
       Loop
   Next
   ```

5. How many times will the MsgBox statement in the following code be executed? Specify your answer as a formula if possible.

   ```
   For J = 1 To N
       For K = 1 To M
           MsgBox("Count me")
       Next
   Next
   ```

6. Write a code segment that performs the following tasks: It should first ask the user to enter the number of items in a sales transaction. The code should then ask the user to enter the price and quantity sold for each item in the transaction set. It should sum the extended price (price times quantity) during this process. When all the items have been processed, the total price (the sum of extended prices) should be displayed to the user.

7. Consider the following code segment:

   ```
   For i = 1 To N Step X
       MsgBox(i)
   Next
   ```

Explain how the loop will behave if
a.   X is greater than 0.
b.   X is less than 0.
c.   X is equal to 0.

8. Assume you are presented with a situation for which a Do While…Loop is appropriate. Could one use a Do Until…Loop equivalently in this situation, without any qualifications? Explain.

9. What is the main difference between a ComboBox and a ListBox ?

10. Explain how a ListBox typically reacts to a click and how it typically reacts to a double-click.

Programming Problems

1. A check digit is a value associated with an identifier such as a bank account number. The purpose of the check digit is to help detect errors in data entry, such as transposing two digits of the account number or entering the wrong digits.

The check digit is derived from the account number using a specific procedure and is then appended to the account number. Subsequently, data entry personnel are required to enter both the account number and the check digit whenever the account number is needed. To check whether the account number was entered correctly, the check-digit calculation is recomputed using the entered account number, and the result is compared to the entered check digit. If they do not match, it is assumed that an error has been made in entering the account number.

For example, suppose that the account number is 436518 and the check digit calculation applied to it yields 6. Subsequently, data entry personnel enter the account number and check digit in the form 436518-6. If the account were entered incorrectly as 436618-6, the check digit calculation applied to 436618 would yield 2. Since the calculated check digit (2) is not equal to the entered check digit (6), the error would be detected.

There are several procedures used to derive check digits. The procedure just described is called the modulus-11 check-digit procedure. It works as follows:

a.   Associate weights with each digit of the original number. The weights are the integers 2, 3, 4, . . ., with the 2 being associated with the rightmost digit. For the account number 436518, the weights and their association with the digits are shown here.

Account No.	Weight
4	7
3	6
6	5
5	4
1	3
8	2

b. Multiply each digit times its weight. Sum these products.

Account No.	Weight	Digit x Weight	Sum
4	7	28	
3	6	18	
6	5	30	
5	4	20	
1	3	3	
8	2	16	115

c. Divide the sum by 11 and find the remainder. In this case, the remainder after dividing 115 by 11 is 5.

d. Subtract the remainder from 11. In this case, $11 - 5 = 6$. This is the check digit. In the case where the result is 10, make the check digit an X; and in the case where the result is 11, make the check digit a 0 (zero).

Using this information, compose a developer-defined function that takes an account number as a parameter, then computes and returns the check digit. To test your function, create a form that contains a TextBox, a Button, and a Label. The user enters an account number in the TextBox and then clicks the button, which should invoke your check-digit function and display the check digit in the label.

2. Write a developer-defined function that computes the factorial of a whole number. The factorial of a number, N, is defined as the product of the numbers from 1 to N. For example, 4 factorial (written as 4!) is defined as $1 \times 2 \times 3 \times 4 = 24$. Create a test form that allows the user to enter a number in a TextBox and click a button to request that the factorial be calculated. Display the answer in a Label. Be aware that factorials get large quickly. Use data types that support large numbers, but be prepared for possible overflow errors.

3. Create an application that computes the future value of an investment at the end of each year. The user should be able to specify the initial amount, the interest rate, and the number of compounding periods per year. The interest rate should use a drop-down ComboBox with values ranging from 5 percent to 12 percent in 1 percent increments. Periods per year should use a simple ComboBox with 1, 4, 12, and 365 as the valid values. The user also should be able to specify the first and last year to be displayed. Use a ListBox to display the yearly values. A sample solution is shown on page 325.

Use Visual Basic .NET's built-in FV() function to perform the calculations. See online help for details on the use of this function. Note that in this application, the payment argument for the FV() function will be zero.

4. Create a depreciation calculator. Your calculator should be able to compute both straight-line depreciation and sum-of-the-years' digits depreciation (SYD). Use Visual Basic .NET's built-in SLN() and SYD() functions to perform the actual calculations. Use option buttons to specify the depreciation method, a ComboBox to specify useful life, and TextBoxes for the remainder of the input parameters. Display your depreciation schedule in a ListView. A sample user interface is shown on page 325.

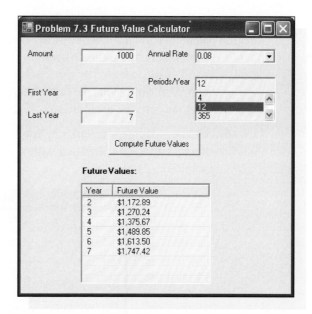

Programming Problem 3

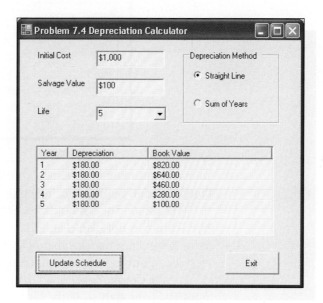

Programming Problem 4

This year's book value is defined as last year's book value minus this year's depreciation. For year 1, use the initial cost as last year's book value.

5. Write a developer-defined function that determines how long it will take for an investment amount to double in value. For example, if you invest $1,000 today at a given interest rate, how many years will it take for the investment to equal $2,000?

   The value at time period t can be calculated using the following formula:

   $$\text{Value}_t = \text{Value}_{(t-1)} * (1 + \text{InterestRate})$$

   Assume that compounding is performed annually. Therefore, the value returned by your function will be the first year in which the investment is at least twice as large as the initial amount.

Create a test form that allows the user to enter an investment amount and an annual interest rate. Provide a Button that, when clicked, invokes your function to determine the answer, then displays the answer in a message box.

Extra Credit: Write your solution so that it is not restricted to annual compounding. That is, let the user specify the number of compounding periods per year in addition to the other parameters.

6. Create a payment calculator. Your calculator should compute monthly payments for a loan calculated with a variety of different interest rates. A sample solution is shown here.

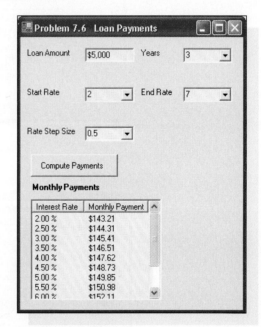

Your solution should use Visual Basic .NET's Pmt() function. Be aware that the Pmt() function requires decimal interest rates (e.g., 0.10 for 10%).

Your solution also should check to be sure that a loan amount is provided (the TextBox is not blank) and that the first interest rate is less than or equal to the last interest rate. If either of these conditions is not met, display an error message informing the user of the problem.

For the ComboBoxes, load the numbers 2 through 10 in the Number of Years list, 1 through 10 in the First Interest Rate list, and 2 through 12 in the Last Interest Rate list. Include Interest Rate Step Sizes of 0.1, 0.5, 1.0, and 2.0.

The ListView should be cleared before a new set of payments is displayed. That is, do not add a new set of payment calculations to the end of the current set.

ACCESSING DATA

Processing Databases

The programs we have written so far have demonstrated Visual Basic .NET's controls and programming language, as well as application design considerations and good programming techniques. But as business application programs, they fall short because of their limited ability to access data. To get data into these programs, we either included the data as part of the program itself or we designed the program so that users could key in information. But the data that even a small business must process into reports, customer invoices, or employee paychecks are far too extensive to be coded into a program or to be rekeyed by a human every time the program is run.

The way to efficiently manage data is to store them in files on disk. The data files and program are separate. When the program is executed, the user provides the name of a file that contains data to be processed, and the program reads and uses these data. Since data files are not part of any program, they never appear in a Visual Basic .NET project window. A data file simply exists on disk, ready to be used by any program that can correctly interpret its contents.

This practice is superior to making data part of the program for two reasons. First, the program need not be modified when the data change—only the data file needs to be modified. Second, different programs can share the same data files; this eliminates the need to replicate the data, and hence reduces data redundancy. Data redundancy has several negative effects, including excessive storage, the need to update data in more than one place, and the possibility that not all duplicate data items will get updated, resulting in inconsistent values for the same data item.

Managing large amounts of related data that are processed by different programs can be difficult unless the data and relationships are organized carefully. Most businesses achieve this by placing their data in a database. **A *database* is an organized collection of data describing entities (things) and relationships that exist between entities.** (Relationships and entities will be defined and discussed in detail in this chapter.) You can think of a database as a large data file on disk that contains related data organized in a particular way. An example of a noncomputer "database" is the phone book, which stores names, addresses, and phone numbers in a structured manner for many individuals; if you imagine such a list on a computer disk, you will begin to understand the arrangement and order of data in a database.

A business typically uses a program called a *database management system (DBMS)* to create and maintain a database that contains the company's data. After the database has been created, many different programs can access the data it contains. Commercially available DBMSs include Microsoft Access, Micrsoft SQL Server, and Oracle Corporation's Oracle.

Because databases are so widely used, Visual Basic .NET provides tools for developers to build database-access capability into their programs. In this chapter we explore some of these tools. To give you the background needed to understand how programs could work with databases, we begin with a discussion of database structure and use. We then turn to a discussion of ADO.NET, which provides the classes to support database access within the Microsoft .NET framework. Visual Basic .NET uses the various classes defined in ADO.NET to access and modify databases. Following this, we discuss how to write programs in Visual Basic .NET that access databases using ADO.NET objects. Finally we look at several helpful tools available within Visual Basic .NET that help us work with various database components.

We address two related topics in Appendix C. This appendix talks about configuring and using Microsoft's MSDE Server and also provides a brief introduction to the SQL Select statement.

Objectives

After studying this chapter, you should be able to

- Understand and use relational databases.

- Understand a subset of the ADO.NET object model including data providers, data adapter, connections, and datasets.

- Apply the ADO.NET object model within Visual Basic .NET to access databases.

- Use the properties and methods of the DataGrid control to display records from a dataset.

- Write SQL Select queries to extract data from a database.

- Bind controls such as TextBoxes and Labels to a dataset.

- Create Master/Detail datasets.

- Use several tools within Visual Basic .NET to manage and use databases.

8.1 A Relational Database Primer

The first step in writing programs that access data in a database is to understand how the database is arranged, and this section discusses these fundamentals. Since most databases in current use share a common structure, once you master the general principles you can quickly surmise what you need to know about any database in order to write programs that work with it.

Entities and Relationships

Every database contains two kinds of information:

1. *Entities*, **which are any of the things of interest to a business and about which the business collects data,** such as products, employees, suppliers, customers, purchases, and sales.

2. *Relationships,* **which express real-world associations between entities.** Examples of relationships among entities are products purchased by customers and employees responsible for particular sales.

Because a database can include a large number of entities and relationships, database designers often use an *entity-relationship diagram (ERD)* to document a database's structure.

The simple ERD in Figure 8.1 shows three entities: Publisher, Title, and Author. The data stored about a Publisher might include a publisher identifier, name, and address. The data stored about a Title might include the International Standard Book Number (ISBN), title, and publisher. The data stored about an Author might include an author identifier, name, and year born.

A relationship is represented in an ERD by a line joining two entities. The symbols at the ends of the line show an important fact about the relationship: "how many" of the entity at one end can be related to "how many" of the entity at the other end. The term *cardinality* is used to describe **the number of one entity that can be related to another entity.** Figure 8.2 shows the cardinality symbols and their meanings.

To interpret a relationship appearing in an ERD, you must read it in both directions: once from left to right and once from right to left. When you read from left to right, ignore the symbol at the left end of the line, and when you read from right to left, ignore the symbol at the right end of the line.

Let's interpret the relationship between Publisher and Title in Figure 8.1. When read from left to right, it means "a publisher can be related to zero or more titles." When read from right to left, it means "a title can be related to one publisher." Combining the interpretations from reading in both directions, we say that this is a one-to-many relationship. In the abstract language of the ERD, it says "one publisher is related to many titles and a title is related to one publisher." Common sense tells us that it expresses the real-world fact that any given publisher may publish many different titles, but any given title is published by a single publisher.

How about the relationship between Title and Author in Figure 8.1? When read from left to right it means "a title can be related to one or more authors." When read from right to left it means "an author can be related to one or more titles." This is a many-to-many relationship. The diagram indicates that any given title has at least one author (maybe more) and that any given author has written at least one title (maybe more).

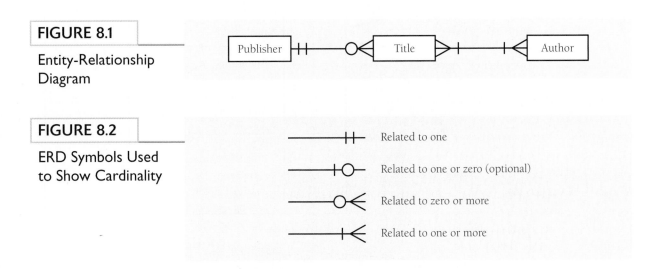

FIGURE 8.1

Entity-Relationship Diagram

FIGURE 8.2

ERD Symbols Used to Show Cardinality

Relational Database Tables

A database stores both the data describing the entities and the relationships that exist between the entities. Several approaches are used to store this information but the most common is the relational database. A *relational database* **stores the data for each entity in a table with rows and columns.** We use the relational database approach in this chapter because of its popularity and because it is compatible with Visual Basic .NET.

Figure 8.3 shows an example table that stores data about the Author entity. Note the alternative terms for the parts of relational database tables. The columns in the table are called either fields or attributes. The rows are referred to as either rows or records.

Each table in a relational database can have a *key field,* **which consists of a specific field or combination of fields guaranteed to be unique from one row to another.** In the Author table in Figure 8.3, Au_ID is the key field. Thus, you would not see two rows in this table that have the same value of Au_ID. **A key field that is a combination of two or more fields is called a** *compound key.*

From the ERD in Figure 8.1 we know that the Author entity and the Title entity are related to each other. Observe in Figure 8.3 that the Author table contains only data about authors; specifically, it does not contain any data that establish the relationship between "authors" and their "titles." The way we store data about a relationship depends on the cardinality of the relationship. We will return to this issue shortly.

Figure 8.4 shows example data from the Publisher and Title tables. Notice that the field PubId exists in both of these tables. In the Publisher table this field uniquely identifies the records; that is, each publisher has a different PubId. Therefore, PubId is the Publisher table's key field. In contrast, in the Title table

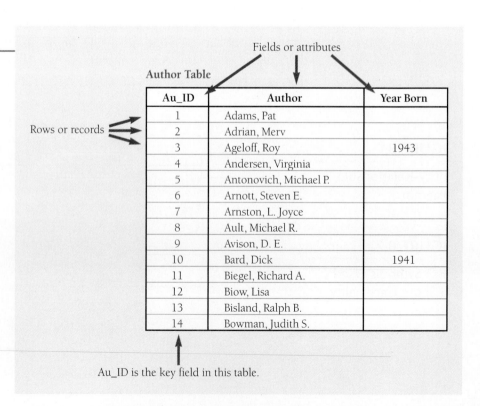

FIGURE 8.3

Author Table in a Relational Database

Author Table

Fields or attributes

Rows or records

Au_ID	Author	Year Born
1	Adams, Pat	
2	Adrian, Merv	
3	Ageloff, Roy	1943
4	Andersen, Virginia	
5	Antonovich, Michael P.	
6	Arnott, Steven E.	
7	Arnston, L. Joyce	
8	Ault, Michael R.	
9	Avison, D. E.	
10	Bard, Dick	1941
11	Biegel, Richard A.	
12	Biow, Lisa	
13	Bisland, Ralph B.	
14	Bowman, Judith S.	

Au_ID is the key field in this table.

(a) Publisher Table

PubId	Name	Address	City	State	Zip
1	ACM	11 W. 42nd St., 3rd flr.	New York	NY	10036
2	Addison-Wesley	Rte 128	Reading	MA	01867
3	Bantam Books	666 Fifth Ave	New York	NY	10103
4	Benjamin/Cummings	390 Bridge Pkwy.	Redwood City	CA	94065
5	Brady Pub.	15 Columbus Cir.	New York	NY	10023
6	Computer Science Press	41 Madison Ave	New York	NY	10010
7	ETN Corporation	RD 4, Box 659	Montoursville	PA	17754-9433
8	Gale	835 Penobscot Bldg	Detroit	MI	48226-4094
9	IEEE	10662 Los Vaqueros Circle	Los Alamitos	CA	90720
10	Intertext	2633 E. 17th Ave.	Anchorage	AK	99508
11	M&T Books	501 Galveston Dr	Redwood City	CA	94063-4728
12	Macmillan Education	175 Fifth Ave	New York	NY	10010
13	McGraw-Hill	1221 Ave of the Americas	New York	NY	10020
14	Microsoft Press	One Microsoft Way	Redmond	WA	98052-6399
15	Morgan Kaufmann	2929 Campus Dr, Suite 260	San Mateo	CA	94403

(b) Title Table

Title	Year Published	ISBN	PubId
Guide to ORACLE	1990	0-0702063-1-7	13
The database experts' guide to SQL	1988	0-0703900-6-1	10
Oracle/SQL; a professional programmer's guide	1992	0-0704077-5-4	13
SQL 400: A Professional Programmer's Guide	1994	0-0704079-9-1	52
Database system concepts	1986	0-0704475-2-7	13
Microsoft FoxPro 2.5 applications programming	1993	0-0705015-3-X	61
First look at—dBASE IV, version 1.5/2.0 for DOS	1994	0-0705107-5-X	80
Applying SQL in Business	1992	0-0705184-2-4	13
Database design	1977	0-0707013-0-X	13
Introduction to Oracle	1989	0-0770716-4-6	13
SQL—the standard handbook; based on the new SQL standard	1993	0-0770766-4-8	52
Paradox; the complete reference	1988	0-0788139-0-5	13
Paradox	1988	0-0788140-4-9	13
Paradox made easy	1988	0-0788141-3-8	16
Using dBASE IV	1988	0-0788147-5-8	16

FIGURE 8.4

Some Records from the Publisher and Title Tables

you can see more than one title with the same PubId. The PubId field is a non-key field in the Title table.

One-to-Many Relationships

When one table's key field appears in a second table and is not the key field in the second table, it is called a *foreign key* in the second table. Foreign keys link, or associate, the rows in the two tables. Specifically, foreign keys implement one-to-many relationships. The relationship is established by placing the key field of the "one" entity's table into the "many" entity's table as a foreign key.

Study the placement of the key and nonkey fields in the Publisher and Title tables. The first row of the Title table shows a book titled *Guide to ORACLE* published in 1990 by PubId 13. Using this value for PubId, we search the Publisher table to find a match. We find the match at row 13 and discover that the publisher is McGraw-Hill. The common field (PubId) allows us to link the two rows of the two tables; we can then use the combined fields of both rows to produce reports or to answer user questions about books and publishers.

Since PubId is unique in the Publisher table, we would expect to find only one match when we search this table for PubId = 13. This agrees with the ERD, which showed that a title can be related to one publisher. But if we search the Title table for PubId = 13, we find many matches. This also agrees with the ERD, which showed that a publisher can be related to many titles.

Many-to-Many Relationships

We also can link tables to establish many-to-many relationships. If you scan the Author table (Figure 8.3), you'll see that it contains no information to associate it with the Title table. Similarly, the Title table (Figure 8.4b) contains no information to associate it with the Author table. Many-to-many relationships are not established by foreign keys. So how do we implement a many-to-many relationship? The answer is by constructing an entirely **new table, called a *correlation table,* or *intersection table,* that contains the key fields from both tables for the entities in the many-to-many relationship.**[1] Figure 8.5 shows such a table, named Title/Author.

Verify the many-to-many relationship by looking down the ISBN column of the correlation table in Figure 8.5. Note that book 0-0702063-1-7 is associated with three authors (26, 65, and 104). Similarly, looking down the Au_ID column you can see that author 59 is associated with two titles (0-0704077-5-4 and 0-0704079-9-1).

Some correlation tables include additional data fields. These additional fields contain facts related to both entities. For example, in the Title/Author table we might want to store the royalties paid to each author for a specific book. In this way we could record different royalty amounts for each author/book combination.

FIGURE 8.5

Title/Author Table Used to Support a Many-To-Many Relationship

Title/Author Table

ISBN	Au_ID
0-0131985-2-1	13
0-0238669-4-2	113
0-0280042-4-8	11
0-0280042-4-8	120
0-0280095-2-5	171
0-0702063-1-7	26
0-0702063-1-7	65
0-0702063-1-7	104
0-0703900-6-1	96
0-0704077-5-4	59
0-0704077-5-4	99
0-0704079-9-1	59
0-0704079-9-1	74
0-0704079-9-1	99

[1] Correlation tables are described in Sally Shlaer and Stephen J. Mellor, *Object-Oriented Systems Analysis: Modeling the World in Data* (Englewood Cliffs, N.J.: Yourdon Press, 1988).

A correlation table that includes additional fields beyond the two key fields is called an *associative object.*

Normalized Databases

This text will not teach you to design databases. You will, however, have to write code to access data from databases, so you will encounter foreign keys, correlation tables, and associative objects. You may be curious as to how database designers decide where to place information. **The process of deciding what data go into each table is based on the desire to eliminate or reduce potential problems, and is called *normalization*.**[2]

One problem that normalization solves is excess data redundancy, that is, storing the same information more than once in a database. For example, suppose you are storing employee addresses. Without proper planning, you might store this information once in a payroll table and again in a human resources table. Obviously this redundancy requires extra storage space, but more importantly, it can lead to data inconsistencies. If an employee moves and notifies the payroll office, payroll will correct the address. However, unless the payroll department notifies the human resources department, the old address may remain in the human resources table. Now there are two different addresses for the same person.

The precise process associated with normalization is beyond the scope of this text. However, a simple rule can be used to judge whether a table is in satisfactory form, known as *third normal form*: **a table is in third normal form if the nonkey fields depend on the key field, the whole key field, and nothing but the key field.**[3]

In a normalized database each nonkey field must be determined only by the key field. A table with Employee Number (key field), Employee Name, Department Code, and Department Name is not in third normal form because Department Name can be determined by the Department Code (which is not the key field). That is, if you know what the Department Code is, you can tell what department you are talking about, so you know the Department Name. We would normalize this table by splitting it into two tables: one table with Employee Number (key field), Employee Name, and Department Code, and a second table with Department Code (key field) and Department Name.

In addition, if you have a compound key (two or more fields), then each nonkey field should be determined by all the fields that make up the compound key, not just some of them. For example, a table with Student Number and Course Identifier as the compound key, and Student Name and Grade as nonkey fields, is not in third normal form. The problem is that the Student Name can be determined by just part of the compound key, the Student Number.

---

[2] The inventor of relational databases, Edgar F. Codd, coined the term *normalization*: "We all have trouble organizing even our personal information. Businesses have those problems in spades. It seems to me essential that some discipline be introduced into database design. I called it normalization because then-President Nixon was talking a lot about normalizing relations with China. I figured that if he could normalize relations, so could I." [Matthew H. Rapaport, "A 'Fireside' Chat," *DBMS* 6, no. 13 (1993), pp. 54–60.]

[3] Data are said to be unnormalized (bad), in first normal form (1NF—better), in second normal form (2NF—better yet), or third normal form (3NF—reasonably good). There are forms beyond 3NF, but they generally solve relatively rare problems within the data.

Again, we would normalize this table by splitting it into two tables. The first would include the original compound key Student Number and Course Identifier, plus the Grade (which needs both fields to determine its value). The second table would include the Student Number (key field) and Student Name.

Exercise 8.1

For each of the following tables, indicate if they are normalized (third normal form) or not normalized. If they are not in third normal form, describe why this is true. The notation TableA = { field1 + field2 + field3 } means that the table (TableA) includes three fields (field1, field2, and field3) and the underline means that field1 is the key field. Clearly indicate any assumptions you are making.

   a. Employee = { EmplNo + Name + Address}

   b. Product = { ProdNo + Desc + Price + QuantityOnHand }

   c. Book = (BookId + AuthorID + Title + AuthorName }

   d. Transcript = { StudentNo + CourseId + Date + Grade }

Exercise 8.2

Referring to Exercise 8.1's instructions, determine if the following table definitions are either normalized (third normal form) or not normalized.

   a. Product = { ProdNo + Desc + CustNo + CustName + Price }

   b. Customer = { CustNo + Name + Address + PhoneNo }

   c. Transaction = { ProdNo + CustNo + Date + Quantity }

   d. SalesPerson = { EmplNo + EmplName + DeptCode + DeptName }

Database Queries

A relational database is made up of tables, each focusing on a single entity. But what happens when we want to use the database to answer questions, called queries in database terminology? Often the data needed to answer the query come from more than one table. Thus, with a relational database, one must be able to combine data from several tables in order to provide useful information to the user.

Most relational database systems use a query language called **structured query language (SQL) to specify how to combine data in related tables and how to select only the desired data.** Visual Basic .NET uses SQL, which we discuss in greater detail in Appendix C. Let's look at a simple query now, to complete our introduction to relational databases.

Suppose that you have a database with the three tables shown in Figure 8.6. Suppose, too, that the user of this database wants to query the database by asking for a list of all students who completed BA 420. The user wants the list to include the student number (StNo), student name (StName), course identifier (CourseId), course name (CourseName), and grade (Grade). The data needed to answer this query come from all three tables. The common fields in the three tables make it possible to determine which rows are appropriate to answer the query.

The computer answers the query by searching the tables for the data it needs. In this case, it starts out in the Course table and finds a match for BA 420 in row 2. The computer now has access to the correct course name. Then the computer searches the Transcript table row by row looking at the CourseId field. Each time it finds a match with BA 420 (rows 2, 3, and 4), it uses the value of

FIGURE 8.6

Sample Database
with Three Tables

Student Table

StNo	StName
123	Jim
543	Sue
333	Joe

Course Table

CourseId	CourseName
BA 310	Programming
BA 420	Database Design
BA 430	Systems Analysis

Transcript Table

StNo	CourseId	Grade
123	BA 310	A
123	BA 420	B
543	BA 420	A-
333	BA 420	B
333	BA 430	B-

the student number to search the Student table. For example, the first match, found in row 2 of the Transcript table, yields student number 123. This student number is found in row 1 of the Student table and the name Jim is extracted. The computer now has all the information it needs to produce one line of output (the first student it found who took BA 420). This process continues with the second match for BA 420 in the Transcript table (row 3), and then again for the next match (row 4).

The process of searching tables and matching common fields is the general solution employed by the computer to answer relational database queries. There are additional options and types of queries, but the basic idea is the same.

It should be pointed out that using a query language is different from the procedural programming we have seen so far. With query language code, you do not tell the computer how to reach a goal, but instead pass a request to the DBMS. The DBMS then determines how to accomplish the task. The developer's role with a query is to determine how to phrase the request so that the desired result is returned by the DBMS.

8.2   An Introduction to ADO.NET

In order to manage data in a database, Visual Basic .NET uses the technology provided by ADO.NET. *ADO.NET* (ActiveX Data Objects) **is a comprehensive technology that includes an extensive set of classes to manage data.** It is very complex and entire books have been published dealing exclusively with the various aspects of the technology. Our intent in this chapter and in Chapter 9 is to provide a foundation for using the ADO.NET technology in the context of Visual Basic .NET, but there will be many features that will not be covered due to extensive nature of the technology.

In this chapter we cover the foundations of ADO.NET and how this technology can be used in the context of relational databases. We also cover some of the wizards and tools available within Visual Basic .NET to work with relational databases. In Chapter 9, we cover how ADO.NET can be used to manage data in a format known as XML (e**X**tensible **M**arkup **L**anguage).

An Overview of ADO.NET

A simplified model[4] of the classes we will be using from ADO.NET is shown in Figure 8.7.

Let us walk through Figure 8.7 to see how everything works within the ADO.NET model. We start with the actual database. This could be a Microsoft SQL Server database, a Microsoft Access database, an Oracle database, or practically any other type of database. A Visual Basic .NET application does not actually manage the database—it calls on the appropriate DBMS by passing it commands typically using SQL (structured query language). This point is important to understand because it means that our Visual Basic .NET application is relatively independent from any specific DBMS. If one decides to change from one DBMS to another, it requires changing very few statements in the Visual Basic .NET application.

As you can see in the Figure 8.7, ADO.NET uses a **DataProvider object to interact directly with the database and its DBMS.** The DataProvider class has two classes to help in the interaction. The first is the Connection class. **A Connection object makes the physical connection to the database.** To do this, it needs to know information such as where the database is located and the appropriate technology that is needed to make this physical connection. The second class is the **DataAdapter** class. This class's **primary responsibility is to act as an intermediary between the database and a dataset** (discussed next). It is also responsible for managing how any changes in the dataset should be reconciled against the actual database.[5]

In addition to the DataProvider, ADO.NET uses the DataSet class to hold the actual data. The easiest way to think about **a DataSet is as a collection of one or more tables.** In order for these tables to be related, the dataset also has a

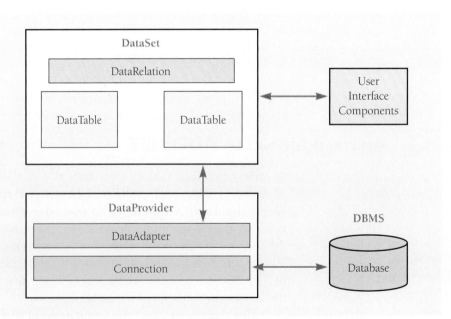

FIGURE 8.7

Classes to Be Used from ADO.NET

---

4   As we mentioned earlier, this is not a complete description of the ADO.NET object model. However, it does accurately depict the classes that we will be covering in this chapter.

5   There is also a Command class that is involved in this process. However, we will not be working directly with any objects from the Command class.

DataRelation class. **Objects from this class include information on how two tables are related including the fields common in the two tables that are used to relate one to the other.**

User interface components such as TextBoxes, ComboBoxes, and DataGrids can work directly with a DataSet object for displaying and modifying data that are managed by the dataset.

In summary, assume that you want to show a list of state abbreviations in a ComboBox and that these abbreviations are stored in a database. Starting with the ComboBox, it would need to be associated with a dataset that contained a table with 50 rows, one for each state abbreviation. In order to get these data, the dataset would need to be associated with a DataAdapter that in turn was associated with a Connection. Finally this Connection would talk directly with the DBMS where the abbreviations were originally stored.

In the sections that follow, we will use a wizard to help us create our Data-Adapter and Connection objects. We also will use Visual Basic's Generate Dataset tool to help build the dataset component(s). We will begin with datasets that have a single table and later move to more complex datasets that have multiple tables and a DataRelation to associate the tables.

8.3   Using ADO.NET with Visual Basic .NET

Now that we have seen the components needed to support relational database access using ADO.NET, we turn our attention to how we use this technology within Visual Basic .NET. We will look at four different applications and will be using the "pubs" database that comes with Visual Basic .NET. We also will be using the Microsoft Data Engine (MSDE) that also comes with Visual Basic .NET. MSDE is a desktop version of Microsoft's SQL Server. To see information on using MSDE and to install MSDE (if not already installed), see Appendix C.

Data Access Using the DataGrid Control

The *DataGrid* **control provides a method of displaying records from a database in a grid-like manner.** By setting several properties of this control, it is very easy to associate it to the records in a dataset. However, before discussing the DataGrid, we need to build a DataAdapter and DataSet. We assume that a new Windows Application project has been created. When we are done, we will have a DataGrid on our form that will display records from the publishers table in the "pubs" database.

Building the DataAdapter

Visual Basic .NET provides a wizard to help create a DataAdapter. We will take advantage of this wizard to simplify the process and minimize the amount of code we have to write.

If you look at the Data tab on the Toolbar, you will see a control labeled OleDbDataAdapter. Figure 8.8 shows this tool. Since we are using the MSDE server, we could also choose the SqlDataAdapter, which is optimized for working with SQL Server 7.0 or later. We will use the OleDbDataAdapter because it is more generic, providing ADO.NET access to any OLE DB-compatible data source.

If you place an OleDbDataAdapter on the form, the Data Adapter Configuration Wizard starts automatically. After displaying an Introduction page, the next page is used to establish a connection to the actual database. Figure 8.9 shows this page.

As you see in Figure 8.9, a connection already exists on the computer that the example is running on. If a connection has not been created, you need to click on the New Connection… button. Doing so brings up a dialog box like the one shown in Figure 8.10.

As shown in Figure 8.10, you need to complete the information in three areas. The first is the name of the database server. In this example, the server is named PICO\NetSDK. The name of the server on the computer can be found by placing the cursor over the icon of the server manager on the Start bar. Figure 8.11 shows how the name of the server is displayed when the cursor is placed over the server manager icon.

The second thing you must specify is information needed to log on to the server. You should select "Use Windows NT Integrated security" unless instructed to do otherwise by your instructor.

Finally you need to specify the database. The drop-down list shows all the databases installed on the server. You should see the database named "pubs" and you should select this and then click on OK. Note that if no databases are shown or if you see an error message, this means that something is wrong in either step 1 or 2.

After completing the Data Connection page and clicking on Next, you will see the Query Type page. As shown in Figure 8.12, you should select the "Use SQL statements" option.

The next page, shown in Figure 8.13, is used to specify the SQL query. **SQL (Structured Query Language) is the industry standard way of specifying**

FIGURE 8.8

The OleDbDataAdapter Tool

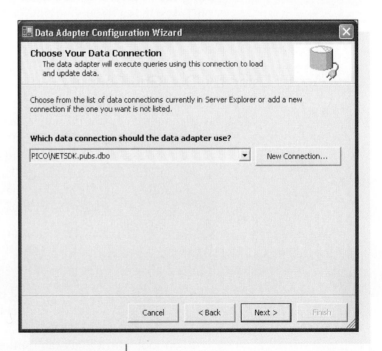

FIGURE 8.9

The Data Connection Page of the Data Adapter Configuration Wizard

FIGURE 8.10

Setting Up a
Connection to a
Database

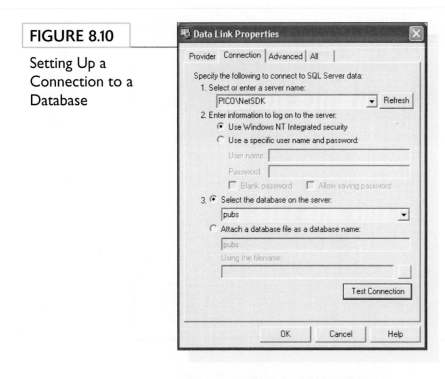

FIGURE 8.11

Determining the
Name of the Server

FIGURE 8.12

Specifying the Query
Type

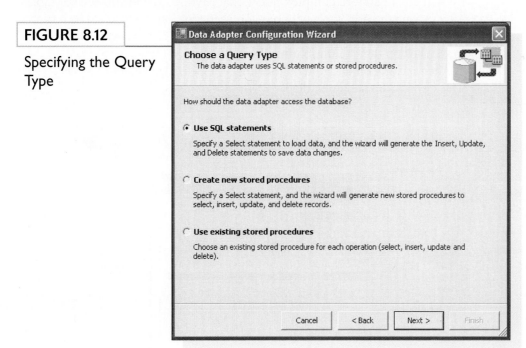

the data that you want to extract from the database. Appendix C provides details on the syntax of the SQL select statement that is used to perform an SQL query. However, this wizard provides a Query Builder tool that automates the creation of an SQL Select statement.

FIGURE 8.13

Specifying the SQL
Query

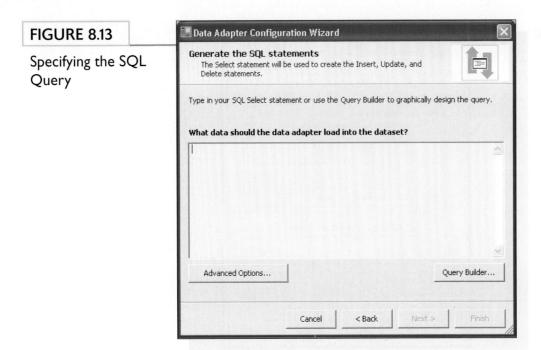

If you click on the Query Builder... button, you will see the dialog box shown in Figure 8.14. In this initial dialog, you must specify the table(s) that contains the data you want to query. For this example, we want to query the "publishers" table so we select it and then click on Add and then on Close. Later we will create a more complex query that involves data from several tables. After closing the Add Table window, you need to select the fields to be retrieved by clicking on the appropriate check boxes. For this case we want all the fields, so we click on the "* (All Columns)" check box (see Figure 8.15).

After clicking on OK, you will see the SQL Select statement that was created by the wizard, as shown in Figure 8.16.

FIGURE 8.14

Selecting the
Publishers Table to
Be Used in a Query

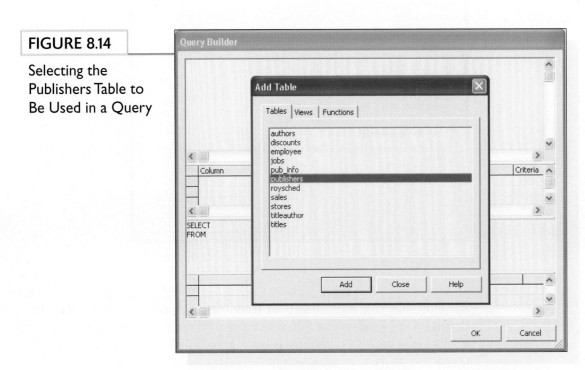

FIGURE 8.15

Selecting "* (All Columns)" from the Publishers Table

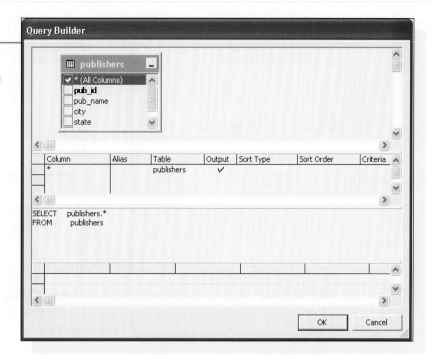

FIGURE 8.16

The SQL Select Statement Created by the Wizard

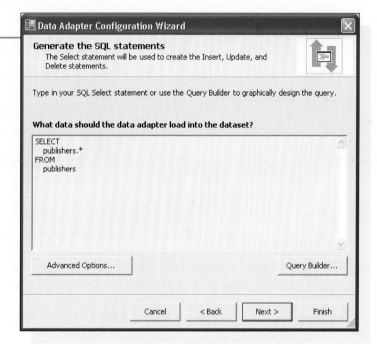

Click on Next and you will see a summary of the actions performed by the wizard. As seen in Figure 8.17, the wizard generates Select, Insert, Update, and Delete statements. Thus, you not only have the ability to see the selected records, you also have the ability to insert new records and update or delete an existing record.

Clicking on Finish completes the process. As you see in Figure 8.18, an OleDbDataAdapter and OleDbConnection have been added to the project and are shown in the tray below the Form Designer.

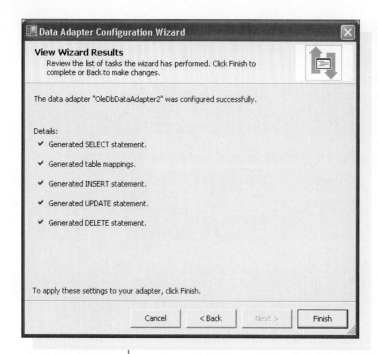

FIGURE 8.17

A Summary of the Actions Performed
by the Wizard

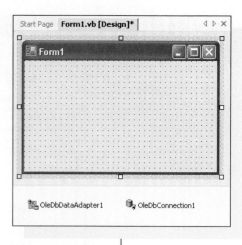

FIGURE 8.18

The OleDbDataAdapter1 and
OleDbConnection1 Added to
the Project

Building the DataSet

Now that we have created a DataAdapter, we need to create a DataSet. Be sure
that the Form Designer is selected and then select Generate Dataset... from the
Data menu. A dialog box like the one shown in Figure 8.19 will be displayed.
As seen in this figure, a new dataset is being created with the name "dsPublishers". This dataset is associated with the publishers table and SQL Select
statement as defined in OleDbDataAdapter1 that we created earlier. The Check-
Box labeled "Add this dataset to the designer" also should be checked.

After clicking on the New radio button, adding the dataset name "dsPublishers", and ensuring that "Add this dataset..." is checked, click on OK. You
should now see the dataset added to the designer (Figure 8.20). Note that the
name in the designer is DsPublishers1, not dsPublishers as shown in Figure
8.19. This is because you are creating a class named dsPublishers in the Create
Dataset window (Figure 8.19). In Figure 8.20 you are seeing an object named
DsPublishers1 that was instantiated from the class dsPublishers and placed in
the design tray by Visual Basic .NET.

Adding the DataGrid

We are now ready to add a DataGrid to the form and set its properties to connect it to the DataAdapter and DataSet. The DataGrid is found on the Windows
Forms tab in the Toolbox, as shown in Figure 8.21.

Place a DataGrid on the form. After doing so, set the DataSource and
DataMember properties as shown in Figure 8.22. These two properties are the
only properties you need to set to establish the relationship between the
DataGrid and the actual dataset.

FIGURE 8.19

Creating a Dataset

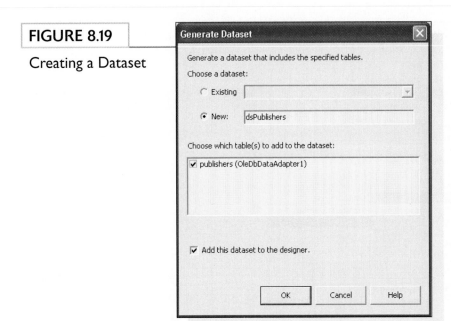

FIGURE 8.20

The DsPublishers1
DataSet Added to
the Form Designer

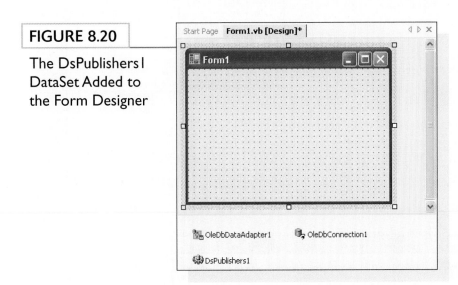

FIGURE 8.21

The DataGrid in the
Toolbox

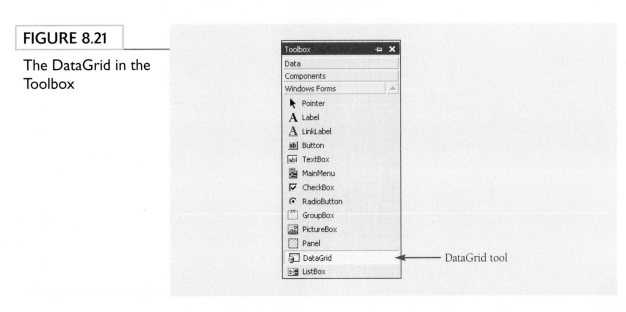

FIGURE 8.22

Selecting the
DataSource and
DataMember
Properties for
the DataGrid

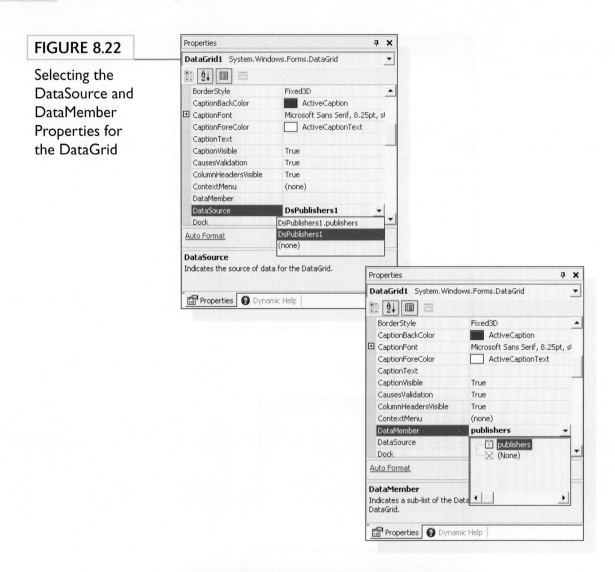

FIGURE 8.23

The DataGrid
after Setting the
DataSource and
DataMember
Properties

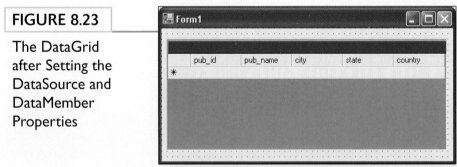

The DataGrid on the form will show the fields you specified in the SQL Select statement as column headings (see Figure 8.23).

If you run the application at this time, you will see the DataGrid but no data will be displayed (the values "(null)" will be displayed). The reason for this is because the dataset has not been "filled" with the data from the DataAdapter. Add a Button to the form and then create a Click event like the one shown in Figure 8.24.

The statement **DsPublishers1.Clear()** clears the DataSet (DsPublishers1) of any data by removing all rows in all tables. Then the statement **OleDbDataAdap-**

FIGURE 8.24

Code to Fill the
DataGrid with Data

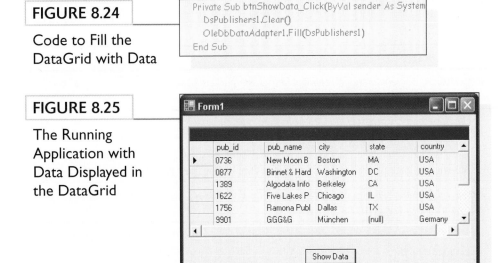

```
Private Sub btnShowData_Click(ByVal sender As System
    DsPublishers1.Clear()
    OleDbDataAdapter1.Fill(DsPublishers1)
End Sub
```

FIGURE 8.25

The Running
Application with
Data Displayed in
the DataGrid

ter1.Fill(DsPublishers1) adds or refreshes rows in the dataset to match those in the data source (database) with which the dataset is associated. When you run the application and click on the Show Data button, you should see the records as shown in Figure 8.25.

The DataGrid Control

As we just saw, the DataGrid control is designed to display the data stored in a dataset (as well as other data sources not covered here). It is an extremely flexible control and somewhat complex with many useful properties and methods. In addition to displaying the rows from a table, if the DataGrid is bound to data with multiple related tables, the grid can display expanders in each row. **An expander allows navigation from a parent table to a child table.** Clicking on a node displays the child table, and clicking the Back button displays the original parent table. In this fashion, the grid displays the hierarchical relationships between tables. We will see an example of this later.

Properties

Some of the most common properties of the DataGrid control are shown in Table 8.1. We will illustrate many of these properties in examples.

Methods

There are a number of methods that can be used to change the appearance of the DataGrid as well as associate it to a dataset at run time. Table 8.2 shows the common methods of the DataGrid control and explains what they do.

Exercise 8.3

Create a Windows Application like the one that was just described except display all the fields in the titles table from the "pubs" database. Use a DataGrid to display the records from the table.

Table 8.1 Properties of the DataGrid control

Property	Value
Name	(grd) *Gets or sets the name of the control.*
AllowSorting	*Gets or sets a Boolean value indicating whether the grid can be resorted by clicking on a column header.*
AlternatingBackColor	*Gets or sets the background color of alternating rows for a ledger appearance. By default, all rows have the same color (the BackColor property of the control). When you set the AlternatingBackColor to a new color, every other row is set to the new color. To reset the alternating background color to its default value, set the property to Color.Empty.*
BackColor	*Gets or sets the background color of the grid. The BackColor property determines the color of rows in the grid.*
BackgroundColor	*Gets or sets the color of the nonrow area of the grid. The BackgroundColor determines the color of the nonrow area of the grid, which is only visible when no table is displayed or if the grid is scrolled to the bottom, or if only a few rows are contained in the grid.*
BorderStyle	*Gets or sets the grid's border style. Available styles include BorderStyle.None, BorderStyle.FixedSingle, and BorderStyle.Fixed3D.*
CaptionBackColor	*Gets or sets the background color of the caption area.*
CaptionFont	*Gets or sets the font of the grid's caption.*
CaptionForeColor	*Gets or sets the foreground color of the caption area.*
CaptionText	*Gets or sets the text of the grid's window caption.*
CaptionVisible	*Gets or sets a Boolean value that indicates whether the grid's caption is visible.*
ColumnHeadersVisible	*Gets or sets a Boolean value indicating whether the column headers of a table are visible.*
CurrentCell	*Gets or sets which cell has the focus. Not available at design time. Uses a DataGridCell class to set the current cell. For example, to set the current cell of the DataGrid grdDemo to row 1 and column 1, you would say grdDemo.CurrentCell = New DataGridCell(1,1).*
CurrentRowIndex	*Gets or sets index of the selected row. The DataGrid uses zero-based indexing with the first row and first column having the index value 0.*
DataMember	*Gets or sets the specific list in a DataSource for which the DataGrid control displays a grid. If a DataSource contains multiple sources of data, you should set the DataMember to one of the sources. For example, if the DataSource is a DataSet that contains three tables named Customers, Orders, and OrderDetails, you must specify one of the tables to bind to.*
DataSource	*Gets or sets the data source for which the grid is displaying data.*
Enabled	*Gets or sets a Boolean value indicating whether the control can respond to user interaction.*
FirstVisibleColumn	*Gets the index of the first visible column in a grid.*
ForeColor	*Gets or sets the foreground color (typically the color of the text) property of the DataGrid control.*
GridLineColor	*Gets or sets the color of the grid lines.*
GridLineStyle	*Gets or sets the line style of the grid. Options include DataGridLineStyle.None and DataGridLineStyle.Solid.*
HeaderBackColor	*Gets or sets the background color of all row and column headers.*
HeaderFont	*Gets or sets the font used for column headers.*

continued

Table 8.1 *Continued*

Property	Value
HeaderForeColor	*Gets or sets the foreground color of headers.*
ParentRowsBackColor	*Gets or sets the background color of parent rows.*
ParentRowsForeColor	*Gets or sets the foreground color of parent rows.*
ParentRowsVisible	*Gets or sets a Boolean value indicating whether the parent rows of a table are visible.*
PreferredColumnWidth	*Gets or sets the default width of the grid columns in pixels.* Set this property before resetting the DataSource and DataMember properties or the property will have no effect.
ReadOnly	*Gets or sets a Boolean value indicating whether the grid is in read-only mode.*
RowHeadersVisible	*Gets or sets a Boolean value that specifies whether row headers are visible.*
RowHeaderWidth	*Gets or sets the width of row headers.* The default is 50.
SelectionBackColor	*Gets or sets the background color of selected rows.*
SelectionForeColor	*Gets or sets the foreground color of selected rows.*

Table 8.2 Methods of the DataGrid control

Method	Behavior
Collapse(*row*)	*Collapses child relations, if any exist for all rows or a specified row.* The argument *row* indicates the number of the row to collapse. If set to −1, all rows are collapsed.
Expand(*row*)	*Displays child relations, if any exist, for all rows or a specific row.* The argument *row* indicates the number of the row to expand. If set to −1, all rows are expanded.
IsExpanded(*row*)	*Gets a Boolean value that indicates whether a specified row's node is expanded or collapsed.*
IsSelected(*row*)	*Gets a value Boolean indicating whether a specified row is selected.*
Select(*row*)	*Selects a specified row.*
SetDataBinding(*dataSourceObject, dataMemberString*)	*Sets the DataSource and DataMember properties at run time.*
UnSelect(row)	*Unselects a specified row.*

Example 8.1

USING A COMPLEX QUERY

Note: **For this and the remaining examples that deal with databases, please read the ReadMe documents that are included with the examples. This document provides information on setting up the examples to connect to the MSDE on your computer.**

In this example we use a DataGrid to display the records from several tables. The "pubs" database includes three tables (among others) named authors, titleauthor, and titles. These tables are related to each other as shown in the ERD in Figure 8.26.

We will create a query that displays the author's last name and phone number; the book's title, price, and year-to-date sales; and the author's royalty percentage for a specific book. We begin by creating a new Windows Application project. As described previously, we first need to build an OleDbDataAdapter that is connected to the "pubs" database. When we get to "Generate the SQL statement" dialog, click on the Query Builder button, add the three tables, and select the six fields as shown in Figure 8.27.

After completing the Data Adapter wizard, view the code generated by Visual Basic .NET for OleDbAdapter1 by right-clicking on this component and then selecting View Code. Open the region titled "Windows Form Designer generated code" by clicking on the + sign to the left of the region box and scroll down until you see the SQL statement autogenerated by Visual Basic .NET. Figure 8.28 shows this code.

Unfortunately this SQL Select statement is not what we want. Visual Basic .NET added four additional fields that we did not ask for.[6] We can easily correct the situation by simply removing the extra code. The code we need to delete is highlighted in Figure 8.29.

Highlight this code and delete it. Now we need to build the dataset. Select Generate Dataset… from the Data menu and create a New DataSet named dsAdvancedQuery (remember that you must have the Form Designer selected). The authors table should already be selected.

FIGURE 8.27

The Query Builder
Dialog Showing the
Tables and Fields for
Our Query

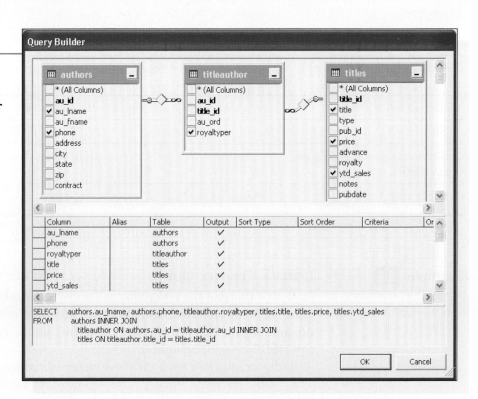

---

6   Microsoft may change this either in a future Service Release or the next major release. Thus, you may not have to make the edit to the SQL described above.

```
'OleDbSelectCommand1
'
Me.OleDbSelectCommand1.CommandText = "SELECT authors.au_lname, authors.phone, titleauthor.royaltyper, titles.title, tit" & _
"les.price, titles.ytd_sales, authors.au_id, titleauthor.au_id AS Expr1, titleaut" & _
"hor.title_id, titles.title_id AS Expr2 FROM authors INNER JOIN titleauthor ON au" & _
"thors.au_id = titleauthor.au_id INNER JOIN titles ON titleauthor.title_id = titl" & _
"es.title_id"
```

FIGURE 8.28

The SQL Select Statement Generated by Visual Basic .NET

```
'OleDbSelectCommand1
'
Me.OleDbSelectCommand1.CommandText = "SELECT authors.au_lname, authors.phone, titleauthor.royaltyper, titles.title, tit" & _
"les.price, titles.ytd_sales, authors.au_id, titleauthor.au_id AS Expr1, titleaut" & _
"hor.title_id, titles.title_id AS Expr2 FROM authors INNER JOIN titleauthor ON au" & _
"thors.au_id = titleauthor.au_id INNER JOIN titles ON titleauthor.title_id = titl" & _
"es.title_id"
```

FIGURE 8.29

Code That We Want to Delete from the Autogenerated SQL Statement

Add a DataGrid to the form and set its DataSource property to DsAdvanced-Query1 and its DataMember property to authors. Finally create a Form_Load event and add the code shown in Figure 8.30.

When you run the application, you should see the form shown in Figure 8.31. The DataGrid on this form has its AlternatingBackColor property set to DarkKhaki and its ReadOnly property set to True. The user also has clicked on the au_lname heading to sort the rows by this field.

FIGURE 8.30

The Form_Load Event That Populates the DataGrid

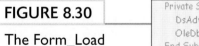

```
Private Sub Form1_Load(ByVal sender As System.Obje
    DsAdvancedQuery1.Clear()
    OleDbDataAdapter1.Fill(DsAdvancedQuery1)
End Sub
```

FIGURE 8.31

Example 8.1 at Run Time

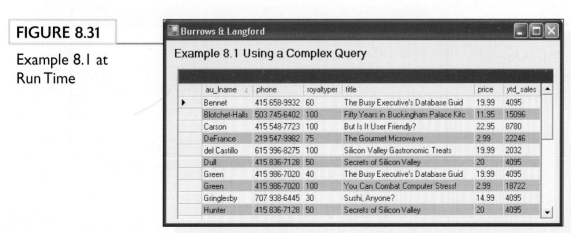

Exercise 8.4

Modify Example 8.1 so that it displays the author's state and the title's price in addition to the fields already displayed.

Exercise 8.5

Using the sales, titles, and stores tables in the pub database, create a Windows Application that uses a DataGrid to display the quantity sold at each store for each title. Include the qty, title, stor_name, and state (from the stores table) as fields in the DataGrid.

Example 8.1a

USING A COMPLEX QUERY WITHOUT USING THE DATA ADAPTER CONFIGURATION WIZARD

In the first two applications (the simple and complex queries), we used the Data Adapter Configuration Wizard to configure an OleDbDataAdapter. Some people prefer not to use wizards because of the argument that the underlying details of the process are hidden. By hiding these details, it then becomes more difficult to set up configurations that are not supported by the wizard.

In this variation of Example 8.1, we manually configure the DataAdapter using the Properties window. Once the data adapter is configured, the remaining steps of Example 8.1 continue unchanged. We will assume that a new connection must be created as well as a new data adapter.

We begin by first creating a new project and then dragging an OleDbDataAdapter to the new form. When the Data Adapter Configuration Wizard appears, we click on Cancel. The Form Designer with the new data adapter in the designer tray should appear as seen in Figure 8.32.

With the data adapter selected, we need to modify some properties in the Properties window. The Properties window for the OleDbDataAdapter1 is shown in Figure 8.33.

We first change the name to odaAuthorTitles. We then click on the SelectCommand plus sign (expansion symbol) to view the SelectCommand properties. Figure 8.34 shows the expanded SelectCommand.

We first need to define a Connection. Click on the Connection property's value box, click on the drop-down arrow, and then select New from the list of choices. Figure 8.35 shows this drop-down list.

After selecting New, a new Data Link Properties dialog box just like shown in Figure 8.10 will be displayed. Complete this dialog box as shown in Figure 8.36.

FIGURE 8.32

Example 8.1a with the OleDbDataAdapter Added to the Designer Tray

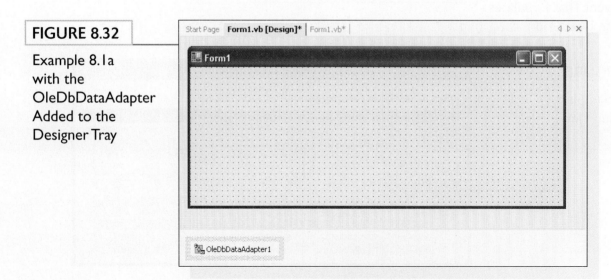

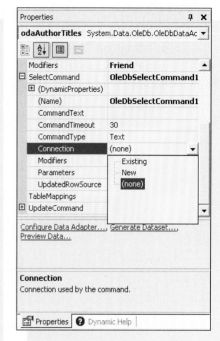

FIGURE 8.33

Properties Window for the OleDbDataAdapter1 Component

FIGURE 8.34

Expanded SelectCommand Property

FIGURE 8.35

Choices Available for the Connection Property of the SelectCommand

FIGURE 8.36

The Data Link Properties Dialog Box Used to Define the Connection

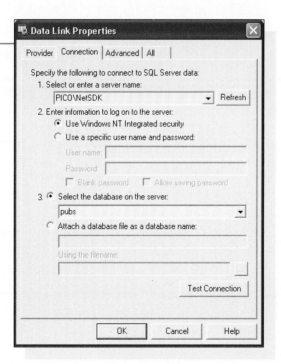

Next we need to define the CommandText property. Click on this property and click on the ellipses and a Query Builder window will be displayed. Fill this out like that shown in Figure 8.27 (except do not select price). When you are done it should look like that shown in Figure 8.37.

FIGURE 8.37

Building the SQL using the Query Builder Tool

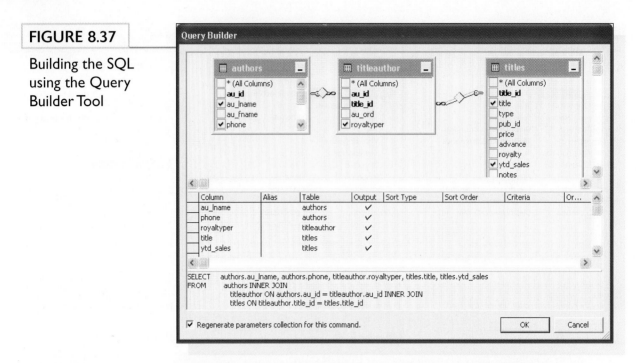

FIGURE 8.38

Example 8.1a at Run Time

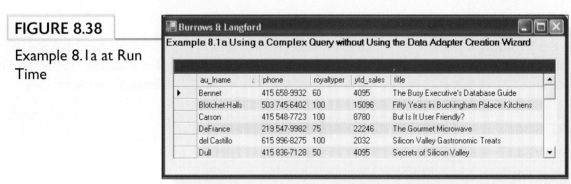

From this point on, the process is the same as discussed in Example 8.1. You need to create a dataset and add a DataGrid to the form and set its DataSource property equal to DsAuthorTitle1._Table. You then add a Form_Load event with code like that shown in Figure 8.30. The running application is shown in Figure 8.38.

Note that using this approach generated SQL that did not need to be modified as was the case with the SQL created within the Data Adapter Configuration Wizard. In addition, only an SQL Select statement was defined. If you want to define an SQL Insert, Delete, or Update command, you would need to modify the CommandText properties for these three properties of the data adapter.

In the examples that follow, we will use the Data Adapter Configuration Wizard but feel free to experiment with setting the values manually as was done in Example 8.1a.

Updating a Table

ADO.NET supports the updating of the original data source if you want to include that capability in your application. As the user changes data in a Data-Grid, for example, the in-memory copy of the data stored in the DataSet object also is changed. The data adapter can then cause the original data source to be changed by using its Update method. This method examines every record in the specified data table in the dataset and, if a record has changed, sends the appropriate Update, Insert, or Delete command to the database.

Example 8.2

UPDATING A DATABASE

This example allows the user to make changes to records in the authors table in the "pubs" database. The data are automatically loaded into a DataGrid when the form is loaded. When the user wants to save changes, she clicks on the Save Changes button. Figure 8.39 shows Example 8.2 at run time. In this example, a new record has been added (au_id = 111-11-1111) and the phone number for Heather McBadden has been changed.

For this example we have created an OleDbDataAdapter with an SQL statement that includes all the fields from the authors table. A dataset was then created using the DataAdapter and the authors table. Finally, a DataGrid was added with its DataSource property set to DsAuthors1 and the DataMember property set to authors.

The code for the form's Load event and the Click event for the Save Changes button is shown in Figure 8.40. In this code you can see the use of the Update method that causes contents of the DataSet DsAuthors1 being used to update the actual database data associated with the data adapter (OleDbDataAdapter1).

Exercise 8.6

Modify Exercise 8.3 so that it has the ability to save changes.

Exercise 8.7

The DataSet component has a property named HasChanges that is a Boolean property set to true if the dataset includes values that have been changed and differ from the data in the underlying database. Modify Example 8.2 by removing the Save Changes button and replacing it with an Exit button. The Click

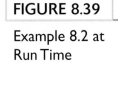

FIGURE 8.39

Example 8.2 at Run Time

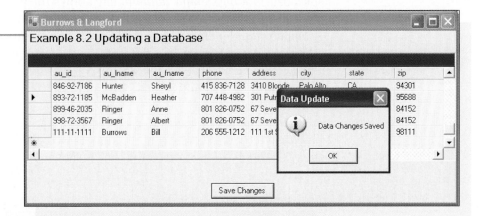

FIGURE 8.40

Code for Example 8.2

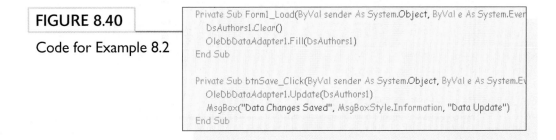

```
Private Sub Form1_Load(ByVal sender As System.Object, ByVal e As System.Even
    DsAuthors1.Clear()
    OleDbDataAdapter1.Fill(DsAuthors1)
End Sub

Private Sub btnSave_Click(ByVal sender As System.Object, ByVal e As System.Ev
    OleDbDataAdapter1.Update(DsAuthors1)
    MsgBox("Data Changes Saved", MsgBoxStyle.Information, "Data Update")
End Sub
```

event for the Exit button should use the HasChanges property to determine if any changes have been made in the dataset. If they have, the message "Changes have been made. Do you want to save them?" should be displayed in a message box. If the user clicks on Yes, then save the changes and then exit the application. If the user clicks on No, exit the application without saving the changes.

Parameterized Queries

Often users want to specify information that will be used as the basis for a query. For example, the user might want the data displayed in the DataGrid in Example 8.2 to be limited to authors in a particular state. The user would specify the appropriate state code and this would then be used to select the matching records from the database. In this case, the **state code the user enters is referred to as a** *parameter* **of the query.**

We will look at two examples that use parameters in their queries. These examples differ in the way they display the results to the user. In our first example (Example 8.3), we present the results of the query in TextBox controls one record at a time. In the second example, the results of the query are presented in a DataGrid control.

Example **8.3**

PARAMETERIZED QUERY USING TEXTBOX CONTROLS

In this example, we "bind" TextBox controls to a dataset. *Data binding* **refers to the process of associating one or more properties of a Visual Basic .NET control to a specific data source** such as a dataset. For example, it is very common to bind the Text property of a TextBox control to a specific column (field) in a dataset. As a result, the value of the field for the currently active row in the dataset will be displayed in the Text property of a bound TextBox.

There are two types of data binding available: simple data binding and complex data binding. *Simple data binding* **allows the property of a control to be bound to a single data element such as a single field within a dataset.** *Complex data binding* **allows the property of a control to be bound to more than one data element in a dataset.** For example, we already have seen how the DataGrid control can display many columns and many rows from a dataset. Other controls, including ComboBox and ListBox controls, also support complex data binding.

In this example, we ask the user to enter a state abbreviation into a TextBox and then retrieve records from the authors table that match the state abbreviation. The application at execution time is shown in Figure 8.41.

FIGURE 8.41

Example 8.3 at Run Time

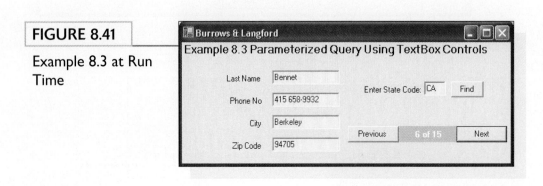

In creating this example, we need to add an OleDbDataAdapter and DataSet as in the previous examples. However, there is a difference in the SQL generated within the OleDbDataAdapter wizard from what we have already seen. The SQL Select statement that we need would be similar to the following.

SELECT au_lname, phone, city, zip FROM authors WHERE (state = 'CA')

However, there is a problem with the Select statement above; we do not know at design time that the user will want to see authors in California ('CA'). SQL has a solution for our problem called a parameterized query. The SQL statement we want to use is

SELECT au_lname, phone, city, zip FROM authors WHERE (state = ?)

At run time, the "?" is replaced with a value provided by the user by calling the appropriate methods of the data adapter.

To create the SQL statement using the OleDbDataAdapter wizard, we bring up the Query Builder, select the au_name, phone, city, and zip fields and enter "= ?" in the Criteria field for the state field. Figure 8.42 shows the Query Builder panel including this entry. If you look at the Select statement in the lower part of the panel, you will see how the "WHERE" clause has been created with the criterion (state = ?). Also note two other things. First, observe that the state field does not have a checkmark next to it in the Output column. We need this field for selecting records from the dataset but we do not need it for display purposes. Second, notice the symbol to the right of the field "state" in the authors table at the top of the panel. This icon indicates that records are "filtered" based on this field. **The term** *filter* **is used to describe the process of selecting a subset of records from the original set.**

After creating the data adapter, a dataset and other components need to be added to the project. Note that there is a label between the Previous and Next buttons. This label has a blue-green background with white forecolor, making the font white.

FIGURE 8.42

Using the Query Builder to Build a Parameterized Query

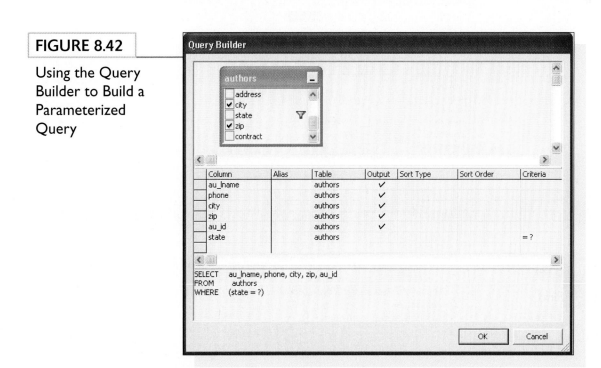

To bind the four TextBox components (Last Name through Zip Code), you need to go to the Properties window and open the (DataBindings) property by clicking on the + sign and then binding the Text property to the appropriate field in the dataset. Figure 8.43 shows the process of binding the au_lname field to the TextBox named txtName.

After binding the four TextBox controls to their associated fields, we need to write the code to show the selected records as well as navigate from record to record. To begin, we write the code for the Find button. Figure 8.44 shows the Click event for this button.

There are two statements that need explaining. The first is

OleDbDataAdapter1.SelectCommand.Parameters("state").Value = state

This statement searches the parameter collection for the Select command associated with the data adapter to see if the parameter, "state" in this case, exists. If it does, a value (on the right of the equal sign) is assigned to the parameter. That is, it replaces the question mark in the original Select statement,

SELECT au_lname, phone, city, zip FROM authors WHERE state = ?

with the value of the expression on the right-hand side of the assignment statement. There may be more than one parameter in the Select statement and if there are, you would need to assign a value to each parameter.

The second statement that needs explaining is the procedure **showPosition()**. This procedure, whose code is shown in Figure 8.45, updates the record status in the label between the Previous and Next buttons.

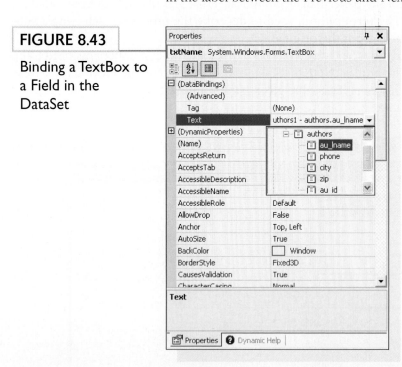

FIGURE 8.43

Binding a TextBox to a Field in the DataSet

FIGURE 8.44

Code to Find Records for a Specific State

```
Private Sub btnFind_Click(ByVal sender As System.Object, ByVal e As Syste
    Dim state As String = txtState.Text
    OleDbDataAdapter1.SelectCommand.Parameters("state").Value = state
    DsAuthors1.Clear()
    OleDbDataAdapter1.Fill(DsAuthors1)
    showPosition()
End Sub
```

FIGURE 8.45

Code for the showPosition() Procedure

```
Private Sub showPosition()
   Dim tot, curPos As Short
   tot = Me.BindingContext(DsAuthors1, "authors").Count
   If tot = 0 Then
      lblRecStatus.Text = "(No records)"
   Else
      curPos = Me.BindingContext(DsAuthors1, "authors").Position + 1
      lblRecStatus.Text = curPos & " of " & tot
   End If
End Sub
```

This procedure first determines the total number of records in the dataset. If the total is zero, it places the text "(No records)" into the label. Otherwise it determines what the current record index is and creates the text similar to "3 of 15" where the "3" is the current position and the "15" is the total.

The two references

```
Me.BindingContext(DsAuthors1, "authors").Count
Me.BindingContext(DsAuthors1, "authors").Position
```

need explanation. The reference to "Me" is a reference to the form object where the code exists. Each form has a **BindingContext** object associated with it. This object **keeps track of all the data sources associated with the form.** The parameters (DsAuthors1, "authors") are necessary because it is possible for a form to have more than one data source associated with it. The parameters are used to find the correct data source.

One final explanation relating to the Position property is necessary. The records in the dataset are numbered beginning with zero. So if there are 5 records (the Count property would be equal to 5), the records are indexed with the numbers 0, 1, 2, 3, and 4. If the current record index were 2 for example, it would be the third record. If we didn't add one to the Position property when we displayed the status information, we would end up saying "2 of 5" when we are referring to the third record.

Finally we need to write the code for the Previous and Next buttons. This code is shown in Figure 8.46. In this code we are again referencing the Position property of the data source like we did in the showPosition() procedure. Here we either increment or decrement the value of this property moving forward or backward one record. The system also controls the value of the Position property to be sure it stays legal ($0 \le$ Position $<$ Count). That is, if Position equals 0 (the first record) and the user clicks the Previous button, the value of Position will not go negative.

FIGURE 8.46

Code for the Previous and Next Buttons

```
Private Sub btnPrevious_Click(ByVal sender As System.Object, ByVal e As S
   Me.BindingContext(DsAuthors1, "authors").Position = _
               Me.BindingContext(DsAuthors1, "authors").Position - 1
   showPosition()
End Sub

Private Sub btnNext_Click(ByVal sender As System.Object, ByVal e As Syst
   Me.BindingContext(DsAuthors1, "authors").Position = _
               Me.BindingContext(DsAuthors1, "authors").Position + 1
   showPosition()
End Sub
```

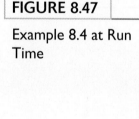

Exercise 8.8

Modify Example 8.3 so that it finds records that match a specific zip code entered by the user instead of a state code.

Exercise 8.9

Modify Exercise 8.5 so that it displays records based on a state code entered by the user at run time.

Our second example dealing with parameterized queries is very similar to Example 8.3. It differs in that it provides the user with a ComboBox component filled with all the state codes found in the database. This makes the application more user friendly in that the user simply selects the state he is interested in and does not have to remember what the valid codes are.

Example 8.4

PARAMETERIZED QUERY WITH COMBOBOX AND DATAGRID CONTROLS

Figure 8.47 shows this example at run time. The ComboBox on the left is populated with state codes from the database. When the user selects a code, the DataGrid on the right is filled with records from the database that match the user-selected state code.

We must create two datasets using two different data adapters. We begin by creating an OleDbDataAdapter just like the one we created for Example 8.3. This data adapter will be used to retrieve the records from the database to fill the DataGrid. The SQL for this provides for a parameterized query with the expectation that the user will supply the code used to select the set of state-specific records. Figure 8.48 shows the Query Builder window that is used to create the SQL.

After creating the OleDbDataAdapter (named OleDbDataAdapter1), a new DataSet object is created (named DsAuthors1).

The second OleDbDataAdapter is used to extract a unique list of state codes from the authors table to fill the ComboBox. However, there is a little problem that needs to be overcome. If we just select the state codes from the authors table, we end up with potential duplicates. For example, there are a total of 15 authors from California who all have "CA" as their state code. SQL has a way to solve this problem by adding the keyword **Distinct** to the query. **This keyword results in a set of records that are unique,** that is, if there are any duplicate rows, then they are reduced to a single row. Figure 8.49 shows the Data Adapter Wizard for our second OleDbDataAdapter object. The Query Builder does not have a way to designate Distinct, so we need to enter the SQL statement directly as you can see in the figure.

FIGURE 8.47

Example 8.4 at Run Time

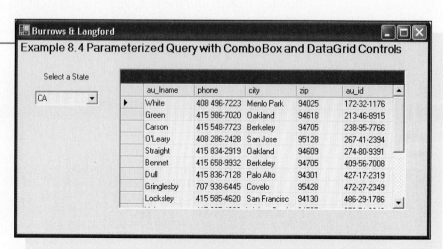

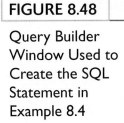

FIGURE 8.48

Query Builder
Window Used to
Create the SQL
Statement in
Example 8.4

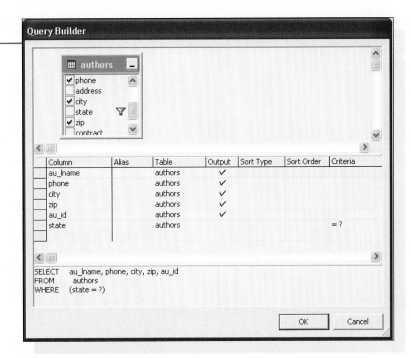

FIGURE 8.49

Specifying a Distinct
Select Query

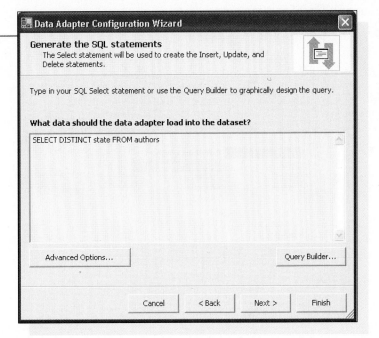

After creating the second OleDbDataAdapter, named OleDbDataAdapter2, we create a new DataSet named DsStates1. You need to be careful to associate this new Dataset with the second OleDbDataAdapter. Figure 8.50 shows this action.

After adding the ComboBox and DataGrid controls to the form, we need to bind them to the appropriate data sources. For the ComboBox, we need to set its DataSource property equal to the DataSet DsStates1 and its DisplayMember to authors.state. We also set the ComboBox's DropDownStyle property to DropDownList. Figure 8.51 shows these settings.

For the DataGrid control, we set its DataSource property to DsAuthors1. authors. Figure 8.52 shows the choices Visual Basic .NET provides for this control's DataSource property. You may find this list a bit confusing and are wondering

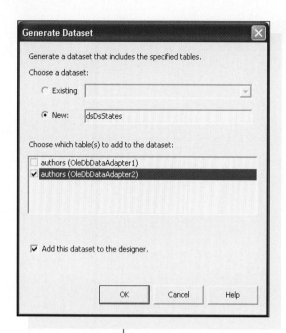

FIGURE 8.51

Setting Property Values for the DataSource, DisplayMember, and DropDownStyle Properties

FIGURE 8.50

Creating the Second DataSet Associated with a Distinct List of State Codes

FIGURE 8.52

Choices of Values for the DataGrid's DataSource Property

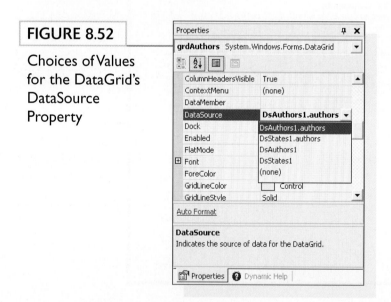

how to decide which of the choices is appropriate, so let's go over each option. The choice DsStates1.authors refers to a dataset that contains just a list of state codes extracted from the authors table. We know this because the DsStates1 DataSet is associated with the OleDbDataAdapter2 data adapter (that includes the SQL Select Distinct query for state codes). We know that this is not correct for the DataGrid.

The choice DsStates1 is probably not tempting (it relates only to state codes, not the fields shown in the DataGrid). This leaves the two choices DsAuthors1. authors and DsAuthors1 (without a table qualification). A dataset can include more than one table. However, our DataGrid can display only information from one table. If we chose to associate the DataSource property to DsAuthors1 (without a table qualification), we would not be providing enough information

FIGURE 8.53

Code to Populate the ComboBox with State Abbreviations

```
Private Sub Form1_Load(ByVal sender As System.Object, ByVal e As System.E
    DsStates1.Clear()
    OleDbDataAdapter2.Fill(DsStates1)
    ' The following causes the combo box selected index to be changed
    ' This forces the datagrid to be filled when application starts
    cboStates.SelectedIndex = 1
    cboStates.SelectedIndex = 0
End Sub
```

FIGURE 8.54

Code to Populate the DataGrid when the User Selects a New State

```
Private Sub cboStates_SelectedIndexChanged(ByVal sender As Object, ByVal
    Dim state As String = cboStates.Text
    OleDbDataAdapter1.SelectCommand.Parameters.Item("state").Value = state
    DsAuthors1.Clear()
    OleDbDataAdapter1.Fill(DsAuthors1)
End Sub
```

because the DataGrid wants to know which table in the dataset it should be bound to. This is true even in our case where our dataset contains only one table. So the correct choice for our purpose is DsAuthors1.authors.

After binding the two controls to the correct datasets, we need to write the code to fill the ComboBox and DataGrid. The ComboBox is populated when the form first loads so we place the code in the form's load event. Figure 8.53 shows this code.

This code first clears the DataSet object and then fills it with data as defined in the SQL statement in the data adapter. The last two statements are included to guarantee that the DataGrid is populated when the application first starts. As you will see next, we use the ComboBox's SelectedIndexChanged event to populate the DataGrid. Changing the selected index in the Form1_Load event forces the ComboBox's SelectedIndexChanged event to be called.

The code for the ComboBox's SelectedIndexChanged event is shown in Figure 8.54. The code for the selected state is taken from the ComboBox and then used to set the parameter value in the parameterized query associated with OleDbDataAdapter1. Finally, the dataset is cleared and then filled from the SQL statement associated with OleDbDataAdapter1.

Exercise 8.10

Modify Example 8.4 so that the ComboBox displays (distinct) zip codes instead of state codes. The user then selects records based on zip code values.

Exercise 8.11

Modify Exercise 8.5 so that it displays records based on a state code chosen by the user from a ComboBox at run time. Be sure that the state codes are unique within the ComboBox.

Master/Detail Record Display

In all of our previous examples we have worked with a dataset that had a single table. Example 8.4 had two datasets but each had only a single table associated with it. Example 8.2 used a complex SQL query that involved three tables, but the result of the SQL query was a single table. Here we look at using a dataset that includes two tables that are related with a common field.

When you have more than one table in a dataset, you have what is called a *master/detail dataset.* This **defines a relationship where each master record (from one of the tables) is related to zero or more records from the second table.** For example, assume that you have one table called Department. Each record in this table has information on a specific department in an organization. You also have a table called Employee that lists all the employees in the organization. Each record in the Employee table includes a field named DeptCode that indicates to which department the employee is assigned. Here the master record would be a record from the Department table and it would be associated with zero or more detail records from the Employee table. As an alternative to the terms *master* and *detail,* we sometimes use the terms *parent* and *child.* Using this terminology, the departments are the parent records and the employees are the child records.

Example 8.5

CREATING A MASTER/DETAIL RECORD DISPLAY

In this example, we look at the publishers in the SQL "pubs" database and their employees. The master (parent) records will be the publishers and the detail (child) records will be a list of employees for each publisher.

Figure 8.55 shows the application at run time. You can see the + expander symbol in the left-most column in the table next to each master record. Clicking on the + drops down a link to the master's detail records. In Figure 8.55, publisher number 0877 has revealed a link to its employees.

If you click on the detail link, you will see the screen shown in Figure 8.56. In this figure you see the 10 employees of publisher 0877. You also can see the publisher details on the top of the DataGrid control. Note that there are two icons on the upper-right corner of the DataGrid. The left arrow (←) causes the details to be collapsed and the master (publisher) records will be displayed. The other icon, which looks like a rectangle with up and down arrows under it, is used to show/hide the master record detail at the top of the grid.

As explained earlier, to create a master/detail record display like this, one must create a dataset that includes two related tables. We need to create two data adapters, one for the publishers table and a second for the employee table. We then need to create a dataset that includes both of these tables and also has a relationship to link them together.

FIGURE 8.55

Example 8.5 at Run Time with One Master Record's Detail Record Link Exposed

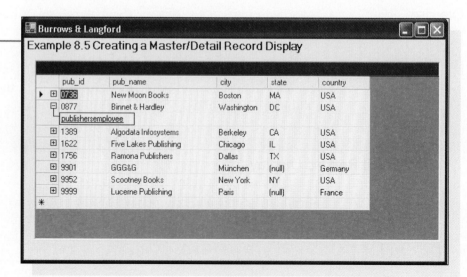

FIGURE 8.56

Example 8.5 with a Publisher's Details Displayed

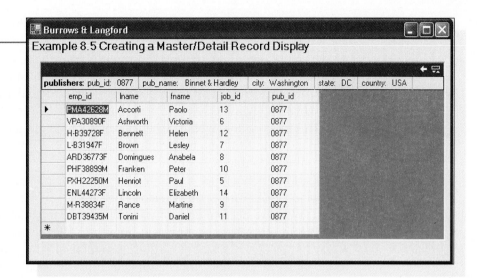

We start by creating two OleDbDataAdapters. Figure 8.57 shows the Query Builder for constructing the SQL for the publishers table and the employee table. There is nothing new here: just two separate data adapters (OleDbDataAdapter1 and OleDbDataAdapter2), each using a different table from the database.

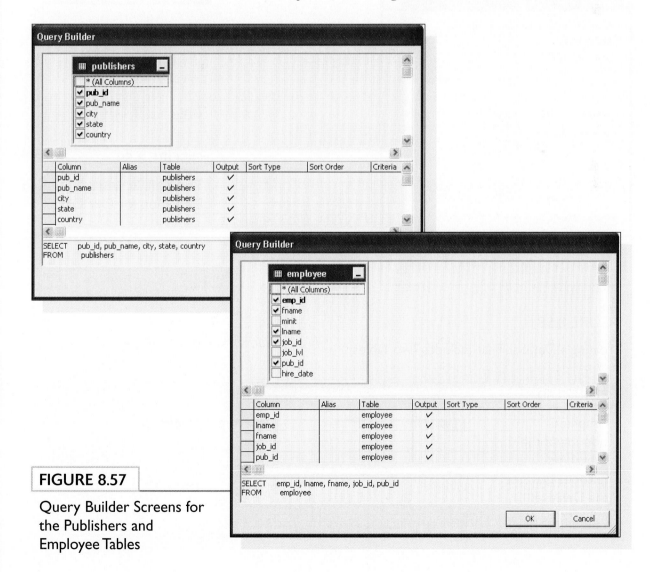

FIGURE 8.57

Query Builder Screens for the Publishers and Employee Tables

We next need to create a dataset that includes the two tables. We start out as before by selecting Generate Dataset... from the Data menu. Figure 8.58 shows the window used to supply appropriate information to generate the dataset. Note that we include both the employee and publishers tables in this dataset.

After clicking on OK, you should see a new entry in the Solution Explorer. As shown in Figure 8.59, there is now an entry titled dsPublishersEmployees.xsd. This file contains an **XML S**chema **D**efinition (hence the extension xsd). We talk more about XML and its various supporting technologies in the next chapter.

If you double-click on the dsPublishersEmployees.xsd entry in the Solution Explorer, you will see something like that shown in Figure 8.60 in the Designer window. You can see the two tables that are part of the previously defined dataset.

What we need to do next is establish a relationship between the two tables. Dragging a Relation component from the XML Schema Toolbar to the Designer window does this. Figure 8.61 shows the Relation component in the Toolbar.

We drag the Relation component from the Toolbar to the table that will be the detail (child) table in the relationship. In our case this is the employee table. So we drag the Relation component to the employee table on the left.

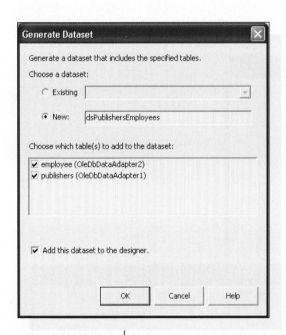

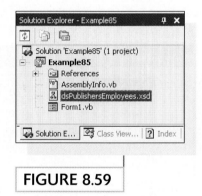

FIGURE 8.59

The XML Schema Definition for Our DataSet

FIGURE 8.58

Creating a DataSet That Includes Two Tables

FIGURE 8.60

A Graphical Rendering of the dsPublishers-Employees DataSet in the Designer Window

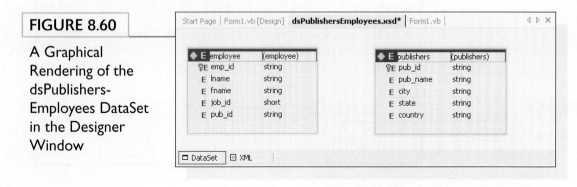

FIGURE 8.61

The Relation
Component in the
XML Schema
Toolbar

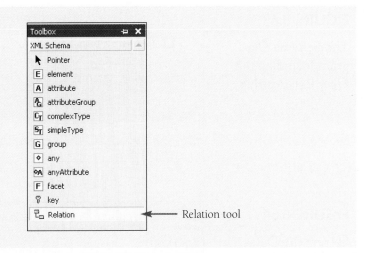

After doing this, an Edit Relation dialog box like the one in Figure 8.62 will
be displayed. Here we specify the Parent (master) and Child (detail) elements.
We also define the field in each table that will be used to link the two tables
together. In this case, this is the pub_id field common to each table.

After clicking on OK, you should see an updated schema diagram showing
the relationship between the two tables. This is shown in Figure 8.63.

The next task that we need to perform is to place a DataGrid on the form and
associate it to the appropriate data source. As seen in Figure 8.64, we do this by
setting the DataSource property to equal DsPublishersEmployees1.publishers.
We set the property to this value so that the publishers records are shown as the
master records. If we had chosen instead to set the DataSource property equal
to DsPublishersEmployees1.employee, then we would initially see employee

FIGURE 8.62

Defining the Rela-
tionship between
the publishers and
employee Tables

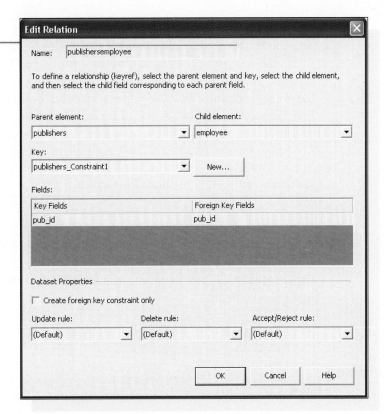

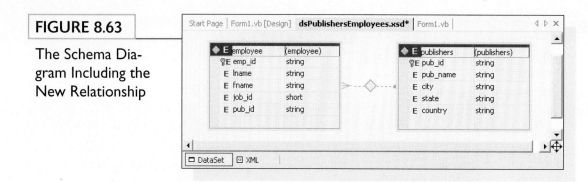

FIGURE 8.63

The Schema Diagram Including the New Relationship

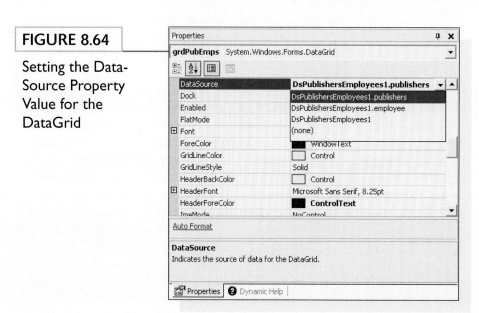

FIGURE 8.64

Setting the DataSource Property Value for the DataGrid

records when the application starts, but since these have no detail records associated with them, we could never see the publisher information. If we chose the third option, DsPublishersEmployees1, the initial DataGrid would show no records, but instead a + expander allowing the user to expand either the publishers table or the employee table. While this is not the behavior we want for this application, it could be useful for other applications.

The final task is to add the code necessary to populate the datasets. We do this in the form's Load event. Since the dataset is associated with tables defined in two data adapters, we need to fill it from two sources. As seen in Figure 8.65, we do this with Fill() methods for each data adapter.

Exercise 8.12

Create a Windows Application similar to Example 8.5 that uses the "pubs" database and shows a DataGrid with records in the publishers table as the master records (you choose the fields to display) and records from the titles table as the detail records. For the detail records, display the title, price, advance, royalty, and pubdate fields.

FIGURE 8.65

Code for Example 8.5

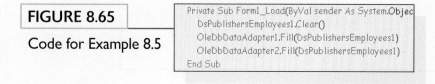

```
Private Sub Form1_Load(ByVal sender As System.Objec
    DsPublishersEmployees1.Clear()
    OleDbDataAdapter1.Fill(DsPublishersEmployees1)
    OleDbDataAdapter2.Fill(DsPublishersEmployees1)
End Sub
```

Exercise 8.13

Create a Windows Application similar to Example 8.5 that uses the "pubs" database and shows a DataGrid with records in the stores table as the master records (you choose the fields to display) and records from the sales table as the detail records. For the detail records, display the ord_num, ord_date, and qty fields.

8.4 | Additional Visual Basic .NET Database Tools

In this section we look at using the Server Explorer (available under the View menu if it is not already visible) to work with databases. The Server Explorer (see Figure 8.66) provides easy access to both servers as well as Connections. In Figure 8.66, we see several Data Connections including the connection to the "pubs" MSDE Server database we have been working with in the previous section. We also see one server (the MSDE server that comes with Visual Basic .NET) named "PICO" (the author's computer).

In this section, we show how to add a data connection to the server and then use this connection to create a data adapter and dataset. In this case we add a data connection for a Microsoft Access 2000 database instead of an SQL Server database. We use an example (Example 8.6) to demonstrate working with the Server Explorer.

Example 8.6

USING THE SERVER EXPLORER TO PROCESS AN ACCESS 2000 DATABASE

This example displays records from a Microsoft Access 2000 database named Listings.mdb, a database that stores real estate listings. Figure 8.67 shows this application at run time.

We begin by opening a new Windows Application project. Next we add a new data connection using the Server Explorer. Make sure the Server Explorer is visible by selecting Server Explorer from the View menu. Right-click on Data Connections and select Add Connection... from the pop-up menu, as shown in Figure 8.68.

You will next see the Data Link Properties dialog box as shown in Figure 8.69. Click on the Provider tab and select the "Microsoft Jet 4.0 OLE DB Provider". The "Jet" database engine is the technology used by the MS Access DBMS to manage its databases. If this provider is not displayed, then this means you will not be able to use MS Access databases on the specific computer.

After specifying the data provider, you next click on the Connection tab to specify the actual database information. As seen in Figure 8.70, the database (including its path) must be provided in box #1. Click on the ellipses (...) button to browse to find the database. If the database needs a user name and password,

FIGURE 8.66

The Server Explorer

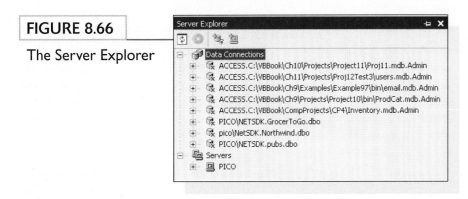

FIGURE 8.67

Example 8.6 at Run Time

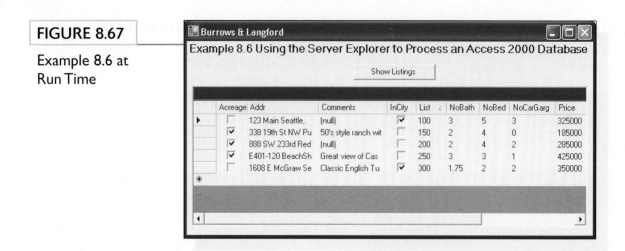

FIGURE 8.68

Pop-up Menu Generated by Right-Clicking on Data Connections

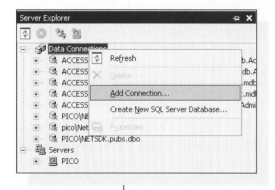

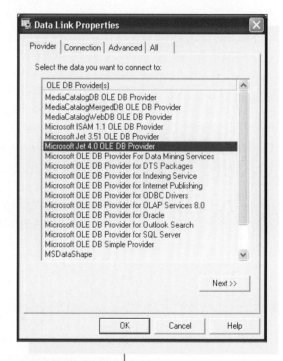

FIGURE 8.69

Selecting the Access Data Provider

use box #2 to specify this information. When you are done, click on the Test Connection button to confirm that the connection parameters are correct. Click on OK when you are done.

When you are done, you should see that the connection has been added in the Server Explorer. Figure 8.71 shows what you should see.

You can use the Server Explorer to see how your database is designed. If you expand the data connection by clicking on the + symbol, you see more and more detail. Figure 8.72 shows the detail down to the field name level of the table named Listings.

After you create the data connection, drag and drop it on your form in the Designer window. This adds the connection to your form. You should see the data connection in the tray below the form in the designer window as shown in Figure 8.73.

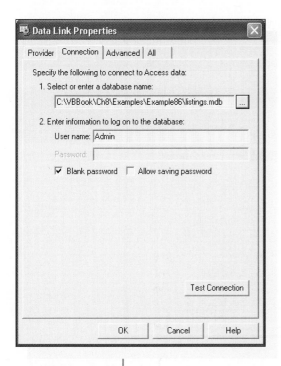

FIGURE 8.70

Specifying the Actual Database for the Connection

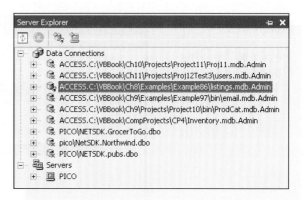

FIGURE 8.71

The New Connection as Seen in the Server Explorer Window

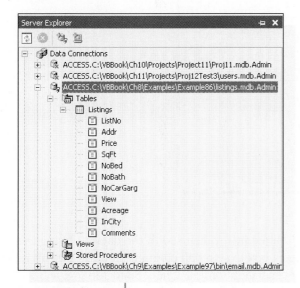

FIGURE 8.72

Viewing Details by Expanding the Data Connection

FIGURE 8.73

The Data Connection in the Designer Tray

Once we have a connection established, it's time to create a data adapter and dataset just as we have done previously. We start by creating an OleDbData-Adapter using the Data Adapter Configuration Wizard. When we get to the Data Connection page, we choose the data connection just created, as seen in Figure 8.74.

FIGURE 8.74

Selecting the Data
Connection

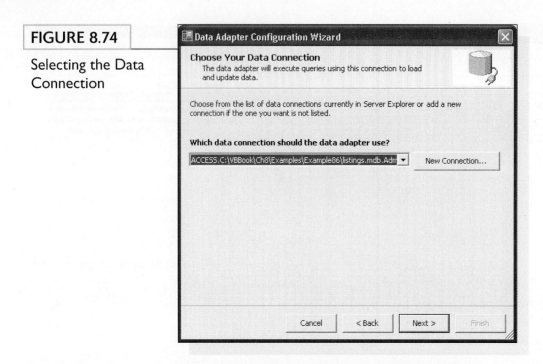

FIGURE 8.75

Selecting All the
Columns from the
Listings Table

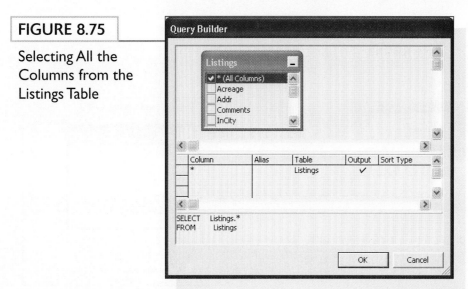

We again use SQL to select the records to be used in the dataset. Using the
Query Builder, we select the check box to select all columns. You can see this as
well as the SQL Select statement generated from the Query Builder in Figure 8.75.

After the OleDbDataAdapter is created, we need to create a new dataset
named dsListings by selecting Generate Dataset… from the Data window.

After creating the dataset, we need to add a DataGrid and Button component
to the form. The DataGrid's DataSource property value should be set equal to
DsListings1.Listings.

Finally we need to write the code for the Show Listings button. Figure 8.76
shows the now familiar two lines that first clear the DataSet object and then fill
it using the OleDbDataAdapter.

There is another very useful feature called the Data Adapter Preview tool that
you might find useful. This tool allows you to display the data associated with

FIGURE 8.76

Code Used to Fill
the DataSet Object

```
Private Sub btnShow_Click(ByVal sender As System.Obj
    DsListings1.Clear()
    OleDbDataAdapter1.Fill(DsListings1)
End Sub
```

FIGURE 8.77

The Generate
Dataset and Preview
Dataset Links at the
Bottom of the
Properties Window

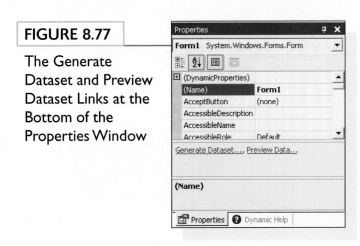

any dataset defined for your project. Figure 8.77 shows two links at the bottom of the Properties window named "Generate Dataset" and "Preview Dataset".

Clicking on the Preview Dataset link brings up the Data Adapter Preview window as shown in Figure 8.78. You can use this to choose a data adapter (if your project has more than one) and a target dataset and table.

Clicking on the Fill Dataset button then fills the dataset and uses the Results grid to display the contents of the dataset. Figure 8.79 shows this.

FIGURE 8.78

The Data Adapter
Preview Window to
See the Contents of
a Dataset

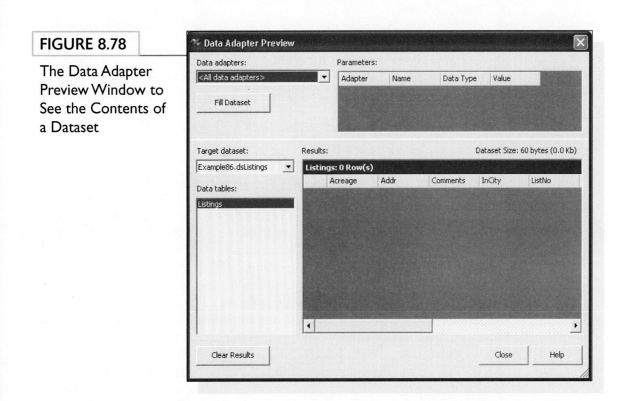

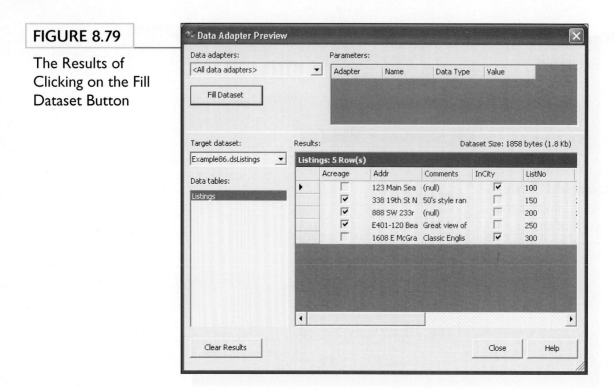

FIGURE 8.79

The Results of
Clicking on the Fill
Dataset Button

8.5 Project 9: Real Estate Listings Database Application

Note: **This project introduces new concepts related to database processing including adding new records and editing and deleting existing records. It also includes information on how a form can access data values found on another form.**

Many database applications provide support for a company's operations. In this project we describe a database application that a real estate agent might use to access information on listings (properties and homes available for sale). This realistic example not only demonstrates database principles discussed in this chapter, but also employs many of the controls and techniques covered in earlier chapters.

Description of the Application

Real estate agents require access to a large amount of data to perform their daily tasks. They often need to access this information from different locations—their office, their home, or the properties they are showing to clients. A laptop computer makes it possible for them to carry a computer-based database. What they need is an application that makes it easy to access the data.

Figure 8.80 shows such an application. It displays information about each listing (address, price, square feet, etc.) on the left side of the form. Controls on the right side allow the user to browse through the database record by record. Controls on the bottom allow the user to perform standard database maintenance functions as well as display the payment calculator. Figure 8.81 shows the dialog box used to get information on a new listing and Figure 8.82 shows the calculator that is displayed when the user clicks the Compute Monthly Pmnt button.

FIGURE 8.80

Real Estate Listings
Application at Run
Time

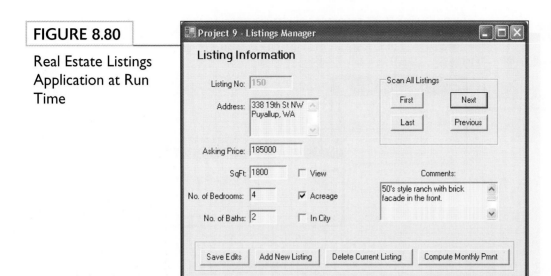

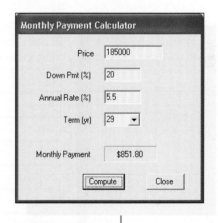

FIGURE 8.82

Monthly Payment Calculator at
Run Time

FIGURE 8.81

Add New Listing Dialog at Run Time

In addition to the three functional forms shown previously, the application also shows a number of confirmation messages. Figure 8.83 shows message boxes with these confirmation messages.

Design of the Application

The application is built around a single-table database created with Microsoft Access. This database is called Listings.mdb and its single table is called Listings. Table 8.3 shows the fields in the Listings table. Note that the "Access Type" column indicates the type as defined within Microsoft Access, not Visual Basic .NET. You will need to create a connection for this database (see Section 8.4). The main form for the application has an OleDbDataAdapter associated with the Listings.mdb connection and an SQL Select statement that accesses all the fields from the Listings table. It also has a dataset that is associated with the data adapter. All the data are presented via bound controls (see Example 8.3). The check boxes (View, Acreage, and In City) are bound to fields that are type

FIGURE 8.83

Various Confirmation Messages

Database Field	Access Type	Description
ListNo	Text	Listing number
Addr	Text	Address
Price	Currency	Asking price
SqFt	Integer	Number of square feet
NoBed	Integer	Number of bedrooms
NoBath	Single	Number of bathrooms
NoCarGarg	Integer	Garage space for cars
View	Yes/No	Is there a view
Acreage	Yes/No	Is there acreage
InCity	Yes/No	Is house in the city
Comments	Text	Misc. comments

Table 8.3 Fields in real estate Listings table

Yes/No in the Microsoft Access database. The values Yes and No in Access are the same as the Boolean values True and False in Visual Basic .NET.

Let us turn our attention to the Scan All Listings command buttons on the right side of the form. These controls move through the records of the database as indicated by the button captions.

- **First**: Sets the Position property of the dataset to the first record (a value of 0).

- **Last**: Sets the Position property of the dataset to the last record (a value equal to the Count property minus 1).

- **Next**: Increases the value of the Position property by the value 1 (see Example 8.3).

- **Previous**: Decreases the value of the Position property by the value 1 (see Example 8.3).

In addition to the main form, you should create a second form (dialog box) that enables the user to add a new listing (see Figure 8.81). This form needs to include a way for the information entered by the user to be available to the main form where database management activities take place. We will facilitate this by adding some public functions that return the values. We also need to be able to tell which of the two buttons (OK or Cancel) was clicked from the main form so we know what to do when the user is finished with the Add New Listing dialog box. These tasks are discussed later.

Finally, you should create a third form that enables the user to calculate the monthly payments for a loan (see Figure 8.82). The Price field should be taken from the Asking Price text box on the main form. That is, the Text property of the Price text box should automatically be set before the form is shown. Recall from Chapter 3 that to access a control on another form, you must qualify the control name with the name of the form on which it resides. For example, if you are writing code for frmMain that has a TextBox component named txtPrice and you want code in frmMain to store the value of txtPrice's Text property in the component txtCost that is on the form referenced by ObjCalc, then you could enter the following:

ObjCalc.txtCost.Text = txtPrice.Text

The Close button hides the form. The Compute button takes the purchase price, down payment percentage, annual interest rate, and the term from the TextBox components and drop-down ComboBox component, then computes and displays the monthly payment. The interest rate and down payment percent are entered as whole numbers; for example, 20 is entered for 20%. This means that your code needs to divide these two values by 100 to move the decimal point to the right location (20/100 = .20). Compute the loan amount by subtracting the down payment from the purchase price. Then use the Pmt() function to compute the monthly payment.

Payment = -Pmt(IntRate / 12, Term * 12, LoanAmt, 0, 0)

The Term ComboBox should include the values 10, 15, 20, 25, 29, and 30 set up at design time.

Construction of the Application

Start by creating a Windows Application. You then need to add the connection, data adapter, and dataset. (See the "ReadMe" file for this project for information on the database Listings.mdb.) See Example 8.6 for details on this step. Next add a few of the bound text boxes like the ones for the listing number and address. Set their (DataBindings) Text property to the appropriate field from the dataset (see Example 8.3). Using the form's Load event, add the code to fill the data adapter and then run the application. You should see the values from the first record in the database displayed in these bound controls.

When you get the first few bound controls working, add a few more and get them working. Continue by setting up the remainder of the controls that are bound directly to the database.

Now turn your attention to the navigation controls on the right side of the form. Again, add one button (the First button in the Scan All Listings section would be a good place to start), then code and test it. Continue, one button at a time, to add and test. Use the descriptions provided earlier to guide you in writing the code.

Remember, limit what you do at each step and thoroughly test what you've done before you proceed. The strategy of doing a little coding and then testing will limit the number and complexity of the problems you encounter. It also increases the chances you'll be able to correct the problem quickly.

Once you have the navigation buttons working, it's time to work on the functionality of the database maintenance buttons and the monthly payment compute button at the bottom of the form. We start with the Save Edits button. The user can make changes to any of the fields except the Listing Number (that text box should not be enabled). As these changes are made, the underlying dataset is also changed because of the controls that are bound to it. However, to cause these changes to be made to the actual database, the data adapter must execute its Update method. For example, if the data adapter is named OleDbDataAdapter1 and the dataset is named DsListings1, then the statement

OleDbDataAdapter1.Update(DsListings1)

should cause the database to be updated. However, before this works, the system must move to a new different record. Instead of having the user move to a different record, we add that logic to the code for the Save button's Click event. Figure 8.84 shows this navigation code as well as the Update method.

Next we turn our attention to the Add New Listing button. This button causes the Add New Listing dialog box, shown in Figure 8.81, to be displayed. The tricky part about this task is providing the mechanism for the main form to be able to get the data entered by the user on the dialog box. One strategy is to add a set of public functions (methods) to the class definition for the Add New Listing form that provide the access to the TextBox components. For example, consider the code in Figure 8.85. This function returns the value the user entered in the TextBox txtListNo on the Add New Listing form.

You need to add a function like this for all the components used by the user to define a new listing such as the asking price, square footage, and so forth. In the main form you can use these functions such as

ListNo = ObjNewListing.getListNo

to get the value (assuming the Add New Listing form is referenced by the object reference ObjNewListing).

To determine which button the user clicked, you can use a variable and set it equal to one of two values depending on which button was pressed. Consider the

---

FIGURE 8.84

Code to Update an Existing Record

```
Private Sub btnSave_Click(ByVal sender As System.Object, ByVal e As System.Event
    Dim Current As Short
    Current = Me.BindingContext(DsListings1, "Listings").Position
    Me.BindingContext(DsListings1, "Listings").Position = 0
    Me.BindingContext(DsListings1, "Listings").Position = Current
    OleDbDataAdapter1.Update(DsListings1)
    MsgBox("Update Complete", MsgBoxStyle.Information, "Update Confirmation")
End Sub
```

FIGURE 8.85

Public Function That Returns the User-Entered Value in txtListNo

```
Public Function getListNo() As String
    Return txtListNo.Text
End Function
```

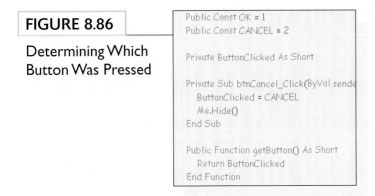

FIGURE 8.86

Determining Which
Button Was Pressed

```
Public Const OK = 1
Public Const CANCEL = 2


Private ButtonClicked As Short


Private Sub btnCancel_Click(ByVal sende
    ButtonClicked = CANCEL
    Me.Hide()
End Sub


Public Function getButton() As Short
    Return ButtonClicked
End Function
```

code in Figure 8.86. In this code the variable **ButtonClicked** is set to either the constant OK (=1) or CANCEL (=2) in the btnOK_Click or btnCancel_Click events. The function getButton can then be used to return the value of the variable.

In the main form the getButton function can be used to determine which button was clicked, as the segment of code below shows.

If (ObjNewListing.getButton() = ObjNewListing.CANCEL) Then Exit Sub

The btnOK_Click event should verify that the data are complete and that the numeric fields contain valid numbers. Use message boxes to notify the user if an error is detected (see Figure 8.87).

Once the user has correctly filled out the Add New Listing form and clicked on the OK button, a new record needs to be added to the database. Using the dataset's Add method followed by the data adapter's Update method does this. Figure 8.88 shows the code that performs these two steps.

Be aware that the code

DsListings1.Listings.AddListingsRow(…)

is formed using the name of the database table associated to the dataset. In the case above, the table is named "Listings". If the table had been called "Stuff", the statement would have been

DsListings1.Stuff.AddStuffRow(…)

FIGURE 8.87

Message Boxes
Indicating Missing
Data or
Nonnumeric Values
on the New Listing
Form

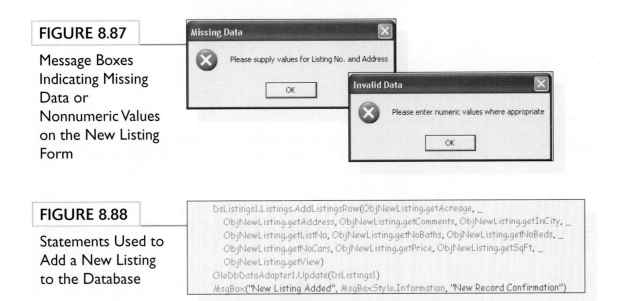

FIGURE 8.88

Statements Used to
Add a New Listing
to the Database

```
DsListings1.Listings.AddListingsRow(ObjNewListing.getAcreage, _
    ObjNewListing.getAddress, ObjNewListing.getComments, ObjNewListing.getInCity, _
    ObjNewListing.getListNo, ObjNewListing.getNoBaths, ObjNewListing.getNoBeds, _
    ObjNewListing.getNoCars, ObjNewListing.getPrice, ObjNewListing.getSqFt, _
    ObjNewListing.getView)
OleDbDataAdapter1.Update(DsListings1)
MsgBox("New Listing Added", MsgBoxStyle.Information, "New Record Confirmation")
```

FIGURE 8.89

Code Used to Delete the Current Record

```
Current = Me.BindingContext(DsListings1, "Listings").Position
DsListings1.Listings.Rows(Current).Delete()
OleDbDataAdapter1.Update(DsListings1)
MsgBox("Listing has been deleted", MsgBoxStyle.Information, "Deletion Complete")
```

The final button we need to add is the Delete Current Record button. To delete the current record, you first need to determine the index of the current record by accessing the Position property of the dataset. This value is then used to delete the record from the dataset. Finally, the database is updated using the data adapter's Update method. Figure 8.89 shows the code to perform these tasks.

Chapter Summary

1. A database is an organized collection of data and relationships that describe entities of interest to a business. An entity is a thing, such as an employee, a customer, a product, or a part. Examples of relationships are (a) the parts used to assemble a product and (b) the set of customers an employee is responsible for. Databases are a very important part of most business data processing, and Visual Basic .NET is a very important tool used by businesses to access the data in their databases.

2. An entity-relationship diagram (ERD) documents entities and their relationships. This diagram indicates cardinality—the number of one entity that can be related to another entity. For example, an ERD might indicate that a customer is related to one employee and an employee is related to many customers. This would be an example of a one-to-many relationship.

3. Visual Basic .NET supports the relational database approach for organizing data about entities and their relationships. In a relational database, the data for each entity are stored in their own two-dimensional table. Each table may include a key field that has unique values from one record to another. Relational databases use foreign keys and correlation tables to link tables according to the relationships between the entities.

4. Database designers use a process called normalization to place data items into tables in a way that minimizes the problems of redundant data while maintaining the correct relationships between the entities. The data stored in several related tables of a relational database can be used to answer a question using an SQL (structured query language) query.

5. Visual Basic .NET uses ADO.NET as the technology to access and manage databases. The ADO.NET object model includes the data provider classes for DataAdapters and Connections. It also provides the DataSet class that contains a set of tables that are associated with data providers. These classes provide the ability to select existing records for display, deletion, and modification as well as to add new records to a database.

6. The DataGrid control is a control that can be bound to a specific dataset. It provides a row and column display of records and fields from a dataset and also provides a rich set of properties that control the appearance of the data displayed in the grid.

7. Parameterized queries provide for the ability to determine how records will be selected at run time. The use of parameterized queries allows values entered by the user as the program executes to be used to find a set of records from the database.

8. Many of Visual Basic .NET's controls can be bound to a dataset and its fields. Simple data binding allows the property of a control to be bound to a single data element such as a single field within a dataset. Complex data binding allows the property of a control to be bound to more than one data element in a dataset.

9. ADO.NET supports master/detail record relationships where one master record is associated with zero or more detail records. The DataGrid supports this type of relationship by including an expander symbol, +, to expand and collapse detail records.

10. The Server Explorer provides access and management tools for connections and servers.

Key Terms

ADO.NET	DataGrid	key field
associative object	DataProvider	master/detail dataset
BindingContext	DataRelation	normalization
cardinality	DataSet	parameter
complex data binding	DBMS	relational database
compound key	Distinct	relationships
Connection	entities	simple data binding
correlation table	entity-relationship	SQL
DataAdapter	diagram (ERD)	structured query
database	expander	language
database management	filter	third normal form
system	foreign key	
data binding	intersection table	

End-of-Chapter Problems

1. Describe the association between entities and relationships. Give examples of each.

2. A table consists of rows and columns. What type of column is used in a source table to provide a one-to-many relation? What type of column is used in a destination table to reference a value in the source column?

3. Name and describe the statement that is used to retrieve current data and place it in a dataset. What statement is used to send modifications made to the dataset back to the data source?

4. Classify the following controls as simple bound controls or complex bound controls: TextBox, ComboBox, ListBox, CheckBox, RadioButton, and DataGrid. Explain the difference between the two types of controls.

5. Name the two properties that must be set on a DataGrid control to establish a relationship to the data source and describe the function of each.

6. How is an intersection table used in a complex query?

7. Can the Query Builder be used to create a query that contains a relationship between two or more tables? If so, does it provide the SQL code that represents this relationship that may be edited?

8. The DataGrid control can be used to display the Master and Details of a dataset. Explain what a master/detail relation represents. Provide an example.

9. What does the acronym SQL stand for? Write out the SQL Select statement generated by the Query Builder used to return all of the data from the publishers table.

10. Would use of the Distinct keyword affect the dataset returned by a query? Explain.

Programming Problems

1. Create a simple Visual Basic. NET database application that displays the titles of books available in the pubs database using a DataGrid control. From the titles table, display the columns for title id, title, price, notes, and publication date in the grid. You will need to create a connection and an SQL data adapter and generate a dataset. Your Form_Load event should initialize the dataset and fill the data adapter.

2. The flexible display nature of the DataGrid control provides the perfect method of browsing several tables on a data source. Create a form that contains a ComboBox control with selections for the authors, employee, and publishers tables. The user selection in the ComboBox should fill the DataGrid with the appropriate information.

You will need to create three DataAdapters and three datasets, one for each table reference. The SelectedIndexChanged event of the ComboBox control can be used to reassign the properties of the DataGrid to display the proper table. Setting the DataGrid to a specific table requires modification of the same properties that you've set manually with the Properties window in this chapter. For example, to view the authors table, the program would set the DataSource property of the grid to equal DsAuthors1 and the DataMember property to equal "authors", clear the dataset, and then fill the data adapter.

3. In this chapter, you learned how to display a master/detail relationship using a DataGrid. With a little extra work, it is possible to show the master records in a ListBox and allow the user to select a ListBox item that displays the detail records in a DataGrid on another part of the form. Create an application that displays the titles of all of the books in the pubs database in a ListBox and allows the user to select a title to display all of the sales records associated with that title in a grid.

You will need a form that holds a ListBox control and a DataGrid control below it. Data adapters for the sales and titles tables will be needed. When you generate a dataset that includes both of these tables, an XSD file will be created. You will need to set a relation between these tables as demonstrated in the chapter except that when the relation dialog is displayed, set the Parent element ComboBox to titles and the Child element to sales.

The DataSource property of the ListBox control should be set to the dataset and the DisplayMember property to the title column of the data (titles.title). To connect the DataGrid to the current record selected in the ListBox, set the DataSource property of the grid to the DataSet (DsTitleSales1) and the DataMember to the name of the relation between the two source tables (titles.titlessales). Make sure that the Form_Load event clears the dataset and then fills both data adapters from it.

4. Many database applications, particularly financial, use information from a data source to generate a report that includes calculations and summary data. Create an application that displays fields for book title, price, royalty, advance, and year-to-date sales from the titles table that are bound to read-only TextBox controls.

   From the information in these TextBoxes, calculate the Total Author Earnings on the book so far this year and the Amount of Credit that remains to be paid to the author and display these figures in label controls. To obtain the total earnings, you will need to multiply the royalty percentage by the price of each book and then multiply that number by the number of books sold in the year to date. From the earnings figure, subtract the advance already paid to the author to determine the amount currently owed. Some of the books in the pubs database do not have values entered for price, royalty, and so forth, so be sure to include error trapping so your calculations don't cause a fatal exception. Also add Next and Previous buttons to the form to allow the user to page through the available title records.

5. Create an application that allows the user to edit name, address, city, state, zip, and phone of records from the authors table displayed in TextBox controls. Include buttons for Update, Discard Changes, Next, and Previous. By default, the Update and the Discard buttons should have their Enabled properties set to False. The activation of the TextChanged event on any of the TextBox controls should enable these buttons.

   The Update button should use the EndCurrentEdit method (**Me.BindingContext(DsAuthors1,"authors").EndCurrentEdit()**) to store the changes to the dataset, execute the Update method on the data adapter, and disable this button and the Discard button. The Discard button can use the CancelCurrentEdit method on the binding context and then disable itself and the Update button. Both the Next and the Previous buttons should cancel the current edit (just in case changes were made), change the position of the current record, and then disable the two modification buttons (since the position change will execute the TextChanged events).

6. When a search of records fails (no records meet the search criteria), the application usually warns the user that no records were found. Create an application that uses a parameterized query on the publishers table to allow the user to determine which publishers are located in a specified state. Accept the two-letter state abbreviation input from a TextBox control and use the parameterized query to fill a DataGrid control. If no records were returned by the query, make the DataGrid invisible (using the Visible property) and display a message box alerting the user to the search failure. If records have been returned, make the grid visible to display the records.

   To determine the number of records generated by a query, the Fill method returns an Integer value of the number generated by the fill when it completes execution. You can write a simple statement to catch the result of this method (**num = daPublishers.Fill(DsPublishers1)**) and then check if that result is zero. *Note:* The parameterized query example in the chapter works perfectly for an OleDB data source, but if you use the SqlAdapter, you will need to give the query parameter a specific name (such as "@state") in the Select statement (**WHERE (state = @state)**). Set the named parameter in the same manner as shown in the chapter (such as **.Parameters("@state").Value**).

Using XML

T he *eXtensible Markup Language* (*XML*) **is a language used to represent data in a form that does not rely on any particular proprietary technology.** The technology-neutral language is defined by standards set up by the World Wide Web Consortium (w3c.org) and has rapidly become the standard for data exchange using the Internet. Not only is XML technology neutral, but it also is based on simple character formatting (it is human-readable like HTML) and thus is compatible with the network protocols (TCP/IP) that manage data transmission on the Internet.

In addition to XML, a number of associated technologies have evolved that make XML even more useful. One of these is the XML Schema[1] Language. This language provides a way of defining how an XML document should be formed. Since XML can be easily customized for a specific application, an *XML Schema* **provides a way of defining and validating XML documents to be sure that they follow the rules of the schema**. Business partners can agree upon a specific XML Schema for XML documents that they exchange. In this way they are sure that the documents they exchange include all the data they expect in a format they can understand.

Another useful technology associated with XML is the *eXtensible Stylesheet Language* (*XSL*) and *eXtensible Stylesheet Language Transforms* (*XSLT*). **XSLT provides a means of transforming one XML document into another XML document.** This capability is useful because it provides a way to take a single XML document and transform it into a variety of different versions (including HTML) that are specialized for specific uses.

In this chapter we first take a closer look at XML and its related technologies. We then see how Visual Basic .NET works with XML, XML Schemas, and XSLT. A number of classes within Visual Basic .NET provide methods that work directly with XML. In fact, Microsoft's .NET initiative uses XML as its foundation data technology. Specifically, we will see how Visual Basic .NET can work directly with XML, how it can take data from a relational database and convert it into XML, and how an XML document can be transformed into other XML documents.

Objectives

After studying this chapter, you should be able to

- Understand what XML is and how it is used within business-to-business transactions.

- Understand XML Schemas and XSL Transforms and how they are used within the context of XML.

---

[1] Generically, a schema, pronounced "skeema," is the definition of an entire database. It defines the structure and the type of contents of each data element within the database. (Source: TechWeb.com.) An XML Schema defines the content used in an XML document.

- Read and process data that are stored in an XML document.

- Read data from a relational database and transform them into their equivalent XML.

- Transform one XML document into a new XML document using an XSLT document.

9.1 An XML Primer

What Is XML?

As the Internet became more popular and businesses starting using it to support a variety of commercial applications, both business-to-consumer (B2C) and business-to-business (B2B), it became clear that the Hypertext Markup Language (HTML) had a number of shortcomings. **HTML is a language that focuses on the presentation of information for human consumption.** That is, it is designed to transform data into a form that makes it easy for humans to understand. Consider the Web page shown in Figure 9.1.

It should be fairly clear what the meaning (semantics) of the information displayed on the website is. We see information on three products that includes the Product Number, Description, and Price. If you were asked to determine the price of the product with a Product Number equal to 54321, you would have no difficulty coming up with a price of $0.02. In fact, this task is so easy that you could do it without any thought. This is because you are intelligent and are able to attach a meaning to the visual information you process.[2]

What happens if another machine were to process the same data? First of all, another machine would likely not process the image as shown in the browser.

FIGURE 9.1

Typical Web Page Formatted Using HTML

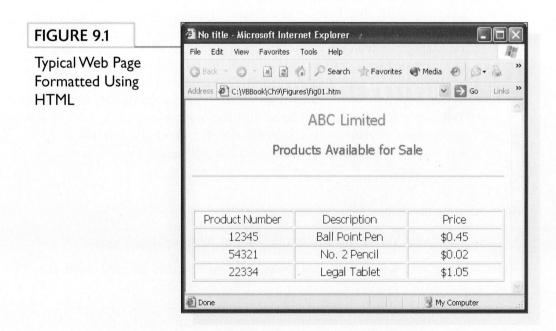

Product Number	Description	Price
12345	Ball Point Pen	$0.45
54321	No. 2 Pencil	$0.02
22334	Legal Tablet	$1.05

2 Note that some people with certain learning disabilities might have difficulty with the question posed because their ability to process a visual display is not developed as expected.

Instead, the machine would most likely see the data in their original form, that is, the HTML that was used by the browser to create the display in Figure 9.1. What does this HTML look like? Figure 9.2 shows the HTML that was rendered by the browser in the previous figure.

You may not understand HTML, but the symbol <tr>, known as a tag, means the start of a table row while the tag </tr> means the end of a table row. Within a table row, each new column is defined within the pair of tags <td> </td>. Figure 9.3 shows just one table row definition.

We will focus on the third line of Figure 9.3, which defines one table column using the following HTML:

<font face="Tahoma">12345</font>

What does this mean? The **<p>** tag defines a new paragraph and **</p>** defines the end of the paragraph. Within the paragraph tag we see an attribute named align that is equal to the string "center". This means that the contents of the

FIGURE 9.2

The HTML Used to Create the Browser Rendering in Figure 9.1

```
<html>
<head>
<title>No title</title>
</head>
<body bgcolor="white" text="black" link="blue" vlink="purple" alink="red">
...
<table border="1">
    <tr>
        <td width="299">
            <p align="center"><font face="Tahoma">Product Number</font></p>
        </td>
        <td width="299">
            <p align="center"><font face="Tahoma">Description</font></p>
        </td>
        <td width="299">
            <p align="center"><font face="Tahoma">Price</font></p>
        </td>
    </tr>
    <tr>
        <td width="299">
            <p align="center"><font face="Tahoma">12345</font></p>
        </td>
        <td width="299">
            <p align="center"><font face="Tahoma">Ball Point Pen</font></p>
        </td>
        <td width="299">
            <p align="center"><font face="Tahoma">$0.45</font></p>
        </td>
    </tr>
...
</table>
</body>
</html>
```

FIGURE 9.3

The HTML Definition for One Row in a Table

```
<tr>
    <td width="299">
        <p align="center"><font face="Tahoma">12345</font></p>
    </td>
    <td width="299">
        <p align="center"><font face="Tahoma">Ball Point Pen</font></p>
    </td>
    <td width="299">
        <p align="center"><font face="Tahoma">$0.45</font></p>
    </td>
</tr>
```

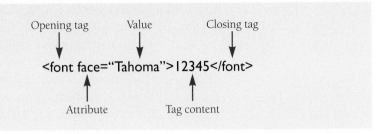

paragraph will be centered. The **<font>** tag defines the font to be used as indicated with the face attribute (Tahoma in this case). Finally, within the paragraph tag, between the **<font>** and **</font>** tags, we see 12345. This is defined as the content, which is in a centered paragraph using Tahoma font. It should be clear that HTML deals with the display of information. Figure 9.4 summarizes the terminology we just used. We should also add that the terms "tag," "node," and "element" might be used interchangeably.

We now ask, what does tag content 12345 mean? From the HTML, we know how it should look, but we have no clue what it means. Again, referring to Figure 9.1, we know that its meaning is a product number because we see it under the column heading "Product Number." But strictly from the HTML, it would be hard to draw that conclusion.

This demonstrates the major shortcoming of HTML: it does an excellent job describing how to display content, but it does a very poor job communicating the meaning of its content. How does this shortcoming impact our applications? First of all, applications like search engines end up giving you some useless information because they generally search content without any application of semantics. Assume you want to search for the table of elements used in chemistry and you enter the search criteria "element table". Figure 9.5 shows the results of such a search.

You can see some "hits" and some "misses" because the semantics of "element table" have a number of different interpretations. In an application like this we again rely on the human to decide which "hits" are valuable and which ones are

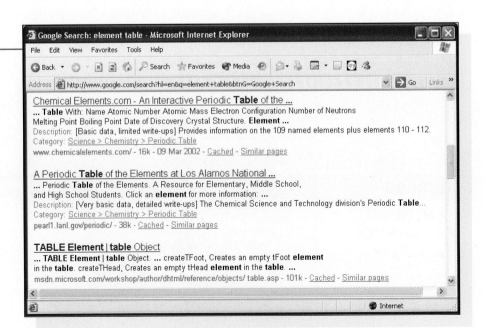

junk. Most humans are able to make this decision but having a computer make the decision is difficult at best.

What if the HTML shown in Figure 9.2 were replaced with the data shown in Figure 9.6? Note that the tags are now using terminology that is directly relevant to the data being stored. If the question is "What does the content 'Legal Tablet' mean?" we can easily see that it is a product description (it's in the Description tag that is inside a Product tag, so it's a product's description). In Figure 9.6 you are looking at the definition of a product list using the Extensible Markup Language or XML (www.w3c.org). Where did the tags such as **<Product>** and **<Price>** come from? The authors made them up. That's the meaning of *extensible*—**one is free to "extend" any XML freely as long as a few simple rules that we will cover later are followed.**

However, you may be observing that the data don't look as good as the HTML rendering. You are correct, but you need to understand that with XML, we separate the data content from the data presentation. Using several different techniques, we can present the same XML in a number of different ways. Figure 9.7 shows two different renderings of the XML from Figure 9.6

Both renderings in Figure 9.7 use the same XML file. Here you can see the power associated with separating data content from presentation—the same data can be rendered in any way that is useful. For example, one rendering might be HTML destined for a desktop browser (like that shown in Figure 9.7), another rendering might be WML (Wireless Markup Language) destined for a wireless device, and a third rendering might be the original XML destined for a wholesaler's electronic catalog. There is no practical limit to the number of different renderings possible for one XML file. One of the best examples is the use of XML in the newspaper industry. Many major newspapers have both a printed and a Web version of their paper. By storing their news articles in XML, they can use the same information as the basis of both versions of their paper (since both are electronically rendered). This makes the publication of multiple formats very efficient.

As you might guess, XML is rapidly becoming the data format "standard" for the exchange of data on the Internet. Computer-to-computer data transfers are possible because the computers can be programmed to find particular tags (such as **<Price>**) and use their content as appropriate. Standards such as

FIGURE 9.6

XML Equivalent to the HTML Content in Figure 9.2

```xml
<?xml version="1.0" encoding="UTF-8"?>
<?xml-stylesheet type="text/xsl" href="prodDesc.xslt"?>
<ProductList>
    <Product>
        <ProductNumber>12345</ProductNumber>
        <Description>Ball Point Pen</Description>
        <Price>0.45</Price>
    </Product>
    <Product>
        <ProductNumber>54321</ProductNumber>
        <Description>No. 2 Pencil</Description>
        <Price>0.02</Price>
    </Product>
    <Product>
        <ProductNumber>22334</ProductNumber>
        <Description>Legal Tablet</Description>
        <Price>1.05</Price>
    </Product>
</ProductList>
```

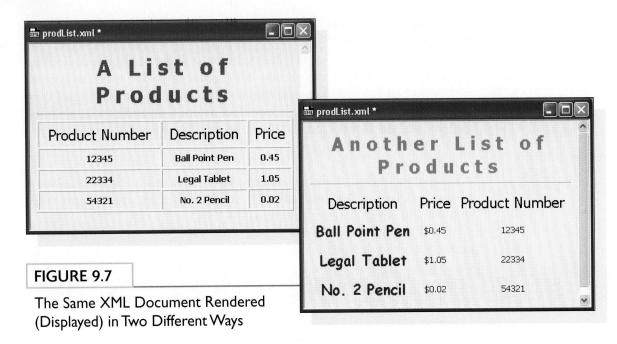

The Same XML Document Rendered (Displayed) in Two Different Ways

ebXML[3] (electronic business XML) for business-to-business transaction processing are already being used. In addition, companies are finding that the ability to transform XML data into a form that can be displayed in a browser, that is, transformed into HTML, makes it possible to create dynamic and current content.

XML data represent what is called a tree. A *tree* **is a data structure that is characterized by a single "root" with branches and leaves.** For example, the XML we saw previously in Figure 9.6 can be drawn as a tree, as shown in Figure 9.8.

In Figure 9.8 "ProductList" is the root node, "Product" represents a branch node, and "ProductNumber", "Description", and "Price" are leaf nodes. The textual content of elements (string or numeric) is usually associated with leaf nodes. It is also possible to assign some content values to nonleaf nodes using "attributes," which will be discussed later.

In addition to having just one root node, a nonroot node (branch and leaf) can be associated only with a single node above it (a child node can have only one parent). Thus, it would not be legal for a specific ProductNumber leaf node to be a child of more that one product.

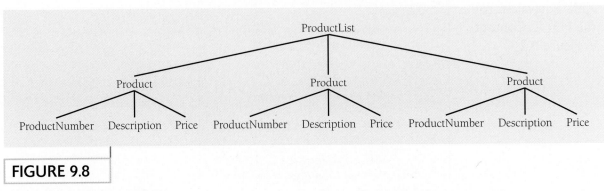

FIGURE 9.8

The "Tree" View of XML

3   For more information on ebXML, see www.ebxml.org/.

To summarize, XML provides a way of storing structured data that is self-describing, that is, the content meaning is more apparent due to the use of "tags" that are meaningful in the context of the application. It is useful for exchanging data on the Internet either through computer-to-computer communications or as a source to be transformed into a display for use by people. This ability to transform the "view" of the data for the particular viewer is a very important capability.

XML Syntax

XML syntax involves understanding and following a few straightforward rules. These include

- The language is case sensitive. This means that the tags `<price>` and `<Price>` do not refer to the same thing.

- There is one and only one root node.

- All elements must have both a start tag and an end tag. This means that if you have `<price>` as a starting tag, you must have a corresponding closing tag. The closing tag could be `</price>`, that is, the same as the opening tag except a slash (/) must precede the tag name. There is a shortcut that can be used for leaf nodes if they have empty content. For example, if the `<price>` element had no content, you could say `<price/>` and this would be considered both the starting and ending tag for the "price" tag. Thus, `<price></price>` and `<price/>` are identical.

- Tags must be nested correctly. That is, one tag may be inside another tag ("nested"), but its starting and ending tags must be within the starting and ending tags of the surrounding tag. The following is legal:

```
<product>
    <price> 1.25 </price>
</product>
```

In this example, "price" is nested in "product". Illegal nesting is shown in the next example:

```
<product>
    <price> 1.25 </product>
</price>
```

This is not legal because the price element's starting and ending tags are not both within the product element's starting and ending tags.

- If an element has an attribute, the attribute value must be quoted. **Attributes are values associated with a node.** For example, you might see the following XML fragment:

```
<product hazardous="true">
    <name> nitroglycerin </name>
</product>
```

In this example, the product element has an attribute named hazardous. Each element can have zero or more attributes defined for it. The value of attributes must be enclosed in either single or double quotes.

You are free to make up element and attribute names. They must start with a letter or an underscore and can contain any number of letters, numbers, hyphens, periods, or underscores. However, keep the element names short and descriptive just like you have been doing with variable names.

If you follow theses rules, your XML document is characterized as being *well formed*. **This simply means that there are no syntax violations within the document**. There is another way to characterize XML documents. This is known as being "valid." We will discuss valid documents later, but for the time being understand that a document may be well formed but not valid.

Namespaces

What if you receive an XML document from a furniture supplier that has a **<table>** tag and you also get a different XML document from a tax advisor that also has a **<table>** tag? In the first document, **<table>** referred to a piece of furniture (like a table and chairs) while in the second document, **<table>** referred to a row/column-oriented display of information (like the itemized deductions table). How can you resolve the dual meaning for the same element tag? You might be able to resolve the meaning by looking at the content of the two tags, but this could be difficult or perhaps not possible. XML has a solution for this type of situation. The solution is to use something called a namespace (www.w3.org/TR/REC-xml-names/). **A *namespace* simply defines a point of reference.** In the furniture supplier's namespace, we know what **<table>** means and in the tax advisor's namespace, we also know what **<table>** means and we know the two do not mean the same thing.

How do we use namespaces within an XML document? We simply change the element tag by adding a prefix and a colon to the tag. Using the examples from above, we might say **<furn:table>** and **<tax:table>** to differentiate the two types of elements. Be aware, however, if the two tags did not appear in the same XML document, then there might not be a problem, because the two documents themselves might be sufficient to establish the context.

Namespaces serve another function in addition to differentiating two tags within the same document. This second function allows XML parsers (a parser is a program that processes the XML to determine its content) to understand the context of a particular tag even if the tag itself is unambiguous in the specific document. For example, we will see later the XML statement

```
<xsl:sort select="ProductNumber"/>
```

Here the namespace "xsl" stands for eXtensible Stylesheet Language. When an XML parser sees this namespace, it knows that it must perform the sort function as defined within XSL.

How do we establish namespaces for our documents? To define a namespace, you add an xmlns (**xml n**amespace) declaration as an attribute within any element. All descendents of the element may then use the namespace. If you want the namespace available within the entire XML tree, you could place the xmlns declaration as an attribute of the root node. The declaration has the following syntax:

```
xmlns:name = "uri"
```

where you make up the name. The **uri (*Uniform Resource Identifier*) is a unique identifier and is often, but not necessarily, a url (Uniform Resource Locator).** We will say more about the uri later.

FIGURE 9.9

XML with a
Namespace
Definition

```
<?xml version="1.0"?>
<ipo:purchaseOrder xmlns:ipo="http://www.altova.com/IPO" >
...
    <Items>
      <item partNum="833-AA">
         <productName>Lapis necklace</productName>
         <quantity>1</quantity>
         <price>99.95</price>
         <ipo:comment>Want this for the holidays!</ipo:comment>
         <shipDate>1999-12-05</shipDate>
      </item>
    </Items>
</ipo:purchaseOrder>
```

Figure 9.9[4] provides an example of creating a namespace definition and then using it later as part of a tag in the definition of a node. In this example the root node is the **<purchaseOrder>**. An attribute has been added to the definition of this node (**xmlns:ipo="http://www.altova.com/IPO"**). The name "ipo" could be any name. Note that the name is added to both the root node's starting and ending tags (**ipo:purchaseOrder**) as well as the comment node's starting and ending tags (**ipo:comment**).

The uri in the example (which is actually a URL) is "http://www.altova.com/IPO". If you were to go to this site with a browser, you would get an error because there is no HTML content there. The sole purpose of this uri is to be sure it is unique. Since the company Altova, Inc., owns the URL www.altova.com, it has full control of the URL and no other firm can use this. Thus, as a matter of convenience, the uri, which must be unique, is often created using a URL.

Sometimes the uri is not constructed using a URL, but in this case there is usually an international standards organization that guarantees the uniqueness of the uri. In addition, when a URL is used as the uri, some organizations put content at the URL that documents the namespace. We should add that "uniqueness" is only necessary within a document; that is, two different and unrelated entities may by chance choose the same uri. As long as the two uris do not appear in the same document, there will be no problem.

Document Prolog

The *document prolog* indicates that the document is XML as well as indicating other things such as document type, entity definitions, and other processing instructions. Here we cover just the XML declaration and not entity definitions or other processing instructions.

The first line in any XML document indicates that the document is XML and declares the version of XML being used. An example is

<?xml version="1.0"?>

There are additional attributes available besides the version attribute. These include how the document is encoded (the character set used) as well as an indication of other files that this document needs to have loaded for it to operate correctly. Note the special starting and ending tags for this entry (**<?** and **?>**). These tags are used to

---

4   This is taken from an example by Alexander Falk that comes with XML Spy v4.0 (Altova, Inc.).

define a *processing instruction* (sometimes referred to as PI), that is, **information used by the XML parser and not part of the actual data content.**

XML Schemas

Suppose two business partners decide to exchange data using XML documents. How do they communicate what is legal in the documents and how can they verify that a document they receive from the other follows the rules? Imagine if there were no rules, then each partner would be free to make up tags that the other partner would not expect or not even understand. In addition, the two partners also would be free to use different tags for the same content. One might use **<po>** for purchase order and the other might use **<purchOrder>** for the same thing. You can imagine how difficult communication would be without an agreed-upon set of rules for valid XML documents.

XML has two ways of defining the rules for valid XML documents: Document Type Definitions (DTD) and XML Schemas (www.w3c.org/XML/Schema). The DTD was the original tool used for this purpose. However, it is rapidly being replaced with the newer, and by most accounts much better, XML Schema. We will not cover the DTD but will focus instead on the XML Schema, because it is considered better and is the standard used by Microsoft in Visual Basic .NET.

Consider the XML we saw earlier in Figure 9.6 (reproduced in Figure 9.10). An XML Schema would define what was legal as far as elements and tags are concerned as well as what the content would consist of. Figure 9.11 shows an XML Schema that would support the XML document in Figure 9.10.

This discussion is not intended to provide the degree of detail needed so that you can become an expert at creating XML Schemas. In Section 9.2 we discuss some tools available within Visual Basic .NET that help you build a schema without having to know all the syntax rules. In fact, the schema code shown in Figure 9.11 was created with one such tool. However, it would be helpful here to talk about the schema code in Figure 9.11 to enhance your understanding.

FIGURE 9.10

The XML from Figure 9.6

```xml
<?xml version="1.0" encoding="UTF-8"?>
<?xml-stylesheet type="text/xsl" href="prodDesc.xslt"?>
<ProductList>
    <Product>
        <ProductNumber>12345</ProductNumber>
        <Description>Ball Point Pen</Description>
        <Price>0.45</Price>
    </Product>
    <Product>
        <ProductNumber>54321</ProductNumber>
        <Description>No. 2 Pencil</Description>
        <Price>0.02</Price>
    </Product>
    <Product>
        <ProductNumber>22334</ProductNumber>
        <Description>Legal Tablet</Description>
        <Price>1.05</Price>
    </Product>
</ProductList>
```

FIGURE 9.11

XML Schema
Definition

```xml
<?xml version="1.0" ?>
<xs:schema id="ProductList" targetNamespace="http://tempuri.org/prodList.xsd"
    xmlns:mstns="http://tempuri.org/prodList.xsd" xmlns="http://tempuri.org/prodList.xsd"
    xmlns:xs="http://www.w3.org/2001/XMLSchema"
    xmlns:msdata="urn:schemas-microsoft-com:xml-msdata" attributeFormDefault="qualified"
    elementFormDefault="qualified">
  <xs:element name="ProductList" msdata:IsDataSet="true" msdata:EnforceConstraints="False">
    <xs:complexType>
      <xs:choice maxOccurs="unbounded">
        <xs:element name="Product">
          <xs:complexType>
            <xs:sequence>
              <xs:element name="ProductNumber" type="xs:string" minOccurs="0" />
              <xs:element name="Description" type="xs:string" minOccurs="0" />
              <xs:element name="Price" type="xs:float" minOccurs="0" />
            </xs:sequence>
          </xs:complexType>
        </xs:element>
      </xs:choice>
    </xs:complexType>
  </xs:element>
</xs:schema>
```

First note that an XML Schema is in fact just an XML document (you can see this in the document prolog in the first line of the schema). This means that you already know the basic syntax rules associated with writing the schema. The second through sixth lines are the root element that defines the schema **<xs:schema ...>**. In addition to defining the root node, this statement also defines the id, targetNamespace, attributeFormDefault and elementFormDefault attributes. Finally, it defines four namespaces including the namespace "xs" that qualifies the remaining tags in the definition. Do not worry about all this detail at this time. In fact, this element definition, as generated by Visual Basic .NET, is actually more complex than it need be. Often, when a tool creates code, it produces a very general version that is more verbose than well-designed custom code would be.

The schema then defines an element named ProductList as a complex type. **A complex type is one that consists of additional elements.** The ProductList element is made up of an unbounded number of elements that are chosen from the list of Product elements. Again this "choice" element is really not necessary when you are selecting from a choice of one element, but for a general solution, the choice element is provided. The Product element is defined as a complex type that consists of a sequence of elements named ProductNumber, Description, and Price. These final three elements store content of type string, string, and float, respectively.

This is not the only way to write the schema. That is, there are generally several ways to write a schema for the same XML document. There are additional tags that can be used within the schema definition. We will see some additional tags in Section 9.2 when we develop some XML and XML Schemas.

Once an XML Schema has been developed for an XML document, that document can be validated against the schema. That is, the XML document is compared to the rules defined in the schema and if any rule is broken, then the XML document will be considered as invalid. Note that it can still be well formed, that is, it does not violate any of the syntax rules outlined earlier in this section, but it still can be invalid. Well formed refers to basic syntax rules while **valid refers to a well-formed document following some set of additional rules controlling how the elements are arranged within the document.**

Finally, a number of industry and standards groups are developing XML schemas that define documents specific to their industry or specialized needs. For example, *ebXML* **(electronic business XML—www.ebxml.org) provides a set of schemas for various transactions and other common documents that are used in electronic business.** Another example is *XBRL* **(Extensible Business Reporting Language—www.xbrl.org).** Through the adoption of these open standards, business partners can exchange documents via XML with the assurance that others will be able to understand and process them.

Styling XML

In Figure 9.7 we saw two different renderings of the same XML document. This was done with the help of Extensible Stylesheet Language Transforms (XSLT— www.w3.org/Style/XSL). XSLT provides a means of transforming one XML document into a second XML document. Figure 9.12 shows how this transformation process works.

As you can see in Figure 9.12, an XML document and XSLT instructions are processed by an XSLT processor to create a new XML document. In our case, the new XML document was also an HTML document. Note that HTML is legal XML as long as it follows the rules we defined earlier. This is a common transformation process by which we can transform an XML document into any valid XML document. Other documents that are valid XML include the Wireless Markup Language (WML) and HTML Basic that support wireless devices. XSLT processors are available in a variety of software products. For example, Internet Explorer includes an XSLT processor that can transform and render XML documents into HTML for display. Visual Basic .NET includes classes and methods that also have the ability to process XML using an XSLT processor. There are also a number of XSLT processors available for free as both open source and freeware products. We will be using Internet Explorer and Visual Basic .NET for our processing of XML and XSLT.

We must repeat again the caution that XSLT, like the XML Schema, is very complex and our coverage here is just an overview to show you some examples and provide you with a high-level awareness of the technology and its applications. XSLT provides the means to take the original XML document (remember, it is a tree structure), and select the entire tree or any subtrees (called pruning) and format or rearrange the nodes of the new tree into a new XML document.

Figure 9.13 shows our original XML and the Internet Explorer–rendered version of the transformed XML (transformed into HTML using an XSLT document). Note that in the second line of the XML document you see the statement

<?xml-stylesheet type="text/xsl" href="prodDesc.xslt"?>

FIGURE 9.12

Overview of the XSLT Transformation Process

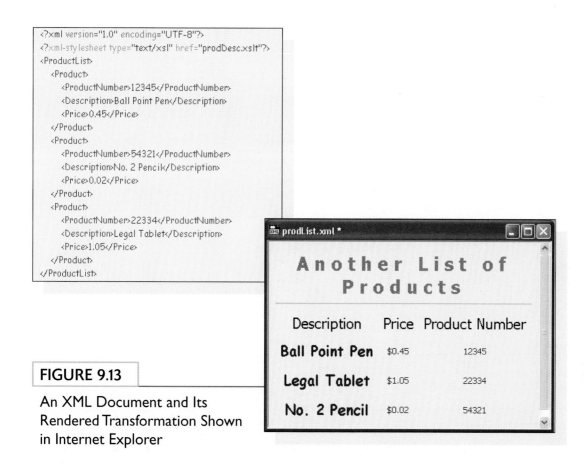

```
<?xml version="1.0" encoding="UTF-8"?>
<?xml-stylesheet type="text/xsl" href="prodDesc.xslt"?>
<ProductList>
   <Product>
      <ProductNumber>12345</ProductNumber>
      <Description>Ball Point Pen</Description>
      <Price>0.45</Price>
   </Product>
   <Product>
      <ProductNumber>54321</ProductNumber>
      <Description>No. 2 Pencil</Description>
      <Price>0.02</Price>
   </Product>
   <Product>
      <ProductNumber>22334</ProductNumber>
      <Description>Legal Tablet</Description>
      <Price>1.05</Price>
   </Product>
</ProductList>
```

FIGURE 9.13

An XML Document and Its Rendered Transformation Shown in Internet Explorer

This statement is a directive telling the browser that a stylesheet has been defined for it and that stylesheet is found in a file named prodDesc.xslt. Figures 9.14a and 9.14b show the contents of the XSLT document stored in the prod-Desc.xslt file.

Let's look at the XSLT to try to see what is going on. First note that the prolog (first line of code) defines this as an XML document, so just like XML Schemas, XSLT documents are also XML. The second line defines the stylesheet element. This includes the definition of the appropriate namespace (xsl) plus setting the version attribute value. Line 3 defines the output element that is used by the XSLT processor to determine what type of output to generate. In this case, the method attribute indicates that XML will be the output type.

The sixth line, **<xsl:template match="ProductList">**, starts the definition of a template element. Templates are the primary method used by XSLT to define how the transformation should look. You may have used templates for drawing. Drawing templates define the basic shape of an object and you use the template with a pen or pencil to draw the object on paper. **XSLT *templates* work in a similar way—they define the basic shape of the resulting document and what "parts" of the original XML tree to include in this new document.**

To understand the XSLT, we need to review the tree structure of the original XML document. Figure 9.15 shows this tree.

Now look at the XSLT in Figure 9.14 and you will see four templates (**xsl: template**). Each of these templates has a match attribute. The first template matches "ProductList," the second matches "Description," the third "Product-Number," and the fourth "Price." The first template, the one that matches "ProductList," is a template that applies to the entire tree (because it matches the root). The other three templates each apply to one specific leaf node.

FIGURE 9.14a

First Part of the
XSLT Document
Used to Transform
the XML into HTML

```xml
<?xml version="1.0" encoding="UTF-8"?>
<xsl:stylesheet version="1.0" xmlns:xsl="http://www.w3.org/1999/XSL/Transform">
<xsl:output method="xml" version="1.0" encoding="UTF-8" indent="yes"/>


<!-- Template #1 -->
<xsl:template match="ProductList">
 <html>
  <body>
    <div style="font-family:Tahoma,Arial,sans-serif;
           font-size:20pt; color:red;
           text-align:center; letter-spacing:8px;
           font-weight:bold">
      Another List of Products
    </div>
    <hr />
    <table width="100%" cellpadding="5" border="0"
           style="font-family:Tahoma,Arial,sans-serif;
           font-size:16pt; color:black;
           text-align:center">
      <tr>
        <td>Description</td>
        <td>Price</td>
        <td>Product Number</td>
      </tr>
    <xsl:for-each select="Product">
    <xsl:sort select="Description"/>
      <tr>
        <xsl:apply-templates select="Description" />
        <xsl:apply-templates select="Price" />
        <xsl:apply-templates select="ProductNumber" />
      </tr>
    </xsl:for-each>
    </table>
    <div style="font-family:Arial,sans-serif;
           font-size:8pt; margin-left:10px">
    </div>
   </body>
  </html>
</xsl:template>
```

FIGURE 9.14b

Remainder of the
XSLT Document
Used to Transform
the XML into HTML

```xml
<!-- Template #2 -->
<xsl:template match="Description">
 <td style="font-family:Comic Sans MS, Arial,sans-serif;
        color:darkblue; font-size:16pt;
        font-weight:bold">
  <b><xsl:value-of select="."/></b>
 </td>
</xsl:template>


<!-- Template #3 -->
<xsl:template match="ProductNumber">
 <td style="font-family:Tahoma,Arial,sans-serif;
        font-size:10pt">
  <xsl:value-of select="."/>
 </td>
</xsl:template>


<!-- Template #4 -->
<xsl:template match="Price">
 <td style="font-family:Tahoma,Arial,sans-serif;
        font-size:10pt">
  $<xsl:value-of select="."/>
 </td>
</xsl:template>
```

FIGURE 9.15

The Tree Representation of the Original XML Document

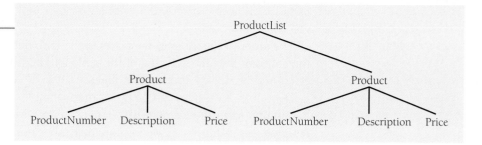

The template that applies to the entire tree should be considered the "master" template in that it controls the overall structure of the new XML document (tree). You may recognize that the first few lines within the first template contain HTML. This HTML will be part of the new tree (remember that HTML that follows our XML rules is also XML). The first XSLT code within the first template is shown in Figure 9.16.

The first statement (**xsl:for-each**) is very much like a Visual Basic .NET For Each…Next Structure loop. In the case of XSLT, we are building a loop that will be repeated for each Product node in the XML document. Our document has three product nodes (Product numbers 12345, 54321, and 22334) so the loop will iterate three times, once for each product node. The next statement (**xsl:sort**) does exactly what it says: it sorts the nodes in the resulting tree in order by their Description field. You then see the HTML definition of a table row (**<tr> ... </tr>**). This means that the three **xsl:apply-templates** instructions will generate content that will be within an HTML table row. The three **xsl:apply-templates** statements, each with different select attribute values, will search for a corresponding template and apply it to generate content.

The first **xsl:apply-templates** statement selects the Description node. The template for that node is shown in Figure 9.17.

Here we see that an HTML table column definition is being created (**<td> ... </td>**). Within this table definition, the xsl statement

<xsl:value-of select="."/>

is found (enclosed in the HTML bold tag (**<b> ... </b>**)). The **select="."** attribute means to select the content at the current node. Since the current node is the

FIGURE 9.16

The XSLT Code within the First Template

```
<xsl:for-each select="Product">
<xsl:sort select="Description"/>
    <tr>
        <xsl:apply-templates select="Description" />
        <xsl:apply-templates select="Price" />
        <xsl:apply-templates select="ProductNumber" />
    </tr>
</xsl:for-each>
```

FIGURE 9.17

Template for the Description Node in the XML Tree

```
<!-- Template #2 -->
<xsl:template match="Description">
    <td style="font-family:Comic Sans MS, Arial,sans-serif;
        color:darkblue; font-size:16pt;
        font-weight:bold">
    <b><xsl:value-of select="."/></b>
    </td>
</xsl:template>
```

Description node, the content is whatever is stored at this leaf node, for example, "Ball Point Pen".

The order of the **xsl:apply-templates** in the loop determines the order in which the columns within each row of the table will be filled (Description first, then Price, and finally the ProductNumber).

Of course, XML trees can be much more complex than our example, so XSLT has many additional capabilities than we see here. We encourage you to research this important topic in more depth but hope that at this point the general ideas associated with transforming one XML document into another XML document are clear.

Exercise 9.1

Can an XML document be valid but not be well formed? Explain.

Exercise 9.2

Write an XML document that describes the books in a library. When describing a book, include just three or four elements. For your example, put information for three books.

Exercise 9.3

Given the following XML document, construct a tree that represents the underlying structure.

```
<?xml version="1.0"?>
<StudentList>
    <Student>
        <StNo>1111</StNo>
        <Name>Skippy</Name>
        <Class>1</Class>
    </Student>
    <Student>
        <StNo>2222</StNo>
        <Name>Karen</Name>
        <Class>2</Class>
    </Student>
    <Student>
        <StNo>3333</StNo>
        <Name>Joe</Name>
        <Class>3</Class>
    </Student>
</StudentList>
```

Exercise 9.4

Why would you use an XML Schema and why would you use an XSLT document?

Exercise 9.5

Assume you have information on a student that includes a student number, name, address, and courses taken. The address is made up of street address, city, state, and zip. Information on a course includes course number, description, credit hours, and grade received.

Given this information, create a tree that correctly models these data and write a short XML document that is consistent with the tree. Populate the XML document with information on two students who each have taken at least three courses.

9.2 Creating XML Documents and XML Schemas Using Visual Basic .NET

Now that we have seen the basic ideas behind XML and XML Schemas, we turn our attention to Visual Basic .NET and the tools it provides that allow us to design schemas and then use them to build XML documents. Visual Basic .NET includes an XML Schema design tool that allows us to create XML Schemas using a graphical tool while it creates the actual schema code in the background. As with most graphical tools, the schema code generated in the background may not be as good as code written by a person who is an expert in XML Schema design. However, since our intention is not to teach you XML Schema design in depth, the graphical design tool is more than adequate. Since you can see the schema code generated by the tool, this can be effective in helping you understand the schema code.

Creating an XML Schema

We will first create a very simple schema that defines the information we might store regarding a student. The information relating to our student will include a student number, name, address, and age. To keep things simple, we will start with a definition for a single student (not a list of students).

We begin by creating a new Visual Basic .NET project and choosing a new Windows Application. After creating the new project, we need to add an XML Schema to the project by selecting Add New Item... from the File menu. The ensuing dialog box, shown in Figure 9.18, shows that the XML Schema icon has been chosen. Give this schema a new name if you like (we will leave the name as XMLSchema1.xsd).

After clicking on Open in the Add New Item dialog box, Visual Basic .NET will display the schema in the Designer window. Figure 9.19 shows what you should see. Note that you can now drag items from either the Server Explorer or the Toolbox to create your schema design.

FIGURE 9.18

Add a New XML Schema to the Project

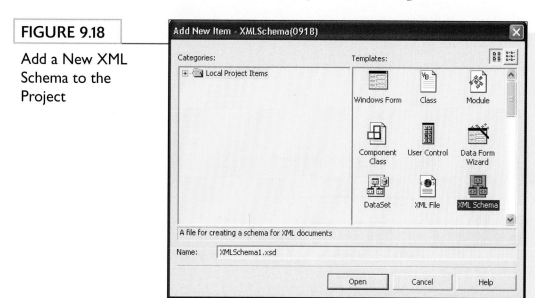

FIGURE 9.19

The Designer Window for a New XML Schema

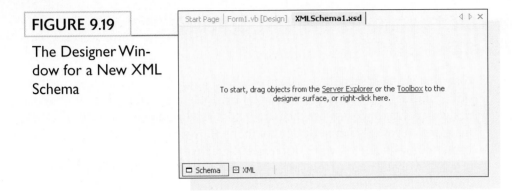

We will create our schema using the tools in the Toolbox. If you open the Toolbox, you will see some new components designed exclusively for XML Schemas. Figure 9.20 shows what this Toolbox should look like.

For our student example, we need to create an element. Our element will store four facts (student number, name, address, and age) for the student. Drag an element component to the Designer window. A new element (element1) will appear in the Designer as shown in Figure 9.21.

The box in the top row next to the (E) icon should include the name of the element. In our case we should change this to Student. Starting in row 2, you need to define each child node of the Student tree. The first column is used to indicate the category of each node. In our case these are also elements. The second column is used to hold the name of the node, and the third column defines the type of the node. Figure 9.22 shows the drop-down lists for the first and third columns.

FIGURE 9.20

The XML Schema Toolbox with the Element Tool Selected

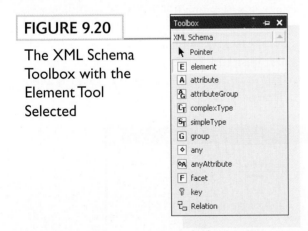

FIGURE 9.21

The Element Component in the Designer Window

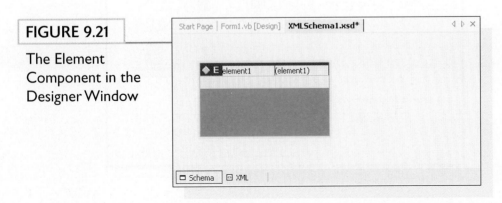

FIGURE 9.22

Choosing a
Category and Type
of a Node

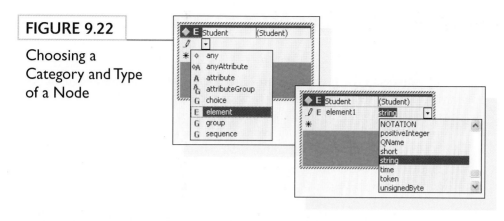

FIGURE 9.23

The Final Schema
Design

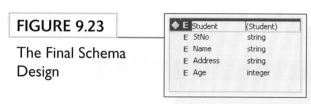

When you finish, you should see the Schema definition of the element named Student as shown in Figure 9.23.

Before we proceed, *it is important to save the Schema definition.* Before we can work with the Schema definition, it must exist as a file on disk, not just as a document within the Visual Basic .NET development environment.

We can see the actual schema code by clicking on the XML tab at the bottom of the Designer. Figure 9.24 shows this code. Even though we have not covered the XML Schema language in depth, the XML code in the figure should be fairly clear. After defining the XML prolog and the schema element, we see an element named Student that includes a complexType that consists of a sequence of elements named StNo, Name, Address, and Age that are all string type except for Age, which is an integer type. The complexType element was added so that the Student element could contain nodes, not just content. That is, the Student element is the root node and includes four additional elements (leaf nodes) named StNo, Name, Address, and Age.

FIGURE 9.24

The XML Schema
Code for Student

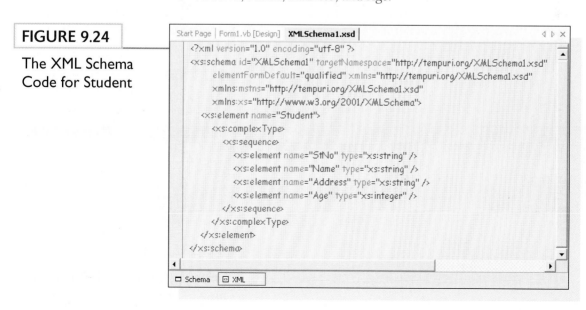

Creating an XML Document

Now that we have a schema and it has been saved on disk, what can we do with it? One thing is to use it to create an XML document. Go to the File menu and select Add New Item…. In the Add New Item dialog box, click on the XML File icon, name it Student.xml, and then click on Open (see Figure 9.25).

After opening the new XML file, you should see a blank XML document. The only XML code in this file is the initial prolog statement that makes this an XML file. Figure 9.26 shows this new XML file.

We next want to associate the schema we just defined with this new XML file. To do this, be sure the XML file is active in the Designer and click on the targetSchema property in the Properties window. Then select the correct XML Schema file from the drop-down list, as shown in Figure 9.27.

FIGURE 9.25

Opening a New XML File

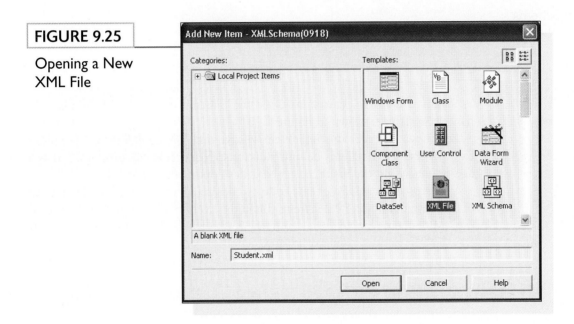

FIGURE 9.26

The New XML File

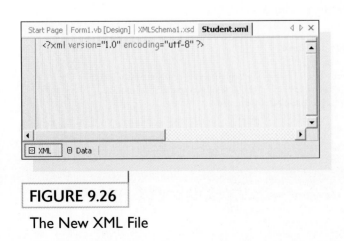

FIGURE 9.27

Selecting the Target Schema for an XML File

At this point you should see the XML code modified to include the root node (Student) as well as a reference to the XML Schema. If you click on the Data tab at the bottom of the Designer, you should see the XML displayed as a table. Figure 9.28 shows these two views.

Using the Data view, add several students to the table. After doing so, check the XML view and you should see that their data have been formatted and entered into the XML file surrounded by the appropriate tags. Figure 9.29 shows both the XML and Data views after entering some data.

We have seen a simple example of creating an XML Schema and a related XML document. We now focus on some more complex examples. We assume that you understand the mechanics of creating the XML Schema and XML file, so in the example we focus on the schemas and the type of relationships they

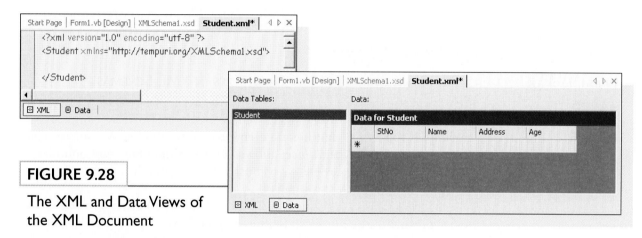

FIGURE 9.28

The XML and Data Views of the XML Document

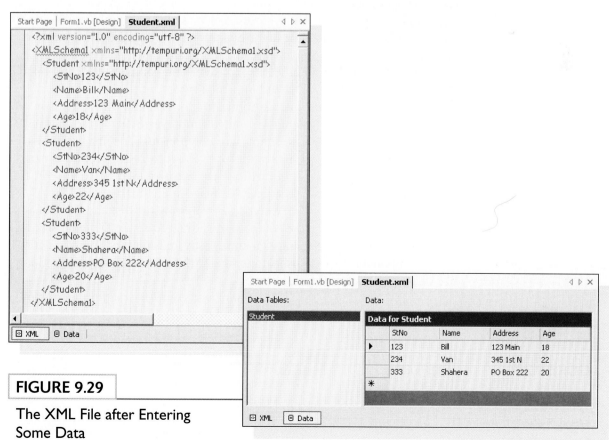

FIGURE 9.29

The XML File after Entering Some Data

support. The context for these examples is twofold. The first relates to creating XML Schemas to validate an XML document. Microsoft includes a validation command (Validate XML Data under the XML menu item) as well as methods to perform this validation at run time. However, validating XML documents against an XML Schema at run time is too complex for this text, but you are encouraged to investigate the capability. The second is using XML Schemas to facilitate the conversion of a relational database query to and from an XML document. In this latter context, Microsoft has added some additional elements (in their own namespace) to facilitate this translation between ADO.NET and XML. We will see some more on this in Example 9.3.

Exercise 9.6

Notice that in Figure 9.29, the second line of the XML document shows the element named **XMLSchema1** with a squiggly line under it. First, what function does this element fulfill? Second, why has the XML Designer placed the squiggly line under it?

Example 9.1

USING SIMPLE AND COMPLEX DATA TYPES IN XML SCHEMAS

In this example we create a schema for an Employee element. The schema will include a number of simple types as well as one explicit (named) complex type. **A *simple type* is one that has no elements or attributes.** We can associate facets with a simple type. **A *facet* allows you to define limits and boundaries on data values**. For example, we will use a facet to limit the number of characters in a state code to a maximum of 2.

Our schema also will include a named complex type. **A *complex type* is one that may include attributes and other elements.** We use the term *named complex type* because there are also unnamed complex types. A named complex type can be defined once and used many times, while an unnamed complex type can only be used one time in the definition of an element. The Student element we just looked at is an example of an unnamed complex type. The XML Schema Toolbox includes both the simpleType and complexType components and these support both named and unnamed types.

We begin with a new Windows Application project and first add a new element selecting an XML Schema we named EmployeesSchema.xsd. Using the new XML Schema, we add two simpleType components. The first one is named StateCode of type string with a length facet (F) set to 2. The second is named ZipCode of type positive integer with a maxInclusive facet set to 99999. The XML Schema design should look like the image in Figure 9.30.

Next we add a named complex type that will store the first and last names of an employee. A complexType component is dragged to the Designer window and named "Name". Two string elements, LastName and FirstName, are added to the component. When this is done, the XML Schema designer should look like that shown in Figure 9.31.

The final step involves creating an unnamed complex type for the Employee element. To do this, an element is dragged to the Designer window and named

FIGURE 9.30

Two simpleType Components in the XML Schema

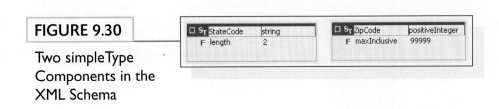

FIGURE 9.31

XML Schema Design with the complexType Name Added

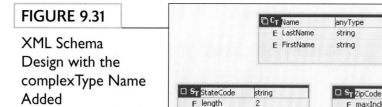

Employee. To this we add a string element named EmpNo and then an element named EmpName. When we click on the type cell for EmpName, we choose the Name complex type defined earlier. We continue by adding two string elements named Street and City, and then finish by adding a State and Zip element. For these final two elements, we again choose the simpleTypes StateCode and ZipCode we defined earlier. The final schema design is shown in Figure 9.32. Notice that since the EmpName is a complex type, the Designer has added a specific instance of the Name type (named EmpName) and linked it to the Employee element. Be sure that the schema is saved before you start working on documents that will reference it.

Finally we need to add a new XML File item to our project. When you select Add New Item… from the File menu and select XML File, name it something meaningful—we named ours EmployeeXML.xml. After adding the XML file, set its targetSchema property value equal to the schema just created. If you then click on the Data tab, you should see a table similar to the one in Figure 9.33. Here we have already added employee 1234 to the table.

Clicking on the expand detail symbol (+) on the left of the row opens up an area to enter the name. This is similar to the master/detail record display we saw

FIGURE 9.32

The Final XML Schema Design for the Employee Element

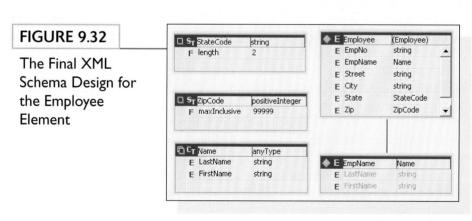

FIGURE 9.33

The XML Data View with One Employee Added

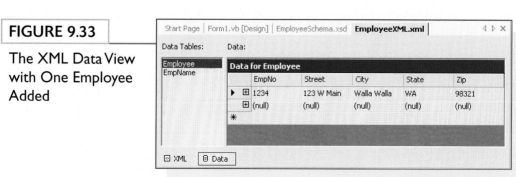

FIGURE 9.34

Expanding the
EmpName Table to
Add a Name

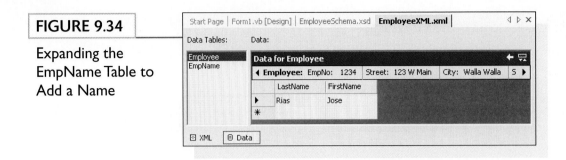

in Chapter 8 with the DataGrid control bound to a master/detail dataset. Figure 9.34 shows this.

In this example you have seen how to create an XML Schema by first creating simpleType and complexType components and then adding them to another element definition. This gives you the ability to create types of your own using the primary data types available within the XML Schema specification.

Exercise 9.7

Modify Example 9.1 so that it includes a named complexType named Address that consists of the City, State, and Zip. Use the StateCode and ZipCode simpleTypes in this new type. Add a new XML file and fill it with some data according to the new definition in the XML Schema.

Example 9.2

CREATING NESTED RELATIONSHIPS IN AN XML SCHEMA

In this example we create a Customer element and a Product element and establish a nested relationship with the Customer as the parent element and Product as the child element. This data design allows us to keep track of the products purchased by customers.

We begin with a new Visual Basic .NET Windows Application project and add an XML Schema. We define two elements, Customer and Product, as shown in Figure 9.35.

We have defined key fields for each table (note the little key glyph). To do this, drag a key component from the XML Schema Toolbox and drop it on an element where you want to define the key. An Edit Key dialog box like the one in Figure 9.36 will be displayed. In this example we dragged the key component onto the Product element. We then named the key ProductKey (you may name it anything you want) and verified that it was being applied to the Product element and was using the ProdNo field. Finally we checked the "Dataset primary key" checkbox. This means that the values for the key must be unique. We performed similar tasks for the Customer element.

FIGURE 9.35

The Initial Two
Elements in the
XML Schema Design

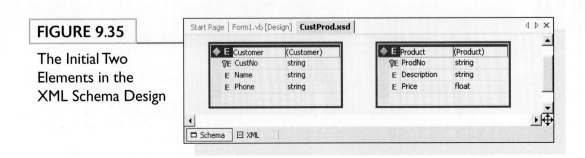

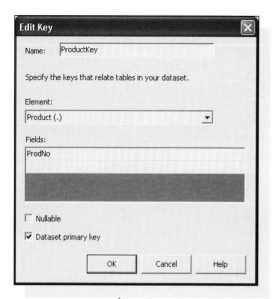

FIGURE 9.36

Creating a New Primary Key Field for
an Element

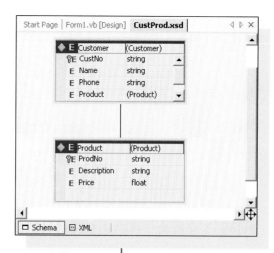

FIGURE 9.37

XML Schema Designer Showing
Parent/Child Relationship between
Customer (Top Element) and Product
(Bottom Element)

FIGURE 9.38

Data Entered into an
XML File Using the
Nested Relationship
between Customer
and Product

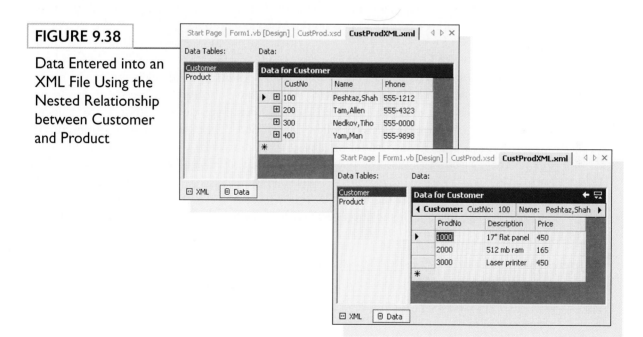

Following this we need to establish the parent/child relationship between the
two elements. To do this we drag the child element (Product in our case) and
drop it on the parent element (Customer in this example). This establishes a
relationship such that for each parent (master) element, there can be many children elements (many Products). The XML Schema Designer should now reflect
this relationship with a line between the two elements as shown in Figure 9.37.

After saving the schema, we can now add an XML File to our project and use
its Data tab to fill the XML file with some data. This is shown in Figure 9.38 in
both the unexpanded and expanded views.

Exercise 9.8

Create a new project similar to Example 9.2 but create an XML Schema that has a Product as the parent element and Parts as the child element. Make up the elements that are used to describe Product and Part. Include at least one element for Product and Part that uses a facet that is appropriate given your design.

Example 9.3

CREATING TABLES WITH RELATIONSHIPS IN AN XML SCHEMA

In this example we show how to create an XML Schema that includes **Data-Relation objects that are used by the database management system to navigate between tables in the database.** We will build the XML Schema for the database that is described in the entity-relationship diagram shown in Figure 9.39.

We begin by creating a new Visual Basic .NET Windows Application and then add an XML Schema item to the project. Using the XML Schema Toolbox, we create three elements, as shown in Figure 9.40.

The only thing done in this schema that we have not seen before is establishing the compound key in the Transcript table. We do this by selecting two fields when we drag the key component to the Transcript table. Looking at Figure 9.41 you can see that we have added both StNo and CourseId fields to the key. When you click on a row in the Fields grid, you will be able to use a drop-down arrow to select the field you want to include as part of the key.

Now that we have the elements defined, we need to define the relationships between the elements. Dragging the Relation component from the XML Schema Toolbox and dropping it on the *child* element does this. In our case we need to first drag a Relation component to the Transcript element (the child element for both Student and Course). You should see an Edit Relation dialog box like that in Figure 9.42. Be sure that the correct parent and child elements are selected as well as the correct key field. We also have chosen the Cascade option for the Update and Delete rules. These mean that if you delete a Student, that student's transcript records also will be deleted under the assumption that a transcript for a student not in the database is not desirable. Of course, one might argue against this assumption, but that is what we have chosen here.

We also need to add another relation with the Course element (parent) and Transcript element (child). You will likely have to change some of the default values for this relation because the defaults may still be set up for the Student-

FIGURE 9.39

Entity-Relationship Diagram Used as the Basis for the XML Schema

FIGURE 9.40

The Three Elements in the XML Schema

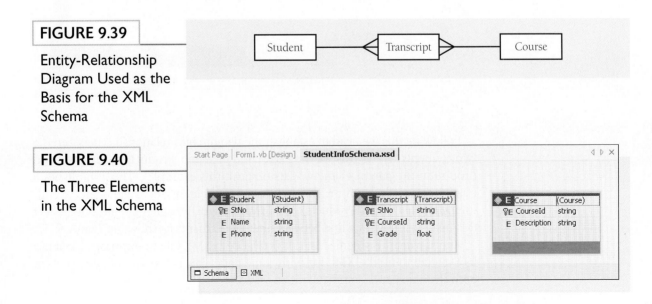

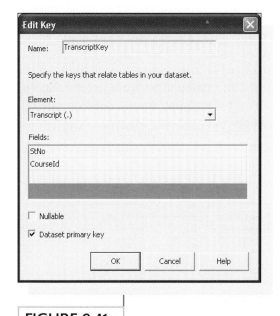

FIGURE 9.41

Selecting Several Fields for the Key

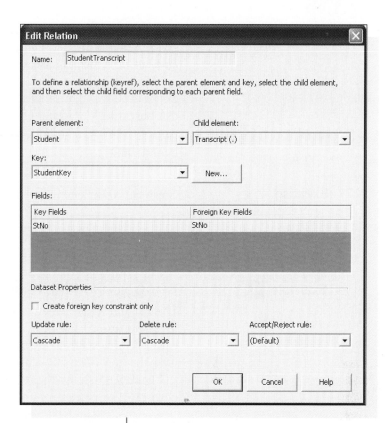

FIGURE 9.42

Creating the Relation between the Student and Transcript Elements

Transcript relation. When you finish, you should see a design like that shown in Figure 9.43.

As a final note, let's look at a little of the actual XML that was created by Visual Basic .NET and relate this to the namespace concept discussed earlier. The XML statement

<xs:key name="StudentKey" msdata:PrimaryKey="true">

shows two namespace prefixes, **xs** and **msdata**. If we look at the namespace declarations in the code we see

xmlns:xs=http://www.w3.org/2001/XMLSchema
xmlns:msdata="urn:schemas-microsoft-com:xml-msdata"

The first namespace, **xmlns:xs=http://www.w3.org/2001/XMLSchema,** includes the schema definitions based on the W3C specification; thus, any processor that

FIGURE 9.43

The Final XML Schema Design for Example 9.3

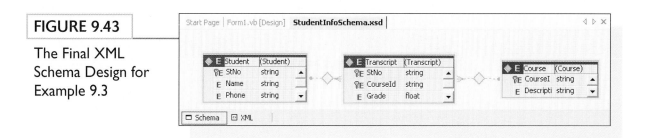

complies with this specification can validate any XML document against any giving schema created using this namespace. The second namespace, **xmlns: msdata="urn:schemas-microsoft-com:xml-msdata"**, is defined by Microsoft and is used to add attributes and elements (such as the PrimaryKey attribute in the example above) that provide ADO.NET the ability to bridge between relational database and XML data. Understand, however, that these extensions are not part of the W3C standard, so one might find that non-Microsoft XML parsers ignore them.

Exercise 9.9

Create an XML Schema for the following entity-relationship diagram:

Example **9.4**

TRANSFORMING XML USING XSLT

This example demonstrates how you can transform an XML file into a new XML file using an XSLT specification. We will use the XML and XSLT files we saw earlier in this section and generate a new file in HTML format. You then can view the new file using a browser to confirm that the transformation worked.

Figure 9.44 shows the original XML file and Figure 9.45 shows the first part of the XSLT file (the entire XSLT file was shown earlier in Figure 9.14).

A Visual Basic .NET Windows Application has been created with a single form. The form has only one Button control that holds the code to perform the transform. To make things easier, we have placed the two files prodList.xml and prodDesc.xslt in the bin folder of the project. This allows us to write code to access the files without having to include the entire file path (by default, Visual Basic .NET looks in its bin folder for any files referenced in the executing code).

The code for this example is shown in Figure 9.46. Notice that we have added an Imports statement to the start of the code. This statement is necessary to get access to the namespace (set of classes) that support the XSL behavior. All Imports statements must be at the very beginning of the code. If you left this Imports statement out, the Dim statement in the Click event would not be valid (the reference to the XslTransform class would not be valid).

FIGURE 9.44

The Original XML File

```xml
<?xml version="1.0" encoding="UTF-8"?>
<ProductList>
    <Product>
        <ProductNumber>12345</ProductNumber>
        <Description>Ball Point Pen</Description>
        <Price>0.45</Price>
    </Product>
    <Product>
        <ProductNumber>54321</ProductNumber>
        <Description>No. 2 Pencil</Description>
        <Price>0.02</Price>
    </Product>
    <Product>
        <ProductNumber>22334</ProductNumber>
        <Description>Legal Tablet</Description>
        <Price>1.05</Price>
    </Product>
</ProductList>
```

FIGURE 9.45

The First Part of the XSLT File

```xml
<?xml version="1.0" encoding="UTF-8"?>
<xsl:stylesheet version="1.0" xmlns:xsl="http://www.w3.org/1999/XSL/Transform">
<xsl:output method="xml" version="1.0" encoding="UTF-8" indent="yes"/>

<!-- Template #1 -->
<xsl:template match="ProductList">
  <html>
    <body>
      <div style="font-family:Tahoma,Arial,sans-serif;
            font-size:20pt; color:red;
            text-align:center; letter-spacing:8px;
            font-weight:bold">
        Another List of Products
      </div>
      <hr />
      <table width="100%" cellpadding="5" border="0"
            style="font-family:Tahoma,Arial,sans-serif;
            font-size:16pt; color:black;
            text-align:center">
        <tr>
          <td>Description</td>
          <td>Price</td>
          <td>Product Number</td>
        </tr>
        <xsl:for-each select="Product">
        <xsl:sort select="Description"/>
          <tr>
            <xsl:apply-templates select="Description" />
            <xsl:apply-templates select="Price" />
            <xsl:apply-templates select="ProductNumber" />
          </tr>
        </xsl:for-each>
      </table>
```

FIGURE 9.46

Code for Example 9.4

```vbnet
Imports System.Xml.Xsl

Public Class Form1
    Inherits System.Windows.Forms.Form

    [Windows Form Designer generated code]

    Private Sub btnApplyXSLT_Click(ByVal sender As System.Object, ByVal e As Syst
        Dim MyXslTransform As XslTransform = New XslTransform()
        Try
            MyXslTransform.Load("prodDesc.xslt")
            MyXslTransform.Transform("prodList.xml", "transformedHTML.html")
            MsgBox("Transformed file sucessfully created", MsgBoxStyle.Information)
        Catch except As Exception
            MsgBox("Exception found: " & except.ToString())
        End Try
    End Sub
End Class
```

The actual transformation process is really very straightforward due to the power of the XSL methods available in Visual Basic .NET. We first declare an object reference **MyXslTransform**:

Dim MyXslTransform As XslTransform = New XslTransform()

We then use the Load() and Transform() methods available to XslTransform objects to perform the actual transformation.

MyXslTransform.Load("prodDesc.xslt")
MyXslTransform.Transform("prodList.xml", "transformedHTML.html")

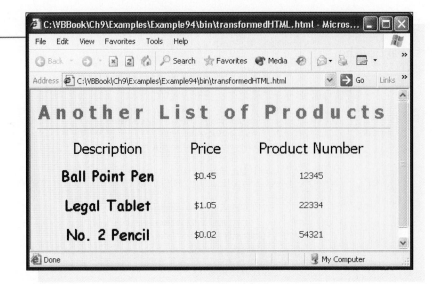

The Load() method loads the XSLT code (see Figure 9.45) from the file named prodDesc.xslt located in the project's bin directory. The Transform() method then uses the XSLT code to transform the XML file (prodList.xml) into a new file (transformedHTML.html). If you look at the transformed file (it also will be stored in the project's bin directory) using a browser, you should see what is shown in Figure 9.47.

Exercise 9.10

Modify Example 9.4 so that the HTML document shows details for each product with the product number first, followed by the description and price.

Exercise 9.11

Create an XML document for a Student element that consists of a Student Number, Name, and Phone Number. Then modify the XSLT in Figure 9.45 so that it processes your XML document and shows, for each Student, the three elements in the order defined (Student Number, Name, and Phone Number).

9.3 Using ADO.NET with XML

ADO.NET provides a number of useful classes and methods to work directly with XML documents. This should not be a surprise since a DataSet component uses XML as its internal data representation. Thus, data are already in XML form and all we are doing with the various XML-related ADO.NET classes is getting access to the XML that has already been created.

In this section we provide a number of examples that demonstrate some of the XML capabilities of the ADO.NET framework. We begin with an example that reads XML data directly instead of reading data from a relational database. This would be useful if a company kept its data in raw XML form or if they needed to process some XML that was sent to them by one of their business partners. We then look at an example where we read data from a relational database and convert it into equivalent XML. We finish with an example that reads data from a relational database, converts it into XML, and then uses an XSLT document to reformat the data.

For these examples we assume that you have read Chapter 8 and are familiar with ADO.NET and its associated components such as a connection, data adapter, and dataset.

Example **9.5**

PROCESSING AN XML DOCUMENT

In this example we see how you can create a dataset from an XML document. You then can use the dataset to display its contents in a DataGrid control. We also see how you can generate an XML Schema from within a running application once the XML document is processed. Figure 9.48 shows the example as it is running and Figure 9.49 shows the XML Schema.

The XML document used in this example is an expanded version of the product list XML document we have seen earlier. Figure 9.50 shows a portion of this document.

In this example we create a DataSet object directly in the code. This is because we are not using a database connection or data adapter like we did in Chapter 8. Objects instantiated from the DataSet class have a method called ReadXML(). This method reads an XML document directly from a file and uses

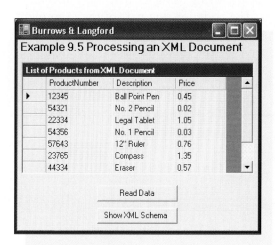

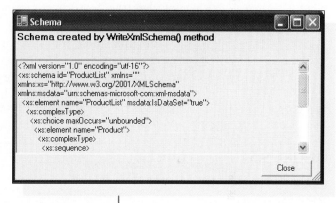

FIGURE 9.49

Example 9.5 with the XML Schema Displayed

FIGURE 9.48

Example 9.5 at Run Time

FIGURE 9.50

A Portion of the XML Document Used in Example 9.5

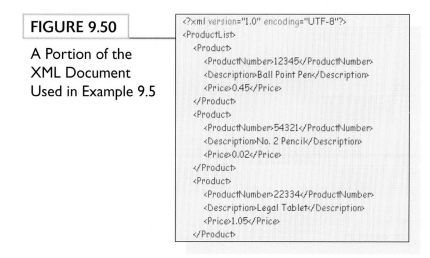

the contents of the document to fill the dataset. Once the DataSet is created and filled with data, it is used to populate a DataGrid component. Code to perform these tasks is shown in Figure 9.51.

The Dim statement creates the DataSet object reference named **dsProducts**. This object reference then uses its ReadXml() method to read the XML document from a file named prodList.xml. This XML document must be in the project's bin directory for it to be found. Following this, the DataSource property value is set equal to the DataSet **dsProduct**. Finally, the grid's DataMember property value is set equal to "Product" because the XML document uses **<Product> ... </Product>** as the main tag to identify each row of the dataset.

To show the XML Schema, we create a second form and display it with the code shown in Figure 9.52.

This form includes one TextBox component with its Multiline and ReadOnly property values set to True. It creates and uses a DataSet object to read the XML document just like we saw before. It also uses the dataset's WriteXmlSchema() method to develop and show an XML Schema that describes the XML document. The code also uses a StringWriter object that is initially used to store the XML Schema generated by the dataset's WriteXmlSchema() method. The StringWriter object is then turned into a String using its ToString() method to populate the TextBox component. The code for this part of the example is shown in Figure 9.53.

Note that after the Text property of the TextBox is set, the TextBox's SelectionStart and SelectionLength property values are set. If this were not done, then all the text in the TextBox would be selected and we want to avoid this behavior because it would look strange to the end user.

FIGURE 9.51

Code to Process the XML Document and Then Fill a DataGrid

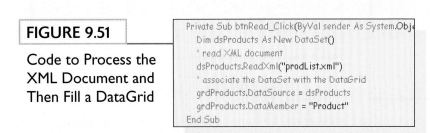

```
Private Sub btnRead_Click(ByVal sender As System.Obj
    Dim dsProducts As New DataSet()
    ' read XML document
    dsProducts.ReadXml("prodList.xml")
    ' associate the DataSet with the DataGrid
    grdProducts.DataSource = dsProducts
    grdProducts.DataMember = "Product"
End Sub
```

FIGURE 9.52

Form and Code to Display the Form That Will Show the XML Schema

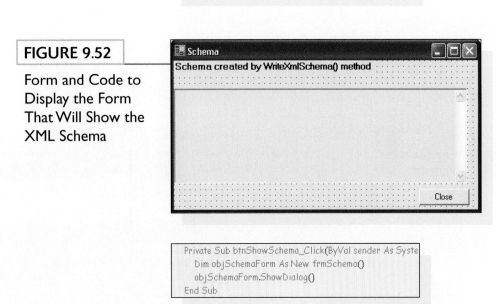

```
Private Sub btnShowSchema_Click(ByVal sender As Syste
    Dim objSchemaForm As New frmSchema()
    objSchemaForm.ShowDialog()
End Sub
```

FIGURE 9.53

Code to Display
XML Schema
in TextBox
Component

```
Private Sub btnClose_Click(ByVal sender As System.Object, By
    Me.Hide()
End Sub

Private Sub frmSchema_Load(ByVal sender As System.Object,
    Dim dsProducts As New DataSet()
    Dim XmlStringWriter As New System.IO.StringWriter()
    dsProducts.ReadXml("prodList.xml")
    dsProducts.WriteXmlSchema(XmlStringWriter)
    txtSchema.Text = XmlStringWriter.ToString
    ' move the selection so no text will not be selected
    txtSchema.SelectionStart = 0
    txtSchema.SelectionLength = 0
End Sub
```

Exercise 9.12

Modify Example 9.5 so that it uses the XML document defined in Exercise 9.11.

Example 9.6

CONVERTING RELATIONAL DB DATA INTO XML

The objective of this example is to demonstrate how you can read data from a conventional relational database and, after you get the results, you can transform the results into an XML document. For example, this might be useful if you store your data in a conventional database but need to send some information to a business partner using XML. Another example might be the need to place the data on a remote Web server that does not have the database software installed on it.

In this example we take data from the pubs database and re-create Example 8.5. In addition, we add the code to generate and display the XML document for the results of the query used to create the dataset displayed in a DataGrid. We also add code to generate and display the XML Schema for the data in the dataset like we did in Example 9.5. Figure 9.54 shows the application at run time. Note that Example 8.5 demonstrated how to create a master/detail dataset. The + expander symbols can be used to see the employees of a specific publisher.

Clicking on the Convert to XML and Display button shows a form like that in Figure 9.55 and clicking on the Show XML Schema button shows another form like that in Figure 9.56.

FIGURE 9.54

Example 9.6 at Run
Time

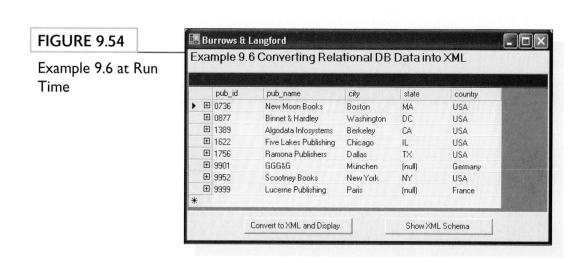

FIGURE 9.55

The XML Document
for the Dataset
Shown in Figure 9.54

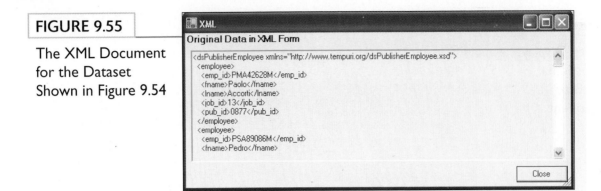

FIGURE 9.56

The XML Schema
for the XML Shown
in Figure 9.55

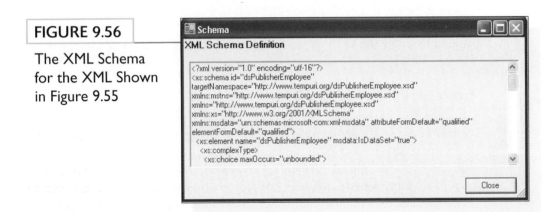

We start by creating the project described in Example 8.5. Using that as the
starting point, we add two new buttons to the main form, one to display the
XML document in a new form and another to display the XML Schema in
another new form. The code for displaying the XML is shown in Figure 9.57.

In the code in Figure 9.57, the DataSet **dsPublisherEmployee** was created using
the instructions given in Example 8.5 (Figures 8.58 and 8.62). The dataset represents the data as shown in Figure 9.58.

FIGURE 9.57

Code to Display the
XML Document in a
New Form

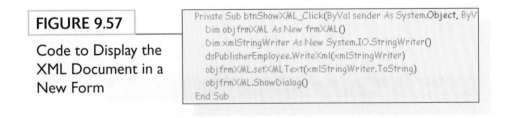

```
Private Sub btnShowXML_Click(ByVal sender As System.Object, ByV
    Dim objfrmXML As New frmXML()
    Dim xmlStringWriter As New System.IO.StringWriter()
    dsPublisherEmployee.WriteXml(xmlStringWriter)
    objfrmXML.setXMLText(xmlStringWriter.ToString)
    objfrmXML.ShowDialog()
End Sub
```

FIGURE 9.58

The Data Design
Used to Create the
Data Stored in
dsPublisherEmployee

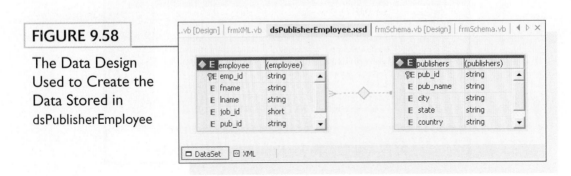

```
Public Sub setXMLText(ByVal XmlText As String)
   txtXML.Text = XmlText
End Sub
```

FIGURE 9.59

Code for the Method setXMLText() on
the Form frmXML

```
Private Sub btnShowSchema_Click(ByVal sender As System.Object,
   Dim objfrmSchema As New frmSchema()
   Dim xmlStringWriter As New System.IO.StringWriter()
   dsPublisherEmployee.WriteXmlSchema(xmlStringWriter)
   objfrmSchema.setSchemaText(xmlStringWriter.ToString)
   objfrmSchema.ShowDialog()
End Sub
```

FIGURE 9.60

Code to Create the XMLSchema and Display It
on a New Form

In addition to having a WriteXmlSchema() method, the DataSet class also has a WriteXml() method that is used in the code in Figure 9.57. This method writes the XML document to a StringWriter as was done in Example 9.5. The new form, an instance of frmXML, contains a TextBox and Close button. We call the new form's setXMLText() method and pass the String equivalent of the StringWriter object. Figure 9.59 shows the code for frmXML's setXMLText() method.

The code used to create the XML Schema and display it on another form is shown in Figure 9.60. We create the schema like we did in Example 9.5 and we fill the new form's TextBox like we just filled the XML form's TextBox.

Exercise 9.13

Using Microsoft Access, create the database described in Exercise 9.9. After populating this database with a few sample records, modify Example 9.6 so that it works with the new database.

Exercise 9.14

Modify Example 9.6 so that it uses the authors, titles, and titleauthor tables in the pubs database.

Example 9.7

**USING XML AND XSLT TO TRANSFORM DATA
FROM A RELATIONAL DATABASE[5]**

This example brings everything we have seen in this chapter together and also adds some additional capabilities we have not seen in the past. We start with a hypothetical database that contains email messages. We read the records from this database and convert them into an XML document. We then allow the user to specify whether to see just the email "headers" or the entire email document. We use two different XSLT documents to convert the XML into HTML depending on their choice of display format. Finally we use a component on the Windows Form that renders and displays the HTML for the user. Run-time images of the example are shown in Figure 9.61 (email headers only) and Figure 9.62 (full view).

As you can see in Figure 9.62, there is a View menu item that includes two subitems "Headers Only" and "Full View." Recall that Section 6.8 covered the details of using the MainMenu control.

---

5   The example is based on a Walkthrough titled "Displaying an XML Document in a Web Forms Page Using Transformations" that is provided with Microsoft Visual Studio .NET.

FIGURE 9.61

Example 9.7
Showing the Email
Headers

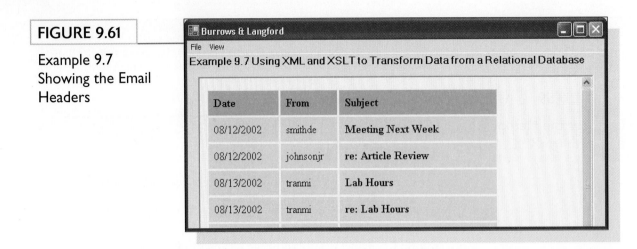

FIGURE 9.62

Example 9.7
Showing the
Complete Email
Message

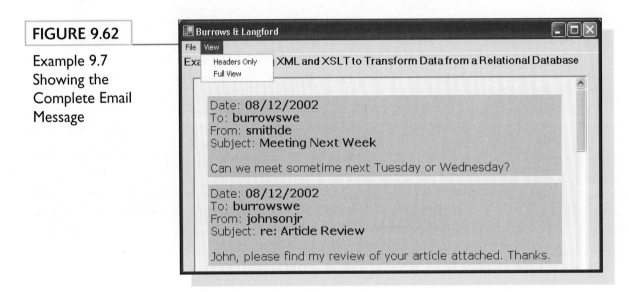

When we prepare examples, we try to choose situations that are realistic but do not present any unexpected problems as far as coding the solution is concerned. While creating this example, we found a little problem. This involved the XML created by the dataset's WriteXML method. The problem meant that the XSLT that we were using to render the XML document into HTML would not work. Instead of throwing the example out or changing it to eliminate the problem, we chose to program a "fix."[6] Our rationale was very simple: in real-life programming, it is not unusual to find little problems, so we think it is important to show an example of this and how we got around it.

The database is a Microsoft Access database named email.mdb consisting of a single table. Figure 9.63 shows the table and its field definitions.

This database is added to the Server Explorer (see Example 8.6) and a connection is established. We then create an OleDbDataAdapter named **odaEmail** and a DataSet named **dsEmail**. This gets us ready to start the project code.

---

6   We actually had two choices for our "fix." One would involve modifying the XSLT to take into account the namespace defined in the XML document. While this would be a relatively easy fix, we chose to use the programming approach because it allows the introduction of some file-processing code and a short example of some useful string manipulation.

FIGURE 9.63

The emailList Table in the Database

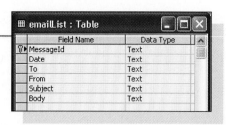

The coding begins with a Form_Load event. This event's primary function is to process the database and convert it into an XML document. However, this is where we encountered our little problem. The WriteXml() method of the DataSet class adds a namespace specification to the opening of the XML document (see the first line in the XML document shown in Example 9.6's Figure 9.55). There is nothing wrong with doing this except for the fact that when we later transform the XML into HTML, the XSLT code fails because of this namespace specification. So we need to write some code to remove it.

Instead of writing the XML to a StringWriter as we have done in the past, we need to write it to a file on the disk. To do this we'll see some new code that deals with reading and writing files on the disk without the aid of a database management system. Given this background, the overall logic of the Form_Load event is

1. Fill the dataset using the data adapter.

2. Create a temporary disk file to store the XML.

3. Write the XML from the dataset to the temporary disk file.

4. Copy each record from the temporary disk file to another disk file to be used later. This new disk file will contain the XML from the temporary file but will not include the namespace specification that caused the problem.

5. Close all the files and delete the temporary disk file.

Step 4 is the step that "solves" our problem. The code for the Form_Load event that covers steps 1–3 is shown in Figure 9.64.

The only part of the code in Figure 9.64 that we have not seen before relates to the temporary file: the FileOpen() and FileClose() methods. The FileOpen() with the OpenMode.Output parameter creates a new file if one does not exist. If

FIGURE 9.64

Code for Steps 1–3 of the Form_Load Event for Example 9.7

```
Private Sub Form1_Load(ByVal sender As System.Object, ByVal e As S
    ' clear then fill the DataSet
    dsEmail.Clear()
    odaEmail.Fill(dsEmail)
    ' now open/close the file
    ' this ensures that a file with the name "tempData.xml" will exist
    Try
        FileOpen(1, "tempData.xml", OpenMode.Output)
    Catch ex As Exception
        MsgBox("File error: " & ex.ToString, MsgBoxStyle.Critical)
    Finally
        FileClose(1)
    End Try
    ' now write the XML version of the DataSet to the file
    dsEmail.WriteXml("tempData.xml")
```

one exists, it just "opens" it, meaning that we can write data into the file if we want to. We are ignoring the situation where the file already exists; we are only taking advantage of the fact that a new file will be created if it does not already exist. The file will be created in the project's bin directory by default. Files are identified by number inside the code, so we are calling this file #1 in the FileOpen() and using "1" in the FileClose(). When the code in Figure 9.64 is done, the XML document (with the problem namespace specification) is in the file named tempData.xml stored in the project's bin directory.

Now we need to fix the problem. The code in Figure 9.65 (a continuation of the Form_Load event) shows how we performed the fix.

This code begins by opening two files: file #1 is a new file named data.xml that will store the corrected XML and file #2 is our temporary file that contains the original problematic XML. It then enters a loop until the function EOF(2) becomes True. EOF stands for End of File, so we are going to process the records in file #2 until we come to the end of that file. Inside the loop we first get the next line (record) from the temporary file (#2). We then search this line for a namespace specification that looks like

<dsEmail xmlns="http://www.tempuri.org/dsEmail.xsd">

If we find the String "xmlns", we need to remove everything up to the closing ">" symbol. In the code above, "xmlns" is found starting in position 10 of the string. So we replace the **NextLine** string with the original nine characters on the left followed by a ">" character. The result looks like

<dsEmail >

Regardless if we find the bad line or not, we then use the PrintLine statement to write the string **NextLine** to file #1 (our correct XML document file).

When the loop terminates, all the lines of the temporary file have been transferred to the new file (including the corrected line). We then close both files and

FIGURE 9.65

Continuation of the Code for Example 9.7's Form_Load Event

```vb
dsEmail.WriteXml("tempData.xml")

' remove the namespace specification because it breaks the XSLT
' read the temporary file and copy it (sans the namespace) to the file data.xml
Try
    FileOpen(1, "data.xml", OpenMode.Output)
    FileOpen(2, "tempData.xml", OpenMode.Input)
    Dim NextLine As String
    Dim NameSpaceLoc As Short
    Do Until EOF(2) ' read to the end of the temporary file
        NextLine = LineInput(2)
        NameSpaceLoc = InStr(NextLine, "xmlns") ' find the xmlsn attribute
        If NameSpaceLoc <> 0 Then ' if xmlsn attribute found, remove it
            NextLine = Microsoft.VisualBasic.Left(NextLine, NameSpaceLoc - 1) & ">"
        End If
        PrintLine(1, NextLine) ' print line to new file
    Loop
Catch ex As Exception
    MsgBox("File error: " & ex.ToString, MsgBoxStyle.Critical)
Finally
    FileClose(1)
    FileClose(2)
    ' delete the temporary file
    System.IO.File.Delete("tempData.xml")
End Try
End Sub
```

delete the temporary file (tempData.xml) using the Delete() function in the System.IO.File namespace.

We now have the data from the database successfully corrected and transferred to the file named data.xml. A portion of that XML document is shown in Figure 9.66.

Before we go any further, we need to point out two lines of code added to the form that are outside any events. These are shown in Figure 9.67. There are two Imports statements that are needed so we can perform the XSL transforms and find out the name of the directory where our application is currently running. We know that our application will be running in the Project's bin directory, but we need to know the complete path; there is a method called getCurrentDirectory() in the System.IO namespace that does this.

Now we turn our attention to translating the XML into HTML and displaying it on the Windows Form. If we were displaying it on a Web form using a browser, there would be no difficulties. However, we want to display the HTML on a Windows Form and there is not a Visual Basic .NET component to do this. We can, however, add an ActiveX component to our Toolbox and use it as long as Internet Explorer is installed on the computer. To add a new component to the Toolbox, right-click on Windows Forms and select Customize Toolbox… from the pop-up menu, as shown in Figure 9.68.

In the Customize Toolbox dialog box, scroll down until you can see the "Microsoft Web Browser" component, as shown in Figure 9.69. Select this by selecting the check box and then click on OK.

FIGURE 9.66

A Portion of the
XML Document

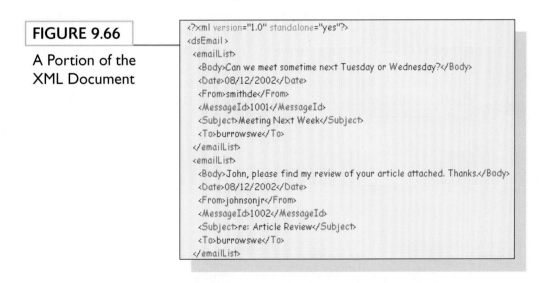

```xml
<?xml version="1.0" standalone="yes"?>
<dsEmail >
 <emailList>
  <Body>Can we meet sometime next Tuesday or Wednesday?</Body>
  <Date>08/12/2002</Date>
  <From>smithde</From>
  <MessageId>1001</MessageId>
  <Subject>Meeting Next Week</Subject>
  <To>burrowswe</To>
 </emailList>
 <emailList>
  <Body>John, please find my review of your article attached. Thanks.</Body>
  <Date>08/12/2002</Date>
  <From>johnsonjr</From>
  <MessageId>1002</MessageId>
  <Subject>re: Article Review</Subject>
  <To>burrowswe</To>
 </emailList>
```

FIGURE 9.67

The Imports
Statements Needed
in the Project

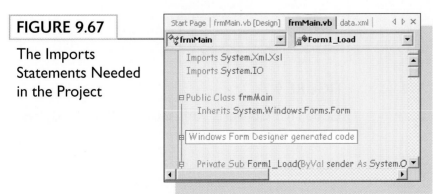

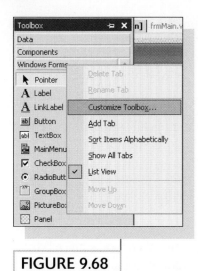

FIGURE 9.68

Pop-Up Menu Used to Add a New Component to the Toolbox

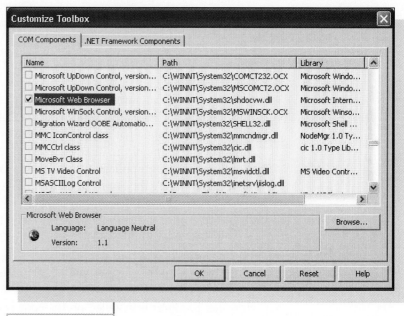

FIGURE 9.69

Dialog Box for Adding a New Component to the Toolbox

When the dialog box closes, you should see the new component in the Windows Forms toolset. The new component will be called Explorer and will likely be at the bottom of the toolset. Figure 9.70 shows the new Explorer component. You use the ▼ icon on the lower right of the figure to scroll through the components in the Toolbox. We added this component to our form and named it "brwMail".

We now turn our attention to the code needed to convert the XML into HTML and display it in the Explorer component. The code that shows the email header information is shown in Figure 9.71.

We have worked with the XslTransform class in previous examples. We create a new XslTransform object and then use the Load() and Transform() methods to load an XSLT document and transform the XML document, using the XSLT, into an HTML document. The XSLT for this process is shown in Figure 9.72.

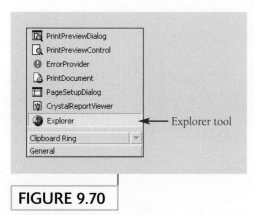

FIGURE 9.70

The Explorer Component in the Windows Forms Toolbox

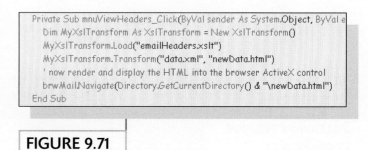

```
Private Sub mnuViewHeaders_Click(ByVal sender As System.Object, ByVal e
    Dim MyXslTransform As XslTransform = New XslTransform()
    MyXslTransform.Load("emailHeaders.xslt")
    MyXslTransform.Transform("data.xml", "newData.html")
    ' now render and display the HTML into the browser ActiveX control
    brwMail.Navigate(Directory.GetCurrentDirectory() & "\newData.html")
End Sub
```

FIGURE 9.71

Code That Converts XML into HTML and Displays it in the Explorer Component

FIGURE 9.72

The XSLT Used to Show the Email Headers

```xml
<?xml version='1.0'?>
<xsl:stylesheet xmlns:xsl="http://www.w3.org/1999/XSL/Transform" version="1.0">
<xsl:template match="dsEmail">
<HTML>
<BODY>
<TABLE cellspacing="3" cellpadding="8">
 <TR bgcolor="#AAAAAA">
   <TD class="heading"><B>Date</B></TD>
   <TD class="heading"><B>From</B></TD>
   <TD class="heading"><B>Subject</B></TD>
 </TR>
 <xsl:for-each select="emailList" >
 <TR bgcolor="#DDDDDD">
   <TD width="25%" valign="top">
     <xsl:value-of select="Date"/>
   </TD>
   <TD width="20%" valign="top">
     <xsl:value-of select="From"/>
   </TD>
   <TD width="55%" valign="top">
     <B><xsl:value-of select="Subject"/></B>
   </TD>
 </TR>
 </xsl:for-each>
</TABLE>
</BODY>
</HTML>
</xsl:template>
</xsl:stylesheet>
```

The last statement in Figure 9.71 uses the Explorer component (**brwMail**) and its Navigate() method to load the HTML file and display it. The code

Directory.GetCurrentDirectory() & "\newData.html"

finds the path of the project's bin folder and concatenates the name of the HTML file using a "\" to separate the directory path and the file name. This is then used by the Navigate() method to find the HTML.

The code for showing all the email content is almost identical to the code used for showing the headers only. The difference is the XSLT filename, and more important, the XSLT contents. Figure 9.73 shows the code and Figure 9.74 shows the XSLT.

Exercise 9.15

Modify Example 9.7 so that the "complete" email view shows the elements as:

Date:<Date>	To:<To>
Subject:<Subject>	From:<From>
Message:<Body>	

FIGURE 9.73

Code Used to Display All the Email Content

```vb
Private Sub mnuViewFull_Click(ByVal sender As System.Object, ByVal e As
    Dim MyXslTransform As XslTransform = New XslTransform()
    MyXslTransform.Load("emailAll.xslt")
    MyXslTransform.Transform("data.xml", "newData.html")
    ' now render and display the HTML into the browser ActiveX control
    brwMail.Navigate(Directory.GetCurrentDirectory() & "\newData.html")
End Sub
```

FIGURE 9.74

The XSLT Used to
Show the Entire
Email Content

```
<?xml version='1.0'?>
<xsl:stylesheet xmlns:xsl="http://www.w3.org/1999/XSL/Transform" version="1.0">
<xsl:template match="dsEmail">
<HTML>
<BODY>
<FONT face="Verdana" size="2">
<TABLE cellspacing="10" cellpadding="4">
  <xsl:for-each select="emailList">
  <TR bgcolor="#CCCCCC">
  <TD class="info">
     Date: <B><xsl:value-of select="Date"/></B><BR></BR>
     To: <B><xsl:value-of select="To"/></B><BR></BR>
     From: <B><xsl:value-of select="From"/></B><BR></BR>
     Subject: <B><xsl:value-of select="Subject"/></B><BR></BR>
     <BR></BR><xsl:value-of select="Body"/>
  </TD>
  </TR>
  </xsl:for-each>
</TABLE>
</FONT>
</BODY>
</HTML>
</xsl:template>
</xsl:stylesheet>
```

Exercise 9.16

Modify Example 9.7 so that the "header" view shows the email headers in order by the <From> element.

This concludes our discussion of XML and its associated technologies. As mentioned earlier, XML has very quickly become a very important part of many applications. Its basic understanding is essential for anyone entering the information technology field and advanced knowledge will likely be very valuable. We encourage the reader to try to learn as much as possible about this important data technology.

9.4 Project 10: Product Catalog Application

Description of the Application

Most companies that sell products have a document called their "product catalog" that shows information on the products they sell. More than one audience might use this catalog. These could include their customers, as well as internal users such as the sales and order department as well as the warehouse. Of course, the different audiences would likely be interested in different information about a product. This project involves accessing the product information from a relational database and then, using XML and XSLT, transforming the information for two audiences: customer and inventory views. Figure 9.75 shows the overall transformation process performed by this project.

The two views seen by the users are shown in Figure 9.76. Note that the customer view shows the products ordered by their description and the inventory view shows the products ordered by product number.

Design of the Application

The Access database, named ProdCat.mdb, includes one table. This table includes six fields, as shown in Figure 9.77.

FIGURE 9.75

The Transformations
That Project 10
Performs

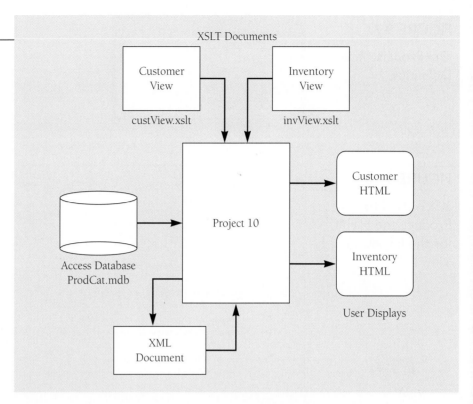

FIGURE 9.76

The Two Views
Generated by
Project 10

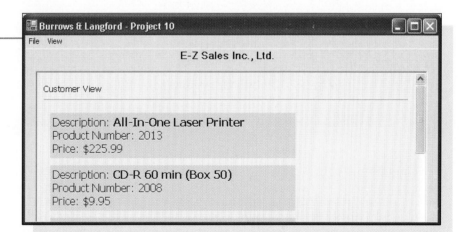

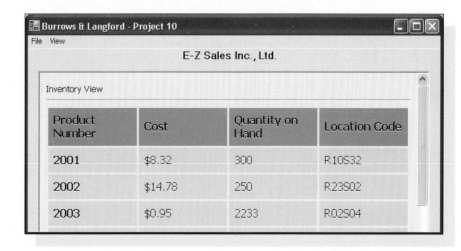

FIGURE 9.77

The ProdList Table
Definition

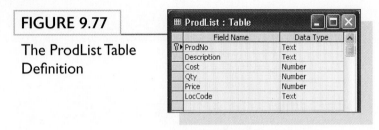

FIGURE 9.78

XSLT Used to
Produce the HTML
for the Inventory
View

```xml
<?xml version='1.0'?>
<xsl:stylesheet xmlns:xsl="http://www.w3.org/1999/XSL/Transform" version="1.0">
<xsl:template match="dsProdCat">
<HTML>
<BODY>
<FONT face="Tahoma" size="2">
Inventory View<hr></hr>
<TABLE cellspacing="3" cellpadding="8">
  <TR bgcolor="#00CCCC">
    <TD class="heading"><B>Product Number</B></TD>
    <TD class="heading"><B>Cost</B></TD>
    <TD class="heading"><B>Quantity on Hand</B></TD>
    <TD class="heading"><B>Location Code</B></TD>
  </TR>
  <xsl:for-each select="ProdList" >
  <TR bgcolor="#CCFFCC">
    <TD width="25%" valign="top">
      <b><xsl:value-of select="ProdNo"/></b>
    </TD>
    <TD width="25%" valign="top">
      $<xsl:value-of select="Cost"/>
    </TD>
    <TD width="25%" valign="top">
      <xsl:value-of select="Qty"/>
    </TD>
    <TD width="25%" valign="top">
      <xsl:value-of select="LocCode"/>
    </TD>
  </TR>
  </xsl:for-each>
</TABLE>
</FONT>
</BODY>
</HTML>
</xsl:template>
</xsl:stylesheet>
```

You will need to write code that converts the records in this database table
into an XML document and write this document to a file for later processing. Be
aware of the potential problem with the namespace attribute as discussed in
Example 9.7.

Once the XML document is available for processing, you need to apply the
appropriate XSLT to transform it into HTML. The XSLT for producing the
inventory view is shown in Figure 9.78. We leave the design of the XSLT for the
customer view as a part of the project. What you have seen so far regarding
XSLT examples and the XSLT for the inventory view should provide you with
enough information to build the XSLT for the customer view.

FIGURE 9.79

Menu Options for
Project 10

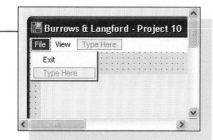
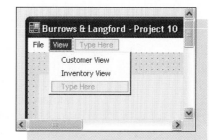

Construction of the Application

Construction of the application is straightforward. You will need to add the Explorer ActiveX component to your Windows Forms Toolbox if you have not done so already (see Example 9.7). Your code uses the Navigate() method of this control to link to the HTML you generated to render and display it.

Add a MainMenu component and set its menu options as shown in Figure 9.79. Use the Click events for the menu to generate the appropriate views from the XML using the appropriate XSLT document.

Chapter Summary

1. XML, the e**X**tensible **M**arkup **L**anguage, provides a technology-neutral way of representing data that has rapidly become the data representation standard of the Internet. XML stores data in a tree relationship with a single root node, where the nonroot nodes are related to one and only one parent. Leaf nodes, nodes that have no children, are usually used to store content. Nonleaf nodes also can store content by using attributes. The data are stored in character format and are thus compatible with the data transmission protocols of the Internet.

    The tags of an XML document can be anything the designer of the XML document wants them to be. This allows documents to be designed that are described as "self-documenting" in that the tags relate directly to the problem-domain underlying the data. When you see a **<Student>** tag in the context of a school, it is obvious what is being described.

2. It is possible to define a special set of rules, called an XML Schema, that control what is valid or not valid as far as the corresponding XML document is concerned. For example, if the XML Schema states that a particular tag, for example, a **<Course>** tag, can occur only one time, then any document that conforms to that XML Schema must follow that rule.

    An XML Schema is itself an XML document, so it must follow the rules associated with all XML documents.

3. An XML document can be well formed and also valid. A well-formed document follows the basic rules of all XML documents. There must be a single root node, a closing tag must exist for every opening tag, tags must be correctly nested, and all attribute values must be enclosed in quotes (either single or double quotes). The tags within an XML document are also case sensitive.

    A document is valid if it is well formed and it conforms to the XML Schema definition it is associated with.

4. Because tags are made up by the designer, it is possible to have two or more identical tags that have different meanings. To solve this problem the XML standard allows for the use of a namespace. The namespace is associated with a unique uniform resource identifier (uri) and tags associated with the namespace are prefixed with a unique character string associated with the namespace.

   Namespaces also are used to identify some predefined tags used by software such as XML parsers. This category of software analyzes the XML tree and determines its content. Some namespaces, such as those defined by the extensible stylesheet language (XSL), are used by the processor to perform the processing task identified by the XSL instruction.

5. eXtensible Stylesheet Language Transforms (XSLT) provide a way of transforming one XML document into a new XML document. This capability is extremely useful in the context of transforming XML into HTML so that the data can be formatted and displayed within a browser.

6. Visual Basic .NET includes classes that define methods to work with XML and its related technologies. For example, the DataSet class includes the WriteXml() and ReadXml() methods that process XML data directly and the XslTransform class includes the Load() and Transform() methods to load XSLT and transform XML into another form using the XSLT document. Visual Basic .NET also includes a number of methods that work with XML Schemas.

Key Terms

attributes	eXtensible Stylesheet	Uniform Resource
complex type	Language	Identifier
DataRelation objects	Transforms	uri
document prolog	facet	valid
ebXML	HTML	well formed
extensible	namespace	XBRL
eXtensible Markup	processing instruction	XML
Language	simple type	XML Schema
eXtensible Stylesheet	template	XSL
Language	tree	XSLT

End-of-Chapter Problems

1. What function does the use of namespaces serve in the context of an XML document? Provide an example of namespace definition.

2. Explain the difference between a well-formed and a valid XML document. A document can be well formed but not be valid. Can a document be valid but not well formed?

3. A university uses qualifications to determine a student's quarterly tuition. These qualifications include class standing (undergraduate, graduate, or professional) as well as residency status (in-state or out-of-state). Draw a tree representation of an XML document that would store this information uniquely for each student. Label the root, branches, and leaves of the tree.

4. Explain the difference between an XML Schema document and an XSLT document. What is the function of an XSLT processor?

5. In the definition of an XML Schema, when would you use a simple type and when would you use a complex type? Give an example of using each. For the complex type, describe when you would use a named or unnamed complex type.

6. Why are nested relationships needed in XML? Are key fields required to create a nested relationship?

7. Are the relationships created for XML Schemas used in the same manner as the relations that link databases in the last chapter?

8. How are XSLT transformations performed with Visual Basic .NET code? Write the code that would perform a transformation of an XML file called studentList.xml using a transformation file named attendanceForm.xslt.

9. What would be the purpose of using the FileOpen() method (with the OpenMode.Output parameter) immediately followed by the FileClose() method? Write a statement line to store in a string variable the proper path to the file "studentList.xml" if it was located in the current directory.

10. Name and describe the three primary methods that can be executed on a DataSet object to perform XML operations.

Programming Problems

1. Use Visual Basic.NET to create an XML Schema that can hold information about your CDA (CD Audio) collection. Create an element in the schema and name it CDA. Columns for the element should include CD id, title, artist, number of tracks, and total running time. Define the cd_id field as an integer and make it the primary key. After you've created the schema, create an XML file from it, add five records, and save the data.

2. XML can be used to support hierarchical data in a nested dataset. In Chapter 1 you learned about the hierarchical nature of classes and how inheritance could be used effectively to handle employee data. Create a Visual Basic .NET application that contains the schema for a Store database that has hourly and salaried employees. You will need to define a Store element, an HourlyEmployee element, and a SalariedEmployee element. The Hourly-Employee element should contain fields for an employee number, a name, an hourly rate, and hours worked. The SalariedEmployee element should contain fields for an employee number, a name, and a salary. The Store element should contain fields for the store ID and location. When you parent the Store element to the other two elements, it also will contain fields for the two employee types.

   Save the schema and create an XML file with some employee data. When you examine the XML of the data file, the beginning should appear to be something like this:

```
<?xml version="1.0" encoding="utf-8"?>
<EmployeeSchema xmlns="http://tempuri.org/EmployeeSchema.xsd">
    <Store xmlns="http://tempuri.org/EmployeeSchema.xsd">
        <storeid>0</storeid>
        <location>San Diego</location>
        <HourlyEmployee>
            <employeenum>0</employeenum>
```

continued

```
            <hourlyrate>8.5</hourlyrate>
            <hoursworked>42</hoursworked>
            <name>John Doe</name>
        </HourlyEmployee>
        <SalariedEmployee>
            <employeenum>0</employeenum>
            <salary>42000</salary>
            <name>Jane Doe</name>
        </SalariedEmployee>
    </Store>
```

3. Contact databases often are created that hold only two telephone numbers: business and personal. The increase in communications has increased the needs to an unknown number of related phone numbers from pagers to cell phone. Create an XML Schema for a contact database that connects two elements (Contact and Telephone) with a one-to-many relation. Define the Contact element with the fields contactid, name, address, city, state, and zip. Set the contactid as the Primary DataSet key. Define the Telephone element with fields contactid, type, phonenum, and notes. Set the contactid field as a key field. Add a relation between the two elements that allows many telephone number records for each contact. Create an XML data file from the schema.

4. An XML complex type can be very helpful when you need to reuse a number of element fields in a schema. Create an XML Schema with a complex type named FullAddress that contains fields for address, aptnum, city, state, and zip. In the schema, add a new element named billto and set the type to FullAddress. As soon as you set the type, you should see all of the fields of the complex type appear as dimmed text in the body of the element. Create another element named shipto using the same method as the billto element. Create an Order element that contains shipto and billto elements. Save the schema and create an XML data file from it.

5. Create an application that can read an XML file into a dataset and display it in a DataGrid control. Use a form that has a TextBox control, two Button controls, and a DataGrid control. The text box should be used to allow the user to enter the path and filename of the desired XML file. For one of the buttons, set the Text property to '…' and place it directly to the right of the filename text box. This button will activate the OpenFile dialog box to allow the user to browse for the appropriate file.

   In the Toolbox, you will find a component named OpenFileDialog. Double-click it to add it to the current form, where it automatically will be named OpenFileDialog1. You will need to add code to your Browse button to use this dialog. The code should first set the Filter property to only display XML files (**OpenFileDialog1.Filter = "XML files | *.xml"**). Then use the ShowDialog() method you learned in Chapter 6 to display the window. Finally, the filename and path that the user selected can be obtained from the FileName property of the dialog. Store this value in the text box on the form.

   To complete the application, use the second button you created on the form to read the XML file (specified in the TextBox) into a DataSet object and display it in the DataGrid as shown in the chapter. It would be a good idea to add some error trapping in case the user selected an invalid XML file. To test the application, use the XML file of your CDAList that you created in Programming Problem 1.

6. As mentioned in the chapter, a DataSet object not only can read an XML file, but can write it from a current DataSet object as well. The WriteXML() method can be used in the same manner as the ReadXML() method except the supplied filename is the output destination (**WriteXML("c:\stores.xml")**). Since Internet Explorer 6 can display any XML file complete with color highlighting and a collapsible hierarchy, the Microsoft Web Browser control can be used to show an XML file that has been written to file storage.

Create an application that reads the stores table from the pubs database, writes an XML file with all of the data in it, and displays this XML file on a form with the Microsoft Web Browser component. Don't forget to fill the data adapter in your Form_Load event or the XML file that is written will be empty of data.

I magine a mail-order company that sells products to customers from all 50 states in the United States. This company is required to charge sales tax on sales to customers in many states, and the sales tax rate varies from state to state. How do we represent these sales tax rates in a program? If we store them in variables of the kind we have seen so far, we will need 50 variables with names like NYTaxRate, NJTaxRate, and CATaxRate. Then the program will require a Select…Case or If…Then…Else statement to identify a customer's state of residence and determine the corresponding tax rate variable to use in the calculation of the sales tax. Because of the large number of variables, this statement will be very long.

Storing a set of related values, such as 50 sales tax rates, in separate variables is tedious at best. However, such situations are common. To resolve this problem, Visual Basic .NET provides another kind of variable called an array. **An *array* is a variable with a single symbolic name that represents many different data items.** This chapter describes how to declare arrays and how to use them to solve some common processing tasks.

In addition to traditional arrays, Visual Basic .NET also provides a number of classes that manage collections of objects. A *collection* **of objects is like an array in that one collection is associated with many objects. These classes "manage" the objects in a number of different ways.** These management techniques differentiate the collection classes. This chapter covers three of these classes: the ArrayList, the Hashtable, and the SortedList collections.

Objectives

After studying this chapter, you should be able to

- Explain why arrays are needed to solve many types of problems.

- Construct an array to store multiple related data values.

- Use ArrayList, Hashtable, and SortedList collections to store and process data values.

10.1 Solving Problems with Arrays

Since we are now introducing arrays, we need a term to describe the ordinary variables we have used prior to this point. We will use the term **simple variable to mean a variable that can store only one value.** We first examine a problem whose solution is very inefficient when we use simple variables. We then show how arrays improve our solution. As we solve the problem, we introduce the structure of arrays.

The Problem

A financial analyst has calculated last year's rate of return[1] for 10 different companies and would like a program to display the names of those companies whose rate of return exceeded the average of the group. What processing steps must we perform to display this information?

The Solution Using Simple Variables

Using the programming techniques we've employed in earlier programs, we might begin to solve this problem by writing the following pseudocode.

> *Compute the average rate of return for the group of ten companies*
> *Display the names of companies whose rate of return exceeds the average*

We first have to compute the average. This requires accessing each individual company's rate of return and adding it to a cumulative total. We can refine the pseudocode for this step as follows:

> *For each company*
>   *get a rate of return and a company name*
>   *add the rate of return to the sum*
> *Next company*
> *Compute the average by dividing the sum by the number of companies*

Once we have the average, we must go back through the rates of return, comparing each to the average. If a rate of return exceeds the average, we display the company name. The pseudocode for this step might be

> *For each company*
>   *If the company's rate of return is greater than the average Then*
>   *display the company's name*
>   *End If*
> *Next company*

This problem requires two passes through the data: one pass to compute the average and a second to compare the average with each rate of return. There is no other way to solve this problem.

Now think about how you would convert this pseudocode to actual code. You would have to store each rate of return in a variable because each is used twice: first to compute the sum, then later to compare to the average. If the

---

[1]   *Rate of return* is a measure of profitability.

company names are input into the program at the same time as the rate of return values, then the company names also will have to be stored in variables. Thus, if we had 10 companies, we'd need 20 variables.

Let's look at some code, assuming that we have only three companies instead of 10. The following code might be found in a Click event procedure for a button captioned "Find Best Companies".

```
Private Sub btnFindBestCompanies_Click(...)
    Dim CompAReturn As Decimal, CompAName As String
    Dim CompBReturn As Decimal, CompBName As String
    Dim CompCReturn As Decimal, CompCName As String
    Dim Average As Decimal
    Dim Sum As Decimal
    CompAReturn = InputBox("Enter Rate of Return for Company A")
    CompAName = InputBox("Enter Company A Name")
    Sum = Sum + CompAReturn
    CompBReturn = InputBox("Enter Rate of Return for Company B")
    CompBName = InputBox("Enter Company B Name")
    Sum = Sum + CompBReturn
    CompCReturn = InputBox("Enter Rate of Return for Company C")
    CompCName = InputBox("Enter Company C Name")
    Sum = Sum + CompCReturn
    Average = Sum / 3
    If CompAReturn > Average Then
        MsgBox CompAName & " exceeds the average rate of return"
    End If
    If CompBReturn > Average Then
        MsgBox CompBName & " exceeds the average rate of return"
    End If
    If CompCReturn > Average Then
        MsgBox CompCName & " exceeds the average rate of return"
    End If
End Sub
```

This solution approach works, but it is not a good general solution. Imagine if you had 30, or 300, or 30,000 companies. You would be writing code for the rest of your life. There must be a better way.

You can spot two places in the code where statement blocks are "nearly repeated" three times. We would like to use loops but are prevented from doing so because each value is stored in a different variable and each variable has a different name. For example, we'd like to have something like the following loop:

```
For K = 1 To 3
    CompAReturn = InputBox("Enter Rate of Return for Company A")
    CompAName = InputBox("Enter Company A Name")
    Sum = Sum + CompAReturn
Next
```

Although the sum would be computed correctly, the problem with this loop is that there is no way to store and preserve the individual rate of return and name for each company. Each iteration of the loop updates the value in **CompAReturn**, destroying the previous rate of return as it obtains the next value needed to accumulate the sum.

FIGURE 10.1

An Array

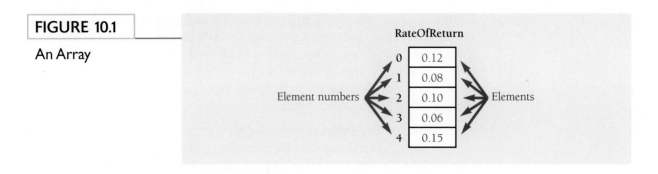

The Structure of an Array

What we need is a different kind of variable—one that has a single name but can store more than a single value. This new kind of variable is known as an array. Figure 10.1 depicts an array named **RateOfReturn** that stores five values. **Each element of an array is like a simple variable.** We can store a different company's rate of return in each element. The entire set of elements shares the name **RateOfReturn**.

The elements in an array are numbered, starting at zero, as shown in Figure 10.1. To access an individual element, we append its number to the array name. For example, in the array depicted in Figure 10.1, the third element is referred to as **RateOfReturn(2)**,[2] and it currently holds the value 0.10. **The element number is called the *subscript*. An alternative term for an element number is the *index value*.** For this reason, **another term that is sometimes used for an array is *subscripted* or *indexed variable*.** The array depicted in Figure 10.1 is a ***one-dimensional array* because each element is referenced using a single subscript value.** You can also create **two-, three-, and higher-dimensional arrays, called *multidimensional arrays*.**

The syntax for referencing a specific element in a one-dimensional array is

> *ArrayName(SubscriptValue)*

where *SubscriptValue* is a numeric expression.

The Solution Using Arrays

If we store the rates of return in an array like the one shown in Figure 10.1, we can design a better solution to the problem. A procedure can process the contents of an array element just as it processes any other variable. For example, the following statement adds the values in elements 0 and 1 of the array.

> *Sum = RateOfReturn(0) + RateOfReturn(1)*

The result stored in the variable **Sum** is 0.20. However, using constants as subscripts this way is almost never done. The reason is simple: using constants as subscripts in your code is no different than using simple variables. That is, the constant fixes the reference to a specific element just as the name of a simple variable refers to a specific storage location.

If we don't use constants as subscripts, then what do we use? The answer is a numeric variable, or a numeric expression containing a variable. For example, the

---

2   Note that since the array numbering system starts at zero, when we speak of the *n*th element of the array, it will be numbered ($n-1$); for example, the fourth element of the array is element number 3.

following statement, in which **K** is an Integer variable, is typical of statements that refer to array elements.

    Sum = Sum + RateOfReturn(K)

Which element in the array does this refer to? You don't know unless you know the value of the subscript **K**. This is very important. If **K** holds the value 2, then the statement above refers to the third element. If **K** holds 3, then the very same statement refers to the fourth element. Thus, we can write a For...Next loop that processes each array element in turn by using the loop's counter variable as the array subscript, as follows:

    For K = 0 To 4
        Sum = Sum + RateOfReturn(K)
    Next

Figure 10.2 illustrates the execution of this code.

If the array had 5,000 elements instead of 5, what change would you have to make to this code? You would simply have to change the For statement so that it starts at 0 and ends at 4,999.

    For K = 0 To 4999

A drawback of our first solution to this problem was that the number of lines of code would increase proportionately if the number of companies that we needed to analyze increased. However, with the array approach shown in Figure 10.2, the number of lines of code is independent of the number of companies.

The number of lines of code you write should not have to be increased in proportion to the number of items to be processed. If you find that this is happening, you probably need to use an array instead of simple variables.

To make the loop

    For K = 0 To 4
        Sum = Sum + RateOfReturn(K)
    Next

even more useful, it would be a good idea to not restrict it to processing only five elements. How can we remove this restriction? Consider the following:

    For K = 0 To NumOfElements - 1
        Sum = Sum + RateOfReturn(K)
    Next

FIGURE 10.2

Summing the Elements of an Array Using a For...Next Loop

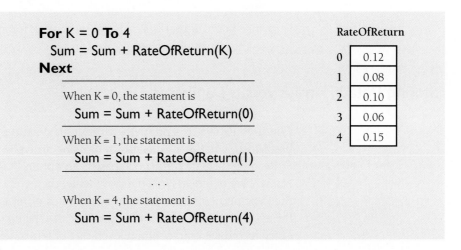

FIGURE 10.3

Arrays for Rate of
Return Problem

	RateOfReturn		CompanyName
0	0.12	0	ABC Inc
1	0.08	1	L2 Inc
2	0.10	2	XYZ Tires
3	0.06	3	Delta
4	0.15	4	FOG Inc

Now we can control the number of elements included in the summing process simply by setting the value of the variable **NumOfElements** prior to the For statement. Again note that since the subscripts start at zero, the largest subscript value will be one less than the number of elements; for example, if there are 10 elements, the range of the subscripts is 0...9.

Let's return to our problem of finding the average rate of return and displaying the company names that exceed the average. We'll add one more array to store the company names, as shown in Figure 10.3.

Observe that the elements of the two arrays are coordinated. That is, the rate of return in element number 0 of the **RateOfReturn** array corresponds to the company name in element number 0 of the **CompanyName** array. This technique is often used when the data types of the two arrays are different; in the present case, **RateOfReturn** holds numeric data (Decimal, most likely) and **CompanyName** holds string data. When the data types of the arrays are the same, an alternative approach is to use a two-dimensional array, which we will discuss shortly.

Consider the following code segment for the rate of return problem. It assumes that the two arrays already exist and the number of companies has already been stored in the variable **NumberOfCompanies**.

```
For K = 1 To NumberOfCompanies - 1
    Sum = Sum + RateOfReturn(K)
Next
Average = Sum / NumberOfCompanies
For K = 1 To NumberOfCompanies - 1
    If RateOfReturn(K) > Average Then
        MsgBox CompanyName(K) & " exceeds the average"
    End If
Next
```

Convince yourself that this solution will work for any number of companies as long as the arrays have been created and correctly initialized with values.

Storing Data in Arrays versus Databases

Could you solve this problem without arrays if the data were stored in a database? If so, what is the advantage of using arrays?

Reading the data from a database is an option. If Rate of Return and Company Name were two fields in a database table, then you could read every record from the table and compute the sum of the rates of return. You could then compute the average. Finally, you could move back to the first record of the table and read every record again to compare each rate of return to the average.

Arrays are variables and, like all variables, they exist in random access memory (RAM). Data stored in RAM are accessed quickly, typically in nanoseconds (billionths of a second). But storage for arrays is limited because RAM is relatively expensive and is needed for other uses such as storage of the operating system.

Databases are stored on disk. The computer must transfer database records to RAM in order to process them and, as a result, access to database records is relatively slow—it is typically measured in milliseconds (thousandths of a second). But storage for databases is less constrained because disk storage is considerably less expensive and a computer typically has much more disk storage than RAM storage.

When the same data items are accessed multiple times during processing, using arrays can produce a superior program. The factors that must be considered when deciding which approach to use include (1) execution speed, (2) the amount of data that needs to be processed, and (3) the clarity of the code that accomplishes the task. If the amount of data is very large (too large for RAM), then directly accessing the database would be the only feasible solution even though it might execute more slowly. If the amount of data is relatively small, then reading the data from the database and storing it in an array for processing can improve execution speed. The speed advantage of the array solution will be greater the more times the data are accessed during processing.

Finally, as RAM gets less expensive, the distinction between databases and arrays gets less clear. Database technology tries to store as much of the data being processed in RAM as it can so as RAM capacity increases, the database technology uses high-speed RAM just as arrays do. If speed is a critical factor, you would store data in RAM regardless of whether it is managed by a database management system or is stored in an array.

Multidimensional Arrays

The number of dimensions an array has is called its *dimensionality*. A one-dimensional array uses one subscript to refer to an element. The array **RateOf-Return** is a one-dimensional array. One-dimensional arrays are useful when the data to be stored in the array are similar to a list of numbers or a list of names.

A two-dimensional array uses two subscripts to refer to a single element and is sometimes called a *matrix* or *table*. Figure 10.4 shows a two-dimensional array. All 12 elements are collectively referred to by the single name **Quantity**. Supplying the values of the specific row and column, the subscripts, identifies an individual element. For example, the reference **Quantity(3, 1)** refers to the element in row number 3 and column number 1 (which holds the number 62 in this case). The first value between the parentheses is the row number and the second is the column number. This is easy to get mixed up; for example, does **Quantity(1, 2)** refer to the value 13 or the value 21? It is row number 1, column number 2, not column number 1, row number 2, so it refers to the value 13.

The general syntax for referencing a specific element in a two-dimensional array is

ArrayName(RowSubscriptValue, ColumnSubscriptValue)

where *RowSubscriptValue* and *ColumnSubscriptValue* are numeric expressions.

For what purpose might we use a two-dimensional array like the one in Figure 10.4? Well, the rows might represent products (four products) and the columns might represent warehouses (three warehouses). Then the values

FIGURE 10.4

A Two-Dimensional Array

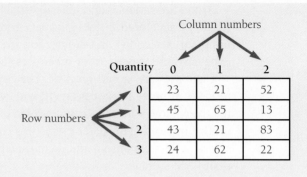

stored in the array could represent the inventory count of a particular product in a particular warehouse (the quantity of product number 3 in warehouse number 1 is 62).

You are not limited to two dimensions. You can create three, four, or more. However, using subscripts slows down the execution of any program. The more subscripts an array has, the slower the execution, so you should always use the minimum number of subscripts necessary to solve the problem.

Exercise 10.1

Suppose you are writing a program that will continually retrieve and update inventory counts for four products at three warehouses. Your program contains three simple Integer variables named **Stock**, **ProdNo**, and **WareNo**. **ProdNo** currently holds a valid product number (0, 1, 2, or 3) and **WareNo** currently holds a valid warehouse number (0, 1, or 2). Assume you have the array depicted in Figure 10.4. Write the statement that stores in the variable **Stock** the inventory count of the product specified by **ProdNo** at the warehouse specified by **WareNo**.

10.2 Declaring Arrays

Arrays can help you solve many kinds of problems like the one discussed in Section 10.1. As with simple variables, in order to use arrays in a program, you must declare them. In this section we examine how to declare arrays, and we discuss subscript bounds.

Arrays can store Integer, String, Decimal, or any other data type just as simple variables can. However, every element of an array must have the same data type.[3] That is, if an array is declared as type Integer, all of its elements store integers. You cannot create an array that has some elements of type Integer and some elements of type Decimal.

Use the Dim (or the Static or Public) statement to declare arrays just as you do for simple variables. But for an array, in addition to specifying the variable name and type, you must also specify the number of subscripts (number of dimensions) and their maximum values. The general syntax of the Dim statement for an array is

Dim *ArrayName(subscripts)* As *Type*

---

3   If an array is declared as type Object, then each cell can store different types, for example, Strings and numbers. This is because the type Object can include any other type.

FIGURE 10.5

Array Dimensions

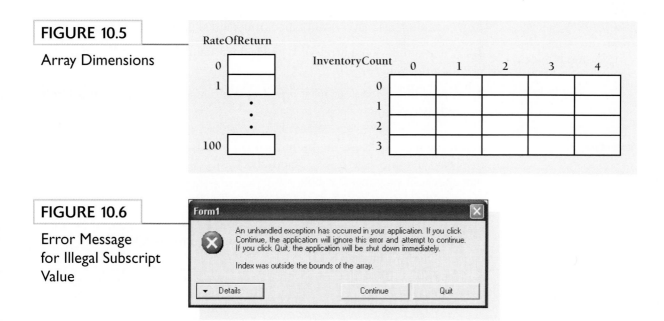

FIGURE 10.6

Error Message
for Illegal Subscript
Value

The *subscripts* portion of the definition is simply a constant for each dimension, separated by commas if there is more than one dimension. These constants define the maximum value of each subscript. For example, you can write

```
Dim RateOfReturn(100) As Decimal
Dim InventoryCount(3, 4) As Integer
```

to create the arrays depicted in Figure 10.5.

The first Dim statement creates a one-dimensional array with 101 elements numbered 0 through 100. The second Dim statement creates a two-dimensional array with four rows and five columns (a total of 20 elements). Notice that the minimum value for each subscript is zero (0). Some people find it odd that the first element number is 0, not 1. After all, if you want to store information on 100 rates of return, it would make the most sense to start at element 1 and end at element 100, not start at element 0 and end at element 99. But with Visual Basic .NET, as well as many other languages, the first element is numbered zero.

Visual Basic .NET has a very nice feature: it will tell you when you use a subscript value that is **outside the range—called the *subscript bounds*—specified by the Dim statement.** For example, suppose the **RateOfReturn** array is declared with maximum subscript value 100. Suppose also that **K** and **NumberOfCompanies** are simple variables of type Integer. If the value stored in **NumberOfCompanies** is greater than 100, executing the loop

```
For K = 0 To NumberOfCompanies
    Sum = Sum + RateOfReturn(K)
Next
```

will cause a run time error—a System.IndexOutOfRangeException—when **K** equals 101. Figure 10.6 shows the message that Visual Basic .NET displays when your program exceeds the bounds of an array. You can write a Try/Catch block to handle a situation like this.

Finally, variable scope is the same for arrays as for simple variables.

Exercise 10.2

For each of the following cases, write the declaration statement that creates the specified array.

1. A one-dimensional array of type String named **Cities**, with 500 elements.

2. A one-dimensional array of type Decimal named **Price**, with a maximum subscript value 98910.

3. A two-dimensional array of type Decimal named **Sales**, with twenty rows and six columns.

Exercise 10.3

When the user clicks on the button named btnArrayQuiz, the following code displays three message boxes. Hand-check this code and show the numbers that appear in each message box.

```
Dim A(6) As Integer

Private Sub btnArrayQuiz_Click(...) Handles btnArrayQuiz.Click
    Dim J As Integer
    A(0) = 10
    A(1) = 7
    A(2) = -3
    A(3) = 4
    A(4) = 1
    A(5) = -4
    A(6) = 2
    DisplayArray()
    A(3) = A(2)
    A(2) = A(3)
    A(6) = A(5)
    A(5) = A(4)
    A(0) = A(1)
    DisplayArray()
    For J = 1 To 6
        A(J - 1) = A(J)
    Next
    DisplayArray()
End Sub

Private Sub DisplayArray()
    Dim K As Integer
    Dim Message As String
    For K = 0 To 6
        Message = Message & " " & A(K)
    Next
    MsgBox(Message)
End Sub
```

Example 10.1

POPULATING AN ARRAY FROM A DATABASE

Arrays are capable of holding large quantities of data, and it is unlikely that the user will be willing (or able) to type in a large amount of data every time a program is executed. In actual business applications, the data for populating an array are typically obtained from a database instead of from the user.

In this example, the Form_Load event procedure performs the task of populating two class-level arrays named **CompanyName** and **RateOfReturn**. There is a third class-level variable named **NumRows** that stores the number of rows in the dataset. A DataSet named DsCompInfo1 and OleDataBaseAdapter named odaCompInfo establish a connection to a table named CompInfo in the Access database named Comp.mdb (remember to use the Server Explorer to make the connection to the Comp.mdb database). The two fields in the table are named **CompName** and **RateOfReturn**. The code for this example is in Figure 10.7. Figure 10.8 shows the user interface after the user has clicked the Review Array Contents button.

Note that the arrays have fixed upper bounds: the Dim statements fix the maximum subscript value at 99 (100 total values). Since the database table could conceivably have more than 100 records, in Form1_Load the value for the number of rows is checked and, if it is too large, the user is informed and the number of rows is adjusted to the array maximum. We will show how to overcome this fixed-size restriction later in the chapter when we introduce collections.

FIGURE 10.7

Code for
Example 10.1

```
Dim NumRows As Integer
Dim CompName(99) As String
Dim RateOfReturn(99) As Decimal

Private Sub Form1_Load(ByVal sender As System.Object, ByVal e As System.EventArgs) Ha
    Dim Row As Integer
    DsCompInfo1.Clear() ' clear and fill the DataSet
    odaCompInfo.Fill(DsCompInfo1)
    NumRows = DsCompInfo1.CompInfo.Rows.Count ' determine number of rows
    ' test for array overflow
    If NumRows > 100 Then
        MsgBox("Not enough array storage for all rows - first 100 will be used", _
                MsgBoxStyle.Information, "Storage Problem")
        NumRows = 100
    End If
    For Row = 0 To NumRows - 1 ' fill the array
        CompName(Row) = DsCompInfo1.CompInfo.Rows.Item(Row).Item("CompName")
        RateOfReturn(Row) = DsCompInfo1.CompInfo.Rows.Item(Row).Item("RateOfReturn")
    Next
End Sub

Private Sub btnReviewArrayContents_Click(ByVal sender As System.Object, ByVal e As Sys
    Dim Row As Integer, NewRow As String
    For Row = 0 To NumRows - 1
        NewRow = CompName(Row) & " - " & RateOfReturn(Row)
        lstArrayContents.Items.Add(NewRow)
    Next
End Sub
```

FIGURE 10.8

Array Contents
Displayed when the
User Clicks on
Review Array
Contents Button

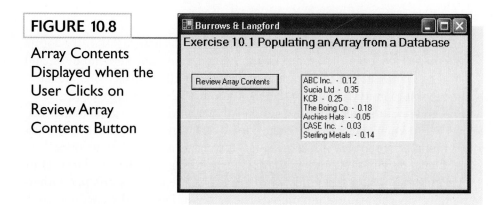

Within the Form1_Load event, we see the loop that actually transfers the data from the dataset into the arrays. This loop includes the following code:

```
For Row = 0 To NumRows - 1 ' fill the array
    CompName(Row) = DsCompInfo1.CompInfo.Rows.Item(Row).Item("CompName")
    RateOfReturn(Row) = DsCompInfo1.CompInfo.Rows.Item(Row).Item("RateOfReturn")
Next
```

Here we see how to access a specific value within a given row and column in the dataset. We start by getting the DataTable associated with the DataSet (DsCompInfo1.CompInfo). Using this, we get a specific row from the Rows collection (Rows.Item(Row)). Now that we have a row, we need to get the specific value from one of the valid columns in each row (Item("CompName") or Item("RateOfReturn")). This is a long statement but you can clearly see how the various objects are used in the decomposition of the dataset. Once the value from the dataset is identified, it is stored in the array in the element indicated by the variable **Row**.

Exercise 10.4

Modify Example 10.1 so that it computes the sum of the rates of return for all companies and then displays the average (sum/count) rate of return using a MsgBox.

Exercise 10.5

Modify Example 10.1 so that it displays the name of the company with the largest rate of return value.

Example 10.2

SEQUENTIALLY SEARCHING AN UNORDERED ARRAY

Searching an array involves checking the values of the array's elements to see if a certain value, called the target, exists within the array. The way we go through the elements, that is, the order in which they are searched, determines the type of the search.

A *sequential search* works by examining each element of the array individually and in turn. The search begins at the first element, proceeds to the second element, then the third, and so on, continuing until the program finds the target or comes to the end of the array. **Sequential search is sometimes also called *linear search*.**

For this sequential search example, we use the two-dimensional array created by the following statement:

```
Dim PriceTable(4,1) As Decimal
```

We populate the array with the values shown in Figure 10.9 in the form's Load event. The values in the first column represent unique item numbers, and the values in the second column represent corresponding prices. Thus, we interpret the values in row 0 to mean that item number 324 has a price of $2.34.

Let us use our search procedure in the following way: given an item number, we want to know the corresponding price. The target for our search will be an item number, and once we locate the target we can easily retrieve its price.

When the values in an array are in ascending (smallest to largest) or descending (largest to smallest) order, we say the array is *ordered*. Otherwise, we say the array is *unordered*. The values in Figure 10.9 are unordered.

FIGURE 10.9

A Two-Dimensional Array for Testing Search Techniques

PriceTable	0	1
0	324	2.34
1	423	3.23
2	254	1.95
3	321	0.34
4	132	2.25

Our sequential search uses a simple loop.

For rows 0 To the last row
If the item number in column zero of the current row equals the target Then
we found a match; remember the row number and exit the loop
Else
do nothing; let loop continue with next iteration
End If
Next row
If we reached the end of the array Then
conclude that the item we are searching for does not exist
End If

We write our solution in the form of a Click event. The search begins in row 0 of the array. If it finds the target, it sets **FoundLoc** equal to the row number where the target is located; if the target does not exist, **FoundLoc** will still be equal to its initial value –1.

Figure 10.10 shows the code for the form's Load event and the button's Click event.

FIGURE 10.10

Code for the Sequential Search in Example 10.2

```
Dim PriceTable(4, 1) As Decimal

Private Sub Form1_Load(ByVal sender As System.Object, ByVal e As System.Event
    ' this "brute force" method of populating an array is
    ' generally only valid for demonstration purposes
    PriceTable(3, 0) = 324 : PriceTable(3, 1) = 2.34
    PriceTable(4, 0) = 423 : PriceTable(4, 1) = 3.23
    PriceTable(1, 0) = 254 : PriceTable(1, 1) = 1.95
    PriceTable(2, 0) = 321 : PriceTable(2, 1) = 0.34
    PriceTable(0, 0) = 132 : PriceTable(0, 1) = 2.25
End Sub

Private Sub btnSearch_Click(ByVal sender As System.Object, ByVal e As System.E
    Dim Row As Integer
    Dim FoundLoc As Integer = -1
    Dim Target As Integer = txtItemNumber.Text
    For Row = 0 To 4
        If PriceTable(Row, 0) = Target Then
            FoundLoc = Row
            Exit For
        End If
    Next
    If FoundLoc <> -1 Then
        MsgBox("Price for item #" & Target & " is $" & PriceTable(FoundLoc, 1))
    Else
        MsgBox("Item #" & Target & " not found in table")
    End If
End Sub
```

Finally, it is possible to define and initialize an array just as one can do with simple variables. For example, consider the following two Visual Basic .NET statements:

```
Dim a() As Integer = {1, 2, 3, 4, 5}
Dim b(,) As Integer = {{1, 2}, {3, 4}, {5, 6}}
```

In the first statement, the array **a** is declared as an Integer type and stores the five values shown in the braces. The array's legal index values range from **a(0)** to **a(4)** (a total of five values). In the second statement, a two-dimensional array is declared and initialized to the values shown in the braces. The inner set of braces each represents a new row in the array **b**. Thus the array has three rows and two columns. Sample values from this array include **b(0,0)** = 1, **b(1,1)** = 4, and **b(2,0)** = 5. Note that, in both examples, the actual size of the array is determined by the number of values shown after the equal sign. It is not possible to use this technique to declare an array that has more cells than the number of given values.

As you can see, arrays provide a powerful way of representing data. There are numerous algorithms that can be programmed using arrays including more complex (and faster) searches, and sorting data into ascending or descending order. In the past the developer would often write this complex and hard-to-debug code. However, Visual Basic .NET provides a number of specialized classes that make the job of working with arraylike structures much easier and more effective for the typical developer.

In the sections that follow, we look at three of these classes, called collection classes, because they are all members of the System.Collections namespace. We will cover the ArrayList, SortedList, and Hashtable collections. In addition to these three classes, there are a number of additional collection classes available within Visual Basic .NET.

Exercise 10.6

Modify the data in Example 10.2 so that they are stored in the array in order by product number. Then, using these newly ordered data, modify the search so that it will be more efficient if the user enters a nonexistent product number. By "more efficient," we mean it potentially goes through the loop fewer times.

10.3 The ArrayList Collection

The *ArrayList* collection class is like a one-dimensional array in that it is indexed using a zero-based indexing system. You can reference individual elements by using a subscript just as with an array. What is different is the capacity of the ArrayList—it provides a dynamic resizing ability. Its capacity (size) grows automatically as items are added. Although it is limited to one dimension, each element can store references to other objects so you could, for example, store a reference to another ArrayList object in each element. This would give you the ability to simulate a multidimensional array.

Properties

The most common properties available to objects of the ArrayList class are shown in Table 10.1

It is generally a good idea to leave the Capacity property alone. The ArrayList object can manage this property very well and probably better than the developer.

Table 10.1 Common properties of the ArrayList class	
Property	**Action**
Capacity	Gets or sets the number of elements that the ArrayList can contain.
Count	Gets the number of elements actually contained in the ArrayList.
Item	Gets or sets the element at the specified index.

The Count property tells you how many elements are actually being used in the ArrayList. Because the indexing starts at zero, the legal index values are 0 ... (Count − 1). The Item property is used to reference a specific element. For example, if you have an ArrayList named **CityName**, you would reference element number 2 by saying:

> **CityName.Item(2)**

Methods

The most common methods available to objects of the ArrayList class are shown in Table 10.2.

The Add and Insert methods are used to place new values into the ArrayList. Add places elements at the end of the ArrayList while Insert places a new element at a specific index value. When inserting, the element at the current index location and the elements after this one are shifted down one location to make room for the inserted element.

Table 10.2 Common methods of the ArrayList class	
Method	**Behavior**
Add	Adds an object to the end of the ArrayList.
BinarySearch	Uses a binary search algorithm to locate a specific element in the *sorted* ArrayList.
Clear	Removes all elements from the ArrayList.
Contains	Determines whether an element is in the ArrayList. Returns True or False.
IndexOf	Returns the zero-based index of the first occurrence of a value in the ArrayList.
Insert	Inserts an element into the ArrayList at the specified index.
Remove	Removes the first occurrence of a specific object from the ArrayList.
RemoveAt	Removes the element at the specified index of the ArrayList.
Reverse	Reverses the order of the elements in the ArrayList.
Sort	Sorts the elements in the ArrayList.
ToArray	Copies the elements of the ArrayList to a new array.
TrimToSize	Sets the capacity to the actual number of elements in the ArrayList.

FIGURE 10.11

A Sample ArrayList
Named Words

ArrayList Words	
Item	Value
0	"Good"
1	"Bad"
2	"Ugly"
3	"Hello"
4	"Goodbye"
5	"Candy"

Remove and RemoveAt remove elements from the ArrayList. RemoveAt takes an index value and removes the element at that index location. Remove takes an object and removes the first element storing that object. In Figure 10.11 you see a sample ArrayList named **Words**. If you say **Words.Remove("Hello")**, then the value at item 3 ("Hello") would be removed. Using the RemoveAt method, you would say **Words.RemoveAt(3)**.

Contains and IndexOf are similar to Remove and RemoveAt. Contains searches for an occurrence of a value. **Words.Contains("Hello")** would return True. IndexOf returns the actual index value. **Words.IndexOf("Hello")** returns 3.

The BinarySearch method performs a search of the ArrayList (that must first be sorted using the Sort method). **A binary search is a very fast search method** (much faster than the sequential search we saw in the previous section). In a binary search, you start your search by checking the middle value (if you had 11 values, you would start by checking element 5, assuming the first element is numbered zero). If you find what you are looking for you are done. However, if you do not find what you are looking for, you only need to search the top or bottom half of the ArrayList. This is because the data are sorted. If your values are integers and they are sorted, and you are looking for the value 104, if you find the value 110 at location 5, you know that all values after location 5 are greater than 110. Thus, the value you are searching for cannot be in locations 6 through 10 and you would eliminate those elements from any further searching. In the remaining locations (0 through 4), you would again try the middle value and so on. The approach is called a binary search because you keep reducing the search space by one-half. This gets you very quickly to the target location. If you have 1,000 values, numbered 1 … 1000, the locations you would search might be: 500, 250, 125, 62, 31, 15, and so forth. Note that after only six tries, you have limited the search area to only 7 locations out of 1,000.

Exercise 10.7

Explain why a binary search requires the data to be ordered (sorted) for it to work.

Exercise 10.8

You are given the following list of numbers: 10, 20, 22, 34, 45, 46, 50, 66, 70, 78, 79, 80, 85, 92, and 98. Show how a binary search would work if you were searching for the value 80. Show how a binary search would work if you were searching for the value 21. How can you determine when to stop a binary search?

Example 10.3

POPULATING AN ARRAYLIST FROM A DATABASE

In this example, we redo Example 10.1 except we use two ArrayLists instead of arrays to store the data from the database table. This example demonstrates the

FIGURE 10.12

Code for
Example 10.3

```
Dim NumRows As Integer
Dim CompName As New ArrayList()
Dim RateOfReturn As New ArrayList()

Private Sub Form1_Load(ByVal sender As System.Object, ByVal e As System.EventArgs)
    Dim Row As Integer
    DsCompInfo1.Clear() ' clear and fill the DataSet
    odaCompInfo.Fill(DsCompInfo1)
    NumRows = DsCompInfo1.CompInfo.Rows.Count ' determine number of rows
    For Row = 0 To NumRows - 1 ' fill the array
        CompName.Add(DsCompInfo1.CompInfo.Rows.Item(Row).Item("CompName"))
        RateOfReturn.Add(DsCompInfo1.CompInfo.Rows.Item(Row).Item("RateOfReturn"))
    Next
End Sub

Private Sub btnReviewArrayContents_Click(ByVal sender As System.Object, ByVal e As
    Dim Row As Integer, NewRow As String
    For Row = 0 To NumRows - 1
        NewRow = CompName.Item(Row) & " - " & RateOfReturn.Item(Row)
        lstArrayContents.Items.Add(NewRow)
    Next
End Sub
```

dynamic nature of the length of the ArrayList. Figure 10.12 shows the code for this example.

If you compare Figure 10.7 with Figure 10.12, you can first see that the variables **CompName** and **RateOfReturn** are declared as new ArrayList objects in Figure 10.12. Then, in Form1's Load event, you see no need to check on the number of rows because the capacity of the ArrayList is dynamic and will grow as needed. You also see the use of the ArrayList's Add method used within the loop that processes rows of the dataset.

In the Click event of btnReviewArrayContents, you see the use of the Item property to get access to the values stored within the ArrayList so that they may be transferred to the ListBox component.

Example 10.4

PERFORMING A BINARY SEARCH

As discussed previously, the binary search is a very fast search method, especially when the number of items to be searched is large. In this example, we fill an ArrayList with an unordered set of fruit names and then provide a search function. Figure 10.13 shows the application at run time. Notice that the original values displayed in the ListBox component are not ordered, that the Sort button is enabled, and that the Search button is not enabled. Since the binary search works only on an ordered list, the Sort button must first be clicked, which causes the items in the ArrayList to be sorted and then used to refill the ListBox. In addition, the Search button is enabled. Finally, as you can see in the figure, a successful search indicates where the item was found (remember that we start at item number zero).

The code for the form's Load event is shown in Figure 10.14. In this code, we fill the ArrayList by just entering some fruit names. In reality the data would more likely come from a database. Once the ArrayList is filled, the ListBox component is filled.

The code for the sort is very simple. The Sort method for the ListArray is executed, the ListBox is cleared and then refilled from the now sorted ArrayList, and

FIGURE 10.13

Example 10.4 at
Run Time

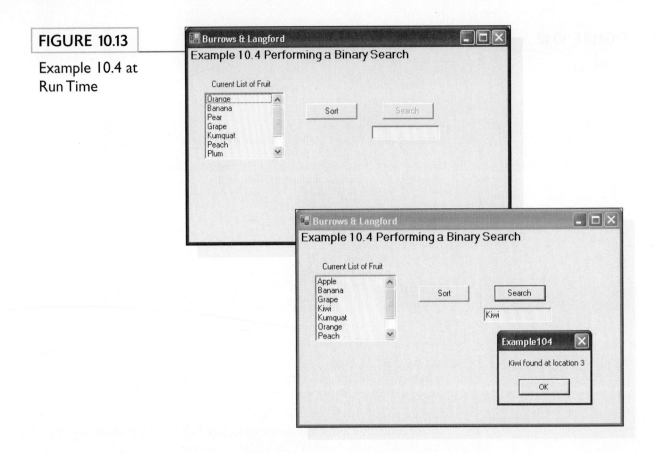

FIGURE 10.14

The Form's
Load Event for
Example 10.4

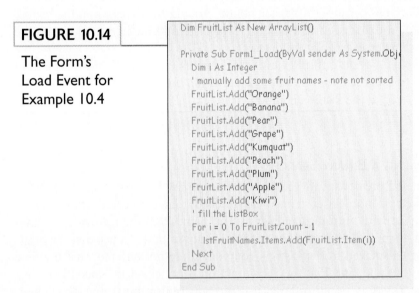

```
Dim FruitList As New ArrayList()

Private Sub Form1_Load(ByVal sender As System.Obj
  Dim i As Integer
  ' manually add some fruit names - note not sorted
  FruitList.Add("Orange")
  FruitList.Add("Banana")
  FruitList.Add("Pear")
  FruitList.Add("Grape")
  FruitList.Add("Kumquat")
  FruitList.Add("Peach")
  FruitList.Add("Plum")
  FruitList.Add("Apple")
  FruitList.Add("Kiwi")
  ' fill the ListBox
  For i = 0 To FruitList.Count - 1
    lstFruitNames.Items.Add(FruitList.Item(i))
  Next
End Sub
```

the Search button is enabled. The search code is also very straightforward. The
BinarySearch method is executed and returns an integer value indicating where
it found the target value. If this return value is less than zero, the search failed
(the actual value that is returned changes, but a failed search will always return a
negative number). Figure 10.15 shows the code for these two Click events.

Exercise 10.9

Modify Example 10.4 so that the user can perform a search without first sorting
the array. What happens when you do this?

FIGURE 10.15

The Click Event
Code for
Example 10.4

```
Private Sub btnSort_Click(ByVal sender As System.Object,
    Dim i As Integer
    FruitList.Sort()
    ' refill the ListBox
    lstFruitNames.Items.Clear()
    For i = 0 To FruitList.Count - 1
        lstFruitNames.Items.Add(FruitList.Item(i))
    Next
    btnSearch.Enabled = True
End Sub

Private Sub btnSearch_Click(ByVal sender As System.Obje
    Dim target As String, FoundLoc As Integer
    target = txtTarget.Text
    FoundLoc = FruitList.BinarySearch(target)
    If FoundLoc < 0 Then 'not found
        MsgBox("Sorry, " & target & " not found.")
    Else
        MsgBox(target & " found at location " & FoundLoc)
    End If
End Sub
```

Example 10.5   **PERFORMING MULTIPLE RESULT SEARCH**

In this example, we use the IndexOf method to find and count the number of times a specific word exists in an ArrayList of words. Figure 10.16 shows the example at run time.

The ArrayList is filled and then used to fill the ListBox component in the form's Load event as in the previous examples. The code for the Search button is shown in Figure 10.17. This code uses the IndexOf method very much like you might use the InStr() function. It begins by searching for the target word starting in item zero. If this search fails, it returns a value of −1. The searching continues as long as it succeeds (return values >= 0). Each new search starts in the next item following where the previous search succeeded.

FIGURE 10.16

Example 10.5 at
Run Time

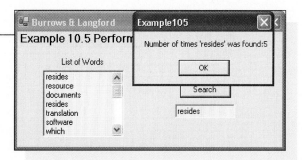

FIGURE 10.17

The Search Code
for Example 10.5

```
Private Sub btnSearch_Click(ByVal sender As System.Object, ByVa
    Dim target As String = txtTarget.Text
    Dim count As Integer
    Dim loc = WordList.IndexOf(target, 0)
    Do While loc >= 0
        count = count + 1
        loc = WordList.IndexOf(target, loc + 1)
    Loop
    MsgBox("Number of times '" & target & "' was found:" & count)
End Sub
```

10.4 The Hashtable Collection

A *Hashtable* is a data structure that supports very fast access to information based on a key field. For example, if you want to store information on students, you could use the student number as the key field. Later, when you wanted to find information on a particular student, you would specify the specific student number and the Hashtable would find the corresponding information based on the value of the student number.

The details of how a Hashtable works are rather complex and beyond the scope of this text. However, the general concepts are fairly easy and worth discussing because they help explain when a Hashtable makes sense to use and when it does not make sense. The secret behind a Hashtable is something called the hash function. The ***hash function* takes a unique key field (part number, student number, social security number, etc.) and transforms it into a new value called a bucket number**. We can describe this symbolically as:

$$f(keyField) \rightarrow bucketNo$$

where f represents the hash function. There are a number of different hash functions, but a commonly used one uses the modulus (remainder) function. In this case, the key field is divided by a constant and the remainder becomes the bucket number.

Once a bucket number is generated, the information related to the key field (such as student name, address, etc.) is stored in that bucket. Later, when you want to get the information related to the key, you specify the key field, it is transformed into a bucket number, and then you go to that bucket to find the information. Figure 10.18 shows information on six students including their student numbers and names. The student numbers are the key fields. The bucket number is calculated by dividing the student number by 11 and using the remainder. Note that if you divide a number by 11, the remainders range from 0 to 10.

You can see from Figure 10.18 that the values "hash" into buckets in a random fashion. That is, there is no relationship between the order in the buckets and either the original order of the student records or the value of the student

FIGURE 10.18

An Example of Hashing Six Students into Buckets

Student No. (key)	Bucket No. (key mod 11)	Name
3243	9	Bill
1244	1	Sue
4362	6	Joe
8741	7	Jill
2351	8	Jose
9334	6	Alice

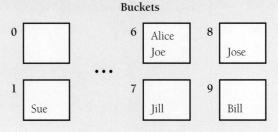

numbers. This is an important characteristic of the *hashing process*—**it results in storing information in a random order.** Also note that two different keys can end up being hashed to the same bucket (see bucket 6). The Hashtable has the ability to handle this.

Once the values are "hashed" to their buckets, performing the hashing process again later provides access to the information. If you want to know the name of student number 2351, you would apply the hash function to 2351, get bucket number 8, and go directly to bucket 8 to find the name. Unlike search methods such as the binary search, hashing can generally find the correct value in one or two tries.

As developers, we can use the Hashtable class available in Visual Basic .NET that handles all the details for us. The important things we need to remember regarding the use of Hashtables are

- They support very fast access to a record given the key field.

- They store the records randomly in the buckets.

- It is difficult to access the entire set of records one after the other.

- You must use the exact key to access the value as you used when the value was first stored. This means that searches for partial key matches, such as all names that start with "Smi", are not possible.

The last point above is a result of the randomization process. You can go through the buckets sequentially, but if you do, the order of the records will be random. For example, the order of the records (by name) using the data in Figure 10.18 would be Sue, Alice, Joe, Jill, Jose, and Bill.

Now that we have some understanding of the Hashtable and its operation, we turn our attention to the common properties and methods.

Properties

Recall that a Hashtable is based on the key field and value(s) associated with it. Microsoft calls this the key/value pair. You can see the most common properties of the Hashtable class in Table 10.3.

The most commonly used property is the Item property. This property gets the value associated with a key. Its syntax is

.Item*(key)*

For example, if you had a Hashtable named **Students** and you wanted to get the value associated with student number 1234, you would say:

String Name = Students.Item("1234")

Table 10.3 Common properties of the Hashtable class

Property	Action
Count	Gets the number of key/value pairs contained in the Hashtable.
Item	Gets or sets the value associated with the specified key.
Keys	Gets a collection containing the keys in the Hashtable.
Values	Gets a collection containing the values in the Hashtable.

If there is a record in the Hashtable with a key matching "1234", then the student's name would be returned (assuming that is what was stored in the first place). If there was no record associated with the key "1234", then the special value Nothing would be returned. Typically you follow a reference to the Items property with an If statement to see what happened, as follows:

```
String Name = Students.Item("1234")
If Name = Nothing Then
    ' no match
Else
    ' match
End If
```

Methods

The common methods associated with the Hashtable class are described in Table 10.4.

The syntax of the Add method is

MyHashtable.Add(key, value)

where *key* is used in the hash function to find the bucket number and *value* is what you want to associate with the key. The key cannot be anything—it must be from a class that implements a method called GetHashCode. Fortunately, the String class implements this method, so we can use Strings for keys. Like the ArrayList, the capacity of the Hashtable is dynamic—its capacity grows as needed as new elements are added.

If you want to get all the values from a Hashtable, you must use the GetEnumerator method. This method returns an IDictionaryEnumerator object. The term "to enumerate" can be defined as "to specify one after another." **An *enumeration* therefore is a list of items one after the other.** The IDictionaryEnumerator object is a list of all values one after the other. The IDictionaryEnumerator class has a method called MoveNext. When the enumeration is first created, the

Table 10.4 Common methods of the Hashtable class

Method	Behavior
Add	Adds an element with the specified key and value into the Hashtable.
Clear	Removes all elements from the Hashtable.
Contains	Determines whether the Hashtable contains a specific key. Returns True or False.
ContainsKey	Determines whether the Hashtable contains a specific key. Returns True or False.
ContainsValue	Determines whether the Hashtable contains a specific value. Returns True or False.
GetEnumerator	Returns an enumerator that can iterate through the Hashtable.
Remove	Removes the element with the specified key from the Hashtable.

"current" item is pointing before the first item, so you have to execute the MoveNext once to get to the first item. After that, MoveNext moves to the next items one after the other. The MoveNext method returns a Boolean value True if the process of moving next finds a next record. It returns a Boolean value False if the process of moving next comes to the end of the list.

The IDictionaryEnumerator class has two properties, Key and Value, that store the key and the value of the current item. Assuming you have a Hashtable named **Students**, you could get and process an enumeration with the following code:

```
Dim AnEnumerator As IDictionaryEnumerator = Students.GetEnumerator
Do While AnEnumerator.MoveNext
    ' here you could reference AnEnumerator.Key and AnEnumerator.Value
Loop
```

Exercise 10.10

You are given the following set of student numbers: 2132, 4365, 3864, 1649, 9342, 5477, 1992, 1032, 7493, and 2299. Create a set of buckets numbered 0 to 10 and store the student numbers into their proper bucket using the modulus-11 method (bucket number = remainder after dividing by 11). Then, using the value 5477, show how you would find the student number in the set of buckets.

We now turn our attention to two examples that work with Hashtables.

Example 10.6

POPULATING A HASHTABLE FROM A DATABASE TABLE

We again return to our example that processes a database table and stores the records in a Hashtable. The example also creates and displays an enumeration from the Hashtable. Figure 10.19 shows Example 10.6 at run time. Note that the original order of the records is different than the order shown in the enumeration. This should not surprise you because of the randomization process associated with converting the key values into bucket numbers.

The code for the example is shown in Figure 10.20. In the form's Load event, you can see the Add method using the company name as the key and rate of return as the value. The loop that processes the dataset also adds items to the ListBox **lstOriginal**. This list box shows the items in the order they were stored in the dataset.

The Click event creates an enumerator and then goes through it item by item, accessing the enumerator's Key and Value properties to get and display the company name (key) and rate of return (value).

FIGURE 10.19

Example 10.6 at Run Time

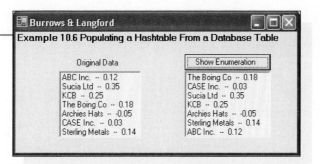

FIGURE 10.20

Code for
Example 10.6

```
Dim NumRows As Integer
Dim ROR As New Hashtable()

Private Sub Form1_Load(ByVal sender As System.Object, ByVal e As System.EventA
    Dim Row As Integer
    Dim Key As String, RateOfReturn As Decimal
    DsCompInfo1.Clear() ' clear and fill the DataSet
    odaCompInfo.Fill(DsCompInfo1)
    NumRows = DsCompInfo1.CompInfo.Rows.Count ' determine number of rows
    For Row = 0 To NumRows - 1 ' fill the array
        Key = DsCompInfo1.CompInfo.Rows.Item(Row).Item("CompName")
        RateOfReturn = DsCompInfo1.CompInfo.Rows.Item(Row).Item("RateOfReturn"
        ROR.Add(Key, RateOfReturn)
        lstOriginal.Items.Add(Key & " -- " & RateOfReturn)
    Next
End Sub

Private Sub btnShowEnumeration_Click(ByVal sender As System.Object, ByVal e As
    Dim AnEnumerator As IDictionaryEnumerator = ROR.GetEnumerator
    Do While AnEnumerator.MoveNext
        lstEnumeration.Items.Add(AnEnumerator.Key & " -- " & AnEnumerator.Value)
    Loop
End Sub
```

Exercise 10.11

Modify the code in Example 10.6 so that the values for the enumeration are shown in alphabetic order based on the company name. The ListBox component should just show the company names, not the rates of return. Consider using an ArrayList object in your solution.

Example 10.7

SEARCHING A HASHTABLE

The primary value of the Hashtable is its ability to find a record quickly given a key value. This example demonstrates this feature. Figure 10.21 shows the example at run time.

The code for the Click event for this example is shown in Figure 10.22 (the form's Load event is the same as that in Example 10.6). You can see that this event gets the value entered by the user in the TextBox component and uses this to access the Item property to get the value associated with the key. The value returned is tested to see if it is equal to "Nothing" to determine if the value entered by the user exists as a key in the Hashtable.

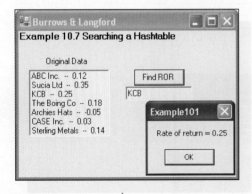

FIGURE 10.21

Example 10.7 at Run Time

```
Private Sub btnSearch_Click(ByVal sender As System.Objec
    Dim key As String = txtCompNo.Text
    Dim RateOfReturn As Decimal = ROR.Item(key)
    If RateOfReturn = Nothing Then
        MsgBox("Sorry, company " & key & " not found.")
    Else
        MsgBox("Rate of return = " & RateOfReturn)
    End If
End Sub
```

FIGURE 10.22

Code for the Click Event for Example 10.7

Exercise 10.12

Modify Example 10.7 so that it computes the average rate of return (sum of rates of return divided by the number of rates of return). Place this code in a new button's Click event.

Exercise 10.13

Modify Example 10.7 so that it finds and prints the company name for the company with the largest rate of return. Place this code in a new button's Click event.

ArrayList versus Hashtable

It is important to understand the main differences between the ArrayList and the Hashtable. The ArrayList is an *index-based data structure*, **that is, it uses indices (subscripts) to access information it holds (just like a regular array).** On the other hand, the Hashtable is not index based; it stores information based on the value of a key field.

With index-based data structures, the developer has control of the order in which the information is stored. It is also possible to go directly to an item based on the subscript value. For example, you can go directly to item 10. The difficulty is you cannot go directly to the item that stores information on product 3000 (unless product 3000 is stored in element number 3000). This is why the ArrayList class includes the BinarySearch method. You can, however, access items one after the other by using index values such as 0, 1, 2, ...

The *key-based data structures* **like the Hashtable provide fast access to information based on the key value.** However, the developer has no control over the order in which the values are stored. In addition, one must use an enumerator to access all the values one after the other.

You need to keep these factors in mind when deciding what type of collection you should use for your applications.

We now turn our attention to a third type of collection known as the SortedList. As you will see, this data structure provides some of the advantages of both the index- and key-based data structures.

10.5 The SortedList Collection

A *SortedList* **is a hybrid between a Hashtable and an ArrayList.** When an element is accessed by its key using the Item property, it behaves like a Hashtable. When an element is accessed by its index using GetByIndex or SetByIndex, it behaves like an ArrayList.

A SortedList internally maintains two arrays to store the elements of the list; that is, one array for the keys and another array for the associated values.

The elements of a SortedList are ordered by the value of the keys. A SortedList does not allow duplicate keys. It is also not possible to sort the items of a SortedList by its values.

Operations on a SortedList tend to be slower than operations on a Hashtable because of the sorting. However, the SortedList offers more flexibility by allowing access to the values either through the associated keys or through the indices.

Properties

The common properties of the SortedList class are shown in Table 10.5.

As with the Hashtable, the Item property can be used to get a specific value based on value of the key. The syntax is

> **.Item***(key)*

If there is an item matching the *key*, the value associated with that item is returned, otherwise Nothing is returned.

Methods

The commonly used methods of the SortedList class are shown in Table 10.6.

As you can see from the list of methods, there are some that are index-based, like those found in Table 10.2 for the ArrayList, and others that are key-based,

Table 10.5 Common properties of the SortedList class

Property	Action
Count	Gets the number of elements contained in the SortedList.
Item	Gets and sets the value associated with a specific key in the SortedList.
Keys	Gets the keys in the SortedList as an ICollection.
Values	Gets the values in the SortedList as an ICollection.

Table 10.6 Common methods of the SortedList class

Method	Behavior
Add	Adds an element with the specified key and value to the SortedList.
Clear	Removes all elements from the SortedList.
ContainsKey	Determines whether the SortedList contains a specific key.
ContainsValue	Determines whether the SortedList contains a specific value.
GetByIndex	Gets the value at the specified index of the SortedList.
GetEnumerator	Returns an IDictionaryEnumerator that can iterate through the SortedList.
GetKey	Gets the key at the specified index of the SortedList.
IndexOfKey	Returns the zero-based index of the specified key in the SortedList.
IndexOfValue	Returns the zero-based index of the first occurrence of the specified value in the SortedList.
Remove	Removes the element with the specified key from SortedList.
RemoveAt	Removes the element at the specified index of SortedList.
SetByIndex	Replaces the value at a specific index in the SortedList.
TrimToSize	Sets the capacity to the actual number of elements in the SortedList.

like those found in Table 10.4 for the Hashtable. This reinforces the idea that the SortedList is both an index- and key-based data structure.

The GetKey and GetByIndex are the primary methods used to get the key and value at a particular index location. Both require you to supply an index value.

The Add method is similar to the Hashtable's Add method, using both a key and a value. However, unlike the Hashtable's Add method, the key does not have to belong to a class that implements the GetHashCode method. This means that it is somewhat more flexible as far as keys are concerned. Like both the ArrayList and Hashtable, the capacity of the SortedList is dynamic and grows as new elements are added.

The SortedList class also includes a GetEnumerator method. Once you get the enumeration, you process it as was described in Section 10.4.

EXAMPLE **POPULATING A SORTEDLIST FROM A DATABASE TABLE**

We return a final time to our example that populates a collection; in this case we populate a SortedList. Figure 10.23 shows the example at run time. You can see that in addition to populating the SortedList, an enumeration is created and displayed and the SortedList is displayed by index. You can see that both enumeration and indexed display are ordered by the key, which is the company name in this case.

The code for the Form_Load event is shown in Figure 10.24. Except for the declaration of the SortedList:

> Dim ROR As New SortedList()

FIGURE 10.23

Example 10.8 at Run Time

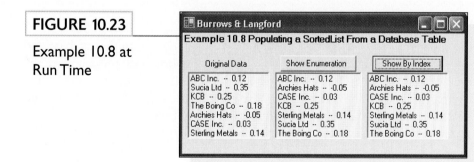

FIGURE 10.24

Code for Example 10.8's Form_Load Event

```
Dim NumRows As Integer
Dim ROR As New SortedList()

Private Sub Form1_Load(ByVal sender As System.Object, ByVal e As System.EventArg
    Dim Row As Integer
    Dim Key As String, RateOfReturn As Decimal
    DsCompInfo1.Clear() ' clear and fill the DataSet
    odaCompInfo.Fill(DsCompInfo1)
    NumRows = DsCompInfo1.CompInfo.Rows.Count ' determine number of rows
    For Row = 0 To NumRows - 1 ' fill the array
        Key = DsCompInfo1.CompInfo.Rows.Item(Row).Item("CompName")
        RateOfReturn = DsCompInfo1.CompInfo.Rows.Item(Row).Item("RateOfReturn")
        ROR.Add(Key, RateOfReturn)
        lstOriginal.Items.Add(Key & " -- " & RateOfReturn)
    Next
End Sub
```

FIGURE 10.25

Code for the Two Click Events in Example 10.8

```
Private Sub btnShowEnumeration_Click(ByVal sender As System.Object, ByVal e As
    Dim AnEnumerator As IDictionaryEnumerator = ROR.GetEnumerator
    lstEnumeration.Items.Clear()
    Do While AnEnumerator.MoveNext
        lstEnumeration.Items.Add(AnEnumerator.Key & " -- " & AnEnumerator.Value)
    Loop
End Sub

Private Sub btnShowByIndex_Click(ByVal sender As System.Object, ByVal e As Sy
    Dim r As Integer
    lstShowByIndex.Items.Clear()
    For r = 0 To ROR.Count - 1
        lstShowByIndex.Items.Add(ROR.GetKey(r) & " -- " & ROR.GetByIndex(r))
    Next
End Sub
```

this code is identical to the Form_Load event for the Hashtable in Example 10.6. That is, the Add method looks the same; it is only different in its internal operation.

The code for the two "display" methods is shown in Figure 10.25. The code that shows the enumeration is unchanged from the Hashtable example. This is because both are based on an enumerator and once you have an enumerator, it is processed the same way regardless of where it came from. The only difference is the order of the items in the enumerator due to the random nature of the Hashtable and sorted nature of the SortedList.

In Figure 10.25, the ShowByIndex code uses an index **r** to go through the SortedList based on the index value. This code uses **GetKey(r)** and **GetByIndex(r)** methods to access the key and value pair for element **r**.

EXAMPLE 10.9

FINDING AVERAGE RATE OF RETURN

In this example we read the company rate of return data from the database and store it into a SortedList. We then go through the SortedList and compute the average rate of return. Finally we go back through the SortedList and place the company names of the companies whose rate of return exceeds the average into a ListBox. Figure 10.26 shows Example 10.9 at run time.

The form's Load event is identical to that in Example 10.8. The Click event that computes the average and fills the list box is shown in Figure 10.27. Note that this code implements the pseudocode discussed in Section 10.1. It first goes through the SortedList and finds the sum of the ROR values. It then calculates the average ROR. Finally, it goes through the SortedList a second time comparing each company's ROR with the average and adding the company name to a ListBox for those whose ROR exceeds the average.

FIGURE 10.26

Example 10.9 at Run Time

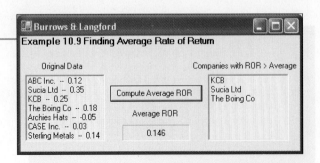

FIGURE 10.27

Code for Example 10.9's Click Event

```
Private Sub btnComputeAvgROR_Click(ByVal sender As System.Object,
    Dim Sum As Decimal, Item As Integer, Average As Decimal
    ' sum the ROR values
    For Item = 0 To ROR.Count - 1
        Sum = Sum + ROR.GetByIndex(Item)
    Next
    Average = Sum / ROR.Count
    lblAverageROR.Text = Format(Average, "0.###")
    ' now fill list box with companies who have above average ROR
    lstAboveAverage.Items.Clear()
    For Item = 0 To ROR.Count - 1
        If ROR.GetByIndex(Item) > Average Then
            lstAboveAverage.Items.Add(ROR.GetKey(Item))
        End If
    Next
End Sub
```

Exercise 10.14

Modify Example 10.9 so that it finds and prints the company name for the company with the largest rate of return. Place this code in a new button's Click event.

10.6 Project 11: Order Entry Application

Description of the Application

Note: In addition to using arrays, this project also introduces additional features associated with the DataSet and DataGrid controls.

This project simulates an order entry system. It displays a list of products and provides the user with the ability to build an order by choosing products from the list. The user can display the contents of the order at any time.

The main user interface for the project is shown in Figure 10.28. The form shows a list of products. The user may select any product in this list and then click on the Buy button to add the product to the order.

When the user clicks on the Buy button, a new dialog box is displayed that asks the user for a quantity. This dialog box is shown in Figure 10.29. The user must enter a valid number for the quantity. If the user does not do this, then an error dialog is displayed. This error dialog is also shown in Figure 10.29.

In this version of the project (there is a more complex version in the Comprehensive Projects Section), the user cannot order the same product more

FIGURE 10.28

Main Form for Project 11

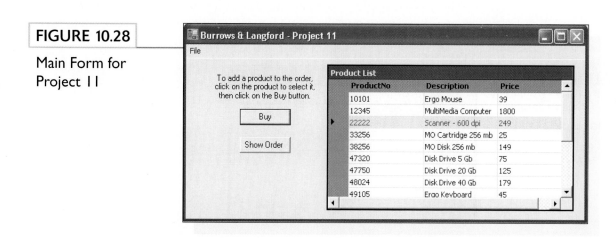

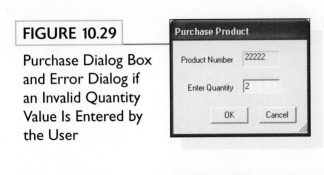

FIGURE 10.29

Purchase Dialog Box
and Error Dialog if
an Invalid Quantity
Value Is Entered by
the User

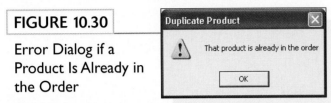

FIGURE 10.30

Error Dialog if a
Product Is Already in
the Order

than one time. If the user tries to do so, an error message, shown in Figure 10.30, is displayed.

The user can click on the Show Order button at any time. When clicked, the current products that have been ordered are displayed. Figure 10.31 shows an example of this display.

Design of the Application

This is a challenging project because it incorporates material from Chapters 7 and 8 as well as some new material. References to relevant material in prior chapters are made throughout the following discussion. It is likely that you will have to review that material.

The overall design of this project involves a database containing product information that is used to populate the DataGrid component on the main form. When the Buy button is clicked, there needs to be a way of recording the product and its quantity. This is necessary because the product information for ordered products must be saved for display purposes on the Order Details dialog box. The information on this dialog box is displayed using a ListView component.

The database for this project is an Access database named Proj11.mdb. This database contains a single table named Product. The design information for this table is shown in Figure 10.32.

This table is used to populate the DataGrid component. A connection, data adapter, and dataset must be created in order to do this. The actual code should

FIGURE 10.31

The Order Details
Dialog Box

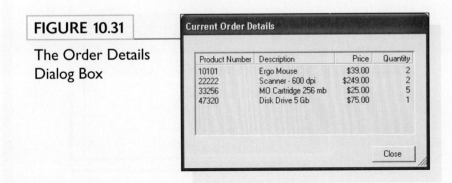

FIGURE 10.32

The Product Table in the Proj11.mdb Database

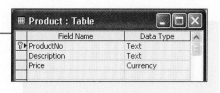

be placed in the form's Load event so that the product information is displayed when the application first starts.

When the user clicks on the Buy button, there must be a way to determine which product was selected at that time. This can be done by first finding the row number of the current cell and then using that information to get the value of the Product Number for the product in that row. You can find the current row by using the DataGrid's CurrentCell and RowNumber properties. Assuming you have a DataGrid named grdProducts, the code would be

> Dim Row As Integer = grdProducts.CurrentCell.RowNumber

Once you have the row number of the current row, you can get the value of any cell within that row using the DataGrid's Item property. Since the Product Number is in the first column of the DataGrid, its column number is zero. The code to get the value out of the row identified by the variable **Row**, column zero, is

> Dim ProdNo As String = grdProducts.Item(Row, 0)

At this point the user needs to be asked for the quantity of the product he wants to order. A new form must be displayed to do this (see Figure 10.29). Before the form is displayed, the Product Number must be stored in a Label component on the Buy form. This can be done by creating a new method in the Buy form named something like **SetProdNo**, which stores a String value into the label. The following is a sample of what might be created:

> Public Sub SetProdNo(ByVal ProdNo As String)
>   lblProdNo.Text = ProdNo
> End Sub

This method can first be called and then the Buy form can be shown using the ShowDialog method. This should be done from the main form code using statements such as

> objBuyForm.SetProdNo(ProdNo)
> objBuyForm.ShowDialog()

Within the Buy dialog box, code must be written that provides access to the quantity the user entered as well as which button, OK or Cancel, was pressed. You should review Project 9 where this type of communication is discussed in detail.

When the OK button on the Buy dialog box is clicked, the Product Number and Quantity Ordered should be known. The question to address is how to store this information for later use when the user wants to show the current order details. There are several options. One option would be to write the information to a database table (not the Product table in the Proj11 database). Another option would be to add the information to an array. The later option is the one we will use here.

The next questions are: what should be stored in that array and what type of array should be used? To answer the first question, we will just store the Product Number and Quantity in the array. If we have the Product Number, we can go to the database and get the other information (Description and Price).

FIGURE 10.33

Using a Traditional
Two-Dimensional
Array

"Order" Array

	ProdNo 0	Qty 1
0	10101	3
1	22222	2
2	47750	5
3		
.		
.		
.		
N		

This will simplify what needs to be stored in the array. We have several choices for the type of array to use. One choice is a two-dimensional array such as the one shown in Figure 10.33. This array has two columns; the first column stores the Product Number and the second column stores the Quantity. The problem with this option is determining how many rows to dimension. If we create too many, we waste storage because many rows will be unused. On the other hand, if we create too few, then the user will be limited on the number of products that can be ordered. This is certainly not good.

An alternative is to use one of the array collection classes. The advantage of this is the fact that their capacity is unbounded and can be as large as needed. For this project we will use a SortedList collection. This allows us to use the Product Number as the key and Quantity as the data item or value. We will be able to access an entry in the SortedList by using either the Product Number or index. In this way we can access by index to get each value, one at a time. Later, if we need to access a specific product, for example, to update a quantity value, we can use key access.

Assume we have a SortedList named **ShoppingCart**. Once the user has finished entering the quantity value in the Buy dialog box, we can first check to see if the OK button was clicked and, if it was, add a new entry to the SortedList that includes the Product Number and Quantity. The code below shows how this might be done.

```
If objBuyForm.GetBtnStatus = objBuyForm.OK Then
    Qty = objBuyForm.GetQty
    ShoppingCart.Add(ProdNo, Qty)
Else
    Exit Sub
End If
```

This code makes a reference to the symbolic constant **objBuyForm.OK**. This symbolic constant is defined in the Buy form using a Public statement:

```
Public Const OK = 1
```

Since we are using a SortedList, we cannot add more than one entry that has a specific Product Number. As we saw earlier, the code needs to detect this and handle the exception that would be thrown if one tried to add a duplicate Product Number.

We turn our attention to displaying the current order status. A separate form is used to display the information (see Figure 10.31). This form includes a ListView component that must be populated. The easiest way to do this is to do it from the main form since the main form has access to both the shopping cart SortedList as well as the DataSet component. The code segment below shows code for the Show Order button:

```
Dim objOrderForm As New frmOrder()
populateOrderFormListView(objOrderForm)
objOrderForm.ShowDialog()
objOrderForm.Close()
```

The populateOrderFormListView method is part of the main form's code. It uses the **ShoppingCart** collection plus information from the Product table in the DataSet to add new rows to the ListView component that is stored on the order form.

The populateOrderFormListView method needs to perform the following steps:

1. Set up the ListView (see Chapter 7).
    a. Set the view type.
    b. Get the ColumnHeaderCollection.
    c. Set up the column headings.

2. Perform the steps below for each item in the **ShoppingCart** collection (**For N = 0 To ShoppingCart.Count - 1**).
    a. Get the product number from location **N** of the **ShoppingCart** collection.
    b. Add a new row, with the current product number in the first cell, to the ListView component on the order form.
    c. Get the row from the dataset that matches the current product number.
    d. Extract the description and price from the row retrieved in step c.
    e. Add subitems to the current ListView row including the description, price, and quantity (from the **ShoppingCart**).

Step 1 above should be fairly straightforward—review the material in Section 7.7 on the ListView component.

Step 2 needs some explanation. Getting the product number for item **N** of the **ShoppingCart** is done using the GetKey method. Using this value to add a new row to the ListView component is done using the Add method for the ListView component's Items property. Remember that if you want to access a component on another form, you need to prefix the component's name with the form name, such as

```
Row = objfrmOrder.lvwOrder.Items.Add(ProdNo)
```

where **Row** is declared as a ListViewItem object.

Step c requires accessing the row from the DataSet component that matches the current product number. The DataSet class's Table property has a Select method. The Select method selects a specific record or records based on a *filter,* **which defines the condition that must be met to choose a row.** The following code segment shows how this is done.

```
Dim Filter As String = "ProductNo = " & ShoppingCart.GetKey(N)
Dim DBRow As DataRow() = DsProducts.Tables("Product").Select(Filter)
```

Since product numbers are unique in the DataSet, there will be only one row (row number 0) returned in this case. Step d says to extract a value from the row. This can be done using the Item property of the DataRow class.

```
Dim Desc As String = DBRow(0).Item("Description")
```

Finally the values from the **DataRow**, as well as the quantity from the **Shop-pingCart**, must be added as subitems to the row of the ListView using the Add method for the SubItems class.

```
Row.SubItems.Add(Desc)
```

Construction of the Application

After creating a new Windows Application, you need to add two new forms: one for obtaining the quantity the user wants to buy and another to display the current order status. A connection to the Access database needs to be set up using the Server Explorer. An OleDbDataAdapter with access to all the records in the Product table needs to be added to the main form. A dataset also needs to be added to the main form. Once this is done, a DataGrid can be added to the main form and connected to the data adapter and dataset.

The properties that should be set for the DataGrid (besides the DataSource and DataMember properties) include setting ReadOnly to True and Changing PreferredColumnWidth and PreferredHeaderWidth to appropriate values. The sample solution shown here used 111 and 30 respectively.

In Figure 10.28 you can see that the DataGrid is formatted with a variety of colors and fonts. The DataGrid provides an Auto Format feature that gives you some predefined options. Figure 10.34 shows where this feature is located in the Properties window.

When you click on this link, an Add Format dialog box like the one shown in Figure 10.35 is displayed. The solution shown here used the "Colorful 4" format.

There is not much left besides the code. Remember that the main form needs to communicate with both the Buy form and the Order Details form. The main form needs to tell the Buy form the product number and the Buy form needs to make available to the main form the quantity entered and the button clicked. The main form has to tell the Order Details form the products ordered (**ShoppingCart**) so that it knows what to add to the ListView component. Project 9 includes details on this type of communication.

FIGURE 10.34

The Auto Format Link in the Properties Window

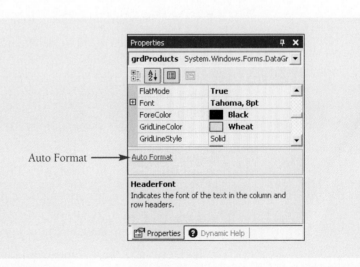

FIGURE 10.35

The Formats Defined for the DataGrid

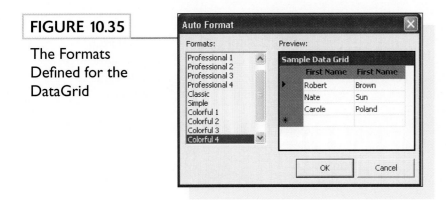

Chapter Summary

1. An array is a variable that stores more than a single value. Arrays make it possible to solve many problems that cannot be solved with simple variables.

2. Like simple variables, arrays need to be declared using a Dim, Static, or Public statement. However, in addition to establishing the variable's name, type, and scope, for arrays the declaration statement also establishes the number of dimensions (the dimensionality) and the upper limits on the subscript for each dimension.

3. To access an element of an array, the programmer specifies both the array name and specific subscript values. Typically, subscripts are specified using variables or more complex expressions containing variables. For example, in the reference **PayRate(K)**, the current value of **K** determines which element of the array **PayRate** is being accessed.

4. As with simple variables, the declaration statement that creates an array initializes all of its elements to zero or the zero-length string. Thus, it is typical for a program to first store data in an array and then use the array to process the data. Storing data in an array is referred to as populating the array. Business applications typically obtain the data to populate an array from a database. The data sometimes come from another, previously populated array.

5. An ArrayList collection is an index-based data structure like an array. However, it does not have a fixed capacity. The capacity of an ArrayList is dynamic and grows as new items are added. The ArrayList class includes methods to sort the elements of the ArrayList (Sort) and search for a specific element (BinarySearch).

6. A Hashtable collection is a key-based data structure that, unlike an array, uses a key field to store and retrieve elements. This provides the ability to access a specific element very quickly without having to do a slow search operation. To access all the elements of the Hashtable, the class provides a method to generate an enumeration. The enumeration allows processing of the element one by one, but the order of the elements is random (due to the randomizing effect of hashing).

7. A SortedList provides both index-based and key-based access to its elements. Thus, it shares the characteristics of both the ArrayList and Hashtable. Accessing an element via an index requires use of the GetByIndex method. Accessing an element by key is done using the Item property. The sorted list also provides a method to generate an enumeration. The order of the elements in the enumeration is based on the sorted order of the key.

Key Terms

array	Hashtable	ordered array
ArrayList	index-based data	sequential search
binary search	structure	simple variable
collection	indexed variable	SortedList
dimensionality	index value	subscript
element	key-based data structure	subscript bounds
enumeration	linear search	subscripted variable
filter	matrix	table
hash function	multidimensional array	unordered array
hashing process	one-dimensional array	

End-of-Chapter Problems

1. Why would an array be used instead of a database? When is it better to use a database than an array? Can they be used together? Why?

2. Explain the difference between an array and a collection. Which structures can hold references to other objects: an array, a collection, or both?

3. What are the advantages of using an array, an ArrayList, or a SortedList? Which of the three types are index-based data structures, key-based data structures, or both? Give an example where each array type (an array, an ArrayList, and a SortedList) would best be used to solve a problem.

4. What is the purpose of a hash table? If you wanted to step through a hash table one element at a time, how would you do it?

5. If a multidimensional array was defined with the "Dim myArray(2,30) As Integer" statement, how many total elements would the array contain? How many rows? How many columns? What are the index numbers of the first row and the first column of this array?

6. If you had to store the ordering information for football jerseys (price, jersey number, and player position), how could three arrays be coordinated to solve the problem? Why not use one array?

7. Describe how a binary search can be used on an ArrayList to locate a value. Why is using a binary search much faster than using index numbers to move through the list testing one element at a time?

8. How are new values added to an existing ArrayList? Provide an example of adding an item to an ArrayList and one of inserting an item before the first element. How can you determine the number of elements in an ArrayList?

9. In an ArrayList, SortedList, or Hashtable, can you use the available search functions to locate a partial string such as all of the string values ending with the ".edu" suffix? Can a database be searched to look for a partial value in a field?

10. What is the function of a database filter? How is a filter used with a database? Is there a SQL language statement that you learned in Chapter 8 that could perform a similar function?

Programming Problems

1. Write an application that creates a one-dimensional array and then copies the items contained in the array into a SortedList object and a Hashtable. Start by placing three list boxes to display the primary array, the ArrayList, and the Hashtable. Then create two buttons: one that fills the list boxes with the current contents of the array, SortedList and Hashtable, and the second to copy the items from the first array into the SortedList and Hashtable.

   The Form_Load event should populate a list of items (such as states, names, foreign language terms, etc.) into the primary array. Transfer all of the values from the array into both the SortedList and the Hashtable.

2. Each telephone keypad has letters that correspond to the various numbers. While advertisers use these letters extensively, you can use an array to enter text to figure out when you're getting a new phone number. Create an application that converts a text string input in a text box into a telephone number. Define two arrays: a letterArray (as an ArrayList so you can use the IndexOf() function) to hold the 24 letters on the phone (the letters "Q" and "Z" aren't included) and a numberArray that relates the keypad number to each element in the letterArray. Use a TextBox for input, a Convert button to activate the conversion, and a label to receive the converted number. For the conversion algorithm you will need to use the Mid() function to retrieve the individual letters from the string and the IndexOf() function on the ArrayList to determine which element that letter represents. Use the following keypad table as a reference for defining the letter/number relation in your arrays:

Letters	Number
ABC	2
DEF	3
GHI	4
JKL	5
MNO	6
PRS	7
TUV	8
WXY	9

3. In this chapter, you learned how to use the Filter option on a dataset to return just the data that you want. Create an application that uses a filter to access the stores table of the pubs database and select only the stores that are located in Washington (**Dim Filter As String = "state = 'WA'"**). Fill a ListBox using the DataRow object with the 'stor_name' field of all the stores that match the filter criteria.

4. One of the common uses of multidimensional arrays in a program is for internal calculation to perform the same types of functions needed in spreadsheets. Tabulating rows and columns of figures is simple and fast using arrays to store the data. Create an application that generates two simple reports:

Total education spending by year (in thousands) and Average education spending by year (in thousands). You will need to define a two-dimensional array (4 × 11) to hold the figures shown in the table below. They are the educational budget amounts from the U.S. Office of Management and Budget for the even years of the 1980s. The figures are broken down into 11 divisions. Provide the users with two ComboBox controls so they may select the year and the report to be displayed. Then allow the user to click a button that will run the computations and display the results in a label. You can use the SelectedIndex of the year ComboBox to select the correct column in the array.

	1980	1982	1984	1986
Elementary and secondary	$4,239,022	$3,802,234	$4,294,269	$4,447,153
School assistance	$812,873	$457,227	$608,791	$677,055
Education of Disabled Individuals	$1,555,253	$2,023,536	$2,416,799	$2,573,399
Vocational/adult programs	$1,153,743	$751,118	$954,320	$1,016,302
Postsecondary assistance	$5,108,534	$6,584,012	$7,478,401	$8,932,803
Direct postsecondary aid	$277,068	$284,467	$311,221	$294,681
Higher education facilities	$268,493	$449,191	$216,893	$206,017
Other higher education programs	$34,927	$38,226	$82,410	$64,032
Public library services	$101,218	$80,074	$107,895	$117,998
Special institutions	$273,860	$251,570	$249,610	$255,297
Department accounts	$277,174	$347,943	$352,089	$355,944

5. One of the important features of arrays is their ability to store lists of other objects. As mentioned in the chapter, these objects even can be other arrays. Create three ArrayList objects, each containing three elements, for a total of nine items (Orange, Apple, Peach, Beef, Fish, Chicken, Water, Milk, and Soda). Create a summary ArrayList with three elements: the three other ArrayLists. Make an application that uses a loop to move through the summary ArrayList and a nested loop to place all of the text of the individual array items from the secondary array to display to a list box. *Hint:* It is probably easiest to create a temporary ArrayList inside the main loop that holds the current array and is used by the nested loop (**tempArray = myALSummary(i)**).

6. Create an application with a hash table of a list of individuals (social security number and name). Use the string containing social security numbers as the key field. Allow the user to enter a key field and click the search button. If the entered value is found, display the name of the user with that SSN. Otherwise, show a display that the key field was not found. *Hint:* You can use the Masked Edit control to enforce the standard SSN format to prevent entry errors. The control is available by right-clicking the Toolbox, selecting the Customized Toolbox option, and adding the Microsoft Masked Edit Control.

CHAPTER ELEVEN

CHAPTER
ELEVEN

USING VISUAL BASIC .NET TO CREATE WEB APPLICATIONS

I n this chapter we change our focus from building Windows Applications to building Web Applications. That is, instead of building applications that run entirely on the user's computer, we look at applications where various parts of the application run on the user's computer (the client) as well as on other computers (servers). Visual Basic .NET provides a powerful set of tools that support the development and testing of Web Applications using Microsoft's ASP.NET technology.

We begin by explaining and contrasting a number of different Web architecture options. We break an application into its three primary functions: presentation (GUI), processing business logic, and data management. We look at how these three functions can be located on the client and servers and evaluate the advantages and disadvantages of the various options.

We then turn our attention to Visual Basic .NET and how it supports the various Web architectures. We look at creating a basic Web Application project and how to run it using the Microsoft IIS Web Server. We look at validating data (both on the client and on the server) using various Visual Basic .NET Validation controls.

We next focus on processing databases in the context of Web Applications where the data are typically located on a server distinct from the client. We present the version of the DataGrid control designed to be processed on the server and look first at a simple example that displays data from a database. Next, we see how the DataGrid control can support field editing with changes coming from the user at the client and the database changes being processed on the server. Lastly, we look at an example that shows how XML and XSLT can be used to transform XML into different views on the server and then rendered for viewing on the client.

We conclude the chapter with a project that shows how two or more Web pages can communicate with each other by sharing data. We first discuss four different options for sharing data between pages and then focus on the use of the Session object that stores name/value pairs on the server. To demonstrate this concept, the project has the user fill in a typical registration form, validate it for accuracy, and then move to a second form. The second form then gets and displays the values entered by the user on the first form, demonstrating that they are able to pass data between them.

Objectives

After studying this chapter, you should be able to

- Explain the various functions of a typical Web Application.

- Explain what is meant by the term "client/server" and how the client/server architecture can be implemented in a number of different ways.

- Discuss the trade-offs associated with various client/server architecture options.

- Build a Web Application using the tools available with Visual Basic .NET.

- Validate user data using the Validation controls supported by Visual Basic .NET.

- Use the Web Form DataGrid control to display a dataset and to edit and update a database.

- Use XSLT documents to transform XML into HTML on the server to then be displayed on the client.

11.1 An Introduction to Functional Web Architectures

A useful way to look at an application is to break it down into three primary functions. These include presentation, business logic, and data management. *Presentation* **involves how the application interacts with the user.** The GUI is part of this presentation function, but presentation also could include audio or video input/output on a variety of devices such as wireless devices, for example, PDAs and cell phones. *Business logic* **involves rules that define how the application handles data and processes them.** This can include very basic rules such as restricting part numbers to numeric characters as well as more complex rules such as determining if a customer should be given credit. *Data management* **deals with databases and software used to manage these databases.**

When an application is designed, the developer has a number of choices as to where these functions should be located. For example, the applications we have seen so far in this text have located all three functions on a single computer. This computer supported the GUI managed by the Visual Basic .NET program, it also supported the logic or business decisions that defined the program's behavior, and, if a database was involved, it was likely managed by the MSDE service. On the other hand, if you use the Internet to buy books or other products, the browser running on your computer supports the GUI, but most of the business logic and data management are done on the seller's computer. We use the term *architecture* **to describe how these three functions are allocated to various computers.**

We now turn our attention to each of these functions and investigate the advantages and disadvantages of various architecture options. In this discussion, we will use the terms *client* and *server.* The term *client* **means the computer (or other intelligent device) that the user is using.** The term *server* **refers to another computer that is distinct from the client and may be located anywhere in the world.** There may be more than one server involved in the overall solution architecture. If there is **one server involved, this is generally referred to as** *two-tier architecture* (the client is one tier and the server is the second tier). If there are **more than two servers involved, the term** *n-tier architecture* **is used.**

Presentation

If there are no servers involved, then the client can support the presentation function within the same program that supports the other two functions. However, with the advent of the browser, it is possible to support the presentation function distinct from the other two functions. Here we focus on the client/server solution with the assumption that the browser, running on the client computer, will be rendering HTML (or XML)[1] into the content seen by the user. We will look at two options here.

Option 1: Pure HTML.

In this option, any changes seen on the browser need to be sent to the browser from the Web server. For example, the application might use a drop-down menu or might have font that changes color when the user places the cursor over it. If this is the case, then an entire new Web page would need to be sent from the server to the browser for each change seen by the user. Consider, for example, a menu on the user interface that drops down, showing five menu items. If the user causes the menu to drop down, and then moves the cursor down the list of five items with each one changing color, this would require five or six different Web pages to be sent from the server when the menu first drops down and as each item changes color.

The primary disadvantage of this option is the large amount of **network traffic (called *bandwidth*)** associated with downloading so many pages. In fact, the time it takes to download so many pages would result in a very unsatisfactory user experience. Thus, this option is unacceptable.

Option 2: Script within the Browser

In this option, **small segments of program code called *script*** are embedded within the HTML code sent from the server to the browser. The browser then executes this code when certain events are detected. For example, if the user clicks on a menu, then a Click event could be executed that drops the menu down for the user to select a choice. With this option, a rich GUI could be supported without having to go back to the server. The term ***client-side script* is used to describe script that is executed within the browser on the client machine.** In contrast, any **script executed on the server is referred to as *server-side script*.**

The most popular scripting languages are JavaScript (also called JScript)[2] and VBScript (a variation of Visual Basic). Both of these languages are interpreted, not compiled into actual machine language. The main impact of this is speed— interpreted languages are not as fast as compiled languages. However, given the speed of today's typical personal computer, this is not really a very significant factor. JavaScript is a Java-like language from a syntax perspective, but it is not the same as the Java programming language. The two main browsers, Internet Explorer and Netscape Navigator, both support JavaScript.[3] However, VBScript is supported only on the Internet Explorer. For this reason, most client-side script is written using JavaScript.

A small script written in JavaScript is shown in Figure 11.1. This script displays an alert box (similar to a MsgBox) that is also shown in the figure.

---

1   We are not limited to HTML or XML. For example, we also could use WML (Wireless Markup Language) to render content on a cell phone. HTML will be used to represent all possible markup languages.

2   Both JavaScript and JScript implement a standard known as ECMAScript created by the European Computer Manufacturer's Association.

3   Early versions of both Microsoft Internet Explorer and Netscape Navigator did not support JavaScript.

FIGURE 11.1

JavaScript and
Its Output

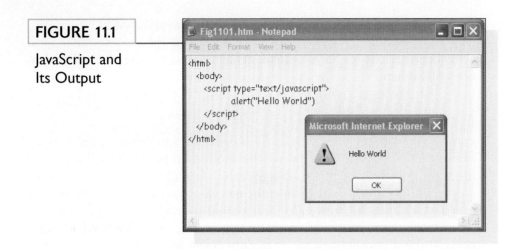

This option creates very powerful user interfaces using significantly less bandwidth than option 1. The only disadvantage is the added complexity associated with writing and maintaining the script in addition to the HTML. Visual Basic .NET helps alleviate this problem by allowing the developer to add client-side script to a Web application.

Business Logic

As stated previously, the term *business logic* is used to describe the rules and policies associated with an application. These can range from very simple, for example, requiring that a field not be left blank, to complex, for example, determining the amount of credit to be extended based on historical payment information. In this section we provide four different options regarding where and how the code associated with business logic should be executed.

Option 1: All Client

This model is similar to what we have been doing with our Windows Applications: the application runs exclusively on the client computer. We have seen applications that validate user input, for example, by ensuring that the data are numeric, by verifying that data fall within certain ranges, and so on. Our applications also have performed more complex business logic such as calculating loan payments or retrieving data from a database based on various criteria.

An advantage of this option is its low (perhaps zero) bandwidth requirement since a network connection is generally not needed. This means that if one computer fails, other computers that also have the application installed can continue running. This option has been available ever since the personal computer was developed. This option continues to be used for most productivity software such as word processing and spreadsheets. Most computer owners have software that runs on their computer regardless of whether they are connected to a network.

While the advantage of this option is significant, for medium and large organizations, with hundreds or thousands of desktop computers, this option can be very difficult to use. The problems revolve around installation and maintenance. Installing hundreds or thousands of copies of software on different computers and then keeping each copy current with the latest version can be a monumental task. It is possible to perform "network installs," where all the software is updated via a network, but this can be a problem if, for example, a computer user has turned off the machine. Things get even more complex if users are all over the world and connected via the Internet. As a result of these difficulties, most organizations are limiting their use of this option for processing business logic.

Option 2: Embed Business Logic in a Web Page Using Client-Side Scripting

This option involves using scripts (VBScript or JavaScript) that are interpreted in the browser. It is like the second presentation option, except the script is processing business logic, not appearance. Figure 11.2 shows an example where a user tries to submit some information to a server and a message is displayed indicating that the missing information must be supplied before the submission can take place.

The code that is executed when the user clicks on the "Submit Info" button is shown in Figure 11.3. This code, written in JavaScript, first checks the length of the HoldersName text box to see if it equals zero. If the length is zero, the text box has been left blank and error text is added to the **message** variable. It then checks to see if the length of the CardNumber text box is less than 16. If it is, additional error text is added to **message**. Finally, the CardNumber text field is tested to see if it is not a number (isNaN). If it is not a number, then additional error text is generated. Finally, if an error was found (the variable **message** not empty), an alert box is displayed.

This option clearly overcomes the installation and maintenance issues associated with Option 1. Every time users download the page to their browser, they get a fresh version of the HTML and its embedded scripts. If a revision is made to the page on the server, then everyone who downloads the page after that gets the revised version. There is some extra network overhead associated with sending the script as well as the HTML, but this is generally minimal.

The problem with this option is the user's ability to view the script. There is no way to prevent this with today's technology. In the situation above, this is probably not an issue. However, there are times when the business logic is proprietary or contains sensitive information. In these cases, this option is not acceptable.

FIGURE 11.2

Alert Indicating that Complete and Valid Data Are Required for Submission

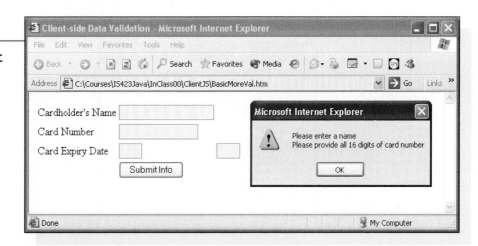

FIGURE 11.3

JavaScript Used to
Validate User Input

```javascript
<script language="JavaScript">
  function checkForm()
  {
    var message = "";
    // verify nonblank carholder name
    if (document.CardForm.HoldersName.value.length == 0)
    {
      message = message + "Please enter a name\n";
    }
    // check account number
    if (document.CardForm.CardNumber.value.length < 16)
    {
      message = message + "Please provide all 16 digits of card number\n";
    }
    if (isNaN(document.CardForm.CardNumber.value))
    {
      message = message + "Please enter digits only for card number\n"
    }
    if (message.length != 0)
    {
      alert(message);
      return false;
    }
    else
    {
      return true;
    }
  }
</script>
```

Option 3: Embed a Client-Side Component in the Web Page

In this option, a software component, not script, is embedded in the Web page
and downloaded each time the page is accessed. Software components such as
Java Applets and Microsoft ActiveX components can be used in this scenario.
Figure 11.4 shows a sample Web page that computes gross pay (hours times
rate) using a Java Applet component. The component is downloaded with the
page in a form where the coded business logic is difficult or impossible for the
user to examine or copy.

Figure 11.5 shows part of the HTML code that computes the gross pay. The
<APPLET> tag near the bottom identifies a class named Applet1 that has the
name "payComp". The computePay() function uses this component's setHours()
and setRate() methods to store values from the hours and rate text boxes. The

FIGURE 11.4

A Web Page That
Computes Pay Via a
Java Applet

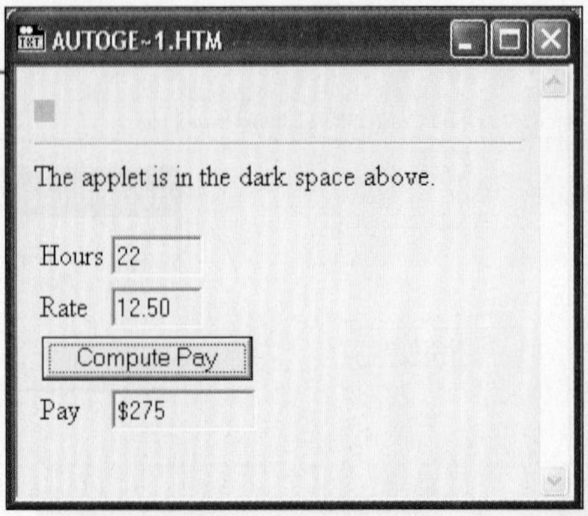

AUTOGE~1.HTM

The applet is in the dark space above.

Hours 22

Rate 12.50

Compute Pay

Pay $275

FIGURE 11.5

HTML Code That
Uses the Java Applet

```
<HTML>
<HEAD>
<TITLE>Applet/JS interaction</TITLE>
<script language="JavaScript">
function computePay()
{
    document.payComp.setHours(document.myForm.hours.value);
    document.payComp.setRate(document.myForm.rate.value);
    var pay = document.payComp.computePay();
    document.myForm.txtPay.value = "$" + pay;
}
</script>
</HEAD>
<BODY>
<APPLET CODE="Applet1.class" archive="aTest.jar"
    WIDTH="12" HEIGHT="12" name="payComp" VIEWASTEXT>
</APPLET>
```

function then uses the Applet's computePay() method to compute the pay and store the results in the variable **pay**.

This option shares the advantages of Option 2 and overcomes the problem of making the actual logic for the business rule visible to the user. However, it has its own set of new problems. One problem is network bandwidth: these software components can get rather large and take a long time to download. Another is the fact that not all browsers support the environment to execute applets or ActiveX controls.

The second and potentially most significant problem with this approach is security. A software component is just a small program. Many people are rightfully leery about downloading an executable program onto their computer for fear it contains a virus, a Trojan horse, or something else that could damage the computer. To overcome this concern, Java restricts its applets to run only with the browser. An applet cannot access any resources (like file systems) that are outside the browser. While this has been fairly effective in terms of security, it has limited what applets can do on the client computer. The term *security sandbox* **is used to describe the situation where code is contained within a specific application that limits the code's access to the general resources of the computer.**

Instead of restricting the component to the browser, Microsoft uses the concept of a *trusted application*. **In this model, the software vendor has a third party certify that they are legitimate.** This third party's certificate of authenticity is included with the component when it is downloaded. The user is given the option of accepting the component or rejecting it based on the certificate displayed. If the component is accepted by the user, it is downloaded to the client machine and has few restrictions on what it can do. Some users, however, do not like this approach because there have been reports of hackers who can "fake" the certificate of a legitimate organization. The user is then fooled into believing the component comes from a reliable source.

Option 4: Process Business Logic on the Server

In this option, the business logic is processed on the server, not on the client. Figure 11.6 shows the cycle involved in this option. In this figure, step 1 shows the user requesting a Web page from a Web server using a URL such as http://www.demo.com/form.html. The Web server then sends the requested page to

FIGURE 11.6

Cycle Involved in
Server-Side
Processing

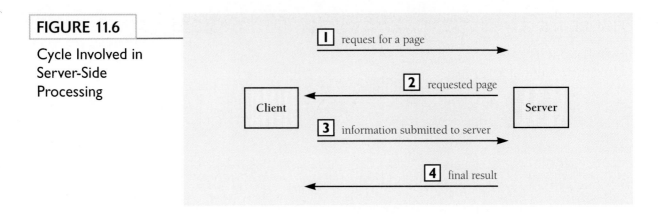

the user's browser (step 2). The user enters information on the page and then presses the Submit button. This causes the information entered by the user to be sent back to the server along with the name of a page to execute on the server (step 3). The server then processes the requested page and executes any embedded script using the information provided by the user. This process creates a new page that is then sent back to the user (step 4). **These fours steps are collectively referred to as a *round trip* between the client and server**.

As an example, Figure 11.7 shows a page requested by the user (the result of steps 1 and 2 in Figure 11.6). The user enters the information in the text box (.10) and clicks on the Compute FV Factors button. This causes the browser to send the value .10, as well as the name of a new page, to the server.

When the server receives the request from the browser, it gets the requested page and processes any script associated with this page. Figure 11.8 shows this page and its code. Within this page, the JavaScript code is highlighted in yellow. The remaining code is HTML. The HTML, as well as the output from the script generated from the Response.Write("whatever") statements, is sent back to the client (step 4).

The client's browser then renders the HTML for presentation. Figure 11.9 shows the results of this rendering.

This option is implemented using Microsoft technology known as *Active Server Pages* (ASP). **The name is derived from the fact that pages on the server are not passive, but instead include script that is executed on the server to dynamically determine what is sent back to the user.** In the Java world, this option is implemented with Java Server Pages (JSP). From a high level, these two technologies are conceptually very similar.[4] In addition,

FIGURE 11.7

The User Enters
the Required
Information in the
Page FVFactor.htm

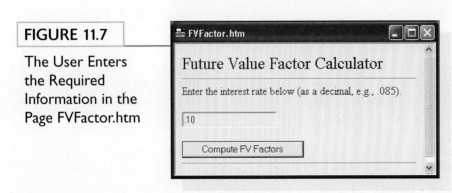

---

4   Internally, there are a number of differences between the two technologies. These details are beyond the scope of this text.

FIGURE 11.8

JavaScript Executed
on the Server

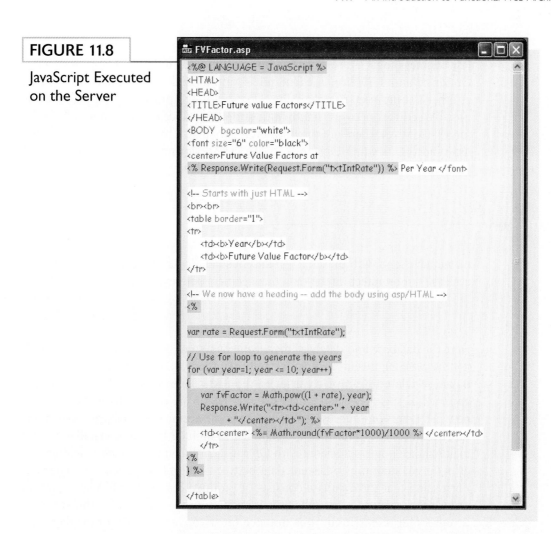

FIGURE 11.9

Final Results
Rendered by the
Browser

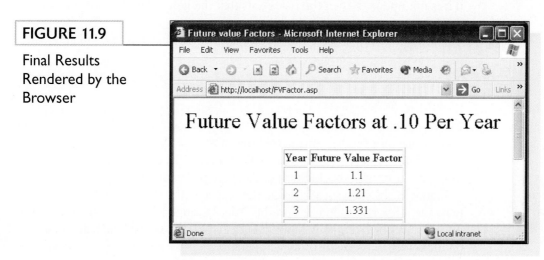

Microsoft's ASP.NET technology (presented in the next section) is different than
the generic ASP technology just discussed.

This option includes all the advantages of Option 3 without the disadvantages of potential large bandwidth from the component or the security issues
associated with "trusted" relationships.

Summary

For business logic, the most common model used today is a combination of Options 2 and 4. Option 2, client-side script, is used for data validation as well as other nonproprietary processing. Doing as much processing on the client as possible reduces network bandwidth and also reduces processing load on the server. However, there are times when it is not wise to expose the script to the user and this is when Option 4, server-side script, makes sense. In addition, Option 4 is ideal for database support, as we will see next.

Data Management

As we have seen with presentation and business logic, there are several options available for architecting the data management activity.

Option 1: Client-Side Only

Here the database and database management system both reside on the client. If you have MSDE installed on your computer, then you used this option with the database-related examples earlier in the text. The obvious advantage of this approach is speed. Since the database and DBMS are on the client, there are no network issues or issues when multiple people access the database concurrently. The drawbacks, and they are significant, include the same installation and maintenance issues associated with Option 1 for business logic as well as another issue: maintaining consistent data between multiple copies of the database. For example, if the database consists of product inventory information for an order entry system, then when an item is sold by one person, the adjusted inventory for that item must be updated on all the other copies of the database. If it is not updated, then the risk exists that the item could be sold a second or third time.

Due to the difficulties of database consistency, installation, and maintenance, this option is generally not feasible.

Option 2: Server-Side Only

In this option, the database and DBMS both reside on a server. Note that this may or may not be the same server that hosts the Web pages. The database is accessed from code that exists on the Web server. The cycle is the same as shown in Figure 11.6, with the addition of database processing between steps 3 and 4.

Figure 11.10 shows a Web page that expects that the user will enter a company identifier and then click on the Delete Company button. Clicking on this button sends the company identifier to the server as well as the name of a page on the server to process the delete operation.

Figure 11.11 shows the page that is executed on the server. The code is JavaScript and is highlighted in yellow. You can probably read the code and figure out most of what it does. It begins by creating a connection (**oConn**) to the database. Once this is done, it executes an SQL Select statement searching for a record in the database that matches the company identifier sent to this page from the client browser:

```
var compId = Request.Form("txtCompId");
```

FIGURE 11.10

Page Used to Specify a Company to Be Deleted from the Database

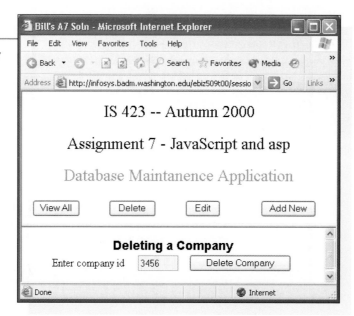

FIGURE 11.11

Code That Executes on the Server to Delete a Database Record

```
<%@ LANGUAGE = JScript %>

<HTML>
  <HEAD>
    <TITLE>Delete Company</TITLE>
  </HEAD>

<BODY BGCOLOR="White" topmargin="10" leftmargin="10">
    <center>
<font size="4" face="Arial, Helvetica"><b>

    <%
        var oConn;
        var oRs;
        var filePath;

        // Map Comp database to physical path
        filePath = Server.MapPath("Comp.mdb");

        // Create ADO Connection Component to connect database
        oConn = Server.CreateObject("ADODB.Connection");
        oConn.Open("Provider=Microsoft.Jet.OLEDB.4.0;Data Source=" + filePath);

        // See if the company exists
        var compId = Request.Form("txtCompId");
        var oRs = oConn.Execute("Select * from Company where CompanyId='" + compId + "'" );
        if (oRs.eof)
        {
            Response.Write("Delete failed -- company " + compId
                + " does not exist.");
        }
        else
        {
            // Delete record
            oConn.Execute ( "Delete from Company where CompanyId='" + compId + "'" );
            Response.Write("Company " + compId + " deleted.");
        }
    %>
```

FIGURE 11.12

Confirmation that
Company Record
Was Deleted

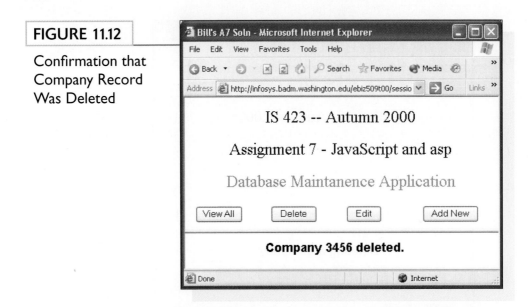

The code then checks to see if the set of records matching the company identifier include at least one record (oRs.eof checks to see if the record set called **oRs** is at its end of file). If there are no records, the "Delete failed..." message is displayed.

If a record was found, then an SQL Delete statement is executed, again using the company identifier in the Delete statement's Where clause. The message "Company ... deleted" is then displayed. Figure 11.12 shows this.

The only drawback of this approach is the fact that to do anything with the data, a request must be sent to the server for processing. Consider a typical Web purchase search where you might request to see all computers that are priced at $2,000 or less. Assume there are 50 computers that meet this criterion. Typically the server would send back the first 10 records and you would click on the Next 10 button to see records 11 through 20. This requires another trip to the server and perhaps even a new database query. Further, assume that from the computers that are priced at $2,000 or less, you want to see those that have 256 MB or more of RAM. With the server-side solution, this will require another trip to the server and another database select. The next option attempts to solve this problem.

Option 3: Send a Set of Records to Client for Further Processing

This option is similar to Option 2 except that instead of formatting the HTML on the server and sending the data back to the browser as part of the HTML, the data are sent back in a form that can be processed directly by the browser. Thus, if the initial request was for computers that are priced at $2,000 or less, all 50 records would be sent to the browser. These records would be in a form that could be processed locally. If the user asked for computers from this set of 50 that have 256 or more MB of RAM, the browser, not the server, would process the 50 records and only display those that also met this additional requirement.

At the time of this writing, this type of processing is supported only by the Internet Explorer. IE can process either XML or structured data sent to it from the server.

Summary

As we can see, there are many different options for processing the presentation, business logic, and data management functions of a typical application. The choice of options is critical in the overall success of an application. The number of choices has increased since the advent of the Internet and browser technology.

In the next sections we introduce Microsoft's ASP.NET technology and how it is supported in Visual Basic .NET. As we cover various topics, we will make references back to this architecture discussion. Hopefully that will help solidify your understanding of these choices.

Exercise 11.1 From your experience, discuss a specific business rule that would be best processed using client-side script.

Exercise 11.2 From your experience, discuss a specific business rule that would be best processed using server-side script.

Exercise 11.3 Assume that a company wants to allow customers to purchase products from them directly using a Web browser. Provide a Web architecture that could support this application. Clearly state which activities should take place on the client and which should take place on the server(s).

Exercise 11.4 Discuss how using a client/server architecture helps reduce the problems associated with processing business logic solely on the client.

11.2 ASP.NET Web Applications

In this section and Section 11.3 we introduce some of the fundamental controls and concepts associated with ASP.NET and Visual Basic .NET. This coverage will not be exhaustive and instead will provide a glimpse into the world of Web Applications using ASP.NET. In order to run the examples and work on the project in this chapter, you will need access to both Microsoft IIS 5.0 or newer as well as the MSDE or SQL Server. You should refer to Appendices B and C for more information on these tools including installation and configuration options. The code in this chapter uses a local version of both IIS 5.0 (localhost) and MSDE.

Creating a Simple Web Application

To start, we need to understand the basic structure of a Web Application. Visual Basic .NET provides a template to create a new Web Application project using the same steps as we have already used while creating Windows Applications. We start a new project by bringing up the New Project dialog box as shown in Figure 11.13. However, unlike previous projects, we select the ASP.NET Web Application template. The location box must refer to a valid directory registered in the IIS server. When the new project is created, Visual Basic .NET automatically creates a new Web directory for you. In Figure 11.13 we see the URL

http://localhost/Demo1

When you first start using Visual Basic .NET, you will likely see the URL

http://localhost/WebApplication1

This second URL is referring to the default site created on the IIS server. We have changed "WebApplication1" to "Demo1" in Figure 11.13 so that the Web directory has a more meaningful name.

After clicking on OK, a new Web Application project will be created. The actual directory structure for this new application will be

c:\Inetpub\wwwroot\Demo1\

The Inetpub and wwwroot folders are the standard default folders used for storing Web Applications associated with the IIS server.

Figure 11.14 shows the Web Form. This is similar to the Windows Form that we have been using in previous chapters. The difference is the underlying code is HTML. You can see the HTML tab at the bottom of the window.

As with Windows Forms, you can drag and drop components from the Toolbox. With Web Forms, some of the tabs in the Toolbox differ from those in Windows Forms. Figure 11.15 shows a segment of the Web Forms tab. You can see many of the same controls that exist in Windows Forms (although, as we will see, the names of some of their properties will differ).

If we look at the Solution Explorer, we also see some differences. Figure 11.16 shows the Solution Explorer for our Web Application. Notice that the file extension for the Web Form is ".aspx". This extension is very important and

FIGURE 11.13

Creating a New
ASP.NET Web
Application

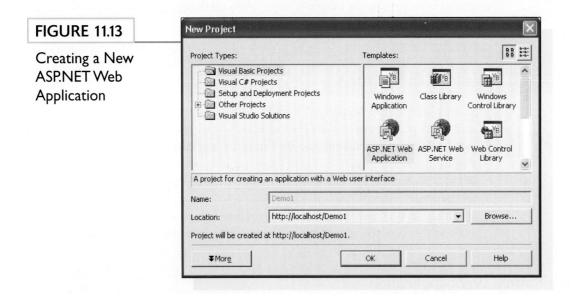

FIGURE 11.14

The Web Form Used
to Create an HTML
Page

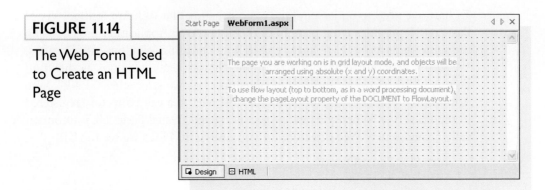

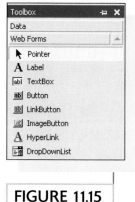

FIGURE 11.15

Some of the Web Forms Tools

FIGURE 11.16

The Solution Explorer for a Web Application Solution

should not be changed. It is used by the server to indicate that the content of the files includes script that must be executed on the server.

We strongly recommend that you take one additional step that will make it easier to move your Web project from one developer's computer to another. This involves moving the solution file (.sln) into the Web folder. Visual Basic .NET initially saves the solution file in the Documents and Settings folder on the C: drive. This works fine as long as you do your work on the same computer. However, if you move your project to another computer, you will need the solutions file as well as all the other files shown in Figure 11.16. To move the solution file to the Web folder, click the Solution entry at the top of the Solution Explorer window (Demo1 in this example), then select "Save Demo1.sln As..." from the File menu. Be sure you select Save As..., not just Save. In the Save dialog box that is then shown, navigate to the Web Application root (**c:\Inetpub\ wwwroot\Demo1** in this example), and save the solution file there. In this way, you can copy the Demo1 folder to another computer and you will have all the files that are needed. See Appendix B for more information on moving a Web Application from one computer to another for development purposes.

For this simple application, we will place Button and Label controls on the Web Form. When the user clicks on the button, some text will be displayed in the label. Figure 11.17 shows the Web Form with the button and label. Note the little green glyphs in the upper-left corner of each control. This indicates that the control is a Web Control.

We need to change the value of several properties for the two controls. Table 11.1 shows the property names and their values. Note that some of the names of the properties differ from the equivalent properties for Windows Forms.

FIGURE 11.17

The Web Form with a Button and a Label

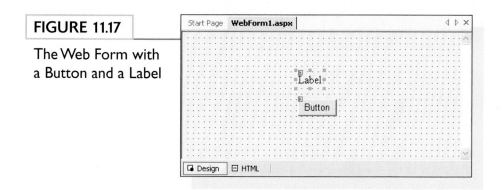

Table 11.1 Property value settings		
Type	Property	Setting
Button	(ID)	btnClickMe
	Text	Click Me
Label	(ID)	lblWords
	Text	""

We next create a Click event for the Button component. To do this, double-click on the button and the Code window will open. Inside the Click event, we add code to set the Text property of the label. Figure 11.18 shows the entire class definition. Notice that the code is stored in an "aspx.vb" file. This is the Visual Basic .NET code associated with the specific "aspx" file.

We can run the application one of two ways. The first way is to right-click on the Web Form in the Solution Explorer and select "Build and Browse" from the pop-up menu. This will add another tab to the Designer window, as shown in Figure 11.19. This figure shows the Web Application after the user has clicked on the Click Me button. To stop the application, simply right-click on the Browse tab and select Hide from the pop-up menu.

The other way to run the application is to click on the Start tool in the Toolbar (or select Start from the Debug menu). This will cause Internet Explorer to be launched and the page to be loaded.[5] Figure 11.20 shows this.

FIGURE 11.18

Code for the Button's Click Event

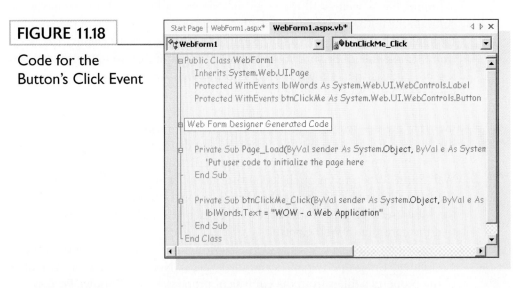

FIGURE 11.19

The Web Application in Browse Mode

---

5   It may be necessary in some cases to first use the Build and Browse method to display the Web page before displaying it using the Internet Explorer.

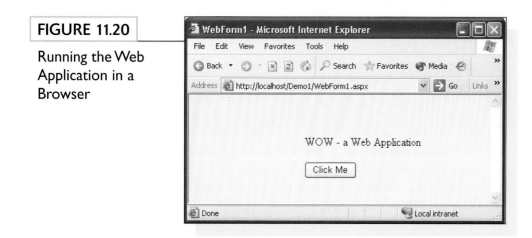

FIGURE 11.20

Running the Web
Application in a
Browser

When the Click Me button is pressed, the Web Form is sent to the server, the Click event is executed, which causes the Label's Text property to change, and then the updated page is sent back to the browser. When running within the browser, you can briefly see the status bar at the bottom of the Browser window flicker as it sends the page to the server and the server sends the updated page back. Note that, unlike a Windows Application, where a Click event is processed by the computer where the application is running, a Web Application's code is executed on the server no matter where the server is located. In this case the server is running locally, but it makes no difference where the server is running as long as the client browser has access to the network.

Finally, you can look at the HTML that is generated by the system by clicking on the HTML tab. Figure 11.21 shows the HTML. You probably will not have to modify the HTML, but if you do modify it, the changes will appear on the Design window when you click back on the Design tab. Also, if you click on a tag in the HTML, such as on the **<form ...>** tag, the Properties Editor will be set to that component.

FIGURE 11.21

Showing the HTML
by Selecting the
HTML Tag

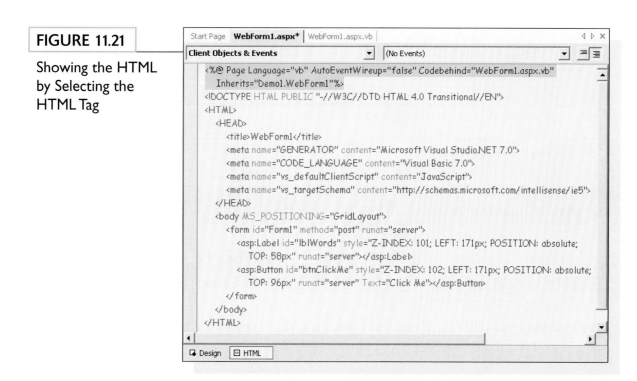

Example **11.1**	**SIMPLE WEB APPLICATION**

This is a very simple example that computes gross pay based on hours worked and an hourly rate. Figure 11.22 shows the application after the user has clicked the Compute Gross Pay button.

The application at design time is shown in Figure 11.23. You can see that there are two text boxes for user input, a label that is used to display the gross pay, and a button to initiate the calculation. In addition, there are a number of labels used to identify the text boxes and the result. These are placed on the Web Form design just as was done with the Windows Form. From this perspective, the process of creating a Web Form in Visual Basic .NET is identical to creating a Windows Form. The difference is we are using a Web Application template and taking the controls from the Web Forms Toolbox.

The code for the Button control is shown in Figure 11.24. This too is just like the code that you would write for a Windows Form.

Note that the code for the button does not do any checking for valid numeric values or for empty text boxes. If the user tries to run the application with an empty text box, the output shown in Figure 11.25 is displayed. With your background, the error is fairly easy to identify. However, you would never want an application to generate an error like this for the end user, who would certainly be confused. We next turn our attention to preventing such problems.

FIGURE 11.22

Example 11.1 as It Runs

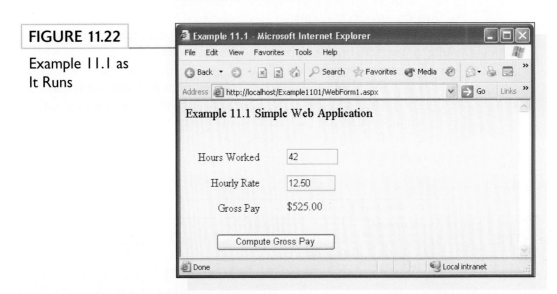

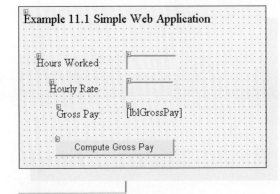

FIGURE 11.23

Example 11.1 at Design Time

```
Private Sub btnGrossPay_Click(ByVal sender As System.O
    Dim Hours As Decimal = txtHours.Text
    Dim Rate As Decimal = txtRate.Text
    Dim Gross As Decimal = Hours * Rate
    lblGrossPay.Text = Format(Gross, "Currency")
End Sub
```

FIGURE 11.24

Code for Example 11.1

FIGURE 11.25

Output Generated when an Empty Text Box Is Involved in the Calculation

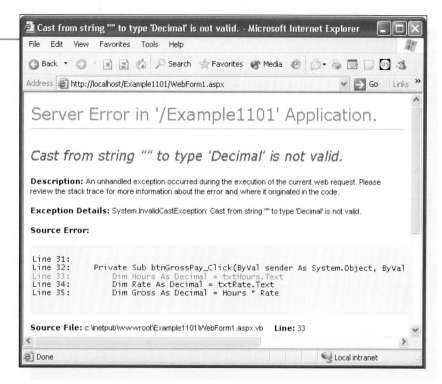

Exercise 11.5

Modify Example 11.1 so that it also calculates and displays net pay. Calculate net pay by applying a payroll tax of 6.5 percent to gross pay.

Exercise 11.6

Modify Example 11.1 so that it reports a data error if the hourly rate is less than $6.25 (assumed to be the minimum wage). Use the lblGrossPay label for the error message.

Validating User Input

Microsoft has provided a set of **Validator controls for Web Forms that provide the means for checking (validating) the contents of other controls.** These controls are described in Table 11.2. In addition, a control named Validation-Summary is used to provide a summary of errors for the user.

Each input control can have zero or more validators associated with it. These validators can perform both client-side as well as server-side validation. As was discussed in Section 11.1, the ability of a Web Application to perform client-side validation reduces network bandwidth. With the Validator controls, client-side validation is performed by default as long as the browser hosting the application supports client-side scripting. To turn off client-side validation, a control's EnableClientScript property should be set to False.

If client-side validation is enabled, then any validation errors detected on the client prevent the Web page from being sent to the server for processing. In this way, the Web Application reduces its use of the network and server. If all validation rules are passed with a client-side check, then the page is sent to the server for processing. Regardless of whether client-side validation was enabled or disabled, the server performs the validations too. This is viewed as an extra security check to be sure that the validation rules on the client have not been compromised.

Table 11.2 The validation controls available for Web Forms		
Type of Validation	Control to Use	Description
Required entry	RequiredFieldValidator	Ensures that the user does not skip an entry.
Comparison to a value	CompareValidator	Compares a user's entry against a constant value, or against a property value of another control, using a comparison operator (less than, equal, greater than, and so on).
Range checking	RangeValidator	Checks that a user's entry is between specified lower and upper boundaries. You can check ranges within pairs of numbers, alphabetic characters, and dates.
Pattern matching	RegularExpressionValidator	Checks that the entry matches a pattern defined by a regular expression. This type of validation allows you to check for predictable sequences of characters, such as those in social security numbers, email addresses, telephone numbers, postal codes, and so on.
User-defined	CustomValidator	Checks the user's entry using validation logic that you write yourself. This type of validation allows you to check for values derived at run time.

Assume we have three text boxes on a Web Form as shown in Figure 11.26. We want to enforce the following set of rules for the three text boxes.

1. All three fields are required—the user must supply data in these fields.

2. Phone number must be formatted according to U.S. phone number syntax.

3. Zip code must be formatted according to U.S. zip code syntax.

To enforce these rules, we need to add appropriate Validator controls. We first add a RequiredFieldValidator and place it next to the text box for the name. In design mode, the form should look like that in Figure 11.27. After placing the Validator on the form, we need to modify some its properties. Table 11.3 shows the properties we need to change and their new values

After changing the property values, the form should look like the one in Figure 11.28. Notice that the Text property ("**x**") shows up on the form. This will be invisible on the form unless it is determined that the field is invalid (empty). If it is empty when the form is submitted, the "**x**" will appear and the

FIGURE 11.26

A Web Form with Three Text Boxes

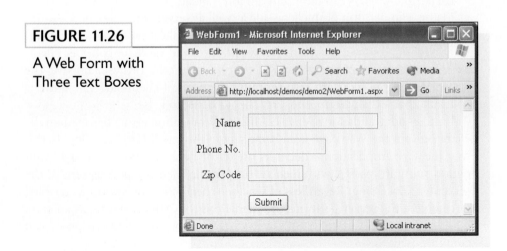

FIGURE 11.27

Adding a Required-
FieldValidator to the
Web Form

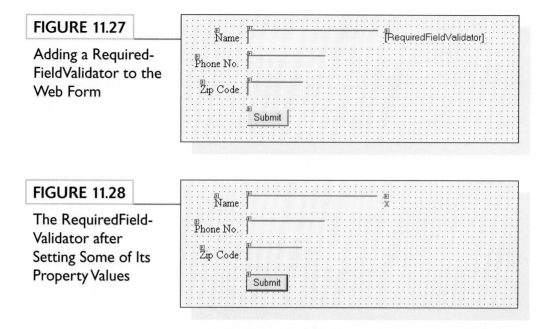

FIGURE 11.28

The RequiredField-
Validator after
Setting Some of Its
Property Values

Table 11.3 New property values for the RequiredFieldValidator

Property	Value
Text	"x"
ControlToValidate	txtName (the name of the text box)
ErrorMessage	"Name is required"

Font
  Bold
  Name
	
	True
	Arial

form will not get submitted (due to the client-side validation). The value of the ErrorMessage property will be used later when we set up a ValidationSummary component.

We add two more RequiredFieldValidator controls for the phone number and zip code text boxes and set their property values accordingly (the ControlTo-Validate and ErrorMessage property values will differ).

Next we add a RegularExpressionValidator control to the form next to the phone number text box. A regular expression is a special string that includes a number of characters that describe the valid syntax of another string. For example, the regular expression "\d{5}(-\d{4})?" defines the valid syntax for a U.S. Zip Code. The first part—**d{5}**—indicates that 5 digits are required. The second part—**(-\d{4})**—indicates that, optionally, one can add a dash followed by four more digits. Regular expressions can get quite complex and are beyond the scope of this text. However, a number of predefined expressions are available within Visual Basic .NET.

Table 11.4 shows the property values for the RegularExpressionValidator control for the phone number text box. A second RegularExpressionValidator control must be added to the Zip Code text box. The ValidationExpression for this Validator should be "U.S. Zip Code". When all the Validators have been added to the Web Form, it should look like the form in Figure 11.29.

Table 11.4 New property values for the RegularExpression Validator	
Property	Value
Text	"x"
ControlToValidate	txtPhone (the name of the text box)
ErrorMessage	"Invalid phone number syntax"
ValidationExpression	U.S. Phone Number
Font	
Bold	True
Name	Arial

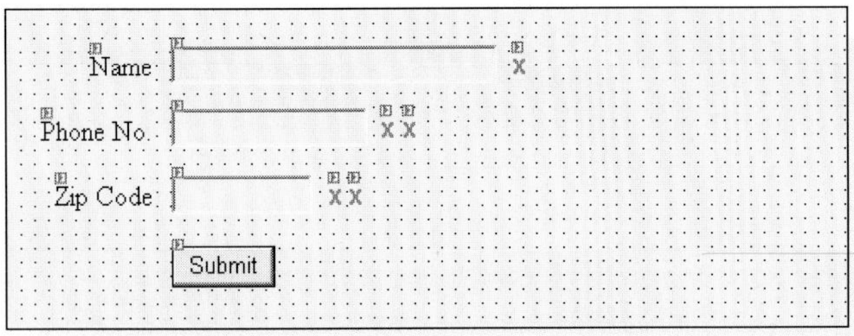

FIGURE 11.29

All Five Validator Controls on the Web Form at Design Time

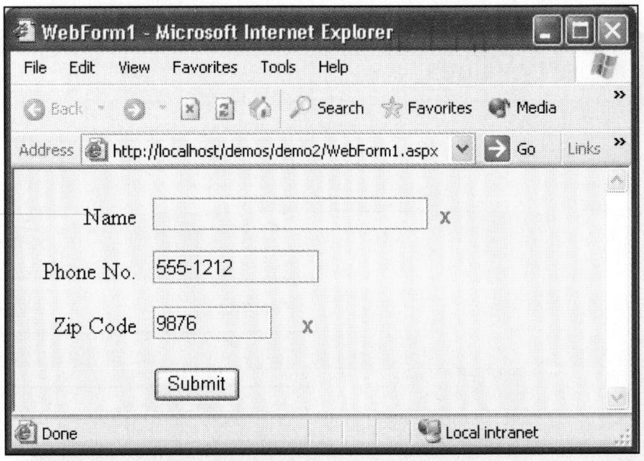

FIGURE 11.30

The Web Form as Shown in the Browser

Figure 11.30 shows the Web Form as seen in the browser. The user has just clicked the Submit button and **x**s can be seen next to both the Name and Zip Code text boxes. These are a result of client-side validation finding that the required Name field is missing and the Zip Code is syntactically invalid. Remember that since a client-side validation detected an error, the form was not sent to the server for processing.

One thing to note in Figure 11.30 is the fact that the symbol **x** may not be sufficient to help the user understand the nature of the problem. To solve this, we can add a ValidationSummary control to the form. This is shown in Figure 11.31. This control displays the value of the ErrorMessage properties for all the errors that are detected on the Web Form. There are two properties of this control that deserve mentioning: these are the DisplayMode and MessageBox properties. The value of the DisplayMode property controls how the error messages are displayed within the control. Choices include bullet list, list, and single paragraph. The MessageBox property values (True or False) control whether a message box is displayed if client-side errors are detected.

Figure 11.32 shows the running application with the ValidationSummary control in place. In this figure, the user has just clicked the Submit button. You can see the values of the ErrorMessage properties are displayed in a bullet list (as well as the **x** next to the text boxes that contain errors).

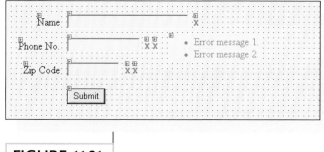

FIGURE 11.31

The Web Form with a ValidationSummary Control Added

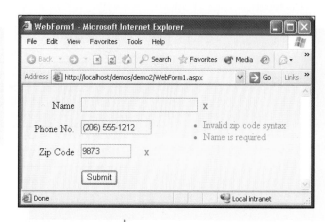

FIGURE 11.32

ValidationSummary Control Displaying Errors at Run Time

Example **11.2**   **VALIDATING USER INPUT**

This example demonstrates a sample form that might be used by someone to enroll in a service provided for people who are affiliated with an educational institution. The Web Form is shown displayed in a browser in Figure 11.33.

The validation rules for the fields are described in Table 11.5.

All of the Validator controls have their Font set to "Webdings" and "Bold" and they all have their Text property set to "r". This creates a ✗ symbol to be displayed if a validation error is detected. The Web Form with some errors is displayed in Figure 11.34. You can see that in addition to the Validator controls, there is also a ValidationSummary component that displays a summary of the errors by showing the values of their ErrorMessage properties.

FIGURE 11.33

The Web Form for Example 11.2

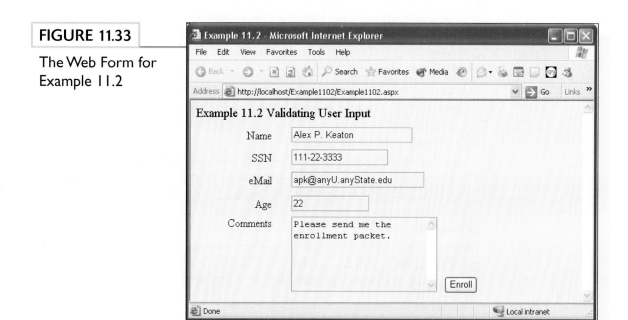

Table 11.5 Validation rules for Example 11.2	
Field	**Validation Rule**
Name	Required
SSN	Required Validated as SSN
eMail	Required Validated as eMail
Age	Required Integer Valid range 0–99 inclusive
Comments	None

FIGURE 11.34

Example 11.2 with Some Validation Errors

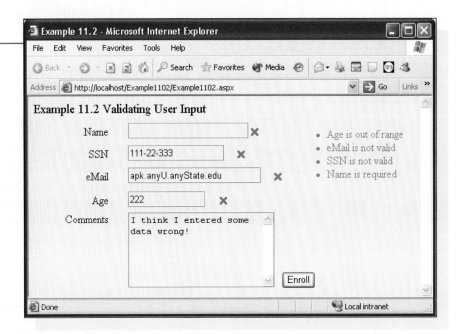

The SSN and eMail text boxes are validated using a RegularExpression-Validator. As we saw earlier, this control has a property named Validation-Expression that includes some predefined values. These predefined values include "U.S. Social Security Number (ID Number)" and "Internet E-mail Address". These are set for the appropriate text boxes.

The Age text box includes two Validator controls in addition to the Required-FieldValidator. One is a RangeValidator and the other is a CompareValidator. Table 11.6 shows the values that have been set for these properties.

In addition to the validation process, the Enroll button should be programmed to scan the email field and determine if it is an ".edu" type. This is a simulation of what might be done to determine the eligibility of the applicant (people affiliated with educational institutions). It also attempts to determine if the applicant is a student or staff member by looking at the age.[6] This "guess" is

---

6   This is not very realistic, but it does provide a demonstration of working with the numeric value on the server.

Table 11.6	Property values for the RangeValidator and CompareValidator controls for the Age text box	
Validator	**Property**	**Value**
RangeValidator	MaximumValue	99
	MinimumValue	I
	Type	Integer
CompareValidator	Operator	DataTypeCheck
	Type	Integer

FIGURE 11.35

Web Form after Being Submitted to Server

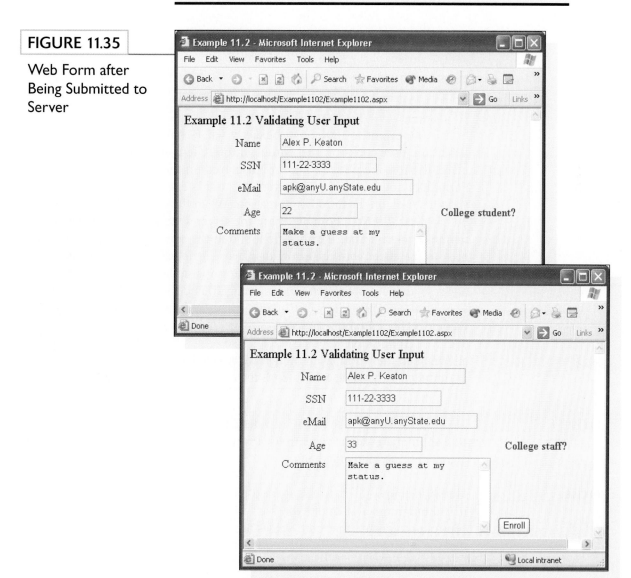

displayed on the Web Form after the user presses the Enroll button. Figure 11.35 shows two screens with different values for the Age text box.

The code for the Enroll button is shown in Figure 11.36. You can see that we search the email text box for the string "edu". The type and age are then compared against parameters established by the hypothetical organization in charge of the application and the appropriate message is placed into the label on the Web Form.

FIGURE 11.36

Code for the Enroll Button for Example 11.2

```
Private Sub btnSubmit_Click(ByVal sender As System.Object, ByVal
    Dim Age As Integer, EduFound As Boolean
    Dim Email As String = txtEmail.Text
    ' check for edu
    If Microsoft.VisualBasic.Right(Email, 4) = ".edu" Then
        EduFound = True
    Else
        EduFound = False
    End If
    ' prepare response
    Age = txtAge.Text
    If EduFound And Age < 25 Then
        lblStatus.Text = "College student?"
    ElseIf EduFound And Age >= 25 Then
        lblStatus.Text = "College staff?"
    Else
        lblStatus.Text = "Not a college account"
    End If
End Sub
```

It is important to understand exactly what's happening in this example. When the user clicks on the Enroll button, client-side data validation takes place. If errors are present, they are displayed on the Web Form and the Web Form does not get sent to the server. The user is expected to correct the errors and then click on the Enroll button again. When the client-side validation finds no problems, the Web Form is sent to the server. On the server, the data validation takes place again. If errors are found at the server, the Web Form is sent back to the client with the errors displayed. If no validation errors are found, the Click event is processed. The Web Form is updated with any changes (in our case, the label's Text property is changed) and then sent back to the client. This is a cooperative effort between the client and the server and demonstrates the key architectural differences between Windows Applications (client only) and Web Applications (client/server). Also remember that the server could be anywhere in the world, even though we are testing the application with a server running on the same computer as the client browser runs.

Exercise 11.7

Modify Example 11.2 so that it includes a text box to obtain the user's zip code. Add appropriate Validator control(s) to ensure that the field is not left blank and it contains only numeric digits.

Exercise 11.8

Modify Example 11.2 by adding two text boxes that store the minimum and maximum number of credits the user wants to take. Add appropriate Validator control(s) to ensure that both values are included, that they are numeric, and that the minimum is less than or equal to the maximum.

11.3 Using Databases with Web Applications

As we discussed in Section 11.1, with Web Applications the location of the database can be either on the same computer as the Web server or on a different computer that is called the database server. When the Web server and database server reside on the same computer, this is referred to as two-tier architecture. If a database server is on another computer, the architecture is called three-tier. For the discussions in this chapter, we will be using a two-tier solution. Our IIS

Web server and the MSDE database server will be on the same computer, the local computer. If we were using a different arrangement of servers, the only difference in our solutions would be identifying the various servers using URLs in our Connection objects (for the database server).

For database access, we will be using data adapters and datasets just as we did earlier. We also will be using the DataGrid component. However, there are some differences that we need to keep in mind. First, the data adapter and dataset will exist in the code running on the Web server, not the client. Second, the DataGrid component we will be using on the server-side is not the same as the DataGrid we used earlier on the client. It is very similar but does not behave exactly the same; for example, it does not support master/detail datasets we saw back in Section 8.3.

Since we already have covered the use of data adapters, datasets, and the DataGrid component, we will present the use of the components via a set of examples.

EXAMPLE 11.3   **USING A DATAGRID TO DISPLAY DATA ON A WEB FORM**

In this example we create a very simple application that displays a dataset created from the Suppliers table in the Northwind database. The output of this example is shown in a browser in Figure 11.37.

After creating a new Web Application project, an OleDbDataAdapter named OdaSuppliers is created. This data adapter is connected to the Northwind database. The SQL Select statement used in the data adapter is

SELECT SupplierID, ContactName, City, Country, Phone FROM Suppliers

A DataSet named DsSuppliers is created next using the Suppliers table from the data adapter.

After the data adapter and dataset are created, a DataGrid is added from the Web Forms tab on the Toolbox. The property settings for this DataGrid component are shown in Table 11.7.

To fill the DataGrid component, code is added to the WebPage's Page_Load event (see Figure 11.38). This event is called when the page is first loaded on the server. The two statements that are used to fill the DataGrid are

```
OdaSuppliers.Fill(DsSuppliers)
grdSuppliers.DataBind()
```

FIGURE 11.37

Example 11.3 Shown in the Browser Window

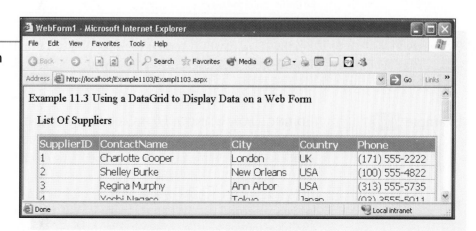

Table 11.7 DataGrid property settings for Example 11.3

Property	Setting
BorderColor	Salmon
BorderStyle	Double
BorderWidth	4
DataMember	Suppliers
DataSource	DsSuppliers
Font	Tahoma
HeaderStyle BackColor Font ForeColor	Red Tahoma White

FIGURE 11.38

The Code for Example 11.3

```
Private Sub Page_Load(ByVal sender As System.Object, E
    'Put user code to initialize the page here
    If Not IsPostBack Then
        OdaSuppliers.Fill(DsSuppliers)
        grdSuppliers.DataBind()
    End If
End Sub
```

Just as in Chapter 8, the Fill method fills the DataSet (DsSuppliers) with data from the database using the SQL statement defined in the OleDbDataAdapter. The second statement binds the data grid to the dataset. By binding the dataset to the DataGrid control, the information in the dataset is displayed in the DataGrid control.

The term *PostBack* **is used to describe the process of the Web page being sent back to the server for processing.** For example, this happened in Example 11.2 when the Enroll button was clicked by the user. The property IsPostBack is a Boolean property that is equal to True if the page is being posted back to the server. It is equal to False if the page is being created for the first time. The If statement in Figure 11.38 is checking to see if the page is being posted back to the server. If it is, the data grid does not have to be filled again since it is already filled. This makes the application more efficient by not doing unnecessary refills.

Exercise 11.9

Modify Example 11.3 so that the suppliers are listed in the DataGrid in alphabetical order based on Country and within a country based on City.

Example 11.4

EDITING DATA USING A DATAGRID COMPONENT

The DataGrid for the Web Form includes the ability to add buttons to each record so that one can edit data within a record. This example demonstrates how to do that. Figure 11.39 shows the Web page as it is first displayed in the browser.

When the user clicks on one of the Edit buttons, the page is sent back to the server to be updated. When the page is sent back to the client from the server, the page looks like that shown in Figure 11.40. You can see that the Edit button

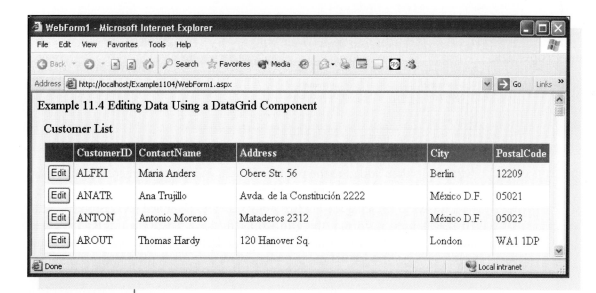

FIGURE 11.39

The Initial Web Page for Example 11.4

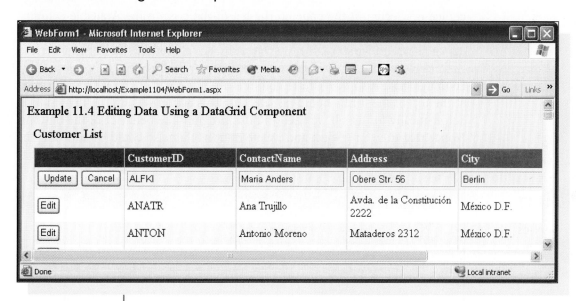

FIGURE 11.40

Example 11.4 after the User Has Clicked on an Edit Button

has been replaced with Update and Cancel buttons. In addition, the information in each field for the selected row has been placed in a TextBox control. If the user edits any one of the text boxes and then clicks on the Update button, the page is sent back to the server where the field values are used to update both the dataset and the underlying database. The page is then sent back to the client with the DataGrid updated to reflect the edited data. In addition, the two buttons in the row that was edited are replaced with a single Edit button.

After creating a new Web Application project, an OleDbDataAdapter is added to the project. It is connected to the Northwind database and defines the following SQL select statement used to extract records from the Customers table.

SELECT CustomerID, ContactName, Address, City, PostalCode FROM Customers

FIGURE 11.41

The Data Properties
for the DataGrid
Control

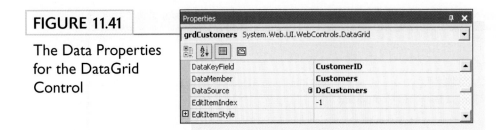

A dataset is then added to the project. The data adapter is named odaCustomers and the dataset is named DsCustomers.

A DataGrid is then added to the Web Form and is named grdCustomers. Auto Format is used to format the grid using the "Classic 2" option. Figure 11.41 shows the values of the Data properties. The DataKeyField property is set equal to the CustomerID field. This property must be set so that the appropriate row in the dataset, as well as the database, can be found for the update operation.

Finally, we need to add the special column on the left of the DataGrid that holds the various buttons. To do this, we modify the Columns collection property of the DataGrid. We first select the Columns property and click on the ellipses to open the Properties dialog box, as shown in Figure 11.42. The "Columns" choice is selected in the pane on the left of the box. In the Available columns box, we click on the + expander for the "Button Column" choice. When this is expanded (see Figure 11.43), we select the "Edit, Update, Cancel" option and then click on the arrow button (>) to move the selection to the "Selected columns" box. Also the "Create columns automatically at run time" check box at the top of the form should be selected. This action sets up the first column automatically for us; all we need to do is program the behavior of the buttons. Notice that there are Select and Delete buttons that also could be added to the column if we wanted that functionality.

FIGURE 11.42

The Properties
Dialog with the
Columns Option
Selected

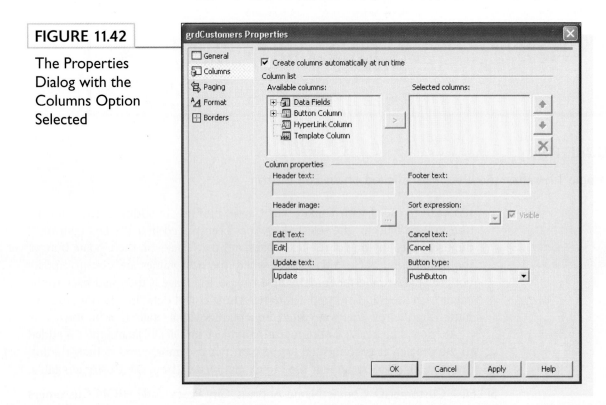

FIGURE 11.43

FIGURE 11.43

Moving the Edit,
Update, Cancel
Buttons from the
Available to the
Selected Columns
Boxes

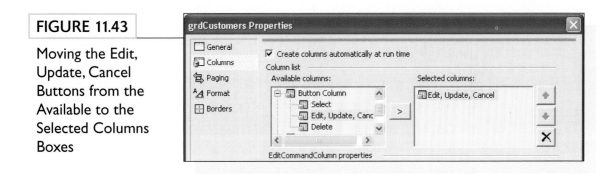

FIGURE 11.44

Example 11.4's
Page_Load Event

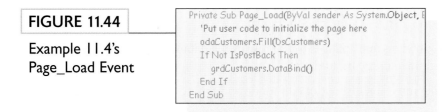

```
Private Sub Page_Load(ByVal sender As System.Object, E
    'Put user code to initialize the page here
    odaCustomers.Fill(DsCustomers)
    If Not IsPostBack Then
        grdCustomers.DataBind()
    End If
End Sub
```

We need to write code that initially fills the DataGrid with records from the dataset. The code for this is located in the Page_Load event procedure as seen in Figure 11.44. Unlike Example 11.3, where both the Fill and the DataBind methods were not executed if the page was being posted back to the server, here the Fill method is executed each time. Data binding must be done every time the data change so the DataBind method will be called from the events that actually modify the data.

Next we need to write code for the three buttons. The code will be part of events defined for the DataGrid: the CancelCommand, EditCommand, and UpdateCommand events. The DataGrid's CancelCommand event is shown in Figure 11.45. In this procedure, editing is turned off by setting the index of the DataGrid's item (row) being edited to –1.

    grdCustomers.EditItemIndex = -1

Following this, the DataGrid is bound to the dataset so that it accurately reflects the contents of the dataset.

The code that supports the Edit button is shown in Figure 11.46. In this code, the parameter **e** contains information on which row the user clicked. This information is used to set the EditItemIndex property of the grid, which places that row into edit mode. Edit mode causes the Update and Cancel buttons to be displayed and also causes the cells of the row to be displayed in text boxes. After this is done, the DataGrid is rebound to its data source.

```
Private Sub grdCustomers_CancelCommand(ByVal source
    grdCustomers.EditItemIndex = -1
    grdCustomers.DataBind()
End Sub
```

```
Private Sub grdCustomers_EditCommand(ByVal source As
    grdCustomers.EditItemIndex = e.Item.ItemIndex
    grdCustomers.DataBind()
End Sub
```

FIGURE 11.45

Code That Is Executed when the User
Clicks on the Cancel Button

FIGURE 11.46

Code That Is Executed when the User
Clicks on the Edit Button

Finally we need to add code for the Update button. This code is more complex than the prior two event procedures. The following pseudocode helps understand what needs to be done.

1. Find the index of the row that was updated.

2. Get the key from the row whose index was found in step 1.

3. Get the (potentially) changed values from the text boxes in the row where the edits took place.

4. Find the row in the dataset to be updated. Since we know the value of the key (step 3), it is used to find the row in the dataset.

5. Write changes to the row in the dataset.

6. Apply the same changes to the row in the database. Now both the database and the dataset are updated.

7. Take the DataGrid out of edit mode and rebind it to the data source.

The Visual Basic .NET code that implements the pseudocode is shown in Figure 11.47. We will take a look at each segment of code since most of it is new.

To get the value of the key field, we need to determine which row was selected for editing and then get the key value associated with that row. The code to do this is

```
' find the index of the row that was updated
Dim RowIndex As Integer = e.Item.ItemIndex
' get the key from the row
Dim KeyValue As String = grdCustomers.DataKeys(RowIndex).ToString
```

FIGURE 11.47

Code That Is Executed when the User Clicks on the Update Button

```
Private Sub grdCustomers_UpdateCommand(ByVal source As Object, ByVal
    ' find the index of the row that was updated
    Dim RowIndex As Integer = e.Item.ItemIndex
    ' get the key from the row
    Dim KeyValue As String = grdCustomers.DataKeys(RowIndex).ToString
    ' get the (potentially) changed values
    Dim Name As String, Addr As String, City As String, PostZone As String
    Dim TxtBox As TextBox
    TxtBox = CType(e.Item.Cells(2).Controls(0), TextBox)
    Name = TxtBox.Text
    TxtBox = CType(e.Item.Cells(3).Controls(0), TextBox)
    Addr = TxtBox.Text
    TxtBox = CType(e.Item.Cells(4).Controls(0), TextBox)
    City = TxtBox.Text
    TxtBox = CType(e.Item.Cells(5).Controls(0), TextBox)
    PostZone = TxtBox.Text
    ' find the row in the dataset to be updated
    Dim dsRow As dsCustomers.CustomersRow
    dsRow = DsCustomers.Customers.FindByCustomerID(KeyValue)
    ' write changes to the dataset row
    dsRow.ContactName = Name
    dsRow.Address = Addr
    dsRow.City = City
    dsRow.PostalCode = PostZone
    ' apply changes to database
    odaCustomers.Update(DsCustomers)
    ' take data grid out of edit mode and update it
    grdCustomers.EditItemIndex = -1
    grdCustomers.DataBind()
End Sub
```

We first get the index of the row selected for updating by using the parameter **e** (as we did earlier). Once we have the index of the row to be updated, we access the DataKeys property using the index value. Recall earlier we set the DataGrid's Data-KeyField property. This is used by the DataGrid to create the DataKeys collection.

Next we need to get the changed values from the text boxes on the row to be updated. Recall from Figure 11.40 that all the fields in the selected row were displayed as text boxes when the user clicked on the Edit button. There is no easy way to determine which field(s) were changed, so we just assume they were all changed and process each field. Let's look at the code for handling the CustomerName field. The code for this is

```
Dim Name As String, Addr As String, City As String, PostZone As String
Dim TxtBox As TextBox
TxtBox = CType(e.Item.Cells(2).Controls(0), TextBox)
Name = TxtBox.Text
```

The Dim statements define String variables for each of the fields (note that we are not going to change the key field value (CustomerID)—this is generally not possible without a great deal of effort). We next declare a variable (**TxtBox**) that can reference a TextBox. We need to get access to the specific TextBox within the row that is being updated. To do this, we again use the parameter **e**. The Cells collection stores the fields within a row. Cells(0) stores the buttons, Cells(1) stores the CustomerID, and Cells(2) stores the ContactName. The remaining cells (3–5) store Address through PostalCode. The Controls collection stores information about the control. Element zero (Controls(0)) stores the data associated with the DataGrid control (the TextBox in this case). The CType() function casts the control into a TextBox type so the assignment to **TxtBox** is legal. Finally the Text property of the text box is accessed and stored into the String variable **Name**. The code then continues with the remaining three text boxes.

Once the new values from the text boxes are stored in String variables, we need to find the row in the dataset that matches the key value and then store the values into the dataset's variables for the specific row.

```
' find the row in the dataset to be updated
Dim dsRow As dsCustomers.CustomersRow
dsRow = DsCustomers.Customers.FindByCustomerID(KeyValue)
' write changes to the dataset row
dsRow.ContactName = Name
dsRow.Address = Addr
dsRow.City = City
dsRow.PostalCode = PostZone
```

To do this we declare a variable that can store a row of a dataset. We then use the dataset's FindByCustomerID method to access the row that matches the **Key-Value** variable. Once this is done, the specific fields of the dataset row are assigned the values stored in the String variables (that store the values from the TextBox controls).

Finally we need to change the data in the database associated with the dataset and then take the DataGrid out of edit mode.

```
' apply changes to database
odaCustomers.Update(DsCustomers)
' take data grid out of edit mode and update it
grdCustomers.EditItemIndex = -1
grdCustomers.DataBind()
```

To update the database we use the data adapter's Update method, passing it the now-updated dataset. We then take the DataGrid out of Edit mode by setting its EditItemIndex to –1. Finally we rebind the DataGrid to the data source to be sure that updated information is displayed in the DataGrid when the Web Form is sent back to the client.

Exercise 11.10

Using Example 11.4 as a model, create a Web Application that provides the edit capability for the Supplier table in the Northwind database. Make the application display the SupplierID, ContactName, and HomePhone fields. The ContactName and HomePhone fields should be editable.

Example 11.5

USING XML AND XSL WITH WEB FORM

For this final example we are going to redo Example 9.7, where we used two XSL documents to transform an XML file with email information into a display by headers or a display of complete email messages. This solution will actually be easier because of a Web Form control called the Xml control. In addition, we will be using an XML file on the server directly rather than creating an XML document from a database like we did in Example 9.7. You could do the same thing that was done in Example 9.7 if you want to start with a database instead of XML.

Figures 11.48 and 11.49 show the two different displays for this example. Note that a check box has been added to the form to allow the user to choose the appropriate view. When the value of this check box is changed by the user, the page is sent to the server, the value of the check box is determined, and the appropriate XSL document is used to transform the XML. This transformed document is then sent back to the client for viewing.

After creating a new Web Application project, we first add an HTML table. In addition to a Web Forms tab, the Toolbox also has an HTML tab. We use this tab to select a Table component. This table will have two rows and one column and will be used to hold the check box and Xml components. Figure 11.50 shows the Web Form in design mode where the table can be seen.

The HTML table initially shows three rows and three columns. If one right-clicks on a row or column of the table, the pop-up menu that follows includes

FIGURE 11.48

Example 11.5 with Headers View

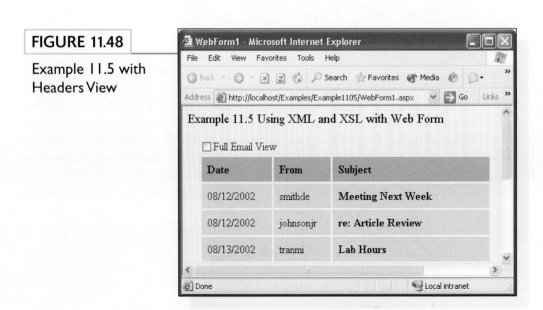

FIGURE 11.49

Example 11.5 with
Full View

FIGURE 11.49

Example 11.5 with
Full View

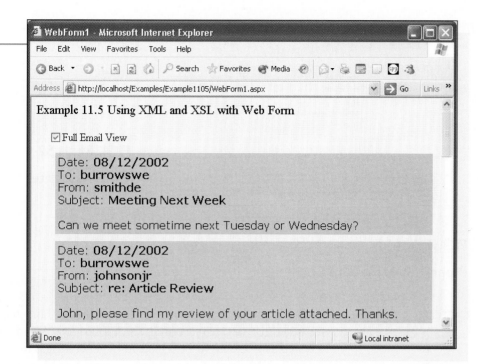

FIGURE 11.50

Example 11.5 Shown
at Design Time

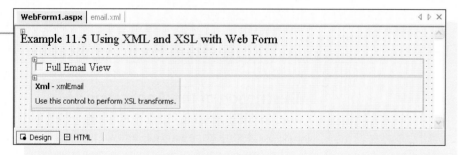

an option to delete a row or column. This is used to reduce the table to one column and two rows. In addition, the "border" property of the table is set to 0 so that it does not show at run time.

Using the Web Forms tab in the Toolbox, a CheckBox control is placed in the first row of the table and an Xml control is placed in the second row. The Text property of CheckBox is set to "Full Email View". *In addition, the AutoPostBack property is set to True. This setting is particularly important because it causes the form to be posted back to the server when the user clicks on the CheckBox to change its status.* The properties of the Xml control are show in Figure 11.51. The two files, email.xml and emailHeaders.xslt, are stored in the main project folder (Example1105 in this case). In addition, this folder also holds a file named emailAll.xslt that is used to transform the xml into full content view.

The Xml component does all the work. It takes the xml and xsl files and performs and displays the resulting transformation. The only code that needs to be written for this application is code relating to the user clicking on the check box. This code is shown in Figure 11.52. In this event, the value of the Checked property is tested and, depending on its value, it sets the TransformSource property to either emailAll.xslt or emailHeaders.xslt.

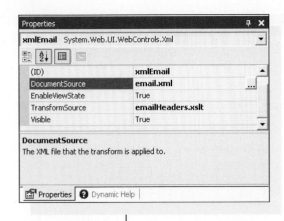

FIGURE 11.51

Properties of the Xml Component

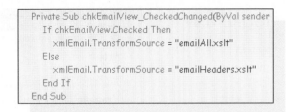

FIGURE 11.52

Code Associated with the Check Box

Exercise 11.11

Using Example 11.5 as a model, redo Project 10 in Chapter 9 so that it is based on a Web, rather than a Windows, Application. Assume that the XML is already created as in Example 11.5 instead of generating it from a database as was done in Project 10.

11.4 Project 12: A Web Registration Form Application

Description of the Application

Note: In addition to using concepts presented earlier in this chapter, Project 12 also covers a mechanism that allows two pages to share information.

This project gathers information on a user who wants to register for the services of a hypothetical company. The user first enters information on a registration form and presses the Validate button. This is shown in Figure 11.53.

If all the fields are valid, the Validate button is replaced with a "Next Page" button (see Figure 11.54). Clicking on this button brings up a new Web page that simply shows the data entered on the first page. This can be seen in Figure 11.55. The intention of this second page is to show how one page can pass information to another page.

The data on the form should be validated using the following set of rules:

1. The Name, email, and two Password fields are required.

2. The email field must be formed correctly.

3. The two Password fields must contain the same text.

Error messages should appear next to the field values where problems are detected. Figure 11.56 shows the Web page with several user errors present.

Design of the Application

Much of the design of the application has been covered in previous sections. To verify that the two Password fields are the same, a CompareValidator is used. The ControlToCompare and ControlToValidate properties are set equal to the two password text boxes and the Operator property is set to "Equal".

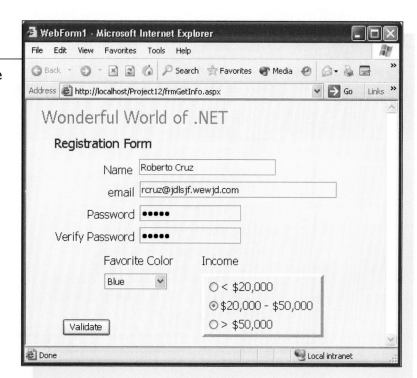

FIGURE 11.53

The Initial Web Page for Project 12

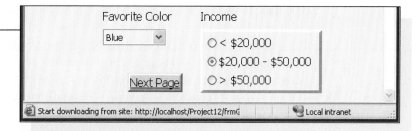

FIGURE 11.54

The Next Page Button That Is Displayed after the Form Is Validated

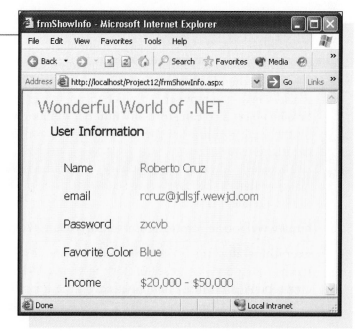

FIGURE 11.55

The Second Web Page Showing the Information Entered by the User

FIGURE 11.56

Project 12 with Data
Validation Errors
Displayed

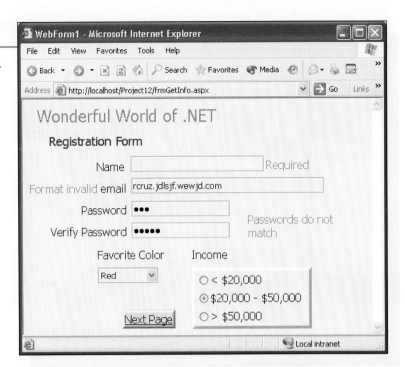

The two Web pages need to communicate with each other in order to share some data. However, the HTTP is a stateless protocol, which means that each time a page is requested from the server, a new connection is established. The impact of this means that a Web server does not know whether a set of requests comes from a specific client. Thus, a client that makes several requests to complete a transaction poses a problem. This problem can be overcome in several ways. One solution is to use "cookies." **A *cookie* is a small packet of information (a small file) stored on the client computer.** This cookie can store information such as product numbers and quantities of items being purchased by a shopper. The cookie is sent to the server with each page request and in this way the server can be kept aware of what the user is doing. **The process of accumulating information as the user moves from page to page is called *session tracking.***

Another method used to support session tracking is using a Session object. When a client first accesses a page, a unique session identifier is created on the server. This is stored in the Session object and is sent back to the browser in the response. When the browser sends another request to the server, the Session Id is also sent so the browser can relate this new request to the prior request. **The *Session object* also can store any number of name-value pairs.** These are used by the code running on the server to store and retrieve information from request to request.

There are additional ways for pages to communicate including placing information within the URL and using Hidden fields on a Web page. You may have seen a URL like the following:

http://www.google.com/search?hl=en&q=Adams+Apple&btnG=Google+Search

Everything after the "?" is name-value pairs, for example, q=Adams+Apple means the query was to search for the words "Adams Apple". HTML Hidden components are simply fields placed on the form that cannot be seen by the user. However, the code can read/write from/to these fields and thus maintain session state that way.

In this project we will be using the Session object. The main difference between using Session objects and cookies is where the information is stored. Cookies are stored on the client machine. They can stay there for a very short time (expire when the browser stops) or a very long time (forever).[7] Since they exist on the client, they allow a user to extend a transaction over a several-day period. In contrast, the Session object exists on the server. It persists for a much shorter period of time (the default time is 20 minutes). Some users do not like cookies being written to their computers and a Session object overcomes this concern.

For this project we use the Session object. This object has two methods that we will use: the Add and Item methods. The Add method's syntax is Add(*Name, Object*) where *Name* is a String used to identify the item being stored and *Object* is the actual item being stored. For example,

> Session.Add("username","Joe")

would store the string **"Joe"** into the Session object and would be identified with the identifier **"username"**. To access this later, one could write

> Dim Name As String = Session("username")

Here the variable **Name** would be set equal to "Joe". The Session object can store an unlimited number of name-value pairs. Each name is typically unique. For this project, we will store the registrant's name, email, password, favorite color, and income bracket. This will be done as the data are validated. The Session object will then be available to the second page and will be used to display the information from the Session object.

Construction of the Application

A new Web Application project must first be created. To this is added a second Web Form (Project → Add Web Form…). The first Web Form gathers the Registration information and the second displays the user's input. Figure 11.57 shows the first form at design time. You can see the text boxes as well as the

FIGURE 11.57

Registration Form at Design Time

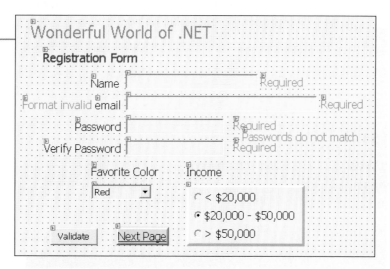

---

7   Edward Rice, a Business Economics professor at the University of Washington, was fond of saying that "forever is a very long time!" It would be more accurate to say a cookie can stay on the client machine until the cookie file is erased (for whatever reason).

value of the ErrorMessage properties of Validator controls associated with each text box. Also note that the value of the TextMode property of the password text boxes is set to "Password". This causes the characters typed by the user to be replaced with "dots" on the form.

The DropDownList component is populated at design time by adding color names to its Items collection property. The RadioButtonList component is populated at design time also using its Items collection property. The second item ($20,000 - $50,000) has its Selected property set to True.

The component that shows "<u>Next Page</u>" in its Text property is a HyperLink component. Its BorderStyle property is set to Outset and its NavigateURL property is set to refer to the second page in the project. When the user clicks on the HyperLink component, the server accesses the page defined by the NavigateURL property, executes any code in that page on the server, and then sends the completed page back to the client.

The Validate button should store the values of the registrant's name, email, password, favorite color, and income bracket into the Session object as name-value pairs. The choice of names is up to the developer. For example, the following line of code might be used to store the applicant's email address into the Session object:

```
Session.Add("email", txtEmail.Text)
```

Similar statements are needed for the other name-value pairs.

Initially the **Next Page** button is not visible. When the Validate button is clicked, its Visible property should be set to False while the Visible property of the **Next Page** button should be set to True.

The second form is very simple. It is shown in Figure 11.58. The five Label components need to be populated with values from the Session object. A good place to do this is in the form's Page_Load event. Here the Session object is accessed and its Item method is used to extract information stored earlier by the first Web Page. For example,

```
lblEmail.Text = Session.Item("email")
```

extracts the value associated with the name **"email"** and stores this value into the Text property of the Label named lblEmail.

FIGURE 11.58

The Second Web Form Shown at Design Time

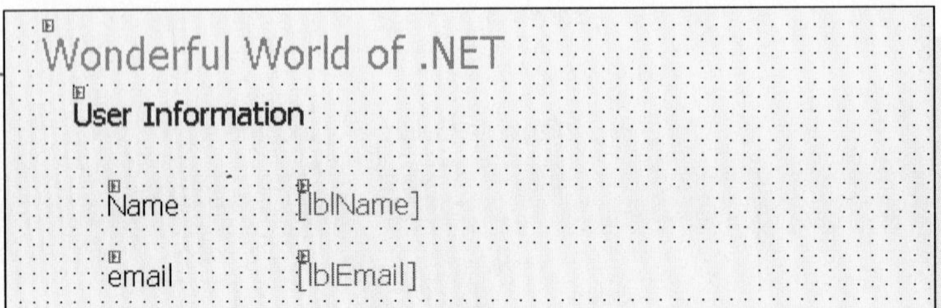

Chapter Summary

1. When thinking about applications on the Web, it is valuable to consider the three primary functions of any application—presentation, business logic, and data management—and then where these functions could be located to be most effective.

2. With Web Applications, presentation is almost always managed on the client using a browser to manage the rendering of HTML into an attractive user interface. The processing of business logic can be done on the client or on the server. Processing simple business rules such as data validation is best done with embedded script on the client. This is efficient and reduces the workload placed on both the network and the server. Complex and/or proprietary business logic typically should be done on the server. Since client-side script is viewable by the user, it should not be used for proprietary code processing. Servers are often more powerful than a typical client, so they also might be better for complex processing activities. Data management is typically done on a server located on a computer other than the client. The server can reside on the same computer as the Web server or a separate machine (the database server).

3. Visual Basic .NET supports Web Application projects. The Web Form is the primary component in this type of application. The developer builds an application using tools from the Web Forms and HTML tabs of the Toolbox using a drag-and-drop paradigm just like building Windows Applications.

   Although the Web Form looks like a typical Windows Application Form, it is different because underlying it is HTML code that is created automatically by Visual Basic .NET.

4. Web Forms include a number of Validator controls that can be added to the project. These controls perform a number of common validation tests such as requiring the user to complete a field, limiting the user to a certain type or range of values, and so on. The validation is automatically carried out in the browser on the client via script. If a problem is found, an error message is displayed and the page does not get sent to the server. If no errors are found, the page is sent to the server for processing. The first step on the server is a repetition of the validation rules. This is done to ensure that the client-side checks have not been compromised. Following this processing, any additional processing defined by the developer is completed and the page is sent back to the client.

5. The DataGrid control for the Web Form supports the display of datasets just as the DataGrid component for Windows Applications. However, the Web Form version, which executes on the server, supports different functionality. For example, it allows a new column to be added at run time that supports a number of data editing functions.

6. The Xml component available for the Web Form is a component with methods that support XML processing and display as well as transformations using XSLT documents.

7. To maintain a session within ASP.NET, one can use cookies stored on the client, a Session object stored on the server, hidden fields stored in Web pages, or URL encoding where name-value pairs are added to the URL as pages are posted to the server and sent back to the client. All of these methods are

available within Visual Basic .NET. The Session object includes the Add and Item methods that are used to add and get name-value pairs as different pages are accessed by the user during a session.

Key Terms

Active Server Pages	data management	server
architecture	*n*-tier architecture	server-side script
bandwidth	PostBack	Session object
business logic	presentation	session tracking
client	round trip	trusted application
client-side script	script	two-tier architecture
cookie	security sandbox	Validator controls

End-of-Chapter Problems

1. How is a Web Application different from a standard Windows Application?

2. What is a two-tiered application? What is a three-tiered application? If the Web server and the database server are located on the same computer, how many tier application is that considered?

3. Describe the difference between client-side and server-side execution. What are the advantages and disadvantages of client-side execution? What are the advantages and disadvantages of server-side execution?

4. Explain the purpose of using an applet. What are the advantages of using an applet over client script code? What are the disadvantages? Does an applet have more robust security settings?

5. If there is client-side validation of user data, why validate it again on the server?

6. Describe the process of PostBack. Explain the function of the AutoPostBack property of Web controls.

7. What is a security sandbox? What is a trusted application? Which method is used by a Java applet?

8. What is the purpose of the Validator controls? Name each of the four primary types of Validator controls and describe the purpose of each. Can multiple Validator controls be used on a single TextBox control?

9. Can JavaScript code and VB Script code run on either Microsoft or Netscape browsers?

10. Is there a limit to the number of session variables that may be defined? Where are session variables stored? How long do variables defined in the Session object last? What other method is available to store user-related variables for a longer time?

Programming Problems

1. The ancient Maya chose December 21, 2012 (A.D.), as the end of their Long Count calendar. Create an application that accepts a birth date entered by the user and then displays how old that user will be on the end date in years and days. You can use the DateDiff() function to determine the number of days between two dates (**DateDiff("d","8/24/79","12/21/2012")**) and then use the division and modulus operators to calculate the years and days, respectively. Add a RangeValidator control to ensure the entered birth date is not before a reasonable date (such as 1850) or after the end of the Mayan calendar. Be sure to set the Type property of the RangeValidator so the date is evaluated properly.

2. Create a simple database application that presents all of the records of the stores table via the Web browser. Bind the table found in the pubs database to a DataGrid control for display.

3. Many eCommerce solutions divide entry of user data into several pages. Often, general information is entered into an unsecured page while a separate Web page (usually on a secure server) is used to take confidential information such as a credit card number. Create a three-page solution that uses session variables to maintain information across them. On the first page, allow the user to enter general shipping information including name, address, city, state, zip code, and phone number (optional). On the second page, allow the user to enter credit card information by including a Combo-Box for credit card type (Visa, MasterCard, or American Express, etc.), a TextBox for the cardholder name as printed on the card, a TextBox for the credit card number, and a TextBox for the expiration date. The third page should show all of the information entered on pages 1 and 2 for summary display. Be sure to include validation controls on the first two pages to be sure that none of the fields are empty.

   Since the values the user entered must be copied from the text boxes into session variables, a simple hyperlink to move from one page to another cannot be used. To solve this problem, you may create a Validation button as shown in the chapter and then display a Next Page hyperlink after the validation is complete. Alternately, you can use a standard Button control and in the Click event, after the data have been stored to the session variables, use the Redirect() method of the Response object to move to the next page (**Response.Redirect("CreditCard.aspx")**).

4. The code executed on a Web server may be every bit as robust as a standalone Visual Basic .NET application although the user interface presentation is different. The results of the processing in a Web Application may be sent to the user with the Write() method of the Response object. Create an application that allows the user to enter a number between 1 and 20. When the user clicks the Compute button, execute a nested loop routine to display the factorials of every number up to the one selected. For example, if the user entered the number 3, the Web Application would return

   ```
   1 = 1
   1 * 2 = 2
   1 * 2 * 3 = 6
   ```

   For the TextBox control, add a required field validator and a range validator to make sure the number the user entered is between 1 and 20. To provide line breaks, you can use the HTML line break tag **
** (**Response.Write (factor & "<br>")**).

5. In Chapter 9, you extensively studied how an XSLT file could be used to generate an HTML presentation from XML data. If your presentation needs are simple, however, the DataGrid control may be used on a Web Form to

display XML data. Create an application that uses the ReadXML() function to load an XML file (perhaps the CDAList.xml from Chapter 9) into a DataSet object and then binds the dataset to the grid. You can set the DataMember property of the grid by obtaining the first table name of the XML dataset (**grdXML.DataMember = dsXML.Tables(0).TableName**) to allow any XML file to be displayed.

6. Write an application that shows the names of three of the tables from the pubs database in a ComboBox control. When the user selects a table, fill a Label control with text explaining how many records are available in that table. Set the AutoPostBack property on the combo box to True so any change in user selection will be reflected in the label display. Make sure that you check the IsPostBack property in the Form_Load event to make sure that you don't reset the variables and refill the data adapters each time the user makes a selection. You can store the number of records in session variables when the form first loads so the values may be displayed quickly.

Comprehensive Projects

The projects in this section provide an opportunity to build solutions that generally include features from a number of chapters in the text. In some cases, they include features not covered in the text but, instead, require self-learning using the documentation supplied by Microsoft. The goal of these projects is to challenge the reader and provide the opportunity to work in an environment that more closely matches reality. Each project description includes less detail and specific instruction than the projects in the chapters. As a result, these projects should be viewed as having a relatively high degree of difficulty.

Comprehensive Project 1: Multiple Forms, Menus, and Logical Decision Making

The main form for this project is shown in Figure CP.1. It consists of a set of menus and a label that is used to display the status of user-selected settings (set on another form).

The menu structure is shown in Figure CP.2. You should look in Chapter 6 for information on how to use the menu editor to create menus and how to code menu item Click events.

When the user selects Options... from the Tools menu, an options form (shown in Figure CP.3) should be displayed. You should create this form by adding a new form to your project. Review the use of multiple forms discussed in Chapter 3. When the Options form is shown, have it displayed as a modal form (see Section 6.7 on modal and modeless forms).

As an example, the dialog box in Figure CP.3 shows that the user has selected "Prompt to Save Changes" when the program stops. In addition, the window settings call for "Drag and Drop Editing" and "Full Module View". Finally, a path of "c:\whatever" has been specified for the Temporary Directory.

After the user clicks on the Close button, the user can select what to see by using the View option from the Tools menu and selecting the appropriate submenu option.

The code should be able to handle any combination of boxes checked in the Window settings frame (*hint:* review the use of the vbCrLf—see Example 4.11). This should include the fact that no check boxes may be selected. If no selections

---

FIGURE CP.1

The Main Form for the Project

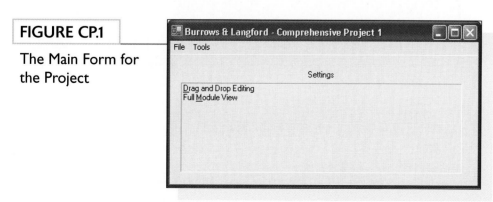

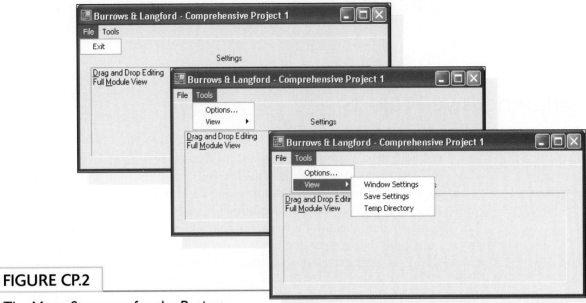

FIGURE CP.2

The Menu Structure for the Project

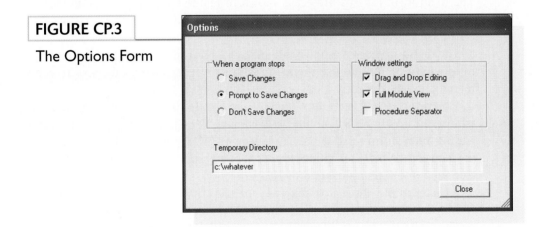

FIGURE CP.3

The Options Form

FIGURE CP.4

Settings Window
when the User Has
Made No Selections

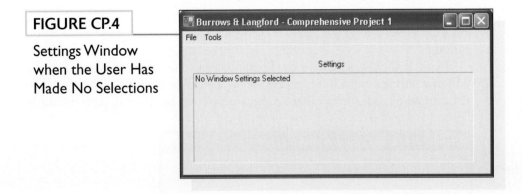

are made, then the Settings label should indicate this situation (see Figure CP.4).
All three of the View submenus should display what the user has selected from
the appropriate sections of the Options form.

Remember that you can access the controls on another form by using the syntax

formName.control.property

Comprehensive Project 2: Economic Order Quantity Calculator

The objective of this project is to provide exposure to general function procedures, arguments and parameters, data validation, code modules, and the KeyPress event for a TextBox control.

You are required to create a project that can be used to compute the economic order quantity (EOQ). A sample application is shown in Figure CP.5.

The formula for computing the EOQ is

$$EOQ = \sqrt{\frac{2RS}{kC}}$$

where S is the cost to prepare an order
R is the annual demand (in units)
C is the cost per unit
k is the cost rate of carrying \$1 of inventory per year

Your solution must include a code module where you define a general function procedure that is passed the four variables and computes and returns the EOQ. This function procedure also should check to see if either k or C is equal to zero. If this is found to be true, then the function should return the value −1. Your calling code should check this return value and if a −1 is detected, an appropriate message should be displayed to the user.

Your solution should also enforce some input validation rules for the text boxes on the form. First, all text boxes should restrict the user to entering the digits 0 to 9, a backspace, and a decimal point. In addition to these general restrictions, the cost to prepare an order (S) and cost per unit (C) should allow dollar signs and commas and the annual demand (R) should allow commas. The cost rate of carrying \$1 of inventory per year (k) should be limited to a number between 0 (exclusive) and 1 (inclusive), that is, $0 < k \le 1$. This limit check is best made when the user moves focus away from this text box. If a value outside this range is detected, an appropriate message should be displayed and then focus moved back to the text box.

Your solution also should check for empty text boxes and if any are found, an appropriate message should be displayed to the user. Figure CP.6 shows what happens when the annual demand value is left blank.

Your File menu should include an Exit option that terminates the application. The Help menu should include an option to display an About box similar to the one shown in Figure CP.7.

FIGURE CP.5

Comprehensive
Project 2 at Run
Time

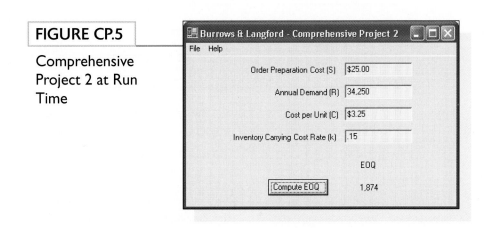

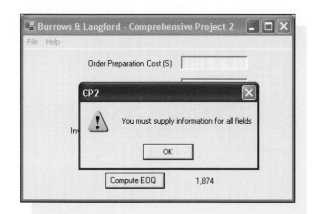

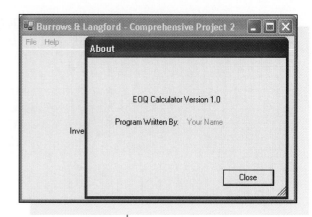

FIGURE CP.6

A Message Box Telling the User that All Fields Are Required

FIGURE CP.7

The About Box for the Project

The About box should be a separate form that is displayed as a modal form. Be sure that you include a Close button to hide the About box.

Comprehensive Project 3: Order Policy Simulation

The objective of this project is to provide exposure to loops, the ComboBox control, and the ListView control. It also provides experience writing a simulation.

Consider the following problem.[1] Karen is the owner of a fish stand located in the Pike Place Market and wants to evaluate the policy she uses to determine order amounts. She currently purchases salmon at $2.20 a pound and sells it for $4.60 a pound. She sells only fresh salmon and places an order at the end of each day for the next day's sales. Any fish not sold by the end of the day are frozen and donated to a local food bank.

Karen has kept careful sales records over the years and knows that the daily demand for salmon ranges from 30 to 70 pounds. The following table shows the relative frequency of these sales.

Daily Demand (pounds)	Relative Frequency
30	10%
40	10%
50	30%
60	40%
70	10%

Karen's current ordering policy is to order the average amount (computed from the historical data above) each day. The average is computed as follows:

$$30 \times .10 + 40 \times .10 + 50 \times .30 + 60 \times .40 + 70 \times .10 = 53$$

---

[1] This problem is based on a problem described in Richard B. Chase and Nicholas J. Aquilano, *Production and Operations Management,* 5th ed. (Homewood, IL: Richard D. Irwin, 1989).

She wants to evaluate an alternative policy whereby the order for tomorrow is set equal to today's demand. These two order policies can be summarized as

$$\text{Policy 1: } Q_n = \text{Historical average}$$
$$\text{Policy 2: } Q_n = D_{n-1}$$

where Q_n = Amount ordered on day n
D_{n-1} = Amount demanded the previous day

Karen is interested in seeing which policy results in the largest profit. She computes profit as

$$P_n = (S_n \times p) - (Q_n \times c)$$

where P_n = Profit on day n
S_n = Amount sold on day n
p = Selling price per pound
Q_n = Amount ordered on day n (as defined above)
c = Cost per pound

Using this information, you are required to create a project that simulates daily demand for a number of days and displays the results. Figure CP.8 shows the main form that allows the user to specify simulation parameters and Figure CP.9 shows the results of a simulation run.

FIGURE CP.8

Comprehensive Project 3 at Run Time

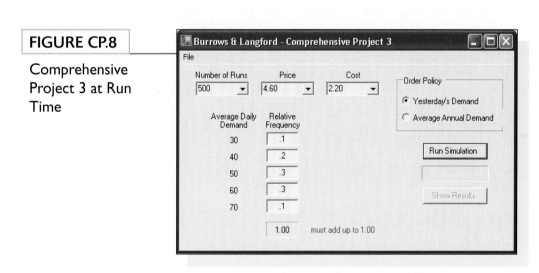

FIGURE CP.9

The Results of the Simulation

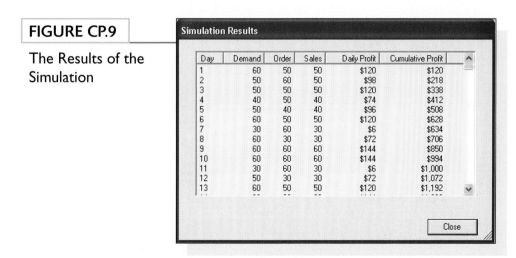

On the parameter form (Figure CP.8), you should provide combo boxes that the user may use to specify the number of days (runs) in your simulation as well as the price and cost of salmon. For the Number of Runs combo box, include the values 100, 250, 500, and 1000. For the Price combo, include the values 4.30, 4.40, …, 4.90. Finally, include the values 2.10, 2.20, …, 2.60 for the Cost combo box. In addition, the user should be able to enter any other value in these combo boxes. The user should use the option buttons in the Order Policy frame to indicate which of the two order policies should be used in the simulation.

The user should be able to enter the relative frequencies for each demand amount. You should limit input in these text boxes to digits and backspaces. The user should be able to enter a decimal point (but should not be able to enter more than one). Also, the total in the label below the last frequency should automatically update as the user enters frequencies in the text boxes above it. This update should occur each time the contents of a text box change.

Note that the Show Results command button is not enabled. The user has to first click on the Run Simulation button before the results can be displayed. When the user clicks on Run Simulation, a check should be made to ensure that all the parameters have been defined. In addition, the relative frequencies should be summed and, if they do not add up to 1.00, the user should be informed of the problem.

You can see a rectangular bar between the Show Results and Run Simulation buttons. This is a ProgressBar component that is used to indicate to the user the relative progress of the simulation. The bar is initially empty. Its shading should progress from left to right as the simulation goes from day 1 to the final day of the simulation. The ProgressBar component can be found in the Windows Forms tab in the ToolBox. Be sure that it fills in proportion to the simulation's progress; that is, if the simulation is half over, the bar should be half filled.

The Simulation Results form shows the results of the simulation with one row per day. For each day, it should display the day number, the daily demand (a random value discussed later), the order amount (determined by the policy chosen by the user), sales (the minimum of demand and order amount), daily profit, and, finally, the cumulative profit. You should use a ListView control to display the results.

The Simulation

The simulation uses the Monte Carlo simulation method to generate demand using random numbers. Basically, a random number between 0 and 1 is generated and compared to the demand frequencies defined by the user on the parameter form. For example, consider the relative frequencies shown in Figure CP.10.

Assume that the random number generated was .25. If this were the case, then you would select a demand of 50 (because .25 is between .20 and .50).

FIGURE CP.10

Example Relative Frequencies for Demand

Daily Demand (pounds)	Relative Frequency	Cumulative Frequency
30	10%	0.10
40	10%	0.20
50	30%	0.50
60	40%	0.90
70	10%	1.00

On the other hand, if the random number generated were .85, the corresponding demand would be 60 (because .85 is between .50 and .90). Using this technique, demands would be generated that follow the relative frequencies. For example, if you generate 1,000 random numbers and use this approach to generate demands, you would expect about 10 percent of the demands to equal 40.

Following is pseudocode that outlines the major steps involved in performing the simulation:

1. Validate user input as required.

2. Get values for cost and price from the user interface.

3. Set the variable "demandYesterday" equal to 50 (an arbitrary amount at the midpoint of the possible demand values). This value must be set here so that step 5a below works correctly for day 1 of the simulation.

4. Compute the average annual demand by finding the sum of the demand figures times their relative frequency.

5. Repeat the following for each day of the simulation:
    a. Set order amount according to the user choice on the user interface.
    b. Set demand using the Monte Carlo method described above.
    c. Set sales equal to the minimum of demand and order.
    d. Compute the daily profit.
    e. Compute the cumulative profit.
    f. Place the day's results into the ListView component located on the Results form.
    g. Set demandYesterday equal to demand.
    h. Update the progress bar.

6. Enable the button to allow the user to show the results.

Comprehensive Project 4: Order Entry Application Revisited

This project extends Project 11 in Chapter 10. You should read and understand Project 11 before you attempt to complete this project.

The first change you need to make in this project compared to Project 11 is to allow the user to purchase the same product more than one time. In Project 11, attempting to do this would result in an error message being displayed indicating that the product had already been entered on the order. For this version of the project, you should accept a second (or more) purchase for the same product and simply increase the quantity by the new amount the user enters. Figure CP.11 shows the order details with Product Number 10101 and a quantity of two units.

FIGURE CP.11

Current Order Details with Two Units Ordered for Product Number 10101

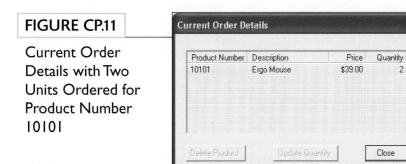

Product Number	Description	Price	Quantity
10101	Ergo Mouse	$39.00	2

Delete Product   Update Quantity   Close

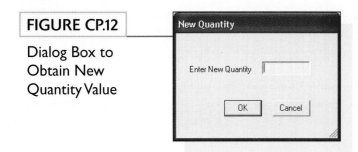

FIGURE CP.12

Dialog Box to
Obtain New
Quantity Value

If that product is selected again with an order quantity of three, then the quantity on the Current Order Details dialog box should show a new quantity of five units.

To accomplish this, you will need to investigate the SortedList class's ContainsKey() method. This will tell you if an entry with the given key already exists in the SortedList collection. If it does exist, you should delete it and replace the entry with one that has the updated quantity value. Note that the SortedList class also has a Remove() method.

If you look at Figure CP.11 you can see two new buttons (compared to Project 11). The Delete Product button removes a product from the order and the Update Quantity button changes the quantity on the order. Note that both buttons are not enabled on the form in Figure CP.11. These two buttons do not get enabled until the user clicks on a product in the ListView component. Use the ListView's Click event to enable the buttons.

To either delete a product or update its quantity, you need to know which row in the ListView component was selected. This can be done by using the SelectedItems() property of the ListView control. This property has an Items collection that stores the Items in the row. In this project, there should be only one selected item (set the ListView's MultiSelect property to False). The code below will get the product number from the selected row and store it in the variable **ProdNo**.

ProdNo = lvwOrder.SelectedItems.Item(0).Text

Once you know the product number for the selected row, you can use the SortedList's Remove() method to remove the product. To update the quantity value, you first need to display a dialog box to get a new quantity value (see Figure CP.12). You can then remove the current entry for the product in the SortedList and add a new entry for the product with a new quantity value.

Be sure that you have included code to make sure that user errors are handled. For example, be sure that the new quantity value is a valid number.

Comprehensive Project 5: Real Estate Listings Database Application Revisited

This project is an extension of Project 9 in Chapter 8. You should read and understand Project 9 before you attempt to complete this project. Project 9 provided the ability to manage real estate records in a database. It would most likely be used by a real estate firm to manage the database. This project is focused on the customers of the firm and provides features useful for them.

Figure CP.13 shows the main form for this project. All the listings are shown in the DataGrid like they were in Project 9. However, there are four "selection" buttons at the bottom of the user interface that provide the user with the ability to display the listing by various criteria. For example, if the user clicks on the Acreage radio button, the DataGrid should display only those listings for that category. Figure CP.14 shows this.

FIGURE CP.13

The Main Form for Comprehensive Project 5

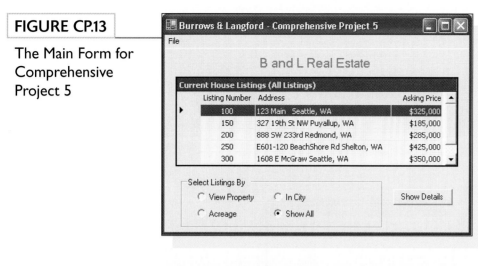

FIGURE CP.14

Acreage Listings Only Being Displayed

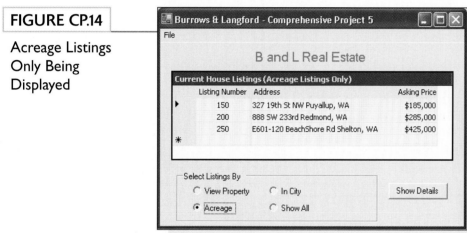

When the user clicks on a listing, the Show Details button should become enabled. If the user then clicks on this button, a new form should be displayed that shows all the information on that specific listing. Figure CP.15 shows an example for Listing Number 200.

The database for this project is an Access database named HouseDB.mdb. Figure CP.16 shows the fields for the Listings table stored in the database. Most

FIGURE CP.15

Details for Listing Number 200

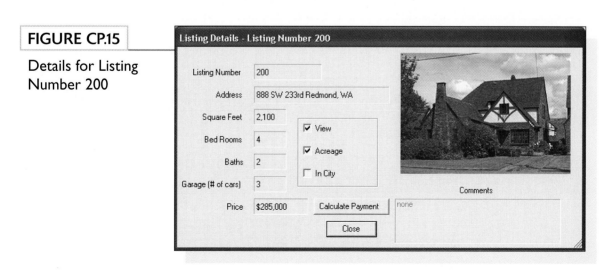

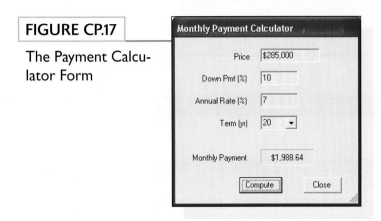

FIGURE CP.16

Fields in the Listings
Table of the
Database

FIGURE CP.17

The Payment Calcu-
lator Form

of the same fields were in the database for Project 9. The exception is the field named PicFileName. This Text field stores the name of the file that stores the picture of each house being listed. The actual picture files should be stored in the Project bin directory.

The Calculate Payment feature is identical to that described in Project 9. When the button is clicked, a new form like that shown in Figure CP.17 should be displayed.

Coding Details

When the user clicks on one of the selection criteria radio buttons at the bottom of the form, the code needs to detect this (a Click event) and then assign the DataGrid to a different dataset. For this project, you can define five OleDbData-Adapters and corresponding datasets. Four of the data adapters are related to the four views ("Where" clauses are used in the SQL to select the appropriate records). The fifth contains all the records and all the fields. This last adapter and dataset are used in displaying the information on the Details form.

To change the set of records displayed in the DataGrid, you should first clear the dataset and then refill it from the data adapter. Then you need to set the DataGrid's DataSource and DataMember properties. Finally, you need to execute the DataGrid's Refresh() method to cause the new records to be displayed.

To fill the Details form, you need to complete the following steps:

1. Clear the dataset that will contain all the records and all the fields. Then fill this from the appropriate data adapter.

2. Get the selected row from the DataGrid using the CurrentRowIndex property. Use this property and the grid's Item property to get the Listing Number from column zero of the selected row.

3. Get the row from the dataset that matches the Listing Number from step 2. For example, if the dataset is named DsAllFields, you could enter

```
Dim Filter As String = "ListNo = " & ListingNo
Dim DBRow As DataRow() = DsAllFields.Tables("Listings").Select(Filter)
```

4. Once you have the current row, you can use the DataRow's Item property to extract and store the field values. For example, to get the address, you could say

```
Dim Addr As String = DBRow(0).Item("Addr")
```

Note that the three "Yes/No" type database fields should be defined as Boolean in Visual Basic .NET to work correctly.

5. After getting all the field values, store their values into the appropriate components on the Details form. In most cases this is straightforward. For example, to store the address you could say

```
objDetailsForm.lblAddr.Text = Addr
```

The picture of the house is shown using a PictureBox control. This class has an Image property that stores the image file name. Assuming that you stored the image file name from the database in a variable named PictureURL, the following code would load the picture into the PictureBox control named picHouse:

```
objDetailsForm.picHouse.Image = Image.FromFile(PictureURL)
```

6. After filling all the components on the Details form, the form should be shown as a dialog box.

Two considerations need to be kept in mind on the Details form. First, the PictureBox has a property named SizeMode. This property should be set to Auto-Size. Second, the user should not be able to change the value of the check boxes by clicking on them. To prevent this from happening, set each CheckBox's AutoCheck property to False.

Debugging

In the process of coding computer applications you will inevitably make mistakes. Some will be readily apparent, as when Visual Basic .NET halts execution of the running application and displays an error message. Others may go unnoticed for a long time until a processing problem occurs. When you do discover a mistake—a *bug* in a program—your task will be to locate its source and fix it. This task is known as *debugging*.

We begin this appendix by categorizing programming errors. We then discuss the strategies and tools for locating the source of problems and fixing them. Finally, we discuss the debugging tools provided by Visual Basic .NET.

Categories of Errors

There are three categories of errors that can arise in programs: compile errors, run-time errors, and logic errors. The category of the error is determined by the type of mistake you make and the way you find out that a problem exists. Knowing to which category an error belongs helps you determine how to begin your attack on the problem (that is, finding and fixing the error).

Compile Errors

Compile errors are also called *syntax errors* because they occur when you violate syntax rules; for example, you misspell a keyword or use a valid statement in the wrong context.

Compile errors are not hard to discover: Visual Basic .NET informs you of them by underlining and displaying an error message when you type the statement. In fact, the program will not execute until you have fixed all compile errors.

Visual Basic .NET checks each new line of code for correct syntax when you enter it in the Code window. Figure A.1 shows this kind of error message.

Fixing a compile error generally requires reviewing the correct syntax for the statement; confirming that you have correctly spelled variable names, control names, or property names; and checking that you have not omitted statements altogether.

Run-Time Errors

As the name suggests, *run-time errors* occur while the program is running. They occur when the computer attempts to execute a statement and finds that it is unable to because a situation has arisen that prevents the statement from performing

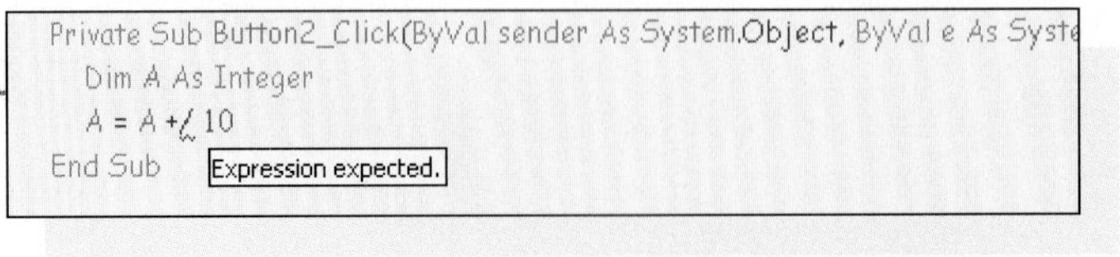

FIGURE A.1

An Example Syntax Error

```
Private Sub Button2_Click(ByVal sender As System.Object, ByVal e As Syste
    Dim A As Integer
    A = A +  10
End Sub    Expression expected.
```

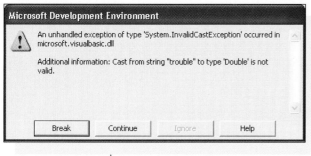

FIGURE A.2

An Example Run-Time Error

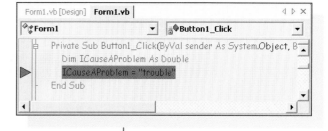

FIGURE A.3

Code Window with Offending Statement Highlighted

properly. Run-time errors can result when the developer fails to anticipate certain situations that may arise at run time, overlooks important details of how statements work, or has produced a flawed design for the application.

When a run-time error occurs, the user cannot miss it: Visual Basic .NET halts execution of the program and displays an error message dialog box.

As an example, suppose you have the following statements in a procedure.

```
Dim ICauseAProblem As Double
ICauseAProblem = "trouble"
```

Since the String constant "trouble" cannot be stored in a variable of type Double, Visual Basic .NET halts execution of the program, then displays the error message dialog box shown in Figure A.2.

If you click on the Break button in the error message dialog box, Visual Basic .NET displays the Code window with the statement that failed to execute highlighted, as shown in Figure A.3.

End users don't like run-time errors. One reason is that they cause execution of the program to terminate. Another is that when the user restarts the program, he or she will probably have to redo some of the work done before the run-time error occurred. Not surprisingly, software development companies find they cannot sell programs that frequently terminate with run-time errors.

A program may be used successfully for a long time before any run-time errors occur. For this reason developers expect that even programs that have been used successfully for years still have within them any number of bugs that have not yet been discovered.

Logic Errors

The last type of mistake is the logic error, which is a flaw in the program design. If the developer is lucky, a logic error will cause a run-time error to occur, which serves as a clue that something is wrong with the program. If the developer is unlucky, the program will appear to run successfully but will produce incorrect results. For example, if the program miscalculates the total charge on an invoice, the customer will be paying either too much or too little. When this mistake is discovered, someone will be unhappy about it.

Logic errors are generally the most difficult to deal with because the computer does not find them and notify the developer as it does with compile and run-time errors. Instead, the developer must attempt to discover any logic errors by thoroughly testing the program.

Correcting Mistakes

If a program aborts or runs incorrectly, the world hasn't come to an end. You can view a problem as a challenge. With a good attitude, a strategy to tackle the problem, and debugging tools, you have the ability to locate the error and correct it.

Attitude

The first, and some say most important, aspect of debugging is approaching the task with the right attitude. Debugging can be tedious and frustrating. Not knowing why the computer is rejecting your syntax or not being able to find a logic error can upset the best of developers. However, by using a good strategy and the right tools, and by adopting a "detective" attitude, you can actually enjoy the process of debugging. After all, there can be a great deal of satisfaction in solving a difficult puzzle.

Think of a problem in your code as a mystery novel. Your task is to determine "who done it." You will be given a number of obvious clues such as error messages or incorrect results. You also will have to find some rather subtle clues that can be investigated with the help of Visual Basic .NET's debugging tools. At times you will follow a clue that is deceptive and is no help at all. After some practice, you might become quite accomplished at debugging.

Strategy

Developers use many different approaches to debug code. The following are approaches that we have found helpful.

Debug in Small Increments. Do not write the code for the entire application before attempting to run it the first time. Instead, write a small amount of code, run it, and debug it. When you get that code "clean" (no apparent bugs), then write a little more code, run it again, and debug it again.

Visual Basic .NET naturally segments your code into small event procedures. Take advantage of this fact and debug each event procedure as you code it. Of course, there will be times when you cannot debug one procedure until another one is working. However, with a little forethought you can often choose wisely the order in which to create procedures: first create those procedures that are needed by the largest number of other procedures. This will help make it possible to debug small segments of code rather than large ones.

Carefully Select Test Cases. When a program appears to run successfully, you cannot just assume that it produces correct results. Always bear in mind that a program may contain logic errors that cause it to produce incorrect results while appearing to run successfully. The only way to gain confidence that the program is producing correct results is to test it. That is, you need to enter test data into your application and determine if the application is handling these data correctly.

How should you select the data to use in testing? First, select data that would typically be expected for the application. For example, if your application computes monthly mortgage payments, enter 30 years and an interest rate of 8.7 percent. Manually compute some results and check to see if your application produces the same answers.

In addition to using typical test data, you should also use unexpected values. Users often do unexpected things when they interact with an application, and your application needs to be able to handle these things. For example, what does your application do if the user enters 8.7 for the interest rate when you expected .087? Try to imagine every possible variation of input values and test each one.

As another example, suppose that your code searches a list of employee numbers to find a target value entered by the user. To test the search code, you should enter an employee number that exists and another employee number that does not exist. These should clearly result in different behaviors by your application. If the employee numbers are ordered from smallest to largest in your list, then try to find the first one and then the last one. Also try to find an employee number that is smaller than the first one and another that is larger than the last one. Called "testing at the extremes," this process often identifies places where code fails.

Peer Examination. A final strategy is to show your code to someone else. How many times have you written a term paper and proofread it carefully, only to have your instructor circle spelling and grammar errors? Errors creep in because we see what we think is there, not what is actually there. You are likely to encounter this same problem when you write code. When you are debugging, you see what you intended to write, not what you actually wrote. Someone else reading your code will often find the error quickly because he or she reads literally what is there.

It is also helpful to explain your code to another person. As you do this, you often start to explain a line of code only to ask yourself why you wrote it.

Tools. Most sophisticated programming environments, including Visual Basic .NET, provide debugging tools that make it easy to suspend execution of code at any statement so that you can look at the values stored in variables. As an example of the value of such tools, consider the following. As developer you know the intended effect of each procedure in your project. By examining the values of variables right before a procedure call, then executing the procedure, and then examining the values of variables again, you can check whether the procedure affects the variables as you intended. This provides a quick way of uncovering clues to the source of problems.

Visual Basic .NET's Debugging Tools

In the remainder of this appendix we describe Visual Basic .NET's debugging environment, discuss the various tools it provides, and give examples of how the tools are used in the debugging process.

Modes

Recall that at any given time, a Visual Basic .NET project exists in one of three modes: design mode, run mode, or break mode. In design mode, your application is not running, and you can create controls and write code. In run mode, your application is controlling the system, and so you are interacting with your application, not directly with Visual Basic .NET. Break mode is when your application is running but "suspended." Visual Basic .NET's debugging tools work in break mode. Many debugging tools "look into" your code and tell you what is going on in memory.

It is easy to tell which mode you are in by looking at Visual Basic .NET's Title bar. Figure A.4 shows the three different modes as indicated by the Title bar.

You can force your program to enter break mode while your program is running by entering the [CTRL]+[BREAK] keystroke (press and hold the [CTRL] key and

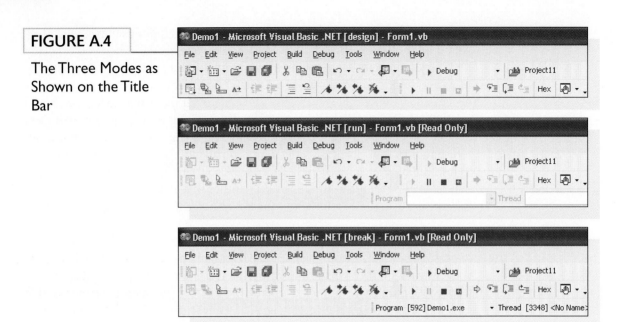

then press the BREAK key). The only way to interrupt an infinite loop (in which your program executes a number of statements repeatedly, forever) is to use the CTRL+BREAK key combination.

Debugging Tools on the Toolbar

Visual Basic .NET has a number of debugging tools that are helpful for finding and diagnosing logic errors in your code. These tools can be accessed by using either the Debug menu or the Debug toolbar. To show the Debug toolbar, select Toolbars from the View menu or right-click on the Toolbar and select Debug from the ensuing popup menu. The Debug toolbar is shown in Figure A.5. The behavior of the various tools is summarized in Table A.1.

In addition to the Debug menu, there are also a number of useful windows that can be displayed. If you click on the Additional Windows tool (see Figure A.5) while the program is in **debug mode**, a menu drops down that shows a number of useful tools. Figure A.6 shows these tools. Many of the tools provide information that is beyond the scope of this text but we will look at the Autos window later.

Breakpoints

Breakpoints cause a program to pause and go into break mode. You can set any statement to be a breakpoint. Visual Basic .NET suspends execution right before it executes such a statement.

FIGURE A.5

Debugging Tools

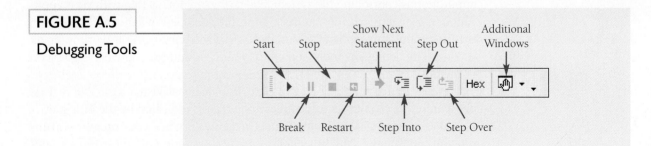

Table A.1 Actions of tools in the Debug Toolbar

Tool	Action
Start	Starts the program running. When in break mode, this becomes the Continue button to resume execution.
Break	Places the program into break mode.
Stop	Stops the program.
Restart	Restarts the program.
Show Next Statement	In break mode, shows the next statement to be executed.
Step Into	Executes the next statement even if it is inside a new procedure.
Step Out	Finishes executing the existing (called) procedure and stops when control returns to the calling procedure.
Step Over	Executes the next statement. If that statement is a procedure, the procedure is executed without stopping.

FIGURE A.6

Additional
Debugging Tools

Breakpoints	Ctrl+Alt+B
Running Documents	Ctrl+Alt+N
Watch	▶
Autos	Ctrl+Alt+V, A
Locals	Ctrl+Alt+V, L
Me	Ctrl+Alt+V, T
Immediate	Ctrl+G
Call Stack	Ctrl+L
Threads	Ctrl+Alt+H
Modules	Ctrl+Alt+U
Memory	▶
Disassembly	Ctrl+Alt+D
Registers	Ctrl+Alt+G
Toggle Disassembly	Ctrl+F11

To set a breakpoint, you can click in the Margin Indicator Bar to the left of a statement where you want the breakpoint to be placed. A round "breakpoint" indicator will be placed there to indicate that the statement is a breakpoint, and Visual Basic .NET will highlight the statement. Figure A.7 shows the result of setting a breakpoint. To turn the breakpoint off, click on the breakpoint indicator in the Margin Indicator Bar. This toggles the breakpoint on and off. Each time you click on the breakpoint indicator, the line of code changes to its opposite state: if it was a breakpoint before the click, it will not be after the click, and if it was not a breakpoint before the click, it will be after the click.

During program execution, when Visual Basic .NET encounters a breakpoint, it suspends execution and shows the Code window with a yellow "current statement" indicator pointing at the breakpoint statement (Figure A.8). At this point the program is in break mode. You can click the Run tool to resume execution at this statement, or click the End tool to stop execution. Alternatively, you can use the debugging tools.

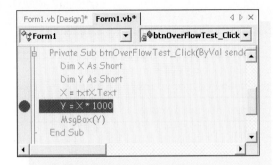

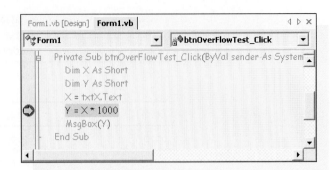

FIGURE A.7

Line of Code Set as a Breakpoint

FIGURE A.8

Program Code with Execution
Suspended at a Breakpoint

Let's suppose you want to see the values of some variables at this point. You can do this in several ways. First, you can simply position the cursor over any variable. Visual Basic .NET will display the current value of the variable next to the cursor, as illustrated in Figure A.9. Second, you can click on the Autos window tab to show the current values of all local variables and GUI components. This is illustrated in Figure A.10.

If you know that the final value of a series of calculations in your program is incorrect, you can set breakpoints at the statements that perform the intermediate calculations and check the intermediate values to see where the error is taking place. You also can use breakpoints and the Step buttons to help you determine the sequence in which statements are being executed. This is particularly valuable when you have If statements and you are not sure whether the True or False clauses are being executed. Not only can you tell which clause is being executed; you can look at the values of the decision variables to help understand why a particular clause was chosen. Note that breakpoints are not saved, so if you close a project and then open it later, any breakpoints will be gone.

With the use of breakpoints, the Autos window, and Step buttons, a great deal of insight can be gained about the program as it processes the data and performs the logic of a procedure or set of procedures.

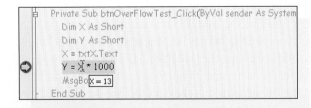

FIGURE A.9

Visual Basic .NET Displaying the Current
Value of a Variable

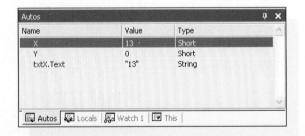

FIGURE A.10

Using the Autos Window to Show the
Value of All Variables

Configuring and Using Internet Information Services (IIS) Server

Visual Basic .NET has extensive support for developing Web-based applications that range from simple HTML pages bound together by scripts to comprehensive e-commerce applications that use elaborate business rules. These applications are built around ASP.NET, which is a technology for developing and deploying applications on a Web server and is an integral part of the .NET framework. These applications run on the Microsoft Internet Information Services (IIS) Web server.

In this appendix we describe the use of the IIS server in Web Applications. We first start with an introduction to the IIS server, followed by a description of the various configurations that will enable you to use an IIS server to host Web-based applications. Visual Basic .NET performs most of the interaction with the IIS server; nevertheless, it is useful to know the working of the server and the various options that are available when building Web Applications. We also present the differences between Web servers on a local machine versus remote servers that are controlled by a central authority.

IIS Web Server Installation

IIS Web Server is the Web server provided by Microsoft for platforms running the various versions of the Windows operating system. It is installed by default and running on server platforms such as NT4 server and Windows 2000 server. IIS Server is not installed by default on workstation platforms such as Windows 2000 Professional, Windows XP Professional, and Windows NT workstation. To install IIS Server on workstation platforms, you need to install it through the additional Windows Components that are available through the control panel. In Figure B.1 we show the installation of IIS Server on a workstation machine.

To access the Windows Components Wizard, you first need to go to the Control Panel, then click on "Add or Remove Programs," and then select "Add/Remove Windows Components." To start the installation you need to check the box adjacent to Internet Information Services (IIS) and then click on "Next >" and follow the installation instructions.

After installation of the IIS Server, it is necessary to check if the server is running on your machine. The easiest way to check for the presence of IIS Server is to use the Internet Explorer browser. To do this, open a Web browser and type **http://localhost** or **http://[machinename]**, where [machinename] is the name of your machine. The website also can be accessed using the IP Address of the machine. Each machine has a unique IP address that is used to identify it on the network. To connect to your local machine using an IP address, type **http://127.0.0.1** on your browser. This is a special address and it is always used to represent the local machine's IP address. By doing this you are trying to access the Web server running on your machine. Figure B.2 shows a snapshot of the screen if IIS Server is running on your machine.

The Installation
Options for IIS
Server on
Workstations

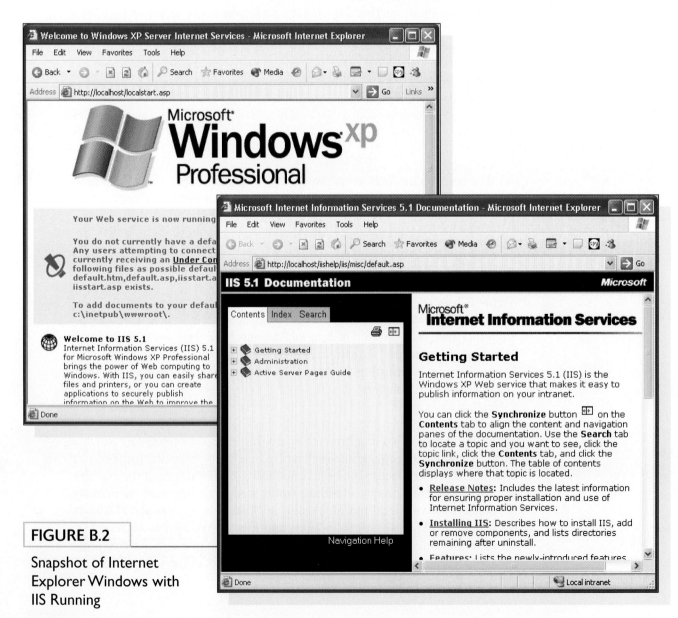

Snapshot of Internet
Explorer Windows with
IIS Running

One of the windows refers to the documentation available with the Web server. The second window brings up a default page that describes the status of the Web server. This page contains information about the default pages that are acceptable to the Web server and the location of the files that belong to the Web server. In most of the cases, website-related files are stored in the "/inetpub/wwwroot" folder on your local hard-drive. If you try to access this Web server from another machine by typing **http://[*machine name*]** on the Web browser, you will see an "Under Construction" page. This is displayed because you have not yet built a Web page that will be displayed automatically to users connecting to your Web server. Later in the appendix we will describe how to add Web pages to the Web server that can be seen by users trying to access your Web server from other machines.

Controlling and Configuring IIS Web Server

To configure the IIS Web server, open the Internet Services Manager from the Control Panel, go to "Administrative Tools," and double-click on "Internet Information Services."[1]

The Internet Services Manager provides configuration options to start or stop the local Web server and to configure the various websites that are available through the Web server. The tool's interface is divided into two adjacent frames. Figure B.3 shows the Default Web Site and other associated files that are initially created when IIS is installed.

At this point it is possible to perform many simple actions such as stopping/starting the server, creating default files for Web pages, and renaming files. These actions can be performed either by clicking on the menu items in the window or by right-clicking on the Default Web Site. Figure B.4 shows how to stop the currently running Web server.

FIGURE B.3

Default Files on a Web Server

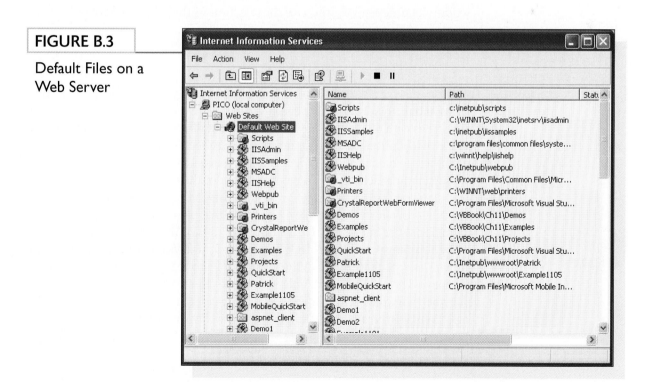

---

[1]   In Windows 2000 this tool is named Internet Services Manager.

FIGURE B.4

Stopping the Web Server on a Local Machine

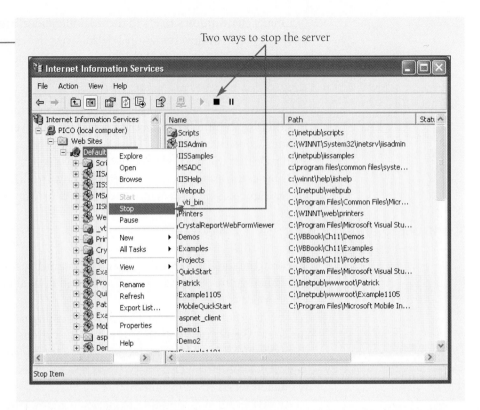

When the Web server is stopped, the website is no longer available for anyone trying to connect to it and, similarly, the Web applications that are developed are no longer accessible to users. Clicking on the Start button restarts the Web server. Note that the options available through the pop-up menu and through the Action menu depend on the current selection in the left pane. For example if you right-click on "local computer," a different menu pops up.

Virtual Directories

A virtual directory is an alias for a physical directory and it supports the creation of websites with different names and in different directories than the default Inetpub/wwwroot directory. This feature increases the security of the Web server by hiding the actual names of the folders, and also allows more flexibility in storing the website on the machine. The default location for the server website (home directory) is Inetpub\wwwroot on the system drive (the drive where Windows is installed—usually the "C:\" drive). Any folder that is created within that folder will automatically be added as a virtual directory to the Web server's default website.

We also can specify the default homepage for the virtual directory, which will allow us to type the address of the virtual directory name without specifying the file name. The following example shows how to create a new folder under the c:\Inetpub\wwwroot, setting up the default page for that virtual directory, and viewing a Web page created in that folder using an http address.

Example B.1

CREATING NEW FOLDER IN "C:\INETPUB\WWWROOT"

We begin by creating a new folder under c:\inetpub\wwwroot called "VDirDemo" using the Windows Explorer. In this folder we place a new file (that can be created using Notepad or another text editor) called "welcome.html" that has the following HTML code:

```
<html>
   <body>
      <h3><center>Welcome to my virtual directory</center></h3>
   </body>
</html>
```

Figure B.5 shows the Windows Explorer with the physical folder structure and the Internet Services Manager. You can see that the VDirDemo folder we created in c:\Inetpub\wwwroot was added automatically to the virtual directories list in the Internet Services Manager.[2]

To set the file named "welcome.html" to be the default page in the VDirDemo virtual directory, use the Internet Services Manager, right-click on the VDirDemo icon, and select "Properties". Then select the Documents tab and click on the

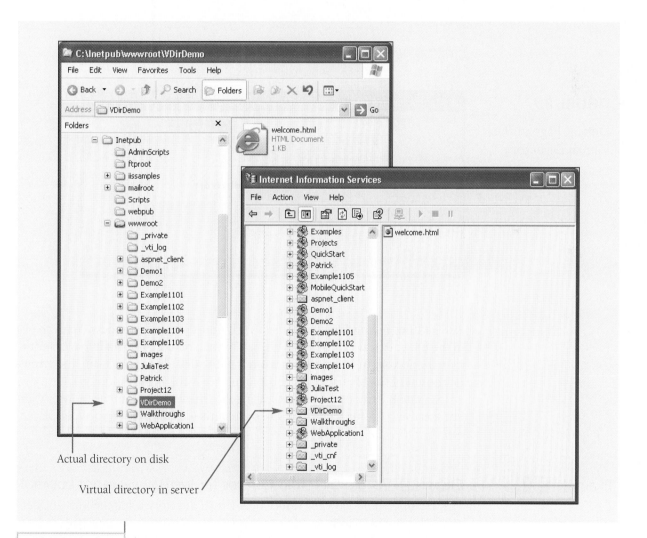

Actual directory on disk

Virtual directory in server

FIGURE B.5

Creation of Virtual Directory

2   In Windows 2000, you may need to select Refresh from the pop-up menu before you see the virtual directory.

FIGURE B.6

Virtual Directory
Properties Window

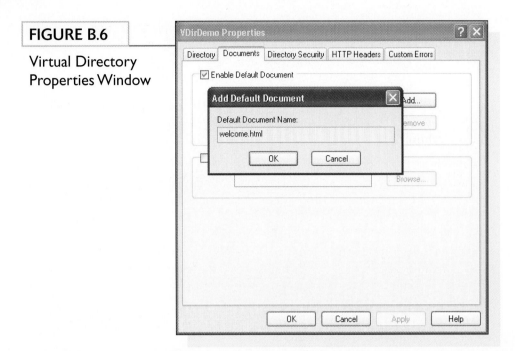

FIGURE B.7

Default Page in the
Virtual Directory

Add button. Figure B.6 shows the VDirDemo Properties window. You can see in the figure that IIS already has file names that are used as default pages for the virtual directory. You can set the priority of the default page by using the arrows on the left of the file names list (top element has the highest priority).

In Figure B.7 we see the result of calling the virtual directory in the browser without specifying the file name. You can see that the default page has been displayed.

Example **B.2**

CREATING A VIRTUAL DIRECTORY OUTSIDE THE INETPUB\WWWROOT LOCATION

This example shows how to create a new virtual directory using the Virtual Directory Wizard and map it to a folder that exists outside of the root path c:\Inetpub\wwwroot. We start by creating a folder named "ActualDir" on the "C:\" drive. We then place in that folder the "welcome.html," which we modify to say "Welcome to my page that is located in "C:\ActualDir"". In the Internet Services Manager, we right-click on the default website folder and select "New" then "Virtual Directory…". In the wizard that is opened for us we choose "VDir" as the alias and "C:\ActualDir" as the location (see Figure B.8.)

FIGURE B.8

Virtual Directory
Creation Wizard—
Selecting Physical
Folder

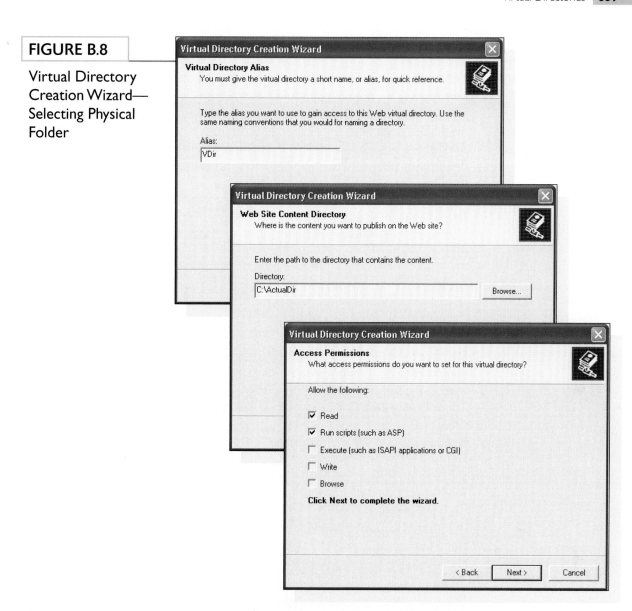

FIGURE B.9

The Default Web
Page in the Browser

Continue to click through the wizard. When it's done, you can view the Web
page you saved (see Figure B.9) in C:\ActualDir using the following address:

http://localhost/VDir/welcome.html

Remote Server Configuration

The Internet Services Manager allows administration of websites located on a remote machine. It is quite common in a corporate network or even in a local network inside a university to have a Web server on a machine different from the local machine. To configure IIS Web server on a remote machine or to deploy Web Applications or Web services, you will need to have administrative privileges on that machine. To configure a remote machine, you will need to connect to that machine; once you are connected, you can perform operations on the remote machine as you did on your local machine. Figure B.10 shows how to connect to a remote machine using Internet Services Manager.

If you have the necessary permissions, the Internet Services Manager provides the entire configuration options that are available on a local machine. Figure B.11 shows a snapshot of the Management window that is connected to two different machines. One of them is a local machine and the other one is a remote machine.

Moving a Web Application to Another Computer

We have found that it is difficult to move a Web Application project to another computer to do development. A number of problems can arise that prevent the moved application from being debugged and run from within Visual Basic .NET. The following describes a procedure that seems to work without encountering any problems.

Assume that you want to move Example 11.1 from Chapter 11 to another computer. To do this, you should first create a new Web Application project on the computer you are moving the project to. This new Web Application should be created in the Inetpub/wwwroot directory (the "localhost"). Figure B.12 shows the project named "NewExample1101" being created.

When the project opens, it will create a new Web Form named Web-Form1.aspx. You need to delete this Web Form and replace it with the Web

FIGURE B.10

Snapshot of Internet
Services Manager to
Connect to a
Remote Machine

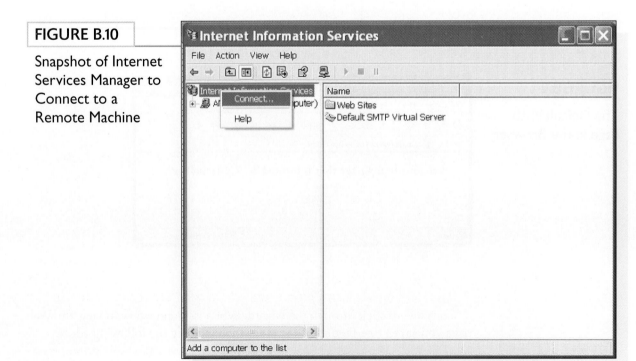

FIGURE B.11

Internet Services
Manager View of
Both a Remote and
a Local Machine
Connection

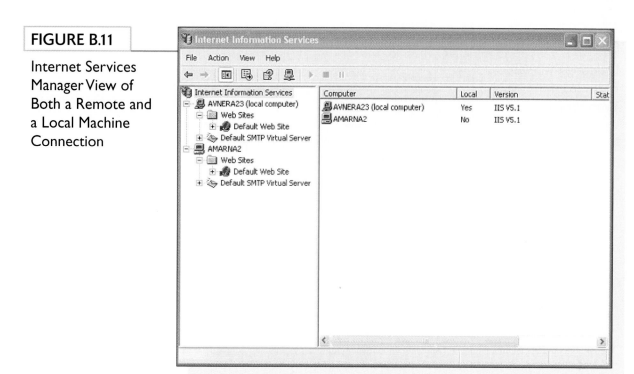

FIGURE B.12

Creating a New Web
Application That Will
Be Used for Moving
Example 11.1

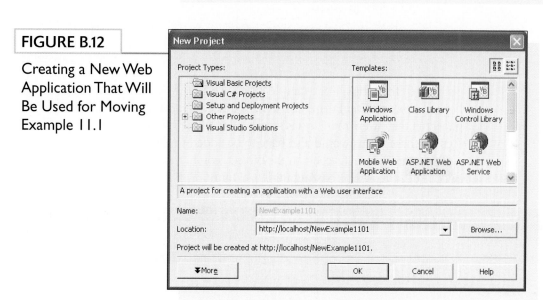

Forms and Visual Basic .NET code that exist with the original application on the computer you are moving the project from.[3] Figure B.13 shows the pop-up menu that is generated when you right-click on the file WebForm1.aspx. From this pop-up menu you should select the Delete option. This will delete the form from the project and the disk.

Once this form is deleted from the new project, you next need to add the Web forms and code from the original project. It is assumed that you have access to the original project; you could have copied it to a floppy disk or to the hard drive of the computer where the project is being moved to. When you open the original project folder, you will see files with the extensions .aspx and .aspx.vb that are asso-

---

3   If the original project used the Global.asax file or any .aspx.resx (resource) files, you need to delete and replace these also.

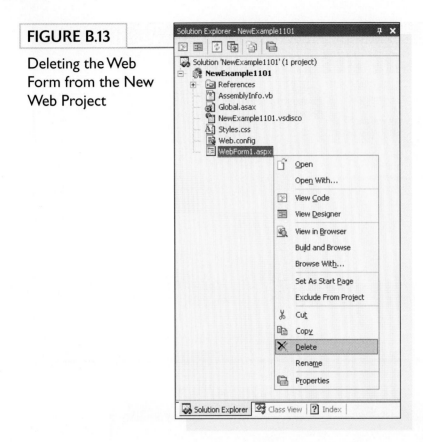

FIGURE B.13

Deleting the Web
Form from the New
Web Project

ciated with the forms. For example, in Figure B.14, you see the files named Web-Form1.aspx and WebForm1.aspx.vb. You need to add these two files to the new project. If there were more forms associated with the project, the .aspx and .aspx.vb files for these forms would also have to be added to the new project

To do this, first right-click on the project icon in the Solution Explorer and then select Add, then Add Existing Item…. Figure B.15 shows this sequence.

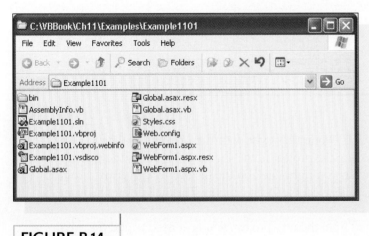

FIGURE B.14

All the Files in the Original Project

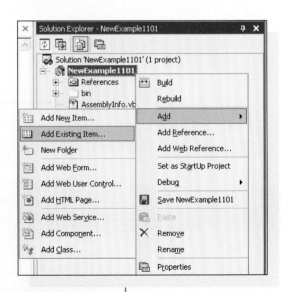

FIGURE B.15

Selecting Add Existing Item… for the
New Project

All the Files
Associated with the
Original Project

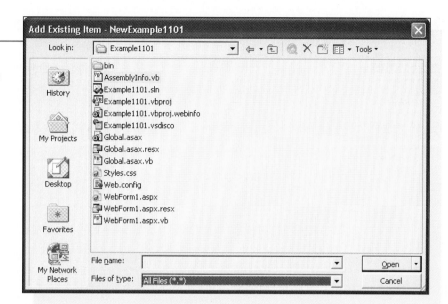

You will see an Add Existing Item dialog box as shown in Figure B.16. Note that in the "Files of type" box at the bottom of the dialog box, "All Files (*.*)" has been selected. If you do not select this option, then you will not see all the files that need to be added.

From this dialog box, you should select the .aspx and .aspx.vb files associated with the Web Form. Figure B.17 shows that these files have been selected. Once they are selected, click on Open to add the files to the existing (new) project. Figure B.18 shows the Solution Explorer with these files shown in the project.

The final step to perform is to set the appropriate form as the form to be shown at startup. You do this by right-clicking on the appropriate form and selecting Set As Start Page from the pop-up menu, as shown in Figure B.19. After doing this, you can save the new project and then run it. As a result, you have successfully moved the project from one computer to another computer. The new project can be seen running in Figure B.20. Note that the URL in Figure B.20, **http://local-host/NewExample1101/WebForm1.aspx**, makes reference to the new project.

Selecting the Files to
Be Added to the
New Project

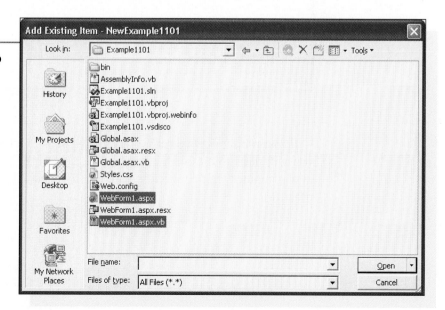

FIGURE B.18

Solution Explorer Showing the Files That Have Been Added to the New Project

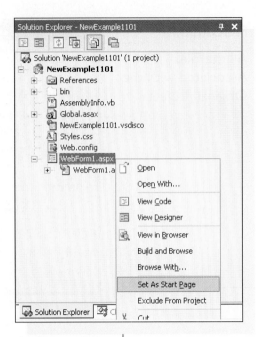

FIGURE B.19

Selecting the Start-Up Form in the New Project

FIGURE B.20

The New Project as It Runs in the Internet Explorer

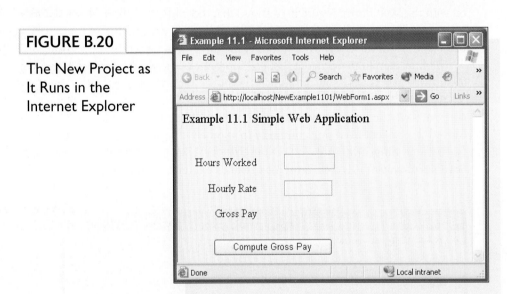

If your project uses a database served with MSDE on the original local computer, you will need to establish a new connection to the MSDE server on the new local computer. This connection will have to be linked to the data adapter for the project.

Configuring and Using MSDE and the SQL Select Statement

In this appendix we provide more information about MSDE (Microsoft Desktop Engine) that supports Visual Basic .NET and elaborate on the SQL (structured query language) that was briefly introduced in Chapter 8. Although SQL queries are automatically generated by the Query Builder when using Visual Basic .NET, it is useful to have an understanding of SQL as it is the de facto language used by almost all commercial relational databases.

MSDE (Microsoft Desktop Engine)

Installation

After installing Visual Basic .NET (or the complete Visual Studio .NET package), you need to install MSDE and the sample databases. To install MSDE, you should find a file named instmsde.exe located in the following folder:

> **C:\Program Files\Microsoft Visual Studio .NET\FrameworkSDK\Samples\Setup\msde**

Figure C.1 shows the file in the Windows Explorer. Note the path that is shown in the title bar of the folder. You need to execute this file by double-clicking on it.

After installing MSDE, you need to install the sample databases. To do this, you run the program named ConfigSamples.exe that should be located at

> **C:\Program Files\Microsoft Visual Studio .NET\FrameworkSDK\Samples\Setup**

Figure C.2 shows the folder and the program you need to run. Double-clicking on the program file should start it executing. When this is done executing, you should see the databases named GrocerToGo, master, model, msdb, Northwind, Portal, and pubs using the Server Explorer.

Double-click here to start installer

FIGURE C.2

Installation File for
the Sample
Databases

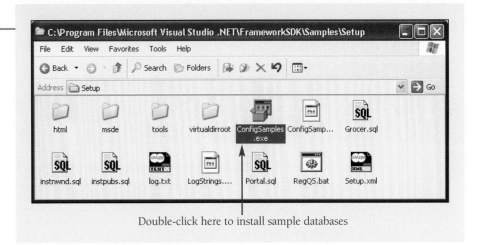

Double-click here to install sample databases

FIGURE C.3

The MSDE Icon on
the Start Bar and
the Server Service
Manager

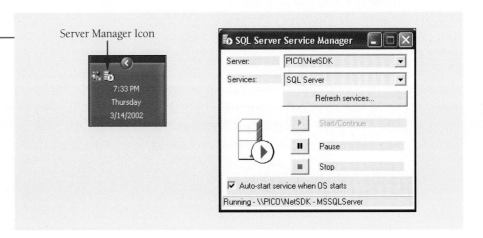

Configuration

Operations such as starting and stopping the server are available through the SQL Server Service Manager. The icon for the service manager for the MSDE server is found in the icons on the Start bar. This icon and the Server Service Manager are shown in Figure C.3. At the bottom of the Server Service Manager window you can see that the server is running. You also can see the machine name (PICO) and the server name (NetSDK). You should expect to see a different name because it is unlikely your computer also is named PICO.

MSDE is a fully SQL Server compliant database engine and can be used for creating desktop and shared database solutions. Applications that use the MSDE server can be built using development environments such as Visual Studio 6 and Visual Studio .NET as well as Microsoft Access.

MSDE and Microsoft Access

A Microsoft Access database is based on what Microsoft calls the Jet technology. It is a file system–based database engine and the databases are stored in individual files. In contrast, MSDE supports client-server architecture, runs as a service on the computer, and provides many of the advantages of a powerful database server like SQL Server. Some of these advantages are that it allows various SQL operations such as creation of stored procedures, user-defined functions, and views inside databases. It allows for creating scalable applications that can be easily migrated to SQL Server without any modifications and, thus, it is ideal for migrating desktop-based applications to the enterprise environment.

MSDE uses a query language that is fully compliant with Transact-SQL (T-SQL). Transact-SQL is a standard language for communicating with a database server defined by ANSI.[1] It defines the way in which queries are written for a database server and allows the use of custom business logic in the query language. Transact-SQL is an augmentation of the core SQL language and most of the statements cited as being SQL, including those in Chapter 8, are actually Transact-SQL statements.

The Jet technology used by Access is not compliant with T-SQL; instead, it uses its own query language with support for functions using Visual Basic for Applications.

A disadvantage of MSDE is that it does not have a user-interface; all the interactions with it can be done only through either Visual Studio .NET, Visual Studio 6.0, or Access.

Database Operations Using MSDE

In Section 8.4 we briefly described some of the operations that are possible using the Server Explorer. In this section we present some of the operations that can be carried out in the pubs database through the Server Explorer. Note that before any of these operations can be performed, connection objects, discussed in Chapter 8, must first be created. Figure C.4 shows a snapshot of the pubs database in the Server Explorer. To perform any operation presented in this section, you need to select the object being discussed and then right-click on it to bring up the appropriate pop-up menu.

For any database, Database Diagrams allow the creation of a new database diagram or modification of an existing diagram. In a database diagram you can create relationships between tables that allow you to enforce data integrity rules.

The Tables folder contains the existing tables in the database and allows creation, modification, and deletion of tables in the database.

FIGURE C.4

The pubs Database in the Server Explorer

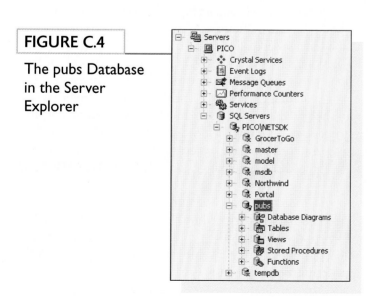

---

1   American National Standards Institute.

The Views folder contains the views in the database. Views are similar to tables as they also are composed of columns and rows, but they are not real tables; they are a saved query that selects fields from different tables in the database. The advantage of creating views is that it is possible to organize data from columns in different tables under a single object in the database; this object can later be referenced in queries like any other table in the database. In the pubs database we have a single view called "titleview". To modify the query that creates this view, select "Design View" from the right-click pop-up menu.

Stored Procedures are a very important part of a database and are used extensively while creating database applications. To perform operations in the databases in Chapters 8–11, you have been creating SQL statements in your program and sending them to the database for processing. An alternative is to store the statements in procedures inside the database and call them from the applications. Such procedures are called stored procedures and they consist of a group of SQL statements compiled together.

Stored procedures are very similar to the concept of functions you have seen in Visual Basic .NET. They are similar as they can have parameters, perform operations on the database, and return values. The advantages of using stored procedures are (1) improved performance, (2) reuse of code across different applications, and (3) separation of the SQL code from the application code. It is considered a good application design to write stored procedures for commonly used queries and tasks in the database.

The example that follows demonstrates creating a stored procedure in the pubs database using the Server Explorer.

Example **C.1**   **CREATING A STORED PROCEDURE**

We start by right-clicking on Stored Procedures for the pubs database and then selecting "New Stored Procedure" from the pop-up menu. Visual Studio .NET opens a Stored Procedure editor and creates a basic structure of the stored procedure.

The commented code provides an example of creating input and output parameters. Comments start with "/*" and close with "*/". We change the name of the stored procedure to AuthorsFromState and add an input parameter named **state** with a data type "char(2)" and a default value of 'CA'. We will not go into detail on MSDE data types, but they are conceptually similar to Visual Basic .NET data types.

We now add the SQL statement. We will explain the various parts of the SQL query in the next section; for now we will just save the new stored procedure. Figure C.5 shows the changes outlined previously. The developer has right-clicked on the Designer tab for the procedure and is selecting the Save option. Note that the name of the file to be saved is shown as "StoredProcedure1". This will be changed by the system to "AuthorsFromState" when the save takes place. Note also that the heading of the procedure will change from **CREATE PROCEDURE** to **ALTER PROCEDURE**.

To run the new stored procedure, place the cursor anywhere in the editor, then right-click and select "Run Stored Procedure" from the pop-up menu. You will be prompted with a window to enter the parameter value. You may enter a state code or click OK (without entering a value) since your parameter in the stored procedure has a default value (in Figure C.6, the value entered was "UT"). You may need to expand the output tab to view the results.

The Server Explorer also enables us to see the Functions inside a database and also create new functions. Functions are similar to stored procedures; they

FIGURE C.5

Creating a Stored
Procedure

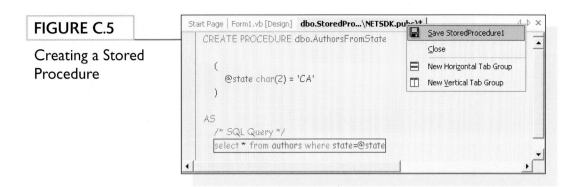

FIGURE C.6

Output from
Running a Stored
Procedure

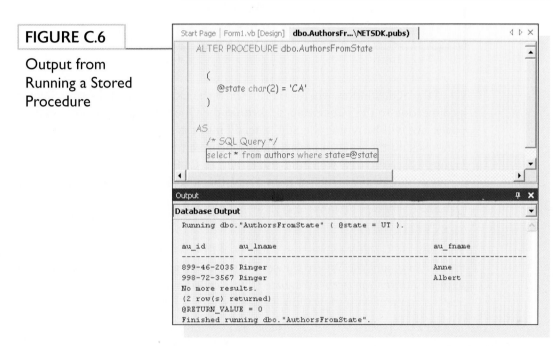

are made of one or more SQL statements and can be used to achieve the reuse of
code. There are many built-in functions in SQL, but SQL also enables developers to create their own functions (called "User Defined Functions"). A Function
can be either a Scalar Function that returns a single data value or it can be a
Table Valued Function that returns a table.

In the following section, we will demonstrate writing SQL queries using the
Query Builder; however, as an alternative, you can create stored procedures and
use them to follow and try the examples.

SQL

SQL can be used to perform operations such as retrieving information from
DBMS (database management systems), inserting data, deleting data, and also
updating the data. The scope of SQL is too extensive to be covered in its entire-
ty here; hence we will be concentrating on the retrieval of data and some interesting operators that allow us to organize the data during retrieval. We also
provide a brief introduction to the SQL language statements that will allow us to
update data.

The samples in this appendix are run in the Query Builder available in Visual Basic .NET. To get to the Query Builder, create a new Windows Application project and add a new OleDbDataAdapter and proceed through the wizard until you

FIGURE C.7

Hiding a Pane within
the Query Builder

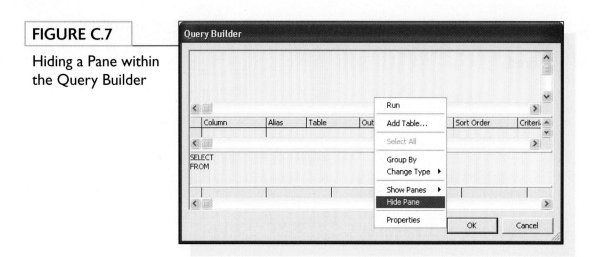

get to the SQL window where you can show the Query Builder. Be sure there is
a connection to the pubs database. Within the Query Builder, hide the top two
panes (we will be typing the SQL directly into the SQL pane). To hide a pane,
right-click on the pane and select Hide Pane from the pop-up menu as shown in
Figure C.7. Note that we could use either an OLEDB or SQL data adapter to
access an SQL database such as pubs. Using the SQL data adapter is more efficient.

SQL Select Syntax

The basic SQL Select expression consists of three clauses: the Select clause, the
From clause, and the Where clause. These clauses are used in a combination to
retrieve information from a database (this is called a query). The syntax of a SQL
Select statement with the various clauses is

SELECT [*select_list*] FROM [*table_list*] WHERE [*search_expression*]

In the syntax, **[*select_list*]** refers to the list of columns that will be included in the
result set, **[*table_list*]** refers to the tables from which the data are coming, and
[*search_expression*] provides search conditions that limit the data range to specific rows in the tables that meet the search condition. Also be aware that all SQL
statements are not case sensitive (like Visual Basic .NET and unlike XML).

In the pubs database there are a number of tables, such as titles, authors, publishers, employees, and so forth, that can be used in SQL queries. While querying
the database, one or more of these tables can be used in the From clause's **[*table_list*]**.
If we choose the authors table, we can only use the columns from the authors
table in the **[*select_list*]**. Let us start with a simple query that will retrieve the author
id (**au_id**), the last name (**au_lname**), the first name (**au_fname**), the phone (**phone**),
and the contract (**contract**) data for all the authors. The SQL query is shown in Figure C.8. If you right-click on the SQL pane in the Query Builder and bring up the
pop-up window, you can then click on Run to run the query and see the database
records that are returned from running the query. Each row will contain one entry
that consists of the all columns that were listed in the Select clause.

The "*" is used to represent all the columns. If we remove the Where clause and
use the "*" in the Select clause, data from all the columns and all the rows are
retrieved; in other words, the entire table data are retrieved. In the next query we
filter the records returned from the authors table to all authors where **contract = 0**.
We use the Where clause to filter the records. If the argument we compare to is
not numeric, we need to wrap it with single quotes. The query in Figure C.9

FIGURE C.8

Simple Query to
Retrieve Information
from Authors Table

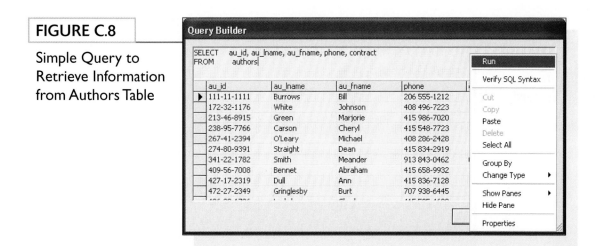

FIGURE C.9

Query Demonstrat-
ing Select Statement
Using "*" Operator

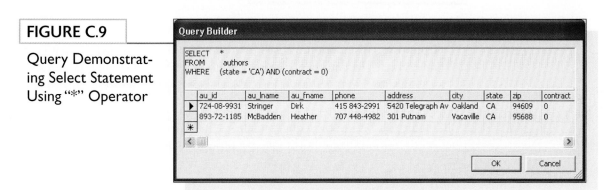

selects all the authors who do not have a contract (**contract = 0**) and who are from California (**state = 'CA'**). Note that since CA is not numeric, we enclose the value in single quotes. The Where clause allows the use of comparison operators such as < and >. It also allows the use of logical operators such as *and, or,* and *not.* The use of comparison operators, logical operators, and parentheses is very similar to Visual Basic .NET.

In the following query, we change from the authors tables and retrieve data from all the columns in the titles table where the price of the title is between 10.0 and 20.0 inclusive:

```
SELECT    *
FROM      titles
WHERE     (price >= 10.0) AND (price <= 20.0)
```

Additional Keywords

There are other keywords provided in the SQL Select statement that enable us to organize the data further. The most commonly used additional keywords are Distinct, Order By, and Group By.

- **Distinct:** This keyword is used to remove any duplicate rows from the retrieved information.

- **Order By:** This keyword is used to sort the results based on the column list specified. It will first sort by the first column and then by the other columns in the order they appear in the Order By clause. The default sort is ascending; to sort in a descending order we add the keyword DESC.

FIGURE C.10

Query to
Demonstrate the
Distinct Keyword

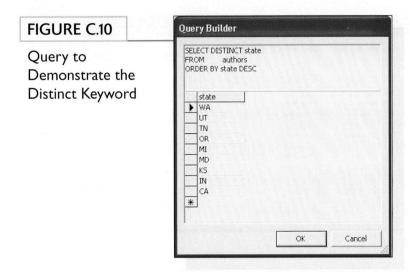

- **Group By:** This keyword is used to group the values returned based on certain criteria. The Group By clause is required if an aggregation function such as Sum is used in the Select clause. We will expand on this in the aggregation function section.

In Figure C.10, we show a query that uses the Distinct keyword to retrieve distinct states from in the authors table; we order the result in a descending order.

String Functions

SQL allows a variety of functions that act on character strings. Some of the commonly used functions are SubString (for extracting substrings), Replace (for replacing strings), and the "||" operator for concatenating strings. There are also other utility functions such as Year and Month that retrieve the year and month from a DateTime data type value. In the following example, we show the use of the SubString function. The syntax of the SubString function is

SUBSTRING *(expression, start, length)*

The arguments of the SubString function are the string from which the substring is extracted (*expression*), the starting point of the extracted string (*start*), and the length of the extracted string (*length*). In the query in Figure C.11, we get the area code by extracting the first three digits of the phone number of the authors in the authors table. The As keyword we see in the Select clause is used to give the resulting substring a name.

Aggregate Functions

Aggregate functions take multiple rows and perform an operation on the values to return a single value of a particular type. The following list includes some of the aggregation functions available with SQL:

- **AVG:** This is used to return the average value from a set of values.

- **COUNT:** This is used to return the count of the set of values.

- **MAX:** This is used to return the maximum value from a set of values.

- **MIN:** This is used to return the minimum value from a set of values.

- **SUM:** This is used to return the sum of the set of values.

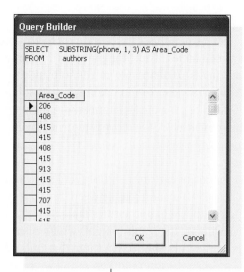

FIGURE C.11

Query That Demonstrates the Use
of String Function SubString

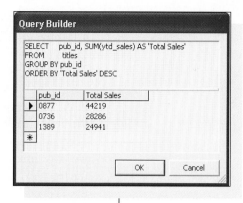

FIGURE C.12

Query that Demonstrates
SUM Function and the Use of
the Group By Clause

The Group By clause determines the set of values to which the aggregation is applied. It must include all columns that are specified in the select clause which are not included in the aggregation functions themselves. Figure C.12 shows the list of distinct publishers (created by the Group By clause) and the sum of sales for each publisher.

In the query in Figure C.12 we again see the use of the As keyword to create a new column name for the SUM column in the result set.

By doing the aggregation on the server, we usually experience better overall performance. It is typically much faster to have the DBMS perform this function rather than querying all the records back to the client as a DataSet and using Visual Basic .NET code to perform the aggregation.

Creating Relationships Using Joins

In Chapter 8 we discussed relationships between entities in an ERD. Special SQL statements are needed to create relationships between different tables that are joined through common fields. The Join keyword is to be used in SQL to create relationships between tables. Joins can be of two types, INNER Join and OUTER Join. We will discuss the difference between these two types of joins in the following sections. In addition to using the Join keyword, we can create a relationship by creating expressions in the Where clause. For example, we can create an inner join relationship between the titles and the publishers tables using the following expression.

> WHERE titles.pub_id = publishers.pub_id

However, since the Query Builder is using the Join keyword, we will continue our discussion on creating relationships using Join syntax:

> FROM table1 JOIN table2 ON table1.field = table2.field
> JOIN table3 ON table3.field = ...

We can join any number of tables with any number of fields.

Inner Join

The inner join creates a new set of records by using the search condition to equate the values in fields that are common between tables. Thus, the query returns only records that have the same value in the fields participating in the join in both tables. Once a join is created, we can return any field from the tables participating in the join using the Select clause. For example, if we create an inner join between the titles and the publishers table on the pub_id field, the records returned by the query will be records where the same pub_id appears in both tables. In Figure C.13, we have modified the query in Figure C.12 to return the publisher name with the total YTD sales. Since the publisher name appears in the publishers table and the YTD sales appear in the titles table, we need to create a join between these tables. In Figure C.13 we see that there are three publishers in the titles table. If we run the query **Select COUNT(pub_id) From publishers**, the result is eight, which means that there are a total of eight publishers in the publishers table (note that pub_id is a primary key in the publishers table). Since the query in Figure C.13 returns only three publishers, there are only three publishers who appear in both tables.

Outer Join

Outer join returns rows that have the same values in the Join fields and, in addition, rows from one of the tables for which there are no matching rows in the other table. The table from which the additional rows are returned depends on the type of the join. The various types of joins that are possible are

- **Left Outer Join:** All the rows from the left table specified in the Left Outer Join clause are returned. Null values are used for unmatched rows from the right table.

- **Right Outer Join:** This is the reverse of left outer join and all the rows of the table on the right of the clause are returned.

- **Full Outer Join:** All the rows from both the tables are returned.

Once we create the Join equality, we determine whether it is a left or right join based on which side of the join the table for which we want to return all the rows is located. Outer joins are especially useful when we want to verify the completeness of the data on which our query is based. For example, in Figure C.14 we would like to include in the publisher sales report all the publishers, including the publishers without any sales so far. We use a right outer join between the publishers table (right table) and the titles table (left table) to retrieve all the publishers and the total YTD sales. In order to avoid returning NULL, which would require

FIGURE C.13

Using Inner Join to Return the Publisher Names

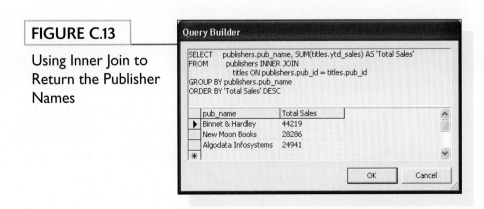

FIGURE C.14

Using Right Outer
Join to Return All
Publishers

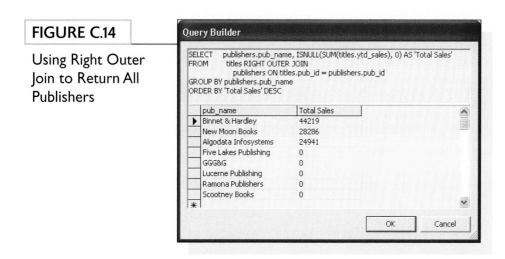

special processing later, we use the ISNULL function to replace the NULL values
with 0. The syntax of the ISNULL function is

ISNULL(*expression, replace value*)

Updating Data Using SQL

SQL also provides the capability to update the data in a table. This can be done
by either inserting new rows, updating existing rows, or deleting existing rows.

Insert

SQL allows insertion of data into tables using the Insert statement. The general
syntax of the Insert statement is

INSERT Into *[table_name]*
COLUMNS(*[col1],[col2], …*)
VALUES (*[col1_val], [col2_val], …*)

In the above, **[table_name]** refers to the table where the data are to be inserted;
the columns list contains the columns that will have values in the Values list. If a
column in the table is not included in the Columns list, then SQL will insert a value of Null (assuming that the database allows the field to be Null). Figure C.15
shows an example of inserting a new row into the authors table. Note that this row
already exists in the table so you will need to delete it before you insert it again.

FIGURE C.15

Inserting a Single
Row in authors Table

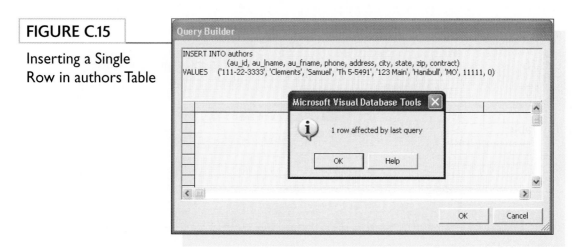

Insertion of new rows into a table can be complicated if the table is related to some other table through a relationship. In such cases, it is not possible to place arbitrary values in a table as some of the columns are constrained by values in the columns in related tables.

There are various other options possible when inserting rows. Some of these include inserting multiple rows, inserting rows from one table to another table, inserting Null values, plus some other options. These additional options are not covered in this appendix.

Delete

The SQL Delete statement has a very simple syntax; however, it is a very powerful statement and you should be cautious when using it since it is difficult or impossible to undo. We advise you to first try a similar Select statement to see how many rows are going to be deleted (the same number selected will be deleted if you next try a delete). Then replace "Select" with "Delete". The Delete statement syntax is

DELETE From *[table_name]*
WHERE *[search_expression]*

You can delete only entire rows; if you want to delete specific values from a row, you should use the Update statement that is described next. Figure C.16 shows an example of deletion of all the records from the titleauthor table where the **royaltyper = 99** (0 records). We chose the value 99 so you would not actually delete records from the sample database.

Update

The SQL Update statement allows us to change the values of a specific column (field) in a group of rows (records) selected by the Where clause. The general syntax of an update statement is

UPDATE *[table_list]*
SET *[value]*
WHERE *[search_condition]*

The Set clause is used to provide the new value for a column in the rows that match the search condition. We also can use an expression to generate the new value as you can see in Figure C.17. In this example, we increased the royalty schedule for **title_id** PC1035 by adding 2 percent.

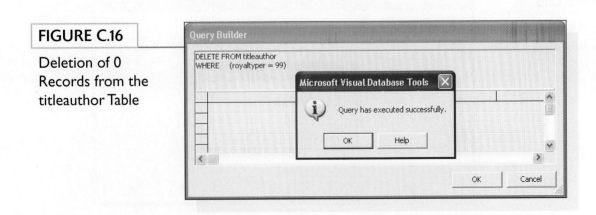

FIGURE C.16

Deletion of 0
Records from the
titleauthor Table

FIGURE C.17

Query Demonstrating Update of Royalty Schedule

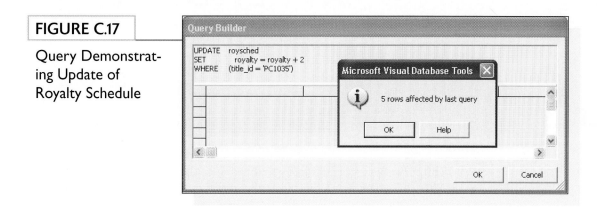

Summary

This appendix has provided a brief overview of SQL with a focus on the SQL Select statement. For additional information, you can consult any number of good reference books on SQL and databases.

XSLT

XSLT is a programming language defined by the World Wide Web Consortium, W3C (http://www.w3.org/TR/xslt), that provides the mechanism to transform a given XML document to another XML document. In this appendix we will explain and provide examples of using XSLT to transform XML documents into HTML, since this is one of the most common uses of XSLT. The language contains many more functions, elements, and mechanisms that are used for transformation than will be covered here due to their complexity. The reader is encouraged to learn more about XSLT from one of many good XSLT references.

In addition to XSLT-specific elements that support the creation of the result document (transformation), the XSLT language implements XPath, which is another language defined by W3C (http://www.w3.org/TR/xpath). XPath defines navigation syntax over an XML document coupled with a very useful set of built-in functions. In this appendix we will not make a distinction between elements, expressions, and functions based on the language where they are defined. Instead, we will treat all syntax as XSLT syntax.

We assume that you gained some knowledge of XSLT while working through Chapter 9 and we will not go through the XSLT elements that were explained in that chapter.

Path and Patterns Expressions

At any given time while a transformation is happening, the XSLT processor is pointing to a specific node in the source XML document. Retrieving the node value, or its sibling, child, parent, or any other node in the document, requires a navigation expression. XSLT uses XPath and patterns to support navigation, selection, and matching nodes in the source XML document.

We will start with a short example to illustrate how the processor reads an XPath expression and selects the applicable nodes from the XML document. For this example, and the following examples throughout this appendix, we will use an XML document that contains the inventory data show in Figure D.1. We also will assume that the current node is the ProductGroup element outlined in red.

Before we go any further, we need to recall that the document in Figure D.1 represents a "tree" structure. This tree is shown in Figure D.2. In addition, each node includes one or more attributes. Attributes allow information to be stored at a node based on an attribute name. For example, the Warehouse node has an attribute named "City" that stores the name of the city where the warehouse is located. Each Product node includes five attributes (name, unit, Quantity, Price, and Amount). These attributes store information about each product.

The "current" node, as identified in red in Figure D.1, can be drawn as the tree segment in Figure D.3.

The XPath expression shown below Figure D.3 will select the Quantity attribute (whose value is 30) and is located in the Product node that has a name attribute with the value "Yogurt".

FIGURE D.1

XML Inventory Document

```xml
<?xml version="1.0" ?>
<Root>
  <Warehouse City="Seattle">
    <ProductGroup name="Dairy Products">
      <Product name="Milk" unit="Quart" Quantity="25" Price="1.05" Amount="26.25" />
      <Product name="Milk" unit="Half Gallon" Quantity="18" Price="1.89" Amount="34.02" />
      <Product name="Butter" unit="LB" Quantity="42" Price="3.62" Amount="152.04" />
      <Product name="Cottage Cheese" unit="LB" Quantity="20" Price="2.00" Amount="40" />
    </ProductGroup>
    <ProductGroup name="Vegetables">
      <Product name="Potato" unit="LB" Quantity="220" Price="0.22" Amount="48.40" />
      <Product name="Parsley" unit="bunch" Quantity="34" Price="0.79" Amount="26.86" />
      <Product name="Onion" unit="LB" Quantity="78" Price="0.29" Amount="22.62" />
    </ProductGroup>
  </Warehouse>
  <Warehouse City="Portland">
    <ProductGroup name="Dairy Products">
      <Product name="Cream" unit="pint" Quantity="21" Price="2.29" Amount="48.09" />
      <Product name="Yogurt" unit="Quart" Quantity="30" Price="2.99" Amount="89.70" />
      <Product name="Cottage Cheese" unit="LB" Quantity="42" Price="1.69" Amount="70.98" />
    </ProductGroup>
    <ProductGroup name="Vegetables">
      <Product name="Potato" unit="LB" Quantity="180" Price="0.19" Amount="34.20" />
      <Product name="Onion" unit="LB" Quantity="105" Price="0.33" Amount="34.65" />
    </ProductGroup>
  </Warehouse>
</Root>
```

FIGURE D.2

Tree Representing XML Document from Figure D.1

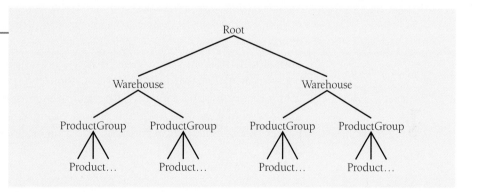

FIGURE D.3

Tree Showing the Current Node (red)

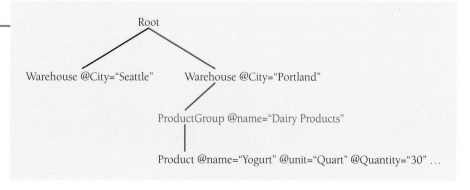

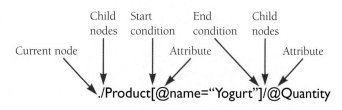

XPath expressions are read from left to right; the dot sign signifies the current node and the single forward slash signifies the child nodes of the current node. Thus, we are currently pointing to the "Product" elements that are the children of the current node. Brackets signify a condition; the "@" sign signifies that we are looking for an attribute named "name" with a value equal to "Yogurt". Since only the second "Product" element satisfies this condition; we select this element. Again the forward slash signifies child nodes (attributes are considered to be child nodes of an element). We thus select the Quantity attribute of the Product node whose **name="Yogurt"**.

Table D.1 contains some XPath expressions in their abbreviated form and patterns in XSLT. These expressions either are relative to the current node or select a node or a node set from the document regardless of the current node.

Functions

XSLT has a core library of functions that are divided into five groups: Nodeset, String, Boolean, Numeric and Other. These functions are similar to functions that are available with Visual Basic .NET. To call a function, we use the function name followed by a set of parentheses that enclose the arguments (if there are any). Table D.2 presents some of the functions and provides an example based on the XML document in Figure D.1. Recall that the current node in Figure D.1 is marked in red.

Numeric Operators

XSLT expressions are evaluated with respect to their context to four basic data types: Node-sets, Boolean, Number and String. Like Visual Basic .NET, addition, subtraction, multiplication, division and mod operators are available to perform calculations during the transformation. If the expression is applied to node values that cannot be converted to a valid number, the result will be **NaN** (not a number). For example, the expression **./@name * 2** will output NaN in the output document since "Dairy Products" (**./@name**) is not numeric. Since the forward slash "/" is heavily used for path expressions, the division operator is **div**; for example, the result of **4 div 2** is 2.

Conditional Statements

XSLT has two elements that provide the ability to perform conditional processing based on the Boolean expressions. The first element is **xsl:if**, which provides a simple if-then functionality. However, unlike Visual Basic .NET's If…Then statement, it does not support the ElseIf or Else clauses. The following example will output **This is the last element in the node-set** when the current node is last in the node-set:

```
<xsl:if test="position()=last()">
    <b>This is the last element in the node-set</b>
</xsl:if>
```

The second element that performs conditional processing is **xsl:choose**. This supports the selection of one choice from several possibilities. It is similar to the Visual Basic .NET Select Case statement. It consists of a sequence of **xsl:when** elements, followed by an optional **xsl:otherwise** element. Each **xsl:when** element has a single attribute, which specifies an expression. When an **xsl:choose** element is processed, each of the **xsl:when** elements is tested in turn, by evaluating the

Table D.1 XSLT Path expressions

Path	Semantics
"@"	Signifies an attribute node
Example:	**@name**
Result:	**Dairy Products**
"."	Selects the current node
Example:	**"."**
Result:	**<ProductGroup name="Dairy Products">**
".."	Selects the parent of the current node
Example:	**../@City**
Result:	**Portland**
"/"	By itself selects the root of the document; also used to provide a step separator for relative path. Child is the default axis. Attributes considered as child nodes of an element.
Example:	**./Product/@Quantity**
Result:	**21**
"//"	Selects all nodes that are descendant-or-self node of the current node. If not preceded with other expression will select all the matching nodes in the document.
Example:	**//Product**
Result:	**<Product name="Milk" unit="Quart" Quantity="25" Price="1.05" Amount="26.25"></Product>** **<Product name="Milk" unit="Half Gallon" Quantity="18" Price="1.89"** **Amount="34.02"></Product>** **<Product name="Butter" unit="LB" Quantity="42" Price="3.62" Amount="152.04"></Product>** **<Product name="Cottage Cheese" unit="LB" Quantity="20" Price="2.00"** **Amount="40"></Product>** **<Product name="Potato" unit="LB" Quantity="220" Price="0.22" Amount="48.40"></Product>** **<Product name="Parsley" unit="bunch" Quantity="34" Price="0.79" Amount="26.86"></Product>** **<Product name="Onion" unit="LB" Quantity="78" Price="0.29" Amount="22.62"></Product>** **<Product name="Cream" unit="pint" Quantity="21" Price="2.29" Amount="48.09"></Product>** **<Product name="Yogurt" unit="Quart" Quantity="30" Price="2.99" Amount="89.70"></Product>** **<Product name="Cottage Cheese" unit="LB" Quantity="42" Price="1.69"** **Amount="70.98"></Product>** **<Product name="Potato" unit="LB" Quantity="180" Price="0.19" Amount="34.20"></Product>** **<Product name="Onion" unit="LB" Quantity="105" Price="0.33" Amount="34.65"></Product>**
"[]"	Predicate expression, similar to a Where clause in SQL. Filters the nodes where the condition expression is true. The following example should be read "Return all the Product nodes where the attribute 'name' is equal to 'Cottage Cheese'".
Example:	**//Product[@name='Cottage Cheese']**
Result:	**<Product name="Cottage Cheese" unit="LB" Quantity="20" Price="2.00"** **Amount="40"></Product>** **<Product name="Cottage Cheese" unit="LB" Quantity="42" Price="1.69"** **Amount="70.98"></Product>**

expression to Boolean. The content of the first, and only the first, **xsl:when** element whose test is true is executed. If none of the **xsl:when** elements are true, the content of the **xsl:otherwise** element is executed. If no **xsl:when** element is true and no **xsl:otherwise** element is present, nothing happens. The following example will

Table D.2 XSLT functions

Function	Semantics	Example	Result
Number **position()**	Returns the position of the current node in the node set. First node position() = 1.	position()	3
Number **count**(*node-set*)	Returns the number of nodes in the argument node-set.	count(//Warehouse)	2
Number **last()**	Returns the number (position) of the last node in the current node's node-set. Since there are four <ProductGroup> nodes, the result is 4.	Last()	4
String **concat**(*string, string, string**)	Returns the concatenation of its arguments. The third or more strings are optional.	concat('The product group is ',../@name,' In ',../@City)	The product group is Dairy Products In Portland
String **name()**	Returns the name of the current node.	name()	ProductGroup
Boolean **contains**(*string,string*)	Returns true if the first argument string contains the second argument string, and otherwise returns false.	contains(./@name,'airy')	true
String **substring-before** (*string, string*)	Returns the substring of the first argument string that precedes the first occurrence of the second argument string in the first argument string.	substring-before(./@name, 'Prod')	Dairy
String **substring-after** (*string, string*)	Returns the substring of the first argument string that follows the first occurrence of the second argument string in the first argument string.	substring-after(./@name, 'Prod')	ucts
String **substring**(*string, number, number?*)	Returns the substring of the first argument starting at the position specified in the second argument with length specified in the third argument. If the third argument is missing, it continues to the end of the string.	substring(./@name,7)	Products
Number **string-length**(*string?*)	Returns the number of characters in the string; if the argument is omitted, it defaults to the context node converted to a string.	string-length(./@name)	14
Boolean **not**(*boolean*)	Returns true if the argument is evaluated to false and false otherwise. You can use '!=' to create the "not equal" expression.	not(last()=5) last() != 5	true
Number **round**(*number*)	Returns the number that is closest to the argument and that is an integer.	round(./Product [position()=1])/@Price	2
Number **sum**(*node-set*)	Returns the result of summing each node in the argument node-set.	sum(./Product/@Quantity)	93
String **format-number** (*number, string*)	Converts its first argument to a string using the format pattern string specified by the second argument.	format-number(1625.726, '$#,###.00')	$1,625.73

apply the color blue as the paragraph background color for each node whose position is even, and the color red as the background color for every other node.

```
<xsl:choose>
    <xsl:when test="(position() mod 2)=0">
        <P style="background-color:blue"></P>
    </xsl:when>
    <xsl:otherwise>
        <P style="background-color:red"></P>
    </xsl:otherwise>
</xsl:choose>
```

Variables and Params

Similar to Visual Basic .NET, you can create variables that are bound to an expression such as a string, node, or node-set. There are two elements that represent variables in XSLT: **xsl:variable** and **xsl:param**. A top-level, variable-binding element declares a global variable that is visible everywhere within the XSLT document. In addition, template variables are allowed anywhere within a template (we will talk about templates soon). In this case, the variable is visible only within that template.

The **xsl:variable** is used mainly to compute values and to select and create nodes for use in other places in the transformation. Global variables are particularly useful when you would like to compute a value from the source XML document and use it more than once during a transformation. Global variables are also useful for declaring constant values. Template variables are useful when you need an intermediate calculation while processing a node-set. Unlike Visual Basic .NET, you cannot use a variable in its own expression. Thus, the Visual Basic .NET statement **x=x+1** is not valid in XSLT.

The **xsl:param** element is used mainly to pass values from another application to the XSLT stylesheet, and from template to template promoting reusability and abstraction. For example, passing user input to a stylesheet using a global param allows creating different reports from the same XML and XSLT documents.

Referring to a variable or param to retrieve its value is done by prefixing the variable or param name with a $. The following demonstrates declaring and retrieving values from variables.

Declare: `<xsl:variable name="x">2</xsl:variable>`
           `<xsl:param name="y">3</xsl:param>`

Retrieve: `<xsl:value-of select="$x * $y"/>`

Result: **6**

Templates (Procedural and Recursive)

XSLT provides two mechanisms for processing the source document to get the result tree. The first is procedural processing, which allows creating a transformation using control structures similar to Visual Basic .NET. To allow procedural-like processing, XSLT provides named templates, which are similar to calling a function or sub procedure in Visual Basic .NET. XSLT also has a for-each element that supports looping through a node-set. Named templates are invoked by the **<xsl:call-template>** element, which can pass params to the called template.

The **<xsl:for-each>** element supports the processing of a node-set directly within the template. The following example demonstrates processing of all the Products nodes that are child nodes of the ProductGroup nodes. It uses a for-each element and a named template whose name is **ProcessProducts** (not shown) to control the processing.

```
<xsl:for-each select="ProductGroup">
    Do something here (optional)
    <xsl:call-template name="ProcessProducts">
        <xsl:with-param name="CurrentProduct" select="./Product"/>
    </xsl:call-template>
    Do something here (optional)
</xsl:for-each>
```

The second mechanism for processing the source document is recursive processing where a list of nodes is selected from the source tree by using an **<xsl:apply-templates select="">** instruction. When the processor encounters an **<xsl:apply-templates select="">**, it searches for the best matching template to process the nodes. The template that best matches the node list may contain additional node list selections for processing and is instantiated with a current node and source node list. The process of matching the node list by template, applying the template rules, and selecting new node list will continue recursively until no new source nodes are selected for processing. The select attribute in the apply-templates element is optional since the selecting of the child nodes is the default selection of nodes by the processor.

The following template will process all the Products nodes that are child nodes of the ProductGroup nodes by finding a template that matches "Product". It will produce the same result as the previous example. The select attribute, although redundant in this case, is added for clarity.

```
<xsl:template match="ProductGroup">
    Do something here (optional)
        <xsl:apply-templates select="Product"/>
    Do something here (optional)
</xsl:template>
```

Transforming an XML document recursively using **<xsl:apply-templates>** elements can be a complex and sometimes difficult task; however, many XSLT programmers consider it as a more natural way to transform and process an XML document.

Finally, you can combine the procedural and recursive approaches to create the desired transformation. For example you can replace the call to a named template in the first example with an **<xsl:apply-templates>** instruction in the second example to get the same results.

Creating an HTML Inventory Report from an XML Document Using XSLT

The following example will combine many elements and expressions of the XSLT language to create an HTML report from the Inventory XML document in Figure D.1. We will show how to create the same report using two stylesheets. The first uses a named template and for-each elements to perform procedural processing similar to Visual Basic .NET programs. The other uses an apply-templates element to recursively process the XML tree to create the same report. Figure D.4 shows the results of the transformed XML as a rendered HTML document. As you can see, the

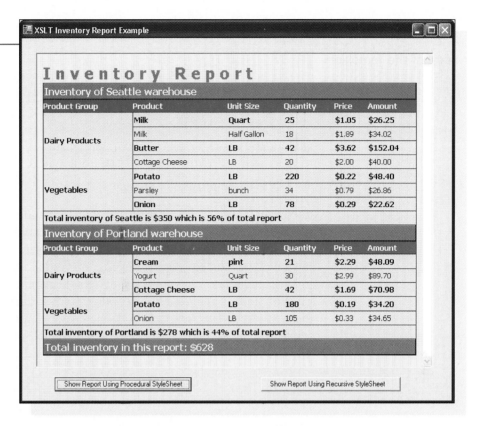

report is fairly complex in terms of appearance and style. The XSLT document is responsible for adding the appropriate HTML tags to achieve this appearance.

XML Declaration and Global Variables

We start by creating a new XML document and adding the XSLT namespace. Both XSLT stylesheets use the same set of global variables to define the report formatting. Defining the formatting definitions as global variables allows us to change the report appearance by changing a value in only one place. Figure D.5 shows the XML document declaration and the definition of the first of seven global variables (**ColHeader**) included in the actual document (the other six global variables define

```xml
<?xml version="1.0" encoding="UTF-8"?>
<xsl:stylesheet version="1.0" xmlns:xsl="http://www.w3.org/1999/XSL/Transform">
<!-- Declare global variables -->
<xsl:variable name="ColHeader">
{
    BORDER-BOTTOM: 0.08em solid #3f0600;
    BORDER-TOP: 0.08em solid #3f0600;
    PADDING-TOP: 0.15em;
    PADDING-BOTTOM: 0.15em;
    PADDING-LEFT: 0;
    FONT-SIZE: 0.8em;
    COLOR: #ffffff;
    BACKGROUND-COLOR: #00aadd;
    FONT-WEIGHT: bold;
}
</xsl:variable>
```

FIGURE D.6

Start of the Template

```
<xsl:template match="/">
<HTML>
  <Body>
    <Div style="{$ReportHeader}">Inventory Report</Div>
    <Div>
    <Table style="{$TablFormat}" cellspacing="0" cellpadding="0" width="100%">
```

additional styles and are not shown here). Later we use these variables to define the style attribute of the table cell **TD**, using syntax like the following:

<TD style="{$Variable Name}">

The curly braces signify that during transformation, the value of the attribute needs to be evaluated to the result of the XSLT expression.

We then proceed and create the starting template that processes the root element of the document signified by the "/" symbol. Although it is not mandatory to have a template that processes the root element, it is a highly recommended practice since it defines a clear starting point for processing the source document. It also allows us to easily define a root element in the result document (the **HTML** tag in our example). We will use an HTML table with its tags (**Table**, **TR**, **TD**) to display the report. Figure D.6 shows the start of the first template.

Approach 1: Using for-each and call-template to Process the Source Document

In the first (procedural) stylesheet, we are using three nested for-each loops to iterate through each level of the tree to create the report table. The outer loop iterates through the Warehouse nodes and creates a table row for each warehouse. An inner loop iterates through each product group. Within this inner loop is a third loop that iterates through each product for the product group. If you look back at Figure D.4, you can see the impact of these three loops. After the inner loops finish, but before the outer loop repeats, a new row is created to show the total inventory for that warehouse and the percentage of total inventory represented by the warehouse. The Sum function and the div operator (for division) are used to accomplish this task. Finally, we format the result using the format-number function:

```
<xsl:value-of select="concat('Total inventory of ', ./@City,' _is ',
format-number(sum(.//@Amount),'$#,###'),' which is ',
format-number(sum(.//@Amount) div sum(//@Amount),'#0%'),' of total report')"/>
```

The inner loop that creates a row for each product group uses the rowSpan attribute of the TD element to merge the first cell in the ProductGroup row and the product rows that are created in the product inner loop. To calculate the number of rows to merge, we use the following statement:

rowspan="{count(./Product) + 1}"

This statement counts the child nodes of each ProductGroup and adds an additional row to account for the heading.

Within the product group loop, where the current node is a ProductGroup node, we call a named template and pass the current node using the Current() function as a param:

```
<xsl:call-template name="displayProductGroup">
    <xsl:with-param name="prodGroup" select="current()"/>
</xsl:call-template>
```

FIGURE D.7

Embedding for-each
Loops and Creating
the Table

```
<xsl:for-each select="//Warehouse">
  <TR>
     <TD colspan="6" style="{$WHouse}">
        <xsl:value-of select="concat('Inventory of ', ./@City,' warehouse')"/>
     </TD>
  </TR>
  <TR>
     <TD style="{$ColHeader}">Product Group</TD><TD style="{$ColHeader}">Product</TD>
     <TD style="{$ColHeader}">Unit Size</TD><TD style="{$ColHeader}">Quantity</TD>
     <TD style="{$ColHeader}">Price</TD><TD style="{$ColHeader}">Amount</TD>
  </TR>
  <xsl:for-each select="./ProductGroup">
     <TR>
        <TD rowspan="{count(./Product) + 1}" style="{$ProdGroup}">
           <xsl:value-of select="./@name"/>
        </TD>
     </TR>
     <xsl:call-template name="displayProductGroup">
        <xsl:with-param name="prodGroup" select="current()"/>
     </xsl:call-template>
  </xsl:for-each>
  <TR>
     <TD colspan="6" style="{$CellValue2}">
        <xsl:value-of select="concat('Total inventory of ', ./@City,' is ',
                        format-number(sum(.//@Amount),'$#,###'),' which is ',
                        format-number(sum(.//@Amount) div sum(//@Amount),'#0%')
                        ,' of total report')"/>
     </TD>
  </TR>
</xsl:for-each>
<TR>
   <TD colspan="6" style="{$WHouse}">
   <xsl:value-of select="concat('Total inventory in this report: '
               , format-number(sum(//@Amount),'$#,###'))"/>
   </TD>
</TR>
</Table>
```

Figure D.7 shows the XSLT code that includes the outer "Warehouse" loop as well as the embedded "ProductGroup" loop.

Within the inner ProductGroup loop, the displayProductGroup template is called. This template, shown in Figure D.8, includes the loop that iterates through each product.

Approach 2: Using apply-templates to Process the Source Document

In the second stylesheet, we use the **<xsl:apply-templates>** element, which allows us to recursively process the source document. We also replace the named template with three new templates that match the Warehouse, ProductGroup, and Product elements. The XSLT processor starts processing the source document from the root element and looks for a template that matches this element. If it does not find one, it will continue to look for templates that match the child nodes of this element. This process will continue until a matching template is found or until the source document is completely processed and no matching templates for its elements are found. Since our first template matches the root node (**<xsl:template match="/">**), the source document transformation starts with the template shown in Figure D.9. After inserting the **HTML**, **Body**, and **Table** tags into the result document, the processor encounters the **<xsl:apply-templates/>** instruction that starts the processing of the child nodes of the current node.

FIGURE D.8

The displayProduct-Group Template

```
<xsl:template name="displayProductGroup">
  <xsl:param name="prodGroup"/>
  <xsl:for-each select="$prodGroup/Product">
    <TR>
      <xsl:choose>
      <xsl:when test="(position() mod 2) = 0">
        <TD style="{$CellValue}"><xsl:value-of select="./@name"/></TD>
        <TD style="{$CellValue}"><xsl:value-of select="./@unit"/></TD>
        <TD style="{$CellValue}"><xsl:value-of select="./@Quantity"/></TD>
        <TD style="{$CellValue}"><xsl:value-of
                select="format-number(./@Price,'$#,##0.00')"/></TD>
        <TD style="{$CellValue}"><xsl:value-of
                select="format-number(./@Price * ./@Quantity,'$#,###.00')"/></TD>
      </xsl:when>
      <xsl:otherwise>
          <TD style="{$CellValue2}"><xsl:value-of select="./@name"/></TD>
        <TD style="{$CellValue2}"><xsl:value-of select="./@unit"/></TD>
        <TD style="{$CellValue2}"><xsl:value-of select="./@Quantity"/></TD>
        <TD style="{$CellValue2}"><xsl:value-of
              select="format-number(./@Price,'$#,##0.00')"/></TD>
        <TD style="{$CellValue2}"><xsl:value-of
              select="format-number(./@Price * ./@Quantity,'$#,###.00')"/></TD>
      </xsl:otherwise>
      </xsl:choose>
    </TR>
  </xsl:for-each>
</xsl:template>
```

FIGURE D.9

Template That Matches the Root

```
<xsl:template match="/">
<HTML>
  <Body>
    <Div style="{$ReportHeader}">Inventory Report</Div>
    <Div>
    <Table style="{$TablFormat}" cellspacing="0" cellpadding="0" width="100%">
    <xsl:apply-templates/>
    <TR>
        <TD colspan="6" style="{$WHouse}">
        <xsl:value-of select="concat('Total inventory in this report: '
                    , format-number(sum(//@Amount),'$#,###'))"/>
        </TD>
    </TR>
    </Table>
    </Div>
  </Body>
</HTML>
</xsl:template>
```

The child nodes of the Root element are the Warehouse elements, so the processor looks for a template that matches the Warehouse element. That template (see Figure D.10) outputs two rows to the result document before another **<xsl:apply-templates/>** instruction, which causes the processor to look for a matching template for the current element **<Warehouse City="Seattle">** child nodes (ProductGroup nodes).

The template that matches the ProductGroup elements is shown in Figure D.11.

Processing of the child nodes of the ProductGroup elements, that is, the Product elements, will happen when the processor encounters **<xsl:apply-templates/>** in the ProductGroup template. Since the Product template, shown in Figure D.12, does not have any references to other templates, the processor will return

FIGURE D.10

Template That
Processes the
Warehouse Nodes

```
<xsl:template match="Warehouse">
  <TR>
    <TD colspan="6" style="{$WHouse}">
      <xsl:value-of select="concat('Inventory of ', ./@City,' warehouse')"/>
    </TD>
  </TR>
  <TR>
    <TD style="{$ColHeader}">Product Group</TD><TD style="{$ColHeader}">Product</TD>
    <TD style="{$ColHeader}">Unit Size</TD><TD style="{$ColHeader}">Quantity</TD>
    <TD style="{$ColHeader}">Price</TD><TD style="{$ColHeader}">Amount</TD>
  </TR>
  <xsl:apply-templates/>
  <TR>
    <TD colspan="6" style="{$CellValue2}">
      <xsl:value-of select="concat('Total inventory of ', ./@City,' is ',
                  format-number(sum(.//@Amount),'$#,###'),' which is ',
                  format-number(sum(.//@Amount) div sum(//@Amount),'#0%')
                  ,' of total report')"/>
    </TD>
  </TR>
</xsl:template>
```

FIGURE D.11

Template That
Processes the
ProductGroup
Nodes

```
<xsl:template match="ProductGroup">
  <TR>
    <TD rowspan="{count(./Product) + 1}" style="{$ProdGroup}">
      <xsl:value-of select="./@name"/>
    </TD>
  </TR>
  <xsl:apply-templates/>
</xsl:template>
```

FIGURE D.12

Template That
Processes the
Product Nodes

```
<xsl:template match="Product">
  <TR>
    <xsl:choose>
    <xsl:when test="(position() mod 2) = 0">
    <TD style="{$CellValue}"><xsl:value-of select="./@name"/></TD>
    <TD style="{$CellValue}"><xsl:value-of select="./@unit"/></TD>
    <TD style="{$CellValue}"><xsl:value-of select="./@Quantity"/></TD>
    <TD style="{$CellValue}"><xsl:value-of
            select="format-number(./@Price,'$#,##0.00')"/></TD>
    <TD style="{$CellValue}"><xsl:value-of
            select="format-number(./@Price * ./@Quantity,'$#,###.00')"/></TD>
    </xsl:when>
    <xsl:otherwise>
      <TD style="{$CellValue2}"><xsl:value-of select="./@name"/></TD>
      <TD style="{$CellValue2}"><xsl:value-of select="./@unit"/></TD>
      <TD style="{$CellValue2}"><xsl:value-of select="./@Quantity"/></TD>
      <TD style="{$CellValue2}"><xsl:value-of
            select="format-number(./@Price,'$#,##0.00')"/></TD>
      <TD style="{$CellValue2}"><xsl:value-of
            select="format-number(./@Price * ./@Quantity,'$#,###.00')"/></TD>
    </xsl:otherwise>
    </xsl:choose>
  </TR>
</xsl:template>
```

to the ProductGroup template and from there to the Warehouse template. This
process will continue recursively until there are no more nodes that match one of
these templates in the source document.

Summary

XSLT is an extremely powerful language for transforming an XML document into other XML documents. Similar to Visual Basic .NET, it has a set of operators and functions as well as conditional and iteration statements. In addition, it supports recursion that provides a very natural way of processing an XML tree. An XSLT developer can design stylesheets that are procedural or recursive or combine both methodologies to create the same transformation documents.

XSLT is a key technology in the XML world. While XML is a data format that is easily transferable between different computer systems and between organizations, XSLT provides the means to transform these data to useable format. In addition to transforming XML documents into HTML, it enables scenarios where two organizations can exchange XML data, and, using XSLT, transform the data into the appropriate format so that the data may be inserted into each organization's databases.

Answers to Selected Exercises

Chapter 1

Exercise 1.2

Example pseudocode is

1. *Put contents of Box A into Empty Box 1.*
2. *Put contents of Box B into Box A.*
3. *Put contents of Empty Box 1 into Box B.*

Exercise 1.4

For Word or Excel, the application responds to clicking on the main menu (menu items drop down), to double-clicking on text (text is selected), to placing the mouse over a misspelled word and clicking on the right mouse (suggested changes pop up), to placing the cursor over a toolbar icon (it highlights), and to holding the cursor over a toolbar icon (a tool tip appears).

Exercise 1.6

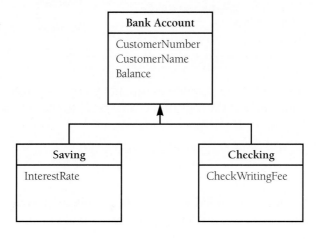

Exercise 1.8

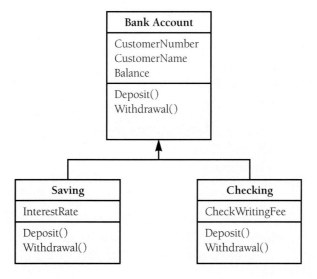

- Deposit Method (Bank Account): Does nothing—an abstract method.

- Deposit Method (Saving/Checking): Increases Balance by an amount provided to the method.

- Withdrawal Method (Bank Account): Does nothing—an abstract method.

- Withdrawal Method (Saving): Decreases Balance by an amount provided to the method.

- Withdrawal Method (Checking): Decreases Balance by an amount provided to the method and also subtracts the CheckWritingFee.

Exercise 1.10

In both applications we see menus, buttons, toolbar icons, drop-down lists, and check boxes. The figure below shows these objects:

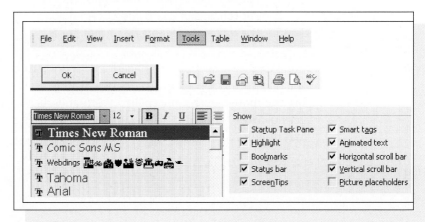

The menu items respond to the cursor hovering over them; the buttons react to being clicked; the toolbar icons respond to the cursor hovering over them; the drop-down list items react to being clicked, as do the check boxes.

Chapter 2

Exercise 2.4

No, it is not a good idea. The Text property is what the user sees on the user interface. It should describe the function of the button for the user. Using a text like btnDoIt is not descriptive. Also, the three-letter prefix, btn, means nothing to the user (its value is to the developer and is used in the Name property).

Exercise 2.8

```
Private Sub btnTopToBot_Click(ByVal ...)
    txtTop.Cut()
    txtBottom.Paste()
End Sub

Private Sub btnBotToTop_Click(ByVal ...)
    txtBottom.Cut()
    txtTop.Paste()
End Sub
```

Exercise 2.10

```
Private Sub btnShowMsgBox_Click(ByVal ...)
    MsgBox("I did it!!", MsgBoxStyle.Exclamation + _
        MsgBoxStyle.OKOnly, "Not that hard")
End Sub
```

Chapter 3

Exercise 3.2	Const OURNAMES = "Joe, Bill" Valid

Const OURNAMES = "Joe, Bill" Valid
Const TIRATE = 1,544,000 Invalid (remove the commas)
Const ANNSOFFICEPHONE = 555 – 1234 Valid (does subtraction)
Const MAX SPEED = 55 Invalid (space between X and S)
Const COMPOSER = Ludwig Van Beethoven Invalid (enclose name in quotes)
Const STARTINGCHECKNUMBER = 100 Valid

Exercise 3.4

.00001234568

Exercise 3.6

The type Short will not work for a zip code because the maximum value that can be stored in a Short is 32767 and zip codes can be bigger than this. Type Integer will work for a nine-digit zip code because the maximum zip code (999999999) is smaller than the maximum value that can be stored in an Integer type. If the nine-digit zip code included a dash between the fifth and sixth characters, then you would have to use a String type because the embedded dash makes the value invalid as a number.

Exercise 3.8

The computer first reports in a dialog box that "There are build errors. Continue?" If you click on No, then the message "Type 'Decimal' is not defined." is displayed in the Task List.

Exercise 3.10

X = X + 1 means to increase the value of the variable X by 1. Take the old value of X, add 1, and then store the new value (1 bigger than the old) back into the variable X.

Exercise 3.12

−11

Exercise 3.14

FullName = FirstName & " " & LastName

Exercise 3.16

Single: 1.111111
Decimal: 1.1111111
Long: 1
Double: 1.1111111

Exercise 3.18

The program stops with an error message "An unhandled exception of type 'System.ObjectDisposedException' occurred in system.windows.forms.dll. Additional information: Cannot access a disposed object named "frmTestB"." It appears that clicking on the Close button does more than "hide" the form. Instead, it appears that the form object is destroyed (disposed), so trying to show it again cannot be completed.

Exercise 3.22

Ideally, the only procedures that would be allowed to access a variable are those procedures that require access to it in order to function properly. This would prevent other procedures (i.e., procedures that really do not require access to the variable) from corrupting its value. Using the smallest scope that will suffice reduces the number of procedures that can change the value stored in the variable, and makes it easier to locate the source of the problem when its value does get set improperly.

Since the value of a constant does not change, inadvertent corruption is not a problem with a constant. If a symbolic constant is global, then its name represents the same unchanging value throughout the program. In contrast, one could have two or more local symbolic constants with the same name but representing different values; then the same symbolic constant name would represent different values at different places in the program, which could be potentially confusing.

Exercise 3.24

Suppose the project is divided up by assigning each team a different set of forms to create. Since multiple forms share global variables, it may be that two or more teams will be writing code that uses the same global variables. It will help them immensely to agree in advance (in the design stage) on the names for these global variables. Otherwise, the teams may choose different names for the same variable, possibly causing a lot of confusion when they combine their forms to test the project.

It also could be that two or more teams are assigned to create different event procedures for the same form. In this case, it will be advantageous for them to agree in advance on the names of module-level variables for the form, because these names will occur in more than one event procedure.

Chapter 4

Exercise 4.2

53

Exercise 4.4

5
35
16.5
6
7
6

Exercise 4.6

```
Static C As Integer
C = (C Mod 4) + 1
lblCycle.Text = C
```

Exercise 4.8

```
Private Sub btnEx48_Click(ByVal ...)
    lbltest.Text = Microsoft.VisualBasic.Left(lbltest.Text, _
            Len(lbltest.Text) - 1)
End Sub
```

Exercise 4.10

Zero.

Exercise 4.12

```
Private Sub btnEx412_Click(ByVal ...)
    Dim Letter As String
    Letter = txtCiphertext.Text
    lblCiphertext.Text = lblCiphertext.Text & Letter
    lblPlaintext.Text = lblPlaintext.Text & Chr(Asc(Letter) - 3)
End Sub
```

Exercise 4.14

```
Private Sub btnEx414_Click(ByVal ...)
    Dim Letter As String
    Dim PositionInAlphabet As Integer
    Dim RotatedPosition As Integer
    Dim RotatedLetter As String
    Letter = txtCiphertext.Text
    lblPlaintext.Text = lblPlaintext.Text & Letter
    PositionInAlphabet = Asc(Letter) - 65
    RotatedPosition = (PositionInAlphabet + 3) Mod 26
    RotatedLetter = Chr(65 + RotatedPosition)
    lblCiphertext.Text = lblCiphertext.Text & RotatedLetter
End Sub
```

Exercise 4.16

1. Write down the whole plaintext string.

2. Take the first letter of the plaintext string.

3. Locate the current letter in the ANSI table.

4. Find the letter that is in the ANSI table three places below the location from step 3.

5. Append the letter you found in step 4 to the ciphertext string.

6. Take the next letter of the plaintext string.

7. Repeat steps 3 through 6, until you reach the end of the plaintext string.

Exercise 4.18

The event procedure does not perform as it should when the user is between 3 and 9 years old, inclusive, or between 100 and 199 years old, inclusive. The string value "3" is greater than the string value "20", because "3" has a higher ANSI value than "2" (i.e., "3" comes after "2" in the ANSI table). Likewise, "100" is less than "20" because "1" has a lower ANSI value than "2".

Exercise 4.20

True

Exercise 4.22

If the programmer types Or instead of And, the message box will display "Between ten and twenty? True" regardless of the value of **Age**.

Why is this? Suppose **Age** holds a number that is greater than or equal to 10; then the comparison (**10 <= Age**) will be True, so (**10 <= Age**) **Or** (**Age <= 20**) will be True. Now suppose Age holds a number that is less than 10; then the comparison (**Age <= 20**) will be True, so (**10 <= Age**) **Or** (**Age <= 20**) will be True. Either way, the result of the expression (**10 <= Age**) **Or** (**Age <= 20**) is True.

Exercise 4.24

FalseFalseTrue

Chapter 5

Exercise 5.2

If we move the statement **Target = 1 + Int(6 * Rnd())** out of btnGuessMe_Click and into the Form_Load event procedure, then the random target is generated only once, when program execution first begins. This means that the target is fixed, so the user should never guess the same number twice. The user should employ Strategy B.

Exercise 5.4

```
Private Sub Ex54_Click(ByVal ...)
    Dim Target As Integer
    Dim Guess As Integer
    Static NumGuesses As Integer
    Target = I + Int(6 * Rnd())
    Guess = txtGuess.text
    NumGuesses = NumGuesses + I
    If Guess = Target Then
        Beep()
        MsgBox("Correct -- congratulations!")
        MsgBox("Number of guesses taken = " & NumGuesses)
        End
    Else
        MsgBox("Incorrect -- bummer!")
    End If
End Sub
```

Exercise 5.6

Here's the complete event procedure, with no variables. This code is harder to read than that in Example 5.1, partly because it lacks the descriptive names provided by the variables and partly because the If statement's condition is so long.

```
Private Sub btnGuessMe_Click()
    If txtGuess.Text = (I + Int(6 * Rnd())) Then
        Beep
        MsgBox ("Correct -- congratulations!")
    Else
        MsgBox ("Incorrect -- bummer!")
    End If
End Sub
```

Exercise 5.8

One statement block that works is as follows:

```
If (X < Y) And (Y < Z) Then
    BlankOrNot = ""
Else
    BlankOrNot = "Not"
End If
```

A shorter solution is as follows:

```
If Not ((X < Y) And (Y < Z)) Then
    BlankOrNot = "Not"
End If
```

A still shorter solution uses IIf().

```
BlankOrNot = IIf((X < Y) And (Y < Z), "", "Not")
```

Exercise 5.10

If the user enters "male" instead of "Male" in response to the first input box, the code will use the risk rate for females. This happens because the condition **Sex = "Male"** will be False, so the computer executes the statement block following Else.

One possible way to improve the code is to change the condition of the If statement as follows:

```
If (Sex = "Male") Or (Sex = "male") Then
```

But this solution does not handle the case where the user enters "MALE". A better solution is to use Visual Basic's UCase() function, which returns an uppercase version of its argument, as follows:

```
If UCase(Sex) = "MALE" Then
```

Exercise 5.12

```
Private Sub Ex512_Click(ByVal ...)
    Const MINTHRESHOLD = 20
    Const MINFRACTION = 0.02
    Dim Balance As Decimal
    Dim MinimumDue As Decimal
    Balance = txtBalance.Text
    If Balance < 0 Then
        MinimumDue = 0
    ElseIf Balance <= MINTHRESHOLD Then
        MinimumDue = Balance
    Else
        MinimumDue = IIf(MINTHRESHOLD>MINFRACTION * Balance, _
            MINTHRESHOLD, MINFRACTION * Balance)
    End If
    MsgBox("The minimum amount due is " & _
        Format(MinimumDue, "Currency"))
End Sub
```

Exercise 5.14

You can include access keys for the radio buttons to give the user a keyboard alternative to positioning and clicking the mouse. This should be better than using a text box, which opens up the possibility of typographical errors.

Exercise 5.16

```
TotalA = 5
TotalX = 15
```

Exercise 5.18

One way to do this is to place the last message box statement inside its own If statement, so that this message is displayed only if the value of DaysInMonth is greater than 0.

```
If DaysInMonth > 0 Then
    MsgBox (MonthAbbr & " has " & DaysInMonth & " days.")
End If
```

Exercise 5.20

Experienced programmers, who are used to working with ranges that use the keyword Is and that overlap, find the following Select Case statement more readable. The redundant data in the Select Case statement in Figure 5.25 sets off alarms for an experienced programmer, who knows he or she has to be wary of gaps between the ranges (and looking for such gaps is tedious).

```
Select Case Rnd()
Case Is < 0.2
    Target = 1
Case Is <= 0.3
    Target = 2
Case Is <= 0.6
    Target = 3
```

continued

```
            Case Is <= 0.75
                Target = 4
            Case Is <= 0.9
                Target = 5
            Case Else
                Target = 6
        End Select
```

Exercise 5.22

The following solution to Exercise 5.12 is more readable than the solution using If. The decision has multiple outcomes that depend on a single expression.

```
Private Sub btnMinimumAmountDue_Click()
    Const MINTHRESHOLD = 20
    Const MINFRACTION = 0.02
    Dim Balance As Decimal
    Dim MinimumDue As Decimal
    Balance = txtBalance.Text
    Select Case Balance
        Case Is < 0
            MinimumDue = 0
        Case Is <= MINTHRESHOLD
            MinimumDue = Balance
        Case Else
            MinimumDue = IIf(MINTHRESHOLD>MINFRACTION*Balance, _
                    MINTHRESHOLD, MINFRACTION * Balance)
    End Select
    MsgBox ("The minimum amount due is " & _
            Format(MinimumDue, "Currency"))
End Sub
```

Chapter 6

Exercise 6.5

```
Dim WageRate As Decimal
Dim MonthsOfService As Integer

Private Sub ComputeWageRate()
    If MonthsOfService < 3 Then
        WageRate = 9.75
    ElseIf MonthsOfService < 6 Then
        WageRate = 10.25
    ElseIf MonthsOfService < 12 Then
        WageRate = 11
    ElseIf MonthsOfService < 24 Then
        WageRate = 12.5
    Else
        WageRate = 14.75
    End If
End Sub

Private Sub btnLookupWageRate_Click()
    MonthsOfService = txtMonthsOfService.Text
    ComputeWageRate
    MsgBox ("Wage rate is " & Format(WageRate, "currency"))
End Sub
```

Exercise 6.6

```
Dim MonthAbbr As String
Dim DaysInMonth As Integer

Private Sub FindNumDaysInMonth()
    Select Case MonthAbbr
    Case "JAN", "MAR", "MAY", "JUL", "AUG", "OCT", "DEC"
        DaysInMonth = 31
    Case "APR", "JUN", "SEP", "NOV"
        DaysInMonth = 30
    Case "FEB"
        DaysInMonth = 28
    Case Else
        MsgBox (MonthAbbr & " is not a valid month abbreviation.")
    End Select
End Sub

Private Sub btnMonthDays_Click(...)
    MonthAbbr = txtMonth.Text
    FindNumDaysInMonth
    MsgBox (MonthAbbr & " has " & DaysInMonth & " days.")
End Sub
```

Exercise 6.8

The message displayed by btnParameterQuiz1_Click is "From short words emerges a short sentence."

Exercise 6.10

The message boxes displayed by btnMultipleParametersTest_Click contain the messages A = 3, B = 8, and C = 1.833333.

Exercise 6.12

```
Private Sub Swap(ByRef X As Single, ByRef Y As Single)
    Dim Z As Single
    Z = X
    X = Y
    Y = Z
End Sub
```

Exercise 6.14

The message boxes will contain "maze", "agin", "busi", and "ness". The actions performed by procedure Rearrange are intricate enough that you probably have to work through the code by hand again, unless you are exceptionally good at identifying patterns.

Exercise 6.16

```
100-25-200
100-100-33
100-100-100
```

Exercise 6.17

```
Private Sub ComputeWageRate(WageRate As Decimal, _
            ByVal MonthsOfService As Integer)
    If MonthsOfService < 3 Then
        WageRate = 9.75
    ElseIf MonthsOfService < 6 Then
        WageRate = 10.25
    ElseIf MonthsOfService < 12 Then
        WageRate = 11
```

continued

```
            ElseIf MonthsOfService < 24 Then
                WageRate = 12.5
            Else
                WageRate = 14.75
            End If
    End Sub


    Private Sub btnLookupWageRate_Click(...)
        Dim WageRate As Decimal
        Dim MonthsOfService As Integer
        MonthsOfService = txtMonthsOfService.Text
        ComputeWageRate WageRate, MonthsOfService
        MsgBox ("Wage rate is " & Format(WageRate, "currency"))
    End Sub
```

| Exercise 6.21 |

From the user's point of view, it is very convenient to have the focus start out in the Username text box each time the login form appears again. That way, the user doesn't even have to look to see which box has the focus; she can start typing her username as soon as the form appears.

To ensure that the Username text box will have the focus when the login form reappears, insert the following statement in the event procedure for the login form's OK button. Note that this statement must be placed above the statement that hides the form, since Visual Basic .NET allows you to set the focus for a form only when the form is showing (i.e., when it is not hidden).

```
        frmLogin.txtUsername.Focus
```

Chapter 7

| Exercise 7.2 |

The following event procedure behaves identically to that in Example 7.5. It is harder to understand because of the statement **Target = 7** just before the loop. This statement ensures that the loop's condition will be True the first time it is evaluated; without it the condition would be False because the Dim statements initialize both **Target** and **Guess** to 0. The drawback of the Do...While loop in this case is that statements like **Target = 7** are necessary, and they don't seem to make any sense.

```
        Private Sub btnGuessMe_Click()
            Dim Target As Integer
            Dim Guess As Integer
            Target = 7
            Do While Guess <> Target
                Target = 1 + Int(6 * Rnd())
                Guess = InputBox("Enter a guess between 1 and 6, " & _
                    "inclusive.")
                If Guess <> Target Then
                    MsgBox ("Incorrect -- bummer!")
                End If
            Loop
            Beep
            MsgBox ("Correct -- congratulations!")
        End Sub
```

The following is an alternative solution that does make sense. Its disadvantage is that the statement Target = 1 + Int(6 * Rnd()) appears in two places.

```
Private Sub btnGuessMe_Click()
    Dim Target As Integer
    Dim Guess As Integer
    Target = 1 + Int(6 * Rnd())        'generate first target
    Do While Guess <> Target
        Guess = InputBox("Enter a guess between 1 and 6, " & _
                "inclusive.")
        If Guess <> Target Then
            MsgBox ("Incorrect -- bummer!")
            Target = 1 + Int(6 * Rnd()) 'generate new target
        End If
    Loop
    Beep
    MsgBox ("Correct -- congratulations!")
End Sub
```

Exercise 7.4

```
Private Sub btnGuidedGuessMe_Click()
    Dim Target As Integer
    Dim Guess As Integer
    Dim Count As Integer
    Target = 1 + Int(127 * Rnd())
    Do Until Guess = Target
        Guess = InputBox("Enter a guess between 1 " & _
                "and 127, inclusive.")
        Count = Count + 1
        If Guess < Target Then
            MsgBox ("Too low")
        ElseIf Guess > Target Then
            MsgBox ("Too high")
        End If
    Loop
    MsgBox ("It took you " & Count & " guesses.")
End Sub
```

Exercise 7.6

If the user enters −1 in response to the input box, the Do Until loop's condition will be True the first time it is evaluated; thus, the loop will terminate immediately and no letters will be displayed.

Exercise 7.8

The following will display the numbers 1 through 10, inclusive:

```
Private Sub btnForNextTest_Click()
    Dim X As Integer
    For X = 1 To 10
        MsgBox (X)
    Next
End Sub
```

Exercise 7.10

```
Private Sub btnCoinTossExperiment_Click()
    Dim NumberOfTosses As Integer
    Dim Toss As Integer
```

continued

```
                    Dim Heads As Boolean
                    Dim HeadCount As Integer
                    NumberOfTosses = InputBox("How many tosses?")
                    For Toss = 1 To NumberOfTosses
                        Heads = (Rnd() <= 0.5)        ' True means heads
                                                      ' False means tails

                        If Heads = True Then
                            HeadCount = HeadCount + 1
                        End If
                    Next
                    MsgBox("Fraction of tosses that came up heads = " & _
                        HeadCount / NumberOfTosses)
                End Sub
```

Exercise 7.12

Event procedure btnAnnoyingLoop_Click displays the number 1 in message boxes, repeatedly, forever. The loop is an infinite loop because the step amount is 0. This happens because the programmer failed to store any value in the variable **StepAmount**. (Remember to use Ctrl+Break to stop a loop like this.)

Chapter 8

Exercise 8.2

a. Product = { <u>ProdNo</u> + Desc + CustNo + CustName + Price }

Not in third normal form. **CustName** can be determined by **CustNo**, which is not part of the key.

b. Customer = { <u>CustNo</u> + Name + Address + PhoneNo }

In third normal form.

c. Transaction = { <u>ProdNo + CustNo + Date</u> + Quantity }

In third normal form.

d. SalesPerson = { <u>EmplNo</u> + EmplName + DeptCode + DeptName }

Not in third normal form. **DeptName** can be determined by **DeptCode**, which is not part of the key.

Chapter 9

Exercise 9.2

```
<Booklist>
    <Book>
        <Title>23 Ways To Leave Your Mother</Title>
        <Author>Woody Ellen</Author>
        <Publisher>Wadsworthless</Publisher>
        <CopyrightDate>1983</CopyrightDate>
    </Book>
    <Book>
        <Title>Bob, Ted, Carol, and Salad</Title>
        <Author>Sid CeasarSalad</Author>
        <Publisher>Green Leaves</Publisher>
        <CopyrightDate>1966</CopyrightDate>
    </Book>
```

```
<Book>
    <Title>Three Blind Mice</Title>
    <Author>Bill Gater</Author>
    <Publisher>MacroHard</Publisher>
    <CopyrightDate>1993</CopyrightDate>
</Book>
</Booklist>
```

Exercise 9.4

An XML Schema is used to verify that a particular XML document is valid, that is, it contains elements that are legal according to the schema. This lets business partners verify that documents sent to them follow some agreed-upon rules.

You use XSLT to transform an XML document into a different XML document. For example, this can be used to transform an XML document into an HTML document (which is also XML if it follows the XML rules).

Exercise 9.6

This element defines a namespace, that is, a prefix that can be appended to an XML element to make it different from an element with the same spelling but in a different namespace. The squiggly line means that the namespace name is spelled incorrectly.

Exercise 9.9

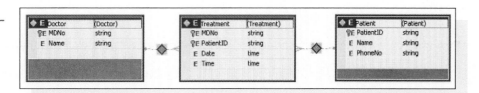

Chapter 10

Exercise 10.1

Stock = Quantity(ProdNo, WareNo)

Exercise 10.3

The values displayed in the three message boxes are:

```
7    -3    4    1    -4    2
7    -3   -3    1     1    4
-3   -3    1    1    -4   -4
```

Exercise 10.5

The following segment of code stores the company name for the company with the largest rate of return in the variable named **MaxRORCompName**.

```
Dim MaxROR As Double = RateOfReturn(0)
Dim MaxRORIndex = 0
For Row = 1 To NumRows - 1
    If RateOfReturn(Row) > MaxROR Then
        MaxROR = RateOfReturn(Row)
        MaxRORIndex = Row
    EndIf
Next
MaxRORCompName = CompName(MaxRORIndex)
```

Exercise 10.7

When you make a guess in a binary search, you want to eliminate all the entries above or below that guess. This is only possible if the elements in the array are ordered. Without an ordered array, you cannot draw the conclusion and cannot eliminate the values.

Exercise 10.9

The search does not return the correct conclusion in all cases. In most cases it reports a failed search even though the item being searched for exists in the array.

Exercise 10.11

```
Private Sub btnShowEnumeration_Click(ByVal ...)
    Dim AnEnumerator As IDictionaryEnumerator = ROR.GetEnumerator
    Dim SortedEnum As New ArrayList()
    Dim I As Integer = 0
    Do While AnEnumerator.MoveNext
        SortedEnum.Add(AnEnumerator.Key)
        I = I + I
    Loop
    SortedEnum.Sort()
    For I = 0 To SortedEnum.Count - I
        lstEnumeration.Items.Add(SortedEnum(I))
    Next
End Sub
```

Chapter 11

Exercise 11.2

A financial consulting company has a proprietary formula for determining the relative risk associated with various stocks. This formula represents the primary intellectual property asset of the firm. This formula should not be sent to the client where it can be seen by the user.

Exercise 11.4

By placing business logic on the server instead of the client, it makes it easier to change the logic with the assurance that everyone who accesses the logic after the change will be using the changed code. It makes the update and maintenance of the code very efficient.

Exercise 11.6

```
Private Sub btnGrossPay_Click(ByVal sender ...)
    Dim Hours As Decimal = txtHours.Text
    Dim Rate As Decimal = txtRate.Text
    Dim Gross As Decimal = Hours * Rate
    If Rate >= 6.25 Then
        lblGrossPay.Text = Format(Gross, "Currency")
    Else
        lblGrossPay.Text = "Hourly Rate must be >= $6.25"
    EndIf
End Sub
```

Exercise 11.9

Modify the SQL using an Order By clause:

```
SELECT SupplierID, ContactName, City, Country, Phone
FROM Suppliers
ORDER BY Country, City
```

INDEX